Dynamics of
Democracy in
TAIWAN

Dynamics of Democracy in
TAIWAN

The Ma Ying-jeou Years

edited by
Kharis Templeman
Yun-han Chu
Larry Diamond

LYNNE
RIENNER
PUBLISHERS

BOULDER
LONDON

Published in the United States of America in 2020 by
Lynne Rienner Publishers, Inc.
1800 30th Street, Suite 314, Boulder, Colorado 80301
www.rienner.com

and in the United Kingdom by
Lynne Rienner Publishers, Inc.
Gray's Inn House, 127 Clerkenwell Road, London EC1 5DB

Library of Congress Cataloging-in-Publication Data
Names: Templeman, Kharis, editor. | Chu, Yun-han, editor. | Diamond, Larry
Jay, editor.
Title: Dynamics of Democracy in Taiwan : the Ma Ying-jeou Years / edited
by Kharis Templeman, Yun-han Chu, and Larry Diamond.
Description: Boulder, Colorado : Lynne Rienner Publishers, Inc., 2020. |
Includes bibliographical references and index.
Identifiers: LCCN 2020014995 | ISBN 9781626379046 (hardcover) | ISBN
9781626379114 (paperback)
Subjects: LCSH: Taiwan—Politics and government—2000 | Democracy—Taiwan.
| Political parties—Taiwan.
Classification: LCC DS799.847 .D86 2020 | DDC 320.951249—dc23
LC record available at https://lccn.loc.gov/2020014995

British Cataloguing in Publication Data
A Cataloguing in Publication record for this book
is available from the British Library.

Printed and bound in the United States of America

The paper used in this publication meets the requirements
of the American National Standard for Permanence of
Paper for Printed Library Materials Z39.48-1992.

5 4 3 2 1

Contents

Illustrations

Tables

Figures

Acknowledgments

We are grateful for the assistance of many individuals and institutions that have helped to make this book possible. The Taipei Economic and Cultural Office (TECO) in San Francisco has been a steadfast supporter of the Taiwan Democracy Project at Stanford University over the past fifteen years. Larry Diamond and Kharis Templeman offer special thanks to Director General Joseph Ma and Director Shannon Shiau for their ongoing commitment to the conferences and other activities of the program; it has been our pleasure to engage with them and their colleagues in the TECO office. We also thank the Center for Democracy, Development, and the Rule of Law (CDDRL), which hosted the original Project on Democracy in Taiwan and the conference on which this book is based, as well as the director, Francis Fukuyama, and the staff of CDDRL.

During the final phase of production of the book, the Taiwan project was based at the Shorenstein Asia-Pacific Research Center (APARC), which (like CDDRL) is part of the Freeman Spogli Institute for International Studies (FSI) at Stanford University. We thank the director of APARC, Gi-wook Shin, as well as the current director of FSI, Ambassador Mike McFaul, for their support and interest in the program, and Ambassador Karl Eikenberry for his leadership of the Taiwan project when it was based at APARC. In addition, the staff of APARC, especially Andrea Brown and Huma Shaik, provided efficient and effective administrative assistance for the Taiwan project during its time at the center.

The themes and conclusions of the book have been greatly influenced by conversations the editors have had over the past several years with many people who participated in or directly observed key events during the Ma presidency. We would especially like to acknowledge Chang Kuor-hsin,

Chao Tien-lin, Chen Wei-ting, Johnny Chiang, Eric Chu, Fan Yun, Fan Chiang Tai-ji, Eric Huang, Jason Hsu, Jiang Yi-huah, Ko Wen-je, David Lin, Lin Fei-fan, Lo Chih-chiang, Ian Rowen, Shen Lyu-shun, Tao Yi-feng, Tsai Ting-kuey, Wang Yu-chi, Wang Jin-pyng, Timothy Yang, Wei Yang, Yao Wen-chih, and Yeh Jiunn-rong. In addition, we are deeply grateful for the opportunities we have had to speak directly with President Tsai Ing-wen and President Ma Ying-jeou, and we thank them for sharing with us their insights about Taiwan politics.

We also thank Lynne Rienner for her creative assistance in helping to frame the volume and for her enduring commitment to quality and affordable publishing of scholarly books in this challenging economic environment. We are also grateful to Nicole Moore and Shena Redmond for their careful management of the editorial process; to Jason Cook for his close reading and copyediting of the text, figures, and tables; and to Catherine Bowman for assembling the detailed index.

Finally, we thank all of the contributors to this collection for their patience and commitment as we saw the project through to completion.

—*The Editors*

1

The Dynamics of Democracy During the Ma Ying-jeou Years

Kharis Templeman, Yun-han Chu, and Larry Diamond

The eight years of the Ma Ying-jeou presidency (2008–2016) are an era of contradictions. In 2008, Ma won the largest share of the presidential vote in the democratic era, yet he later recorded the lowest public approval ratings of any leader of Taiwan. During his time in office, Taiwan's economy went through both the most rapid quarterly expansion and the deepest recession of the past three decades. His Chinese Nationalist Party, or Kuomintang (KMT), held large majorities in the Legislative Yuan, Taiwan's national parliament, yet many of his administration's top legislative priorities were repeatedly delayed or blocked there. Public trust in democratic institutions continued to decline even as support for democratic values and rejection of authoritarianism deepened. Economic and people-to-people exchanges with the Chinese mainland increased dramatically during Ma's time in office, but at the same time public opinion surveys showed a continued rise in an exclusivist Taiwanese identity among the island's people. Most notably, President Ma developed the best relations with Beijing a Taiwanese government has had in a quarter century, even meeting on an equal basis with Chinese Communist Party (CCP) chairman Xi Jinping in Singapore in November 2015—the first-ever meeting between leaders of the Republic of China (ROC) and the People's Republic of China (PRC). But his cross-Strait rapprochement policies also triggered a domestic political backlash, including a student-led occupation of the legislature and the defeat of a trade agreement that left the KMT bruised, battered, and beaten. Taiwan's longtime ruling party ended the Ma era leaderless, out of power, and facing an existential crisis.

Quality of Democracy During the Ma Era

This volume analyzes the legacy of the eight years of the Ma Ying-jeou presidency for democracy in Taiwan. Overall, during this period Taiwan remained one of the most liberal democracies not only in Asia but also among all the third wave democracies of the world, as Table 1.1 and Figure 1.1 show.

Freedom House rated Taiwan "free" for the entire era with an average freedom rating on political rights and civil liberties of 1.5 on a scale of 1 to 7, putting it on a par with Japan as the freest regime in the Asia Pacific and ranking it among the world's more liberal democracies. This overall score, however, hides some important variation within these categories. Taiwan's political rights rating rose in 2010 from 2 to 1 in response to better enforcement of anticorruption laws, including the successful prosecution of the previous president, Chen Shui-bian. But at the same time, its civil liberties rating fell from 1 to 2 due to what Freedom House identified as flaws in the protection of criminal defendants' rights and rising limitations on academic freedom. Only after President Ma left office did Taiwan's overall ranking rise to the highest Freedom House score, a 1 on both 7-point scales, and to a score of 93 on the more detailed 100-point scale that aggregates the raw scores for political rights and civil liberties, depicted in Figure 1.1.

Considered over the full span of Ma's time in office, two kinds of concerns consistently appear in the Freedom House reports.[1] The first is about the rule of law, especially weakness and lack of impartiality of the judiciary

Table 1.1   Freedom House Overall Score for Selected Countries (1–7 Scale), 2008–2018

	2008	2009	2010	2011	2012	2013	2014	2015	2016	2017	2018
Cambodia	5.5	5.5	5.5	5.5	5.5	5.5	5.5	5.5	5.5	5.5	5.5
Chile	1	1	1	1	1	1	1	1	1	1	1
Czechia	1	1	1	1	1	1	1	1	1	1	1
Indonesia	2.5	2.5	2.5	2.5	2.5	2.5	3	3	3	3	3
Japan	1.5	1.5	1.5	1.5	1.5	1.5	1	1	1	1	1
Korea	1.5	1.5	1.5	1.5	1.5	1.5	2	2	2	2	2
Malaysia	4	4	4	4	4	4	4	4	4	4	4
Mongolia	2	2	2	2	2	1.5	1.5	1.5	1.5	1.5	1.5
Myanmar	7	7	7	7	6.5	5.5	5.5	6	5.5	5	5
Peru	2.5	2.5	2.5	2.5	2.5	2.5	2.5	2.5	2.5	2.5	2.5
Philippines	3.5	3.5	3.5	3	3	3	3	3	3	3	3
Poland	1	1	1	1	1	1	1	1	1	1.5	1.5
Singapore	4.5	4.5	4.5	4.5	4	4	4	4	4	4	4
Taiwan	1.5	1.5	1.5	1.5	1.5	1.5	1.5	1.5	1.5	1	1
Thailand	5	4.5	4.5	4.5	4	4	4	5.5	5.5	5.5	5.5

Source: Freedom House.
Note: 1 = highest, 7 = lowest.

Figure 1.1   Freedom House Aggregate Score for Selected Countries, 2014–2019

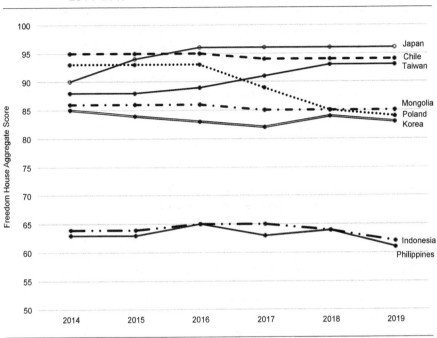

and prosecutors and selective prosecution of corruption. As in previous administrations, judicial scandals were a regular occurrence during the Ma era; in 2010, for instance, both the president and the vice president of the Judicial Yuan resigned after several judges were caught taking bribes to deliver a not-guilty verdict in a high-profile corruption case, and several other senior judges were suspended. Prosecutorial leaks to the media before trial were a recurrent problem as well, most notably in the case of former president Chen. Several cases of potentially improper government use of eminent domain also occurred, prompting the legislature in 2012 to pass amendments requiring that such actions be taken "in the public interest."

The second concern is about media freedom, particularly the rising influence of the PRC on Taiwan's media landscape. This worry was vividly illustrated in 2008 when the China-friendly tycoon Tsai Eng-meng (Cai Yanming), the founder and head of the food manufacturing company Want Wang Holdings, purchased the China Times group, which included one of Taiwan's oldest newspapers and two television channels. The editorial line of the group swung sharply toward the PRC after this takeover, moving the *China Times* from its traditional position in the middle of the political spectrum toward the pro-unification extreme. In 2012, Want Want attempted to purchase additional television cable channels, and at about the same time another investor group that included Tsai's son made a bid for the fiercely independent tabloid newspaper *Apple Daily* and its hard-hitting weekly investigative news magazine, *Next*. Popular protests against the proposed sales called attention to the potential impact on the public sphere, and Taiwan's National Communications Commission eventually set such stringent terms for purchase that both deals fell through.[2] But PRC influence over Taiwan's media environment, including rising self-censorship, pro-Beijing editorial lines, and payments for positive coverage of the Chinese mainland, remained worrisome and a long-term challenge to Taiwan's democratic vitality.

Political Challenges: Executive-Legislative Relations, Cross-Strait Relations, and the Sunflower Movement

Executive-legislative relations were a frequent source of political intrigue during the Ma era. Some conflict between these branches was inevitable: all presidential regimes, with their separate origin and survival of the two branches, are set up to be adversarial, and many are even under unified single-party rule. But the legitimacy and decisiveness of Taiwan's policymaking process has also long been hampered by vague and under-institutionalized procedures for decisionmaking, as well as a massive asymmetry of expertise and capacity that favors the executive at the expense of the legislative branch. The challenges of these arrangements became increasingly obvious during Ma's presidency, as political battles over cross-Strait policy morphed into interbranch institutional conflict.

President Ma's top political priority was to conclude an ambitious set of cross-Strait agreements that ranged from relaxing restrictions on PRC-based investment to cooperation on criminal investigations and extraditions. He began his presidency with a clear mandate behind this agenda: in the legislative elections held in January 2008, KMT candidates captured 72 percent of the seats (and over 75 percent if we include allied independents and People First Party [PFP] legislators), and in the presidential election in March, Ma carried over 58 percent of the vote, the most decisive victory in Taiwan's democratic history. Public opinion, too, initially ran in favor of cross-Strait rapprochement, and Ma quickly set about trying to enhance cross-Strait exchanges. Within days of his taking office, Ma's appointees at the Straits Exchange Foundation (SEF), the semiofficial body set up to handle negotiations with the PRC, were in productive talks with their counterparts at the Association for Relations Across the Taiwan Strait (ARATS) about transit and tourism. These discussions yielded quick results: within two months, dozens of commercial charter flights were crossing the Strait every day, and busloads of Chinese tour groups had become a ubiquitous presence around Chiang Kai-shek Memorial Hall and the National Palace Museum in Taipei.

Nevertheless, the same streamlined approval and implementation process that enabled the quick conclusion of these agreements also came at a political cost: it contributed to rising mistrust of President Ma's motivations and weakened public support for rapprochement. Under the terms of the law governing cross-Strait relations, most deals with Beijing could take effect without positive legislative action, unless a majority could be mustered in the Legislative Yuan to veto them. Of the twenty-three agreements signed during the Ma era, only three required an affirmative vote by the legislature to come into force; the rest were submitted as executive orders "for reference" rather than "for review," meaning that the Legislative Yuan had to act in order to block their implementation.[3] Given the politically sensitive nature of many of these agreements, the quite reasonable need to keep bargaining positions private in negotiations, and the fact that cross-Strait relations were (and continue to be) the most salient political divide in Taiwanese politics, this low threshold for adoption contributed to a legitimacy deficit that eventually triggered a legislative and then popular backlash against the whole political project.

The two most prominent agreements of the Ma era illustrate this problem. On June 29, 2010, the SEF and ARATS signed the key agreement laying out a legal framework for cross-Strait interaction, dubbed the Economic Cooperation Framework Agreement (ECFA). Because this agreement required changes to domestic laws in Taiwan, the Ma administration then submitted the ECFA to the legislature for review.[4] Public support at the time was positive: a TVBS survey in May 2010 found 41 percent of respondents approved of signing the agreement, while 34 percent disapproved.[5] The opposition Democratic Progressive Party (DPP) was able to delay consideration for a month, but with universal support from the KMT caucus and public opinion running in favor, the legislature held a vote and passed the agreement, along with another on intellectual property rights protection, on August 17.

By contrast, the controversial Cross-Strait Services Trade Agreement (CSSTA) was signed and reviewed under much different circumstances. The CSSTA was officially concluded on June 21, 2013, a year into Ma's second term. By that point President Ma's approval rating had slumped to a new low: a TVBS poll that month found only 13 percent of respondents approved of his performance, with 73 percent disapproving. The same poll found 47 percent opposed the CSSTA, with only 30 percent supporting it.[6] Nevertheless, as it had done with all but two other agreements, the Ma administration quickly signaled its intention to send the CSSTA to the legislature as an executive order only "for reference," putting it on a fast track to implementation. Unless the Legislative Yuan took action to block it, it would come into force three months after formal notification. In this instance, however, something rather extraordinary happened before the agreement was delivered to the legislature: after a DPP-led scrum at the speaker's podium prevented the legislature from coming to order on June 25, Legislative Yuan speaker Wang Jin-pyng negotiated a cross-party consensus stating that, once it was received, the CSSTA would not take effect without being reviewed and ratified by the legislature, and that each item in the agreement would be voted on separately. In other words, the legislature, run by Ma's own KMT, had changed the rules to make passage of the CSSTA almost impossible.[7]

These new conditions were major concessions to the opposition DPP, but they also reflected increasing uneasiness within the KMT's own legislative caucus about some of the terms of the agreement amid falling public support for rapprochement with the PRC. By negotiating a cross-party consensus, Speaker Wang provided some political cover for those in the ruling party who did not support the CSSTA but did not want to go public with their opposition to the agreement, the party leadership, and President Ma.[8] As a consequence, the Ma administration could no longer count on Speaker Wang as a reliable ally in pushing through cross-Strait agreements, and Wang became directly embroiled in the political conflict over Ma's cross-Strait policies.

The next phase of this conflict erupted in September 2013, when the Special Investigative Division (SID) of the supreme prosecutor's office recorded Speaker Wang on a wiretap attempting to pressure a local prosecutor's office not to appeal a court ruling in favor of DPP party caucus leader Ker Chien-ming. Huang Shih-ming, the prosecutor-general and director of the SID, reported this allegation directly to President Ma, who quickly went public with the accusations. At the same time, Ma used his position as party chairman to attempt to strip Wang of his KMT membership and remove him from the Legislative Yuan, which would allow Ma to replace him as speaker with someone more loyal to his administration. Wang countered by filing his own lawsuit against Ma, alleging that he could not be expelled from the party without due process, and in an unexpected ruling a lower court agreed with Wang and issued a temporary injunction blocking Ma's action. The effect of the ruling was that Speaker Wang kept his party membership, and his job leading the legislature, for the rest of the term. Ma was dealt a costly political setback, and the ensuing uproar over the failed purge left the KMT even more divided than before.[9]

Nevertheless, the Ma administration continued to prioritize winning approval of the CSSTA, and it insisted that the KMT caucus should use its legislative majority to hold an up-or-down vote and pass the agreement. Though Speaker Wang had pledged not to bring it to the floor until a series of twenty public hearings had wrapped up, President Ma repeatedly pressured the Legislative Yuan caucus, without success, to convene a special session to take action earlier. When the last of these hearings finally concluded on March 10, 2014, the DPP attempted to use its control of the Internal Affairs Committee convener's chair for the week to begin the line-by-line review of the agreement. The KMT in turn argued that this move violated an unwritten Legislative Yuan norm: any item of discussion placed on the agenda by one convener should not be discussed while the other convener was presiding. Since KMT legislator Chiang Chi-chen had chaired the first hearing on the CSSTA the previous July, the KMT asserted that the DPP could not bring up the CSSTA that week. The DPP countered that the review was a separate item from the hearings, and that they were entitled to place the line-by-line review on the committee agenda while DPP legislator Chen Chi-mai held the chair for the week. Thus the DPP pushed ahead with committee meetings to review the agreement on March 12 and 13, which quickly descended into chaos as KMT and DPP legislators repeatedly argued over procedures and scuffled with each other. The review was then postponed yet again until the following week, when the KMT's Chang Ching-chung was due to take over the convener's role.

Over the weekend, President Ma publicly called on KMT legislators to step up their efforts and show up at the Legislative Yuan for a final showdown to pass the CSSTA. Then, on Monday, March 17, DPP and Taiwan Solidarity Union (TSU) legislators occupied the committee room to prevent Legislator Chang from presiding, arguing that he did not have the right to oversee the review because the DPP had introduced it to the agenda—much like KMT legislators had done the week before. Finally, after a daylong standoff, Chang suddenly called the meeting to order and announced to no one in particular that, because the three-month time limit for reviewing an executive order had already passed, the review was complete and the CSSTA was advanced out of committee for a final vote at a plenary session of the Legislative Yuan on Friday, March 21. At about the same time, a group of protesters—many of them college students and civil society activists—had gathered outside to demonstrate against the CSSTA, staging a sit-in near the entrance to the legislature. As news spread of Chang's unilateral announcement, the crowd grew over the next twenty-four hours, and during a much larger demonstration the next evening, March 18, protesters suddenly broke through the Legislative Yuan's main gates and pushed into the central chamber, occupying the floor and barricading the doors shut to prevent security from removing them.[10]

They remained there for over three weeks, demanding that the CSSTA be withdrawn, bringing all legislative business to a halt, and attracting widespread media coverage in Taiwan and abroad. Someone brought in sunflowers to hand to some of the demonstrators, and the protest got its iconic name: the Sunflower Movement. The Ma administration condemned the occupation and threatened to send in riot police to forcibly remove the demonstrators,[11] but backed down in the face of objections from Speaker Wang, who found himself playing dealmaker once again: on March 20 he personally guaranteed the safety of the protesters in the face of the administration's mobilization of police from around the island, and then on April 6 he promised that the vote on the CSSTA would not be held, and its review would be delayed, until after legislation strengthening oversight and monitoring of cross-Strait negotiations was passed. The leaders of the movement then announced they would end the occupation and leave the legislature on April 10, which they did.

The Sunflower Movement's Mixed Legacy for Democracy in Taiwan

As the chapters in this book demonstrate, interpretations of the Sunflower Movement and the legacy it has left for Taiwan are no less divided now than they were at the time. It was without a doubt the seminal moment of the Ma era, one that could have sent Taiwan down a much more worrisome political trajectory. But we do not view the Sunflower Movement as either a critical event that saved Taiwan's democracy or one that fatally damaged it. Its impact is too complicated for such a stark, Manichean judgment. What can be said with the benefit of hindsight is that the movement occurred because of enduring weaknesses in Taiwan's political institutions: incomplete rule of law, unclear procedures for resolving divisive political conflicts, disproportional representation in the legislature, a polarized media environment that allowed rumors and partisan vendettas to flourish, and widespread distrust of nonpartisan state agencies. Those weaknesses remain today, and they should be of deep concern to anyone who cares about Taiwan's survival as a liberal democracy.

Nevertheless, on a more positive note, the occupation of the Legislative Yuan was also eventually resolved peacefully: the Ma administration backed down, riot police stepped back, and a quiet and orderly departure of the demonstrators was negotiated. Crucially as well, the broader social protest movement was eventually channeled into electoral competition within the established democratic system. Rather than attempt to radically reshape Taiwan's political institutions via an extra-constitutional "people power" revolution, most of the activists and demonstrators instead dedicated their energies over the following months and years to electoral organizing and campaigning. Protest leaders joined the opposition DPP or founded new political parties, and interest surged in the next local elections, held in November 2014. Taiwan's democratic institutions were strained, but with some timely action by key players, political elites on the whole shied away from steps that might have triggered violent conflict. Instead they respected shifts in public opinion and accepted the ultimate electoral verdicts delivered by voters in 2014 and 2016. In the end, Ma's agenda for cross-Strait rapprochement ran up against a decisive shift in public opinion away from support for engagement and toward greater concern about the PRC—and this shift eventually halted the project.

Taiwan's formal democratic "hardware"—its constitutional structure, its nonpartisan agencies, its judiciary and legal institutions—did not function especially well during this period. But its democratic "software" remained surprisingly strong and resilient: despite deep political divisions, elites and ordinary Taiwanese alike demonstrated an enduring commitment to democratic norms of peaceful coexistence, debate, and negotiation, and they ultimately accepted the resolution through the electoral process of the many political conflicts of this era. Despite intense polarization over the China question during the Ma Ying-jeou years, democracy in Taiwan muddled through.

Taiwan's Economic Challenges and Opportunities at the Beginning of the Ma Era

As Ma and his advisers plotted a course for his first presidential term, the strategic environment they faced presented both formidable challenges and unique opportunities. The foremost challenge was the state of the domestic economy. Taiwan's economic performance in the preceding decade appeared underwhelming to most Taiwanese. The economy averaged annual growth of 4.9 percent from 2000 to 2007, a respectable number for a maturing economy with slowing population growth and a rapidly aging society, but significantly lower than the 6.6 percent average of the 1990s and the 8.2 percent of the 1980s.[12] Ma centered his first presidential campaign on a promise to reinvigorate the economy, arguing that the domestic ideological conflicts and hostile cross-Strait relations of the Chen Shui-bian years[13] had acted as a serious drag on growth. Ending these domestic fights, privileging economic liberalization, and improving the cross-Strait political climate, he promised, would allow Taiwan's economy to reach its full potential again. Ma made this promise explicit with a so-called 6-3-3 pledge: that his administration would achieve annual gross domestic product (GDP) growth of 6 percent, per capita income of US$30,000, and unemployment below 3 percent by the end of his time in office.[14]

Another important trend reshaping Taiwan's external economic environment was shifts in the trading regime of the Asia Pacific. Up through the 1990s, trading rules and practices in the region were under-institutionalized: cross-border trade relied heavily on informal business relationships and the vertical integration of multinational corporations (MNCs) with domestic partners. But by the early 2000s, interminable delays in the Doha Round of World Trade Organization (WTO) negotiations led to increasing frustration and impatience among the leaders of many Asian economies, and several began to pursue bilateral trade accords, both with other Asia Pacific partners and with countries outside the region. Leading the way was South Korea, which concluded agreements with the Association of Southeast Asian Nations (ASEAN), China, the United States, the European Union, and over a dozen other individual countries. The resulting explosion in the number of such agreements led to an increasingly complex "noodle bowl" of trade rules and regulations in the region: since each accord was unique, firms had to adjust to a different set of rules for each bilateral relationship. As a consequence, the Asia Pacific region moved in little more than a decade from an under- to over-institutionalized environment, with many agreements having overlapping membership and different requirements.[15]

That sparked further moves to expand these bilateral agreements by adding additional partners, harmonizing regulations and standards, and moving toward a truly regional trade regime. The most notable of these efforts was the Trans-Pacific Partnership (TPP). The forerunner of the TPP began in 2005 as a four-country economic partnership between Singapore, New Zealand, Brunei, and Chile (known informally as the P4). By 2009, eight other countries had joined discussions to expand the arrangement, including Japan and the United States. In 2012, several ASEAN member states put forward the idea of an alternative trade regime, the Regional Comprehensive Economic Partnership (RCEP), which would have significant overlapping membership with the TPP but include China and India and exclude the United States and other North and South American members.[16]

This trend toward bilateral and then regional trade agreements posed a major threat to Taiwan's economic prosperity. Highly trade-dependent, Taiwan had long been a major player in the global economy, but it was at a disadvantage in negotiating similar agreements because of its diplomatic isolation and the increasingly effective pressure brought to bear by Beijing against Taiwan's trading partners. These obstacles were most obvious in the case of negotiations for the RCEP, in which China was an initial participant. But they were also present for the TPP: because each member state had to approve negotiations with any new participants, and because several TPP members (especially Vietnam and Malaysia) were quite vulnerable to PRC diplomatic and economic pressure, Taiwan's accession to the next round of TPP negotiations could be effectively vetoed by Beijing. If either the TPP or the RCEP were concluded without Taiwan's participation and without a clear path to eventual membership, the impacts on Taiwan's trade-dependent economy and long-term prosperity could be severe.[17]

A third trend presented a strategic opportunity: the mainland Chinese economy was booming. In 2007, it was near the peak of its reform-era expansion and posting official GDP growth rates of 10–14 percent a year. The intoxicating allure of PRC growth was reinforced by the many visible manifestations of rising prosperity apparent to any regular visitor: the rapid construction of ambitious new infrastructure projects, including a nationwide high-speed rail system, highways, metro systems, and dozens of new ports and airports; the forests of construction cranes and new buildings dotting the glittering skylines of major Chinese cities; booming stock markets in Shanghai and Shenzhen; and the massive increases in Chinese tourists, first internally and then, increasingly, to other countries in the region and beyond. The sheer size of China's population, combined with a rapidly growing wealthy elite and middle class with disposable income, promised enormous new markets for Taiwanese businesses if they could expand their operations on the mainland. And it presented an obvious way to improve Taiwan's long-term trajectory: hitch the Taiwanese economy to the Chinese growth engine right across the Strait, and let it be pulled along.[18]

Ma's Grand Strategy: Opening Through Accommodation

These concurrent trends—economic sluggishness in Taiwan, competitive trade liberalization in the Asia Pacific, and a booming mainland Chinese economy—together powerfully shaped the opportunities facing the Ma administration at the beginning of his tenure. In hindsight, it appears almost inevitable that President Ma would risk his presidency on a grand strategy of accommodation with the PRC to reap economic and diplomatic benefits for Taiwan. This strategy had four major components.

First and foremost, Ma had to find diplomatic language to describe the cross-Strait relationship that was acceptable to Beijing, yet did not foreclose the ROC's claims to independent sovereignty or require taking a position unpopular with the Taiwanese voting public. The formula that his advisers hit upon was to skirt the sovereignty question by referring to a "consensus" on a "one-China principle" implicitly agreed upon at the first meeting between the semiofficial SEF and ARATS in November 1992 in Hong Kong. The consensus was that both sides would agree that Taiwan was "part of China," but could state their own respective interpretations about what "China" was.

The KMT's position at this meeting was that "China" referred to the ROC, which it still upheld as the rightful government of all of China, including the mainland Chinese territories that had been outside its control since 1949. The CCP's position was that "China" referred only to the People's Republic of China, and that the ROC did not exist as a separate sovereign state. This difference had up to that point been irreconcilable, as the PRC side refused to move on to substantive matters without first receiving an explicit endorsement of its version of the one-China principle. But in this case, a diplomatic sleight of hand allowed talks to proceed. PRC representatives accepted a KMT proposal that the two sides "make respective statements [about the one-China principle] through verbal announcements," and they then made no comment on the "respective interpretations" part of the Taiwanese position. In their subsequent communications with KMT leaders, Beijing's representatives followed the practice of simply ignoring the "respective interpretations" clause, neither endorsing nor rejecting it.[19]

The term "1992 Consensus" itself did not come into use until years later, when KMT strategist Su Chi suggested it as a convenient shorthand for the version of the one-China principle endorsed at the 1992 SEF-ARATS meeting. The political value in this ambiguous phrase was that the PRC also accepted it: Beijing's representatives let it be known that they would not raise objections if Ma simply stated, in response to questions about the nature of the cross-Strait relationship, that he "accepted the 1992 Consensus." Once Ma took office, this became the password that unlocked the door to cross-Strait talks on matters of real, practical concern.[20]

The second component of Ma's grand strategy was to emphasize economic and cultural exchanges in the cross-Strait relationship, and to focus on reaping as many concrete gains as quickly as possible from greater integration with the mainland Chinese economy. The first and most conspicuous of these changes was to the tourism industry. Less than a month after his inauguration, Ma's team signed their first two agreements with the PRC side: one set the terms under which mainland tourists could come to Taiwan, and the other established rules for direct, cross-Strait charter flights that would bring those tourists to the island. Shortly after, the first flights started to arrive, and Chinese tour groups, with their distinctive hats, tour leader flags, and mainland accents were soon a common sight around the island. Subsequent agreements eased the way for better direct transportation and mail connections and established a mechanism for cooperation on inspection of food imports.

The third component of this strategy was to seek greater space to operate in the diplomatic arena. A crucial goal of accommodation with Beijing was to create room for Taiwan to join other regional trading arrangements, potentially including both the TPP and RCEP. Beijing's influence in the region was already too great for Taiwan to overcome its open opposition, but with a cooperative relationship in other domains the Ma administration could hope for acquiescence on Taiwan's independent participation in regional trade negotiations. Ma also sought to obtain a moratorium on the costly and unseemly competition for diplomatic recognition, as well as meaningful participation in other regional and international bodies. The first he managed to secure quite quickly, as the PRC immediately halted the open wooing of Taiwan's diplomatic allies that it had engaged in during the Chen era. Any countries with which the ROC maintained formal relations at the beginning of the Ma era would no longer be enticed to switch; in fact, in one case Beijing even refused to establish diplomatic ties with Gambia after it unilaterally ended recognition of Taipei. The Ma administration had more limited success in securing a seat at the table in international bodies, but it could still point to tangible improvements: beginning in 2009, it was granted observer status at the World Health Assembly (WHA) under the name "Chinese Taipei," and in 2013 it was granted the same at the International Civil Aviation Organization (ICAO).

The final component of Ma's grand strategy was to implement structural reforms of the domestic economy. These ranged from changing laws and rules to encourage foreign direct investment, to lowering corporate income tax to entice multinational corporations to domicile on the island. Initially at least, this part of the agenda also included privatization of some of Taiwan's remaining state-owned enterprises and liberalization of the banking system, although the spread of the global financial crisis quickly caused the Ma administration to backtrack on many of the boldest of these reforms.[21]

Dangerous Shoals: How Ma's Grand Strategy Foundered

Ultimately, Ma's grand strategy did not deliver the intended transformation of Taiwan's domestic economy and international opportunities. Many of the economic challenges that worried critics in Taiwan were as serious at the end of Ma's eight years in office as they had been at the beginning: stagnant wages, high youth unemployment, widening wealth and income gaps, low foreign direct investment, sluggish new business creation and growth, and offshoring of industrial production. The strategy that the Ma administration had developed to address these concerns depended on several assumptions: that Taiwan would pick up momentum by riding the latest wave of global economic expansion, that the economic benefits of cross-Strait rapprochement and opening would be large and quite visible, that these benefits would be widespread, and that they could be obtained without compromising Taiwan's sovereignty or its security. On each of these dimensions, Ma's strategy came up short.

The Modest Economic Benefits of Cross-Strait Rapprochement

First, the overall record of economic growth during the Ma years ended up no better than that of the Chen Shui-bian era (see Figure 1.2). The "6-3-3" targets that Ma had emphasized in his first presidential campaign were very ambitious, even before the global financial crisis hit with full force in 2008–2009 and threw Taiwan's economy into a sharp recession. In 2008, Taiwan's nominal per capita GDP was below US$20,000, as Figure 1.3 shows; reaching $30,000 by the end of Ma's second term, as he later clarified was what he had meant, would require annual per capita growth in income (not merely the size of the economy) of about 6.5 percent over the following eight years. His target growth rate for the economy of 6 percent was less fanciful, but still would have required returning to a pace of economic expansion that had not occurred regularly in Taiwan since 1995. The onset of the global financial crisis and the ensuing Great Recession pulled the rug out from under the feet

Figure 1.2   Annual GDP Change in Taiwan by Quarter, 2000–2019

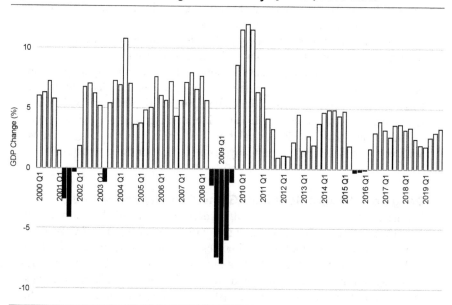

Source: Directorate General of Budget, Accounting, and Statistics, Republic of China (Taiwan).

of Ma's economic team, and the international economic downturn made his original growth target appear even more unrealistic.

Taiwan's unemployment rate had also remained well above 4 percent for the entire previous administration (see Figure 1.4), which suggested that reducing it below 3 percent would require more than just a few quarters of rapid economic expansion. This headline number also hid great heterogeneity and a widening gap across age cohorts: while total unemployment in 2007 was at 4 percent, the rate was significantly higher among those aged twenty-four to twenty-nine at over 6 percent, and the rate among those aged twenty to twenty-four ranged between 10 and 12 percent. This gap had grown considerably over the previous eight years, so that unemployment challenges appeared to be more and more concentrated among young workers. The disparity continued to worsen during the Ma era.

The silver lining in these disappointing headline numbers is that by comparison to other peer economies, Taiwan's performance was quite respectable. The implicit assumption behind Ma's "6-3-3" pledge—that Taiwan had seriously underperformed its economic potential and was lagging behind—is not self-evident in the economic data. Critics could point to more rapid GDP growth in Singapore and Hong Kong, two of the other Asian Tigers—but these were small city-states without rural hinterlands

Figure 1.3   Nominal GDP per Capita in Asia, 2000–2018

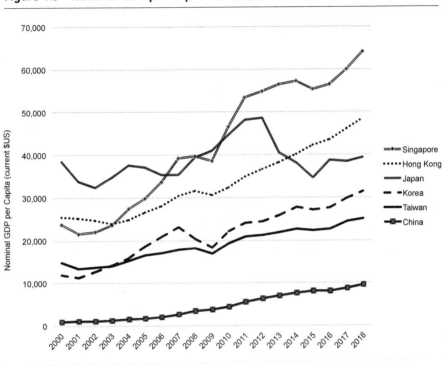

Source: IMF WEO Database, April 2019.

that also were major tax havens, and thus made a very imperfect comparison. A better peer to measure Taiwan up against is South Korea. The use of GDP in current US dollars to compare per-capita incomes across countries, as Ma did in the campaign, can be a bit misleading; while South Korea's per capita income was US$5,000 higher than Taiwan's in 2007, Korean prices were also much higher, as any Taiwanese who has attempted to buy a latte in Seoul is well aware. At purchasing power parity (PPP), as Figure 1.5 shows, Taiwan's adjusted per capita GDP was actually about 18 percent higher than Korea's in 2007. Strikingly, it was also rapidly approaching the level of Japan's, which it passed for the first time in 2009. This gap has continued to widen in subsequent years, so that Taiwan's PPP-adjusted per capita GDP is now about 10 percent higher than Japan's, and 15 percent higher than Korea's—a fact that is often overlooked in discussions of Taiwan's supposed economic stagnation. It is only in comparison with rapid economic growth in the PRC—which is growing from a much lower per capita level—that Taiwan's economic performance looks weak.

Figure 1.4   Taiwan's Official Monthly Unemployment Rate, 2000–2020

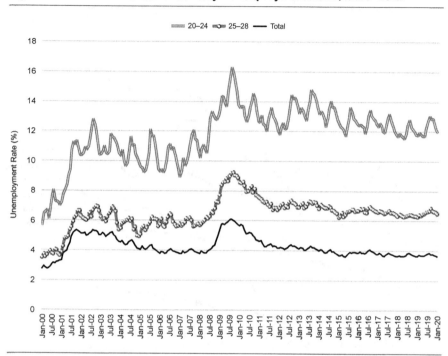

Source: Directorate General of Budget, Accounting, and Statistics, Republic of China (Taiwan).

Who Benefits? Widening Inequality During the Ma Era

As in much of the industrialized world, growing wealth and income inequality became a salient political issue in Taiwan during the Ma era. In industrialized countries, greater integration into the global economy has brought along greater returns to education and an erosion of opportunities for high-paying blue-collar work. In addition, trade agreements almost always produce both domestic winners and losers, and they typically contribute to increases in inequality in the short run. The political consequences of this economic bifurcation—of geographic places and social classes increasingly plugged into the global economy, and those isolated from it and in danger of being left behind—have been especially stressful for democracies.[22] One can point to many cases in the 2010s of sharp political upheavals that can be traced in part back to rising inequality, ranging from the Brexit vote in the United Kingdom to the rise of Marine Le Pen in France to the election of Donald Trump in the United States.

Taiwan was also vulnerable to this kind of political reaction by those "left behind." For its part, the Ma administration consistently tried to avoid

Figure 1.5   Purchasing Power Parity–Adjusted GDP per Capita in Asia, 2000–2016

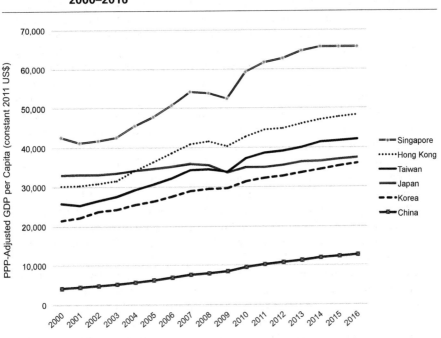

Source: MF WEO Database, April 2019.

discussion of the downsides of trade agreements with the PRC, and it was not effective at identifying and promising compensation for those who might lose out under greater economic openness. The "early harvest" of cross-Strait agreements produced clear benefits, but these proved in many cases to be concentrated narrowly, in specific sectors of the economy and even specific firms. Critics of the Chinese tourist trade, for instance, noted that a handful of well-connected companies captured the majority of this business, bringing tourist groups en masse to the same handful of restaurants, shops, and hotels in return for payoffs from those businesses.[23] Independent travelers from other countries, by contrast, tended to visit and spend money at a much wider array of establishments, diffusing the benefits of tourism more broadly throughout the economy.

The Ma administration also made little effort to mitigate rising inequality. During the 1970s, Taiwan had one of the lowest income gaps in the world—one component of the "economic miracle" that had both produced rapid growth and shared the gains of that growth widely among the Taiwanese people. But beginning in the early 1980s, Taiwan's measures of income and wealth inequality began a steady rise, one that halted only during recessions, and only temporarily.[24] Moreover, Taiwan's income gap data, which are drawn from government surveys of households rather than tax returns, also significantly underestimate inequality: in other countries where both kinds of data are available, the richest respondents massively underreport income and wealth on surveys.[25] Thus, by the time Ma Ying-jeou took office, the gap in opportunities between white- and blue-collar workers, the increasing gains to be had by investing in the real estate market relative to hourly employment, and the regional disparities between rural and urban areas and between greater Taipei and the rest of the island, all combined to make inequality a potentially salient political issue.[26]

Taiwan's tax structure contributed to this problem as well: it taxed income and sales heavily, and capital gains lightly or not at all.[27] Salaried workers, for instance, faced a progressive income tax rate that topped out at 40 percent, while investors in the stock market paid only a "transaction tax" on purchases or sales of stock and did not face additional taxes on capital gains. Other investment income was also taxed very lightly, including rental income and gains from buying and selling real estate, and property taxes were also relatively low. The additional pillars of the tax system were a business tax and a value-added tax (VAT).[28] The latter was especially regressive in its effects: the poor paid more of their income in VAT than did the rich. The overall effect of this system was that the Taiwanese government captured only 12 to 14 percent of GDP in a given year in tax receipts—a ratio that put it well below its contemporaries in Japan (31 percent) and South Korea (28 percent), and even slightly below the Philippines (18 percent).[29] Even if we include mandatory health insurance premiums paid by most Taiwanese, they added up to at most another 5 percent of GDP, so that the Taiwanese state's sources of revenues were surprisingly limited relative to the vibrancy of its economy and its administrative capacity.

A serious attempt to address rising inequality would have had to address this unbalanced tax system. But President Ma showed little interest in attempting that kind of political fight. His own attempts to reform the tax system initially moved it in the opposite direction: in an effort to boost the economy during the recession, his administration instead lowered business, inheritance, and stock transaction taxes in 2009–2010.[30]

A final contributing factor to rising social discontent came from an unlikely source: unemployed college graduates. In the 1990s, Taiwan's political leaders enthusiastically supported a massive expansion of higher education, founding new universities and upgrading vocational schools to four-year colleges throughout the island. The effect of this expansion was to rapidly cheapen the value of a Taiwanese university degree, which had previously been accessible only to those high school students with high test scores, and thus was a strong signal of elite pedigree. By the late 2000s, however, most anyone who wanted to attend college could get admitted somewhere; combined with a dramatic demographic crunch, universities began to struggle to meet enrollment targets, and eventually many of the less prestigious ones were forced to merge or close as their student numbers dropped. The political consequences of this expansion were complex, but one effect was, paradoxically, to worsen the employment prospects of students admitted to the best universities in Taiwan in non-STEM (science, technology, engineering, and mathematics) disciplines. For instance, one study found that students from the humanities and social sciences at National Taiwan University were among the most overrepresented of all Sunflower Movement participants.[31]

The net effect of these trends, and the Ma administration's unwillingness or inability to tackle rising income inequality and a widening wealth gap, eventually undermined confidence in the larger political project of cross-Strait rapprochement.

Rising Dependence on the PRC: Threats to Sovereignty and Security

The third key assumption that Ma's grand strategy rested on was that Taiwan could reap the benefits of greater economic integration without making concessions to either its sovereignty or its security. Ma's team was confident that the PRC threat could be managed, and they were willing to err on the side of greater openness in order to reap economic benefits.

There were obvious political and security concerns about this strategy. But it is easy now to forget that the political trends in the PRC did not look nearly as problematic in 2008 as they did a decade later, at the time of this writing. Hu Jintao was still CCP general party secretary, and the political views of successor-in-waiting Xi Jinping remained a mystery to the outside world. Under Hu, if one looked closely one could see signs of a regime engaging in political experiments and moving, however tentatively, in the direction of greater political openness and institutionalization. One of Hu's signature reforms, for instance, was to promote greater transparency and procedural fairness in the political system: local governments were encouraged to post laws and regulations online, hold public hearings and conduct public opinion surveys about major policy changes, and even commence experiments in deliberative democracy.[32] Another Hu-era reform was to introduce competition for local people's congresses, requiring that more than one candidate contest each available seat.[33] Despite repeated crackdowns, civil society organizations expanded during the Hu era as well, including activist groups such as human rights lawyers and feminists that took on increasingly sensitive political issues. There is evidence of increasing independence and professionalism of Chinese courts during this period, particularly in commercial cases that did not touch on sensitive political issues.[34]

And China's media industry, too, became more and more commercialized, leading to greater competition for scoops and harder-hitting reporting that, though it had to steer clear of sensitive topics and could never criticize the top party leadership, nevertheless managed to break critical exposés of local government malfeasance that led to higher-level intervention.[35]

Only later, starting around 2010, were these reforms visibly stalled or reversed, and organizations and spaces independent of CCP control or monitoring closed off again. Thus, for a leader like Ma, who was predisposed to pursue friendly relations with the authorities in Beijing, the political problems of working with the CCP and of integrating Taiwan's economy more closely with the Chinese mainland seemed, if not simple, at least manageable. And if the security and sovereignty threats could be mitigated, Taiwan's preexisting geographical, cultural, historical, and economic ties made it better-placed than any other country in the region to take advantage of Chinese economic growth. Taiwanese businesses had rapidly increased their investments in the PRC during the Chen Shui-bian era, despite the combative cross-Strait political relationship. But deeper economic integration would require relaxing trade and investment barriers, encouraging people-to-people exchanges, and removing numerous practical hurdles to bilateral exchange—steps that Ma was willing to take for the sake of his economic agenda.

In hindsight, this bet, too, failed to pay off. Ma's cross-Strait integration efforts coincided with two fundamental political shifts in the PRC that left his approach looking obsolete by the end of his second term. The first of these was increasing CCP confidence, bordering on triumphalism, about the relative decline and dysfunction of Western democracies after the global financial crisis.[36] The PRC's ability to stave off an economic meltdown due to its party-state control over financial institutions, and its ability to supply enormous amounts of liquidity into its financial system, produced a better policy response to this downturn than in the West, and it gave critics of greater economic liberalization the upper hand in internal CCP debates. The share of economic output produced by state-owned enterprises began to rise again, and they maintained their privileged access to domestic capital through the state-run banking system. The financial crisis also made China an indispensable partner in the global economy in a way that it had not been before. The PRC's behavior in the interstate system changed significantly after this moment, including its rapid expansion of artificial islands in the South China Sea, greater assertiveness in international organizations, and a concerted effort to expand its economic might and influence abroad through the One Belt One Road (OBOR) project (later rebranded in English as the Belt and Road Initiative [BRI]) and the creation of the Asian Infrastructure Investment Bank (AIIB).[37]

The second shift in the PRC was, paradoxically, a rising paranoia among CCP leaders about domestic threats to their rule, and deep suspicion of any spaces in the political system and civil society where independent actors could still operate. (The ascension of Xi Jinping to power as the general party secretary of the CCP coincides with this trend, but should probably be seen as a trailing indicator rather than a cause of the change, given that the crackdown on independent actors outside the party clearly preceded Xi.)[38] Along with continued tightening of party control over domestic spheres of communication, Xi doubled down on CCP efforts to influence public opinion abroad. An increasing share of Chinese-language media in many Western democracies, for instance, came under the ownership of pro-Beijing businesses and became less critical of the PRC. Chinese embassies and consulates stepped up efforts to keep tabs on and influence ethnic Chinese communities abroad, and the expansion of Confucius Institutes and rising dependence on the tuition dollars that Chinese students paid narrowed or eliminated the discussion on many university campuses of topics that the CCP held to be verboten—including the political status of Taiwan.[39]

These fundamental shifts in the PRC changed the nature of the regime that the Ma administration sought to work with: the China of 2016 was far different from the China of 2008. Ma found it increasingly hard to defend an image of the government in Beijing as one that, while rigidly committed to Taiwan's eventual unification with the mainland, was otherwise mostly benevolent in its actions toward the island's people. The continued tightening of CCP control over Chinese society and the economic system increased the salience of sovereignty and security concerns among the Taiwanese public, and it ultimately made Ma's task of selling rapprochement much more difficult.

Outline of the Book

The chapters in this volume provide a variety of perspectives on politics in Taiwan during the Ma Ying-jeou years. Together they cover four aspects of Taiwan's democratic development: party politics and elections; democratic institutions and governance; public opinion and civil society; and looking outward.

Part 1: Party Politics and Elections

Part 1 covers the major elections of 2012 and 2016 and developments in Taiwan's party politics.[40] In Chapter 2, Shelley Rigger leads off with an analysis of the 2012 presidential and legislative elections, in which Ma Ying-jeou and the KMT legislative majority were reelected in the face of a strong challenge from Tsai Ing-wen and the DPP. The debates, controversies, and outcomes of these elections, Rigger argues, were a reflection of both Taiwan's maturing democracy and its narrowing options for changing its international status. Twelve years under Chen Shui-bian and Ma Ying-jeou had made clear just how tight the constraints on Taiwan's policy choices had become. Both Beijing and Washington had resisted Chen's efforts to expand Taiwan's international space, and while both initially rewarded Ma's more constrained and accommodating policy direction, Beijing's long-term goal of unification did not change. For Taiwanese voters, these external forces were part of a set of difficult questions about how best to improve the island's economic trajectory, as post-industrialization and globalization reshaped social relations in ways that left many Taiwanese deeply dissatisfied.

Ma's landslide victory in 2008 was driven in part by excessive expectations about what he could deliver for the economy. As these deflated and the global financial crisis threw Taiwan's economy into a sharp recession, Ma's public approval ratings slumped into the low thirties, and he appeared vulnerable to defeat by a reinvigorated DPP led by chairwoman Tsai Ing-wen (perhaps aided by a third-party run by former KMT member and PFP chairman James Soong). But in the end, the 2012 election campaign was tempered by realism, and boiled down to a contest of credibility between candidates and parties that Taiwanese voters already knew well. Both the KMT and DPP kept their promises modest, and both leading presidential candidates sought to portray themselves as guardians of the status quo, although they defined that status quo differently. While the race was hard-fought and both sides landed some stinging blows, the campaign's respective visions focused more on practical problems and realistic solutions, moving the election away from the pattern of ideological polarization that characterized previous contests.

Ultimately, Rigger argues, the majority of voters decided that giving Ma Ying-jeou a second term was the safer choice. Ma carried 51.6 percent of the vote to Tsai Ing-wen's 45.6 percent, a much narrower margin than in the previous contest, but still a clear win. (Soong's third-party spoiler campaign drew little support in the end as voters concentrated on the Ma-Tsai contest.) In the Legislative Yuan contests, the KMT lost a net total of 8 seats but retained a majority of 64 seats in the 113-seat body. After gaining 6 seats in by-elections in 2009–2010, the DPP continued its recovery from its disastrous 2008 showing, picking up an additional 7 seats to put it at 40. Under Legislative Yuan rules, this increase to above one-third of the seats ensured the DPP could win co-convener positions on most legislative committees, giving the party considerably more influence over the legislative process. And the PFP and TSU, both minor parties that had been shut out in the 2008 elections, each managed to obtain enough party-list votes to cross the 5 percent threshold; both held three seats in the new legislature, giving them each the right to form a party caucus and participate in cross-party negotiations.[41] Thus, although the KMT retained its majority, it faced a much more challenging legislative environment in Ma's second term than in his first.

One of the most surprising and consequential political developments during this period was the rapid revival of the DPP. After its devastating setbacks in the 2008 elections, the former ruling party appeared hopelessly defeated, divided, and demoralized. The DPP's presidential candidate Frank Hsieh had won under 42 percent of the vote, and the party retained less than a quarter of the seats in the Legislative Yuan under a new, more majoritarian electoral system. Some observers thought it would take a generation or more for the party to recover as a serious electoral force, if it ever did. Yet within two years the DPP was again running competitive campaigns for most local offices and had recovered considerable ground in public opinion.

A key element in this rapid turnaround was the emergence of Tsai Ing-wen as party chairwoman. Prior to her entry into the contest for chair in 2008, Tsai was an outsider to the DPP leadership, without either a power base inside the party or much of a public profile. Thus it is a bit perplexing how she managed not only to win the chair's position but also gradually to build up a position of dominance within the DPP that cleared the field for her to be the party's presidential nominee in both 2012 and 2016. In Chapter 3, Austin Wang explains the resurgence of the DPP, and Tsai Ing-wen's emergence as its clear-cut leader, as the consequence of four factors. First, the depth of the DPP's 2008 defeat led to a consensus in the party that something fundamental had to change, and Tsai offered a clean break with the past: she was a moderate, not linked to any faction, relatively young (fifty-one at the time) and a woman, and had never run for political office on her own before. She had joined the party only four years before, and her most recent previous political experience was as deputy premier under Su Tseng-chang from 2006 to 2007. In the party chair's election in May 2008, she won a decisive 57 percent of DPP member votes, besting the much older, pro-independence firebrand Koo Kwang-ming. Second, because Tsai did not belong to any faction, she emerged as a compromise candidate acceptable to all the major DPP power-brokers. Her consensus-oriented personality and management style also won over critics and allowed her gradually to centralize authority within the party without openly threatening the position of party heavyweights. Third, Tsai managed to push through several institutional reforms that improved the party's electoral prospects: she replaced closed primaries with public opinion surveys to choose district legislative and council candidates, personally negotiated who the party would put up in local executive races rather than holding intraparty competitions, and centralized nominations for the legislative party list. When the DPP won several legislative by-elections in a row and actually obtained more votes than the KMT did in local elections in 2009–2010, many party members were convinced that the DPP was on the right path under Tsai's leadership and would be competitive in 2012 and beyond. Finally, Tsai and the DPP headquarters invested considerable resources in developing a centralized and sophisticated social media campaign for the 2012 and 2016 general elections, providing a standardized set of recommendations about branding, website design, microtargeting, and live-streaming events for all the party's candidates. The centralization of the DPP's online campaign resources further strengthened Tsai's influence over the party's messaging and tactics.

Tsai retained these strengths within the DPP even after she lost the 2012 presidential race to Ma Ying-jeou. Though she had to resign as chairwoman, she was returned to that role after the Sunflower Movement sparked a wave of criticism of her successor, Su Tseng-chang. By the time of the 2016 campaign, Tsai's grip on the party was quite firm, and she had no challengers for the DPP nomination. Wang argues that the DPP was effectively "presidentialized"— with power centralized in the hands of the party's presidential candidate— even before Tsai Ing-wen was inaugurated as president in May 2016.

A similar transformation into a "presidentialized" party occurred within the KMT. As Nathan F. Batto explores at length in Chapter 4, Ma Ying-jeou's dominance over the KMT eventually reversed the traditional direction of accountability in that party: rather than the party leader serving at the pleasure of party elites and grassroots members and pursuing the KMT's collective goals, the president instead set the political agenda and used the party as a tool to serve his own political purposes. Batto focuses on two episodes that were critical to redefining the KMT's party image: the battle in 2013–2014 to pass the Cross-Strait Services Trade Agreement, and the debate in 2015 over whether to move away from the 1992 Consensus. In both of these episodes, grassroots KMT politicians resisted moves by President Ma to move the party in a more pro-China direction. Facing pressure from an electorate that was trending in the opposite direction, these politicians needed the KMT's position on cross-Strait relations to be attractive to the median voter, not to the party's deep-Blue base. Ma had a different calculation. After winning reelection in 2012, his focus was on implementing policies that would deepen the integration of Taiwan's economy with the Chinese mainland's, regardless of public opinion, and he proved willing to spend a tremendous amount of political capital to try to win passage of the CSSTA.

After Ma resigned as party chair following the KMT's sweeping defeat in the 2014 local elections, the ruling party was left without a clear leader—an unfamiliar situation for a presidentialized party, and one that touched off a struggle for primacy among Ma, new party chair Eric Chu, Legislative Yuan speaker Wang Jin-pyng, and the party's 2016 presidential nominee Hung Hsiu-chu, among other players. The battle over the KMT's China discourse took place in the midst of this power struggle. Hung, who came from the KMT's deep-Blue Chinese nationalist wing, moved away from the party's carefully crafted 1992 Consensus position and toward the PRC's preferred formulation of "one China, same interpretation," and she appeared indifferent to how her Chinese nationalist rhetoric would be received by the electorate. Most of the rest of the party resisted her rhetorical moves, but they dared not completely repudiate the views of someone they had nominated to be their presidential standard-bearer. Only in October 2015 did other party elites finally step in and execute a late switch of candidates, replacing Hung with the more moderate and experienced Chu, who duly returned to the party's previous messaging. But by then, the KMT appeared headed for certain defeat in the presidential race, and increasingly likely to lose its majority in the legislature as well. The repeated moves of its leaders—first Ma, then Hung—in a pro-Beijing direction had the effect of repositioning the party much further from the median voter on cross-Strait issues in 2016 than it had been in 2008 or 2012. Thus, the unprecedented repudiation of the party at the ballot box in 2016, Batto argues, had much to do with the failure of KMT leaders to follow shifts in public opinion on cross-Strait relations.

The 2016 elections were unprecedented in other ways as well. In the legislative elections, the DPP won a majority of the seats for the first time in its history, sweeping out many KMT incumbents whose long records of constituent service and dense political networks proved to be no match for the national anti-KMT wave. A record eighteen parties registered for the party-list vote, including several new parties that sprang up in the wake of the Sunflower Movement and the 2014 local elections. The most successful of these, the New Power Party (NPP), managed not only to cross the 5 percent party-list threshold but also to win three district seats, making it the third-largest party in the new legislature. As a sometime ally of the DPP, the NPP effectively replaced the TSU, which failed to cross the threshold and lost its three seats. Many commentators interpreted the 2016 election campaign as marking a fundamental break with the previous party system and expected the results to usher in a critical realignment around issues such as economic redistribution, labor rights, same-sex marriage, and environmental protection—issues unrelated to the China question that had long divided all parties in the legislature.

However, as Kharis Templeman argues in Chapter 5, this critical realignment did not actually happen. Taiwan's party system during the Ma years was remarkably stable and well-institutionalized for a young democracy: electoral volatility was low, partisanship was high, and both elites and masses were broadly committed to the legitimacy of electoral competition to decide who governs. In addition, Taiwan's two leading parties both featured strong party organizations with distinctive brands, clear differentiation of positions on Taiwan's relationship with the PRC, and loyal followings in the electorate.

Despite the striking headlines, Templeman argues that the 2016 elections did not mark a major realignment away from the long-standing pattern of Blue-versus-Green electoral competition, but rather a sharp swing toward the DPP and away from the KMT. The relative success of the NPP depended crucially on pre-electoral coordination with the DPP, whose voters supported its three winning district candidates at about the same rate that they did DPP nominees elsewhere. By contrast, all the other new "third force" parties that did not cooperate with the DPP and attempted to run on issues unrelated to the China cleavage fared much worse, all failing to win enough party-list votes to cross the 5 percent threshold for seats. Overall, there was little evidence to suggest that 2016 was a "critical election" that fundamentally reordered the previous pattern of party competition. The implication was that future elections, especially national-level ones, were still likely to feature a DPP-KMT duopoly and to turn on each party's positioning on the all-important China question.

And indeed, that pattern held true over the next four years. Tsai and the DPP suffered from a steep decline in popularity that began shortly after her inauguration, as many erstwhile supporters became increasingly disillusioned and frustrated with the Tsai administration's reform priorities. This dissatisfaction culminated in a shocking defeat for the DPP in the November 2018 local elections, when the party lost seven of the thirteen local executive positions it held—including the southern special municipality of Kaohsiung, a deep-Green city that most political observers had assumed would never elect a KMT candidate. Most noteworthy, however, is that the biggest beneficiary of the DPP's struggles in these elections was not the social movement–linked "third force" parties, but instead the KMT, which swept right back into power in many cities and counties that it had lost in 2014. Reports that the KMT was in terminal decline after the 2016 elections, it turned out, were greatly exaggerated, and the party again looked like a serious threat to unseat the DPP in 2020.

In the wake of the DPP's local election losses, Tsai was forced to resign as party chairwoman, and her path to reelection in January 2020 looked narrow and perilous. Yet she and the DPP enjoyed their own remarkable political turnaround in only a year's time—mostly thanks, once again, to the increasing salience of the China issue. Tsai's response to a speech on Taiwan given by Xi Jinping in January 2019 was widely lauded in the media and online, and it gave her approval ratings a much-needed boost. The sudden emergence in June of a new protest movement in Hong Kong against PRC political restrictions on the territory also heightened concerns in Taiwan about Beijing's intentions, and the CCP's tone-deaf response further eroded what little appeal remained of the one-country, two-systems model that Xi had offered as the formula for unification.

Tsai also won a contested DPP primary for the presidential nomination against her former premier, William Lai. Though this challenge at first looked like it might fatally damage the DPP's electoral chances, Tsai rallied the party behind her and eventually even added Lai to the ticket as the vice presidential candidate, helping the party to close ranks in time for the elections. Tsai was also helped when two prominent political figures who had flirted with an independent run decided not to enter the race: Taipei mayor Ko Wen-je instead founded a new political party, the Taiwan People's Party, and Terry Gou, chairman of the manufacturing giant Foxconn, decided to back the PFP instead. Thus the presidential election once again turned into a straight-up Blue-versus-Green contest. Finally, the KMT nominated as its presidential candidate Han Kuo-yu, a populist-styled politician who had pulled off the stunning upset victory in the Kaohsiung mayor's race in 2018. Han began his term as mayor with high popularity ratings, and polls taken in the early spring showed him leading Tsai Ing-wen by twenty percentage points or more. But Han made no concessions in his rhetoric about cross-Strait relations even as the Hong Kong protests ignited, instead doubling down on Ma's talk about opening up to the PRC and making vague promises that Taiwan would have economic prosperity without compromising its security under his watch. With relations between the United States and the PRC at their rockiest in decades, and a rising sense of political doom engulfing young generations in Hong Kong, Tsai increasingly looked like the safer choice to protect Taiwan's sovereignty and security. Han's support in the polls steadily declined, and by the late fall he appeared almost hopelessly behind.

In the end, Tsai Ing-wen won reelection with 57 percent of the vote—an even greater share than she had carried in 2016, and on much higher turnout—and the DPP held on to its majority in the legislature. Han's rhetoric excited and mobilized the deep-Blue KMT base to turn out in high numbers, but his failure to articulate a credible vision for how to protect Taiwan's security in the face of a rising threat from the PRC made him unappealing to much of the rest of the electorate—especially to the "naturally independent" generation of voters under age forty, who also turned out at high rates to support Tsai. The 2020 election results thus provided further evidence that the China issue in Taiwanese politics was not fading away, and that the party system would continue to be structured around how best to manage the island's fraught and complicated relationship with the PRC.

Part 2: Democratic Institutions and Governance

The chapters in Part 2 cover the performance of Taiwan's core political institutions during the Ma era. One of the most perplexing patterns of the Ma presidency was his struggle to win approval for his ambitious policy agenda, despite enjoying a huge KMT majority in the legislature, a resounding electoral mandate for a shift in policy, and an enormous concentration of formal institutional power in his hands. Over Ma's two terms, only about half of all bills that the Executive Yuan introduced to the legislature were actually adopted in some form. In Chapter 6, Yun-han Chu and Yu-tzung Chang explain these struggles as a consequence of the decline of governing capacity of the political system. A wide range of factors—structural, institutional, and ideological—combined to create daunting challenges for the Ma administration in most areas of policy. Taiwan's eroding international competitiveness, aging population, and worsening fiscal capacity limited the resources available to Ma's government to advance new initiatives. The legislature turned out to be hard to control even under "unified" one-party rule, as the opposition DPP, Legislative Yuan Speaker Wang Jin-pyng, and individual legislators all found ways to delay, block, or significantly modify priority legislation introduced by the Executive Yuan. The legislature's greater role in policy formation also created many new access points for stakeholders to object to policy change, or to carve out exceptions for individual interest groups, industries, or firms. The capacity and autonomy of the vaunted "developmental state" bureaucracy that had overseen Taiwan's postwar economic miracle had also declined, and Ma oversaw a collection of ministries that were constrained by unprecedented scrutiny from civil society groups and legislators, additional accounting and ethics rules, and other burdensome checks on their freedom of action. They also faced a media industry dominated by either openly partisan or excessively sensationalist outlets, and the growth of social media use further undermined the traditional Taiwanese deference to expertise and objective policy analysis. Finally, a new cohort of "young rebels" who had been educated under the new Taiwan-centric educational curriculum emerged on the political scene during Ma's second term, and they became especially effective at social mobilization and symbolic politics. Together, these factors caught the Ma administration off-guard and left it at a loss for how to respond to the opposition to the CSSTA that burst into the open in 2013–2014. As a consequence, Chu and Chang argue, the governing capacity of the political system became so degraded during the Ma era that it was simply no longer able to respond effectively to the many international and domestic policy challenges that Taiwan faced.

One of the key constraints on rationalized policymaking in Taiwan is the ascendance of the Legislative Yuan and its unusual structure and organization. Curiously, winning a majority *in* the legislature does not guarantee a party complete control *over* the legislature (a fact that is not well understood even by most who are acquainted with Taiwanese politics). As Isaac Shih-hao Huang and Shing-yuan Sheng explain in Chapter 7, the Legislative Yuan is quite decentralized in comparison to most other representative assemblies around the world. Neither the government nor the majority party is consistently able to set the legislative agenda. Bills drafted and introduced by the Executive Yuan are given no special priority on the docket over any other proposed legislation. The majority party cannot block opposition parties from submitting their own bills and, under some conditions, bringing these up for review in committee instead of majority versions. Thus, individual legislators and opposition parties are provided with multiple points of access in the legislative process. Political party caucuses, too, no matter how large or small, are given equal bargaining rights in a peculiar institution known as the party negotiation mechanism (PNM), which functions as a kind of "super-committee" of last resort to resolve interparty disputes of all kinds. Agreements struck within the PNM are binding on all party caucuses and read into the legislative record without a roll-call vote—in effect a form of approval by unanimous consent. During the Ma era, about half of all successful legislation was adopted under these rules, which required agreement from all party caucus representatives. Thus, KMT control over the Legislative Yuan was more mirage than reality for much of the Ma era.

Another critical part of Taiwan's democratic system is its "watchdog institutions"—the Judicial Yuan and Control Yuan, the prosecutor's offices under the Ministry of Justice in the Executive Yuan, and other specialized investigative and ethics bodies. These were the focus of significant public scrutiny and dissatisfaction during the Ma era. In 2010, a major scandal broke when three High Court justices and a top prosecutor were arrested for taking bribes, leading to the resignation of the chief and deputy chief justices of the Judicial Yuan. Ma's response was to create the Agency Against Corruption (AAC), an office within the Ministry of Justice tasked specifically with investigating political corruption. As Christian Göbel details in Chapter 8, this new agency blurred the previous division of labor between other watchdog bodies, most notably the Ministry of Justice's Investigation Bureau and the ethics bureaus embedded into most government branches. Although the creation of the AAC came with considerable fanfare, Göbel argues that it brought little additional benefit to existing anticorruption efforts and imposed significant costs, and it never was able to shake the accusation that its investigations were politically motivated. Wiretapping also increased dramatically compared to the previous Chen Shui-bian administration, including the Legislative Yuan's own phone lines, as the case involving Speaker Wang Jin-pyng revealed. Political accountability in the Ma era did not revert back to the "bad old days" of KMT dominance, when corruption was embedded in the political system to the highest levels; instead, it had much more in common with the previous Chen Shui-bian era. Nevertheless, given high public concern about political corruption and rising distrust of the government, politicians, and political parties, the relatively minor reforms of accountability institutions attempted during the Ma era represent a significant missed opportunity to strengthen their legitimacy, and that of Taiwan's democracy.

Part 2 ends with a critique of Taiwan's economic institutions. Taiwan's economic performance over the past two decades appears disappointing for a couple reasons: its domestic investment as a share of GDP is consistently low, and its foreign direct investment has been at or near the bottom of world rankings for some time. Taiwan's "developmental state" model, based on a high-capacity regulatory state, government control over key "upstream" sectors (such as banking, energy, and transportation), foreign exchange and capital controls, and government-directed investment into strategic growth sectors such as electronics, semiconductors, and biotechnology—all managed by technocrats who operated with little pressure or scrutiny from interest groups or the legislature—had produced an economic "miracle" that featured rapid growth with low inequality. But by the 2000s, this model appeared to have run out of steam. Taiwan's annual growth rates fell significantly, from 6.6 percent for the 1990s to 4.9 percent for 2000–2007. Starting salaries stagnated: adjusted for inflation, college graduates entering the work force in 2016 earned no more on average than their predecessors did in 1997.

In Chapter 9, Pei-shan Lee argues that this economic stagnation can be traced back to the failure to craft a new developmental paradigm, one in which democratic governments could still effectively promote and guide economic growth despite facing new scrutiny and pressure from media, the legislature, and interest groups. The rising influence of groups that objected to elements of the old developmental state model—nuclear energy, environmental degradation, weak labor rights protections, and so forth—made the old ways of directing economic policy increasingly unworkable. But this old model was not replaced by a new economic governance structure that was able to address long-standing economic problems, promote entrepreneurship and dynamism, and provide an effective social safety net while still deepening Taiwan's economic integration with the rest of the world. The Chen Shui-bian administration failed to rise to this challenge, as divided government, polarized politics, and Chen's increasing focus on a symbolic independence agenda hindered the development of a political consensus behind a new economic paradigm. But the Ma administration also failed to craft a new model, despite more politically favorable circumstances. Both administrations suffered from what Lee argues is an "unsuccessful transition" from authoritarian to democratic governance, in which the ascendance of individualistic and group-based policy appeals and a new rights-based political discourse have given rise to an "anti-developmentalist populism" that has blocked creation of a new economic policy consensus for the democratic era.

Part 3: Public Opinion and Civil Society

The chapters in Part 3 cover important trends in Taiwanese public opinion, as well as the origins and patterns of a sharp rise in social activism during the Ma era. In Chapter 10, Yu-tzung Chang and Yun-han Chu draw on several rounds of survey data collected for the Asian Barometer Survey (ABS) project to examine trends in support for democracy. They find a mixed picture. On the positive side, the liberal democratic value orientation of Taiwanese has steadily increased since the late 1990s: public opinion data show rising support for the principles of political equality, popular accountability of leaders, political liberties, checks-and-balances on government officials, and pluralism. They also find consistent increases in the share of respondents saying that democracy is suitable for Taiwan, and expressing what they call "authoritarian detachment"—the rejection of all authoritarian alternatives to democracy. On the negative side, Chang and Chu find evidence of significant and repeated declines in levels of trust in democratic institutions. The large majority of Taiwanese now do not express trust in the president, courts, national government, political parties, and legislature. Trust in the civil service, military, and local governments, while significantly higher, has still fallen over the four ABS waves, and is now below half of all respondents in each case. The only major institution to record increases in public trust over the past two decades is the national police, which saw an uptick to above 50 percent in the most recent survey, in 2014. Overall, these results are consistent with a broader decline in trust in institutions in most democracies around the world, and they raise concerns about the long-term ability of Taiwan's democracy to sustain public support in the face of serious foreign and domestic policy challenges. But unlike in some other regimes threatened with democratic backsliding, the normative commitment to democratic values, and to democracy as the most preferable system of government, is now very high among Taiwanese, and it is highest among the youngest cohorts. Democratic values do appear to have become a part of the Taiwanese citizen's DNA.

In Chapter 11, Ching-hsin Yu examines trends in key public opinion indicators over the Ma era. Taiwan's partisan politics are consolidated around a two-party system centered on the KMT and DPP, and partisanship is relatively high for a young democracy, with between 55 and 60 percent of the electorate expressing a preference for a political party in public opinion polls. But the share of the electorate identifying with one or the other of the major parties shifted significantly during the Ma era: identification with the KMT dropped by nearly twenty points, from a high of 39.5 percent of respondents in 2011 to only 20.8 percent in 2016. Over the same time period, DPP partisans increased by about five points, from 24.9 to 29.9 percent. In addition, despite the KMT's apparent electoral dominance during much of the Ma era, the share of the electorate identifying as exclusively Taiwanese continued to rise over this period, until it leveled off after 2014. Yet the shares of the electorate favoring either independence or unification remained remarkably stable—and clear minorities—in every survey between 2008 and 2016: over the whole era, support for independence, either now or sometime in the future, increased only from 23.1 to 24.9 percent of respondents, and support for unification remained virtually unchanged, at 10.3 versus 10.2 percent. Instead, a large majority of Taiwanese continued to express support for maintaining the cross-Strait status quo. Thus, Yu argues, the increase in Taiwanese identity has had less to do with partisanship, attitudes toward cross-Strait relations, or short-term political competition, and more with the long-run effects of Taiwan's transition to democracy on different generational cohorts. Ma's rapprochement with the PRC did not lead to an increase in support for unification, but neither did it directly cause a rise in pro-independence attitudes.

What the Ma-era rapprochement did cause was a surge in protests and other social movement activities. As Dafydd Fell describes in Chapter 12, the scale, scope, and impact of social movements gradually increased over this period, culminating in the Sunflower Movement opposition to the CSSTA and occupation of the Legislative Yuan. Fell notes that the nature of activism, including who joined protests, changed significantly: during the Chen Shui-bian years, participants in street demonstrations were disproportionately older Taiwanese, but the social movements that emerged during the Ma presidency attracted a much younger set of activists. The targets of protests, too, gradually expanded, from relatively focused demonstrations—such as those against the visit of ARATS chairman Chen Yunlin to Taiwan in 2008 and the proposed construction of the Kuo-kuang Petrochemical Plant in Changhua in 2011—to a much broader coalition of protesters demonstrating about issues that ranged from indigenous land rights and LGBTQ issues to media control and constitutional reform. The members of activist groups gradually learned from one another, built personal relationships, and created a formidable network of grassroots organizations that could be mobilized quickly to demonstrate in the streets, disseminate information, and swing public opinion toward their cause. By the end of the Ma era, polls showed a marked increase in youth interest in politics and activism, and turnout among young voters hit historic highs. Fell argues that this surge in social protest was linked to the Ma administration's open hostility toward civil society groups that had enjoyed a voice in policymaking in the previous Lee and Chen administrations. The KMT suspected that most of these groups were working directly with the DPP, and so shut them out of decisionmaking processes, refused to engage in dialogue, and attempted to close down or to reshape many of the advisory bodies serving various government ministries. With few avenues to influence policy development inside the government, then, members of these groups increasingly directed their energy into the streets as the most effective way to express opposition to controversial decisions by the Ma administration.

In Chapter 13, Min-hua Huang and Mark Weatherall use four waves of ABS data to take a closer look at who these activists were: their ages, social and educational backgrounds, ideological orientations, and expressed motivations for participating in protests and other social movement activities. They find that, in contrast to the Chen Shui-bian era, protesters during the Ma years were younger, better-educated, more likely to believe that elected officials were corrupt, and more likely to express a strong Taiwanese identity, although somewhat surprisingly they were no more likely than the general population to express negative views about Chinese influence on Taiwan. Protest participants were also at least as fervently committed to democratic principles as were other Taiwanese, implying that, while they were directly challenging the legitimacy of some of Taiwan's core democratic institutions (such as the Legislative and Executive Yuans), they did not reject democracy as their preferred political system or express support for authoritarian alternatives. Thus, Huang and Weatherall argue, this deep reservoir of support for democracy helps explain how the Sunflower Movement standoff was ultimately defused peacefully and Taiwan's democratic institutions were able to survive largely intact.

One other distinguishing feature of protests during the Ma era was the widespread use of social media to aid in political mobilization. As Eric Chen-hua Yu and Jia-sin Yu document in Chapter 14, the increase in Internet penetration, prevalence of online news consumption, and use of social media accounts were all associated with an increase in political activism in Taiwan during the Ma years. Indeed, the transformation in how voters got their political news during this period was rapid and profound: in 2008, blogging on websites such as The Wretch was still a significant source of political commentary, including from high-profile political figures, but by 2016 Facebook had become the dominant platform on which to make political statements online. Yu and Yu note that several of the major protest events during the era initially relied mostly on online networks to mobilize protesters, including the Wild Strawberry demonstrations against the visit of ARATS chairman Chen Yunlin in 2008, the White-Shirt Army protests against the death of a conscript in military detention in 2013, and the Sunflower Movement protests against the CSSTA in 2014. Nevertheless, although online networking—or "cyber-mobilization"—made it easier to rally a crowd to turn out to the streets, it could not ultimately substitute for a lack of offline social movement structures. For instance, the Wild Strawberry demonstrations in 2008 eventually petered out because of a flat organizational structure without clear leadership, a small offline presence, and arguments over goals and tactics. It is easy to overlook that the rise in online mobilization during the Ma era also contributed to the more consequential creation of offline networks of activists, as demonstrators met each other and cooperated on protest events, built in-person relationships through shared experiences, and learned from each other about strategy, tactics, and tools. Thus the Sunflower Movement protests were ultimately so large and influential not merely because many of the participants were linked to each other on social media platforms like Facebook, PTT, LINE, or WhatsApp, but also because many preexisting activist groups, as well as political parties, joined the demonstrations and could draw on several years of experience organizing against the Ma administration.

Part 4: Looking Outward

The final part of this volume covers Taiwan's key relationships with the United States, Japan, and above all the People's Republic of China. In Chapter 15, Szu-yin Ho describes the strategy behind Ma Ying-jeou's cross-Strait policies, and the successes and ultimate limitations of the rapprochement that Ma initiated with Beijing. The key diplomatic challenge for Ma was to find a formula to describe cross-Strait relations that would be acceptable to Beijing, without compromising the ROC's claim to sovereignty and a separate, legitimate existence in the interstate system. The ambiguous 1992 Consensus was the result, and when Beijing made it known that it would not object to this formulation, Ma made it the centerpiece of his strategy for improving relations with the PRC. As Ho details, Ma's National Security Council used the 1992 Consensus formula to improve Taiwan's diplomatic position at three levels. First, at the symbolic level, Ma's endorsement of a form of one-China principle—albeit one carefully crafted to emphasize for a domestic audience that he did not intend to pursue unification—allowed his administration to find common ground on which to engage in negotiations about more substantive issues. Second, at the international level, Ma's team worried from the beginning about how Taiwan-PRC rapprochement would affect its other relationships, including the all-important one with the United States, and emphasized to its other partners and allies that Taipei's outreach to Beijing would be beneficial for all. Third, at the practical level, the Ma administration had to walk a tightrope on the many symbolic points of contention with Beijing—on the one hand, choosing its official language carefully, such as referring to the PRC as "mainland China" to be consistent with the ROC constitutional framework, but on the other routinely seeking to move beyond diplomatic hang-ups and get to real "nuts-and-bolts" issues in the cross-Strait relationship. Ho argues that Ma's strategy eventually produced significant benefits for Taiwan: his government was able to sign twenty-three agreements with the PRC, improve relationships with the United States and many other countries in the region, and not lose any more diplomatic allies. In late 2015, Ma was even able to meet on equal terms with CCP chairman Xi Jinping in a historic meeting in Singapore—the first in-person meeting between leaders of the two sides since the founding of the PRC in 1949. But the ultimate limitations of this grand strategy became apparent in Ma's second term, and Ho argues that they were rooted more in domestic factors than international or cross-Strait ones. The opposition DPP sharpened its attacks on rapprochement and reframed them in terms of the effects on the distribution of wealth, and the Ma administration struggled to rebut these criticisms. In addition, the "early harvest" agreements of Ma's first term had been "all gains, no pain"—the PRC lowered tariff barriers on imports much more than Taiwan did—but the CSSTA included concrete concessions by both sides that generated a deep sense of insecurity and sparked fierce opposition from the affected sectors. The politics of trade could also all too easily morph into the politics of identity: the prospect of mainland Chinese publishing houses operating in the Taiwanese publishing industry, for instance, was framed by opponents as an existential threat to Taiwan's distinct culture and its democratic practices and values. Thus, the Ma administration's grand strategy eventually foundered on the shoals of domestic public opinion, despite the considerable early successes it was able to achieve.

The volume concludes with a broad look at Taiwan's strategic environment and how it changed during the Ma era. In Chapter 16, Dean P. Chen argues that the deterioration of Sino-American and Sino-Japanese relations ultimately did as much to undermine Ma's cross-Strait rapprochement with the PRC as did any other factor, even though leaders in both Washington and Tokyo lauded the dramatic improvement of cross-Strait relations that began in 2008. As the rivalry intensified between China, on the one hand, and the United States and Japan, on the other, the KMT's ideological commitment to a single Chinese nation effectively joined Taiwan in a pan-Chinese union with the PRC in international disputes. For instance, the Ma administration's positions on maritime territorial disputes in the East and South China Seas were for the most part identical to those of Beijing's, even though Taipei explicitly refused to cooperate with the PRC to assert these common claims. In contrast, Washington and Tokyo were mostly aligned in their common security interests, and therefore took similar positions on these issues. Though the Obama administration remained firmly committed to the long-standing US "one-China policy" to maintain peace and stability across the Taiwan Strait, the Ma government's China-leaning policy contradicted, at least to some extent, the strategic postures of the United States in the Asia Pacific. Thus, even as the United States and the international community welcomed Ma's conciliatory moves to mend fences with Beijing and promote deeper socioeconomic cooperation across a variety of domains, the increase in Sino-American strategic competition ultimately made Ma's rapprochement efforts less beneficial to US interests.

When Ma Ying-jeou came into office in 2008, he argued that there was room for Taiwan simultaneously to maintain peaceful relations with China, friendly relations with Japan, and close relations with the United States. His grand strategy was premised on the assumption Taiwan could "have it all" and not have to choose sides between the three preeminent powers of the western Pacific. But by the end of his presidency in 2016, the balance of power in the region and each country's perception of national interests and threats looked very different. The rise of the PRC in international stature and power, the deep and alarming authoritarian turn it took under Xi Jinping, and its more assertive and aggressive behavior in all manner of international arenas combined to eliminate much of the space for creative diplomacy that Taiwan enjoyed when Ma first took office. At the end of the Ma years, the greatest reason for pessimism about the future of Taiwan was not Taiwan's contentious domestic politics, its constrained economic decisionmakers, its flawed policymaking processes, or its declining trust in democratic institutions. It was the gradual transformation of the regime across the Strait from an opportunity for Taiwan and its people into a threat.

Notes

1. Annual Freedom House reports for Taiwan are available at the Freedom House website, https://freedomhouse.org.

2. Ebsworth, "Not Wanting Want."

3. One of these "agreements" was actually the signed minutes of talks on cross-Strait charter flights. The three agreements that required a change to domestic laws, and therefore needed to be passed by an affirmative vote in the legislature, were the Economic Cooperation Framework Agreement, the Agreement on Intellectual Property Rights Protection and Cooperation (both approved on September 12, 2010), and the Agreement on Avoidance of Double Taxation and Enhancement of Tax Cooperation (signed in August 2015 but never brought up for a vote). In addition, the two sides issued three other memorandums of understanding and two statements of consensus.

4. The Ma administration reserved the right for itself to interpret whether an agreement required a change to domestic law; given the trouble of securing approval in the legislature, the executive branch attempted to avoid a vote on new cross-Strait agreements whenever possible.

5. See TVBS Polling Center, April 25, 2010, https://cc.tvbs.com.tw/portal/file/poll_center/2017/20170602/yijung-20100426095221.pdf.

6. TVBS Polling Center, June 25, 2013, https://cc.tvbs.com.tw/portal/file/poll_center/2017/20170602/20140117100505510.pdf.

7. The CSSTA was formally transmitted to the Legislative Yuan only on June 27, after this cross-party agreement had already been signed, and then reported to the floor and referred to committee on July 30.

8. Of special note is that in addition to Speaker Wang's intervention, the KMT party whip, Lai Shyh-bao, also signed the consensus agreement as the representative of the KMT caucus. In other words, Wang's deal was also supported by the rest of the KMT leadership in the Legislative Yuan. Speaker Wang also was instrumental in negotiating a subsequent deal on August 5 deciding that there should be another sixteen hearings, each dealing with four items in the CSSTA.

9. At least three aspects of this incident were problematic. First, the SID revealed that it was wiretapping the central telephone switchboard of the legislature without clear legal authority to do so, raising questions about illegal procedure and potential executive-branch intimidation of legislators. Second, the SID was supposed to operate as an independent prosecutorial body, not directly under the control of and reporting to the president. Yet Huang informed Ma as soon as he learned the details of the phone call. Third,

Ma immediately used this information for a transparently political purpose: to try to replace Wang Jin-pyng with someone friendlier to his administration's agenda. SID director Huang was later charged and convicted for his actions in this case, and after he left office Ma was indicted as well for his alleged mishandling of classified information. In a rather ironic twist, the original allegations of "influence peddling" against Wang and Ker were mostly overshadowed in the political uproar, and neither faced any permanent legal or political consequences for their actions. See Horton, "Taiwan's Ex-President Ma Ying-jeou Indicted in Wiretapping Case."

10. On the movement's organization and tactics, see Ho, "Occupy Congress in Taiwan," and Rowen, "Inside Taiwan's Sunflower Movement."

11. The Ma administration did respond with force when a breakaway group of students and activists later broke into the Executive Yuan offices, a short distance away from the Legislative Yuan, on the evening of March 23. That occupation was ended quickly when Premier Jiang ordered riot police to clear the building; though no one died, approximately 150 people were injured, including several who were hospitalized, and some of the protest leaders subsequently faced criminal charges for their actions.

12. Figures calculated from the International Monetary Fund's *World Economic Outlook Database,* https://www.imf.org/external/pubs/ft/weo/2019/02/weodata/index.aspx.

13. For more on the Chen Shui-bian era, see the chapters in our previous volume, Chu, Diamond, and Templeman, *Taiwan's Democracy Challenged.*

14. See Muyard, "Taiwan Elections 2008," pp. 89–91.

15. Aggarwal, "Bilateral Trade Agreements in the Asia-Pacific."

16. See "The Transpacific Partnership and Taiwan's Future Development Strategy," pp. 3–5.

17. Ibid., pp. 62–64.

18. For a representative view from the time, see Chu and San, "Taiwan's Industrial Policy and the Economic Rise of the PRC."

19. For more details on the 1992 meetings to which the "1992 Consensus" refers, see Chapter 15 of this book.

20. It is worth noting here that the DPP has remained implacably opposed to the use of this phrase, to the point that Tsai Ing-wen avoided endorsing it in her otherwise conciliatory presidential inauguration speech in 2016. The DPP has two primary objections to the use of the term "1992 Consensus" to describe the state of cross-Strait relations. First, the 1992 talks were held before either Taiwan's president or its legislature were directly elected, and therefore the ROC delegation at this meeting represented only the KMT and lacked legitimacy to speak for the people of Taiwan. Second, the DPP asserts that the PRC's consistent omission of the "respective interpretations" clause, and the post hoc characterization of the meeting, years after the fact, as having established a "consensus" that neither side endorsed in writing, render it nonsensical.

21. See Wang, Chen, and Kuo, "Restructuring State-Business Relations," pp. 257–260.

22. Rodrik, "Populism and the Economics of Globalization"; Inglehart and Norris, "Trump, Brexit, and the Rise of Populism."

23. Rowen, "Tourism as a Territorial Strategy."

24. Hung, "The Great U-Turn in Taiwan."

25. See Diaz-Bazan, *Measuring Inequality from Top to Bottom.*

26. For instance, see Lin, "Cross-Strait Trade and Class Cleavages in Taiwan."

27. Wu, Hou, and Chang, "Taiwan Needs Radical Tax Reform."

28. Chang, "Taiwan's Unfair Tax System."

29. Numbers for Japan (2017) and South Korea (2018) are from the Organization for Economic Cooperation and Development (OECD) report "Revenue Statistics for 2019," and for the Philippines (2018) from the OECD report "Review Statistics for Asian and Pacific Economies 2019." Taiwan is not an OECD member; the comparable number for revenues collected by all levels of government reported by Taiwan's Directorate-General

of Budgeting, Accounting, and Statistics for 2019 is 13.6 percent; https://eng.stat.gov .tw/point.asp?index=10.

30. Chang, "Taiwan's Unfair Tax System."

31. Kuan, "Generational Differences in Attitudes Toward Cross-Strait Trade."

32. Stromseth, Malesky, and Gueorguiev, *China's Governing Puzzle.*

33. Sun, "Municipal People's Congress Elections in the PRC"; Manion, *Information for Autocrats.*

34. Kinkel and Hurst, "Review Essay—Access to Justice in Post-Mao China"; Wang, *Tying the Autocrat's Hands.*

35. Stockmann, *Media Commercialization and Authoritarian Rule in China.*

36. For instance, see some of the postcrisis examples in Kurlantzick, "Why the 'China Model' Isn't Going Away."

37. For a variety of perspectives on this new assertiveness, see, for example, Rolland, "China's Eurasian Century?"; Feigenbaum, "China and the World"; Minzner, *End of an Era;* and Doshi, "Hu's to Blame for China's Foreign Assertiveness?"

38. On this point, see especially Minzner, *End of an Era,* and Doshi, "Hu's to Blame for China's Foreign Assertiveness?"

39. For examples and evidence of this activity, see Shullman, "Protect the Party"; Diamond and Schell, *Chinese Influence and American Interests;* Cole, *The Hard Edge of Sharp Power;* and Foxall and Hemmings, *The Art of Deceit.*

40. For the 2008 legislative and presidential elections, see Rigger, "Party Politics and Elections," in our previous volume on the Chen Shui-bian years.

41. Taiwan has a multitier electoral system in which voters cast two ballots for the legislature: one for a candidate in one of seventy-three single-member districts, and a second for a national party list, in which thirty-four seats are distributed proportionally to all parties that pass a 5 percent threshold. Indigenous voters elect six representatives of their own from two nationwide constituencies with three members each, using the old single nontransferable vote (SNTV) system.

2

The 2012 Elections

Shelley Rigger

The debates, controversies, and outcomes of the 2012 legislative and presidential elections reflect a maturing democracy's response to narrowing options. For Taiwan to change its international status radically—even, ultimately, to attain formal independence—was never likely, but prior to 2000 such blue sky visions of the island's future still could find an audience. However, twelve years under Chen Shui-bian and Ma Ying-jeou made clear just how tight the constraints on Taiwan's policy choices had become. Not only Beijing but Washington, too, resisted Chen's efforts to expand Taiwan's living space. While Chinese and US officials rewarded Ma's more restrained and accommodating policy direction, Beijing's long-term expectations did not change. For Taiwanese voters, these external forces were part of a larger set of dilemmas that included fundamental questions about the island's economic trajectory, as post-industrialism and globalization reshaped social relations in ways that left many Taiwanese deeply dissatisfied.

Ma Ying-jeou's first term was rocky, but the popular disillusionment reflected in opinion polls was tempered by realism. With the excessive expectations that drove his landslide victory in 2008 deflated, the 2012 election boiled down to a contest of credibility between candidates and parties Taiwanese had come to know well. Both sides kept their promises modest; both presidential candidates sought to portray themselves as guardians of the status quo, although they defined that status quo differently. Ultimately, the voters decided—despite their disappointed hopes—that giving Ma a second term was the safer choice. While the race was hard-fought and both sides landed some stinging blows, the campaigns' respective visions focused on practical problems and realistic solutions, moving the election away from the pattern of ideological polarization that characterized previous contests.

Ma's First Term

It is hard not to see Ma Ying-jeou's 2008 presidential victory as overdetermined, even inevitable, but the 2012 election was a very different story. In the end Ma won reelection by a comfortable margin, but it was less than half of what he had managed four years earlier, and it came with a diminished Kuomintang (KMT) majority in the Legislative Yuan. While his nomination was never in doubt, Ma's popularity ratings were low in the months before the election campaign.[1] Part of the reason was the unrealistic expectations that swept him into office in 2008. Taiwanese were eager to be rid of Chen Shui-bian, but many also were genuinely thrilled by the prospect of having Ma—a man perceived as the most capable and honest of KMT politicians—as their president. Only a few weeks into his presidency, however, Ma's feet of clay began to show.

One immediate challenge facing the new president was the financial meltdown that devastated economies around the world in 2008. Taiwan was far from the worst-hit of nations, but its heavy dependence on exports made it vulnerable. As it turned out, Taiwan's economy recovered more quickly than most (thanks, in part, to Beijing's huge economic stimulus program, which benefited many Taiwanese firms operating on the Chinese mainland), but the recovery was hard to anticipate in the early months of Ma's first term. A devastating typhoon that hit southern Taiwan in August 2009 dealt another blow to Ma's image. The storm took more than 600 lives, and damage to agriculture was estimated at over half a billion dollars. Ma's government faced criticism for preparing inadequately before the storm, responding too slowly in its immediate aftermath, and mishandling international aid in the days afterward. Critics found Ma's interactions with grieving storm victims awkward and wooden, casting doubt on his ability to connect with his people.

The economic crisis and typhoon set the tone for Ma's first term: edgy and anxious. He was increasingly cast as a weak leader, a perception that was reinforced when the legislature repeatedly blocked important initiatives—even though the president's party enjoyed a supermajority. Adding to these concerns were persistent worries about cross-Strait relations. After his inauguration, Ma moved quickly to implement a number of policies Chen had championed but failed to carry out, including opening direct flights between Taiwan and the mainland and easing restrictions on cross-Strait investment. Long-delayed negotiations between the quasi-official Straits Exchange Foundation (SEF) and Association for Relations Across the Taiwan Strait (ARATS) resumed, and the two sides inked a series of economic agreements. In June 2010, they signed the Economic Cooperation Framework

Agreement (ECFA). Ma's administration also won Taiwan more international space. After signing the ECFA, Taipei launched talks with Singapore, New Zealand, and Japan on economic agreements. It also managed to join a number of international organizations as an observer, including the World Health Assembly, from which Beijing previously had blocked its participation, and Taipei and Beijing implemented a tacit "diplomatic truce," suspending their protracted (and expensive) competition for diplomatic recognition.[2]

Overall, Taiwanese supported Ma's cross-Strait policies, and they welcomed the more relaxed environment that accompanied them. They were happy to leave behind Chen-era tensions, which had done nothing to slow the pace of cross-Strait economic exchanges but had left them unregulated and uncoordinated. Nonetheless, the shift in policy unnerved many Taiwanese. In a sense, the public's reaction to Ma's policies was a mirror image of its response to Chen. While Chen's Sinophobic policies were perceived as endangering Taiwan and limiting its economic prospects, Ma was criticized for moving too quickly and risking Taiwan's political and economic autonomy. Even after Taiwan's economy began to recover strongly in 2010, anxiety about the long term remained.

Meanwhile, the Democratic Progressive Party (DPP) added to Ma's troubles by rebounding surprisingly swiftly from its 2008 drubbing. The Chen administration had left DPP supporters and activists disappointed and frustrated; fierce battles over leadership, policy, and Chen's legacy seemed likely to doom the party's recovery. But on the day of Ma Ying-jeou's inauguration in May 2008, the DPP installed Tsai Ing-wen as its chair. Tsai had been a party member for only four years; ironically, her short tenure worked in her favor as a leader, as she was not affiliated with any of the party's factions. Under her leadership, the DPP pulled itself out of its funk to win several legislative by-elections in 2009. Its vote share in that year's municipal elections increased by three percentage points and it picked up an additional local executive seat.

In November 2010, Taiwanese went to the polls to elect mayors and council members in five special municipalities. These large cities include about 60 percent of Taiwan's population, so the elections were an important test of the DPP's new momentum. The KMT won in Taipei, New Taipei (formerly Taipei County), and Taichung. The DPP took the mayorships in Kaohsiung and Tainan, but the results were better for the DPP than these numbers suggest. In total, Democratic Progressive candidates won 400,000 more votes than KMT nominees, capturing just a hair under 50 percent of all the votes cast. In Taichung (a newly created special municipality that merged Taichung City and Taichung County), the DPP's Su Jia-chyuan almost unseated the popular incumbent, Taichung City mayor Jason Hu. These midterm elections showed that the DPP was moving past the trauma of

Chen Shui-bian's meltdown and regaining its footing under Tsai's leadership, altering the outlook for 2012.

The DPP's recovery was aided by new thinking on the policy front. During his eight years in office, Chen Shui-bian experimented with a number of different approaches to cross-Strait relations, ranging from promising not to pursue formal independence in his first inaugural address to advocating a referendum seeking United Nations membership under the name "Taiwan" at the end of his second term. His core goals, however, were consistent: solidify Taiwan's separation from mainland China and strengthen the Taiwanese people's resolve to resist Beijing's unification plans. Under Tsai's leadership, the DPP shifted its policies slightly closer to the center of the political spectrum. After initially opposing the ECFA—signed by the Ma administration and Beijing in mid-2010—Tsai adjusted her position to one of cautious acceptance. As she told an audience in Washington, D.C., in September, "We will conduct regular examinations of [ECFA's] impact on our economy, and if and when revisions are necessary we would follow democratic procedures for handling trade agreements and international obligations."[3] Tsai also retreated from her earlier characterization of the Republic of China (ROC) as a "government in exile" to acknowledge that the ROC is, today, coterminous with Taiwan.

The Presidential Campaign

The DPP formally nominated Tsai in May 2012 based on public opinion polls pitting various DPP hopefuls against Ma. Tsai was an interesting choice for her party. A DPP member since only 2004, the British-educated lawyer came to prominence as a consultant to Lee Teng-hui's Mainland Affairs Council (MAC) in the late 1990s. Many Taiwanese (and many in Beijing) believed she was the brains behind Lee's (in)famous formulation of cross-Strait relations as a "special state-to-state relationship." She headed the MAC under Chen Shui-bian, and also served as a deputy premier and as a legislator. In 2010, she lost a mayoral election in New Taipei, but her competitive campaign and vote share paved the way for her presidential bid.

Tsai was a very different presidential candidate from Chen. Her style was scholarly and serious. Her one-on-one interactions with supporters were warm, but Tsai eschewed the extravagant emotional displays that were the stock-in-trade of most DPP politicians. She also avoided, for the most part, appeals to ethnic politics. While she energetically criticized Ma's cross-Strait policies, her strongest talking points were on the economy. The DPP's strategy in 2012 was to refocus the debate away from growth of gross domestic product (GDP) and cross-Strait progress and toward the economic insecurity plaguing much of Taiwan's society. Tsai foreshadowed these themes in a speech she gave in early 2011:

Another mission of the DPP is to present an economic approach that is different from that of the KMT, to resist the worsening wealth gap in our society. While the KMT is complacent with the GDP growth figures, we will concern ourselves with people's lives, their employment and income. How high the numbers look is irrelevant; they are mere empty figures if the average person does not feel the growth. The DPP must feel what the people are feeling, must provide a secure future for those without economic or social capital. The DPP exists for these people and each day we must remind ourselves that if there were no DPP, who would care for the future of these people? That was the original purpose of the founding of our party, and remains the value we hold firm today and for which we will continue to fight.[4]

The idea that overall economic growth was meaningless because ordinary Taiwanese could not feel it was a central campaign theme in 2012.

The Democratic Progressives adopted "fairness and justice" (*gongping zhengyi*) as their campaign slogan. Tsai and her party's legislative candidates hammered away at problems of economic inequality, unemployment, rising housing costs, weak social justice, and deficit spending. They also criticized the KMT's environmental record and revived a long-standing DPP position opposing nuclear power—a position made more popular by the Fukushima nuclear disaster in Japan following a tsunami in March 2011. Tsai blamed the island's economic problems on its overly eager embrace of globalization and a headlong rush to the Chinese mainland that benefited entrepreneurs but left Taiwanese workers jobless.

The DPP's down-to-earth political style came through clearly in the 2012 campaign. One of its most innovative and effective elements was improvised. At a Tsai rally in Tainan in October, three young children offered the candidate their piggy banks as a campaign donation. The heart-warming gesture became a cause célèbre when election officials threatened to investigate the incident as a violation of a law forbidding nonvoters from donating to campaigns. The Tsai campaign lambasted the hidebound election agency and began distributing plastic piggy banks to collect small donations. DPP sources claimed that almost 150,000 of the banks eventually were returned, containing a total of NT$200 million (about US$7 million).[5] This kind of grassroots campaigning based on activism and small donations was the DPP's hallmark, and the Tsai campaign continued the party's trend.

The Ma campaign defended his administration's economic record while acknowledging the difficulties facing the working class, which it attributed to broad global trends. In Ma's view, Taiwan's challenges would be far worse without the economic outlet and opportunities afforded by the mainland. Although Tsai did not win the election, the issues she raised resonated with voters. For decades, Taiwanese enjoyed steadily rising living standards and a relatively egalitarian distribution of wealth. Aggregate GDP growth could not compensate for the erosion of those achievements, so unless Ma could somehow reverse the trends, the DPP would continue to gain the benefit of its positioning as the party of the "have-nots."[6]

For Taiwan even more than other countries, domestic economic issues are bound up with external relations, particularly cross-Strait policy. No political conversation can long avoid the looming question of what to do about China, and the 2012 presidential election was no exception. The Ma campaign considered the candidate's record on cross-Strait relations a strength, but there was vulnerability there, too. The first big policy controversy of the campaign came in October, when Ma said that Taiwan was likely to face the question of whether to conclude a peace agreement with the People's Republic of China (PRC) within the next ten years. The idea of a peace accord had been on the KMT's to-do list for years; Beijing agreed to work toward such an arrangement in 2005. Nonetheless, the DPP used the issue to paint Ma as a pro-unification ideologue; Tsai accused Ma of setting a timeline for unification talks. The Ma camp seemed unprepared for the intensity of the criticism, and its candidate soon backtracked, saying that any peace agreement would have to be ratified through a popular referendum. The qualification did little to quiet his critics.

The peace accord controversy eventually blew over, but not before raising doubts about the Ma campaign. Observers wondered how Ma and his advisers could have failed to anticipate and prepare for the DPP's attacks. Why bring up such a controversial issue at such a sensitive time? The explanation offered by the campaign was that Ma had promised progress toward a peace accord during his first presidential campaign, and he felt he owed the nation an updated statement of his position. Whatever the reason, the incident raised questions about Ma's readiness to compete in a tight race. According to public opinion polls, it also cut Ma's lead over Tsai substantially.[7] The brouhaha over Ma's remarks also added "peace accord" (*heping xieyi*) to a long list of toxic terms in Taiwanese politics.

The fracas over the peace agreement underscored just how difficult it was for politicians to find the right balance between supporting peace and stability in the Strait—which all Taiwanese wanted—and being accused of catering or surrendering to a PRC leadership still very much determined to bring Taiwan into a unification deal, whether by force, stealth, or seduction. During Chen's presidency, the percentage of Taiwanese who believed the pace of cross-Strait exchanges was too slow consistently exceeded those who said it was too fast. Under Ma, the pattern was reversed (although in both cases a plurality said the pace was just right).[8] This quandary was not unique to Chen Shui-bian or Ma Ying-jeou; it is an inescapable consequence of the rise of China. As China becomes more powerful—economically, militarily, politically—Taiwan faces more pressure to accommodate its demands. Leaders in Taipei face a shrinking menu of options for dealing with Taiwan's relationship with the PRC and other external actors. Voters feel the space for maneuver contracting, but they are not ready to give up the island's autonomous political standing. The result is intense pressure on politicians to find ways to keep Beijing happy (and the benefits of economic interactions flowing) while postponing serious discussion of the two sides' political future.

During the 2012 campaign, Ma Ying-jeou faced a familiar challenge: convincing centrist voters that the DPP's depiction of him as willing (even eager) to enter into political talks with Beijing was inaccurate. The KMT's position on unification was subtle, and the party rarely spoke with one voice. Both of these circumstances created opportunities for critics to paint it as more pro-unification than the electorate. This was an old problem for the KMT, but 2012 saw a new twist on it, as pundits stressed the likelihood that if Ma were reelected the PRC would intensify the pressure on him to enter political negotiations as a first step toward unification. In other words, even if Ma was not interested in starting political talks, his reelection still would increase their likelihood.

The DPP played up the dangers of Ma's Sinophilic outlook and policies, but its candidate had vulnerabilities of her own on the cross-Strait issue. To begin with, she had to carry the burden of the DPP's past, including its reputation as a pro-independence party (support for formal independence is still included in the DPP's charter), the PRC's adamant refusal to engage with DPP politicians, and Chen Shui-bian's record in office. Those factors contributed to concern that a Tsai victory would destabilize cross-Strait relations, putting Taiwan's economy and perhaps even its security at risk. DPP leaders dismissed these fears. They were confident that the PRC's focus on domestic problems—economic and political—would compel Beijing to avoid a rupture in cross-Strait relations, even if a Tsai administration failed to meet its terms for continued dialogue.[9]

The differences between the two candidates on cross-Strait issues crystallized around the so-called 1992 Consensus: Tsai's inability to produce a convincing position on this issue was a critical factor in her defeat, not least because it prompted several influential figures—some of whom had supported the DPP in the past—to denounce her approach in public. The KMT maintained that in 1992, negotiators from the PRC and Taiwan agreed that talks could go forward under the understanding that both sides recognized only one China, although they defined "one China" differently. Their divergent definitions, it was agreed, need not be stated. In Taiwan, the 1992 Consensus is often summarized as "one China, with respective interpretations." The 1992 Consensus is useful because it allows Beijing to claim that one China is intact while Taipei continues to assert a version of one China that does not subordinate Taiwan to the PRC. The DPP maintains there was no consensus in 1992, and that "1992 Consensus" is a phrase invented long after the fact. Whatever its origin, the consensus bridged the conceptual gap between the two sides of the Strait, allowing talks to go forward as long as Ma, who supported the 1992 Consensus, was in office.

Even before the campaign began, it was clear that the 1992 Consensus would play an important role in the election. In December 2010, President Ma challenged the DPP on the issue when he called on Tsai to accept the consensus. At first, the DPP rejected Ma's request through a spokesman, but a few days later Tsai herself spoke out against the idea, which she called a "fabrication." Instead of feigning an agreement they did not really feel, she argued, Taiwan and the PRC should act on the basis of their shared interest in mutual recognition and cooperation. As she put it in a February 2011 speech:

> Taiwan and China are different in our histories, beliefs and values, political systems, and social identities. Yet Taiwan and China share common responsibilities and interests, which are to pursue a peaceful and stable relationship and to grasp the opportunity for prosperity and development. This is what we mean by "peaceful but recognizing differences" and "peaceful and seeking commonality." Therefore I appeal to China, as a large and powerful country, to reexamine the way for long-term development of cross-Strait relations upon this understanding.[10]

As election day approached, the issue of the 1992 Consensus played an increasingly central role in the campaign. Ma repeatedly pressed Tsai to explain how she would preserve and enhance cross-Strait stability while rejecting the consensus. Tsai refused to budge; instead, she raised an alternative approach, which she called the "Taiwan Consensus." According to Tsai, before committing itself to a "consensus" with the PRC, Taiwan needed to arrive at its own internal consensus. She explained her thinking to the *New York Times* in January 2012:

> You need to have a democratic process to form this majority view, or at least a position that is supported by the majority of people here. So that's what I am aiming at, that we need a process. So I have this idea of a Taiwan Consensus, which means people in Taiwan have to get together and form a consensus of their own and that they turn around to talk to the Chinese to form a cross-Strait consensus so we can build a relationship on that consensus. And in my view, that is the right order to do things. And with that we can build a long lasting relationship with China.[11]

She proposed to postpone further negotiations with the PRC while Taiwanese underwent a process of domestic consultation and soul-searching. On its face, the need for a consensus-building process within Taiwan was obvious, but Tsai's proposal came across as vague and utopian.[12]

For the most part, PRC leaders tried to avoid commenting directly on the election, presumably to avoid triggering a backlash. But they could not ignore Tsai's opposition to the 1992 Consensus forever. Asked for comment on Tsai's position, a spokesman for Beijing's Taiwan Affairs Office reiterated the PRC's view that the 1992 Consensus was the basis for continued talks across the Strait; his statement implied that if the DPP failed to uphold the consensus, cross-Strait progress would be significantly curtailed. At the Asia-Pacific Economic Cooperation (APEC) summit in November 2011, Chinese president Hu Jintao told Taiwan's representative, former vice president Lien Chan, that the 1992 Consensus was a precondition for continuing dialogue across the Strait.[13] Other officials made similar statements; some even suggested that if Taiwan's new president failed to endorse the 1992 Consensus, there could be a rollback of existing initiatives—including implementation of the ECFA. Taiwan Affairs Office head Wang Yi compared cross-Strait relations to a multistory building in which the 1992 Consensus was part of the foundation. He said, "If someone calls for the foundation of the building to be demolished, but says that we can continue to add new stories to the building, this is definitely unrealistic and irresponsible."[14] In numerous statements, the Beijing government set forth two preconditions for continued good relations across the Strait: adherence to some version of one China and opposition to Taiwan's independence. Neither was an easy sell to the DPP base.

PRC officials showed a modicum of flexibility by suggesting on some occasions that a different consensus might be possible, but they continued to insist that a "one-China framework" must be the basis for cooperation. For the DPP, the one-China framework, too, was a nonstarter, because the party adamantly opposed the very concept of one China. The party's 1999 Resolution on Taiwan's Future acknowledged that the official name of Taiwan was "Republic of China," but the Democratic Progressives rejected both of the "respective interpretations" attached to the 1992 Consensus, including Beijing's view that Taiwan was part of the PRC and the KMT's opinion that mainland China was part of the ROC. In their view, the ROC was (for the moment, at least) sovereign on Taiwan, and the PRC was sovereign on the mainland. By 2012, this position was too deeply ingrained for Tsai to change it, even if she had wanted to.

Even as some PRC officials were issuing their increasingly stern demands that Taiwan's political leaders embrace the 1992 Consensus, others were unveiling economic initiatives designed to curry favor with sectors of Taiwan's electorate. One of the most publicized of these efforts was a campaign to import milkfish, a Taiwanese specialty, from fish farmers in Tainan County. Tainan is a DPP stronghold, so observers saw political motivation in the decision to import a large quantity of product from one small region. The milkfish campaign was but one example of a much larger campaign by the PRC to give traditional DPP constituencies—especially rural communities in southern Taiwan—a direct interest in promoting cross-Strait economic ties.

Another pro-engagement constituency required little prodding to make its preferences known. For Taiwan's business community, especially those with investments on the mainland, deepening cross-Strait engagement was critical to their continued economic success. Their role in the election became controversial in two ways. As the election approached, a number of high-profile business leaders made public statements endorsing the 1992 Consensus. Lin Yi-shou, the head of the Kaohsiung-based E United Group, called it "the only and best way to narrow Taiwan's south-north growth gap," while Chang Yung-fa of the Evergreen Group called it a "foundation for cross-Strait dialogue."[15] Although most of these statements did not explicitly endorse Ma, it was understood that they were directed against Tsai, who steadfastly rejected the 1992 Consensus.

Another group of Taiwanese whose interests were bound up with cross-Strait relations were those who lived and worked on the mainland. The number of long-term Taiwanese residents in the PRC has been impossible to determine precisely, but most estimates placed it at well over 500,000 during the Ma years. Taiwan does not permit absentee voting, so overseas residents who wished to vote had to return to the island (voters living in Taiwan had to vote where their household registration was recorded, so even many who lived on the island had to travel on election day). Overseas voting has been a factor in Taiwan's elections since the 1990s. At that time, most of the returnees were coming from North America. Both major political parties sponsored campaign events and fundraisers in the United States and Canada to mobilize supporters there. Competition between the KMT and DPP was fierce, with both sides working hard to turn out as many supporters as possible.

Since the early 2000s, the focus of attention on overseas voting has shifted from North America to the Chinese mainland, in part because of the large number of potential returnees, and in part because while voters returning from North American were thought to represent both political parties, those residing in the mainland were perceived (perhaps wrongly) to favor the KMT by a wide margin. Sinoskeptical Taiwanese also worried that the so-called Taishang (Taiwanese businesspeople on the mainland) were inclined to place their own interest in economic opportunity ahead of Taiwan's national interests. The return of voters from the mainland thus brought anxiety to the DPP and hope to the KMT; as a result, pundits devoted considerable attention to estimating and analyzing the likely extent of their participation in the 2012 race. Meanwhile, rumors circulated that Taiwanese companies and even the PRC government were subsidizing plane tickets for Taiwanese going home to vote.[16] In the end, Ma's margin of victory was far too wide for returning voters to have played a decisive role, but the statements from business leaders likely influenced some wavering voters. Taiwanese have a long history of conservative, pro-business voting; taking advice from celebrity entrepreneurs is not at all uncharacteristic.

The participation of mainland-based Taiwanese in the election was a mixed blessing for Beijing. On the one hand, the Taishang were an important constituency who recognized the value of positive cross-Strait relations. On the other hand, their political preferences could only be guessed; no one knew for sure how they would vote. Moreover, some Taiwanese politicians pointed to Taishang political participation as evidence that the PRC government was interfering in the island's politics by inducing the Taishang to speak on its behalf.

Dealing with Taiwan's elections has never been easy for Beijing, but the PRC's role in the 2012 elections was especially fraught. As usual, the Chinese leadership had a preference as to the outcome of the election, but the reverberations for China's domestic politics were abnormally strong that year. Taiwan's presidential election was viewed as a test of President Hu Jintao's policy direction in the run-up to the Chinese Communist Party's (CCP) scheduled leadership transition. Under Hu, the PRC took a relatively soft line toward Taiwan. Although Beijing did not retreat from its near-term goal of preventing any move toward formal independence or its long-term goal of achieving unification, Hu's policy emphasized opportunities for cooperation and sought to minimize sources of conflict. In the months before the election, Chinese sources averred that a Tsai victory would suggest that Hu's approach had failed to rein in "secessionist" tendencies in Taiwan, and was thus a failure. As the election approached, Beijing's efforts to influence the outcome and avoid the backlash that had followed past efforts to sway Taiwanese voters began to seem outright panicky, perhaps because of the added pressure of domestic politics.

Like the PRC, the United States has always taken a keen interest in Taiwanese politics, and the 2012 elections were no exception. Washington's stated position was that it had no preference as to the outcome but was concerned solely that Taiwan's elections be free and fair. Those protestations notwithstanding, a Ma victory seemed especially consistent with the US preference for stability and continued engagement in the Taiwan Strait. Intimations to that effect emerged from an anonymous White House source after Tsai traveled to the United States in September to meet with representatives of the US government. An unnamed official told the *Financial Times* that Tsai "left us with distinct doubts about whether she is both willing and able to continue the stability in cross-Strait relations the region has enjoyed in recent years" and that it was "far from clear . . . that she and her advisers fully appreciate the depth of [Chinese] mistrust of her motives and DPP aspirations."[17]

DPP leaders were furious about the statement, which they viewed as undue interference in Taiwan's democratic process. They were even angrier when, just days before the election, Douglas Paal, a former US diplomat in charge of United States–Taiwan relations, told reporters that most US officials had a strong preference for Ma.[18] A series of policy decisions—including the approval of arms sales, high-level visits by US officials to Taiwan, and the announcement that Taiwanese would likely be given visa-free entry to the United States—reinforced the sense that Washington was seeking to bolster Ma's popularity by painting him as America's favorite. The US government denied any political intention.

Legislative Elections and the James Soong Factor

One novel aspect of the 2012 election season was the decision to hold legislative and presidential elections on the same day. This decision was due in part to the argument by some academics that holding the elections concurrently was more likely to produce a unified government, thereby reducing the chances of reprising the gridlock of the Chen Shui-bian years. Another factor in favor of simultaneous elections was the cost savings, both to the state and to the voters, of organizing for only one election. Meanwhile, both political parties expected to benefit from simultaneous elections. DPP supporters believed a popular presidential candidate would help the party's legislative candidates win election, while KMT strategists hoped that the grassroots organizing techniques favored by their legislative candidates would draw out KMT-leaning voters on behalf of Ma.

The legislative elections were conducted under a formula first used in 2008 that combines seventy-three single-member district (SMD) seats, six seats reserved for indigenous Taiwanese, and thirty-four seats selected through party-list proportional representation (PR) voting. In 2008, the KMT and its allies dominated the SMD and indigenous voting, winning sixty-five out of seventy-nine total seats. Together, the KMT and DPP won all of the PR seats, squeezing out a number of small parties. The new electoral system, which had been adopted in 2005, seemed to strongly benefit the two major parties—especially the KMT.

Perhaps the most intriguing wild card factor in the 2012 elections—one that kept the election exciting right up to election day—was James Soong's candidacy. Soong spent most of his career as a KMT politician, but in 2000 he broke with his party when he lost its presidential nomination to Lien Chan. His independent candidacy in that year captured 37 percent of the vote, far above Lien's 23 percent, but just below Chen Shui-bian's 39 percent. In 2001, Soong founded the People First Party (PFP), which won 46 seats in the legislature (out of 225 seats in total). Soong joined Lien's 2004 presidential ticket in the vice presidential spot; they lost their bid by a fraction of a percentage point. Later that year, the PFP captured 34 seats and 15 percent of the legislative vote, making it a critical ally for the KMT.

After 2008, it looked as though the PFP would be reabsorbed into the KMT, especially with the new, majoritarian electoral rules in place for legislative races, but Soong was not finished yet.[19] In November 2011, Soong announced his intention to run for president. For months, speculation raged as to his real goal. Was he hoping for a spot on the ticket? Appointment to the premiership? Protection for PFP legislative candidates? Given the obvious overlap between KMT and PFP voters, a Soong candidacy seemed destined to reduce Ma's chances of victory, and many observers predicted he would drop out of the race once his demands were met. Soong insisted he was in the race to stay.

As the presidential race wound toward its conclusion, it became clear that Soong meant what he said. Election handicappers predicted that if Soong captured more than about 7 percent of the vote, he could throw the election to Tsai. Pre-election polling suggested such an outcome was not impossible. In the end, Soong received just under 3 percent, leaving Ma with a comfortable margin. If his goal was to win—or spoil—the presidential race, his efforts were unavailing. But Soong's goal may have been something quite different: to provide a flagship and platform for PFP legislative candidates. If that was the case, his candidacy should be judged a success. The PFP won 5.8 percent of the party-list vote, garnering two seats, as well as one seat from the indigenous constituencies. Under the Legislative Yuan's complex rules, three seats is an important threshold, as it is the minimum required to form a party caucus and be included in cross-party negotiations.

Another surprising result in the legislative elections was the three-seat win of the Taiwan Solidarity Union (TSU). The TSU, which split from the KMT in 2001, was the most pro-independence of Taiwan's parties. It nominated no presidential or legislative district candidates, yet managed to win almost 10 percent of the PR vote. One reason for the TSU's success may have been an appearance by its "spiritual leader," former president Lee Teng-hui, at a Tsai Ing-wen rally the night before the election. When Lee said, "I am standing here for the Taiwan I love so much," he was invoking a traditional DPP theme—Taiwanese identity—that Tsai had downplayed in her campaign.[20] Lee's endorsement likely helped improve Tsai's standing among the most Sinophobic voters, but it also reminded listeners that the TSU was an option—one for which the DPP had given its supporters permission to vote.

The two small parties' successes may have been a fluke, but their PR vote shares were large enough to warrant further analysis. One implication would appear to be that Taiwan's voters used their PR votes to indicate "true preferences," even as they followed the logic of strategic voting in the legislative district and presidential balloting. More than twice as many voters chose the PFP's PR list as voted for Soong, suggesting that they used split-ticket voting to balance a "lesser of two evils" presidential vote and a true preference vote in the party list. If that is the case, it reflects a sophisticated understanding of Taiwan's new electoral rules that was not observable in the first round of legislative elections under the new system in 2008. This logic was also evident in 2016 and even more so in 2020.

The TSU's strong showing revealed the extent to which Taiwanese continued to resist and reject the PRC's efforts to limit the island's freedom of action. The TSU unabashedly supported Taiwan's independence, and it was a strong critic of policies that sought to deepen ties across the Strait. It thus competed with the DPP for the deep-Green segment of the electorate. The TSU's 10 percent party vote share (the DPP received 37 percent) recharged the debate within the DPP over whether the party should move toward the center. It also revealed the limits of pro-engagement pragmatism in Taiwan's electorate. It may have been true that the majority of Taiwanese believed that the PRC's rising power required accommodation by Taiwan, but that conviction was not yet a consensus position in 2012 (and many in the DPP would have agreed with the TSU on this point).

Conclusion

Taiwan's 2012 national elections revealed the extent to which democratic procedures had become institutionalized since the democratic breakthroughs of the late 1980s. Every step of the process—from the candidates' nominations through the casting and counting of the ballots—followed well-established routines. The election was more competitive than anyone predicted after the 2008 blowout, proving that Taiwan's democracy was not on the verge of disappearing into a one-party system. The presidential race provided suspense, as the two leading candidates' support rates bounced up and down, with the wildcard third-party candidate and large number of undecided voters keeping pundits guessing right up to the end.[21] The legislative elections were not as suspenseful as the presidential, but still less one-sided than in 2008, suggesting that new electoral rules first implemented in that year had not eliminated legislative competition after all. The emergence of two minor parties with independent legislative influence was another important development.

Although the 2012 elections reflected positively on the development of Taiwan's democracy, their substantive implications were more sobering. After twelve years of extremely rapid growth in cross-Strait economic interactions, Taiwan's economy was deeply entwined with that of the PRC. Setting aside Beijing's preferences was becoming an increasingly risky choice for Taiwan, to the point where a presidential candidate who refused to meet its precondition for dialogue found herself under intense pressure not only from Beijing but also from Washington, from prominent Taiwanese, and from the electorate. Had Tsai Ing-wen conceded on the 1992 Consensus, she might still have lost the election (and she might have lost the support of deep-Green voters, including those who cast their PR ballots for the TSU), but her refusal to yield on the issue turned key constituencies against her.

The 2012 elections thus revealed that although Taiwan's electoral institutions were working well, the range of choices politicians and voters could consider had contracted, leaving the island's leaders with a limited menu of policy options from which to shape its economic and political future. During his second term, Ma too met with increasing popular resistance to his accommodationist approach to cross-Strait relations. As it turned out, Taiwanese voters' appetite for engagement was not unlimited, and the 1992 Consensus was not the magic talisman it seemed to be in 2012. The 2016 elections took place in an entirely different context.

Notes

1. "Dissatisfied" outnumbered "satisfied" in thirteen out of eighteen rounds of polling conducted by the KMT-leaning TVBS during the first three years of Ma's presidency. See TVBS public opinion website, March 15, 2011, https://cc.tvbs.com.tw/portal/file/poll_center/2017/20170602/roggm9ho27.pdf.

2. There is solid evidence that at least one country, Paraguay, was prepared to switch its diplomatic recognition to Beijing, but was discouraged from doing so in order not to upset the diplomatic truce.

3. "Tsai Ing-wen's Remarks at the American Enterprise Institute," September 13, 2011, http://dpptaiwan.blogspot.com/2011/09/tsai-ing-wens-remarks-at-american.html.

4. "DPP Chair Chai [Tsai] Ying-wen's 2011 New Year Statement," http://www.dpp.org.tw/news_content.php?sn=4686.

5. Chris Wang, "DPP's Piggy Bank Donation Campaign Brings in Grand Total of NT$201.2m," January 7, 2012, http://newsroomformosa.blogspot.tw/2012/01/2012-elections-dpps-piggy-bank-donation.html#more.

6. In the 2020 election, the KMT candidate, Han Kuo-yu, adopted precisely this strategy, although without success.

7. The TVBS poll, for example, found Ma's lead over Tsai cut from nine points to six immediately after the announcement. See poll dated October 28–31, 2011, https://cc.tvbs.com.tw/portal/file/poll_center/2017/20170602/sj6y0h4r5u.pdf.

8. See Mainland Affairs Council surveys "The Pace of Cross-Strait Exchanges," https://www.mac.gov.tw/en/Content_List.aspx?n=9157634B03B0E393.

9. Glaser and Billingsley, "Taiwan's 2012 Presidential Elections and Cross-Strait Relations," p. 7.

10. Quoted in Romberg, "The 2012 Taiwan Election," p. 11.

11. "Interview with Tsai Ing-wen," *New York Times,* January 5, 2012, http://www.nytimes.com/2012/01/05/world/asia/interview-with-tsai-ing-wen.html.

12. Jacques DeLisle has observed that the Taiwan Consensus can be viewed as a moderate gesture because it allows for an outcome that is not Taiwanese independence. Instead, it aims at allowing Taiwan's people to decide for themselves what future they wish to pursue; see DeLisle, "Taiwan's 2012 Presidential and Legislative Elections," p. 2. In this sense it is similar to the KMT's official policy, which is that while the KMT itself favors eventual unification, it recognizes that this is but one of Taiwan's possible futures.

13. "Hu, Lien Emphasize Importance of 1992 Consensus to Current Ties," *China Post,* November 13, 2011, http://www.chinapost.com.tw/taiwan/china-taiwan-relations/2011/11/13/322772/Hu-Lien.htm.

14. Quoted in Glaser and Billingsley, "Taiwan's 2012 Presidential Elections and Cross-Strait Relations," pp. 8–9.

15. "Cherishing the '1992 Consensus' Maintains Taiwan's Stability, Development: Entrepreneurs," January 13, 2012, http://news.xinhuanet.com/english/china/2012-01/14/c _131359317.htm.

16. DeLisle, "Taiwan's 2012 Presidential and Legislative Elections," p. 2.

17. Anna Fifield, "US Concerned About Taiwan Candidate," *Financial Times,* September 15, 2011, http://www.ft.com/cms/s/0/f926fd14-df93-11e0-845a-00144feabdc0 .html#axzz20EIgtbg3.

18. Andrew Jacobs, "Former U.S. Diplomat Rattles Taiwan Before Election," *New York Times,* January 13, 2012, http://www.nytimes.com/2012/01/14/world/asia/former -united-states-envoy-remarks-cause-uproar-in-taiwan.html.

19. As it turns out, Soong *really* wasn't finished: he was a presidential candidate again in 2016 and 2020.

20. The quotation is from the *Ballots and Bullets* blog, operated by Jonathan Sullivan at the University of Nottingham, http://nottspolitics.org/2012/01/14/reflections-on-election -night.

21. Even the political futures market operated by National Chengchi University predicted a Tsai victory. Because the futures market had proven more accurate than polls in some earlier elections, its findings propelled a lively debate among election prognosticators.

3

The DPP in Opposition

Austin Horng-En Wang

On January 16, 2016, Democratic Progressive Party (DPP) candidate Tsai Ing-wen won the presidential election in a landslide, capturing 56 percent of the vote to 31 percent for Eric Chu of the Kuomintang (KMT) and becoming the first female leader in Taiwan's history. For anyone who even casually followed the pre-election polls or witnessed the implosion of the KMT's nomination process, the 2016 election result was not surprising. However, if one went back to 2008 and asked a Taiwanese voter on the street, he or she would have been much more likely to bet on the DPP losing for the next twenty years than on a young, nonfactional, and ideologically moderate woman leading the DPP's return to power. How did Tsai Ing-wen emerge as the leader of the DPP and, within eight years, win the presidency?

This chapter reviews Tsai Ing-wen's strategies and her interaction with other DPP politicians, as well as the political context during the eight years of the Ma Ying-jeou era (2008–2016). I highlight four critical factors that shaped Tsai's and the DPP's political strategies during this period: (1) the DPP's interpretation of its 2008 electoral fiasco, (2) the relative balance of power among the temporarily weakened factions inside DPP, (3) the change to concurrent presidential and legislative elections beginning in 2012, and (4) the development of political communication technology.

The first two factors created a unique opportunity for Tsai Ing-wen to emerge and win the DPP chairmanship, for which her moderate position on the cross-Strait issue, "consensus-seeking" personality, lack of affiliation with any particular intraparty faction, and personal background all were advantages. The combination of these four factors enabled Tsai to emerge as the clear party leader, to reform and strengthen the DPP's party

organization, and, as I argue in the following sections, eventually to presidentialize the DPP.[1]

A review of Tsai Ing-wen's failures and successes during the Ma era is
important for both theoretical and practical reasons. First, this case illustrates how a loosely organized opposition party with multiple factions can
be gradually centralized. Second, Tsai's decisionmaking style before her
victory in 2016 sheds light on how she has handled recent policy conflicts
as president. Third, the evolution of the DPP's campaign strategies during
the Ma era provides a demonstration of how the rapid changes in information consumption habits have affected public opinion in Taiwan in recent
years. In the end, the combination of the emergence of Tsai and presidentialization of the party helped the DPP to win back the presidency in 2016,
but it may also have increased the uncertainty about the DPP's future—and
especially the future direction of its cross-Strait policies.

Learning from the DPP's 2008 Electoral Fiasco

In the election held on March 22, 2008, KMT presidential candidate Ma
Ying-jeou won the presidency by an unprecedented margin. Ma received 58
percent of all votes, compared with DPP candidate Frank Hsieh's 42 percent. Two months before this election, the KMT also won an overwhelming
victory in the Legislative Yuan election, taking 81 of 113 seats (72 percent).
This sweeping victory reflected not only the effectiveness of the KMT's
and Ma's campaign strategies but also four fundamental political errors that
the DPP and President Chen Shui-bian had made over the previous eight
years. The party's focus on these errors, and resolve not to repeat them,
then shaped the DPP's decisionmaking process and intraparty politics after
the 2008 elections.

First, the DPP's primary candidate selection method, in which nominees were chosen based on telephone polls that applied a screening question to remove pan-Blue supporters from the sample, did not work well.
After news of President Chen Shui-bian's embezzlement scandal broke in
2006, Chen was sharply criticized by the highly organized New Tide faction, as well as by many other prominent DPP party members. In response,
Chen and DPP chair Yu Shyi-kun established the so-called remove-the-
Blues poll for the county executive and legislative primaries, which was
designed to solicit opinions only from pan-Green respondents to decide on
candidates. By making the primary "Greener," this change benefited nominees who were loyal to the president and successfully prevented New Tide
members from winning the primaries by criticizing Chen. Yu further justified this method by arguing that this remove-the-Blues poll design would
prevent KMT supporters from influencing the DPP's nominations. However, the DPP's humiliating loss in the 2008 legislative election starkly

illustrated the drawbacks of this method.[2] The remove-the-Blues poll primary method tended to result in the nomination of candidates far from the median voter's position for the general election, putting the DPP at a greater electoral disadvantage.

Second, factional competition became more open, fiercer, and much more harmful to the DPP than before. Before Chen Shui-bian became president in 2000, the DPP was made up of a loose coalition of numerous anti-KMT factions and groups. Some of these were composed of victims of the KMT's political repression and the lawyers who helped them, some were labor-movement activists, and some others were overseas advocates of Taiwan's independence.[3] During Chen's presidency, however, these factions spent most of their energy competing with each other for government resources rather than debating policies.[4] Chen deliberately encouraged four party heavyweights—Su Tseng-chang, Yu Shyi-kun, Frank Hsieh, and Annette Lu—to develop their own individual-centered factions in order to achieve a balance of influence within the DPP and to play them off one another. During the 2008 DPP presidential primary, open mudslinging among the four factions was rampant, which was harmful not only to the four of them but also to the DPP as a whole. In addition, the seventh constitutional reform in 2005, which changed the electoral system for the Legislative Yuan, replacing the single nontransferable vote (SNTV) electoral system with single-member districts (SMDs) elected using plurality rule while also cutting the number of seats in the Legislative Yuan in half, further aggravated this factional competition inside the DPP.[5]

Third, during President Chen's second term, the DPP's brand as a "progressive" party became increasingly sullied, and it lost support among the younger generations. As Chen became engulfed in scandal, the proportion of Taiwanese people who considered the DPP to be corrupt increased from 25 percent in 1996 to 45 percent in 2008. (By contrast, the percentage who expressed similar views about the KMT declined from 57 to 44.) Chen had styled himself an anticorruption fighter during his first presidential campaign in 2000, but by 2008 the DPP had lost its advantage among voters who cared most about combating corruption.[6] The factional competition and intraparty mudslinging also damaged the DPP's public image among these groups. Before 2000, college students were strong supporters of the DPP; many of them volunteered for the party's campaign activities and helped build its first online bulletin board system, websites, video games, and online broadcasting system. But as it lost the enthusiastic support of volunteers from the younger generation, the DPP's technological advantage over the KMT declined, so that this gap between the parties was largely eliminated by the time of the 2008 elections.[7] Even the director of the DPP Youth Department for the 2008 campaign complained that he had been unable to hire enough young people to help with campaign activities.

Fourth, in 2008, there was colossal discord over campaign strategies and resource allocations between DPP presidential candidate Frank Hsieh and the party organization controlled by President Chen. The Legislative Yuan election was held in January, while the presidential election was held two months later, in March, which meant that the campaigns for the two elections took place on different schedules. After winning a tough primary, Frank Hsieh had to run his presidential campaign with only the help of his own faction, while President Chen maintained control over the DPP's party headquarters and limited its efforts to the campaign for the legislature.[8] President Chen not only supported the introduction of the remove-the-Blues poll in 2006 but also announced a "Resolution for a Normal Country" in 2007, which stated that the nation should "accomplish rectification of the name 'Taiwan' as soon as possible and write a new constitution." Chen also called for a referendum to join the United Nations under the name of Taiwan, which was set to take place on the same day as the presidential election. Chen's agenda-setting seriously overshadowed Hsieh's campaign, and Hsieh's nearly independent campaign strategy also undermined the DPP's ability to mobilize its supporters to turn out for both elections. Even though Hsieh became the party chairman after the disastrous results of the legislative election, it was all too late for the DPP's chances.

The Rise of Tsai Ing-wen: Balancing Factions and Seeking Consensus

After President Chen left office in May 2008, he faced several criminal investigations, effectively sidelining him from the DPP. Now in opposition, the party needed a new chairman to deal with the four major problems just discussed, but its options were few; as Frank Hsieh stated right after the election, "All DPP elites and anyone with power are responsible for the loss."[9]

Two competing voices emerged during the DPP chairmanship election in May 2008. The fundamentalist camp was initially led by Chai Trong-rong, a seventy-two-year-old faction leader and the founding father of the World United Formosans for Independence in the United States. Chai argued that the DPP needed to push harder for independence, to take a stronger stand against cooperation between the KMT and the People's Republic of China (PRC), and to provide a much clearer ideological stance to attract voters. Later, Chai dropped his bid and cooperated closely with another candidate for chairman, Koo Kwang-ming, an eighty-one-year-old businessman and activist who had previously led the Taiwan independence movement in Japan.

The second group went in the opposite direction and decided to try to position the party closer to the median voter. To address the party's core problems and to regain popular support, some DPP members, mostly young and calling for "generational replacement," believed that the DPP needed a younger chairman with a progressive image who would be an ideological moderate, independent of any faction, and able to mediate between the fractious groups in the party. Moreover, the DPP was under severe financial pressure and facing debts of about US$6 million after the 2008 elections, so the new chairman needed to be able to fundraise for the party as well.

Given these criteria, Tsai Ing-wen seemed to be the only option on the table for this group in 2008.[10] Unlike the old faction leaders, Tsai had not participated in, or suffered during, the pre-1987 democratization movement, so she did not have strong links to any of the factions, and she had only formally joined the DPP four years earlier. Compared with Chai and Koo, Tsai was also much younger, at fifty-one years old, and her gender[11] and highly educated background could help restore the progressive image of the DPP. Tsai was also from an affluent family and held out some promise of stabilizing the party's finances.

Moreover, Tsai's reputation as a consensus seeker implied that she would strive for a more flexible cross-Strait policy, and it made her acceptable to all of the factions, at least in the short run. One of my interviewees who worked closely with Tsai mentioned that she tended not to preclude any viewpoint or make decisions quickly, and she preferred to find a compromise among all relevant actors; she was typically patient enough to wait until a consensus could be reached, even if that took a long time. Tsai's consensus-seeking personality, along with her nonfactional background, enabled her to be the compromise choice among the various DPP factions in the post–2008 election context, especially for those such as the New Tide, who were looking to recover some of their previous influence within the party. Compared with Chai and Koo, Tsai's personal background clearly could help improve the DPP's party image.[12] Nevertheless, her "open-ended" stance on the cross-Strait relationship also troubled many pro-independence DPP members, and it was unclear whether she could secure the chair's position without their support.

In the DPP chairmanship election held on May 19, 2008, about 130,000 DPP members cast ballots, and Tsai won 57 percent of the vote. It was the highest turnout for a party chairmanship election since 1998, and the number of votes Tsai received, 73,865, was also the highest in DPP history. Nevertheless, even though Tsai had received cross-factional support, she did not win overwhelmingly, implying that she was distrusted by many pro-independence party members. The high turnout rate also reflected how critical this election was for deciding the direction the DPP would take in the Ma era: by choosing Tsai to lead the DPP, party members endorsed a strategy of moderation over fundamentalism.

Institutional Reform, the 2012 Elections, and the Presidentialization of the DPP

Centralizing Authority in the Party Chair, 2008–2012

When Tsai was chosen as chairwoman, it was expected that she would not upset the power balance between the party's factions. She initially did not enjoy much independent authority, and her predecessors left her few executive resources except for the party's debts. Therefore, negotiating compromises among the factions was a central feature of Tsai's leadership during her first and second terms as chair (2008–2012). Nevertheless, Tsai and the rest of the DPP learned from the 2008 defeat, and worked to gradually centralize authority and institutionalize the power of the DPP chairmanship. In addition, the decision announced by the Central Election Commission (CEC) to hold the 2012 presidential and legislative elections concurrently, which some KMT campaign staff and DPP legislators believed was done to help Ma's reelection, also helped Tsai consolidate her leadership over the party.

In April 2008, the DPP decided to abolish the remove-the-Blues polling method, since it had contributed to the party's defeat in that year's elections. Two months after becoming the chairwoman, Tsai announced that the party would also eliminate the closed primary for the 2009 and 2010 local elections as well. Instead, the mayoral candidates were to be decided through "negotiations," while the county and city councilor candidates were to be chosen by using telephone surveys that included all respondents. Moreover, potential candidates no longer needed to be a DPP member for at least a year in order to be eligible to be nominated. Tsai justified these changes by arguing that they would prevent fierce intraparty competition and help increase the party's popular appeal.[13] At the same time, Tsai moved to close eighty-four DPP village offices, the lowest level of party office, many of which were particularly corrupt and under the control of nonparty figures.[14] This reform was defended as a cost-saving measure, but it also reduced the possibility that party members would be arrested for corrupt behavior in the closed primaries.[15] These reforms were initially challenged by the pro-independence fundamentalists and the elder party members, but most of the faction leaders expected negotiations for primaries to be beneficial to their own interests, and the telephone survey system appeared as though it would benefit incumbents,[16] so both changes were approved by the party's central committee.

The results of the 2009 and 2010 local elections, in which the DPP did better than expected, increased confidence within the party that its new strategy was effective. Meanwhile, the global economic downturn and President Ma's mismanagement of Typhoon Morakot relief efforts also helped the DPP recover support. The party's rising popularity also helped the DPP and Tsai to fundraise and pay off outstanding debts. After Tsai became the chairwoman in 2008, the large operating deficit forced the DPP to lay off several party staff, cut welfare benefits, close party offices, set fundraising quotas for higher-level party members, and hold a series of fundraising parties. Tsai even used her own personal funds to pay the year-end bonuses for party staff.[17] In September 2011, Tsai mentioned in a fundraising dinner in Los Angeles that the DPP had retired most of the debt, and that "even though the DPP received some support from rich people, most of the funds came from ordinary people's daily income and small donations, such as NTD $100 or $500 (USD $3 or $15)."[18]

In early 2011, the DPP passed three additional important institutional reforms. First, the party's presidential and district legislative candidates (which made up two-thirds of all legislative seats) would be fully decided through simple telephone surveys, rather than through remove-the-Blues polls or closed primaries. Second, the party's definition of a "noncompetitive legislative district" was revised upward, from the DPP receiving 30 percent of votes in the last election to 42.5 percent. Because the DPP chair could directly select candidates for "noncompetitive" districts under the party's nomination rules, this change increased the number of legislative races to which Tsai could assign candidates from thirteen to forty.[19] Third, the DPP's legislative party list (about one-third of all legislative seats) would be fully decided by a nomination committee appointed by the party chair; in 2008, by contrast, the chair could select only one-third of the list, and the rest were decided through the closed primary. These changes were contested by Annette Lu in the DPP's central committee meeting on January 22, 2011, but were supported by over two-thirds of the committee members (227 of 311).

Why did the other factions not protest against this evident centralization of power in the chair's hands? The logic behind these changes was threefold. First, Tsai increased the short-term influence of factions by inviting the faction heads to join the nomination committee or to become candidates themselves. The growing power of the chair over party nominations was, in effect, a "resource" created by Tsai that she could then distribute among the factions.[20] For instance, the DPP's 2012 legislative party list was filled mostly with prominent faction members rather than Tsai allies. Second, at the time of the party's institutional reforms, Tsai had no guarantee that she would be the presidential candidate or remain party chairwoman in the future, so the reform was perceived as fair and not favoring her own interests. For instance, the telephone survey method for choosing the presidential nominee was expected to benefit experienced and already-famous politicians such as Su Tseng-chang and Frank Hsieh more than Tsai. Indeed, Tsai almost failed to secure the DPP presidential nomination in 2011; she received an average support level of 42.5 percent among the five surveys used for the nomination, while Su received 41.2 percent.

Third, Tsai gradually weakened the influence of the DPP's old factions, overseeing the closing of local offices and abolition of the closed primaries. She justified these moves by pointing to the cost savings they generated, as well as the DPP's 2008 presidential loss and the need to reduce corruption among local party members. Time was also on Tsai's side.[21] In interviews that Jui-ming Hsieh conducted in 2011, for instance, most DPP faction leaders (with the exception of the New Tide, Su Tseng-chang, and Frank Hsieh) admitted that they were not cultivating a younger generation to succeed them and that the intraparty competition among factions was not over policy but instead over power and access to resources.[22] Faction heads Su, Hsieh, and Yu Shyi-kun all enjoyed an advantage in raising donations because they had all previously served as premier under Chen Shui-bian, and they had developed fundraising networks from their time in government. While this gave them access to more resources to sustain their factions, these networks could not be easily passed on to successors. Moreover, most of the DPP's factional ties were rooted in shared experiences and collective memories of political repression during the martial law era—and these would inevitably fade away over time as this generation aged out of politics. Though some faction leaders attempted to promote their children as potential successors, their efforts were mostly limited to the local level. In the Legislative Yuan, by contrast, the share of nonfactional DPP legislators increased steadily, from twenty-nine out of eighty-nine (32.6 percent) in 2004, to nine of twenty-seven (33.3 percent) in 2008, and to nineteen of forty (47.5 percent) in 2012.[23] An additional piece of evidence of the weakening influence of factions is that the DPP's institutional reforms survived even after Tsai stepped down as party chair after the 2012 presidential election. She was succeeded by Su Tseng-chang, who together with Hsieh and Yu proposed on May 26, 2013, to scrap the telephone survey and return to the closed primary. However, this proposal was rejected by the majority of DPP central committee members—only 66 of 287 supported the change.

At the same time that Tsai was promoting institutional reform within the party, the CEC announced on January 4, 2011, that it was considering holding the 2012 legislative and presidential elections on the same day. The CEC's public rationale for the change was that it would provide significant cost savings, but it would also require holding the presidential election in January, two months earlier than in 2008. This move was expected to benefit Ma's reelection prospects, since the day of the legislative elections in 2012 was the week of final exams for college students, who would find it hard to return home to vote, and college students tended to support pan-Green candidates.[24] Moreover, as one KMT campaigner suggested, if the DPP gained seats in the 2012 legislative election, it might negatively affect President Ma's vote share two months later.[25] However, Tsai herself did not express strong opposition to holding concurrent elections, and the CEC confirmed the change on May 22, 2011.

In hindsight, holding the presidential and legislative elections at the same time helped Tsai to consolidate her power and presidentialize the DPP.[26] First, in Taiwan the turnout rate for presidential elections has usually been 15 to 20 percent higher than for legislative elections—additional voters are motivated and mobilized by the presidential candidates. For instance, the turnout rate in the 2008 legislative election was 59 percent, while in the presidential election held two months later, it was 76 percent, a 17 percent increase. Second, since both campaigns occurred at the same time, mass media tended to cover the presidential race much more closely than the legislative ones. For instance, in a study of the DPP over this time period, Yen-ting Shih estimated that the average number of news stories about legislative candidates dropped sharply between the two elections, from 187 in 2008 to 122 in 2012 (a 35 percent decline), and 118 in 2016.[27]

The effects of concurrent elections on turnout and media coverage, along with the general lack of independent resources, incentivized DPP legislative candidates to cooperate closely with Tsai, since their electoral fortunes would be decided mainly by Tsai's performance in the campaign rather than their own efforts. In contrast with the discord that characterized the 2008 elections, in 2012 the DPP's legislative candidates mostly followed Tsai's campaign themes and slogans, adopted the same color (yellow) and same design for their campaign materials, and sought out opportunities to campaign with Tsai. This was especially true for those candidates who were less well known to the electorate. Huang and Wang later found empirical evidence of a presidential coattail effect in these concurrent elections.[28] Since Tsai was both the chair of the party and the DPP's presidential candidate at the same time, she was well positioned to coordinate the activities of the individual campaigns, which revitalized the DPP's central campaign organization.

Consolidating Centralized Authority, 2012–2016

By the 2016 campaign, the effect of Tsai's centralization of authority within the DPP was quite evident. After Su, Hsieh, and Yu failed in their attempt to return the DPP to a closed primary system, the Sunflower Movement protests erupted in March 2014. During the movement's occupation of the Legislative Yuan, Su as the DPP chairman was intensely criticized by students and other protesters for the opposition party's failure to block the Cross-Strait Services Trade Agreement (CSSTA) and other agreements that President Ma had signed with the PRC. In May 2014, he resigned, and Tsai reassumed the chairmanship of the party.

By the time of the DPP's 2016 presidential primary, Tsai faced no intraparty challengers to her presidential bid, which gave her additional flexibility to reposition the DPP closer to the median voter. First, she cut off intraparty discussion within the DPP's central party committee about "freezing" the clause in the party charter calling for eventual independence for Taiwan, which could have forced Tsai to clarify her own position.[29]

Second, with the decline in influence of the traditional personal factions, she could exert full control over the nomination process for the 2014 local and 2016 legislative elections. The same rules used in 2010 and 2012, requiring negotiated nominations for difficult races and a chair-appointed nomination committee for the party list, were still in place. This time, however, Tsai did not need to placate the factions, and she did not place any former factional leaders on the party list. Instead, she focused on salient policy issues that the majority of Taiwanese cared about, including food safety, long-term care, daycare, and housing, and then nominated specialists and activists with expertise on these issues.[30] Hence the DPP's party list no longer functioned as a resource to be distributed among the party's factions, but instead became another campaign tool to be used to support Tsai's presidential run.

Third, since the 2016 DPP legislative candidates depended on the party headquarters and Tsai's presidential campaign for resources, she could require candidates and their campaign staff to emphasize specific issues and steer clear of more extreme policies while stumping for votes.[31] Post-election statistical analyses show that Tsai had long coattails in the 2016 elections, and many of the DPP's candidates won because they were closely associated with Tsai.[32]

The Pan-Green Coalition in the 2016 Legislative Elections

By the 2016 elections, Tsai was even powerful enough to force some DPP politicians to step aside in certain districts to make way for candidates nominated by other small parties. For instance, the DPP yielded three district seats to the New Power Party (NPP), a pro-independence party that emerged out of the Sunflower Movement in 2014.[33] One reason that Tsai may have chosen to support the NPP is because it made the DPP seem more moderate. Data from survey experiments conducted in Taiwan suggest that the emergence of more extreme ideological candidates within the same camp can lead voters to perceive mainstream candidates as much more moderate than before, even if their political positions remain unchanged.[34] Additional evidence of this effect comes from a Taiwan National Security Survey conducted in late 2015, which found that 65 percent of Taiwanese did not think tension between the PRC and Taiwan would rise if Tsai and the DPP won the 2016 elections—a major change from previous survey results. Since cross-Strait relations have long been the most critical issue in Taiwanese politics, this survey result provides additional evidence that Tsai's "return-to-the-middle" strategy successfully moderated the DPP's image over the party's eight years in opposition.[35]

Tsai had other reasons as well to cede districts to small parties and non-partisan candidates. One was to ensure they did not run directly against DPP candidates elsewhere, which would have hurt the party's overall performance and could have prevented them from winning a majority. Figure 3.1 shows a scatterplot of the pan-Green camp's vote share in the 2012 and 2016 legislative elections in the seventy-three single-member districts. In 2012, the DPP nominated sixty-nine candidates and ceded one district to the Green Party. In 2016, by contrast, the DPP nominated only fifty-nine candidates (the fifty-nine circles in the figure), and ceded nine districts to the small parties (the three diamonds and six triangles); some small parties also nominated candidates in districts where a DPP candidate was running (the ten squares). The dashed line is the predicted relationship between the DPP's district vote share in 2012 versus 2016 for districts with only a DPP nominee, while the solid diagonal line indicates parity between the DPP's 2012 and 2016 district vote shares.

Figure 3.1 provides several essential insights into the DPP's strategy and Tsai's authority within the party. First, all nine districts that the DPP ceded to small parties were noncompetitive—that is, the DPP received 42.5

Figure 3.1   Pan-Green Camp Vote Share in 2012 vs. 2016 Legislative Elections by Coalition Method

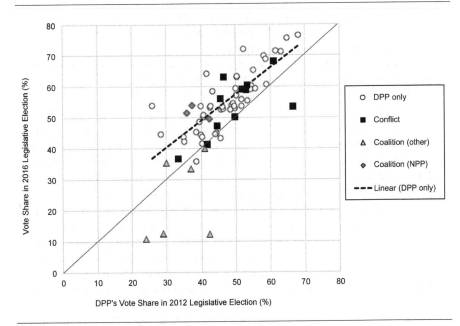

Source: Central Election Commission.

percent or less there in 2012. The average 2012 DPP vote share in the districts in which the DPP also nominated candidates in 2016 was 47.6 percent, while the average share in the nine districts the party ceded was 34.6 percent.[36] Since Tsai set the rule that the party chair could decide who to nominate in these noncompetitive districts, she had the power to cede them to smaller parties.

Second, as the gap between the diagonal parity line and the dashed prediction line in Figure 3.1 shows, the DPP's overall legislative district vote share increased by about 10 percent from 2012 to 2016. In the three districts that the DPP ceded to the NPP, the latter's candidates performed about as well as other DPP candidates. By contrast, all of the other small parties performed relatively worse. This result not only shows that the NPP worked closely with the DPP in the 2016 legislative elections, but also suggests that the social justice issues emphasized by the Green Party and Social Democratic Party were not as salient as the cross-Strait issue. Additional evidence of the primacy of cross-Strait relations to voting behavior in this election comes from Christopher Achen and T. Y. Wang, who found that Taiwanese people's support for or opposition to the Economic Cooperation Framework Agreement was mainly determined by their attitudes toward China rather than their positioning on the left-right ideological spectrum.[37] By the same logic, social justice issues could not mobilize anywhere near as much support as the DPP did by opposing closer relations with the PRC. Evidence from survey experiments, too, suggests that Taiwanese opinions about the Sunflower Movement were determined mostly by respondents' attitudes toward China, rather than views about the possible impacts of trade agreements.[38]

Third, in the districts in which both the DPP and at least one small party nominated candidates, the DPP was hurt by this competition, as the small parties pulled some of the pan-Green vote away from its nominees. In the DPP-only districts, the DPP received on average 55.50 percent of the vote; in districts where at least one small party also ran a candidate, by contrast, the DPP received only 49.96 percent. In other words, the DPP lost about 5 percent of the vote to small parties where they ran directly against DPP candidates in the districts. One can see this difference in Figure 3.1, where seven of the eleven squares are below the dashed line.[39]

In a strategic sense, the DPP's decision not to nominate candidates in some noncompetitive districts was successful. The party still won forty-nine of seventy-three districts in 2016, giving it a large majority in the Legislative Yuan. While most of the candidates from the small parties lost, the NPP was an exception: it won the three district seats that the DPP had yielded to it, in addition to two party-list seats, and became the third-largest party in the legislature (and a frequent critic of the DPP) after 2016. In Taichung's third district, KMT incumbent Yang Chiung-ying had been the legislator since 1999; he had received 58 percent in 2012, while DPP candidate Tong Rui-yang received only 37 percent. With little perceived chance to win, the DPP readily agreed to cede this district to the NPP's Hung Tzu-yung, a young woman who had high name recognition because her brother Hung Chung-chiu had died while in military detention in 2014, leading to a massive protest. In Taipei's fifth district, DPP candidate Yan Sheng-guan had received 42 percent in 2012 and sought the party's nomination to run again in 2016. However, the DPP instead ceded the district to the NPP's Freddy Lim, the lead vocalist of the heavy-metal band Chthonic. Yan did not actively oppose this decision, possibly because both Yan and Lim had worked together under Frank Hsieh during his 2008 presidential campaign.

The most surprising of the three districts was New Taipei's twelfth. According to one of my interviewees, as part of an informal pre-election cooperation agreement, Tsai agreed to let NPP chairman Huang Kuo-chang run in any district he liked. Tsai and the rest of the DPP leadership were confident that Huang would decide to run in New Taipei's eighth district, which was represented by the KMT's Chang Ching-chung, one of the Sunflower Movement's chief villains in the Legislative Yuan. If Huang chose the eighth district, the Huang-Chang battle would undoubtedly attract the spotlight and enjoy nationwide attention. Huang instead surprised the DPP by picking the twelfth district, where he lived. The DPP's leading candidate for that seat, Shen Fa-hui, had run in 2012 and received only 36 percent of the vote; even with the DPP's average improvement of ten points over 2012, he might still not have been able to win if he were the nominee. Nevertheless, he openly opposed Huang's decision when it was announced in June 2015. A month later, however, he apologized, saying that he would "follow the party's decision."[40] This story provides further evidence of how Tsai fully controlled the nomination process and strategically helped the pan-Green coalition to win a majority in the Legislative Yuan for the first time in history.

To sum up, Tsai's institutional reforms of the DPP chairmanship and party organization were initially designed to create a balance between the factions and to reduce the open competition within the party for offices and resources. However, generational replacement within the party gradually weakened the influence of factions, and the switch to concurrent elections strengthened the coordinating role of the party chair. As a result, Tsai, as DPP chairwoman, gradually accumulated additional power that she was able to use to her benefit. In clear contrast to the intraparty mudslinging and discord in 2008 between the DPP headquarters and the Hsieh campaign, Tsai in 2012 and 2016 had firm control of both the party machinery and her presidential campaign, and she was able to create a "Tsai-centered" campaign agenda that steered the DPP toward the median voter.

Information Technology, Campaign Strategies, and Presidentialization of the DPP

One underappreciated aspect of the centralization of authority within the DPP between 2008 and 2016 is the party's adaptation to the rapid development of information technology. The emergence of search engines, personal blogs, smartphones, and social-networking sites fundamentally changed how most Taiwanese voters consumed and responded to political information over this period. Tsai and the DPP undertook two significant top-down institutional reforms, one in 2009, the other in 2015, to take advantage of these emerging communication technologies. With an eye toward the 2016 campaign, they conducted a series of experiments involving microtargeting and micromobilization that not only changed how the DPP ran its campaigns but also reinforced Tsai's leading role within the party.

Over the past two decades, the number of Internet users in Taiwan and their online behavior has changed dramatically. The proportion of Internet users rose from 20 percent of adults in 2000, to 68 percent in 2008, to 82 percent in 2016. The proportion of Taiwanese people who read political news online also increased over this same time period, from 15 percent in 2000, to 35 percent in 2008, to 55 percent in 2016.[41] Yahoo and Google (and their respective email services) also appeared around 2000; personal blogs, YouTube, and Plurk became popular around 2005; and smartphones and Facebook became widespread and quickly transformed how Taiwanese people communicated starting around 2008. Search engines provided opportunities for users to actively search for information rather than passively waiting for news to be reported by traditional media outlets. Personal blogs allowed Internet users to create their own media outlets and disseminate information and commentary on their own. Social-networking sites further increased this two-way transmission of information, and also created more opportunities for "echo chambers" of politically like-minded people to emerge. Smartphones, in turn, massively reduced the physical limitations on sending and receiving information, enabling people to consume and disseminate news even while they were on the street. There is some evidence that the spread of mobile phones throughout the population also helped to reduce the coordination problems inherent in political mass mobilization, and may have contributed to an increase in the number of protests in Taiwan during the Ma years.[42] In short, the advances in information technology during this era fundamentally transformed the capabilities and mobility of Taiwanese citizens, regardless of their generation.

Before 2008, the DPP did not have a comprehensive strategy for online campaigning. Instead, faction heads such as Yu Shyi-kun and Frank Hsieh developed their own "online armies," which fought against one another in the 2008 DPP presidential primary by posting news articles, sending emails, and sharing arguments.[43] These online armies mostly targeted the younger generations. Beyond these factional armies, the DPP's online campaign strategy was run by the Publicity Department and the Youth Department, an indication that the party saw online spaces as an extension of traditional media.[44]

This began to change after Tsai Ing-wen became party chair. Tsai reorganized the former online armies of the factional groups into a new Internet Department within the DPP, which was formally established on February 8, 2009. In my view, the Internet Department played a critical role in Tsai's centralization of authority and the presidentialization of the DPP. First, after the Internet Department was established, it began to provide formal training and advice to all DPP candidates and their campaign staff. According to the teaching materials used in its 2009 training camp,[45] the Internet Department instructed legislators and their staff how to develop their websites and Facebook pages, and it provided professional recommendations about brand-building, design, user flow analysis, collaboration tools, and live-streaming. This shared training also enhanced cooperation between Tsai's campaign and those of other DPP candidates in the 2012 and 2016 concurrent elections.[46]

Second, as early as 2009, the Internet Department recommended that the DPP microtarget a variety of groups online, rather than just young people. To follow Tsai's "return-to-the-middle" strategy and to make the best use of Tsai's personal background, the Internet Department initially focused on young, female, nonpartisan, and absentee voters. The Internet Department believed these groups would be much easier to reach through the Internet—an idea it picked up from US president Barack Obama's 2008 campaign.[47] It was a reasonable strategic change, since Internet users and voters who read political news online in Taiwan had reached a considerable number. Moreover, the Internet Department also successfully predicted the trend toward smartphone use and created the first smartphone-friendly DPP website and app for Tsai and the DPP in 2009 (when only 15 percent of adults had a smartphone).

Third, the effects of online campaigns were empirically tested several times before and during the elections, which introduced the DPP to evidence-based evaluation of campaign messages. For example, Tsai and other DPP candidates held several activities targeted at their personal fans to test how much they could successfully mobilize their online supporters to attend offline events.

The eruption of the Sunflower Movement protests in March 2014 further extended the scope and strategic importance of online campaigning. One month after the Sunflower Movement began, the head of the Internet Department lamented on his blog that the DPP was "totally defeated" by the movement: the party not only had failed to predict the movement's emergence, but also could never hope to mobilize so many people to take to the streets on its own. The DPP also had underestimated the political engagement and willingness of ordinary Taiwanese to mobilize for issues they believed in. The department head then concluded that "the number of fans or website visitors is not at all important; they need to get out and vote."

In a post–Sunflower Movement adjustment, Tsai merged the Internet Department and the Publicity Department together to become the DPP's Media and Creative Center (MCC) in February 2015, and at the same time established a separate News and Opinion Center. There were initially twenty employees in the MCC, and five employees in the News and Opinion Center. According to the head of the MCC, this reform was an indication of the DPP's intention to devote most of its resources to online campaigning, especially microtargeting of potential voters.[48] The idea for the MCC came from the experience of independent candidate Ko Wen-je's campaign for the Taipei City mayoral election in late 2014. Tsai lent half of the Internet Department's staff to Ko and let his campaign test all kinds of microtargeting and mobilization strategies and techniques.[49]

The creation of the MCC was another indication of Tsai's full control over the DPP party organization by this time, and of the top-down nature of the DPP's presidential candidate–centered campaign in 2016. Microtargeting is capital- and labor-intensive and requires long-term preparation. The MCC created, for example, more than eighty campaign videos from the materials the DPP had collected over the previous four years to target a variety of subgroups, which no candidates save the presidential one could afford to do. These videos included one for young people looking for housing, one for pet adoption, one for musicians and artists, one for anime cosplayers and comic book fans, and so forth.[50] After broadcasting the videos, the MCC held a series of meetings with Tsai for each of these groups, focusing on one political issue, or sometimes avoiding political topics altogether. In addition, the MCC not only posted different policy issues using different political frames on different websites and platforms, but also made use of microtargeting tools provided by Google, Facebook, and other Internet services.

Once again, as the 2016 campaign got under way, these materials and tools were shared with other DPP candidates and their staffs. As Tsai's chances of winning the presidency looked better and better, the DPP shifted its goal to winning a majority in the Legislative Yuan, and the party consequently provided more campaign resources and technical help to the DPP's legislative candidates.[51]

Conclusion

Following the DPP's 2008 electoral fiasco, Tsai Ing-wen initially emerged as a compromise candidate supported by all of the party's factions, due to her consensus-seeking personality and "return-to-the-middle" strategy. However, through a series of reforms to the DPP's nomination process and campaign organization, and with the help of the switch to concurrent presidential and legislative elections and advances in information technology, Tsai gradually centralized power within the party, transforming the DPP from a fiercely divided and factionalized organization into a top-down presidential candidate–centered and well-oiled electoral machine. The DPP's recovery during the Ma years demonstrates how a political party can learn from a humiliating defeat, and how both internal and external forces can contribute to its revival.

Reviewing the DPP's transformation and Tsai Ing-wen's emergence over the previous eight years also helps us understand political developments after Tsai was inaugurated as president. First, President Tsai's initial decision to deemphasize highly controversial policies such as same-sex marriage and pension reform, and wait until a consensus had formed within the party and government about how to deal with these issues, is consistent with her previous approach to controversies as party chair while the DPP was still in opposition. One of my interviewees suggested that Tsai would often reset her perception of the "median point" in public opinion about specific policies after witnessing angry protests or reading new poll results. Since Tsai has tended to define her own position as a starting point for discussion rather than as a target to persuade others to move toward, we might expect the number of social movements and protests to increase during her presidency, because they may be effective at changing her perception of where the median in public opinion lies. The huge protests against changes to the labor law, pension reforms, and the legalization of same-sex marriage that occurred during President Tsai's first term make strategic sense, given her political style. This approach has had some drawbacks for her presidency: Tsai's approval rate declined rapidly after she took office, because neither pan-Blue nor pan-Green supporters were very satisfied with her policy decisions. However, it has also been reassuring in some cases: for instance, as long as there is no firm consensus among Taiwanese in favor of altering Taiwan's relationship with the PRC, there is no reason to believe that President Tsai would abruptly shift away from the cross-Strait status quo.

Second, with the decline of the old personalized factions and the institutionalization of inclusive polls for candidate selection, it is likely that the influence of fundamentalist pro-independence members within the DPP will remain limited over the near term. Nevertheless, results from the Taiwan National Security Survey indicate a significant increase in support for Taiwan independence, even at the risk of provoking an attack from the PRC: between 2003 and 2016, the share supporting this option increased from 30 percent to 40 percent.[52] So far at least, the reforms to the DPP's nomination process and Tsai's consensus-seeking approach to intraparty disputes have managed to keep most pro-independence supporters from abandoning the party, while still allowing the DPP to take moderate positions in election campaigns. Nevertheless, it is possible that in the future, more pan-Green supporters could defect to other pro-independence parties such as the Taiwan Solidarity Union, the New Power Party, and the Taiwan Statebuilding Party—if not in Legislative Yuan elections, then at least in local council elections under the more permissive SNTV system.

In the end, it is still not clear whether the DPP's institutional changes will outlast Tsai Ing-wen. The DPP's centralization of authority in the party chair, as well as the presidentialization of the party, depended to a great deal on Tsai's personality (and possibly also her personal resources and political talents). For instance, when Tsai stepped down as chairwoman for the first time after the 2012 elections, many of the staff in the DPP's Internet and Publicity Departments also left the DPP and migrated to Tsai's private think tank. Conversely, after Tsai won the presidency in 2016, she brought many of the party's staff with her to the presidential office, leaving the DPP headquarters half-empty. Thus, even if the institutional changes implemented under Tsai's leadership remain in place over the long term, the chair's ability to set the direction of the DPP will probably be limited by the need to negotiate with the party's other power-brokers.

Notes

1. Samuels and Shugart, *Presidents, Parties, and Prime Ministers;* Passarelli, *The Presidentialization of Political Parties.*

2. Shih, "Timing of Elections, Party Presidentialization, and Party System Nationalization."

3. Negotiations among the factions also appear to have helped the DPP to overcome the coordination problem in legislative elections held under the SNTV electoral system. See Hsu and Chen, "Intra-Party Factional Competition and the Fate of the Party Election."

4. See Hsieh, "Democratic Progressive Party's Factionalism."

5. Chen and the rest of the DPP leadership apparently recognized that factional competition was harmful to the party's image, so the DPP announced in July 2006 that it would dissolve all factions. However, the announcement was widely believed to be targeted at the New Tide faction. Moreover, all factions simply moved underground. Regarding the impact of the constitutional reform, one former DPP legislator admitted that "90% of legislators did not know how switching to SMDs would impact the DPP's future"; see Hsieh, "DPP Factionalism," p. 241.

6. Lin and Yu, "Party Image and Voting Behavior of Taiwanese Voters."

7. Wang, "Democratic Progressive Party's Online Campaigning Strategy."

8. Hsieh, "DPP Factionalism."

9. Ching-shan Liaw, "Frank Hsieh Is Responsible for the Loss," *Taiwan E-News,* April 4, 2008, https://www.taiwanenews.com/doc/liaw20080404.php.

10. Shih, "Timing of Elections."

11. The proportion of Taiwanese female voters supporting the pan-Green camp increased sharply from 1992 to 2004. In 2004, for the first time, female voters were more likely to vote for the DPP rather than the KMT presidential candidate. However, this pattern was completely reversed by Ma in 2008; Ma received broad support from Taiwanese female voters, even among those in the pan-Green camp. See Hsu, "Gender Gap and Voting Behavior," and Yang and Lin, "Do Women Transfer Their Votes to Tsai?"

12. Just one month after Tsai became the new DPP chairwoman, the DPP's approval rate had already jumped from 36 to 58 percent.

13. Chen-kai Yen, "The Pan-Green Camp Is Preparing for the 2009 Local Election," *Apple Daily*, July 11, 2008.

14. Hsieh, "DPP's Factionalism." This reform had also been proposed in 2005, but the chairman at that time, Su Tseng-chang, failed to get it passed.

15. Shih, "Timing of Elections."

16. Chen-kai Yen and Shen-yi Su, "Elder and Younger DPP Members Disagree over the New Nomination Process," *Apple Daily*, January 24, 2010.

17. Chun-hua Ho, "The DPP's Huge Debt," *Business Today*, December 28, 2008.

18. "Tsai's Fundraising Dinner at Los Angeles," *Taiwan Independent Media*, September 21, 2011, http://www.twimi.net/detail.php?mid=201.

19. Shih, "Timing of Elections."

20. Chen-kai Yen, Chia-shan Wu, and Yang-ming Huang, "The DPP's New Party List Nomination Rule Was Attacked As 'Dividing the Spoils,'" *Apple Daily*, January 21, 2011.

21. Min-te Cheng, "Say Good-bye to the DPP's Lawyer Generation," *China Times*, July 18, 2016.

22. Hsieh, "DPP's Factionalism."

23. Batto and Huang, "Executive Competition, Electoral Rules, and Faction Systems in Taiwan," p. 121.

24. However, this change may also have negatively impacted Taiwanese businesspeople who worked in mainland China, a group who tended to support the pan-Blue camp. Since that weekend was one week before the lunar New Year, it was costly for Taiwanese to fly back to Taiwan just to vote.

25. Shih, "Timing of Elections."

26. Ibid.

27. Ibid., p.71.

28. Huang and Wang, "Presidential Coattails in Taiwan."

29. Chia-shan Wu, Hsiu-hui Lin, and Yang-min Huang, "Strongman Tsai Silenced the Discussion About Freezing the Independence Clause in 5 Minutes," *Apple Daily*, July 21, 2014.

30. Hsiu-huei Lin and Shan-yi Su, "Tsai Sets Up 2,000 Fan Clubs Nationwide," *Apple Daily*, July 9, 2015.

31. Shih, "Timing of Elections."

32. Rich, "Coattails and Mixed Electoral Systems."

33. Fell, "Small Parties in Taiwan's 2016 Election."

34. Wang and Chen, "Extreme Candidates as the Beneficent Spoiler?"

35. Achen and Wang, *The Taiwan Voter.*

36. A two-group t-test shows this difference to be significant ($p < 0.01$).

37. Achen and Wang, *The Taiwan Voter.*

38. Chen and Yen, "Who Supports the Sunflower Movement?"

39. Small parties tended to nominate candidates to run against the DPP in two kinds of places: big cities, especially Taipei, where they had the best chances at attracting media attention and popularizing their party brands, and in DPP-dominated districts, especially in the south, where no one expected the KMT candidates to be viable. See Fell, "Small Parties in Taiwan's 2016 National Elections."

40. Fang-ho Su, "Shen Fa-hui Apologized; Huang: 'Never Mind,'" *Liberty Times*, July 20, 2015.

41. Taiwan Election and Democratization Study website, http://teds.nccu.edu.tw.

42. Lin and Su, "Flash-Mob Politics in Taiwan." See also Chapter 14 in this volume.

43. Ling-jia Fang, "Hsieh, Yu, and Su Created 'Online Army' to Attract Young Voters," *United Evening News*, May 29, 2007, p. A15.

44. Wang, "Democratic Progressive Party's Online Campaigning Strategy."

45. Available at http://dppnet.blogspot.com.

46. The training camp continued to be held after Tsai became president. See Fang-he Su, "DPP Provides New Class for 'Ads to the Elder Generation,'" *Liberty Times,* June 16, 2016.

47. Ho-min Lin, "Learning from Obama, DPP Prepares to Establish the Internet Department," *United News,* December 4, 2008, p. A4; Shiu-chiun Lin, "DPP Develops New Platform for Smartphone to Attract Voters," *United News,* June 2, 2011, p. A2.

48. Ke-yong Lin, "The Internet as the New Make-Up for Candidates," *Liberty Times,* February 18, 2016, http://talk.ltn.com.tw/article/breakingnews/1605398.

49. Chen-kai Yen, "DPP Establishes New Departments to Prepare for the 2016 Election," *Storm Media,* January 2, 2015, http://www.storm.mg/article/39783.

50. Li-chien Yen, "Tsai's Online Campaigning: Precision, Micro-Targeting, and Localization," *Business Next,* May 19, 2016, https://www.bnext.com.tw/article/39637/BN-2016-05-19-175914-178.

51. Shih, "Timing of Elections."

52. Austin Horng-En Wang, Wei-ting Yen, Jung-feng Tsai, Greg Sheen, Fang-yu Chen, and Jaw-nian Huang, "Taiwan and Mainland China in Talks? Here Are the 5 Things You Need to Know About What Taiwanese People Are Thinking," *Washington Post,* November 6, 2015, https://www.washingtonpost.com/news/monkey-cage/wp/2015/11/06/taiwan-and-mainland-china-in-talks-here-are-the-5-things-you-need-to-know-about-what-taiwanese-people-are-thinking/.

4

The KMT in Power

Nathan F. Batto

In the 2014 local elections and the 2016 national elections, the Kuomintang (KMT) suffered an unprecedented electoral repudiation. Unlike past defeats, the KMT could not point to renegade candidates splitting the vote or a fortuitously timed assassination attempt to explain away the result. For the first time, the electorate had unambiguously rejected the KMT.

This wave of voters turning away from the KMT was grounded in Taiwan's most fundamental political cleavage: how Taiwan relates to the People's Republic of China (PRC). During President Ma's tenure in office, especially in his second term, the KMT sent out several messages redefining the party's basic orientation on this "China question," repeatedly redefining itself in a more pro-China direction. President Ma had been elected in 2008 as a moderate candidate, promising "no unification, no independence, no war." This promise to maintain Taiwan's de facto independent status made him acceptable to a critical slice of Taiwan's electorate, those who did not consider themselves Chinese but saw potential economic benefit from integrating Taiwan's economy into China's. By the 2016 election, these voters had abandoned the KMT. The KMT was no longer seen as the only party that could maintain cross-Strait peace, and far more voters trusted the Democratic Progressive Party (DPP) to protect Taiwan's interests. Whereas average voters in 2008 had considered themselves to be roughly equidistant from the KMT and DPP on the unification-independence spectrum, by 2016 they considered themselves to be much farther from the KMT.

In this chapter I look in depth at two episodes that were critical in redefining the KMT's image: the battle to ratify the Cross-Strait Services

Trade Agreement (CSSTA) with the PRC, and the debate within the KMT in 2015 over whether to move away from the 1992 Consensus.[1] In both episodes, grassroots KMT politicians resisted efforts by the leadership to move the party in a more pro-China direction. Facing electoral pressure from an electorate that was, if anything, trending in the opposite direction, these grassroots politicians needed the KMT's position to be attractive to the median voter, not to extreme Chinese nationalist voters. The leadership had a different calculation. In his second term, President Ma did not need to run for reelection, and his focus was on implementing policies critical to the central thrust of his presidency—deepening the integration of Taiwan's economy into mainland China's. He proved willing to do almost anything necessary to ratify the CSSTA, regardless of public opinion. In 2015, KMT presidential contender Hung Hsiu-chu, coming from her party's extreme Chinese nationalist wing, seemed indifferent to how her positions would be viewed by the wider public. The rest of the party resisted her discourse, but they dared not completely repudiate the views of a person whom they were about to nominate for the presidency.

Theoretically, I look at these processes through the lens of presidentialized parties. David Samuels and Matthew Shugart have argued that in systems with elected presidents, winning the presidency is such a powerful incentive that parties organize themselves primarily for this task. One result is that presidents, whether prospective or incumbent, take over leadership of the party. Rather than the president pursuing the party's goals, the president uses the party organization as a lever to force party members to serve his or her purposes.[2] During efforts to pass the CSSTA, President Ma repeatedly used the party organization to attempt to bend party members to his will. After Ma resigned as party chair following the 2014 election debacle, the KMT was left without a clear leader, an unfamiliar situation for a presidentialized party. There was a struggle for primacy between the incumbent president, the party chair, and the presumptive presidential nominee, and the battle over the KMT's China discourse took place within this struggle over leadership of the party.

The KMT's Election Debacle

The scale of the KMT's defeat in 2016 was stunning. Eric Chu, the presidential candidate, managed only 31 percent of the vote. Four years earlier, Ma Ying-jeou had won reelection with 52 percent. The KMT was able to win only 35 of 113 legislative seats,[3] down from 64 in 2012. In the district races, where the KMT faced less competition from other parties on the unification side of the political spectrum, it won 39 percent of the vote. On the party-list ballot, where voters had more choices, only 27 percent of voters opted for the KMT. This national-level debacle completed the disastrous electoral cycle that had begun fourteen months earlier with local-level elections. In those elections, the KMT had nearly been swept altogether out of local power, winning only six of twenty-two mayoral positions. Of the six, five were small, rural, and poor counties. At the end of the 2014–2016 electoral cycle, with the notable exception of the New Taipei government, the KMT had been almost entirely expelled from power.

The KMT had suffered electoral defeats before. It lost the presidency in 2000 and 2004, and it was routed in the 1997 local elections when it won only eight of twenty-three local governments, including just two of the ten most populous cities and counties. However, in those previous defeats, the KMT could always comfort itself with the thought that the defeats were due to the KMT's own internal problems rather than a reflection of DPP strength. In 1997 and 2000, the KMT lost because of renegade candidates who split the pan-Blue vote. The greater KMT, including both official and renegade candidates, won far more votes than the DPP. In 2004, the DPP won a razor-thin majority, but KMT sympathizers could comfort themselves with the thought that the dramatic assassination attempt on President Chen the day before the election had swayed the result. The elections in 2014 and 2016 were different. There was no easy way to explain away the defeats.[4] What is more, the electoral results were not out of line with other important indicators, such as party identification or preferences toward independence or unification. For the first time in its history, the KMT had been unambiguously repudiated by the voters.

For longtime observers of Taiwanese politics, the overall numbers are stunning, but some of the more detailed results are nearly unfathomable. For example, consider the Blue north. We have been talking of a Blue north and Green south for nearly two decades, and we have grown used to the idea that the KMT can count on dominating elections there. In 2012, in the thirty-one legislative districts in the Blue north, the KMT won twenty-eight races, exceeded 40 percent of the votes in thirty districts, broke 50 percent in twenty-one districts, and broke 60 percent in seven of the thirty-one districts. In 2016, the KMT won only twelve of the thirty-one districts, and its candidates broke 40 percent in only twenty-one districts. Even more shocking, only two candidates managed (just barely) to exceed 50 percent. None of its legislative candidates in Taipei or Taoyuan managed an absolute majority of votes. The Blue north turned light Green. Similarly, consider Eric Chu's performance in the presidential election. Chu achieved an absolute majority in only the two legislative districts that are technically considered part of Fujian province; he did not achieve 50 percent in any of the seventy-one legislative districts on Taiwan or the Penghu islands. In fact, he managed 40 percent in only seven of those seventy-one. Four years earlier, Ma had broken 40 percent in sixty-eight and 50 percent in fifty-seven of the seventy-one. The Republic of China (ROC) has 368 township-level administrative districts. Chu beat Tsai in only seventy of these. Of the seventy, sixty-three produced fewer than 12,000 votes. Forty were towns with at least 25 percent indigenous voters, and another ten were in Fujian. Most of the remaining towns were rural and heavily Hakka. Finally, consider the indigenous townships. Indigenous voters have long been one of the KMT's most loyal voting blocs. In 2012, Ma Ying-jeou won nearly three out of every four votes in the forty-three townships with at least 25 percent indigenous voters. In those same forty-three townships, Chu won only 50 percent. This was not because Soong took all the votes; 30 percent voted for Tsai. These forty-three townships produced 165,367 total presidential votes, about the same as an ordinary legislative district. If it had been a legislative district, Tsai's 30 percent would have made it her worst district outside Fujian. In comparison, the KMT's worst legislative district was Tainan's second, where it somehow hit the 20 percent trifecta, failing to achieve 20 percent in the presidential, district, and party-list ballots (19.4, 18.7, and 18.6 percent respectively). Those are the types of numbers that the DPP achieved thirty years ago in places they called "democratic deserts." In 2016, the DPP was markedly stronger in indigenous townships than the KMT was in large swaths of the rural south.

Presidentialized Parties

Many studies of political parties start with the assumption that the party's caucus in the national legislature is the heart of the party. This assumption flows naturally from the logic of parliamentary government, in which the national legislature chooses the cabinet and the cabinet must maintain the confidence of the legislature. However, influential studies of US political parties have also made this assumption, even though the United States does not have a parliamentary system.[5] This assumption has never fit Taiwanese politics well. In the longtime ruling KMT, power has always been concentrated in the Central Standing Committee (CSC), and specifically in the party chair. The party chair has never been granted power by the legislative caucus. If anything, the relationship runs in reverse, with the party chair wielding powerful influence over who will be nominated to run for the legislature. Scholars have traditionally explained Taiwan's "unique" party organization with reference to the KMT's authoritarian legacy. Facing oblivion in the early 1920s, Sun Yat-sen reorganized the KMT along Leninist lines. Three decades later, when the KMT relocated to Taiwan and again faced an existential threat, Chiang Kai-shek implemented another reorganization to strengthen party discipline and consolidate his power as party chair. Taiwan democratized in the late 1980s and early 1990s, but the KMT's formal organization remained relatively unchanged. The number of legislators sitting on the CSC increased, but it would be a stretch to suggest that they took over the party or that they were able to determine who was elected party chair.

Taiwan's experience is perhaps not as unique as it appears. Samuels and Shugart argue that parties in systems with elected presidents are different from their counterparts in parliamentary systems in fundamental ways.[6] Because the delegation relationship from the party to the executive is different, parties in presidential systems tend to be dominated by the president.[7] Since their framework is central to this chapter, I will briefly recount the highlights of their theory in this section.

Samuels and Shugart frame their theory in the language of delegation relationships, in which a principal delegates some task to an agent.[8] In a parliamentary system, the legislature delegates executive power to a cabinet. Since the legislature can revoke that delegation at any time through a vote of no confidence, it has a powerful tool to ensure that cabinet remains a faithful agent. Presidents are not chosen directly by the legislature, so the party has to delegate to (meaning nominate) an agent acceptable to the broader electorate as well as to itself. Moreover, the president has a fixed term, so the legislature does not have the power to terminate that delegation at any time. The result is that the president is not necessarily compelled to pursue the policies that the broader party (or the narrower legislative caucus) might prefer.

Because control of the executive branch is such a large prize, parties tend to organize themselves in ways designed to win executive power.[9] Parties thus tend to reflect the constitutional structure, with both a legislative and a presidential branch. This, in turn, leads parties to become "presidentialized," a situation in which parties delegate significant discretion to their leader to shape electoral and governing strategies. Moreover, the president can become so influential that the normal delegation relationship—from legislature to the president—can be reversed. Samuels and Shugart note that in premier-presidential systems, even though the cabinet is constitutionally accountable to the legislature, it is not uncommon for the president to be able to hire and fire the premier.

Accounting for presidentialized parties changes the normal expectation of a balance of powers in a presidential system. In the standard Madisonian logic, the separate origins and interests of the president and the legislature lead them to check one another's power by pitting ambition against ambition. However, Samuels and Shugart argue that this logic holds only across parties, as when a president of one party faces a legislature with a majority from another party. Within parties, the logic of checks-and-balances across branches dissolves. In a presidentialized party, the leader is given significant power to shape the direction of the party, and this includes some disciplinary powers. Thus, while legislators and the president may have different interests, it is the president who generally has more clout within the party to bend the legislative caucus to his or her will.

In the language of delegation, when the party delegates power to the president, the dangers of moral hazard are particularly high. Thanks to fixed terms, the principal has no way of firing an unfaithful agent. In the delegation literature, the assumption is that if the potential costs of delegation are too high, a principal will simply refrain from delegating power. Yet in real life, parties simply do not have that option. Every large party must nominate a presidential candidate, so the risk of a failed delegation is unavoidable.

The KMT as a Presidentialized Party

The notion of the KMT as a presidentialized party invites us to examine the KMT from a different angle. Rather than taking the traditional view of the KMT as a party with a strong authoritarian legacy and focusing on how resistant the old party structure has been to reform in the current democratic era, it may be better to ask how that structure fits into the logic of presidentialism. When the presidency was opened up to electoral competition, the KMT did not need to jettison its old architecture in order to reorient itself toward winning the presidency. The Leninist structure, with centralized power dominated by a strong party chair, fit the new requirements quite well. In fact, the main adjustment was to enhance the power of the legislative branch of the party by increasing the number of legislators on the CSC. However, the unquestioned party leader, who may or may not have been the formal party chair, remained the sitting president or the leading presidential contender.

From the time Ma won the party chair election in July 2005 to the KMT's devastating defeat in the November 2014 mayoral elections, he was the unquestioned leader of the KMT. As its leader, he set the direction of the party and used the tools available to him as party leader in an effort to ensure that the party rigidly pursued his goals. The most important prerogative of the party chair is the power to chair the weekly Wednesday CSC meetings, where the party makes its most important decisions. The chair has the power to set the agenda, guide the discussion, and sum up the consensus of the CSC, putting him or her in a powerful position to dominate the proceedings. However, President Ma did not assume the position of party chair at the beginning of his presidency. Further, the CSC has become somewhat bloated and unwieldy in recent years.[10] To ensure that he would be able to control the CSC, Ma instituted a weekly Chungshan Forum every Tuesday. The Chungshan Forum was attended by the party chair, deputy chairs, secretary-general, party legislative whips, and the heads of the five major party departments—that is, everyone in the CSC other than the ordinary CSC members. The Chungshan Forum served as a planning meeting for the CSC to ensure that everything went according to Ma's designs.[11] In addition to the CSC and Chungshan Forum, Ma also used an even more exclusive platform. On Mondays he convened what the media dubbed the "five-person committee," which included the president, vice president, KMT party chair, premier, and legislative speaker. After Ma assumed the party chair, the party was represented by the secretary-general or deputy chair. At these meetings, the five might discuss whether the party needed to intervene in order to ensure that the legislature carried out the party's directions.[12] Finally, the KMT maintained a legislative party whip organization. While the term "whip" gives the impression of an imperious leadership forcing its membership to obey orders, most successful whip organizations are actually focused on information-gathering. The whip's primary job is to figure out what the members want and how to accommodate as many of those disparate desires as possible. Strong-armed tactics might be used to secure the last few votes, but whips are usually servants of the rank-and-file, not their overlords.[13] In most countries, the party whips are elected by the party's legislative caucus. The two most powerful KMT party whips, however, are appointed by the central party office, and only the third and least-powerful whip is elected by the party members. This inclines KMT whips to act more on behalf of party leaders and less for backbenchers.

Samuels and Shugart suggest that presidents in premier-presidential systems can often use their party powers to exert control over the executive, even though the constitution formally gives that power to the legislature. In Taiwan's parliamentary-presidential system, there is little doubt that the president dominates the executive branch. Taiwanese presidents have further tried to extend their reach into the legislature, using their party powers to bend it to their will. During Ma's first term, the KMT legislative caucus's preferences were mostly aligned with those of President Ma, so this did not cause a crisis. However, in Ma's second term, rifts between what the legislative caucus wanted and what the party leader wanted began to emerge, leading to spectacular political fireworks.

The Political Context

Identity drives Taiwanese politics.[14] In the big picture, there is one question that towers above all others: "Who are we?" In today's Taiwan, identity as a Taiwanese is a consensus value, so the critical question is more specific: "Are we Chinese or not?" While individual voting decisions are tremendously complex, a great deal of Taiwan's electoral history can be explained by this single question. Figure 4.1 takes the national identity trends from the Election Study Center and combines the groups who believe they are exclusively Chinese and are both Chinese and Taiwanese. That is, people who believe they are at least somewhat Chinese are contrasted with people who believe they are exclusively Taiwanese. Overlaid on top of these two national identity trend lines are two lines showing election results over the past quarter century. The aggregate votes for the Blue and Green camps[15] track the national identity lines to a surprising extent. There was a deviation in the early 1990s, when the DPP could still rely on its appeal for faster democratization for some electoral support. There was another deviation in the 2008 and 2012 elections, when the KMT managed to maintain its Chen-era electoral support despite declining Chinese identity. Nevertheless, the fact that Chinese identity had become a clear minority and was continuing to decline should have sent a clear signal of danger to the KMT.

How did the KMT do so well in 2008 and 2012? One obvious answer is that voters were expressing disgust with President Chen's performance in office and that they were voting against the DPP rather than for the KMT. If this is the best explanation, the effect should have faded as Chen faded from the political scene. Another possibility is that the KMT gave voters

Figure 4.1   National Identity and Legislative Election Results, 1991–2016

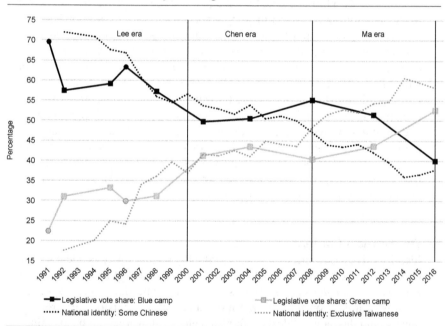

Sources: National identity data from "Trends in Core Political Attitudes," Election Study Center, National Chengchi University, http://esc.nccu.edu.tw/course/news.php?Sn=166. Vote-share data compiled by author using data from the Central Election Commission, https://db.cec.gov.tw/.

Notes: Blue camp includes the KMT, People First Party, and New Party. Green camp includes the DPP, Taiwan Solidarity Union, and New Power Party. For 1992 the Blue camp also includes four independent candidates who became founding members of the New Party in August 1993. Data points for 2008, 2012, and 2016 use party-list election results; earlier data points aggregate votes for all district nominees. Results for 1991 and 1996 are for National Assembly elections (marked with circles).

another compelling reason to vote for it. President Ma's KMT made an economic argument as well as an identity argument. Ma argued that the way to faster growth and shared prosperity was to tap into the vast potential of the Chinese market. To do this, Taiwan would have to deal directly with the Chinese government to rewrite rules and clear away obstacles creating economic inefficiencies, such as excessive red tape, ambiguous legal statuses, and various tariffs or completely closed sectors. Of course, China would not be willing to sit down with Taiwan to renegotiate these new rules without some accession to the one-China framework, making the 1992 Consensus the linchpin of this economic argument.

In fact, many voters with Taiwanese identities who also thought that opening the economy to China would bring economic benefits voted for Ma Ying-jeou. Figure 4.2 shows the presidential vote of six groups of voters, divided by national identity and whether they thought opening to China would help, hurt, or not have any significant effect on Taiwan's economy. In 2008 and 2012, Ma won a clear majority of the voters with a Taiwanese identity and a positive view of economic opening.[16] Among the even larger group with a Taiwanese identity and an ambivalent view of opening, Ma was able to win somewhere around one-third to one-half of the votes.

Some of these voters may have considered economics to be more important than identity, but given the historical primacy of identity in Taiwan, it seems more plausible that Ma persuaded them that economic opening was compatible with a Taiwanese identity. That is, economic opening did not necessarily require that Taiwan commit itself to political integration with China. The 1992 Consensus—one China, each side with its own interpretation—contains just enough ambiguity to convince some voters that it is possible to have both economic integration with China and maintain a separate political status.[17] After all, if there are two sides that both have the internal right to interpret who they are and what China is, in what sense is there only one China? To some extent, the second part of the formula can be seen as negating the first part. So long as the impact of the 1992 Consensus was simply that Taiwan was able to sit down with Chinese authorities and hammer out better economic rules without any impact on Taiwan's de facto sovereignty, there was no need for many voters to make a decision between identity and economic gain.

Survey data reveal just how tenuous support for the 1992 Consensus was. Depending on how it was phrased, it might be electorally viable or it might be completely unacceptable to the general public. Table 4.1 shows just how much difference a slight change in the wording could make. In a January 2016 TISR poll, only 23 percent could accept the "both sides belong to one China," while 30 percent could accept the "1992 Consensus," and 41 percent could accept "one China, each side with its own interpretation." Surveys conducted by the Mainland Affairs Council routinely found

Figure 4.2 National Identity, Opening to China, and Presidential Vote, 2008–2016

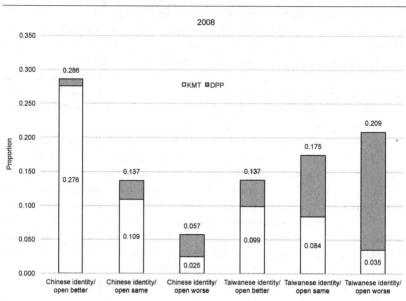

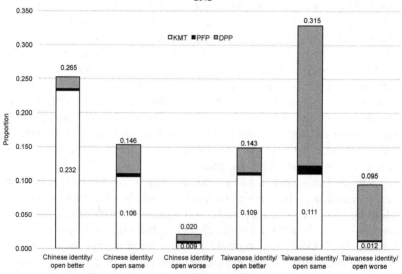

continues

Figure 4.2   Continued

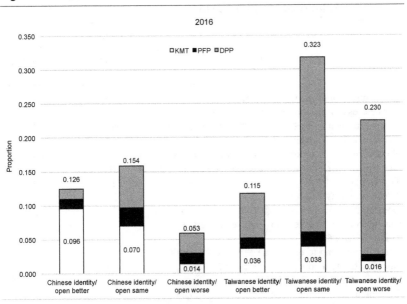

Source: Taiwan's Election and Democratization Study 2008P, 2012, and 2016.

Notes: Label above each bar shows proportion of total valid sample in each category. Label in white space of each bar shows proportion who voted for the KMT's presidential candidate.

Question wordings: 2008, "If the government opens up cross-Strait economic exchanges, do you think the economy will get better, get worse, or stay about the same?"; 2012, "After signing the cross-Strait Economic Cooperation Framework Agreement (ECFA), do you think Taiwan's economy has gotten better, gotten worse, or is about the same?"; 2016, "Since 2008, cross-Strait economic exchanges have intensified. What effect has this had on Taiwan's overall economy? Has it gotten better, gotten worse, or stayed about the same?"

about 50 percent for the 1992 Consensus. In those surveys, the question wordings were even stronger, spelling out and explaining the 1992 Consensus.[18] From a campaign standpoint, as long as Ma could convince the public to think about the 1992 Consensus as the full formula, it was a viable electoral position. However, if the public came to believe that the "real" KMT position was more strident than "each side with its own interpretation," it would not be electorally tenable. Ambiguity allowed both Chinese policymakers and the Taiwanese electorate to hear what they wanted to hear. Any erosion of that ambiguity could destroy the amiable relationship with China or bring electoral disaster.

In 2016, the KMT's inroads into voters with exclusively Taiwanese identity vanished, as those voters opted overwhelmingly to support Tsai Ing-wen. One plausible interpretation is that during Ma's second term,

Table 4.1   Attitudes Toward Various Formulations for Cross-Strait Relations, 2015 and 2016

	Early October 2015 (percentage agreement)	Late January 2016 (percentage agreement)
One country on each side 一邊一國	69.3	74.5
Pursue cross-Strait relations under the ROC constitutional order 在中國民國憲政體制下推動兩岸關係	69.0	74.4
One China, one Taiwan 一中一台	64.8	70.3
No unification, no independence, no war 不統不獨不武	63.8	69.6
One China, each side with its own interpretation 一中各表	36.2	40.6
Two Chinas 兩個中國	25.8	30.4
1992 Consensus 九二共識	27.4	30.4
One country, two systems 一國兩制	28.3	28.9
Change country's name, adopt new constitution 更改國號制定新憲法	—	26.1
Both sides belong to one China 兩岸都屬於一個中國	16.2	23.3
One country, two governments 一國兩府	16.0	19.2
One country, two areas 一國兩區	15.6	17.2
One country, both sides with the same interpretation 一中同表	12.0	12.5
Eventual unification 終極統一	10.5	10.9

Source: Taiwan Indicators Survey Research, http://www.tisr.com.tw/?p=6423.
Note: Question wording: "Below are various descriptions from society of the current or future cross-Strait relationship. Which ones do you find acceptable?"

Taiwanese identifiers were increasingly forced to confront the conflict between their identity and economic integration with China. China's continued pressure for some political progress toward unification led to various departures from the 1992 Consensus, almost always downplaying, omitting, or modifying the second part of the formula—precisely the part that was critical to Taiwanese nationalists. The KMT's 2008 campaign featured the reassuring slogan "no unification, no independence, no war." By the 2016 election, voters had heard KMT leaders suggest "one country, two areas," that the relationship was "not an international relationship," "one China, both sides with the same interpretation," and that the 1992 Consensus had "served its historical purpose." Even when KMT leaders stuck to the 1992 Consensus, they were attacked for only calling it the "1992 Consensus" and being reluctant to say "each side with its own interpretation." Likewise, the upheavals encountered during the efforts to pass the CSSTA, in which President Ma—leader of the Chinese nationalist wing of the KMT—clashed with Speaker Wang—the leader of the nativist wing of the party—and in which students vociferously argued that economic integration with China would have political repercussions, may have persuaded voters that they had to choose between identity and economic opening.

President Ma's Efforts to Pass
the Cross-Strait Services Trade Act

The central theme of Ma Ying-jeou's presidency was a drive to integrate Taiwan's economy more tightly with China's economy. The greatest triumph of his first term was to sign and ratify the Economic Cooperation Framework Agreement (ECFA). The ECFA included some preliminary trade agreements, commonly known as the "Early Harvest" provisions, but its main import was to establish a framework to negotiate future, more substantial agreements between Taiwan and China.[19] The two sides signed dozens of smaller agreements, but the CSSTA, which was signed in June 2013, was to be a major step forward in opening the two economies up to one another.

Unlike the ECFA, the CSSTA did not enjoy public support. Apart from the usual identity-based antipathy toward any move that might draw Taiwan closer to China, there were two major complaints. First, critics charged that government bureaucrats had negotiated the deal without sufficient input from society. Legislators and business groups were largely kept out of the loop. Government spokespeople defended this closed negotiation style as necessary to prevent Chinese negotiators from learning Taiwan's bottom line. Left unsaid was that the government did not want to empower various special interests to defend their sectors' interests for fear that this might turn the agreement into a giant logroll of special interests or even scuttle the entire project. Second, critics claimed that the CSSTA would have a disproportionate negative impact on certain industries. For example, almost immediately after the agreement was signed, senior presidential adviser Rex How began talking about the deleterious impact the CSSTA would have on the publishing industry, and he called for it to be either amended or scrapped.[20] There were also widespread fears that while the CSSTA did not allow Chinese laborers to seek employment in Taiwan, there might be loopholes in some of the clauses that opened up Chinese labor in specific sectors, such as beauty parlors. These two complaints were, of course, closely related. Individual legislators had not been given any opportunities to defend constituents' interests before the deal was signed, and now they had to face criticism from those affected constituents.

Public polling showed that there was substantial public opposition to the CSSTA. Figure 4.3 shows that in several surveys from June 2013 to April 2014, opposition to the pact generally outweighed support by about 10 percent. More specifically, a TISR poll from July 2013 revealed that 62 percent of respondents were not confident that the government would be able to mitigate the negative impacts of the CSSTA, while only 22 percent expressed confidence.[21]

Figure 4.3   Support for the Cross-Strait Services Trade Agreement, 2013–2014

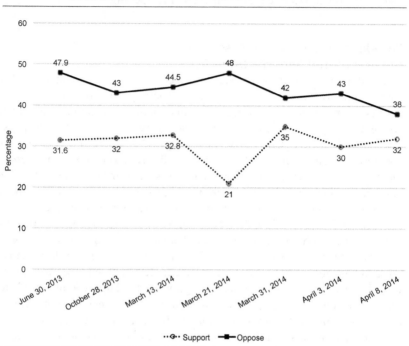

Sources: Data for June 30, 2013, and March 13, 2014, are from Taiwan Indicators Survey Research polling, http://www.tisr.com.tw. The remaining data are from TVBS polling, http://other .tvbs.com.tw/other/poll-center.

The first battle was over how the legislature should review the CSSTA. The executive branch insisted that the agreement could not be amended and it therefore should be considered in its entirety. Any modification would force the government to reopen negotiations with China, something it was loath to do. However, it was possible that once specific clauses were considered individually, the pressure to amend them might be irresistible. In a package vote, a KMT legislator might be able to defend support for an unpopular clause as necessary for passage of the entire pact. In a clause-by-clause vote, that argument would be harder to make. Voting clause-by-clause would significantly raise the danger of the whole bargain unraveling. The executive branch also warned that changes would harm Taiwan's reputation as a bargaining partner with other countries in all future international negotiations. However, legislators rejected the demand for a single up or down vote. In a cross-party negotiation session on June 25, the KMT and DPP caucuses agreed that the legislature would subject the CSSTA to a clause-by-clause review and vote. Speaker Wang pointedly defended the legislature's power, saying: "How the Legislative Yuan handles it is not the Executive Yuan's business. It has been signed. As to how it is handled, we in the Legislative Yuan will work that out ourselves."[22] At the same time, KMT party whip Lai Shyh-bao insisted that the KMT caucus had always been in favor of a clause-by-clause review and vote.[23]

The legislature could not find time for the CSSTA in a special session in July, and several other matters had to be dealt with in the first month of the fall session. This meant that the legislature would not take up the CSSTA until at least November. In the meantime, Speaker Wang, who was not famous for being blunt, continued to make pointed comments criticizing the executive branch. Speaking to a group of senior civil servants in August, Wang complained that the executive branch had a very narrow-minded perspective. He had reminded the Executive Yuan several times to communicate with legislators, but "arbitrary and unilateral" bureaucrats' "inability to accept reasonable and effective suggestions or voices from the outside was an obstacle to the country's progress."[24] A few days later, Wang reiterated his intention for the legislature to exercise real power rather than simply act as a rubber stamp. The legislature had decided how to review the CSSTA, and its priority would be what it considered to be best for the country. The legislature would hold twenty public hearings, at which different business sectors would be able to voice their opinions. Further, Wang warned the executive branch that it had better prepare plans to evaluate and deal with the negative effects of the agreement. While he did not raise the possibility of amending the CSSTA, he effectively threatened to hold up the agreement unless legislators' interests were addressed in supplementary policies.[25]

President Ma struck back in early September, attempting to assert control over the legislature by purging Speaker Wang. While Wang was in a remote Malaysian resort for his daughter's wedding, Ma accused him of influence-peddling over Wang's telephone call to the minister of justice on behalf of DPP legislator and longtime floor leader Ker Chien-ming. Ma went so far as to claim that this case constituted "the most shameful day in the development of Taiwan's democracy," and he demanded that the KMT strip Wang of his party membership.[26] Since Wang had been elected on the party list, this move would have led to the loss of his seat in the legislature and thereby his removal as speaker. In short, Ma was attempting to use his party powers to behead the legislature and bring it to heel.

Ma carefully avoided any public statements linking his attacks on Wang to the ongoing struggles between the executive and legislature over the CSSTA. However, the attacks on lobbying and influence-peddling were part of Ma's larger frustrations with Wang's style of politics, rather than narrowly confined to a specific incidence of interference in one court case.

Wang, on behalf of many KMT legislators, was attempting to use political influence to alter some of the effects of the CSSTA, and Ma saw this as improper and counterproductive. One of the clearest statements of this frustration came in an editorial in the *United Daily News,* a newspaper that strongly supported President Ma. The editorial claimed that Wang had systematically siphoned off public resources to gain complete control over the legislature. In a nutshell, important decisions in the legislature were made in closed-door cross-party negotiations, a mechanism that Wang had institutionalized. As speaker, Wang chaired all these meetings and brokered all deals. In each deal, he siphoned off 20 percent of the social benefits and then used these resources to broker further deals. With his mountain of resources, Wang was in a position to make all the important decisions, even including whether the opposition would be allowed to obstruct proceedings.[27] In this editorial's view, Wang was empowering other KMT legislators to defend their special interests and undermine the general public interest. The CSSTA was not specifically mentioned, but this was exactly the process playing out in what was the most consequential policy fight of the day. Removing Wang would presumably result in a less assertive KMT legislative caucus, a smoother ratification process for the CSSTA, and fewer challenges to Ma's leadership within the KMT and the executive's preeminence within the political process.

The KMT disciplinary committee followed Ma's orders and revoked Wang's party membership. However, the legislature stalled long enough in handling the paperwork for Wang to file a lawsuit and obtain a last-minute injunction. This injunction effectively defeated Ma's gambit, since it meant that Wang would be able to retain his party membership—and his position as speaker—until the court case was settled, a process that promised to drag out for months or even years.[28]

Having failed to remove Wang as speaker, Ma's next move was to try to hollow out Wang's power. Ma had periodically convened meetings of the "five-person committee," of himself, Vice President Wu Den-yih, Premier Jiang Yi-huah, KMT secretary-general William Tseng, and Speaker Wang. Now the committee was to be reconstituted with the KMT party whip, Lin Hung-chih, replacing Wang at these meetings. KMT legislative strategy would thus be funneled through the whip rather than through the speaker.[29] Attempted purge aside, this change empowered the whip—a position selected by central party leaders—at the expense of the speaker—a post elected by the KMT legislative caucus. Again, the presidential branch of the party was attempting to exercise control over the legislative branch of the party.

The CSSTA made little progress in the fall 2013 legislative session, but President Ma was determined to see it passed in the spring 2014 session. As the new session opened, the KMT sent a message to its legislators that defections would not be tolerated by suspending party rights for a member who had voted against the party position in a recent roll-call vote.[30]

The signs were clear that the KMT legislative caucus did not share President Ma's enthusiasm. For example, the KMT had trouble finding someone willing to serve as convener of the Internal Affairs Committee. The convener would be responsible for shepherding the CSSTA through the committee process, and apparently this was not an attractive responsibility. Of the seven KMT members on the committee in fall 2013, three tried to transfer to another committee and two others flatly refused to be convener. Chang Ching-chung, who had been convener in the previous session and whom the KMT leaders had earmarked for the position again, was one of the members trying to move to another committee. Chang said that he was on the committee to work on infrastructure projects and that there were "too many problems" in the committee right now.[31] A day later, facing pressure from party leaders to continue as convener, Chang said he would respect the party caucus but hoped they would "let him off the hook."[32] They did not. The KMT's difficulty in persuading legislators to lead the fight for the CSSTA was a stark contrast with the other side of the aisle, where DPP and Taiwan Solidarity Union (TSU) legislators were eager to stay on or transfer onto the Internal Affairs Committee.[33]

The CSSTA encountered stiff opposition in committee hearings. The DPP employed both regular and irregular tactics, including occupying the podium to prevent proceedings from continuing. Occupying the podium is not strictly legal, but it is a common tactic in Taiwan's legislature.[34] Majorities can defeat this tactic if they can mobilize their full membership to push the minority party off the podium. However, if the majority is not fully committed to the party position, a cohesive minority can successfully obstruct proceedings by occupying the podium. The fact that the KMT caucus did not attempt to recapture the podium and then pass the CSSTA with a roll-call vote is strong evidence that the KMT legislators were much more ambivalent about the pact than the party leadership. Rather than a direct assault on the podium, Convener Chang tried to sidestep the difficulty. Chang revived an idea that had been proposed and rejected several times: since the CSSTA had already been under review for over three months with no decision, the Executive Yuan could declare that it had automatically taken effect. In other words, Chang hoped that the executive branch would assume the political responsibility for passing the CSSTA and relieve him of that burden.[35] Unfortunately for Chang, the party rejected this maneuver.

The KMT party leadership stepped up the pressure on the legislative caucus, making repeated statements that they expected the agreement to be passed. The ultimatum came in the March 12 meeting of the Chungshan Forum. In response to the KMT whip's repeated discussion of the opposition's legislative tactics, President Ma was reported to have replied, "I only care about results. Otherwise, I will hold you personally responsible."[36]

Facing tremendous pressure from the party leadership, intense obstruction by the DPP, and ambivalent support from his own party, Convener Chang had to figure out some way to pass the CSSTA through committee. His solution was, quite infamously, to slink off into a corner during a brawl and simply declare that it had passed. Henceforth, the CSSTA would be the floor's and Speaker Wang's responsibility. This action triggered what would become the Sunflower Movement.

A full treatment of the Sunflower Movement is beyond the scope of this chapter. For current purposes, it is notable that the movement enjoyed substantial public support and that it ended with Speaker Wang promising not to pass the CSSTA until first passing an oversight mechanism. A TVBS poll on March 24, over a week into the protests, found that a 51-to-38 percent majority supported the students continuing to occupy the legislature.[37] A TISR poll on March 28 found that 63 percent thought the students were upholding democracy while only 20 percent thought they were damaging it.[38] A TVBS poll on March 31 found that 59 percent supported the students' position on the CSSTA while only 27 percent supported President Ma's position.[39] A plausible interpretation is that the already-ambivalent support of KMT legislators for President Ma's position simply crumbled in the face of public opinion. An experienced coalition-builder such as Speaker Wang would not have killed the CSSTA unless he could depend on enough support within the KMT caucus to make this position stick.

Perhaps the most surprising facet of this narrative is not that President Ma ultimately failed to pass the CSSTA but rather how long he was able to keep the KMT committed to that goal. He was an unpopular president, with satisfaction ratings hovering in the low teens. The agreement did not enjoy widespread support, and it was hardly the only controversial issue of the day. There were numerous food scandals, an unpopular adjustment to gas and electricity pricing formulas, large protests over the death of a military conscript, anger over the government's response to a major gas explosion in Kaohsiung, and several smaller protests over issues such as the government's use of eminent domain. Perhaps the second most important controversy was over whether to open the Gongliao nuclear power plant (also known as the Fourth Nuclear Power Plant), which had been under construction for almost two decades. The story of that controversy is very similar to the story of the CSSTA, with the executive branch exerting pressure on the legislature to make an unpopular decision. A month after the Sunflower Movement ended, the government surrendered on nuclear power as well, announcing that it would not open the new plant.

Throughout this period, polls showed that the KMT was hemorrhaging popular support. Despite all this, and even after Ma tried to purge the popular speaker, the KMT legislative caucus continued to fall in line, at least superficially. Why did they follow President Ma so far into the dead-end tunnel? The theory of presidentialized parties helps to explain their choice. Even though President Ma insisted on a path that legislators did not completely agree with, his control of the presidency and party empowered him with sufficient resources to compel them to follow him. We can repeatedly see evidence of a presidential and a legislative wing of the party and of the president's efforts to use his control of the party to bring the legislative wing to heel. Samuels and Shugart also point out that parties are more or less stuck with their presidents. Impeachment is rare, and attempted impeachments are rarely successful. Moreover, party rebellions against their presidents usually end in electoral disaster.[40] Once President Ma set the KMT on its course, there were very few good options for unhappy KMT legislators.

If the 1992 Consensus was useful for its ambiguity, this fight over the CSSTA helped to define the KMT's orientation toward China more clearly. On the surface, this was a fight over a trade policy. However, that fight was inextricably intertwined with questions of identity and sovereignty. On the one hand, opponents argued vociferously that the CSSTA would allow Chinese influence to creep into everyday life in Taiwan. Whether by opening the labor market to more Chinese workers, by allowing Chinese censors an avenue—the publishing industry—to stifle freedom of expression in Taiwan, or by passing an agreement from which Taiwan seemed not to have the unilateral legal right to retreat, critics stressed that economics and politics could not be separated. The economic trade deal would have political consequences. On the other hand, Ma's attempts to purge and marginalize Speaker Wang were also related to identity. Wang is often thought of as the leader of the KMT's nativist wing. In other words, he is precisely the type of politician attractive to voters with a Taiwanese identity but who vote for the KMT. Moreover, it is not a coincidence that Ma accused him of corruption. During the KMT's authoritarian past, local Taiwanese politicians won votes by distributing patronage and left policy questions to the bureaucrats in the central government. As a result, the party elite, who tended to be more ideological and professional, and were disproportionately Mainlanders, often looked down on the elected politicians as dirty, corrupt, and unprincipled. By accusing Wang of corruption, Ma was tapping into an old ethnic division within the party and sending a message to a large slice of the electorate that he did not actually value their opinions.

The Lame Duck Period: A Leaderless Presidentialized Party

The November 2014 mayoral elections were a disaster for the KMT. Nationally, the KMT won 41 percent of the votes and six of the twenty-two mayoral spots. The KMT's only significant victory was in New Taipei City, but even that win was somewhat tainted, as Eric Chu, who had been expected to cruise to an easy reelection, had to sweat out a surprisingly narrow victory. The KMT became swamped in what were supposed to be close races in central Taiwan and suffered shocking losses in supposedly deep-Blue cities in northern Taiwan. In the highest-profile race in Taipei City, a longtime KMT stronghold, the bumbling KMT candidate managed to win only 41 percent of the vote. These were historically unprecedented results and a stunning rebuke to President Ma and the KMT. In the aftermath, Ma resigned as KMT chair and his close ally, Premier Jiang, also stepped down.

Samuels and Shugart do not discuss what a presidentialized party would look like in the absence of a leader. They assume that the party must delegate power to a presidential candidate, so the party will be led either by the (formal or informal) presidential candidate or by the incumbent president. This is not what happened with the KMT. Instead, when none of the mainstream politicians entered the KMT presidential primary, there was an opportunity for Hung Hsiu-chu, a politician from the KMT's extreme Chinese nationalist wing, to seize the nomination. However, her position on China proved to be unacceptable to the electorate, and the party was forced to try to rein her in. They first attempted to work through party channels, asserting that the 1992 Consensus was the KMT's official stance. However, in a presidentialized party the presidential candidate's stance matters just as much or even more than the party's official stance. Eventually, in order to avert an electoral disaster or even a party split, the KMT was forced to retract its nomination. Nonetheless, the fight over the party's China discourse helped to define the 1992 Consensus. Since it took place in the context of a presidential election, the KMT could not completely disavow Hung's rhetoric without risking a backlash. By claiming that the 1992 Consensus was compatible with Hung's vision, the 1992 Consensus became a little less acceptable to voters in the middle of the ideological spectrum.

After Ma's resignation as party chair, there were four people frequently mooted as possibilities to take leadership of the party and run in the 2016 presidential election. Of these four, Vice President Wu and former Taipei mayor Hau Lung-bin suffered from low popularity. Repeated survey evidence indicated that they had very little chance of defeating Tsai Ing-wen. Surveys found much more popular support for Speaker Wang and New Taipei mayor Chu.[41] However, President Ma had spent more than a year insisting that his attempted purge was justified by Wang's corruption, and any attempt to nominate Wang would have been strenuously resisted by Ma's wing of the party. Chu was the obvious choice. However, Chu refused to grab the chance. He agreed to serve as party chair, but in his announcement that he would run for that office he also announced that he would not run for president. To the surprise of most observers, he stuck to that position. When the deadline for registering for the KMT presidential nomination arrived in May, only Deputy Speaker Hung Hsiu-chu, widely considered not to be a first-tier candidate, and one other even more obscure aspirant registered.[42] Most observers did not consider the registration deadline to be the final deadline. To win the nomination through the regular process, Hung would have to pass a 30 percent threshold in the polling primary. Because she was an extreme Chinese nationalist without a national profile, this prospect seemed unlikely. However, the backroom negotiations were cut short when the KMT announced that Hung had easily cleared the threshold and would be duly nominated.

In the weeks before the polling primary, Eric Chu held a summit with Chinese president Xi Jinping in Beijing. Under pressure to "go a little further" than the 1992 Consensus,[43] Chu explained that the 1992 Consensus was an agreement reached in 1992 that "both sides belonged to one China" but that the definition and interpretation was different.[44] In the Taiwanese media, the second half of that was widely dropped, and most stories simply reported Chu's position as "both sides belong to one China," a position that did not enjoy tremendous popularity among the general public. Perhaps Chu did not really intend to go beyond the 1992 Consensus but was merely inept at framing his position and clumsily lost control of the public narrative.

In contrast, there was no doubt about Hung Hsiu-chu's stance. As an ardent Chinese nationalist, Hung explicitly wanted to go beyond the 1992 Consensus. While campaigning for the polling primary, she argued that the historical mission of the 1992 Consensus had already been completed, asking: "How long can the KMT just say, 'No unification, no independence, no war'? If the 1992 Consensus doesn't move forward, how much longer can it survive? In the end, isn't it simply an independent Taiwan? Are we going to maintain the status quo forever? What will the cross-Strait relations be? Will they only be limited to economic exchanges?"[45] Her idea of an upgrade from the original 1992 Consensus had three main points. First, Hung called for "one China, both sides with the same interpretation." Like Chu's statement in Beijing, it could be argued that this was less of a departure from the 1992 Consensus than it appeared. She went on to explain that the same interpretation should be that both sides were parts of a "complete China," and that, while cross-Strait relations were not international relations, neither were they simply the internal affairs of either side.[46] As with Chu's formula, almost no one paid attention to her detailed interpretation of her proposal. The formula stressed agreement, and the widespread assumption was simply that Hung must be willing to accept the PRC formulation of one China. Second, she argued that it was time to move on from addressing only easy economics questions. Now it was time to tackle the difficult political questions.[47] Third, the two sides should sign a peace agreement.[48]

Whereas the 1992 Consensus was carefully crafted to give just enough space for Taiwanese nationalists to stay on board the KMT bandwagon,

Hung's blunt statements were indifferent to the sensitivities of that critical voting bloc. She left no doubt that she would actively seek to move the country toward unification much more quickly than Ma had. In fact, her willful blindness to public reaction even extended to what should have been her core constituency. In explaining her concept of one China to the media, she stated that the two shared sovereignty, and therefore "she could not say that the ROC exists, and she could not say that the PRC exists, otherwise there would be two Chinas."[49] After over half a century of KMT education, hearing the KMT's presumptive presidential candidate deny the existence of the ROC was hard to swallow for many party loyalists, even if it was obvious that Hung was not actually disavowing the ROC.

Hung's China discourse was clearly out of line with mainstream public opinion, and the rest of the party, led by Ma and Chu, tried to bring her back in line with the 1992 Consensus. The simplest way of doing this was to deny that her statements conflicted with the 1992 Consensus. For example, Ma suggested that the "same" implied that both sides held the same insistence that there was only one China, though, of course, that meant the ROC. Thus, he explained, her formula was "one China, both sides offering interpretations at the same time."[50] A second attempt to rein in Hung involved changing the party platform. After Hung had passed the polling primary but before she had been formally nominated, Chu moved to formally incorporate the 1992 Consensus into the party platform.[51] Most important, the party put pressure on her through various personal meetings. At two box-lunch meetings with legislators on July 9, nearly all of them expressed hope that she would return to the party's position on the 1992 Consensus.[52] In the next few days, she also had meetings with Ma and Chu, in which they made the same suggestion. Shortly before she was nominated, she agreed to stop talking about "one China, each side with its own position," claiming that her position had been twisted in the public discourse. Instead, she would ask mainland China to formally acknowledge the existence of the ROC government, oppose Taiwan's independence, and seek a peace treaty that would bring lasting stability and peace. At the same time, Chu forcefully stated his insistence on the 1992 Consensus as the KMT's official position.[53] By the time Hung was formally nominated on July 20, the party had more or less pulled her back into the 1992 Consensus.

It is clear that there was widespread pressure on Hung to move back to the 1992 Consensus. It is also clear that Hung's polling numbers were very low during this period. What is not clear is whether there was a rebellion brewing within the KMT. There were certainly rumblings of dissatisfaction. At the end of June, KMT legislator Chang Chia-chun announced that she would not run for reelection because of Hung's "one China, both sides with the same interpretation" position.[54] Even after Hung publicly adjusted her stance, there were still indicators that her Chinese-nationalist image was a problem. As a news story in early August put it, there was a gap between her pro-unification image and the positioning of the nativist faction as "not supporters of independence." As a result, many legislative candidates were planning to "abandon" Hung.[55] Most ominous, there were rumors of nativist faction leaders mulling an outright split. Former Yunlin County magistrate Chang Jung-wei was rumored to be considering joining Soong in the People First Party (PFP),[56] and former Taichung County magistrate Liao Liao-yi was rumored to be considering setting up a new party.[57] As one might expect, both denied these rumors. Nevertheless, these were hints that the efforts to paper over the differences between Hung's position and the 1992 Consensus may not have been entirely successful.

The net effect of all this public discussion was twofold. On the one hand, it confirmed that the KMT was committed to the 1992 Consensus. By grabbing the party's presidential nomination, Hung had been able to challenge the KMT's China discourse. If she had garnered popular support for this, the mainstream KMT might not have been able to resist this challenge. However, Hung proved to be a bad agent in two senses. She not only challenged the party's orthodoxy but also failed in the more important job of appealing to the general public. Because her stance was so toxic with the general public, her candidacy threatened to alienate the KMT's nativist wing and even made a party split possible. It was not sufficient to forcefully restate the party's commitment to the 1992 Consensus. The presidential candidate of a presidentialized party cannot simply be muzzled. Eventually, the party leaders felt it necessary to revoke her nomination altogether. The KMT still lost badly with Chu as the candidate, but at least the party did not split apart.

On the other hand, while the KMT reverted to the 1992 Consensus, it may not have been the same version as the one they took before the electorate in 2008 and 2012. The fight over the party's China discourse took place in the midst of a presidential election, and the winning side could not afford to alienate Hung's supporters only three months before the election. To avert a backlash, they had to insist that her stance fell under the umbrella of the 1992 Consensus. The 1992 Consensus originally covered a wide range of possibilities, and by insisting that Hung's position was not different from the 1992 Consensus, the KMT may have shifted the popular understanding of it in a pro-unification direction. Throughout the 2016 campaign, Ma repeatedly asked, usually with an air of bewilderment, how Tsai could claim to want to maintain the status quo when she did not accept the 1992 Consensus. To him, the status quo was based entirely on the 1992 Consensus. He seemed unaware of the possibility that the KMT had moved away from the version of the 1992 Consensus that the electorate had found acceptable in the previous two elections.

Survey data reveals the extent to which the KMT lost control of the status quo. Two TEDS questions are relevant. First, respondents rated each candidate's ability to maintain cross-Strait peace. Second, respondents rated each candidate's ability to protect Taiwan's interests. These two questions are related to the two halves of the 1992 Consensus. The first half, one China, promises to bring peaceful relations with the PRC. The second half, each side with its own interpretation, implies that the government would insist on asserting Taiwan's interests when appropriate. In 2012, Ma Ying-jeou enjoyed an overwhelming advantage on maintaining peace. Perhaps more significant, more people thought he would be better at protecting Taiwan's interests. The change in 2016 was striking. Cross-Strait peace shifted from an overwhelming KMT advantage to a tie. This seemed to indicate that a significant portion of the electorate rejected the KMT claim that some sort of one-China formula was necessary to maintain peace. The change in judgments about who would better protect Taiwan's interests was also dramatic. Whereas 40 percent felt Ma would be better than Tsai in 2012, only 15 percent expressed the same confidence in Chu in 2016. This plunge was consistent with the idea that the experiences of Ma's second term eroded the strength of "each side with its own interpretation," as Table 4.2 shows.

A second way to see how 2016 was different involves looking at changes on the independence-unification spectrum. In surveys conducted in 2008 and 2016, respondents were asked to place themselves, the KMT, and the DPP on a scale ranging from immediate independence (0) to immediate unification (10). In 2008, slightly more respondents thought they were closer to the KMT than the DPP. If we consider only moderate voters, those who placed themselves between the two parties, the KMT's edge was slightly larger, as Table 4.3 shows. In Ma's first election, the KMT's positioning on Taiwan's future status was not at all out of touch with mainstream public opinion. In 2016, the results were very different. Roughly twice as many respondents considered the DPP's position to be closer to their own as considered the KMT's position to be closer. This was not merely because there were more people on the extreme independence side as on the extreme unification side. The same pattern was found among moderate voters. Of course, much of the change was due to Tsai Ing-wen's efforts in presenting a more moderate image for the DPP. The proportion of respondents placing themselves within two intervals of the DPP rose from 53 percent to 65 percent. However, respondents also simply felt further away from the KMT. In 2008, 52 percent of respondents placed themselves within two intervals of the KMT. In 2016, only 44 percent did so.

Admittedly, these survey data do not directly test whether the KMT lost control of the status quo. Nevertheless, they show that the KMT occupied the median ground in the 2008 and 2012 electorates. In 2016, the DPP was able to seize that middle ground, in part because the KMT was perceived as having become more extreme.

Table 4.2   Maintaining Cross-Strait Peace and Protecting Taiwan's Interests, 2012 and 2016

	Ma/Chu (KMT)	Tsai (DPP)	Same	Number of Respondents
Who is the better candidate? (percentage agreement)				
Maintain cross-Strait peace				
2012	59.2	13.4	15.2	1,603
2016	32.2	31.9	22.8	1,468
Protect Taiwan's interests				
2012	40.1	31.5	17.5	1,628
2016	15.0	50.5	22.1	1,480

Source: Taiwan's Election and Democratization Study, 2012 and 2016 face-to-face surveys.
Notes: In both the 2012 and 2016 surveys, respondents were asked to rate each candidate's ability on different dimensions on a scale of 0 to 10. Only respondents who rated both the KMT and DPP candidates are considered.

Table 4.3   KMT and DPP Positions on the Independence-Unification Spectrum, 2008 and 2016

	KMT	DPP	Same Distance	Number of Respondents
Percentage of Respondents Closer To				
2008				
All respondents	39.4	37.3	23.3	1,557
Moderate respondents	36.7	32.2	31.2	673
2016				
All respondents	27.8	50.8	21.4	1,407
Moderate respondents	23.9	47.2	28.9	502

Source: Taiwan's Election and Democratization Study, 2008P and 2016 face-to-face surveys.
Notes: In both the 2008 and 2016 surveys, respondents were asked to rate their position on the independence-unification spectrum, with 0 representing immediate independence and 10 representing immediate unification. They were then asked to place the KMT and DPP on this same scale. "All respondents" includes respondents who were able to place themselves, the KMT, and the DPP on this scale. "Moderate respondents" includes only those who placed themselves between the DPP on the left and the KMT on the right.

Conclusion

The KMT's 2016 electoral defeat was rooted in the dominant China cleavage. Over the past few years, the electorate has shifted in a more Taiwanese nationalist direction. At the same time, the DPP has worked hard to position itself closer to the middle of the political spectrum. Against these two shifts, the KMT moved to a more extreme Chinese nationalist position, making itself less electorally viable.

In this chapter, I have reviewed two of the most important political episodes of President Ma's second term. In the battle to ratify the CSSTA, Ma demanded that his party follow his lead and approve his trade pact with no amendments. In this fight, Ma clashed openly with the nativist wing of the party, branding their leader as an unprincipled and corrupt political speculator. By pushing so hard for a pact that would tie Taiwan tighter to mainland China, Ma helped to define his ambiguous campaign slogans. In 2008 it might have been easy for a Taiwanese nationalist to imagine that "one China" was an empty slogan, a ritualistic phrase necessary to bring China to the bargaining table but that would not actually commit Taiwan to move any closer to unification. In 2016, after watching Ma push Taiwanese society so hard for a pact that both he and the PRC wanted, it was less easy to believe that "one China" had no consequences or that economic cooperation could be completely independent of political concessions.

In the fight over whether to change the party's official discourse toward China in 2015, the KMT sent more messages to the electorate. In the absence of a clear party leader, there was an opportunity for someone from the extreme Chinese nationalist wing to try to redefine the party's stance. Because no one else ran for the party's presidential nomination, Hung Hsiu-chu was gifted a platform from which she could attempt to pull the party away from the ambiguity of the 1992 Consensus. Her disastrous campaign forced the party first to resist her discourse and then to rescind her nomination. However, because the KMT needed to maintain unity in the midst of an electoral campaign, it had to absorb her discourse into the 1992 Consensus rather than reject it altogether. By insisting that her discourse was compatible with the 1992 Consensus, the party defined the 1992 Consensus as somewhat more pro-unification, thereby depriving it of some of the ambiguity that made it so useful in 2008 and 2012.

This discussion has implications for the KMT's efforts to recover after 2016. Many party figures simply want to return to the 1992 Consensus. However, this may not be electorally viable. Taiwanese public opinion has shifted to a more Taiwanese nationalist orientation. A position that was good enough for the 2008 or 2012 electorates might be too extreme for the 2020 or 2024 electorates. Just as important, years of practical experience have defined the 1992 Consensus and stripped away much of the ambiguity. Since today's understanding of the 1992 Consensus is different from the understanding in 2008, it might be impossible to simply return to the halcyon days of 2008.

The understanding of the KMT as a presidentialized party implies that any redefinition of the party's position toward China will inevitably be framed by the dynamics of future presidential elections. Since the party's orientation to China is the most critical question facing the party, any significant shifts will have to come from the highest level. Even though the KMT is organized as a Leninist party, the party chair is not necessarily the real leader of the party. Power flows from the office of the presidency, and only viable contenders for the presidency will have the authority to redefine the party image. The rank-and-file membership of the KMT may not be clamoring to move the party toward the center of the political spectrum, but the impulse for a new stance may not come from ordinary card-carrying party members. The person who wins the presidential nomination, especially if that person has a reasonable chance to win the election, will assume de facto leadership of the party and determine the party's position.

Notes

1. In this chapter I ignore the controversy over whether a consensus was actually reached in 1992.

2. Samuels and Shugart, *Presidents, Parties, and Prime Ministers.* See also Chapter 3 of this volume for a parallel discussion of this process in the DPP.

3. The number is only this high because the KMT benefited from malapportionment. The KMT won twenty-four district and indigenous seats, which had an average of 210,985 eligible voters. The fifty district and indigenous seats the DPP won had an average of 251,393 eligible voters, 19 percent higher. See Batto, "Sources and Implications of Malapportionment in Taiwan."

4. Some pointed to the lower turnout in 2016, claiming that KMT sympathizers had either voted for Soong or stayed home. However, their claim that there had been no fundamental shift in the political map rests on untenable assumptions. For example, they assume that 100 percent of the people who voted in 2012 but not 2016 would have voted for Chu. Polling data clearly show that such assumptions are incorrect. The election result cannot be explained away by lower turnout. See Batto, "The KMT Coalition Unravels," pp. 14–16.

5. Cox and McCubbins, *Legislative Leviathan;* Aldrich, *Why Parties.*

6. Systems with elected presidents include pure presidential systems as well as semi-presidential systems, in which a premier at least partly accountable to the legislature wields some executive power. In this chapter I use the term "presidential systems" to refer to all systems with an elected president. I refer to systems with an elected president but no premier as "pure presidential systems." To differentiate among various semi-presidential systems, I will follow Matthew Shugart and John Carey's terminology in which systems in which the cabinet is exclusively responsible to the legislature are called "premier-presidential" and systems in which the cabinet is dually responsible to the president and legislature are called "president-parliamentary." See Shugart and Carey, *Presidents and Assemblies.*

7. Samuels and Shugart, *Presidents, Parties, and Prime Ministers.*

8. Alchian and Demsetz, "Production, Information Costs, and Economic Organization"; Kiewiet and McCubbins, *The Logic of Delegation.*

9. See also Hicken, *Building Party Systems in Developing Democracies;* Batto et al., *Mixed-Member Electoral Systems in Constitutional Context.*

10. For example, the CSC in March 2017 included thirty-two elected members, seven appointed members, five deputy party chairs, and the party chair. Since the party secretary-general and the six deputy secretary-generals also attended, there might have been over fifty people in the room.

11. See Chen, "The President's Position-Taking of Bills and His Influence on Legislation Under Semi-Presidentialism." When Ma resigned as party chair after the 2014 election defeat, the new party chair canceled the Chungshan Forum. A party official described it as a transition from "the party serving the government changing back to the party leading the government"; Hsiang-chun Yang, "The Party Leads the Government: Power Returns to the Central Standing Committee," *United Daily News,* January 20, 2015, p. A2.

12. Chen, "The President's Position-Taking."

13. Bowler, Farrell, and Katz, "Party Cohesion, Party Discipline, and Parliaments."

14. Achen and Wang, *The Taiwan Voter.*

15. Admittedly, using the terms "Blue camp" and "Green camp" to describe politics in the 1990s is anachronistic, since they did not enter ordinary political discourse until the Chen Shui-bian era. Nevertheless, the basic cleavage lines developed much earlier than the terminology.

16. Since the TEDS surveys significantly overrepresent supporters of the winning presidential candidate and underrepresent supporters of the losing side, it is perhaps best to look at the broad trend rather the precise numbers.

17. On several occasions, Ma Ying-jeou proudly repeated the description of a visiting member of the US Congress of the 1992 Consensus as a "masterpiece of ambiguity."

18. For example, a July 2014 survey asked, "The government's position on the 1992 Consensus is that the 'one China' in 'one China, each side with its own interpretation' refers to the ROC. Do you support this position?" About 52 expressed support, which was a fairly typical result. Sometimes the MAC preceded this question with other leading questions or employed even more loaded question wordings. For example, a May 2015 survey asked, "Some people say, 'Since 2008, the important result of the government's mainland policy has been to maintain cross-Straits relations and a stable peace.' Do you agree with this statement?" It then asked a confusing question on the 1992 Consensus: "Since 2008, on the foundation of the 1992 Consensus—One China, each side with its own interpretation—One China means the ROC, the government, has steadily promoted cross-Straits negotiations and exchanges. Do you support this position?" About 54 percent expressed support, though some of those respondents may have been expressing support for negotiations and exchanges rather than specifically for the 1992 Consensus. See http://www.mac.gov.tw/public/Attachment/471715371652.pdf and http://www.mac.gov.tw/public/Attachment/5591011390.pdf.

19. Fuller, "ECFA's Empty Promise and Hollow Threat."

20. See "Services Pact: Ministry Seeking to Mollify Publishers," *Taipei Times,* June 23, 2013, http://www.taipeitimes.com/News/taiwan/archives/2013/06/23/2003565466.

21. The question wording was, "Concerning the Cross-Strait Services Trade Agreement signed by Taiwan and the mainland, are you confident that our government can reduce the negative impacts and protect the rights of Taiwan's people?" See http://www.tisr.com.tw/?p=3095#more-3095.

22. Si-hui Lin, Luo-wei Chen, and Yi-yuan Huang, "Legislative Consensus: No Package Votes," *United Daily News,* June 26, 2013, p. A7.

23. Ibid. I cannot find any public opinion data from June 2013, but two polls from March 2014 showed overwhelming public support for a clause-by-clause review. A TISR poll showed 73.7 percent wanted a clause-by-clause review while only 10.2 percent favored a package vote, while a TVBS poll found the gap to be 70 percent to 8 percent. See http://www.tisr.com.tw/?p=3940#more-3940 and http://other.tvbs.com.tw/export/sites/tvbs/file/other/poll-center/20140321224523298.pdf.

24. Wen-hsin Chang, "Wang Jin-pyng: The Executive Should Not Act Unilaterally," *United Daily News,* August 23, 2013, p. A10.

25. Wen-hsin Chang, "Wang Jin-pyng: Review of the CSSTA to Be Guided by National Interest," *United Daily News,* August 27, 2013, p. A2.

26. Stacey Hsu, "Ma Disputes Wang's Claim He Did Not Interfere in Case," *Taipei Times,* September 9, 2013, p. 1.

27. "Editorial: Wang Jin-pyng and the Taipei District Court: The 80/20 Principle," *United Daily News,* September 17, 2013, p. A2.

28. Wang won the first decision, but the KMT appealed the ruling. When Ma resigned as party chair after the 2014 local elections, the new chair dropped the appeal. Wang finished the term as speaker and was elected to a new legislative term on the KMT party list in 2016.

29. Wei-chih Luo and Kuang-tzu Wang, "New Blue Strategy: Leave Wang in Legislature but Watch Him Carefully," *United Daily News,* September 23, 2013, p. A4.

30. Hsiao-kuang Shih, "He Did Not Vote the Party Line on the Land Administration Agent Act: To Ensure Party Authority on the CSSTA, Apollo Chen's Party Membership Is Suspended for One Year," *Liberty Times,* February 28, 2014, https://news.ltn .com.tw/news/focus/paper/758101.

31. Pei-fang Tsai, "Ma Orders CCSTA Passed in March," *United Daily News,* February 17, 2014, p. A1.

32. Nai-ling Chen, Yi-yuan Huang, and Kuang-tzu Wang, "Ma: Try to Pass CSSTA During This Session," *United Daily News,* February 18, 2014, p. A1.

33. Yi-chen Hsu, "CSSTA Battleground: Blue and Green Clash in Internal Affairs Committee," *United Daily News,* February 20, 2014, p. A2.

34. Batto and Tsai, "Storming the Podium." See also Chapter 7 of this book.

35. Wei-lun Sun and An-ni Lin, "Public Hearing Opens: War over CSSTA Begins," *Economic Daily News,* March 11, 2014, p. A4.

36. "Ma Tells Lin Hung-chih Directly: If CSSTA Doesn't Pass, I Will Hold You Personally Responsible," *United Daily News,* March 19, 2014, p. A4. The KMT whip later denied that Ma had used those exact words, but confirmed that Ma had said words with that meaning. Hsiao-kuang Shih, "Ignoring Student Demands, Ma Orders CSSTA Passed This Session," *Liberty Times,* March 20, 2014, https://news.ltn.com.tw/news/focus /paper/763643.

37. Question wording: "The student protesters that occupied the legislature are still continuing their occupation. Do you support the students continuing to occupy the legislature in protest?" See http://other.tvbs.com.tw/export/sites/tvbs/file/other/poll-center /20140324223108658.pdf.

38. Question wording: "The controversies erupting over the legislature's review of the CSSTA have led to many students occupying the legislature to express protest. To this point, do you think these students are upholding the spirit of democracy or are they harming the democratic order?" See http://www.tisr.com.tw/wp-content/uploads/2014 /03/TISR_TMBS_201403_2.pdf.

39. Question wording: "The students want the CSSTA to be returned to the Executive Yuan, and after an oversight mechanism for cross-strait agreements is legislated, the legislature can then review the CSSTA. President Ma believes the legislature should continue with a clause-by-clause review and clause-by-clause vote of the CSSTA. Do you support the students' demands or President Ma's view?" See http://other.tvbs.com.tw/export /sites/tvbs/file/other/poll-center/20140401141358351.pdf.

40. See Samuels and Shugart, *Presidents, Parties, and Prime Ministers,* pp. 94–122.

41. For example, a TVBS poll from February 5, 2015, showed Tsai defeating Wu by 60 to 17 percent, Hau by 55 to 21 percent, Wang by 45 to 31 percent, and Chu by only 43 to 41 percent. See http://other.tvbs.com.tw/export/sites/tvbs/file/other/poll-center /20150210102659516.pdf.

42. The other aspirant, former cabinet member Yaung Chih-liang, could not collect enough party members' signatures to qualify for the polling primary. I can only speculate as to why none of the top four potential candidates registered. The following are some of the main explanations suggested in the media. First, Hau, Wu, and Wang wanted to run

but because they were all opposed by factions within the party, they wanted the party to draft them by universal acclaim rather than actively fight for the nomination. Second, Hau, Wu, and Wang feared they would not pass the polling threshold, so they needed to be drafted rather than go through the normal primary process. Third, Chu did not want to resign as New Taipei mayor. He feared this would be necessary if he spent a year campaigning, especially if he were not drafted. Fourth, since the KMT's likelihood of winning the presidency was very low, they instead tried to position themselves to lead the party after the election.

43. Ko-lun Lin, "Cross Straits Moves to the Next Generation, Depends on Chu-Xi Summit," *United Daily News,* May 4, 2015, p. A3.

44. Ting-yao Lin, "Chu: Cooperation Must Not Be Impeded," *United Daily News,* May 5, 2015, p. A1.

45. Yi Yang, "Hung Hsiu-chu Lobs Shocking Salvo Endorsing Political Dialogue," *China Times,* April 21, 2015, https://www.chinatimes.com/newspapers/20150421000419 -260102?chdtv.

46. Ho-ming Lin, "Hung Hsiu-chu Explains 'One China, Same Interpretation,'" *United Daily News,* May 2, 2015, p. A2.

47. Yi Yang, "Hung Hsiu-chu Lobs Shocking Salvo Endorsing Political Dialogue," *China Times,* April 21, 2015, https://www.chinatimes.com/newspapers/20150421000419 -260102?chdtv.

48. Ho-ming Lin, "Hung Hsiu-chu Explains 'One China, Same Interpretation,'" *United Daily News,* May 2, 2015, p. A2.

49. Chih-hao Chou and Ting-yao Lin, "One China, Same Interpretation Controversy: Ma, Lien Support Hung Hsiu-chu," *United Daily News,* July 3, 2015, p. A4.

50. Ibid.

51. Kuang-yi Lee, "KMT Revises Party Platform, Adds 1992 Consensus," *United Daily News,* June 16, 2015, p. A2.

52. You-hsin Hu, Chih-hao Chou, and Hsiang-chun Yang, "Hung Hsiu-chu Returns to '1992 Consensus, One China, Each Side with Its Own Interpretation,'" *United Daily News,* July 10, 2015, p. A4.

53. Hsiang-chun Yang, Jung-yu Chi, Chih-hao Chou, and You-hsin Hu, "Cross-Strait Discourse Controversy: Hung: I Will Adjust," *United Daily News,* July 18, 2015, p. A2.

54. Ping Cheng, "Chang Chia-chun Considers Quitting Party? Hung Camp Hurriedly Explains to Put Out Fire," *United Daily News,* June 30, 2015, p. A8. Chang was one of nine KMT incumbent district legislators who decided not to run for reelection. Not all of them were protesting Hung's stance, but most of these decisions were expressions of a lack of confidence in the KMT's prospects in 2016.

55. Pei-fang Tsai and Cheng-hai Yang, "Support Hung! Eric Chu Convenes Meeting, Issues Mobilization Order," *United Daily News,* August 11, 2015, p. A4.

56. Chih-hao Chou, "Support Soong? Chang Jung-wei: Emotionally, I Am Still a KMT Member," *United Daily News,* August 6, 2015, p. A4.

57. Pei-fang Tsai, "Liao Liao-yi to Form Party? Consolidate Local Moderate Forces," *United Daily News,* September 29, 2015, p. A4.

5

The Party System Before and After the 2016 Elections

Kharis Templeman

Taiwan stands out among the third-wave democracies for the remarkable stability of its party system.[1] Ever since Taiwan's first fully democratic legislative election was held in 1992, the two leading political parties have remained the same: in 1992, the Chinese Nationalist Party, or Kuomintang (KMT) and the Democratic Progressive Party (DPP) finished first and second, and in 2016 they finished second and first. Despite significant defections from the KMT in the early 2000s, no other party has ever managed to knock either one out of the top two positions.

Taiwan's party system is also unusual among third-wave cases for its unidimensionality. For most of its democratic history, party competition in Taiwan has been oriented around what I will call simply the "China question."[2] Whether we characterize it primarily as a divide over (sub)ethnicity, over national identity, or over competing visions for how to handle cross-Strait relations with the People's Republic of China (PRC), the China question has long been the most salient divide in Taiwanese politics.

Since at least the early 2000s, all significant political parties in the party system have taken distinct positions on the China question.[3] As any observer of Taiwanese politics knows, to the right of the median is the KMT, which has favored a closer, more cooperative relationship with the PRC, and to the left is the DPP, which has been wary of growing cross-Strait ties and has advocated for moves toward de jure or at least maintenance of de facto independence for Taiwan. The KMT has been joined by two breakaway parties, the strongly pro-unification New Party (not to be confused with the New Power Party [NPP]) and the more centrist People First Party (PFP) of James Soong, which together have formed what in Taiwanese political parlance is known as the pan-Blue camp. On the other side, shortly after the 2000 election, the DPP was joined by the Taiwan Solidarity Union (TSU), another group of KMT defectors led by former president Lee Teng-hui, which set up to the DPP's left and took a nativist, anti-China stance. Parallel to the KMT and its more pro-China offshoots, the DPP and TSU together became known as the "pan-Green" camp.

The enduring salience of the China question can also be seen at the individual level. In the past two decades of public opinion research on Taiwanese politics, the single most robust finding is that attitudes toward the China question have increasingly come to determine vote choice in national elections.[4] As the five significant parties repositioned themselves into two camps in the early 2000s, segments of the electorate followed them and re-sorted into the political camp closest to their own views.[5] Ever since, as this body of research has repeatedly shown, the major parties have differentiated themselves primarily through their positions on national identity and cross-Strait relations, and every election has turned at least to some degree on shifts in the median voter's preferences on this dimension.

Was 2016 Different?

It is with this context in mind that questions about a fundamental partisan realignment in the 2016 presidential and legislative elections are so intriguing. In the months before the elections, more than a few observers of Taiwanese politics speculated that this long-standing pattern of Blue-versus-Green competition might at last be in danger of breaking up, and that Taiwan's party system could be headed for a permanent reorientation around something besides the China question.[6]

These expectations were driven in part by developments overseas. After the global financial crisis in 2008–2009 ushered in a deep and prolonged economic recession in most of the world's advanced economies, voting publics in many democracies became increasingly disillusioned with traditional governing elites of all political stripes.[7] New anti-establishment candidates and parties popped up throughout the democratic world on both the traditional left and right, and in many cases they quickly became a serious electoral threat.[8]

This pattern was particularly pronounced in the countries of the European Union, which suffered through an economic downturn that by some measures was worse than the Great Depression of the 1930s. In Greece, for instance, which experienced the longest and deepest economic contraction of any of the members of the eurozone, the two major parties with governing experience both bled votes to challengers through three successive elections, creating an opening for the untested, far-left Syriza party to win a plurality and form a government in 2015. In Spain, the left-wing populist party Podemos, founded on an anticorruption and anti-inequality platform in March 2014, became the third-largest party in parliament in December 2015, and effectively prevented the formation of a stable coalition government there. In Italy, the Five Star Movement, a populist and Euroskeptic party founded by a blogger with no political experience, grew rapidly in prominence and popularity; its candidates won the mayor's elections in Rome and Turin in 2016, and it played a key role in defeating a constitutional referendum in 2016 that led to the resignation of Prime Minister Matteo Renzi. In France, the traditional socialist and Gaullist political camps disintegrated in the run-up to the 2017 presidential election as each faced existential challenges from the political extremes: on the right, Marine Le Pen of the Front National, and on the left, Jean-Luc Melenchon of La France Insoumise. That campaign ended with the election as president of Emmanuel Macron, a former Socialist Party cabinet minister, at the head of La Republique En Marche!, a completely new centrist party that included defectors from parties of both the traditional left and right.

Given the global trend of rising support for new and anti-establishment alternatives, the prospect of a similar development in Taiwan suddenly did not seem so far-fetched. And indeed, there were also some domestic indications that the party system might be headed for a crackup driven by an anti-establishment movement. First, President Ma Ying-jeou's personal popularity and that of his administration turned negative early in his second term, and by 2013 his approval rating was consistently under 20 percent in opinion polls. At the same time, civil society activists led an increase in street protests directed against a wide range of government policies, including the allegedly improper use of eminent domain by local governments in Miaoli County, Taoyuan, and Taipei; proposals to allow imports of US beef and pork; and the negligent death of a conscript in military custody.[9] The surge of social activism culminated in the student-led occupation of the Legislative Yuan for three weeks in spring 2014 to prevent the approval of a trade agreement with the PRC, for which the Ma administration had pushed hard—an event that eventually became known as the Sunflower Movement. Finally, the ruling KMT itself appeared increasingly divided and paralyzed by infighting among its legislative caucus, local officials, and the Ma administration, and buffeted by corruption scandals and rising public opposition to further cross-Strait rapprochement.

The December 2014 local elections put an exclamation point on the swing in public opinion against the ruling party.[10] The KMT was trounced: going into the election, it held fifteen of twenty-two county executive and city mayor seats, but lost nine to either the DPP or independent candidates. The headline result was in Taipei, traditionally a pan-Blue stronghold, where a DPP-supported independent candidate and political novice, Ko Wen-je, handily won the election over KMT nominee Lien Sheng-wen (Sean Lien).

Particularly noteworthy was that Ko positioned himself as a centrist on cross-Strait relations, played down the traditional division between the leading parties, and instead spent much of his campaign emphasizing his outsider status, nonpartisan professional expertise (he was an emergency room physician at National Taiwan University hospital), and concern for local economic and governance issues. When his margin of victory was far larger than any previous DPP candidate had achieved in a Taipei mayor's race, some commentators saw it as proof that Taiwan's party system was headed for a broader realignment around economic and class issues and away from the old Blue-versus-Green competition over cross-Strait relations.[11]

The run-up to the 2016 election raised expectations further that a fundamental change in patterns of political support might be in the offing. In the months after the local elections, several new political parties were founded that claimed to represent a new "third force" in Taiwanese politics, distinguishing themselves from both of the two main political camps by emphasizing distinctive positions on crosscutting social, economic, and cultural issues. The most prominent were three parties that had close links to the social movement groups most active during Ma Ying-jeou's presidency: the New Power Party (NPP), the Social Democratic Party (SDP), and the Green Party Taiwan (GPT).[12] Attempting to capitalize on concerns that they thought the leading parties were ignoring, all three based their campaign appeals on a call to move beyond Blue-versus-Green competition to address other economic and social issues such as labor rights, environmental protection, social welfare policy, and regulation of big business.

These three were joined by at least half a dozen other significant new contestants, including the Republic Party, or Minkuotang (MKT), which began as a personal vehicle for prominent legislator and KMT defector Hsu Hsin-ying but quickly became associated with a Zen Buddhist religious master; the Faith and Hope League, a party appealing to religious conservatives advocating traditional family values; the Military, Civil Servants, Firefighters, Academics [Teachers], and Policemen Party (MCFAP), whose chief issue was the protection of pensions for retired government employees; the National Health Service Alliance, founded by a former minister of health, which advocated for full nationalization of the health insurance system and elimination of for-profit hospitals and clinics, along with a greater emphasis on traditional Chinese medicine; and the Trees Party, another pro–environmental protection party founded by a breakaway group from the GPT. In total, eighteen parties ran their own party lists—a record number for Taiwan. And at least that many nominated candidates at the district level.

But in the end, the disproportionate attention given to these "nontraditional" alternative political parties belied their weakness on election night. Of all the new parties that contested the legislative election, only one, the NPP, managed to win any seats at all; three of its nominees won their district seats, and the party secured 6.1 percent of the party-list vote, enough for an additional two seats. All the others came up short both of the 5 percent threshold for party-list seats and in the scattered district races in which they competed.

Instead, the main shift in the 2016 election was not to upstart "third force" parties at all but from the KMT to the DPP, which won both an easy victory in the presidential race and, for the first time in the party's history, a large majority in the Legislative Yuan. For all the talk about a crackup of the party system, the same two leading parties soon took up their seats in the new legislature, and almost as quickly restarted many of the same familiar partisan arguments that had driven politics for the previous decade and more.

Thus, viewed over a time span of decades, the primary impression one gets of Taiwan's party system is continuity rather than change. At the time of this writing, shortly after the January 2020 elections, the China question is still at the heart of Taiwanese party politics. And despite the staying power of the NPP and the strong showing of Ko Wen-je's newly founded Taiwan People's Party (TPP) in the 2020 elections, the DPP and KMT still remain the primary competitors. Furthermore, Taiwan's party system continues to be exceptionally well institutionalized for a young democracy, with low electoral volatility, high partisanship, broad elite and mass commitment to the legitimacy of elections and party politics, and two leading political parties with strong organizations, distinctive brands, and loyal followings in the electorate. On balance, there is little evidence to support the claim that 2016 was a "critical election" that fundamentally reordered the previous patterns of party competition. I conclude this chapter with some thoughts about how the consistency and stability of Taiwan's party system has contributed to the quality of its democracy and helped buttress the overall legitimacy of the political system.

Party System Institutionalization

We can get a sense of how the stability of Taiwan's party system compares to the rest of the democratic world by looking at some concrete measures of how institutionalized it is. Party-system institutionalization (PSI) is the degree to which the patterned interactions among significant political parties—the issues they advocate for, their membership and bases of support, and the shares of the vote each wins—are stable across multiple election cycles.[13] To operationalize this definition, I follow the influential work of Scott Mainwaring and Timothy Scully, who specify four distinct components of PSI: (1) stability in the nature of interparty competition over multiple election cycles; (2) the "rootedness" of political parties in society; (3) the legitimacy attributed to political parties and the electoral process; and (4) the institutionalization of political party organizations.[14]

Electoral Volatility

The first component of PSI, the stability of interparty competition over time, is typically operationalized as electoral volatility—that is, the change in party vote shares from one election to the next. Electoral volatility is calculated by taking the sum of the net change in the percentage of votes gained or lost by each party i from one election to the next, divided by two—that is: $(\Sigma |v_{it}-v_{it+1}|) / 2$. The resulting electoral volatility index varies from 0 to 100; a score of 0 means the exact same parties receive exactly the same share of votes in elections at time t and $t + 1$, while a score of 100 indicates that the set of parties winning votes at election $t + 1$ is completely different from the set winning votes at election t. The higher the volatility score, the lower is the institutionalization of this component of the party system.

In Table 5.1, I have calculated this measure for Taiwan for each election to the Legislative Yuan from 1992 to 2020; to provide a context in which to situate these scores, Table 5.2 reproduces the electoral volatility scores for the rest of Asia and for party systems in other regions of the world, calculated by Allen Hicken and Eric Kuhonta.[15]

As the data in the tables show, Taiwan's party system has remained fairly stable over its democratic history, with an average volatility score of 14.8. This measure puts Taiwan at the low end of the region; only Singapore and Malaysia, both longtime dominant-party systems, have similar or lower electoral volatility over roughly the same time period. By contrast, average volatility is significantly higher in South Korea (36.5), the democracy to which Taiwan is most often compared, and even slightly higher in Japan (16.5), which has a much longer history of democratic elections and for much of the postwar period was a dominant-party system. And Taiwan is not even in the same ballpark as the leading democracies of Southeast Asia: Indonesia (27.5), the Philippines (38.3), and Thailand prior to the

Table 5.1 Electoral Volatility in Taiwan, 1995–2020

Year	Volatility
1995	13.1
1998	12.4
2001	33.5
2004	10.3
2008	22.9
2012	7.2
2016	8.4
2020	10.6
Average	14.8

Source: Author calculations.
Note: Scale of 0 to 100, with a higher score indicating greater volatility.

Table 5.2   Electoral Volatility in Asia

Regime	Years	Number of Elections	Volatility: First and Second Elections	Volatility: Last Election	Average Volatility
Malaysia II	1974–2013	10	8.6	4.0	10.1
Taiwan	1992–2020	9	13.1	10.6	14.8
Singapore	1968–2011	11	24.6	20.4	15.4
Sri Lanka	1947–2010	14	27.7	9.0	16.6
Japan	1947–2012	24	27.4	16.3	16.8
Philippines I	1946–1969	7	20.4	43.6	18.5
India	1951–2009	15	25.1	11.3	19.2
Cambodia	1993–2013	5	27.9	22.9	24.0
Indonesia	1999–2009	3	25.2	29.8	27.5
Malaysia I	1955–1968	4	38.8	36.4	30.6
Timor Leste	2001–2012	3	49.0	22.5	35.8
South Korea	1988–2012	7	41.9	35.2	36.5
Philippines II	1992–2013	8	57.0	42.9	38.3
Thailand I	1979–1991	4	40.8	32.1	38.4
Thailand II	1992–2011	8	48.7	58.2	42.0

Source: Hicken and Kuhota, *Party System Institutionalization in Asia,* p.12; author calculation for Taiwan.
Note: Volatility scale is 0 to 100, with a higher score indicating greater volatility.

2006 coup (42.0). Allen Hicken and Eric Kuhonta also calculate an average electoral volatility for regions of the world, including Eastern Europe and the post-Soviet states (44.1), Latin America (25.5), and Western democracies including Australia and New Zealand (10.4). Taiwan's electoral volatility score puts it far below the averages in the former two regions and fairly close to the average in the West. In other words, the low electoral volatility of Taiwan's party system makes it appear more like that of a developed democracy than a young third-wave case.[16]

Partisanship
The second component, the "rootedness" of political parties in society, is usually operationalized as partisanship and measured via questions about party identification asked in public opinion surveys of the general population. Figure 5.1 reproduces the well-known data on this question collected regularly since 1994 by the Election Study Center at National Chengchi University.[17]

As one can see from the figure, since 1997 at least half of all respondents in each year have identified with one of the significant political parties in the party system. The share of "partisans" in the electorate has varied quite a bit over this period, ranging from as high as 69.5 percent in 2011 to as low as 50.9 percent in 2018. But, with the exception of a brief period in 2001, the KMT and DPP have retained the largest shares of partisan

Figure 5.1   Partisanship in Taiwan, 1994–2019

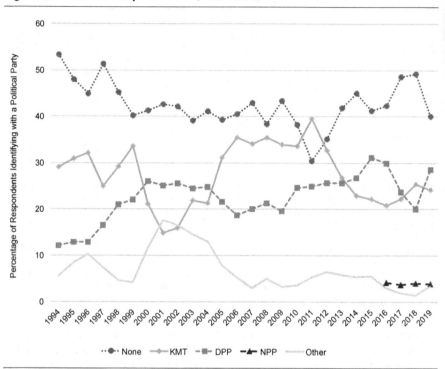

Source: Election Study Center, National Chengchi University.

supporters over Taiwan's entire democratic history, outpacing all other competitors in the party system. Moreover, in recent years declines in partisans
of one of the major parties have been correlated with increases in identification with the other: the surge in identification with the KMT starting in 2005
corresponded to a slump in DPP identification, and a similar drastic decline
in KMT partisans beginning in 2012 was followed by an uptick in DPP partisanship. The pattern repeated itself in the 2016–2020 election cycle, as the
DPP slumped following its high point in 2016 while the KMT showed a
modest recovery, to the point where in 2018 there were more self-identified
KMT partisans than DPP ones in the electorate.

It is also revealing what these data do not show: a rise in third-party
partisanship. In particular, the number of respondents who identify with the
New Power Party has remained small since its founding. The NPP burst
onto the political scene during the 2016 election campaign, winning 6.1
percent of the party-list vote and five seats in the legislature, and its relative
success inspired a fair amount of commentary about a fundamental realign-

ment of Taiwan's party system around issues orthogonal to the China question and a potential end to the old Green-versus-Blue duopoly.[18] Yet the most recent polling data suggest that the NPP remains a niche party in the party system, rather than the usurper and potential future major competitor to the DPP that it was sometimes portrayed as after 2016.[19] After the 2020 elections, similar breathless forecasts are being made about the bright future of Ko Wen-je's new Taiwan People's Party, which won five seats on more than 11 percent of the party-list vote and surpassed the NPP as the third-largest party in the Legislative Yuan. But past experience should lead us to be skeptical of the TPP's staying power, as well: it has no concrete policy positions to speak of and, so far at least, appears to be based solely on the independent electoral appeal of Mayor Ko. Moreover, the success of the NPP and TPP is the exception that proves the rule: for the past two decades, partisanship in Taiwan has remained strong and persistent enough to root the party system into two major camps and to raise a high bar for new third-party challenges—one that only these two parties have managed to overcome since 2001.[20]

Legitimacy of Party Politics

The third component that Mainwaring and Scully define is the legitimacy of political parties and trust in the political system. This dimension has been mostly ignored in subsequent work,[21] so I leave it aside here, although it is worth noting that, with rare exceptions, Taiwanese political parties themselves have accepted electoral competition as the only legitimate path to power, and in public opinion surveys most Taiwanese consistently recognize the right of political parties to contest elections and acknowledge the fairness of the electoral process for choosing political leaders.[22]

Party Organization

The fourth component of party-system institutionalization is party organization. On this dimension, there is wide variation across the parties in Taiwan that have held seats in the legislature during the democratic era. The KMT and DPP are both well-institutionalized: both have robust party organizations that include party branches in almost all local jurisdictions, integrated into a coherent hierarchy, with power concentrated at the top and wielded by a central executive committee and chairperson. Both retain tight party control over their nominations for elected offices, are able to raise and deploy significant financial and personnel resources to aid party activities, and have effective mechanisms for disciplining wayward members including current officeholders. And both are clearly much more than electoral vehicles for the party chairperson or highest officeholder: they have survived long periods in political opposition, rapid rises and falls in political fortunes, and multiple changes in party leadership.[23] This persistence of robust party organizations is particularly noteworthy because Taiwan is a presidential regime, and there is a tendency for presidents to dominate and hollow out the organization of their political parties; when presidents leave office, their political parties sometimes struggle to survive as coherent, meaningful organizations.[24]

The other significant parties in the party system feature much less robust party organizations and have been more clearly associated with a single founding leader: James Soong in the case of the PFP, and Lee Teng-hui in that of the TSU. As both leaders age out of politics, neither party looks like it has a particularly bright future; both were shut out of the legislature in the 2020 elections—the PFP despite James Soong's third-party presidential campaign. The TPP, though new, appears to be in the mold of these earlier parties; so far at least, its image and political positions are inseparable from its founder, Ko Wen-je. The most interesting and uncertain case is that of the NPP, which in its earliest days pledged radical transparency in its policy and strategy deliberations and attempted to foster a more open process of collective decisionmaking among its mostly young, politically inexperienced membership. In the run-up to the 2020 elections, however, two of its five legislators left the party and a third was expelled, and it dropped to only three seats (though it did manage to increase its party-list vote share by about 1.5 points). Having survived this near-death experience, it remains an open question whether the NPP will be able to strengthen its internal organization and to grow into more than a niche party in the system.[25]

Other Evidence for High Party-System Institutionalization in Taiwan

In addition to Mainwaring and Scully's canonical components of PSI, one can also observe other evidence that suggests a high degree of stability in Taiwan's party system. One additional measure is the frequency and consequence of attempts at party-switching, which Dafydd Fell has studied in detail in recent years.[26] Fell finds that while party-switching is not exactly rare, in the legislature it has occurred almost entirely within the pan-Blue camp (i.e., the KMT and allied parties), typically from the KMT to the PFP or New Party and back again. Party-switchers on the Blue side of the spectrum have fared a bit better than those who have attempted to switch to or from the DPP, which has been exceedingly hostile to defectors. But overall, Fell finds very few cases of successful party-switching in which incumbent officeholders manage to win reelection under the banner of another party, suggesting that partisanship and party organizations effectively limit this kind of opportunistic behavior.

One can also look at the fates of new parties in legislative elections, which are an indicator of the party system's "permeability" and thus provide yet another alternative measure of PSI. From 1992 through 2004, Taiwan's legislators were elected using single nontransferable vote (SNTV) in multimember districts, which provided realistic opportunities in some districts for parties winning as little as 5 percent of the vote to capture seats. And since 2008, parties winning at least 5 percent of the separate party-list vote are guaranteed seats from the proportional representation (PR) portion of the electoral system. Thus, Taiwan's electoral system, while not guaranteeing proportionality, has also had a rather low threshold of exclusion for party entry. Yet the vast majority of new parties that have run candidates in legislative elections have had no success. The exceptions have typically been a very specific kind of party: those that took distinct positions on the China question.[27] In 2001, for instance, both the PFP, whose chairman, James Soong, initially took up a position to the right of the KMT, and the TSU, which took up a position to the left of the DPP, managed to win a significant number of seats in the Legislative Yuan elections held that year. Indeed, one can line up on the China-question dimension every single party to hold at least three seats in the legislature since 1992. The parties in the current legislature are no exception. The success of the NPP is in no small part due to the party's positioning itself as a more pro-independence ally of the DPP—a kind of "TSU for young people"[28]—and the TPP's core (some might say only) appeal is that it is between the two major camps on the China question.[29] Thus, the fate of new parties, too, suggests that Taiwan's party system, while permeable enough to allow some replacement of small parties with others, remains deeply rooted in the original cleavage around which it became oriented shortly after democratization.[30]

The 2016 Elections: Realignment or Deviation?

To this point I have argued that Taiwan's party system is notable both for its high degree of PSI and its unidimensionality. The previous evidence suggests that a realignment of the party system in 2016, if it did occur, would have been a rather abrupt departure from previous patterns of party competition, and thus a critical moment in Taiwan's party-system evolution. In this section, I take up the question of whether the 2016 presidential and legislative elections ushered in a lasting partisan realignment, or whether they were instead a temporary deviation from the underlying pattern of partisan competition.

Before tackling that question in earnest, however, we need to agree on some terminology: What exactly is a "critical election" that leads to a "party-system realignment"?[31] Political commentators often use the terms casually, without definition, and most of us have an innate sense of what is meant by it: an election that results in a fundamental, lasting shift in the patterns of party competition and voting behavior, whatever they may be. That definition, however, obscures an important distinction between at least two possible kinds of realignment: what I will call the major and minor versions.

Party-System Realignments: Major and Minor Versions

The major version is what V. O. Key had in mind when he first introduced the concept of a critical election in 1955: it is one in which "the decisive results of the voting reveal a sharp alteration of the preexisting cleavage within the electorate."[32] The key feature here is that a completely new dimension of competition suddenly becomes salient enough that a significant number of erstwhile partisans permanently drop or switch their partisan attachments. The old political coalitions in one or more parties are split apart by this new cleavage, and either a new party emerges to win big chunks of the old parties' voters, or coalitions behind the parties break apart and re-form, with some segments of the electorate in effect "trading places."

For instance, in the 1968 presidential election in the United States, the Democratic Party fractured over the issue of civil rights, and many white voters in the southern states refused to support the Democratic nominee, thus accelerating a period of dealignment from the national Democratic Party and eventual realignment of white southerners toward the Republican Party, while at the same time African American voters swung decisively into the Democratic Party coalition.[33]

By contrast, in the minor version of party realignment, rather than requiring the appearance of a new dimension of competition, the underlying preferences of the electorate can suddenly shift in a way that favors one of the leading parties over others. A significant share of voters who supported Party A (or C or D, or who did not vote at all) in the previous elections now support Party B in the current, "realigning" one. And crucially, *this* shift is both abrupt and lasting: either through the establishment of partisan attachments from formerly unattached voters, through generational replacement, or through wholesale conversion of one party's partisans to another's, the expected share of the electorate who will vote for Party B increases.

For instance, the 1977 Israeli election delivered for the first time a plurality of the vote (33 percent) to the right-wing Likud over the incumbent left-wing Labor Party (26 percent). That vote marked a critical shift in the Israeli party system: Labor (and its predecessor Mapai) had long been the leading party in the electorate and had formed every government since the state of Israel was founded in 1948. The Likud victory in 1977 ushered in the first right-wing government in Israeli history, as well as a new period of relative parity between the left and right blocs in the Israeli electorate and the parliament, and Labor was never again able to regain the dominant position it held prior to that election.[34]

To illustrate more clearly the difference in these two patterns of party-system change, consider the following stylized example. Let us assume a simple, symmetric two-party system with high party identification: both Party A and Party B can each count on the support of 40 percent of the electorate. The remaining 20 percent are swing voters who may alternate their votes between the parties depending on the identities of the candidates, the parties' positions on the issues of the day, the state of the economy, the performance of the party in power, and whatever else affects voting behavior.

In a major critical realignment, a new crosscutting cleavage emerges that divides the coalitions of both parties. Let us take the limiting case for our example: assume this cleavage splits both parties exactly in half, with 20 percent of the electorate on each side in each party, and that this issue is so salient that partisans care more about it than whatever previously divided the two major parties, as Figure 5.2 shows. The party leaders then take opposing positions on this new issue of the day, and the electorate re-sorts into the parties that best correspond to their preferences. After the critical election, the parties enjoy the same proportion of supporters in the electorate—but 40 percent of voters have switched parties.

To be sure, most party-system realignments, even of the major variety, are neither this neat, nor dramatic, nor sudden. In established democracies, partisan attachments tend to be strong and make voters resistant to wholesale party-switching of this kind. So it is more often a completely new party that appears on the scene to scoop up the newly unaligned voters from both camps, as, for instance, the Republican Party did over the issue of slavery in the United States in the 1850s, or the British Labour Party did over class and economic divisions in the 1920s. Regardless, the key feature of the major realignment is not neat, symmetric party-switching, but merely the emergence of a new issue cleavage that leads to a sharp alteration of the preexisting patterns of voting.

Now consider the minor version of a critical realignment, again assuming a symmetric, two-party system with each party enjoying the committed partisan support of 40 percent of the electorate, and 20 percent as swing voters. A minor realignment occurs without the emergence of a new cleavage at all, but simply a lasting defection of some partisans from one camp. In the scenario illustrated in Figure 5.3, 5 percent of the electorate "dealigns" from Party B to become swing voters, while 5 percent of the previous swing voters "realign" with Party A and become committed partisans. After the critical election, the electorate has gone from a perfectly competitive, symmetrically distributed two-party system to one with a pronounced advantage for Party A, which now enjoys a 45-to-35 percent lead among all partisan voters.

Now, note what does not have to occur here: the emergence of a new cleavage. The same issue that separates the two major parties can remain the primary, salient one in the political system, and the two parties that win votes are the same two parties as before. What does have to occur, instead, is a shift in the collective preferences of the electorate, away from Party B's

Figure 5.2   A "Major" Realignment: A New Dimension of Competition Breaks Apart Existing Party Coalitions

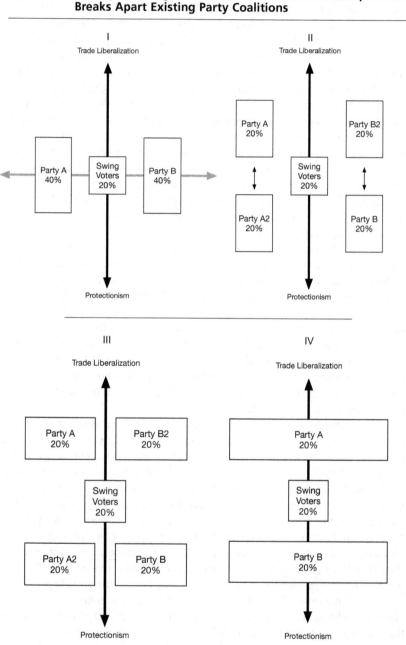

Figure 5.3   A "Minor" Realignment: The Party System Shifts from Parity to an Advantage for Party A

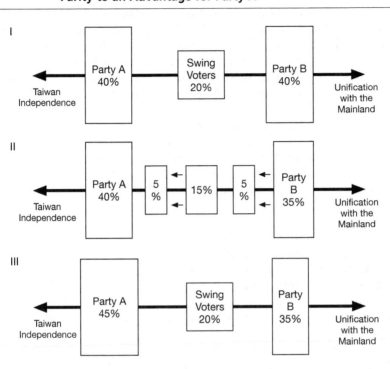

position, and toward Party A's. Either through generational replacement, targeted appeals by Party A (or indifference from Party B), or a true reordering of preferences on the primary dimension of conflict, Party A permanently increases its share of partisans.

Deviating and Maintaining Elections

Finally, a brief comment on two other terms that are sometimes tossed around in the critical elections and realignments literature: "deviating" and "maintaining" elections.[35] Following the stylized example earlier, we can think of a deviating election as one in which there is no change in the underlying partisan balance, but for some reason most of the swing voters break in one direction or the other. If the swing is large enough to look unprecedented, or at least unusual, we might even call it a "surge" election, to use Angus Campbell's term.[36] For instance, if Party B's partisans are only 35 percent of the electorate, while Party A's are 45 percent, as in Figure 5.3 after realignment, then the only way Party B can win an election is if most of the swing voters support it. That is, the electorate as a whole has to deviate from the partisan tendency toward Party A.

Why might voters deviate in this way? Many reasons: an economic downturn is the most likely possibility, but other factors such as an unpopular candidate or party leader, a corruption scandal, a foreign crisis, or general disillusionment with the incumbent are all strong enough to cause these kinds of electoral swings. We need simply observe something that causes a short-term shift in support for one party to another at the ballot box to identify a deviating election.

Last but not least, if none of these changes happens—no critical election, nor a temporary deviation from the established patterns of support—then we have a maintaining election. If, in Figure 5.3 after realignment, the swing voters break half for Party A and half for Party B, then Party A's advantage in the electorate is maintained through that election.

Was 2016 a Critical Election That Launched a Partisan Realignment?

The terms "critical election" and "partisan realignment" come up often in discussions of Taiwanese politics, but the preceding discussion suggests it is worth stepping back and thinking a bit more carefully about what we should observe had a major (or minor) realignment occurred in the party system in 2016.

First and foremost, was there, as a result of an election, a fundamental change in the primary cleavage structuring party competition? This is what we should see to make the case for the major version of a party-system realignment: new cleavage, new electoral coalitions. If no new parties have successfully broken into the system, or if the winning parties are still competing on the same dimensions of conflict, then we have no evidence of a major realignment. The best place to answer this question is to look at the legislative races rather than the presidential one, since it is in the legislative election where new parties ran candidates and attempted to take positions orthogonal to the issue of cross-Strait relations and Blue-versus-Green party competition.

So how did these new, small parties fare in 2016? As Dafydd Fell has argued, they collectively enjoyed a "limited breakthrough" relative to the rather dismal experience of most previous attempts of new parties to compete for seats.[37] Several ran high-profile candidates in the district races as well as for the party-list vote, and one, the New Power Party, ran particularly well in both tiers. The NPP surprised many prognosticators by winning all three district races in which it ran viable candidates, and it came in fourth in the party-list vote with 6.1 percent, winning an additional two seats and narrowly missing out on a third.

But the New Power Party's success is a bit misleading in this context, and we should be skeptical that it represents a "new kind" of politics, for at least two reasons. First, the party deliberately pursued a personality-based campaign strategy. It recruited three candidates with high name recognition to run in the district races: Freddy Lim, a lead singer for the band Chthonic; Hung Tzu-yung, the younger sister of an army conscript who died after harsh punishment while in military detention; and Huang Kuo-chang, a National Taiwan University law professor and one of the public faces of the Sunflower Movement that occupied the legislature in 2014. These candidates helped the party garner a great deal of free media attention, giving it a significant leg up on the other new entrees into the party system.

Second, as Fell notes, the NPP coordinated very closely with the DPP during its campaign.[38] The party went so far as to negotiate a pre-electoral coalition agreement with the DPP not to run candidates in most districts; in exchange, the DPP yielded three winnable districts to the NPP and agreed not to nominate its own candidates there. The DPP even sent Tsai Ing-wen to campaign with the NPP candidates, reinforcing the impression that the NPP was running not as a competitor seeking to split the DPP's base, but as a close pan-Green ally.[39]

We can get a sense of how closely the NPP's fortunes were tied to the DPP's in 2016 by comparing the party's vote shares to Tsai Ing-wen's in the districts. Figure 5.4 shows the vote share won by each district's DPP nominee, plotted against the vote share won by non-DPP candidates endorsed by the DPP. These included the three NPP candidates but also eight other non-DPP candidates, most of whom ran as part of an anti-KMT "Capital Alliance" grouping in Taipei City. The diagonal line represents parity between the district and presidential vote shares; points above the line indicate candidates who ran ahead of Tsai, while points below indicate those who ran behind.[40]

As the figure shows, the three NPP candidates won very nearly the same share of the vote as Tsai did in their districts—their performance looks much like other DPP district candidates. By contrast, the other, non-NPP candidates who were endorsed by the DPP fared much more poorly than Tsai did in their districts. Thus we have an additional piece of evidence that the NPP was not really running an "orthogonal," anti-elite or anti-system campaign, but rather a more conventional, "DPP-lite" one, and that association with Tsai and the DPP was an important component of their success.

Given the close coordination between the NPP and DPP, a better test of the appeal of issues off the primary dimension of competition is the performance of the other "third force" parties, particularly the SDP-GPT Alliance, the Civil Servants party, the Faith and Hope League, and the National Health Service Alliance. So how did they do, as a whole? In the district races, they fared not as well as the NPP, as Figure 5.4 shows—they generally ran behind

Figure 5.4   Tsai Ing-wen District Vote Share Compared to DPP, NPP, and Other Third-Party Candidates in 2016

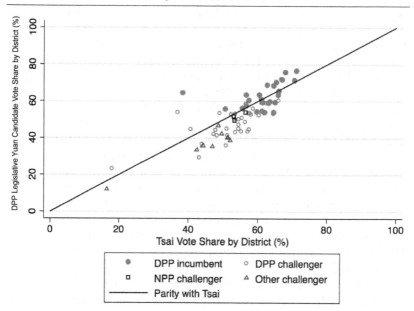

Source: Central Election Commission.

not only Tsai Ing-wen but also the NPP and DPP challengers. But what about the party-list vote? Not well there, either, as Table 5.3 shows. The SDP-GPT Alliance won only 2.53 percent of the party-list vote, despite the distinct ideological space that the party staked out during the campaign. Other parties that highlighted positions off the Blue-versus-Green axis also fared poorly: the Faith and Hope League won 1.69 percent, the MKT won 1.62 percent, and the National Health Service Alliance won 0.42 percent. There is simply no evidence from the party-list vote to support the assertion that a latent, underserved dimension of political conflict suddenly became salient and burst into the open in this election, despite the many attempts by the new political parties to emphasize neglected political issues.

In fact, if we go simply by the parties holding seats in the legislature, the only change to the party system after the election was the replacement of the TSU by the NPP. And after taking office, the NPP positioned itself to the left of the DPP on cross-Strait relations, occupying a roughly similar ideological space to the TSU. Given these facts, it is hard indeed to sustain the case that Taiwan's party system went through a major realignment in 2016, and that the NPP represented the leading edge of a new kind of politics after this election.

Table 5.3   Party-List Vote Shares in the 2016 Legislative Yuan Election

English Name	Chinese Name	Party-List Votes	Percentage	PR Seats Won
Democratic Progressive Party	民主進步黨	5,370,953	44.04	18
Chinese Nationalist Party (Kuomintang)	中國國民黨	3,280,949	26.90	11
People First Party	親民黨	794,838	6.52	3
New Power Party	時代力量	744,315	6.10	2
New Party	新黨	510,074	4.18	0
Green Party– Social Democratic Party Alliance	綠黨社會民主黨聯盟	308,106	2.53	0
Taiwan Solidarity Union	台灣團結聯盟	305,675	2.51	0
Faith and Hope League	信心希望聯盟	206,629	1.69	0
Republic Party (Minkuotang)	民國黨	197,627	1.62	0
Military, Civil Servants, Firefighters, Academics [Teachers], and Policemen Party	軍公教聯盟黨	87,213	0.72	0
Non-Partisan Solidarity Union	無黨團結聯盟	77,672	0.64	0
Trees Party	樹黨	77,174	0.63	0
Chinese Unification Promotion Party	中華統一促進黨	56,347	0.46	0
Health Alliance	健保免費連線	51,024	0.42	0
Free Taiwan Party	自由台灣黨	47,988	0.39	0
Peace Dove Alliance Party	和平鴿聯盟黨	30,617	0.25	0
Taiwan Independence Party	台灣獨立黨	27,496	0.23	0
Great Love Constitutional Reform Party	大愛憲改聯盟	15,442	0.13	0
Total, parties winning seats		10,191,055	83.56	34
Total, parties not winning seats		1,999,084	16.40	0

Source: Central Election Commission.

Was 2016 a Realigning Election or a Deviating One?

While there is no evidence of a reorientation of the party system around a new cleavage in 2016, there was a very clear swing toward the DPP. As noted earlier, Tsai Ing-wen did ten and a half points better in 2016 than in 2012, and she carried into office enough DPP candidates to win over 60 percent of the seats in the Legislative Yuan—the party's first-ever majority. The corollary to the DPP's unprecedented success in this election was the sweeping defeat of the KMT. Its standard-bearer in the presidential race, Eric Chu, won only 31 percent of the vote, a decline of over 20 percent from 2012. The party's legislative candidates fared a bit better in the district vote, winning 38.9 percent (down from 48.1 percent in 2012) but support for the KMT on the party ballot slumped much more dramatically, to only 26.9 percent (down from 44.6 percent in 2012). In the wake of these results, a number of commentators began to speculate that the KMT might never recover from such a comprehensive defeat, and that key segments of the voting public had permanently shifted into the Green camp—that is, to use the preceding terminology, that Taiwan's party system had undergone a minor realignment.

Yet we face a basic challenge in interpreting these shifts: How do we differentiate between a deviating election and a critical one? They are observationally equivalent without other sources of data: the surge in support for the DPP is consistent with either a short-term deviation from the previous pattern of presidential elections, or a long-term shift in the electorate in the direction of the DPP and away from the KMT. Much rides on this question, yet it is the hardest to answer with any degree of certainty. Nevertheless, there are some clues to look for: the level of turnout, generational and regional differences, and the coherence and organization of the parties themselves can all potentially reveal something about whether this election marked the start of a new political era, or whether it instead represented only a short-term deviation from the previous state of play.

With this in mind, there are at least three pieces of evidence that are inconsistent with the claim that this was a critical election that ushered in a lasting realignment, even in the "minor" sense of a simple shift in partisan attachments. First, turnout in this election hit a record low for a presidential race: at 66.3 percent, it was below even the 2014 local elections (67.6 percent), and it fell a full eleven points short of the turnout of 2012 (77.4 percent) and eight of the 2020 election (74.9 percent). That means at least 1 million people who voted in 2012 did not in 2016—and almost 2 million who did not vote in 2016 voted in 2020. One likely reason for the drop in turnout in 2016 is that the presidential election was not expected to be close, and there was very little drama by the end of the campaign, so many voters may not have felt compelled to participate. Another is that the KMT's very late switch of presidential candidate from Hung Hsiu-chu to Eric Chu in October 2015, less than three months before the election, undoubtedly angered some core KMT supporters, and probably further dampened enthusiasm for voting among the pan-Blue side. The latter, at least, is unlikely to recur—indeed, in the 2020 elections the core pan-Blue supporters were energized by KMT candidate Han Kuo-yu, and turned out at much higher rates. Thus, on this count, the 2016 election is best viewed as a deviation to the low side from the "normal" level of pan-Blue support in the electorate.

Second, the KMT's position as the longtime ruling party put it at a distinct disadvantage in this election. Although incumbent president Ma Ying-jeou was not on the ballot, his own low popularity and the widespread dissatisfaction with his government were clearly factors in the KMT's own struggle to run a competitive campaign. The subsequent struggles the Tsai Ing-wen administration has had in confronting many of the same issues that dragged down President Ma are further evidence that the KMT was a more formidable opponent than its showing in 2016 indicated.

Third, incumbency worked against the KMT in 2016 for another reason: a poorly timed economic downturn meant the party was trying to win an election in the middle of a recession—one, furthermore, that was triggered at least in part by a slowdown in the mainland Chinese economy. Because the Ma administration had made closer economic integration with the PRC a central part of its agenda while in office, the KMT was especially vulnerable to criticism that it bore responsibility for this downturn.

Thus, the preponderance of evidence suggests that 2016 was a deviation, not a permanent realignment of the party system, even a minor one. Developments since then are consistent with this interpretation: President Tsai's support slumped dramatically from her initial highs, and in a shocking reversal the DPP was defeated as badly in the 2018 local elections as it had won in 2014. Crucially, the KMT, not the NPP or other third-party alternatives, was the main beneficiary of the DPP's unpopularity. Then, in the 2020 election campaign, cross-Strait relations were once again front and center in the debate between the two parties: Tsai Ing-wen's reputation for caution and skepticism toward Beijing put her much closer to the median voter on this critical dimension of politics, and it ultimately delivered her and the DPP to a decisive win over Han Kuo-yu and the KMT. *Plus ça change . . .*

Conclusion

Viewed over a time span of decades, the primary impression one gets of Taiwan's party system is continuity rather than change. At the time of this writing, shortly after the 2020 elections, the China question remains at the heart of Taiwan's party politics, and the DPP and KMT are still the chief competitors—much as they have been for the past three decades. Taiwan's party system continues to be exceptionally stable for a young democracy, and highly institutionalized: electoral volatility is low, partisanship is high, political elites and masses are both broadly committed to the electoral process as the only legitimate means to win and retain power, and the two leading political parties retain strong organizations, distinctive brands, and loyal followings in the electorate.

It is common in Taiwan to view this exceptional stability through a negative lens, and lament the failure of parties offering clear programmatic platforms distinct from the China question to win seats. There is, indeed, some danger that Taiwan's party system might become too detached from the concerns of an increasing share of the electorate, and that its political elites might become unresponsive to critical issues that do not map neatly onto the independence-versus-unification divide. Such elite drift is probably at least partly to blame for the rise in populist and Euroskeptic parties in Europe, and of Donald Trump in the United States.

Nevertheless, Taiwan's current party system has, so far at least, proven remarkably responsive to shifts in mass public opinion on the China question. When public opinion swung in favor of greater engagement with the PRC during the latter half of Chen Shui-bian's presidency, and the DPP ignored it, it was swept out of office and replaced by a president and party that aggressively pursued cross-Strait rapprochement. When public opinion turned against President Ma's cross-Strait policies, and the KMT attempted to force through additional agreements anyway, it too was swept out of power in the next election. And in 2020, the failure of KMT candidate Han Kuo-yu to reassure voters worried about sovereignty and security threats from Beijing contributed to his comprehensive defeat in the presidential election, even as public opinion polls showed support for the DPP and Tsai Ing-wen to be quite shallow in the months leading up to the elections. In addition, whichever major party is in opposition has shown an impressive ideological flexibility on most issues orthogonal to the China question, as well as a willingness to raise new concerns or reposition itself on old ones for the hope of an electoral advantage—on labor rights, energy policy, and same-sex marriage, for instance. Both parties have also managed to build broad coalitions to return to power. Prior to 2008, for example, the KMT managed to reunite its warring factions and reassimilate much of the PFP into its ranks, and prior to 2016 the DPP brought together a diverse group of critics of the Ma administration and the KMT behind Tsai Ing-wen's candidacy.

From a comparative perspective, democracies with high party-system institutionalization appear to fare systematically better over the long run, in terms of both democratic quality and, more fundamentally, their ability simply to survive, than those with low PSI.[41] Partisanship and Blue-versus-Green competition is the object of much complaining among political observers in Taiwan, but the experience of other young democracies does not provide much evidence that weaker party organizations, a more volatile party system, and less partisanship would improve the representativeness, responsiveness, and accountability of Taiwan's political elite. As boring and predictable as the KMT and DPP's partisan fights may seem to casual observers, they also provide the foundations for a high-quality democracy that, so far at least, compares very well against its peers in the region and beyond.

Notes

1. See Cheng and Hsu, "Long in the Making," pp. 108–135, and the other chapters in Hicken and Kuhonta, *Party System Institutionalization in Asia.*

2. Scholars as a whole have been inconsistent in how they refer to this fundamental cleavage in Taiwanese politics. Rather than defend a particular interpretation, I simply note that there is enough overlap between the identity symbols that each party's core partisans embrace or avoid in their campaigns and public statements, as well as their views on cross-Strait relations, that we can refer without oversimplification to a single dimension of political conflict.

3. Among the many studies making this point over the past two decades, see, for example, Chu, "Taiwan's National Identity Politics and the Prospect of Cross-Strait Relations"; Yu, "The Evolving Party System in Taiwan, 1995–2004"; Hsieh, "Ethnicity, National Identity, and Domestic Politics in Taiwan"; Fell, *Party Politics in Taiwan;* Hsieh, "Continuity and Change in Party Politics in Japan, Taiwan, and South Korea"; Rigger, "Political Parties and Identity Politics in Taiwan"; Cheng and Hsu, "Taiwan's Institutionalized Party System"; Sheng and Liao, "Issues, Political Cleavages, and Party Competition in Taiwan"; and Huang, "Generation Effects?"

4. For an excellent recent summary of this body of research findings, see also Achen and Wang, *The Taiwan Voter.*

5. Yu, "Partisanship and Public Opinion."

6. For some English-language examples, see Wu, "From Identity to Distribution"; Sullivan and Thim, "Here Comes Taiwan's Big Political Realignment"; Sia, "Nationalist Dealignment in 2014, Realignment in 2016?"; Smith, "The Coming Collapse of the KMT?"; and van der Horst, "The Rise of Taiwan's 'Third Force.'" Also relevant here is the post-election discussion in Hsieh, "Taiwan's General Elections of 2016."

7. Armigeon and Guthmann, "Democracy in Crisis?"

8. See, for instance, Kriesi and Pappas, *European Populism in the Shadow of the Great Recession.*

9. For an introduction to these cases and a more general review of protests during the Ma era, see Chapters 12 and 13 of this volume, as well as "Taiwan, America, and Meat Wars," *The Economist,* March 8, 2012, http://www.economist.com/blogs/banyan/2012/03/taiwan-america-and-meat-wars; and "Blooded: A Conscript's Death Has Brought the Young Out on the Streets," *The Economist,* August 10, 2013, http://www.economist.com/news/asia/21583271-conscripts-death-has-brought-young-out-streets-blooded.

10. See Min-hua Huang, "Taiwan's Changing Political Landscape: The KMT's Defeat in the Nine-in-One Elections," Brookings Institution East Asia Commentary Series, December 8, 2014, https://www.brookings.edu/opinions/taiwans-changing-political-landscape-the-kmts-landslide-defeat-in-the-nine-in-one-elections.

11. Wu, "From Identity to Distribution"; Sullivan and Thim, "Here Comes Taiwan's Big Political Realignment"; Sia, "Nationalist Dealignment in 2014, Realignment in 2016?"; Smith, "The Coming Collapse of the KMT?"; and van der Horst, "The Rise of Taiwan's 'Third Force.'"

12. The NPP and SDP were newly founded. The GPT was actually established in the 1990s but gained little traction in elections before the 2016 campaign. On the history of the GPT and the environmental movement, see Fell and Peng, "The Electoral Fortunes of Taiwan's Green Party," Fell, "Small Parties in Taiwan's 2016 National Elections," and Grano, *Environmental Governance in Taiwan.*

13. "Significant" is a vague term, and one could adopt many different cutoffs to distinguish "significant" from "insignificant" parties in the party system. My own preference is to focus on "significance" in terms of policymaking in the legislature; given the outsized power that individual party caucuses have in the Legislative Yuan, I define as significant any party that holds enough seats to form a party caucus.

14. Mainwaring and Scully, *Building Democratic Institutions.*

15. Hicken and Kuhonta, *Party System Institutionalization in Asia,* pp. 11–12.

16. The drop in electoral volatility in the 2012 and 2016 elections may be due in part to the new, more majoritarian electoral system introduced in 2008. Nevertheless, it is not self-evident that Taiwan's low volatility (and high party-system institutionalization) of recent years is related to the change in electoral system. For one, majoritarian electoral systems can also produce extremely high volatility under some conditions, as recent elections in Canada, France, and Malaysia demonstrate. For another, both South Korea and Japan now use systems very similar to Taiwan's to elect their national assemblies, yet have recorded significantly higher electoral volatility over the past decade.

17. Election Study Center, National Chengchi University, https://esc.nccu.edu.tw/main.php.

18. Wu, "From Identity to Distribution"; Sullivan and Thim, "Here Comes Taiwan's Big Political Realignment"; Sia, "Nationalist Dealignment in 2014, Realignment in 2016?"; Smith, "The Coming Collapse of the KMT?"; and van der Horst, "The Rise of Taiwan's 'Third Force.'"

19. Chen and Liao, "The Rise of the New Power Party in Taiwan's 2016 Legislative Election."

20. This is not to say that high PSI prevents successful third-party or independent candidacies in Taiwan, only that they are difficult to pull off and even more difficult to sustain beyond a single election. Skeptics might point to the many independent candidates who have run serious campaigns for local office in recent years, most prominently the current Taipei mayor, Ko Wen-je. Ko, however, is the exception that proves the rule: his election in 2014 relied on the implicit backing of the DPP, which did not run its own candidate and campaigned for him on the stump. When the DPP nominated a challenger in 2018, by contrast, Ko's share of the vote dropped by nearly 20 percent and he barely won reelection, despite high approval ratings for his performance as mayor. Admittedly, the performance of his TPP in the 2020 elections was impressive for a first-time party, and it suggests Ko has considerable independent appeal beyond any partisan considerations. But if he runs for president in 2024, as he now appears to be positioning himself to do, he will eventually have to clarify his stance on cross-Strait relations, and the usual partisan forces will then most likely work against his personal popularity, much as they did in Taipei's 2018 mayoral race.

21. For one important exception, see Croissant and Völkel, "Party System Types and Party System Institutionalization."

22. McAllister, "Democratic Consolidation in Taiwan in Comparative Perspective"; Sanborn, "Democratic Consolidation"; Shyu, "Trust in Institutions and the Democratic Consolidation in Taiwan."

23. On the DPP's organization, see Rigger, *From Opposition to Power.*

24. Samuels and Shugart, *Presidents, Parties, and Prime Ministers.* On the "presidentialization" of party organizations, see also Chapters 3 and 4 of this book.

25. Chen and Liao, "The Rise of the New Power Party," pp. 90–91.

26. Fell, "Should I Stay or Should I Go?"; Fell, "Do Party Switchers Pay an Electoral Price?"; Fell, "Merger and Takeover Attempts in Taiwanese Party Politics."

27. Dafydd Fell, following Paul Lucardie, calls these "purifier" parties. Fell, "Success and Failure of New Parties in Taiwanese Elections," p. 216; see also the discussion in Fell, *Government and Politics in Taiwan,* pp. 115–121.

28. For evidence, see the interviews with NPP activists in Nachman, "Misalignment Between Social Movements and Political Parties in Taiwan's 2016 Election." This characterization of the NPP is my own.

29. The TPP even chose a party color, aquamarine, to highlight its intermediate positioning between the Blue and Green camps.

30. For instance, this is the primary finding of Achen and Wang's *The Taiwan Voter;* see pp. 1–25.

31. Major contributors to the literature on party realignments in the US context include Key, "A Theory of Critical Elections"; Schattschneider, *The Semisovereign People,* pp.

112–125; Burnham, *Critical Elections and the Mainsprings of American Politics;* and Sundquist, *Dynamics of the Party System.* A thorough, although critical, review of this literature can be found in Mayhew, "Electoral Realignments." For a more sympathetic view and defense of the concept, see Carmines and Wagner, "Political Issues and Party Alignments." A good example of research on realignments outside of the United States is Evans and Norris, *Critical Elections.*

32. Key, "A Theory of Critical Elections," p. 4.

33. Stanley, "Southern Partisan Changes."

34. Arian and Shamir, "Two Reversals in Israeli Politics."

35. The fullest discussion and defense of this typology of elections is given in Burnham, *Critical Elections and the Mainsprings of American Politics.*

36. A. Campbell, "Surge and Decline"; J. Campbell, "The Revised Theory of Surge and Decline."

37. Fell, "Small Parties in Taiwan's 2016 National Elections."

38. Ibid., p. 52; see also Nachman, "Misalignment Between Social Movements and Political Parties," pp. 887–889, and the discussion of DPP-NPP coordination in Chapter 3 of this volume.

39. Iok-sin Loa, "Tsai Slams KMT's 'Mudslinging,'" *Taipei Times,* December 14, 2015, p. 3.

40. Note that this comparison does not adjust for the fact that indigenous voters are included in the presidential but not the legislative totals, since they vote in separate constituencies. Because indigenous voters tend to be "Bluer" than the electorate as a whole, Figure 5.4 overstates the divergence in the DPP's party vote share between the presidential and legislative races. This difference is greatest in Taitung and Hualien—the two districts where indigenous voters constitute over 20 percent of the presidential electorate.

41. I develop this argument at length elsewhere. See Templeman, "Blessings in Disguise."

6

The Challenges of Governance

Yun-han Chu and Yu-tzung Chang

When Ma Ying-jeou was inaugurated on May 20, 2008, as the twelfth president of the Republic of China (ROC) (and the sixth since the introduction of the popular vote in 1996), he was entrusted with a strong popular mandate and a unified government. He delivered a convincing win over his Democratic Progressive Party (DPP) opponent in the March election, winning 58.5 percent of the popular vote, while the Kuomintang (KMT) and its political allies grabbed a three-quarters majority of the Legislative Yuan in the election for that body two months earlier.[1]

In theory, the KMT's electoral landslide in 2008 should have brought a conclusive end to the crippling experiences of divided government during Chen Shui-bian's eight-year presidency and put the island back on the track of effective governance.[2] However, this reasonable expectation was unfortunately never fulfilled. In reality, Ma Ying-jeou encountered mounting obstacles whenever he pushed forward major policy initiatives, and he increasingly found himself entrapped in a political quagmire. His public approval ratings nosedived less than six months into his presidency, and they remained depressingly low throughout his the remaining seven and a half years as president. When he left office in 2016, his party suffered a crushing electoral defeat and for the first time had to relinquish control of both the executive and legislative branches to the opposition DPP.

This is not to suggest that Ma accomplished very few things during his eight-year term. He should be given credit for laying a solid foundation for cross-Strait peace by de-escalating military tension, resuming the official dialogues and negotiations interrupted during the previous DPP administration, and concluding twenty-three bilateral pacts with Beijing, covering a wide range of subjects such as civil aviation, investment regulations, and food safety protection.[3] In particular, the signing of the Economic Cooperation Framework Agreement (ECFA) in June 2010 was an important milestone in cross-Strait relations. The ECFA set in motion negotiations on a full-fledged cross-Strait free trade agreement, and it held out the possibility that Taiwan could unleash its full economic potential by exploiting expanding business opportunities in mainland China, which emerged as the new "buyer of last resort" after the 2008–2009 global financial crisis.[4] The agreement also helped put Taiwan back on the map of foreign multinational corporations, which suddenly found new possibilities for incorporating the island into their Greater China strategy. Another path-breaking agreement was the 2012 memorandum of understanding on cross-Strait currency settlement, which created the necessary mechanism for the two sides to settle their bilateral trade in renminbi (RMB), jumpstart cooperation in the financial industry across the Strait, and open up the possibility of developing Taiwan into a second offshore RMB center after Hong Kong.[5]

President Ma should also be given credit for restoring trust and friendship with Taiwan's major allies and trade partners, raising Taiwan's profile in the international arena, and designing a feasible strategy to gain entry into regional free trade blocs. Between 2010 and 2011, Taiwan launched free trade agreement negotiations with Singapore and New Zealand. By the end of 2015, 153 countries and territories, including the United Kingdom, Japan, Canada, the European Union, and the United States, had offered Taiwan citizens visa-free travel status. In 2009, Taiwan was invited by the World Health Organization (WHO) to become an observer (under the name Chinese Taipei) at its annual assembly, and for the first time since the Republic of China had been forced out of the UN in 1971, a cabinet-level public health official from Taiwan was given the official podium at a UN agency.[6] In 2013, the International Civil Aviation Organization made an unprecedented gesture by inviting Taiwan's head of civil aviation authority to be a special guest of its biannual assembly.

Furthermore, Ma's administration should be recognized for its resolve to push two monumental bills for government reorganization through the Legislative Yuan in 2010. The first bill, which was initiated in 1987 but had been shelved for twenty-three years, extensively reorganized the Executive Yuan by eliminating a dozen or so ministry-level agencies and consolidating overlapping governing responsibility into a few super-ministries. The second bill paved the way for elevating some populous county-level cities to special municipalities, typically by annexing their neighboring counties. Under the new bill, four more cities—Xinbei (formerly Taipei County), Taichung, Tainan, and Taoyuan—were promoted to the status of special municipality and joined the ranks of Taipei and Kaoshiung.[7] These four new municipalities together account for almost a quarter of Taiwan's population. As special municipalities, they are now entitled to a larger share of the fiscal transfers from the central government, and thus have enjoyed better basic infrastructure and quality of public services.

Ma probably also deserves some credit for steering Taiwan's economy steadily through the worst global economic crisis since the Great Depression.[8] Like all other export-oriented East Asian economies, Taiwan's dependence on trade through global production networks and export-led growth strategies made the island highly vulnerable to the sharp contraction of demand in the North American and European economies. Taiwan's economy slumped into recession in the second half of 2008. Its real gross domestic product (GDP), following a growth rate of 5.7 percent in 2007, registered a meager 0.7 percent growth in 2008 and contracted by 1.9 percent in 2009 primarily due to a record 19 percent drop in total exports. By the first quarter of 2010, not only did Taiwan exit the recession, but it also recovered the entire loss in output during the so-called Great Recession. Taiwan registered an astonishing 13.6 percent (annualized) growth in the first quarter of 2010 and a remarkable 10.8 percent for the year. This made Taiwan's recovery trajectory superior to that of South Korea, which managed to bounce back at only a 6.1 percent growth rate in 2010.[9]

These accomplishments were enough to carry President Ma through to reelection in 2012. But they still fell far short of what his campaign platform had promised, trailing far behind the high expectations of the great majority of Taiwan's populace. And they were far from adequate to reverse many of the worrisome long-term trends that continue to threaten the island's economic future.

This chapter offers a retrospective analysis of Ma Ying-jeou's poor performance in coping with the challenges of democratic governance during his eight-year presidency, and also explains why his administration was not able to restore effective governance. While deficiencies in his political capabilities and leadership style were clearly responsible in part for Ma's disappointing record, there are many deeper, intractable factors—structural, institutional, and ideological—that are now beyond the grip of its political leaders and that pose formidable obstacles to the restoration of effective democratic governance in Taiwan. In a way, the governing capacity of the political system has been so severely damaged that it is simply not up to the task of responding to the daunting international and domestic policy challenges it faces.

Unfavorable Structural Conditions

Three structural forces—deteriorating international competitiveness, an aging population, and dwindling fiscal resources—have grown to cast a dark cloud over Taiwan's future. Together they severely constrain the scope of any democratically elected government to deliver satisfying socioeconomic outcomes. To begin with, Taiwan has encountered major bottlenecks in its economic growth path over the past two decades and has been unable to overcome them. Taiwan's economy, built on an export-oriented manufacturing sector, was once a powerhouse among Asia's emerging economies. But since the start of the new century, growth in personal income has slowed considerably, and the Taiwanese economic miracle has begun to fade. Its per capita income reached US$8,339 (at current prices) in 1990, and by 2000 it rose to $14,906, a benchmark for a middle-income country. Since then, the pace of economic growth has slowed. Despite its declining birthrate, Taiwan managed to bring its per capita income to only $20,995 by 2012, nominally the lowest among the four so-called Asian Tigers (which also include Korea, Singapore, and Hong Kong).[10]

Over the past two decades, the government has done very little to help Taiwan's private sector retool its business model. Most of Taiwan's export sectors continue to position themselves as low-cost manufacturers in global production networks. Furthermore, Taiwan's exports have become excessively concentrated in electronics and information technology products. This also means that the majority of these exports have suffered from commoditization pressures, with their profit margins shrinking over time. South Korea, on the other hand, has transformed itself into an innovative high-tech country with well-established global brands such as Samsung, LG, and Hyundai, and both Singapore and Hong Kong have become leading providers of global services.[11]

Clinging to this business model anchored on low-cost manufacturing had two dire consequences for Taiwan's income distribution. First, it suppressed wage levels, since Taiwan had to compete with the lower-cost, lower-wage countries entering this space in the global production chain. Most middle- and lower-income families have actually experienced a slow decline in their living standards since the late 1990s. Second, and at the same time, the business community has exerted tremendous pressure on the government for lower tax rates and more generous tax codes for stock options or research-and-development write-offs. In the end, the tax codes have become so skewed that they have aggravated (rather than ameliorated) the problem of widening income and wealth disparity that inevitably comes with globalization.[12]

The rapid rise in the costs of labor and land in mainland China over the past two decades has posed a dual challenge to Taiwan. First, it squeezed the profit margins of Taiwanese firms, as a large proportion of Taiwan's manufacturing activities had already been relocated to mainland China. Second, it compelled mainland Chinese exporters to climb rapidly up the ladder of higher-value-added manufacturing and become direct competitors with Taiwanese firms. In a nutshell, Taiwan's strategy of using mainland China as an export platform to sustain its contract manufacturing business model has run its course. It faces the daunting challenge of carving out an alternative path of sustainable growth.

Taiwan faces a huge social challenge brought about by a rapidly aging population and swiftly declining fertility. Baby-boomers born in 1946 turned sixty-five in 2011, which marked the first year of the twenty-year "aging boom" and the beginning of a wave of retirements. By 2016, the number of seniors in Taiwan exceeded 3 million, out of a population of a little over 23 million. Taiwan's low birthrate has made the challenge of an aging population only tougher. In 2012 the number of newborns in Taiwan was one-third less than that of fifteen years earlier, and in 2011 the fertility rate sank to 1.0, one of the lowest in the world. At this pace it is estimated that in 2020 the size of the labor force will begin to shrink, and one-third of Taiwan's universities will eventually be forced to close or merge. Another implication is that the financial burden of Taiwan's universal health insurance will soon become increasingly unsustainable, and retirement benefits for public-sector employees will soon bankrupt the government—unless they are trimmed back, and soon. Furthermore, the Ma Ying-jeou administration was called upon to deal with these thorny issues in the context of global financial turmoil, slower economic growth, and deteriorating fiscal health, and most of the necessary reforms involving sacrifices, hard choices, and tradeoffs were intrinsically unpopular. In a sense, Ma Ying-jeou was the first elected president since Taiwan's democratization to confront the politics of belt-tightening.

Taiwan's economy has suffered from a growing skills mismatch in the labor market, especially among the younger generation. During the 1990s, the government's education policy was driven both from below, by populist pressure to set up four-year colleges or universities in every conceivable local community, and above, from elite idealism to make college education accessible to all. In the end, the island's higher education system has become oversaturated with 160-plus colleges and universities, most of them underfunded and inadequately equipped and staffed, while vocational education has substantially shrunk. There has been a chronic shortage of manual and semiskilled labor while the labor market is flooded with jobseekers with college and postgraduate degrees. This growing mismatch has suppressed the salary of entry-level white-collar jobs for almost two decades and generated a huge army of underemployed and unemployed young graduates. Increasingly grim career prospects, coupled with rising living expenses in the urban areas, have pushed many frustrated youngsters into anti-globalization and anti-free trade movements.

After years of sluggish economic growth and a series of sweeping tax cuts under DPP rule, the government's fiscal health had steadily deteriorated. By the end of 2008, tax revenue was only 13 percent of GDP, and the government had to raise additional income equivalent to 10 percent of GDP through borrowing, collecting fees and fines, and selling off state-owned assets. When the DPP assumed power in 2000, the central government's total outstanding debt (a narrow definition of accumulated national debt) was less than 24 percent of GDP. By the time Chen Shui-bian left office, the ratio had jumped to 35 percent. If one takes into account the government's legal liabilities for the three public-sector pension schemes—civil servants, military personnel, and teachers—the broad definition of national debt approached 72 percent of GDP at the time that Ma was inaugurated in 2008. Thus, President Ma headed a government with very little spare capacity to borrow and spend. Furthermore, the Ma administration also inherited quite a few headaches that had been swept under the rug for too long. For example, the universal health insurance system had run a deficit for many years due to a politically expedient freeze on monthly fees. The state-owned Taiwan Power Company had suffered huge losses over several years due to a freeze on electricity rates, which did not allow it to offset the rising cost of imported oil and natural gas. In a sense, the DPP government handed over many hot potatoes for Ma Ying-jeou to juggle as soon as he came into office.

When the Ma Ying-jeou government took over in 2008, his economic team initially hoped that it could restore Taiwan's fiscal health over time by revitalizing the economy through measures such as restoring business confidence, liberalizing trade, normalizing cross-Strait economic exchanges, and opening the door to mainland Chinese tourists. But the onslaught of the global financial crisis in late 2008 seriously disrupted if not derailed these efforts to rejuvenate the economy. Instead, the Ma government was forced to adopt a series of short-term emergency measures and a large stimulus package to stabilize the economy and safeguard the banking sector. Most of these measures further damaged Taiwan's fiscal health, at least in the short run. The business community was successful in slipping two controversial tax cuts into the overall economic stabilization package: cutting the corporate income tax rate from 25 percent to 17 percent, which made Taiwan's rate the lowest in East Asia, and drastically reducing the top bracket of inheritance and gift tax from 40 percent to 10 percent.

Two other major decisions announced during Ma's first term also drained the government's fiscal resources over the long run. The first was the decision to end conscription and turn the military into an all-volunteer force by 2016. The second was the extension of free and compulsory basic education from nine to twelve years, which substantially pushed up the cost to public coffers of secondary education. These two major decisions, which could be justified on other grounds, simply made the politics of belt-tightening even harsher. Last but not least, the Ma administration also put off many painful decisions until his second term, such as price hikes for electricity, an increase in health insurance fees, and cutbacks in retirement benefits for public-sector employees and military personnel. As a consequence, even before his second inauguration, Ma Ying-jeou appeared to be condemned to become a very unpopular second-term president because his administration would have to bring many pieces of bad news to the public, in particular to his key constituencies.

Institutional Constraints

Throughout his two terms, Ma Ying-jeou was handicapped by three sets of institutional arrangements. The first set gave the DPP considerable bargaining power (much larger than its nominal share of the Legislative Yuan seats might suggest) to wield over the legislative agenda, and it employed a wide array of tactics to obstruct the KMT government's major initiatives during the legislative process.[13] In the end, the Blue camp's nominal three-quarters majority in the Legislative Yuan turned out to be a mirage. The second set empowered the speaker of the Legislative Yuan, the KMT Legislative Yuan caucus, and maverick KMT legislators to delay or tinker with all major legislative bills initiated by the executive branch. The pendulum of political power swung so decisively toward the legislature that it rendered so-called unified government (under Ma Ying-jeou's concurrent occupation of both the presidency and the KMT chairmanship) largely an illusion. The third set discouraged bureaucrats from being proactive, taking the initiative, and assuming responsibility for meeting policy goals, while also entangling civil servants in cumbersome accounting rules and personnel regulations as well as multiple layers of horizontal accountability.

Being in the minority in the Legislative Yuan throughout Ma's tenure, the DPP developed over the years a rather effective strategy to maximize its influence over the legislative agenda. First, they successfully exploited their position in a peculiar institution known as the party negotiation mechanism (PNM),[14] which has been a part of the legislature's formal procedures since 1999. Any political party or coalition with at least three seats can form a party caucus,[15] and each party caucus can send two representatives to the closed-door negotiation meeting convened by the speaker of the Legislative Yuan.[16] Any party caucus can make a request to send any pending bill or amendment to this negotiation and take it out of the committee stage. Any party caucus attending the negotiation can then request to delay the bill for at least one month. In most cases, the speaker will seek consensus among representatives of party caucuses rather than declaring a breakdown of negotiations. All party caucuses are obligated to make sure that the legislative proposals and amendments coming out of negotiation meetings have a smooth second and third reading on the floor. Only the bills and amendments over which a breakdown in negotiations is declared are then transferred back to the full assembly for a showdown along party lines. The speaker of the Legislative Yuan during the Ma era, KMT member Wang Jin-pyng, would typically cajole his own caucus to compromise with the DPP and other minor parties in order to avoid a showdown on the floor. This enabled the DPP to have a substantial voice in crafting most of the legislative bills and introducing amendments to the budgets that were passed by the Legislative Yuan, even though the opposition initially controlled less than a quarter of the seats.

Many political observers found it very curious that the KMT caucus was willing to restrain itself from taking full advantage of its majority, unlike ruling parties in most parliamentary systems. This is largely because the DPP regularly threatened to use disruptive tactics to block bills that it vehemently opposed.[17] Yet Speaker Wang consistently refused to take disciplinary measures against the opposition for violating the rules of order to paralyze the legislative process. This passivity gave greater credibility to the DPP's threats. Unless the great majority of KMT legislators were willing to pick a fight—often a literal fistfight on the floor of the legislature— the ruling party could not unilaterally determine the contents of any controversial bill. In most cases, KMT legislators were reluctant to go down this unpleasant and ugly route. On a few occasions when both the government and the KMT caucus were desperate to get a particular bill passed, Speaker Wang would ask the KMT caucus to form a human shield to guard the podium to prevent its occupation by the opposition, and he would strike down the gavel in the midst of a tumultuous shouting match.

It is also puzzling why a speaker elected by the KMT majority would simply forgo his disciplinary authority, thus shifting the power balance in the Legislative Yuan decisively in favor of the opposition while preventing his own party from passing legislation that it judged to be in the best interest of the majority of Taiwan's electorate. Another puzzle is why most KMT legislators chose to reelect this speaker repeatedly, and why Ma Ying-jeou as the chairman of the party put up with him for so long. This puzzle calls our attention to the pivotal role that Wang Jin-pyng—who first became the speaker in 1999—played during the post–Lee Teng-hui era, and his complicated relationship with Ma Ying-jeou.

Wang Jin-pyng was Ma Ying-jeou's longtime political rival within the KMT. He ran against Ma during the open contest for party chairman in 2005 and suffered a humiliating defeat. However, he later emerged as the second most influential political figure in Taiwanese politics, after the president, by significantly shifting decisionmaking power to the legislative arena and maximizing the power of the speaker. Most of the peculiar legislative rules and conventions that were introduced after 1999 were tailor-made by him and his followers. For instance, he was the key driver behind the adoption of the PNM, which gives the speaker enormous power in setting the legislative agenda and schedule as well as in crafting the final version of each piece of legislation. Every incumbent premier and virtually all members of the cabinet felt compelled to hurry to his office for help whenever they had an important bill held up in the Legislative Yuan. He invented the unusual convention of allowing legislators to attach a large number of strings and riders to the budget bills. Another new convention that was designed to empower individual members was the rampant and indiscriminate use of the motion to impound (instead of cut) a substantial part of the budget of a given ministry by a standing committee (usually initiated by only two or three legislators on the committee). Under Legislative Yuan–imposed impoundment, the targeted ministry could only use a part of its approved budget to sustain its essential functions until the responsible committee lifted the impoundment, which often happened only after the ministry had met some private or improper demands of individual legislators. These conventions gave every member of the Legislative Yuan, KMT and non-KMT alike, a potent weapon to blackmail executive branch ministries. Speaker Wang also helped encourage the development of a highly questionable convention that empowered the standing committees to pass binding resolutions (without going through the full chamber) that tied the hands of the ministries under their respective purview. As a consequence, it often took only three or four strong-minded legislators to dictate policy demands to a ministry. Over the years, it became a common practice for an individual member to play the role of power-broker by summoning senior officials to his or her office. Ma Ying-jeou and his premiers were politically too timid and feeble either to draw a line and refuse to abide by these conventions or to challenge them at the Constitutional Court.

At the same time, Speaker Wang steadily tended to his own political support among the Legislative Yuan membership to ward off any potential challengers to his position. The DPP was grateful to him for his leniency toward its disruptive tactics and for his skills in brokering political compromises. He was responsive to any legislator who knocked on his door and asked for a favor, either legal or otherwise, and by so doing he collected numerous IOUs from both sides of the aisle. His authority became increasingly entrenched as he wielded the enormous discretionary power and indispensable mediating role of the speaker to exchange favors with business elites, influential mass media commentators, and weighty political figures and prominent political families across party lines. Speaker Wang demonstrated a remarkable capability to exercise delicate balancing acts between stakeholders with conflicting interests. From the beginning, he never made life easy for the Ma Ying-jeou administration, yet he also never pushed his discretionary powers too far.

While President Ma and his cabinet were continually frustrated by Speaker Wang's ambiguous and unhelpful role, they did not muster the nerve to confront him directly in a political showdown until well into his second term. In September 2013, Ma finally attempted to sideline Wang. Ma's prosecutor-general, Huang Shih-ming, announced he had evidence implicating Speaker Wang in an "influence peddling" scheme to exert pressure on senior prosecutors and the Ministry of Justice to acquit Ker Chien-ming, the leader of the DPP caucus, over a criminal charge of embezzlement. The Special Investigative Division in the Prosecutor-General's Office had sought court approval to bug the phone conversation of Ker during an investigation of a bribery case, and this wiretapping operation accidentally uncovered an incriminating conversation between Ker and Speaker Wang about pressuring the minister of justice. The accusations of influence-peddling prompted Ma to initiate the process of kicking him out of the KMT, which would have automatically stripped him of his Legislative Yuan seat as well since he was elected on the KMT's party list. But Wang fought back with a lawsuit, and in a surprising turn of events, he secured a temporary injunction from a district court to suspend the KMT's disciplinary decision. Although it was very unlikely that the injunction would have been upheld by the Council of Grand Justices, Ma then backed down, as he was under tremendous pressure from Speaker Wang's numerous complicit allies within the party and throughout the mass media. While Ma as party chairman continued the lawsuit via a time-consuming civil procedure, he did not file a parallel suit through the Court of Administrative Law, which might have rendered a faster and more conclusive verdict, and Wang remained as the speaker.[18]

From that point on, Ma excluded Wang from all KMT formal meetings and decisionmaking mechanisms, but the standoff lingered on, and Wang ultimately survived with his position and influence in the Legislative Yuan fully intact, and even enhanced. As a consequence, steering the legislative agenda remained a daunting challenge for the Ma administration. At the end of the day, it was impossible for the government to predict what kind of final decision would come out of the legislature's bizarre and opaque lawmaking process, as there were too many players with different hidden agendas, and decisionmaking power was much too dispersed.[19]

Last but not least, the steering wheel of the state bureaucracy also became too slippery to handle. By the time Ma Ying-jeou took office, his administration inherited an economic bureaucracy that had lost much of its prestige, forward-looking vision, and interventionist propensity. Long gone were the days when the government was equipped with a full array of policy instruments and able to chart a farsighted course of industrial upgrading. Instead, after experiencing two rotations of power and endless political bickering between the pan-Blue and pan-Green camps, most senior and middle-ranking civil servants had learned to stay passive and cautious. The political calculations of their appointed superiors were beyond their grasp. They protected themselves with rigid interpretations of relevant statutes and regulations, and whenever in doubt they passed the buck to other agencies or their superiors by asking for written clarifications or instructions. At the same time, their morale became extremely low as they were overburdened by layer upon layer of internal control mechanisms.

During the tumultuous years of polarized conflict between the KMT and the DPP, each camp tried to upstage the other, imposing ever more stringent rules and regulations to show off their resolve to fight corruption and the abuse of power. Each camp initiated one after another set of new standard operating procedures or new restrictions after each incident of embezzlement, falsified documents, or bribe-taking. Numerous internal and external oversight agents were set up to watch over the shoulders of the civil servants—each ministry's own internal accounting department, the civil service ethics department, the Justice Ministry's Agency Against Corruption, the Bureau of Investigation (also under the Justice Ministry), the Inspectors of the National Audit Office, members of the Control Yuan, and individual members of the Legislative Yuan. These overlapping agents of external supervision, along with tedious regulations for internal control, drove most civil servants to develop a new survival instinct: to follow the motto that one cannot be overcautious. Consequently, to push through any major policy objective, most ministers or vice ministers had to pull off the challenge themselves. Each one of them had to act like a solo juggler, keeping many balls in the air at the same time with little proactive support or help from senior civil servants.

The Poisoned Social and Political Soil

The most difficult challenge for the Ma administration was how to navigate through a highly turbulent, volatile, and polarized social and political climate. Beginning with the first party rotation of power in 2000, Taiwan gradually acquired all the elements of an ungovernable society. First, there was a total breakdown of trust and mutual respect between the two contending political blocs, the so-called pan-Blue and pan-Green camps. Their mutual hostility burned all bridges of communication and destroyed even a facade of civility and courtesy in politics. By the time of the Ma administration, the rules of political engagement had led to endless political warfare, and democratic norms and legal procedures were easily twisted or ignored for the sake of partisan gain.

Second, the steady ascendance of the legislative power over the executive branch fed individual lawmakers' growing appetite for advancing their own independent agendas and extorting various government agencies for political gains. These two mutually reinforcing trends created a fertile soil for the mushrooming of fat-cat donors, zealous lobbyists, and single-issue interest groups. Business tycoons and trade associations became keen to use political donations to "adopt" their own legislators in order to safeguard their interests, and whenever possible they lobbied to engineer particularistic tax loopholes or favorable regulatory clauses. Rarely could a government-sponsored bill remain intact when going through this sausage-making machine. Thus the political system and decisionmaking process became increasingly fragmented and gridlocked with veto players. At the same time, leaders of social movements and nongovernmental organizations (NGOs) became increasingly frustrated, as they were largely locked out of this horse-trading process behind closed doors. These developments in turn drove socially and economically disadvantaged groups to take their grievances and demands to the streets, their mobilizing capability enhanced by the rise of social media.

Third, most print and electronic media became either blatantly partisan or excessively sensationalist. Particularly after the Hong Kong–based *Apple Daily* entered the local media market in 2003 and built a large readership, most other media outlets began to resort to tabloid journalism or to become more-or-less "Apple-like" in an effort to compete for market share. Under the suffocating pressure of a shrinking advertising market and saturated competition among eight twenty-four-hour cable news channels (on an island of 23 million people), television channels tried to outcompete one another via vulgar, sensational, and irresponsible "news" reporting and commentary based on half-truths, speculation, and rumors in order to grab viewers' eyeballs for a few minutes. The most cost-effective programs, due to their low costs, were political talk shows. Each of these retained a few pundits, the so-called *mingzui,* or "famous mouths," who pretended to be jacks-of-all-trades, able to comment on any subject matter at any time. These "famous mouths" were prone to overdramatizing the political news, blowing things out of proportion, and making up imaginary conspiracy theories on a whim.

Meanwhile, the explosion of social media turned out to be a double-edged sword. On the one hand, it expanded and enriched the public space, undermining the power of traditional mass media driven largely by commercial interests and media tycoons' personal political agendas. On the other hand, it also opened the floodgates to all kinds of anti-democratic, chauvinist, and racist views and hate messages from a vast array of irresponsible bloggers and online commenters operating from behind the veil of anonymity. With these "famous mouths" and irresponsible "netizens" dominating the media space, there was little room for rational public discourse and sober evaluation of expert opinions. These media dynamics also helped to drive a deeper wedge between Taiwan's two main political camps, as partisans on both sides acted increasingly like the audience at a gladiator fight, baying for blood in scenes worthy of the Roman Empire.

Last but by no means least, at the beginning of Ma's second term there emerged a corps of young rebels who steadily amassed political connections and a tremendous capacity to mobilize demonstrators, which they used to stage large-scale anti-government protests or organize social movements. Their strategy of confrontation rapidly eroded the Ma administration's authority and eventually undermined its legitimacy to govern. His government became increasingly hapless and disoriented, with cabinet ministers and political aides acting like exhausted firefighters being called up to put out fires around the clock.

These young rebels were mostly graduate students or junior-college professors with close ties to DPP politicians, and especially to Tsai Ing-wen,[20] the DPP presidential candidate in 2012 and the winner of the 2016 presidential race. Most of them came of age under the Taiwan nation-building cultural project of the Lee Teng-hui and Chen Shui-bian eras and became ardent Taiwanese nationalists. Most of them were intellectually equipped with a full array of social theories ranging from social justice, anarchism, anti-globalizationism, and environmentalism to variants of leftist ideology. They actively recruited students and out-of-school youngsters who did not hold steady jobs but showed some interest in becoming political activists, and cultivated them into social movement cadres. They instilled in their young recruits a strong sense of moral righteousness as they confronted public authorities using the tactics of civil disobedience and social resistance. They equipped their followers with the know-how to turn social media into a potent weapon of mobilization, and the necessary skills to stage-manage the political agenda online and in the conventional news media. They carefully picked the issues to mobilize around, forged alliances with like-minded groups, and seized critical moments to prop up sympathetic voices, fan popular outrage, galvanize their followers and willing volunteers, and stage one wave of social protest after another until their or their allies' demands were met. They almost always targeted KMT incumbents, central or local, and stayed away from local governments led by the DPP. Over time, they accumulated a vast reservoir of social support, and they were surrounded by an extensive web of financial backers, allies in the mass media and academia, DPP lawmakers, human rights attorneys, rock stars, Falung Gong followers, mainland Chinese dissidents in exile, and even activists of Hong Kong's Occupy Central Movement.

These young rebels learned quickly that Ma's personal weaknesses and his depressingly low approval ratings would simply make him prone to cave in and accede to the demands of a large crowd or determined activists marching in the streets. They also seldom had to worry about legal consequences, because in most cases law-enforcement agencies were too timid to arrest them or press criminal charges. So they pressed on with their agenda with ever more aggressive forms of social protest. At the same time, whenever President Ma caved in to their demands, he further alienated his own key constituencies and emboldened the social movement leaders and their DPP allies.

For instance, in July and August of 2012, the corps of young rebels seized on popular outrage over a dubious case of a young conscript's sudden death a few days before his decommission, allegedly due to disciplinary abuse by a few low-ranking officers. They successfully launched the so-called White-Shirt Army movement, which culminated in two large-scale demonstrations. The movement organizers steadily bid up their demands of the government, which eventually included the total abolition of the power of court-martial and the military justice system, and the transfer of all judicial power from military prosecutors and judges to the civilian judicial system. To quell popular outrage, Ma sacked the minister of national defense and eventually accepted all the White-Shirt Army's demands for reform. In so doing, he dealt a humiliating and demoralizing blow to the armed services, and especially the professional officer corps. Worst of all, his weakness simply invited more disgruntled single-issue groups, ranging from anti–nuclear power activists to laid-off workers seeking unpaid compensation, to stage ever more aggressive and violent street demonstrations. Step by step, Ma became entrapped in a vicious cycle of yielding more and more concessions to the unruly and unpredictable protesters in the street, while also weakening his support from the KMT's key constituencies and alienating more and more of Taiwan's silent majority.

A Perfect Political Storm

In this turbulent and volatile sociopolitical environment, and under the prevailing institutional constraints, the politics of polarization, the divisions over free trade, and the backlash against closer economic ties across the Strait eventually came together to create a perfect political storm with devastating and near-tragic consequences for Ma's presidency and for Taiwan. Ma's agenda for trade negotiations with the People's Republic of China (PRC) and neighboring countries encountered many domestic political roadblocks and moved at a snail's pace. His government was not able to foster a cohesive pro–free trade coalition, nor could it placate the potential losers with material side-payments or moral suasion. Instead, the government was vulnerable to the various and often conflicting demands from all sorts of sector-based interest groups and their surrogates in the Legislative Yuan. In the end, the government could only settle for low-quality free trade agreements that covered only a limited range of products and sectors. This approach of seeking the lowest common denominator allowed Taiwan only to pick the lowest-hanging fruit, such as the initial free trade negotiations with Beijing, which was willing to make unilateral concessions based on political calculations, and Singapore and New Zealand, which did not exert much competitive pressure on most Taiwanese producers. But this approach would certainly not get Taiwan through the much tougher negotiations for entry into the Trans-Pacific Partnership (TPP), the Regional Comprehensive Economic Partnership (RCEP), or free trade agreements with much more demanding trading partners such as India, Indonesia, or Malaysia. As the movement to create super trading blocs gathered momentum on both shores of the Pacific during US president Barack Obama's second term, Taiwan's economic future was increasingly threatened by the risk of being excluded from these agreements and marginalized from new regional trading regimes.

Facing a looming fiscal crisis, alarming demographic trends, and growing frustration among the younger generation, the Ma administration was also unable to foster a social consensus over tax reform and burden-sharing. Instead, the politics of belt-tightening played out like a race to the bottom. The first move to raise the retirement age for hired labor triggered a strong backlash and provoked a popular demand to strip military personnel of many long-running fringe benefits. Then the axe fell on the retirement benefits of public-sector employees. In no time, the reaction to proposed cutbacks grew like a whirlpool, drawing in every major category of middle- and lower-income group, who were seemingly relatively better-off than others. In stark contrast, the groups who had obtained the lion's share of recent economic gains, including big business, white-collar professionals, executives and engineers in the high-tech industry, real estate developers, and stock speculators, were left paying only limited taxes on their incomes and virtually no taxes at all on their capital gains. This irony was familiar to most democratically elected governments that tried to impose austerity measures under prevailing market forces in an era of hyper-globalization.[21] The consequence everywhere was the same: the incumbent government paid a heavy political price for pushing through fiscal belt-tightening reforms.

The most menacing challenge remained the deep-seated polarization over national identity. No matter how hard the Ma administration tried to assuage the fears and anxiety within the pan-Green camp, with multifaceted built-in safeguard mechanisms that came with each step of opening up to mainland Chinese tourists and investors, DPP supporters became increasingly distressed about the stepwise removal of old barriers to exchanges with the PRC, while maintaining suspicions that Ma had a hidden agenda and questioning his loyalty to Taiwan. No matter how sensible and incremental his administration's roadmap for integrating Taiwan into the regional economy and joining trade blocs seemed to be, the pro-independence constituencies stubbornly refused to accept the reality that Taiwan simply did not have a realistic strategy for increasing integration with the regional and global economy that would bypass China.

At the start of his second term, Ma and his advisers did not have any clue that the intensity of anxiety and frustration among these constituencies over the steady acceleration of cross-Strait integration was fast approaching a boiling point, and that the DPP hardliners were waiting on the sidelines for the opportunity to launch an all-out attack on Ma's cross-Strait policy. Despite the efforts by a few DPP presidential aspirants to steer the party's cross-Strait platform closer to the center of the electorate, their followers remained intensely suspicious of the frequent high-level contacts and dialogue between the PRC's top leaders and senior KMT politicians. They were especially alarmed by the takeover of some cable television stations and newspapers by tycoons with huge commercial interests in mainland China, as well as deeply worried about the political consequences of Taiwan's creeping economic dependency on the mainland and the expanding web of cross-Strait social ties. In the meantime, the intensification of strategic competition between Beijing and Washington under Obama's "Pivot to Asia" policy, along with the rapid deterioration of Sino-Japanese relations under Prime Minister Shinzo Abe, also revived the hope of some supporters of Taiwan's independence that the international environment might have turned one more time in a way conducive to a hawkish approach toward China.

Ma and his supporters operated on a very different wavelength. Ma held a strong belief that his administration's progress in the area of cross-Strait relations would become the hallmark of his presidency and his lasting political legacy. After he was reelected in 2012, he threw his remaining political capital behind three policy aims: concluding the free trade agreements with mainland China, amending the existing statutes regulating cross-Strait exchanges to reflect the new realities, and establishing quasi-official representative offices on each side of the Taiwan Strait. At that time, most pundits had little doubt about the political feasibility of this modest policy agenda. As a matter of fact, he was criticized by pan-Blue loyalists for being too conservative and cautious, because his agenda evidently left out the option of opening up official dialogue over political issues or kicking off negotiations over a peace accord.

At the same time, representatives of the business community repeatedly voiced their worry that Taiwan's quest for membership in regional free trade pacts had only inched forward at a snail's pace. In contrast, South Korea, Taiwan's major economic rival, had not only successfully concluded free trade agreements with the United States and the European Union but also jump-started its free trade negotiations with the PRC in 2012. They warned that if Taiwan were locked out of the RCEP, whose potential members were the collective destination for 58 percent of Taiwan's total exports, the country's competitive position in international trade would be severely undermined, and many industries might be forced to move production out of Taiwan. The business community pinned much hope on the signing of the two post-ECFA trade pacts with mainland China, the Cross-Strait Services Trade Agreement (CSSTA) and the Cross-Strait Trade in Goods Agreement (CSTGA). They expected that these two trade pacts would not only help Taiwanese manufacturers defend their market position in the Chinese mainland and enable Taiwan's service providers (especially banking, insurance, brokerage, creativity, logistics, and e-commerce) to expand into mainland markets, but also serve as a steppingstone for Taiwan's entry into the RCEP and possibly the TPP.

The tension between these two political inclinations—one group that could not wait any longer for trade liberalization, another that could not put up with any more opening toward mainland China—finally snapped over the signing of the CSSTA in 2013. This pact, which on the surface promised few economic consequences as it was very limited in scope,[22] ignited a political storm far larger than anything the Ma administration could have imagined. Like all controversies related to cross-Strait relations, facts did not matter and symbolism was everything. DPP politicians and pro-independence political activists, commentators, and bloggers simply blew out of proportion the risk of political infiltration or adverse social impacts that might come with the CSSTA. Nevertheless, their sensationalist messages swamped Ma's attempts to set the record straight. With his approval rate approaching single digits, a majority of the public lost interest entirely in listening to what Ma and his government had to say in defense of the agreement, and Ma-bashing simply became the "in" thing to do among television commentators, artists and writers, bloggers, and student activists.

Two factors compelled DPP leaders to throw all their ammunition behind the battle to stop the CSSTA. First, the DPP heavyweights were competing for the support of the party's core supporters in the forthcoming race for party chair, due to be held in June 2014, and the winner of that contest would have the inside track to the party's presidential nomination for 2016. Second, DPP elites were alarmed by Ma's recent political overtures toward Beijing's new paramount leader, Xi Jinping. In February 2014, Ma sent the head of the Mainland Affairs Council to Nanjing to meet with his counterpart in their official government capacities. This was the first time a formal meeting between official representatives of the two governments since the end of the civil war in 1949 formalized the political division across the Taiwan Strait. Many media pundits speculated that the logical next step would be a summit meeting between Ma and Xi, especially if the CSSTA were ratified in a timely manner.

The prospect of a Ma-Xi meeting was a nightmare for DPP leaders. They were loath to see this kind of historic summit simply out of grave apprehension that it could take cross-Strait relations to a higher level, one that would be beyond their ability to influence. A summit meeting could also help rejuvenate Ma's presidency. They decided to undo their efforts to moderate the DPP's public image on cross-Strait issues, and they launched an all-out war against the CSSTA in the hope that derailing this trade pact would deal a fatal blow to Ma's government and prevent him from getting anything else done during his remaining two years in office.

With the helping hand of Speaker Wang, the DPP caucus had already succeeded in keeping the trade agreement tied up in the Legislative Yuan for six months, since August 2013. In early March of 2014, the bill finally proceeded to the committee review stage. This time the DPP pulled out all their disruptive tactics, paralyzing the committee session for several days. The KMT caucus, which was determined to push the agreement through the legislature during the current session, in turn ambushed the DPP by introducing a motion to skip the committee stage entirely and send the bill directly to a plenary session at lightning speed. This time the DPP caucus was caught by surprise, because Speaker Wang was also kept in the dark, since his party membership was still suspended by the KMT and he no longer had a seat in the party's top decisionmaking circle.

The KMT's legislative ambush immediately sparked outrage among the pan-Green constituencies, and it prompted the corps of young rebels to fight back with one of the most dramatic and disruptive acts of civil disobedience in the history of Taiwan's democracy. On the evening of March 18, they organized hundreds of their supporters and students to break into the Legislative Yuan compound, occupying the main chamber in the name of "defending Taiwan's democracy." They outnumbered the police force guarding the compound and successfully resisted the initial attempts to evict them. Immediately afterward, DPP legislators arrived on the scene to block the entrances and stop riot police from approaching the students. Nearly simultaneously, three DPP legislators started seventy-hour hunger strikes on the grounds that the KMT had broken its promise to subject the trade bill to a clause-by-clause review.[23] Speaker Wang refused to endorse a plan put forward by the police, who had been reinforced overnight, to forcibly evict the student demonstrators. Ma and his cabinet, fearful of the ugly headlines that would be generated if they used force against students, were hesitant to bear sole responsibility for ordering the police to remove them. The next morning, the young rebels declared themselves to be the leaders of the Sunflower Movement, and they mobilized thousands of students to surround the Legislative Yuan compound, leading to a standoff that ultimately lasted over three weeks.[24]

The leaders of the movement immediately launched a blizzard of media campaigns, including creating movement websites on Facebook and taking out a full-page paid advertisement in the *New York Times,* and they effectively dominated public opinion for quite a while. They mobilized many other student groups, even among Taiwanese students studying abroad, to organize sit-ins on various campuses. Initially, the young rebels claimed that they would occupy the Legislative Yuan for only 120 hours, but they extended the protest on the grounds that President Ma had failed to meet their demands, which included asking him to come to the chamber himself to apologize for the way in which his party pushed the trade pact, and sending the CSSTA back to the committee for a clause-by-clause review.

As they enjoyed an upwelling of support from commentators, professors, artists, writers, and rock singers, the young rebels kept increasing their demands: from sending the CSSTA back to the committee stage, to enacting a special law to institutionalize legislative oversight of cross-Strait negotiations, and on to convening a People's Constitutional Convention to reform the constitution. After a splinter group of demonstrators broke into and ransacked the premier's office in the Executive Yuan building on March 23, before quickly being removed by riot police, public opinion shifted somewhat as some in the general public were appalled by the level of lawlessness exhibited by the students. After disappearing from public view for many days, Speaker Wang finally showed up at the Legislative Yuan on April 6, the eighteenth day of the occupation, and offered his personal guarantee, as well as a political pretext sufficient for the young rebels to declare victory, and secured a pledge from the occupiers that they would end the sit-in and withdraw on April 10. In return, Speaker Wang promised that the CSSTA would return to committee for review, and that it would not be considered for a vote until amendments were made to increase legislative oversight of cross-Strait negotiations. Under these terms, the CSSTA effectively had no prospect of approval before the end of Ma's second term.

However, President Ma's political nightmare did not end there. Three weeks later, his government was confronted with another crisis. This time a former DPP chairman, Lin Yi-hsiung, began a hunger strike to press his demand that Taiwan's fourth nuclear power plant, under construction for almost twenty years and nearly ready to open, instead be scrapped. Since Lin was a saintlike figure in the eyes of diehard DPP supporters, he almost single-handedly twisted the arms of the entire DPP leadership stratum to support his cause, as no DPP politician dared to test his resolve to fast until he died. To exert pressure on President Ma, followers of Lin staged another large-scale demonstration demanding that the administration hold a referendum to decide the fate of the fourth nuclear power plant by the end of 2014. This time, Ma felt compelled to consult all the KMT presidential aspirants for 2016, and they reached a unanimous decision to mothball the already-completed first reactor at the plant and suspend the ongoing construction of a second reactor. They also agreed to put the ultimate decision about whether to open the plant to a referendum at an unspecified date in the future. This swift decision defused the time bomb of Lin's hunger strike, but at the same time it wiped out virtually overnight more than US$10 billion from the balance sheet of the state-owned Taiwan Power Company, which technically would have become insolvent had the government officially scrapped the fourth nuclear power plant. It also created a new long-term energy challenge for Taiwan's economy, as the 10 percent of the total power supply that the plant was eventually expected to contribute could not easily be replaced by renewable (and less reliable) energy sources, such as wind and solar.

Sailing in a Raging Sea Without a Captain

The way the Sunflower Movement began and ended carried enormous implications for the remainder of Ma's presidency, as well as for the future of Taiwan's democracy. First, the political furor of pro-independence constituencies manifested in this movement was so powerful that it effectively dashed any remaining hope President Ma had of moving forward with his agenda of cross-Strait rapprochement. Taiwan's government drifted like a ship sailing in a raging sea without a captain for the rest of Ma's presidency. As a weak, isolated, and politically wounded president, Ma could do no more than follow the whim of popular opinion, which was especially capricious and unpredictable in a society prone to overreacting to the moment.

The speed with which this political turmoil reached a crisis also provided a startling demonstration of just how volatile Taiwanese politics can become. In less than six weeks, the government's concessions to demonstrators dealt two severe blows to Taiwan's economic competitiveness. By derailing the CSSTA and shuttering a power plant that was expected to provide up to 10 percent of the island's total electricity supply, protesters left Taiwan facing a grimmer economic future.[25] During that turbulent six weeks, many of the business decisionmakers who collectively held Taiwan's economic future in their hands quietly turned their backs on the island.[26]

The Sunflower Movement also revealed how easily political polarization over cross-Strait relations could trigger a breakdown of democratic norms and procedures. By occupying the most symbolically important building in a representative democracy, the young rebels set a dangerous precedent, transgressing a democratic red line with impunity. But instead of condemnation, they earned instant fame, with well-wishers cheering them on. The movement escalated the lawlessness of Taiwan's street protests to a higher and more dangerous level, with ominous implications for democracy and the rule of law. The political turmoil revealed new and worrying degrees of political intolerance: angry demonstrators chased after journalists whose reporting cast the movement in a less-than-favorable light, annoyed students harassed passers-by who uttered any kind of criticism, fuming bloggers used abusive language to attack highly respected business leaders who had urged the students to go home and called for speedy ratification of the CSSTA, furious movement cadres chanted explicitly racist slogans that demonized President Ma and the mainlander minority,[27] and incensed mobs smashed the windows of KMT lawmakers' cars. Many observers wondered what kind of citizens this movement had created, and it was difficult to tell if Taiwan's young democracy would be able to weather a disputed and inconclusive presidential election like that in 2004, if something similar were to happen again.

Conclusion

When Tsai Ing-wen was inaugurated as president in May 2016, she inherited a deeply divided society in which a democratically elected government could no longer foster a social consensus behind any kind of national political agenda. The old social consensus, anchored on the goal of economic development and a shared vision of how to "catch up," was long gone. The political system was paralyzed by a total breakdown of mutual trust among all key stakeholders due to the nasty political struggle between the pan-Blue and pan-Green camps, the unequal distribution of benefits and risks of economic liberalization and cross-Strait economic integration, and more fundamentally the lack of a common vision for Taiwan's long-term future. She inherited a state economic bureaucracy that had been humiliated and demoralized by its failure to steer Taiwan's manufacturing sector away from an addictive dependence on a supply of cheap water and electricity, subsidized industrial land, and low wages and taxes. She also found herself squeezed between conflicting demands, with little middle ground, in many different policy domains.

On the one hand, in the economic domain she was under pressure to address complaints from business leaders about imminent power shortages, the severe undersupply of skilled labor, the acceleration of a skilled worker "brain drain," lengthy and unpredictable environmental assessment procedures, and the expression of antibusiness sentiments.[28] On the other hand, she felt obliged to fulfill campaign promises to alleviate the grievances of socioeconomically disadvantaged groups, including wage stagnation, runaway housing prices, long working hours, a widening income gap, and an inadequate social safety net. To effectively address any of these socioeconomic challenges would almost certainly dampen business confidence, which was rather fragile already—a fact she learned the hard way as her government stumbled into a political tug-of-war between labor-movement leaders and business owners over the implementation of a five-day workweek.[29]

On cross-Strait relations, she was caught between Xi Jinping's tough stance demanding that the DPP government unambiguously accept the one-China principle, and the pressure to bolster Taiwan's independent statehood exerted by the DPP's younger supporters and by its pro-independence allies in the New Power Party (NPP), which was founded by participants in the Sunflower Movement. The inevitable outcome was a protracted political standoff, something Taiwan could hardly afford, economically and diplomatically.

Beijing was upset by Tsai's inauguration speech, which did not embrace the so-called 1992 Consensus, and the PRC government not only abruptly cut off all channels of official and semiofficial communication with the Tsai administration but also steadily tightened its economic and diplomatic screws on the island while sounding increasingly stark warnings that it would continue to seek unification, including through coercion if necessary. Unfortunately, Tsai found no way out of this dilemma: if she bowed to Beijing's political preconditions for maintaining semiofficial communications, the DPP government would have to be prepared to endure a withering backlash from Taiwanese nationalists and possibly to lose their electoral strongholds to the young rebels and their followers on the polar opposite end of the independence-unification spectrum from Beijing.

Sitting on top of a divided and fractured society, Tsai Ing-wen has quickly discovered how tough it is to govern Taiwan, just as the island is wrestling with many serious short-term and long-term challenges: alarming demographic trends, a looming fiscal crisis, a coming clash over intergenerational justice, and the rising threat of economic marginalization in the region and beyond. Less than two years into her first term, President Tsai's approval rate had sunk below 30 percent, with more than 60 percent of the electorate disapproving of her performance.[30] The many political difficulties that have beset Tsai in her first term, despite her having come into office on the heels of a landslide election victory in 2016 and with a DPP majority in the Legislative Yuan, are an indication that the decline in governmental effectiveness during Ma Ying-jeou's eight years in office were not limited to his presidency.

Notes

1. For a detailed analysis of the outcomes of the 2008 election, see Rigger, "Taiwan's Presidential and Legislative Elections."

2. Wu, "Appointing the Prime Minister Under Incongruence."

3. Chu, "The Political Implications of Taiwan-Mainland Economic Integration."

4. Wei and Chen, "ECFA."

5. Faith Hung, "Taiwan-China Economic Ties to Deepen with Yuan Pact," *Reuters*, September 7, 2013, http://in.reuters.com/article/2012/09/07/taiwan-china-idINL4E8K 52AE20120907.

6. Wang, Lee, and Yu, "Taiwan's Expansion of International Space."

7. Taoyuan's status was elevated in December 2014, four years later than the other three.

8. Chu, "Coping with the Global Financial Crises."

9. Chu, "Unraveling the Enigma of East Asian Economic Resiliency."

10. It is worth noting, however, that according to the International Monetary Fund, Taiwan's gross domestic product per capita based on purchasing power parity reached US$39,767 in 2013, which was higher than that of South Korea at US$33,189.

11. Chen, "Taiwan's Middle-Income Trap."

12. See Milanovic, *Global Inequality.*

13. For a telling insider's account for how the DPP caucus could wield such disproportional influence over the legislative agenda, see the memoir by Ker Chien-ming, the DPP caucus whip, titled *Big Picture, Major Responsibility.*

14. Also sometimes translated as the Cross-Party Negotiation Committee or the Party Caucus Negotiation Mechanism.

15. Before 2008 the threshold was six members; it was reduced to three after the size of the legislature was cut in half in 2008.

16. By law, the negotiations are required to be tape-recorded and subject to public scrutiny, but this requirement was regularly ignored under the reign of Speaker Wang.

17. The repertoire of typical actions included using human chains to block the entrance, locking up the speaker in his private chamber, or ripping out the speaker's microphone and taking away his gavel. These disruptive tactics made Taiwan's legislature infamous around the world for its brawls and unruly behavior.

18. For additional discussion of the events surrounding the Ma-Wang confrontation, see also Chapters 1 and 4 of this volume.

19. On the organization of the Legislative Yuan and its consequences for policymaking, see also Chapter 7 of this volume.

20. The two most visible student leaders, Chen Wei-ting and Lin Fei-fan, were active members of the so-called Youth Corps of Tsai Ing-wen's 2012 presidential campaign. Both of them were also invited by DPP legislators to attend a public hearing at the Committee on Culture and Education at the Legislative Yuan in December 2012. At that public hearing, Chen Wei-ting verbally attacked the minister of education during a live television broadcast. See "Minister of Education Chiang Wei-ning Called a Hypocrite! Tsinghua University's Chen Wei-ting Releases Video and Statement," *ETToday,* December 4, 2012, https://www.ettoday.net/news/20121204/135256.htm.

21. Rodrik, *The Globalization Paradox.*

22. According to an estimate from Taiwan's leading economic think tank, Chung-Hwa Institute of Economic Research (CIER), the CSSTA would lead to an increase of about US$400 million a year in the value of service exports to mainland China, while the increase in the value of imports from mainland China would only be about US$92 million. See "Estimate of the Economic Impact of the Cross-Strait Services Trade Agreement," CIER, July 2013, http://www.ecfa.org.tw/Download.aspx?No=39&strT=ECFADoc.

23. Many insiders viewed the debate over whether the Legislative Yuan should vote on the CSSTA as a single package or review and vote on individual clauses as a moot issue, because a single alteration to any clause would invalidate the whole agreement and send negotiations back to the starting line. The KMT caucus had originally agreed to a clause-by-clause review merely as a token gesture to address the criticism that the legislature had not been able to exercise supervision over the pact.

24. During the standoff, DPP legislators brokered a deal with the police. The deal imposed a limit on the total number of protesters who could stay in the main chamber of the legislature at any point in time, but also allowed the students to rotate in and out and to receive all kinds of supplies, such as food, water, sleeping bags, iPads, and air cleaners. DPP legislators also took eight-hour shifts at the doors to the chamber to provide the protesters some extra protection. During the occupation, the building was well-stocked with all kinds of goodies, virtually anything the protesters requested on social media. For this reason, some cynical commentators dubbed the "Sunflower Movement" the "Student Movement of the Strawberry Generation"—with "Strawberry Generation" being a derogatory term previously applied to young Taiwanese to insinuate that they "bruise easily" in the face of social pressure or hard work, unlike older generations.

25. "Fukushima's Taiwan Fallout," *Wall Street Journal,* May 6, 2014, http://online.wsj.com/news/articles/SB10001424052702304831304579541052029956512.

26. One of us learned via a personal communication that one of Taiwan's largest high-tech giants immediately decided to reverse a recent decision to invest in Taiwan and

instead to move its next research-and-development center to Singapore after seeing protesters ransacking the premier's office.

27. For instance, one sign held by movement cadres read: "Crawl back home, you Chinese beast bastards!"

28. The National Federation of Industry, which represented the entire manufacturing sector, issued a stern warning in its white paper at the end of 2015 that Taiwan's economy was suffering from five shortages: power, land, water, labor, and talents. President Tsai acknowledged publicly that she took note of the issues identified by the white paper. See Lin Wei-feng, "NFI's 'Five Shortfalls' Gets a Hearing, Tsai Ing-wen Receives Wang Wen-yuan and Hsu Sheng-hsiung," *Storm Media,* March 21, 2016, http://www.storm.mg /article/91282.

29. "Taiwan's President Has Upset Both Business and Workers," *The Economist,* May 26, 2018, https://www.economist.com/asia/2018/05/26/taiwans-president-has-upset -both-business-and-workers.

30. Wei-lun Sun, "May 20 Polls Are Out: This Group Gives Tsai the Worst Grades," *CMedia,* May 15, 2018, https://www.cmmedia.com.tw/home/articles/9911.

7

Legislative Politics

Isaac Shih-hao Huang and
Shing-yuan Sheng

In 2008 the Chinese Nationalist Party, or Kuomintang (KMT), won a landslide victory in the presidential and legislative elections. Its charismatic presidential candidate, Ma Ying-jeou, received over 58 percent of the vote, a historic high, and his party grabbed 72 percent of the seats in the Legislative Yuan, Taiwan's legislature. Four years later, Ma was reelected with 52 percent of the presidential vote, and the KMT held on to its majority, winning 57 percent of all seats. With a majority in the Legislative Yuan for Ma's entire presidency, his administration carried a high expectation that the policy changes he had promised during his election campaigns would be approved by the legislature.

Unfortunately, electoral success did not translate into policy success. Many of the Ma administration's legislative proposals were blocked or altered, and his approval rating dropped dramatically. Overall, only 44 percent of the government's bills were approved by the Legislative Yuan during the first parliamentary term of the Ma era (May 20, 2008–January 20, 2012) and 56 percent in the second (February 24, 2012–December 31, 2015).[1] Overall, about half of all executive branch bills failed.[2] These statistics indicate that the KMT government had a difficult time pushing changes to existing laws through the legislature, despite holding a large majority of the seats there. In fact, Ma Ying-jeou's government had only marginally more legislative success than his predecessor, Chen Shui-bian: the success rate for all bills proposed by the Executive Yuan, Taiwan's executive branch, was only 8 percent higher from 2008–2015 than from 2000–2007. This small difference in the success rate between the two presidencies, one with nominal one-party control of both branches, the other facing a hostile opposition majority in the

155

Legislative Yuan, suggests that presidents will struggle to advance their policy agenda in the legislature even under the best of circumstances.[3]

Figure 7.1 further demonstrates the legislative weakness of Taiwan's executive branch in comparative perspective. In many democracies, including both parliamentary and presidential regimes, the government typically manages to enact at least 70 percent of its bills into law. By contrast, in Taiwan the success rate for bills proposed by the executive branch has never reached that level since the transition to democracy. There have been ebbs and flows over the parliamentary terms, but the highest success rate for an entire term of the Legislative Yuan is around 56 percent. By all accounts, in Taiwan the government's agenda has long been vulnerable to defeat in the legislative arena.

An intuitive explanation for these patterns would attribute the executive branch's subpar legislative performance to poor intraparty cohesion, ineffective party leadership, or the minority status of the governing party. While we do not deny that these factors might have played some role during each presidential term, we zero in on a deeper structural issue that better accounts for the long-term patterns of legislative outcomes in Taiwan: the organization of the legislature, which is unusually decentralized by comparative standards. Broadly speaking, the legislative weakness of the executive branch is the tip of the iceberg, and is but one of many symptoms that follow from a decentralized legislature: a large volume of legislative bills, an overall low passage rate of legislation, and a level playing field for each party caucus to attempt to enact policy changes.[4] In particular, a large body of research in legislative studies shows that the degree of (de)centralization of the legislature is a key factor that determines how much power the majority party and the government are able to wield in the lawmaking process.[5]

To be sure, a strong, cohesive majority party may enact certain pieces of legislation by effectively whipping its members to support the legislation. However, whether deploying carrots or sticks, it is extremely costly for the leadership of any party to enforce party discipline, ensure a good turnout, and maintain a high level of party cohesion across many policy issues at all times during the day-to-day grind of legislative activities. When lawmaking powers are widely distributed among legislators, the legislative process can become stuck in an inconclusive and never-ending review of bills, amendments, and motions, and opponents of change can spring procedural ambushes that delay or kill pending legislation at various stages of the process. To counter and remove either expected or unanticipated obstacles to every piece of legislation would impose a huge mobilizational and transactional cost that no party would be able to pay. Thus, even in parliamentary regimes, centralizing legislative authority in the hands of the cabinet or the majority party, and hence constraining the lawmaking rights of others, helps improve overall legislative efficiency.[6] In highly centralized legislatures, the government and the majority party face lower

Figure 7.1 Success Rates of Government Bills in Taiwan and Other Democracies

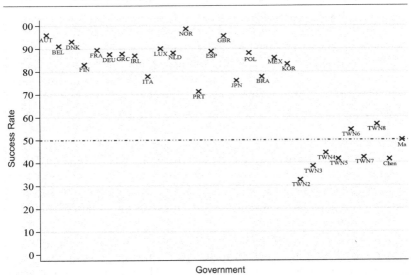

Sources: Data for Taiwan is collected by the authors from the Parliamentary Library of the Legislative Yuan. Data for other countries from Ahn, "A Study of the Determinants Influencing the Legislative Success of a Government-Proposed Bill in Korea"; Andeweg and Nijzink, "Beyond the Two-Body Image: Relations Between Ministers and MPs"; Bowler, "Parties in Legislature: Two Competing Explanations"; Casar, "Executive-Legislative Relations: The Case of Mexico (1946–1997)"; Figueiredo and Limongi, "Presidential Power, Legislative Organization, and Party Behavior in Brazil"; Nalepa, "Party Institutionalization and Legislative Organization: The Evolution of Agenda Power in the Polish Parliament."

Notes: AUT-Austria (1978–1982), BEL-Belgium (1991–2003), DNK-Denmark (1992–2000), FIN-Finland (1945–2002), FRA-France (1958–2002), DEU-Germany (1983–2005), GRC-Greece (1977–2004), IRL-Ireland (1997–2004), ITA-Italy (1948–1996), LUX-Luxembourg (1995–2005), NLD-Netherlands (1978–1982), NOR-Norway (1978–1982), PRT-Portugal (1976–2005), ESP-Spain (1986–2004), GBR-United Kingdom (1995–2004), JPN-Japan (1981–1985), POL-Poland (1997–2011), BRA-Brazil (1989–1997), MEX-Mexico (1997–2000), KOR-South Korea (1988–2016), Ma-Ma Ying-Jeou Administration (May 20, 2008–December 31, 2015), Chen-Chen Shui-bian Administration (May 20, 2000–December 21, 2007). The numbers next to Taiwan labels (TW) indicate the terms of the Legislative Yuan from which the data is taken.

transaction and mobilization costs and are better able to overcome intra-party divisions and pass legislation favored by the leadership.[7]

Taiwan's legislature is so decentralized that the executive branch and majority party have few ways to prioritize their favored legislation and to block other bills from being added to the legislative agenda. Individual legislators and opposition parties are provided with multiple access points to alter legislative drafts and propose new bills of their own. Moreover, power-sharing mechanisms unique to the Legislative Yuan create an unusually equal distribution of legislative rights among the various political actors, who may have starkly different preferences. The most critical of these institutions is the party negotiation mechanism (PNM),[8] a formal, consensus-based decisionmaking procedure that empowers every party caucus to delay and exercise a limited veto over legislation, narrowing the differences in legislative strength between parties.

In this chapter, we are dedicated to showing both the forest and the trees in Taiwan's legislative process during the Ma era. We present patterns of policymaking in Taiwan that cannot be explained away simply by reference to ruling-party size or internal cohesion. That is, we present statistics describing bill-introduction activities, the allocation of committee chairmanships, and the practices of the PNM using data from the seventh and eighth Legislative Yuan terms (2008–2015).[9] We show that the ruling KMT had to deal with a large number of petty bills, share agenda-setting power with minority parties, and spend time negotiating with the opposition in accordance with Legislative Yuan regulations. These features of Taiwan's decentralized legislative organization all contributed to the Ma administration's poor legislative record. In addition, our evidence also indicates that the minority Democratic Progressive Party (DPP) and other small parties got their own bills enacted at a rate comparable to that of the majority KMT. Although it is true that in some cases the ruling party failed to whip its own members into line to support legislation favored by the executive branch, we would be unlikely to observe consistent success rates across parties if legislative authority were not widely distributed. Finally, we offer several case studies of important and salient pieces of legislation to reveal what the success rates do not: that during the Ma era, even executive-branch bills that were eventually approved by the Legislative Yuan passed only after a lengthy process of give-and-take, and the final legislative outcomes often differed significantly from what the Ma administration had initially proposed.

The Policymaking Consequences of Legislative Organization

Policymaking outcomes can be thought of as structure-induced equilibria that are generated not only by the aggregation of preferences via pure majority rule[10] but also by the way in which lawmaking bodies are organized. The organization of a legislature, including the rules under which legislation is considered and the rights and privileges of key power-holders, shapes the distribution of authority in the legislative branch,[11] affects logrolling among legislators,[12] determines the relative bargaining strength of different parties,[13] and influences the efficiency of the lawmaking process.[14]

In particular, legislative organization structures the distribution of resources and parliamentary rights in the lawmaking process.[15] In centralized legislatures, a few privileged groups or individuals with specific powers are able to dominate this process, exerting control over the legislative agenda and regulating and coordinating members' efforts in a way that speeds up action on their own highest-priority bills, and delays or blocks consideration of most other proposals.[16] In decentralized legislatures, by contrast, lawmaking authority is spread widely across parties and individual members,[17] and the legislative process is typically characterized by a fragmented division of decisionmaking responsibility, multiple access points for individual members to influence policy, an absence of seniority rights, and a greater degree of democratization and bureaucratization of legislative staff.[18]

Several important policy consequences follow from legislative decentralization. First, the process of writing new legislation is likely to be less efficient. In Gary Cox's hypothetical evolution of legislatures, for instance, legislators meet in an initial plenary session with equal rights, as if they were in a state of nature when the legislature was founded.[19] In such a state of nature, the legislative process is initially characterized by chaos and inefficiency. To combat this problem, governments in many European democracies have the power to force consideration of their own bills before all others, and nongovernmental bills can be proposed and deliberated for only a limited period of time or only when certain conditions are met.[20] Parliamentary rules in France, for instance, even allow the government to set the parliamentary agenda and preview the content of legislators' bills. When the legislative rights of individual legislators are not constrained, by contrast, there can be a heavy legislative workload that results in a lack of legislative efficiency. Moreover, multiple access points and fragmented decisionmaking authority can incentivize parties and individual legislators to propose narrowly targeted, particularistic bills.[21] As Herman Döring has observed, when individual legislators who have electoral incentives to satisfy the demands of their constituencies are given unlimited rights to propose bills, there can be "an underproduction of highly aggregated collective-benefit bills and an overproduction of many petty bills of a regional or narrow sectional special-benefits character."[22] One implication is that much of the time in decentralized legislatures is spent dealing with a huge number of particularistic bills, rather than the consideration of legislation with broader policy impact.

Second, a highly decentralized lawmaking process tends to equalize the chances of legislative success among various legislative actors, and to reduce the legislative advantages enjoyed by the government and the majority party. Legislative organization determines the rules of the legislative game, and the intrinsic strengths and weaknesses of each actor in the legislative process. When a legislature is highly centralized, even minority governments can use their institutional prerogatives to prioritize the government's agenda and enact new laws with a high degree of success;[23] an internally divided ruling party can bury issues that would ignite intraparty conflicts;[24] and a highly cohesive party can impose its collective will in the legislative arena. However, when a legislature is decentralized, the opposition has many chances to enact the policies it desires and to frustrate the majority or governing party, and individual legislators can take advantage of their formal parliamentary rights to refuse to cooperate with the party leadership, exacerbating the problems of internal party splits and contributing to government weakness in the lawmaking process.[25]

To elaborate, because it can be politically costly to mobilize individual legislators and make them support their party's desired legislation at every moment in the process, the key to ensuring passage is to give institutional priority to specific drafts of legislation and to prevent amendments or alternative proposals from being placed on the legislative agenda. Even in parliamentary democracies that feature a fusion of executive and legislative powers, the lawmaking strength of the government rests on the extent to which legislative institutions empower the executive or the governing party to control the parliamentary agenda and constrain opponents' rights to introduce or amend draft legislation.[26] Empirically, several studies have pointed out that the government and the majority party can enhance their legislative performance by monopolizing agenda-setting power. Gary Cox and Mathew McCubbins demonstrate that the majority party in the US Congress exerts its influence over legislative outcomes primarily by controlling the agenda.[27] Argelina Figueiredo and Fernando Limongi show that the Brazilian government started to enjoy a high rate of legislative success after 1988, when the rules of Congress were revised to favor the executive branch and the leadership of large parties.[28] A similar development occurred in Poland, where the government and ruling party managed to improve their legislative performance by changing the legislative rules so that they were able to choose the legislative speaker, and from there to exercise agenda control.[29]

To sum up, a large and growing body of literature has shown that legislative organization matters a great deal for lawmaking activities and policymaking outcomes. The literature highlights several common features of policymaking when legislatures are decentralized: a large volume of particularistic bills, legislative inefficiency, low passage rates, relative equality of legislative rights across different actors, and reduced advantages for the government and the majority party. In short, when legislative authority is dispersed across many parties and individual legislators, the overall legislative performance suffers, and the government, even when supported by a single-party majority, can struggle to enact significant new laws.

Taiwan's Decentralized Legislature

The key features of Taiwan's decentralized legislative process are shown in Figure 7.2. To become a law, a bill must past through seven major legislative stages in the Legislative Yuan: (1) bill introduction, (2) the procedure committee, (3) the first-reading plenary, (4) standing committees, (5) the

Figure 7.2 Legislative Review Process in the Legislative Yuan

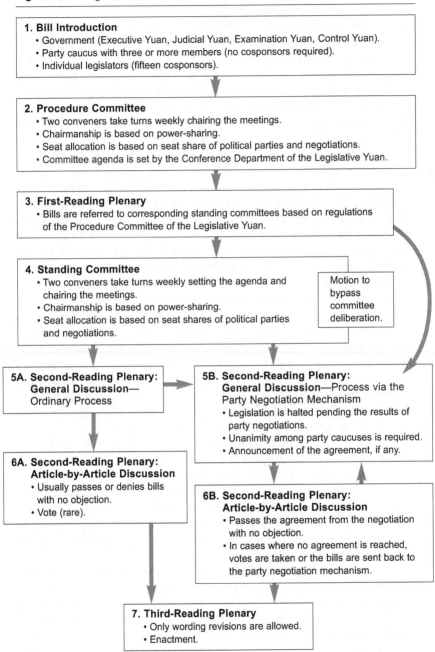

1. Bill Introduction
- Government (Executive Yuan, Judicial Yuan, Examination Yuan, Control Yuan).
- Party caucus with three or more members (no cosponsors required).
- Individual legislators (fifteen cosponsors).

2. Procedure Committee
- Two conveners take turns weekly chairing the meetings.
- Chairmanship is based on power-sharing.
- Seat allocation is based on seat share of political parties and negotiations.
- Committee agenda is set by the Conference Department of the Legislative Yuan.

3. First-Reading Plenary
- Bills are referred to corresponding standing committees based on regulations of the Procedure Committee of the Legislative Yuan.

4. Standing Committee
- Two conveners take turns weekly setting the agenda and chairing the meetings.
- Chairmanship is based on power-sharing.
- Seat allocation is based on seat shares of political parties and negotiations.

Motion to bypass committee deliberation.

5A. Second-Reading Plenary: General Discussion— Ordinary Process

5B. Second-Reading Plenary: General Discussion—Process via the Party Negotiation Mechanism
- Legislation is halted pending the results of party negotiations.
- Unanimity among party caucuses is required.
- Announcement of the agreement, if any.

6A. Second-Reading Plenary: Article-by-Article Discussion
- Usually passes or denies bills with no objection.
- Vote (rare).

6B. Second-Reading Plenary: Article-by-Article Discussion
- Passes the agreement from the negotiation with no objection.
- In cases where no agreement is reached, votes are taken or the bills are sent back to the party negotiation mechanism.

7. Third-Reading Plenary
- Only wording revisions are allowed.
- Enactment.

second-reading plenary-general discussion, (6) the second-reading plenary article-by-article discussion, and (7) the third-reading plenary.[30] Although a small portion of bills may bypass the committee deliberation stage following a motion granted by the floor, most bills have to go through these seven stages before they can be enacted.[31] Importantly, and in contrast to what is observed in many democracies (e.g., the United Kingdom, France, and Switzerland), at none of these stages do the executive branch's bills have legal priority over those proposed by party caucuses or individual legislators. In other words, bills proposed by all types of institutional actors are deliberated together, and the government's bills enjoy no special privilege under the five acts that together govern how the Legislative Yuan operates.[32]

Three other features also make the lawmaking process unusually decentralized in Taiwan. First, there are multiple access points for parties and individual legislators to influence the terms of draft legislation. In many democracies, the bill-introduction rights of parliamentary parties and individual legislators are constrained by various limits, and the government or the majority party can control the plenary agenda.[33] In Taiwan, however, there are few constraints that prevent party caucuses and individual legislators from proposing their own bills, amendments, and motions; the only requirement is that individual members' proposals have to be cosponsored by a certain number of legislators.[34] As long as this cosponsorship requirement is met, there are no other constraints (such as recognition by the legislative speaker) against adding the proposed bills, amendments, and motions to the Legislative Yuan's agenda. By contrast, the executive branch is not allowed to propose amendments and motions. The lack of such provisions, and of a right to propose final amendments at the end of the review process, prevents the Executive Yuan from directly exercising any kind of influence over bills after they have been introduced in the Legislative Yuan.[35]

Moreover, although each party may have its internal rules for the allocation of committee assignments among its membership, Taiwan's legislators are legally allowed to seek assignment to any committee, and to switch between committees once a year. Senior or not, all committee members are eligible to be elected as a "convener," the Legislative Yuan's term for a committee chair (in Chinese, *jiaoji weiyuan*).[36] Hence, individual legislators are provided with equal rights to serve on committees, regardless of seniority or party membership.

Second, several power-sharing mechanisms further equalize the legislative influence of different institutional actors. For instance, the allocation of committee chairmanships is done via a power-sharing rule. Each committee has two co-conveners who chair meetings and set the committee's agenda, and they must alternate every week. Both co-conveners are also elected simultaneously by a vote of committee members, so a party usually has to hold at least two-thirds of the committee seats to place co-partisans in both positions.

Accordingly, in most cases, the majority party, cohesive or not, has to share agenda-setting power in each standing committee with the minority party. Both the majority and minority party thereby have chances to place bills they favor on committee agendas, as well as to "fence out" legislation they oppose.

The third and most unique power-sharing feature of Taiwan's legislature is that the final decisions over legislation are often made via consensus in a small negotiating group made up of representatives from each party caucus.[37] Beginning in the early 1990s, an informal norm emerged in the Legislative Yuan that disputes would go to cross-party negotiation for resolution. In 1996, aiming to improve legislative efficiency, the speaker of the Legislative Yuan, Liu Song-fan, ruled that every bill would be referred to cross-party negotiation after the committee deliberation stage but before the second reading stage at which bills were transferred to the full chamber for general discussion. This negotiation requirement was then written into the Legislative Yuan's organic laws and implemented beginning in 1999. As a result, the party negotiation mechanism is now formally embedded in the second-reading plenary stage of the legislative process.

The second-reading plenary is divided into two sections: the general discussion and the article-by-article discussion (see Figure 7.2). When committee deliberation has concluded, the committee itself can decide to send a bill to the PNM,[38] or if it does not, individual legislators with at least ten cosponsors, or any single party caucus, can file a motion to send the bill to the PNM anyway.[39] These PNM bills go through the procedure detailed on the right-hand side of Figure 7.2 (5B and 6B) at the second reading stage, while the non-PNM bills will be reviewed under the regular procedure shown on the left (5A and 6A).[40] Although the legal minimum is one month, these negotiations often last much longer in practice, as we will show later. Without a unanimous agreement among the party caucuses, bills in the PNM can be bottled up in "negotiations" until the end of the Legislative Yuan term, when they die.

If the party caucuses reach a unanimous agreement in the PNM, the negotiated bills will go through an article-by-article discussion during the second reading (6B), a third reading in plenary session, and then be enacted and promulgated.[41] In other words, agreements negotiated in the PNM can become binding legislation without any further action—not even a final roll-call vote.

By contrast, the bills that are not sent to the PNM pass on through the regular second and third readings in plenary session. Evidence shows that bills sent to the PNM are much less likely to become laws than bills that go through the normal review process.[42] Moreover, given the consensus-based nature of decisionmaking in the PNM, the number of seats a party holds does not determine its legislative success. Even bills proposed by the smallest party in the legislature can become law through the give-and-take of cross-party negotiations, while bills proposed by the executive branch and the majority party can be bottled up indefinitely by opposition in the PNM.

Finally, one might expect that the speaker of the Legislative Yuan, who is elected at the beginning of each term by plurality and so is always from the majority party or coalition, might be able to exercise some authority in the legislative process on behalf of the governing party or majority party. But in fact, there are few formal powers that the speaker has to influence the legislative agenda and legislative outcomes. Under the five acts that govern how the Legislative Yuan operates, the speaker has no authority to appoint the conveners and members of the procedure committee, to allocate convener positions or membership on the standing committees, or to recognize specific bills, amendments, or motions. Bills are sent to the PNM following the decisions of individual committees and motions proposed by party caucuses or legislators, not by the speaker. Moreover, as we show elsewhere, only about a quarter of all negotiation meetings have actually been chaired by the speaker, suggesting that he was not involved in most cases of cross-party negotiation, including during the Ma era.[43] In other words, the speaker of the Legislative Yuan, unlike his counterparts in the United Kingdom, United States, Poland, South Korea, and many other democracies, lacks the necessary institutional tools to steer the legislative review process, control the agenda, or determine the chairmanship and membership of committees.[44]

To sum up, Taiwan's decentralized legislature features multiple access points to influence legislation, as well as power-sharing mechanisms that level the playing field between majority and minority parties. In particular, the executive branch's bills are not legally privileged over other proposals, unlike in many democracies, and the legislative speaker does not possess formal institutional power to dictate the legislative agenda. Considered as a whole, the pattern of policymaking in Taiwan exhibits many classic symptoms of a decentralized legislature: a huge number of petty bills, low rates of passage, relatively even legislative influence across parties, and compromised policy outcomes.

Empirical Implications of Decentralized Legislative Organization in the Ma Era

In this section we draw on the legislative record of over 8,500 bills from the inauguration of President Ma to the end of the eighth Legislative Yuan (May 20, 2008–December 31, 2015) to show empirically some of the symptoms of Taiwan's decentralized legislative organization during the Ma era. The raw data for legislative bills are collected from the archive of the Parliamentary Library of the Legislative Yuan (2015).[45] The Parliamentary Library (*lifayuan guohui tushuguan*) provides complete information about the initiators, content, and progress of each bill. It also provides full transcripts of committee and floor deliberations. By examining such information, we are able to understand how each legislative bill is processed and the overall pattern of policymaking in the Legislative Yuan. The statistics regarding the bill-introduction activities, the allocation of committee chairmanships, the practices of the PNM, and the legislative outcomes demonstrate how the institutional arrangements within the Legislative Yuan shape the influence of different actors over the lawmaking process.

Bill-Introduction Activities

In the Ma era, individual legislators took advantage of the essentially unlimited right to introduce bills to propose an astounding total of 7,067 bills, which accounted for 81 percent of all 8,759 bills submitted to the Legislative Yuan. In comparison to the Chen Shui-bian years, the total number of bills increased by 40 percent during the Ma era, and the number of individual legislators' bills increased by 81 percent. All these prima facie statistics indicate that the workload of the Legislative Yuan skyrocketed during the Ma years, despite the reduced size of the legislature.[46] These numbers also differ from those of many Western democracies, where the government is the main initiator of legislative bills.[47]

Taking the analysis one step further, we look into the scope of bills by initiators (see Table 7.1).[48] Overall, 75 percent of all bills were minor revisions that proposed changes to four or fewer articles in existing laws, 12 percent of the bills proposed completely new laws, and another 11 percent were grand revisions that proposed changes to five or more articles in existing laws.[49] In addition, over 70 percent of the minor revisions proposed changes to only one article. Such one-article bills increased from 1,611 in the seventh Legislative Yuan (May 20, 2008–January 20, 2012) to 2,968 in the eighth (February 24, 2012–December 31, 2015). In both sessions, they accounted for about 50 percent of all bills. Comparing among initiators, 82 percent of the bills proposed by individual legislators were minor revisions, while only 17 percent proposed a new law or a grand revision. Additionally, minor revisions that changed only one article accounted for 60 percent of all individual legislators' bills. Given the multiple access points that party caucuses and individual legislators could use to block or delay legislation, the parties and the executive branch also had incentives to propose bills that were as narrow in scope as possible in order to avoid attracting controversy and to increase the chances of passage. In fact, 70 percent of all the party-caucus and 33 percent of the executive-branch bills proposed only minor revisions. Moreover, more than 70 percent of each party's proposals (including those of both the caucuses and individual party members) were for minor revisions only. The large number of bills introduced during the Ma years that proposed only minor revisions is a classic symptom of decentralized legislative organization. As Keith Kreihbel has noted in the US

Table 7.1   Distribution of Bills, All Ma Years

Initiators	Number of New Laws (%)	Number of Grand Revisions (%)	Number of Minor Revisions (%)	Number of Repeals (%)	Total
Executive branch	338 (27.82)	356 (29.30)	401 (33.00)	120 (9.88)	1,215 (100)
Parties (caucuses)	54 (13.50)	49 (12.25)	281 (70.25)	16 (4.00)	400 (100)
Individual legislators	657 (9.30)	550 (7.78)	5,798 (82.04)	62 (0.88)	7,067 (100)
All	1,049 (12.08)	955 (11.00)	6,480 (74.64)	198 (2.28)	8,682 (100)
KMT	259 (8.31)	207 (6.64)	2,641 (84.73)	10 (0.32)	3,117 (100)
DPP	247 (10.71)	233 (10.10)	1,793 (77.72)	34 (1.47)	2,307 (100)
Small parties	25 (9.58)	27 (10.34)	193 (73.95)	16 (6.13)	261 (100)
Cross-party	180 (10.10)	132 (7.41)	1,452 (81.48)	18 (1.01)	1,782 (100)

Source: Tables in this chapter are author calculations from the Legislative Yuan Bill Tracking System.
Note: Numbers in parentheses are row percentages.

context: "Without parliamentary rights—such as the rights to propose legislation, to debate the content and consequences of legislation, to propose amendments, and to negotiate compromises—a legislator cannot make noteworthy contributions to the legislative product."[50] In other words, even though individual legislators in most parliaments are electorally motivated to propose many of their own bills, they are not able to contribute substantively to the legislative process unless they have something similar to the nearly unconstrained bill-introduction rights that Taiwan's legislators enjoy.

Legislative Performance in Committees

The legislature's heavy workload would be less of a problem if the Executive Yuan and the majority party were able to utilize the committees as gatekeepers to place their favorable bills on the agenda and set others aside. However, according to the rules regulating the procedure committee and standing committees, the two committee co-conveners must take turns chairing the committee meetings, and these two chairs are more often than not from different parties. The leadership of the majority party cannot directly select or hold accountable their co-partisan chair,[51] and the majority party, even if it does exert control over the convener indirectly by selecting a loyalist or by threatening punishment, still must share the committee chairmanship with another party, usually the largest opposition party, unless it holds at least two-thirds of the seats in the committee.[52]

Table 7.2 shows the distribution across parties of committee conveners during the Ma Ying-jeou era. There were eight standing committees in the Legislative Yuan. We count the number of the standing committees whose chairmanship was occupied solely by the KMT and those in which the KMT and the DPP shared the chairmanship. Clearly, even with a majority of seats, the KMT did not exclusively control the chairmanship in each committee except for the first session after President Ma's inauguration. In fact, for the majority of Ma's presidency, the KMT had to share agenda-setting power with the DPP in the Legislative Yuan committees.[53] In the eighth Legislative Yuan, the chairmanship in almost all committees was shared between the two parties, since the KMT held only 57 percent of the seats. By requiring that two co-conveners be elected simultaneously by the committee membership, this institutional arrangement offers opportunities for the largest opposition party to wrest control of the committee agenda for its benefit, and weakens majority-party control over the legislative process.

As far as the DPP was concerned, the chairmanship granted it not only the power to place legislation it favored on the committee schedule but also the chance to block bills favored by the KMT. According to the Organic Law of Committees of the Legislative Yuan (Article 4), the deliberations over any specific piece of legislation can be chaired by the same convener. In addition, there is a strong unwritten norm that any bill that has been

Table 7.2   Distribution of Committee Chairmanships, Ma Years (September 19, 2008–December 18, 2015)

	Number of Standing Committees	
Term and Session	KMT Only	KMT + DPP
7th term		
2nd session	8	0
3rd session	7	1
4th session	6	2
5th session	7	1
6th session[a]	3	4
7th session	5	3
8th session	4	4
8th term		
1st session	2	6
2nd session	0	8
3rd session	2	6
4th session	0	8
5th session	1	7
6th session	0	8
7th session	1	7
8th session	1	7
Total	47	72

Note: a. One convener was not from either of the two major parties.

placed on the agenda by one convener cannot be brought up for deliberation by another. In other words, a committee chair can bury bills by placing them on the agenda in one meeting and never bringing them up again.

It should not be surprising, then, that the Ma administration's bills were more likely to pass through the committee deliberation stage in the seventh Legislative Yuan, when the KMT had full control over most of the committee chairs, than in the eighth, when control over the chairmanships was always split. And in fact, that is exactly what we observe: in the seventh Legislative Yuan, executive-branch bills that had been referred to committee passed through the committee deliberation stage at a rate of 84 percent, while this rate dropped to 75 percent in the eighth. In general, when the ruling party does not exercise complete control over committee agendas, some Executive Yuan–sponsored legislation is likely to be delayed or blocked at the committee deliberation stage.

Party Negotiation Mechanism

Even if a bill survives the committee deliberation, it might be delayed or blocked in the PNM. The record from the Ma years shows that 93 percent of all bills that passed the committee stage and were not sent to cross-party negotiations were approved at the third reading, while only 59 percent of the PNM bills were. In other words, around 40 percent of bills that went to the PNM became stuck in negotiations and were never acted on. During the Ma era, the PNM is where controversial legislation most often died.

In order to demonstrate how the PNM affected policymaking during the Ma years, we first list in Table 7.3 the number of bills that went through the PNM, a voting procedure, or both.[54] As noted earlier, committees have the legal authority to send bills directly to the PNM, and any single party caucus or group of ten individual legislators also has the right to redirect bills to the PNM when they arrive at the second reading in plenary session. A glance at Table 7.3 tells us that voting was seldom used to decide the fate of bills during the second reading. Among all 4,307 bills that reached the second reading, only 4 percent, or 190 bills, were voted on, while about 54 percent (2,332 bills) were instead sent to the PNM. Moreover, 50 percent of all bills that reached the second reading were sent to the PNM and were never voted on. The other 46 percent of all bills did not go through either of these two procedures, and were instead either enacted or rejected with no objections. These numbers clearly show that when there were disagreements, cross-party negotiation, rather than voting, was much more frequently used to make decisions. At least in theory, the majority party, and the executive branch if it is supported by a legislative majority, should benefit the most from holding votes. During the Ma era in Taiwan, however, cross-party negotiation, instead of voting, was the primary way that decisions were made in the final stage of the legislative process. By implica-

**Table 7.3   Decisionmaking Mechanisms for Bills at the Second Reading,
Ma Years**

Mechanism		Number of Bills (%)		
PNM	Voting	7th	8th	All Ma Years
Yes	Yes	104 (6.29)	75 (2.83)	179 (4.16)
Yes	No	809 (48.94)	1,344 (50.64)	2,153 (49.99)
No	Yes	4 (0.24)	7 (0.26)	11 (0.26)
No	No	736 (44.53)	1,228 (46.27)	1,964 (45.60)
Total		1,653 (100)	2,654 (100)	4,307 (100)

Note: Numbers in parentheses are column percentages.

tion, most bills approved by the Legislative Yuan were supported by a cross-party consensus, and it was rare for a bill favored by the majority party but opposed by the minority to pass.

In general, when a head-counting procedure can be frequently replaced with a consensus-based negotiation, the majority party and the executive branch are likely to be frustrated by the lengthy negotiation process. By statute, bills referred to the PNM have to go through a one-month negotiation period.[55] Each party's approval is required in order to make a decision. If no consensus is reached, the bills will be sent to the floor, and the floor has to decide how to proceed. In practice, during the Ma era the negotiations often took much longer than one month, because the floor would often decide to continue cross-party talks. Table 7.4 shows how the PNM operated in practice. Six outcomes are possible once a bill is sent to the PNM. First, there might be a happy ending where a cross-party consensus is reached within the one-month negotiation period. Among all bills sent to the PNM in the Ma years, only 19 percent were dealt with this way. This outcome occurred even less frequently in the seventh Legislative Yuan, when the KMT had a larger majority. Second, the parties might agree to hold a vote to make a decision before the end of the negotiation period. Less than 1 percent of the PNM bills ended in this result. In total, only 20 percent of the PNM bills were in negotiation for less than one month before they were acted on.

For the remaining 80 percent of bills sent to the PNM, the negotiations took longer than one month. The third possible outcome of these bills was that the negotiations took longer than one month, but a cross-party consensus was finally reached before the end of the legislative term. During the Ma years, around one-third of the bills sent to the PNM were approved this way. A fourth outcome occurred only rarely, and only in the seventh Legislative Yuan, in which negotiations took longer than one month, and the

Table 7.4 Outcomes of Negotiation, Ma Years

	Count (%)		
Outcome	7th	8th	All Ma Years
Consensus reached within one month	121 (13.25)	316 (22.27)	437 (18.74)
Voted within one month	13 (1.42)	2 (0.14)	15 (0.64)
Negotiation over one month, consensus reached	330 (36.14)	430 (30.30)	760 (32.59)
Negotiation over one month, proceeded without consensus	20 (2.19)		20 (0.86)
Negotiation over one month, voted	88 (9.64)	70 (4.93)	158 (6.78)
Negotiation over one month, no further progress	341 (37.35)	601 (42.35)	942 (40.39)
Total	913 (100)	1,419 (100)	2,332 (100)

Note: Numbers in parentheses are column percentages.

bills under negotiation proceeded to the second and third reading without any on-record consensus or any vote and were approved without objection. Less than 1 percent of all bills sent to the PNM had such luck. The fifth possible outcome for PNM bills was that the negotiations lasted for more than one month, and the floor then decided to vote on the bill. In the seventh Legislative Yuan, 10 percent of the bills sent to the PNM were finally decided by a floor vote, while this percentage dropped to 5 percent in the eighth. Sixth and finally, the worst-case scenario for a bill sent to cross-party negotiations was that discussions continued without any further progress until the end of the term, and the bills expired without being acted on. The plurality of all bills in the PNM during the Ma years were "buried" this way: 40 percent of the total met this fate.[56]

To further compare the consequences for the bills sent to the PNM, we separate all the PNM bills by type of initiator (Table 7.5). About 42 percent of the executive-branch bills were buried in the negotiation process. This rate was 36 percent and 43 percent for the KMT's and DPP's bills, respectively. Although KMT bills were more likely to be discharged from negotiations and proceed to the next stage, the executive branch did not have a clear advantage over the opposition party in the negotiation process.

These analyses demonstrate that the PNM to a great extent prevented the KMT and the Ma administration from carrying out their policy goals. A significant portion of executive-branch bills that passed through the committee deliberations were buried in the cross-party negotiation process. The evidence speaks for itself that the hands of the Ma administration were tied by the PNM, since it was difficult, if not impossible, to reach a unanimous consensus on controversial legislation. Of course, the KMT could force a

Table 7.5   Outcomes of Negotiation by Initiator, Ma Years

| | Count (%) | | |
Outcome	Executive Branch	KMT	DPP
Consensus reached within one month	70 (14.49)	196 (20.85)	144 (19.33)
Voted within one month	5 (1.04)	4 (0.43)	4 (0.54)
Negotiation over one month, consensus reached	168 (34.78)	329 (35.00)	215 (28.86)
Negotiation over one month, proceeded without consensus	4 (0.83)	6 (0.64)	7 (0.94)
Negotiation over one month, voted	31 (6.42)	64 (6.81)	53 (7.11)
Negotiation over one month, no further progress	205 (42.44)	341 (36.28)	322 (43.22)
Total	483 (100)	940 (100)	745 (100)

Note: Numbers in parentheses are column percentages.

vote after the legally required one-month period of negotiation had ended, and then whip its members to support the executive branch's proposed legislation. As we discuss later, this undoubtedly was how several important pieces of legislation desired by the Ma administration were approved by the Legislative Yuan. Nevertheless, using this method also imposed huge transaction and mobilization costs on the ruling party, and so it was not a common occurrence given the thousands of bills on the legislative agenda. Because the PNM provides the opposition parties with limited veto power and opportunities to avoid taking a vote, the KMT and Ma administration could not fully exploit the legislative advantage that would be expected given their large seat share in the Legislative Yuan.

Overall Legislative Success

The end product of decentralized legislative organization is a low chance of success for any given piece of legislation.[57] In particular, given the Legislative Yuan's multiple access points to influence legislation and its power-sharing decisionmaking mechanisms, all legislative actors have opportunities to advance their own policy goals, while no single one is unilaterally able to approve legislation that it desires.

The success rate for all bills submitted during the legislative term was 25 percent during the seventh Legislative Yuan, 29 percent during the eighth, and 28 percent for the entire Ma era. Thus, only about one-fourth of all bills were enacted. Table 7.6 provides an overview of passage rates for bills introduced by the executive branch, party caucuses, and individual legislators. The executive branch performed better than party caucuses and individual legislators. This finding is consistent with previous research that attributes the government's legislative advantage as the result of a resource and information asymmetry between the executive and legislative branches.[58] However, even with this advantage, the Ma administration succeeded in winning passage of only 44 percent of the bills it submitted during the seventh Legislative Yuan and 57 percent in the eighth. The administration's success rate was 50 percent for the entire Ma era. (See Figure 7.1.) In other words, half of the Ma administration's bills were never approved, even though the KMT held a large majority in the Legislative Yuan for this entire period. This result is at odds with the expectation that a president whose party holds a majority in the legislature should be able to exert control over the legislative process and get his policy priorities enacted into law.

However, individual legislators and small parties were also able to get some of their desired policies enacted. In fact, while only 608 executive branch proposals were approved, 1,668 bills of individual legislators succeeded, accounting for 70 percent of the total. Comparing across parties, the KMT (including both the caucus and individual legislators) fared only slightly better than the DPP: 25 percent versus 21 percent. This near-parity in legislative success was not reflective of the KMT's much larger share of seats.[59] The disproportionality of seats to legislative success rate is even more obvious if we compare between the KMT and small parties. The People First Party (PFP), Taiwan Solidarity Union (TSU), Non-Partisan Solidarity Union (NPSU), and other small parties held fewer than twenty seats between them, yet they were able to enact 17 percent of their bills. Moreover, many bills proposed by legislators from the small parties ended up with cross-party sponsorship. These cross-party bills were as likely to be enacted as the KMT's, and in the first part of Ma's first term they were even more likely to succeed. Clearly, small parties were able to enact more bills

Table 7.6 Success Rates of Legislative Bills by Initiator, Ma Years

Initiators	Success Rate (Count)		
	7th	8th	All Ma Years
Executive branch	43.57 (271)	56.83 (337)	50.04 (608)
Parties (caucuses)	31.31 (31)	20.60 (62)	23.25 (93)
Individual legislators	19.88 (494)	25.62 (1,174)	23.60 (1,668)
All	24.83 (796)	28.73 (1,573)	27.29 (2,369)
KMT	20.12 (314)	30.46 (474)	25.28 (788)
DPP	19.46 (115)	21.27 (365)	20.81 (480)
Small parties	18.92 (7)	16.96 (38)	17.24 (45)
Cross-party	22.53 (89)	25.8 (359)	25.14 (448)

Note: Bills proposed by the Judicial Yuan, the Control Yuan, and Examination Yuan are not included. The numbers in the parentheses are the number of enacted bills.

than their share of seats implied, and bills with sponsors across party lines were more likely to succeed than those initiated by only the majority party. These are classic features of policymaking in a decentralized legislature. The KMT's lack of cohesion might explain part of its legislative failures, but it cannot explain why the opposition DPP and small parties enacted their bills at a rate comparable to the majority party's bills.

Table 7.7 shows the success rates for bills with different scopes. Overall, one-fourth of the bills proposing only minor revisions were enacted. Although the success rate for this group was low overall, all legislative actors managed to win approval for at least some of their bills by proposing many different particularistic bills. The Legislative Yuan enacted 1,623 minor revisions in total, and among these, 1,341 bills (83 percent) were proposed by individual legislators. In addition, the Ma administration proposed and won passage of quite a few bills that repealed existing laws, or parts of laws, in the eighth Legislative Yuan, which in part explains why the overall success rate for executive-branch bills was higher during this term than it was previously.

Our findings demonstrate that individual legislators' petty bills constituted a vast majority of the policymaking outputs of the Legislative Yuan; each party had an almost equivalent chance to enact their bills; and it was important to obtain support across party lines in order to enact legislation. Finally, the legislative advantage of the executive branch and the majority KMT was small during the Ma years.

Beyond Legislative Success: Compromising to Succeed

A low chance of legislative success alone is not sufficient to fully describe the frustration experienced by the KMT and the Ma administration. Another classic feature of decentralized legislatures is the need to resort to compromise to win approval for government-sponsored legislation.[60] Accordingly, in this section we present case studies of important legislation to demonstrate that the Ma administration often had to compromise on its policy goals.

We examine ten signature policy proposals of the Ma era. These policies were either major planks in Ma's presidential campaign platforms or policies that he had publicly advocated. For each bill related to a draft piece of legislation, we identify its position and assign it a score based upon its distance from the status quo. In each piece of legislation, the status quo is given a score of 0, and the scores for bills can range from −3 to 3. A positive value means that the bill is more liberal than the status quo, while a negative value means that it is more conservative.[61] On the cross-Strait relationship and national identity issues, a positive value means that a given bill promotes greater cross-Strait openness than the status quo, while a negative one means that the given bill proposes to further restrict cross-Strait interaction. On all

Table 7.7   Success Rates by Scope of Bills, Ma Years

Initiators	Success Rate (Count)			
	New Laws	Grand Revisions	Minor Revisions	Repeals
Executive branch	39.35 (133)	49.72 (177)	53.37 (214)	70.00 (84)
Parties (caucuses)	14.81 (8)	28.57 (14)	24.91 (70)	6.25 (1)
Individual legislators	24.66 (162)	29.64 (163)	23.13 (1,341)	3.23 (2)
All	28.88 (303)	37.28 (356)	25.05 (1,623)	43.94 (87)
KMT	24.32 (63)	28.02 (58)	25.26 (667)	— (0)
DPP	21.46 (53)	28.76 (67)	20.02 (359)	2.94 (1)
Small parties	12.00 (3)	25.93 (7)	17.62 (34)	6.25 (1)
Cross-party	28.33 (51)	35.61 (47)	24.04 (349)	5.56 (1)

Notes: Bills proposed by the Judicial Yuan, Control Yuan, and Examination Yuan are not included. Numbers in parentheses are numbers of enacted bills.

issues, a bill is assigned a score of 0 when it does not differ from the status quo.[62] (A caveat is that the scores should be interpreted in a relative sense and should not be directly compared across different pieces of legislation.) The goal of this analysis is to compare the executive branch's original draft legislation with the enacted laws in order to gauge whether and to what extent the Ma administration's policy goals were compromised.

As shown in Table 7.8, most of the executive branch's high-priority bills went through a lengthy legislative process. For example, the legislation permitting the acceptance of mainland Chinese students and People's Republic of China (PRC) educational qualifications at Taiwanese universities took twenty months to be approved, despite the fact that President Ma had explicitly advocated for this policy on multiple occasions.[63] The decision to send the executive branch's bill to the relevant committees was stonewalled by the DPP for about five months. The committees then took another year to review and discharge the bill, as well as a counterproposal introduced by a DPP legislator, Kuan Bi-ling. This legislation stayed under negotiation for the next two months and was finally approved without a vote in 2010. For Ma's signature policy proposals, the average duration before approval was twelve months, and the average length of negotiations was just under five months.

In addition to facing a lengthy legislative process, the Ma administration frequently had to accept a compromise to get legislation approved. Eight out of the ten cases ended up with a policy outcome significantly different from the executive branch's original proposal. In some cases, the outcomes were closer to the status quo than the executive-branch drafts, indicating that the administration obtained less than what it wished for. The legislation concerning Chinese educational qualifications is an example. The Ma administration wanted to accept all Chinese educational qualifications without any legal constraints. However, the enacted legislation

Table 7.8 Compromised Outcomes in High-Priority Legislation

Legislation	Issue	Executive	Outcome	KMT	DPP	Other[b]	Negotiation	Vote	Duration	Timeframe
Economic Cooperation Framework Agreement (ECFA)	Approval of agreement	2	2		0		1 month	Yes	1 month	July 8, 2010–Aug. 17, 2010
Act Governing Relations Between the People of the Taiwan Area and the Mainland Area	Acceptance of Chinese students and Chinese educational records	3	2			1	2 months	No	20 months	Dec. 19, 2008–Aug. 19, 2010
Rural Rejuvenation Act	Rejuvenating rural areas	1.5	2	1.5 to 2	2.5	3	7 months	No	28 months	Mar. 7, 2008–July 14, 2010
Statute for Industrial Innovation	Tax exemption for industries	-2	-1			-1.5	10 months	Yes	11 months	May 1, 2009–Apr. 16, 2010
National Pension Act Revision	Delink farmers' health insurance and national pension policy	-2.5	-2.5		-1	-1.5 to -2.5	< 1 month	Yes	21 days	June 27, 2008–July 18, 2008
National Pension Act Revision	Enlarge the pool of insured pensioners	1.5	2			1 to 3	6 months	No	8 months	Oct. 10, 2010–June 13, 2011
Act Governing Food Sanitation	Importation of US beef, lifting ban on ractopamine	0.5	1	1	1 to 2	0.5 to 3	3 months	Yes	5 months	Mar. 2, 2012–July 26, 2012
Income Tax Act	Changes to capital gains tax	2	0.5	0.5 to 1	2.5	0.5 to 3	2 months	Yes	2 months	May 4, 2012–July 25, 2012
Act Governing Food Sanitation	Preventing edible-oil contamination	1	3		2	0.5 to 2	1 months	No	7 months	Apr. 18, 2014–Nov. 18, 2014
Long-Term Care Services Act	Creating long-term care service fund	1.5	2	2	2.5	0.5 to 3	16 months	Yes	38 months	Mar. 2, 2012–May 15, 2015

Notes: a. A range of −3 to 3, with 0 indicating the status quo. Positive value means a bill is more liberal, and negative means more conservative. b. Other parties and individual legislators.

excluded medical education and imposed a restriction regarding national examinations, though these constraints were weaker than ones outlined in Legislator Kuan's bill. Hence, the enacted policy received a score of 2, which was between the two rival proposals just outlined. This outcome can also be observed in the legislation concerning the Statute for Industrial Innovation and the Income Tax Act.

In other cases, the outcomes were even more distant from the status quo than the Ma administration's draft legislation. This occurred when legislators wanted to bring pork back to please their voters or to impose strict regulations on things unpopular among the public. For example, in the legislation to enlarge the pool of the insured in the national pension program, the executive branch's bill scored 1.5, and individual legislators proposed numerous alternative bills whose scores ranged from 1 to 3. After the negotiation, the outcome policy scored 2, which was more distant from the status quo than the executive's original bill. Similar examples include the Long-Term Care Services Act, Act Governing Food Sanitation, National Pension Act, and Rural Rejuvenation Act. In both scenarios, the policy outcomes were the result of give-and-take among the executive branch, the KMT caucus and opposition parties, and individual legislators.

Although the Ma administration could still enact many of its policies, it often had to accept significant compromises despite the fact that Ma's KMT was the majority party in the Legislative Yuan. In most cases, the executive branch had to make concessions to the opposition to win approval for high-priority legislation.

Lawmaking in the Tsai Ing-wen Era

While previous research has argued that the minority status of the DPP led to the weakness of the Chen Shui-bian administration,[64] the findings in this chapter imply that lawmaking under a DPP president with a DPP legislative majority would not look dramatically different. Taiwan's decentralized legislative process makes it hard for governments to pass priority legislation whether or not the president's party controls a majority in the Legislative Yuan. We can test this implication by examining the legislative achievements of President Ma's successor, Tsai Ing-wen. Like Ma and the KMT did in 2008, President Tsai and the DPP won a landslide victory in the 2016 presidential and legislative elections. For the first time in Taiwan's history, the DPP became the majority party in the Legislative Yuan, winning 60 percent of the seats. Since the DPP's legislative caucus was more cohesive than the KMT's, it was expected that the Tsai administration would be better able to hold sway over the Legislative Yuan and advance its top legislative priorities.

The legislative record from Tsai's first term, however, suggests that her administration's policy initiatives have also been somewhat stymied by the decentralized policymaking process in the Legislative Yuan. Although we are not yet able to measure the success rates for the ninth Legislative Yuan at the time of this writing, we can still examine the raw enactment rates to gauge how effective each legislative actor has been at pushing forward its bills through the three readings of the legislative process. Unlike the success rates reported in the previous sections, the raw enactment rates do not account for whether the content of each bill is incorporated into an enacted law, but only measure what share successfully passed through the three readings. The raw enactment rates tend to be higher than the overall success rates.

These data show that, while the Tsai administration has succeeded in winning approval of some legislation by effectively whipping DPP legislators, its overall enactment rate has not differed much from that of the Ma administration. During Tsai's first year, 49 percent of executive-branch bills introduced to that point were enacted.[65] The raw enactment rate for executive-branch bills proposed between President Tsai's inauguration (May 20, 2016) and the end of the ninth Legislative Yuan (January 10, 2019) was about 63 percent—a significantly better rate than during the Ma administration (58 percent). However, if party size and cohesion are what matter most during the legislative process, a large and cohesive DPP majority should have been able to get almost all, if not all, of its bills enacted. Instead, Tsai appears to have faced difficulties similar to Ma. The decentralized organization of the Legislative Yuan undercuts the legislative advantage that the ruling party might expect to enjoy if legislative authority were more centralized.

If we compare legislative performance across different parties during President Tsai's first term, the preliminary statistics show that the raw enactment rates were virtually the same between the KMT (31 percent) and the DPP (30 percent), even though the KMT was in the minority during this term. Most striking, however, is that the small parties fared much better than their small size would lead us to predict. The PFP, a party with only three members, saw 40 percent of the bills proposed by its caucus and members enacted. Because of the decentralized organization of the Legislative Yuan, the majority party, whether or not it is cohesive, has not enjoyed a substantial advantage in enacting legislation, and the legislative achievements of each party were certainly not proportional to their seat shares.

Conclusion

The pattern of policymaking during the Ma Ying-jeou era is a textbook case of lawmaking in a decentralized legislature. In the Legislative Yuan, parties of all different sizes, as well as individual legislators, can exert influence over legislation: they have almost unlimited rights to introduce new bills, multiple access points during the lawmaking process, a power-sharing committee system, and a consensus-based party negotiation mechanism. As a result, across different terms, the legislative agenda is typically over-stuffed with petty bills, the overall success rate of proposed legislation is low, influence over legislation is relatively evenly distributed across parties, and the legislative advantage of the executive branch and the majority party is small. We considered quantitative measures of legislative success and examined several qualitative case studies of priority legislation in order to see how major changes in policy proposed by the Ma administration were blocked or altered in the Legislative Yuan, despite the KMT's majority there. We also undertook a preliminary analysis of the legislative performance of the Tsai Ing-wen administration. We found additional evidence that the decentralized organization of the legislature imposes significant constraints on the presidential administration's ability to pass new laws, despite the strength of the majority party implied by its seat share and internal cohesion, and regardless of which party controls the presidency.

In contemporary democracies, governments, especially those with the support of a parliamentary majority, have a significant legislative advantage. Although the 90 percent rule might be an exaggeration (90 percent of legislative activities are initiated by the executive, which gets 90 percent of what it wants), the rate of enactment for government-proposed bills is typically at least 70 percent in most democracies.[66] In contrast, over Taiwan's nearly thirty-year democratic history, the government has proposed less than 40 percent of all bills, of which at least 45 percent have ultimately failed to pass in some form.[67] The legislative weakness of the executive branch limits presidential governing capacity in Taiwan: programmatic policies that tackle critical national problems often cannot be efficiently approved and carried out.[68]

This chapter by no means suggests that majority status, party cohesion, leadership strategies, legislative skill, or occasional parliamentary brawls do not have any influence on legislative performance. We simply hope to draw scholarly attention to how the organization of the Legislative Yuan fundamentally shapes the nature of the legislative game and the policymaking process in Taiwan.

Notes

1. In our analysis, for a bill to be "successful" it not only has to pass through the entire legislative process but its main contents also actually have to be incorporated into the enacted law. The success rate is then calculated as the number of successful bills divided by the number of all bills submitted during a Legislative Yuan term. This rate is close to but different from what we refer to as the raw enactment rate, which is calculated as the number of bills that passed through the three readings divided by the number of all bills proposed during a term.

2. Throughout this chapter, "bill" and "proposal" are used interchangeably. Both terms refer to a formal draft piece of legislation submitted to the Legislative Yuan. Each bill contains a proposal to enact a new law or to revise or repeal an existing law. An amendment is a proposal to revise a bill that is being considered during the committee or floor deliberations. Due to the enormous number of proposed amendments, and considering that the executive branch is not allowed to propose amendments, we do not include amendments in our empirical analysis.

3. The raw enactment rate for the executive branch's bills during the first year after the inauguration was 52 percent for the Ma administration and 49 percent for the Tsai administration. Thus, despite important differences between the KMT and DPP party organizations, both governments had limited legislative success even during their political honeymoons. See Wang and Chang, "Comparison of the Legislative Output of the New President in the First Year."

4. Hedlund, "Organizational Attributes of Legislative Institutions."

5. Cox and McCubbins, *Setting the Agenda;* Figueiredo and Limongi, "Presidential Power, Legislative Organization, and Party Behavior in Brazil"; Nalepa, "Party Institutionalization and Legislative Organization."

6. Cox, "The Organization of Democratic Legislatures."

7. Cox and McCubbins, *Setting the Agenda.*

8. The party negotiation mechanism (in Chinese, *zhengdang xieshang* or *chaoye xieshang*) is sometimes also translated into English as the "cross-party negotiation committee," "interparty negotiation mechanism," or "party caucus negotiation mechanism."

9. We exclude the very last legislative session of the Ma era since it was the first session of the ninth Legislative Yuan, wherein the KMT was no longer the majority party, and the government was only a caretaker. Bills proposed during this transitional period might not be comparable with those introduced in other sessions.

10. Shepsle and Weingast, "Structure-Induced Equilibrium and Legislative Choice."

11. Hedlund and Freeman, "A Strategy for Measuring the Performance of Legislatures in Processing Decisions."

12. Buchanan and Tullock, *The Calculus of Consent;* Fiorina, "Comment: Alternative Rationales for Restrictive Procedures"; Weingast and Marshall, "The Industrial Organization of Congress."

13. Cox and McCubbins, *Legislative Leviathan;* Cox and McCubbins, *Setting the Agenda.*

14. Cox, "The Organization of Democratic Legislatures"; Froman, "Organization Theory and the Explanation of Important Characteristics of Congress"; Hedlund, "Organizational Attributes of Legislative Institutions"; Hedlund and Freeman, "A Strategy for Measuring the Performance of Legislatures in Processing Decisions"; Davidson and Oleszek, "Adaptation and Consolidation."

15. Krehbiel, *Information and Legislative Organization.*

16. Strøm, "Parliamentary Committees in European Democracies."

17. Ibid.

18. Hedlund, "Organizational Attributes of Legislative Institutions."

19. Cox, "The Organization of Democratic Legislatures."

20. Mattson, "Private Members' Initiatives and Amendments."

21. Hedlund, "Organizational Attributes of Legislative Institutions."

22. Döring, "Parliaments, Public Choice, and Legislation," p. 7. For the electoral incentives that motivate bill-introduction activities, see Brunner, *Parliaments and Legislative Activity.*

23. Field, *Why Minority Governments Work.*

24. Cox and McCubbins, *Setting the Agenda.*

25. Rasch, "Institutionally Weak Governments and Parliamentary Voting on Bills."

26. Cox and McCubbins, *Setting the Agenda;* Mattson, "Private Members' Initiatives and Amendments"; Rasch, "Institutionally Weak Governments and Parliamentary Voting on Bills"; Tsebelis, *Veto Players.*

27. Cox and McCubbins, *Legislative Leviathan.*

28. Figueiredo and Limongi, "Presidential Power, Legislative Organization, and Party Behavior in Brazil."

29. Nalepa, "Party Institutionalization and Legislative Organization."

30. The flowchart describes the procedure through which a legislative bill is reviewed, from its introduction to enactment. It matches what one will see in the official reports of the actual legislative deliberations, the *Legislative Yuan Gazette.*

31. According to the Law Governing the Legislative Yuan's Power, Article 8, there is a legal provision for fast-track legislation that allows individual legislators with twenty cosponsors or each party caucus to propose a motion to deliver a bill directly to the second reading plenary. In practice, whenever such a motion is granted by the floor, the bill will bypass the committee deliberation stage and will be referred directly to the party negotiation mechanism.

32. The laws that govern how the Legislative Yuan operates include the Law Governing the Legislative Yuan's Powers, the Organic Law of the Legislative Yuan, the Rules of Procedure of the Legislative Yuan, the Organic Law of Committees of the Legislative Yuan, and the Law Regulating Legislator Behavior.

33. Cox and McCubbins, *Setting the Agenda;* Mattson, "Private Members' Initiatives and Amendments."

34. According to the Rules of Procedure of the Legislative Yuan, the number of cosponsors required to propose a bill is fifteen (Article 8), and the number of cosponsors required for a motion or an amendment is ten (Article 11). In committees, the number of cosponsors required for motions and amendments is one-fifth of that on the floor (Article 57), which means two cosponsors are sufficient. Furthermore, according to the Law Governing the Legislative Yuan's Powers, any party caucuses can propose bills, amendment, and motions without cosponsors (Article 75).

35. Heller, "Making Policy Stick"; Zucchini, "Italy."

36. Shiao, "The Seniority System in the Legislative Yuan in Taiwan."

37. The Organic Law of the Legislative Yuan requires that caucuses have at least three members, so in practice only parties holding at least three seats are represented in the PNM. Independents can also form a caucus; after the 2008 elections, for instance, two independent legislators joined the Non-Partisan Solidarity Union caucus, which gave them collective representation in the PNM along with the KMT and DPP.

38. In practice, no vote is taken to decide whether bills are sent to the PNM, and it is often the committee convener's call. When there is an unresolved dispute over a bill, it will almost always be sent to the PNM by the committee.

39. The bills that bypass the committee deliberation per the floor-granted motions will be referred to the PNM, and they will go through procedures 5B and 6B in Figure 7.2.

40. The current procedure is different from that of the fourth Legislative Yuan (1999–2002). In the fourth Legislative Yuan, the process of the second reading in plenary session would not start before the negotiations reached some kind of agreement. Starting from the fifth Legislative Yuan, the PNM bills may be advanced to the general discussion section of the second reading in plenary session (5B) pending the results of negotiations.

41. According to the Law Governing the Legislative Yuan's Powers, after an agreement is reached and announced on the floor, no legislators except the representatives assigned by the party caucuses are allowed to make any speeches in either stages 5B or 6B, and no objections are permitted in stage 6B (Articles 72 and 73). Legally, in 5B, individual legislators with more than eight cosponsors may file an objection to a cross-party agreement (Article 72). However, in practice this is very rare, since if there exist any objections, the negotiations will continue, and no agreement will be announced until the negotiating parties reach a unanimous deal or decide to take a vote.

42. Huang, "How Formal Parliamentary Negotiation Affects Policymaking."

43. Sheng and Huang, "Party Negotiation Mechanism."

44. Wang Jin-pyng, the longtime KMT speaker of the Legislative Yuan and sometime rival of President Ma, did not originally set up this institutional system. The major components, including the PNM, were actually established before his speakership started in 1999, in the fourth Legislative Yuan. During the Ma years, Speaker Wang was widely viewed as a powerful political figure second only to President Ma in his ability to influence policymaking, but his influence was mostly informal rather than institutional, built up through his personal reputation, long political experience and relationships, and financial resources and networks. Exerting such informal influence to advance divisive policies is more costly than utilizing institutional tools, and it is unlikely that any speaker in the future will be powerful enough to affect a large number of bills in this fashion.

45. Parliamentary Library, *Bill Tracking System,* https://lis.ly.gov.tw/lylgmeetc /lgmeetkm?.c3690837000100000080000100000^0000E001C000000000303C503f26.

46. As part of the 2005 constitutional reforms, the number of legislators was reduced from 225 to 113 beginning with the seventh Legislative Yuan (2008–2012).

47. Brunner, *Parliaments and Legislative Activity;* Olson and Norton, "Legislatures in Democratic Transition."

48. In this chapter, we define party bills to include those proposed by a party caucus and those for which at least 90 percent of cosponsors are from the same party. The bottom row of Tables 7.1, 7.6, and 7.7 presents the counts and percentages for each party calculated on the basis of this typology. The bills proposed by the Judicial Yuan, Control Yuan, and Examination Yuan are excluded from this chapter since our focus is on the comparison between the executive and legislative branches.

49. Minor revisions also include bills that slightly change the wording of more than five articles in preexisting laws.

50. Krehbiel, *Information and Legislative Organization,* p. 2.

51. Shiao, "The Seniority System in the Legislative Yuan in Taiwan."

52. To reiterate, the share of seats held by each party in each committee is in proportion to the party's seat share in the Legislative Yuan. Thus, in practice, unless the majority party holds more than two-thirds of all seats in the legislature, it will usually be unable to elect both committee conveners and will have to rotate control of each committee chairmanship with the opposition.

53. The KMT won over 70 percent of the seats (81 of 113) in the 2008 legislative election, so it initially had the votes in the seventh Legislative Yuan to elect both of the co-conveners in each committee. However, the KMT's seat share started to drop in 2009, because several legislators resigned for various reasons (e.g., running for local office or being charged with vote-buying in the previous election), and the DPP won several of the by-elections to replace them. By February 2010, the KMT held only 66.4 percent of the seats (75 of 113). Since new committee convener elections are held at the beginning of each Legislative Yuan session, the KMT no longer had enough votes to ensure both would be from the KMT, and had to rotate committee chairmanships with the DPP for the rest of President Ma's time in office.

54. The bills that did not arrive at the second reading are not included here because the PNM is applied at the stage of the second reading.

55. See *Law Governing the Legislative Yuan's Powers,* article 71-1.

56. Technically speaking, according to the archive of the Parliamentary Library, the final status of most of these bills at the end of the term was the second reading, general discussion (5B in Figure 7.2).

57. Hedlund, "Organizational Attributes of Legislative Institutions."

58. McCubbins and Noble, *Legislative Leviathan.*

59. The KMT's seat shares at the beginning of the seventh and eighth Legislative Yuan terms were 72 percent and 57 percent, respectively, while the DPP's seat shares were only 24 percent and 35 percent.

60. Davidson, "The Two Congresses and How They Are Changing"; Hedlund, "Organizational Attributes of Legislative Institutions," p. 80.

61. The term "liberal" here means support for a larger role for government and a stronger emphasis on equality, environmental protection, and human rights; "conservative" means support for more limited government and a greater emphasis on economic development over environmental protection and human rights.

62. All the scores were assigned based upon coding by ourselves as well as three research assistants.

63. Chen, "The President's Position Taking of Bills and His Influence on Legislation Under Semi-Presidentialism."

64. Hawang, "Executive-Legislative Relations Under Divided Government."

65. Wang and Chang, "Comparison of the Legislative Output of the New President in the First Year."

66. This "90 percent" rule is from Olson and Norton, "Legislatures in Democratic Transition."

67. Sheng and Huang, "Decentralized Legislative Organization and Its Consequences for Policymaking."

68. Field, *Why Minority Governments Work.*

8

Watchdog Institutions

Christian Göbel

Chen Shui-bian ended his presidency in handcuffs. He and his wife had been found guilty of several charges of serious corruption, and they were initially sentenced to life imprisonment.[1] Chen had been Taiwan's first president not to hail from the Kuomintang (KMT), the political party that had ruled Taiwan uninterrupted for fifty-five years. The KMT was—and for many in Taiwan still is—associated with systemic corruption, and Chen's promise that he would rid Taiwan of the twin evils of organized crime and money politics convinced many swing voters to cast their votes for him. Chen's conviction on charges of corruption had betrayed these hopes, even though the improvement of political accountability represented one of the major achievements of the Chen administration. After all, Chen had been brought to justice by an anticorruption agency that he himself had helped create.

There was much hope that his successor, Ma Ying-jeou, would improve the system further. Ma had been appointed minister of justice in 1993, and it was probably his hard line against the KMT's local clientelist networks that led to his replacement only three years later.[2] However, Ma's reputation as a corruption fighter was seriously tarnished just before he signaled his intention to run as presidential candidate in 2007, when he was also indicted on charges of embezzlement during his time as mayor of Taipei. Ma was eventually acquitted despite the fact that half of his public special expenditure allowance had ended up in his private bank account. His campaign for president ended up unaffected by the accusations, and he and the KMT swept back into office on the crest of an anti–Democratic Progressive Party (DPP) wave in the 2008 elections.[3]

183

Although these issues might suggest that the Ma administration returned to the "bad old days" of KMT rule, when corruption was systemic and a fundamental part of political selection, this was not the case. The indictment of Chen Shui-bian illustrates that a political leader can strengthen watchdog institutions but nevertheless engage in corrupt behavior. It is thus necessary to analyze the development and performance of watchdog institutions on their own merits. This is what this chapter sets out to do.

I draw on information obtained from the websites of Taiwan's watchdog institutions, official statistics, legal documents, and interviews that I conducted with politicians, prosecutors, and agents in October and November 2014 to identify three key trends shaping accountability institutions during the Ma years. First, the Ma administration strengthened Taiwan's watchdog bodies, but also weakened their political and legal accountability. Ma's Ministry of Justice used wiretaps and other tools for gathering intelligence much more extensively than the Chen administration did, and there is evidence that it engaged in surveillance to weaken political opponents.[4] Nevertheless, these measures did not affect political corruption in any discernible way.

Second, anticorruption activities in Taiwan were hampered by functional redundancy—that is, more than one organization was responsible for the same task. Despite the fact that it had the necessary KMT majority in the legislature to reform and streamline anticorruption institutions, the Ma administration instead added yet one more organization to the mix, again without any measurable effect on corruption. By establishing the Agency Against Corruption (AAC), Ma muddled the division of labor between the existing watchdog bodies, most notably the Ministry of Justice's Investigation Bureau (MoJIB) and the intelligence-supplying ethics bureaus embedded into most government organs.[5]

Third, Taiwan's citizens have long been cynical about anticorruption in Taiwan, irrespective of who is in power. As I have shown elsewhere, this cynicism is not justified by either the steady organizational improvements Taiwan's watchdog bodies have made over the years or the significant corruption-fighting achievements they have recorded. Instead, it is primarily because neither governments nor the media have effectively communicated these achievements to the general public. One explanation for this pattern is that Taiwan's deep political divisions prevent officials from acknowledging improvements made by previous administrations, and this partisanship is accentuated by Taiwan's politicized news media. I present another, less intuitive explanation in this chapter: the many organizations that are tasked with fighting corruption all produce their own reports and statistics, and this valuable information is dispersed and therefore hard to find and piece together. What is more, it is frequently not presented in a way that makes it amenable for full text searches or statistical analyses. As a result, it is exceedingly difficult to measure and track trends in anticorruption activities over time, and the data that are available probably present an unduly pessimistic impression of the level of political corruption in Taiwan.

The chapter begins with a brief introduction of the four watchdog institutions with anticorruption responsibilities: the Control Yuan, the Investigation Bureau of the Ministry of Justice, the supreme prosecutor's Special Investigation Division (SID), and the Agency Against Corruption, the last of which was created during the Ma era. The main focus in this section is on the AAC and its uneasy relationship with the MoJIB. Next, based on official data, I document the increased and virtually unchecked use of wiretaps during the Ma administration. In the third section, I analyze how much and what kind of information each watchdog provided to the public, thus substantiating the claim that information on anticorruption in Taiwan is dispersed, varies widely in quality, and, for some organizations, is difficult to locate and process. The fourth and final section considers some of the specific corruption-related controversies and scandals in the Ma era. I argue that the administration did a poor job of responding to accusations of political bias in corruption cases. The perceived lack of impartiality was a major factor undermining the credibility of Taiwan's watchdog institutions, and the Ma administration wasted a chance to improve its image by better explaining and justifying its controversial decisions and policies.

Organizational Redundancy and Its Consequences

In this section, I illustrate the practical problems brought about by redundancy among anticorruption institutions. To better understand the origins of harmful departmental competition, especially between the MoJIB and the AAC, I briefly introduce the other watchdogs the AAC is cooperating and competing with, namely the Control Yuan, the MoJIB, ethics bureaus, and the Special Investigation Division under the supreme prosecutor, before turning to the AAC itself.

The Control Yuan

The most prominent accountability institution in Taiwan is the Control Yuan, one of the five branches of the Republic of China (ROC) government. Besides the legislative, judicial, and executive branches, the ROC constitution provides for two separate branches of government for the selection of civil servants and for government audits. It is not a stretch to say that an anticorruption agency has formed a distinct branch of government since the ROC was founded in 1911. Nevertheless, despite being one of the five branches, or *yuan,* the Control Yuan has not received much academic attention. It is often misunderstood as being little more than an ombudsman—an organization that collects public grievances and presents them to the relevant departments.

However, the Control Yuan exercises its powers not only in a reactive fashion, by responding to complaints, but also by proactively launching its own investigations. Each Control Yuan member is empowered to open formal inquiries on his or her own initiative. If an investigation finds irregular behavior, the Control Yuan has three different courses of action at its disposal. If an infraction was committed by a public servant, it can notify the offender's superiors and ask them to educate and discipline the offender. In the case of an elected politician, it can refer the matter to another disciplinary organ and, depending on how serious the matter is, possibly initiate impeachment. Or, if the investigation yields evidence of a breach of Taiwan's laws, the Control Yuan can refer the case to the police or prosecution, who will initiate proceedings in accordance with criminal law.[6]

The Control Yuan is also an audit organ with multiple areas of responsibility, including internal and external affairs, national defense, finance, education, procurement, and judicial and prison administration. Anticorruption efforts can involve most of these domains, so one of eight Control Yuan special committees is devoted explicitly to the task of monitoring public officials to detect and deter corrupt and unethical behavior. Its main responsibility is the enforcement of the so-called Sunshine Laws: the Public Functionaries Asset Declaration Law, the Conflict of Interest Prevention Law, and the Lobby Law. Infractions against these laws usually result in administrative punishment or, in rare cases, impeachment. As mentioned, corrupt activities that violate the criminal code are not investigated by the Control Yuan, and are instead handled by one of the other watchdog institutions discussed in this section.

The Ministry of Justice's Investigation Bureau

Before the AAC came into being, anticorruption investigations were usually conducted by the MoJIB, which was established in 1956. In theory, prosecutors in Taiwan do not have to rely on agents from the MoJIB for their investigations, but can also recruit police, military police, or the coast guard to help. However, this seldom happens due to a long-standing division of labor between the various enforcement units. MoJIB agents are specially trained to conduct corruption-related investigations, while other units are usually preoccupied with their own specialized assignments.[7] Like the Control Yuan, the Ministry of Justice's Investigation Bureau has many responsibilities and functions that stretch well beyond anticorruption investigations: of the MoJIB's twenty-one units (fifteen offices, five "rooms," and a research commission), only one is devoted solely to fighting corruption, the Integrity Office. (In that sense, its remit is similar to the Federal Bureau of Investigation in the United States, which also has a wide range of responsibilities.)

More than 1,500 ethics bureaus, another type of organization particular to Taiwan, form the third part of what has long been a tripartite anticorruption structure. Ethics bureaus are embedded in government units such as departments, divisions, or public service providers, where they provide another level of oversight over public officials. Ethics officers educate civil servants about what constitutes corrupt behavior and, at least before the AAC was established, also serve as a source of intelligence for MoJIB agents. In practice, ethics officers who discover corrupt acts typically report them to local prosecutors, who then will empower MoJIB agents to investigate the matter, whereby they can count on assistance from the ethics officers.[8]

The Supreme Prosecutor's Special Investigation Division

After the island of Taiwan was returned to the Republic of China after Japan's defeat in World War II, day-to-day anticorruption work was not performed by the Control Yuan but, as in most other countries, by prosecutors. In Taiwan, the prosecutoriate consists of three levels: the supreme prosecutor's office, two high prosecution offices, and district prosecution offices. Prosecutors have the power to authorize individuals and units with "judicial police status" to conduct investigations, detain suspects and witnesses, and gather evidence.

The supreme prosecutor's Special Investigation Division has its origins in the Chen Shui-bian era, when it was founded as a presidential task force designed to tackle corruption. When Chen took office, Taiwan's integrity institutions were still dominated by individuals for whom reform was not a priority, and so he created a new organization to bypass these structures. The Black Gold Investigation Center (BGIC), as it was initially called, was formed in 2001 as an informal task force within the Ministry of Justice, and was regulated only by an executive order. The body consisted of ten prosecutors, handpicked by the minister of justice, whose mandate was to investigate three main kinds of illegal behavior: organized crime, serious political and corporate corruption, and electoral fraud.[9]

In 2007 the organization was made a formal part of the supreme prosecutor's office in Taiwan's High Court, renamed the Special Investigation Division, and given statutory authority through Article 63-1 of the Organic Law of the Judicial Yuan. This article, now abolished, defined the organization's tasks as investigating high-profile corruption cases involving the president or vice president, the heads of the five government branches, ministers, the mayor of Taipei, and high-ranking officers in the military. It was also responsible for investigating electoral fraud and large-scale corporate corruption. The SID was to consist of at least six but not more than fifteen prosecutors chosen by the supreme prosecutor from among the prosecutors offices at the various levels of administration. The structure of the SID mirrored the BGIC in its simplicity: the chairman, appointed by the supreme prosecutor, was in charge of the prosecutors, who in turn could draw on specialists and staff from other offices.

Ultimately, which cases were referred to the SID was a political decision, because the head of the SID was responsible to the minister of justice. In Taiwan, the prosecutoriate is a part of the executive branch, albeit with prerogatives more typical of the judicial branch. On the one hand, prosecutors are required to follow the orders of their superiors, who decide if a case will be handled by prosecutors or referred to the police. On the other hand, prosecutors have the right—and the obligation—to perform their duties in an objective manner and free from external interference.[10]

Out of the twenty-five cases highlighted on the SID's homepage, nine, or more than one-third, represented investigations into the alleged corruption of former president Chen Shui-bian. In addition, the SID also indicted former vice president Lu Hsiu-lien (Annette Lu), former minister of justice Shih Mao-Lin, former vice premier Chiu I-jen, and Taiwan's first democratically elected president, Lee Teng-hui, on charges of embezzlement.[11] All of them were eventually acquitted,[12] and it was widely perceived that these indictments had been political, because Ma Ying-jeou had been acquitted of the same charges just two years earlier.[13]

However, the SID also investigated less controversial cases, such as the organized-crime activities of former KMT legislator Luo Fu-chu, bribe-taking by High Court judge Chen Jung-ho, and embezzlement by Lin Yi-shih, the former secretary-general of the Executive Yuan.[14]

The Agency Against Corruption

Although anticorruption had not been high on Ma's agenda when he ran for president, a number of high-level corruption cases forced him to demonstrate his resolve in fighting political corruption. To this end, the Agency Against Corruption was added to the many accountability organizations that already existed in Taiwan. The better part of the Ma presidency was spent integrating the AAC into the existing corruption-prevention framework, and mitigating the debilitating interagency competition that the ACC's creation caused.

The AAC is similar to the celebrated anticorruption agencies of Hong Kong and Singapore in (its English) name only.[15] Far from being independent, the AAC is in fact an office within the Ministry of Justice. It functions as an addition to the other bodies tasked with anticorruption, and coordinating the activities of all these watchdog institutions became one of the main mandates of the Ma administration's integrity policies.

The AAC was initially established in response to the indictment of three High Court judges for serious corruption. Its stated purpose was the prevention and investigation of political corruption, something the triangle of prosecutors, ethics officers, and MoJIB had previously been in charge of. Of course, the investigation of political corruption was only one among many tasks handled by prosecutors and the MoJIB, and the Ma administration argued that creating yet another new agency was necessary because it would not be burdened with other tasks and therefore be better equipped to fight political corruption. The ethics officers would be required to report to the AAC alone, although the MoJIB would continue to investigate political corruption.[16]

This arrangement posed two immediate problems. First, it was often difficult to distinguish between political and economic corruption. The first would be investigated by the AAC or the MoJIB or both, and the second by the MoJIB alone. Although two separate organizations had been created to investigate two different types of corruption, the fluid boundaries between these types of corruption required the two organizations to cooperate regularly. The fact that the MoJIB had historically resented other organizations' encroachment into what it regarded as its own terrain led in turn to a kind of competition that was not beneficial to the cause of anticorruption work.[17] The second problem was one of resources: a specialized agency might work well if it was adequately funded and staffed, but this was clearly not the case for the AAC, as its budget was comparatively low, and the Ma administration tried to cut costs by borrowing personnel from other organizations, such as the district prosecutors offices.[18]

This practice in turn caused a number of other problems. The creators of the AAC seemingly failed to consider that mixing staff from agencies with strong organizational cultures would result in communication and coordination failures. This challenge was compounded when the AAC—the host organization—did not have its own salary scheme, resulting in a situation where people with similar positions and portfolios had very different incomes. Although equal in the administrative hierarchy of the agency, those with significantly lower salaries perceived themselves to be second-class employees. On a related note, the AAC was viewed by many aspiring civil servants as a dead-end destination for their careers. For one, the AAC's conviction rate was very low, far lower than that of the local prosecutors offices, and since the promotion of prosecutors in Taiwan was linked to successful cases, they tended to dread the prospect of working for the AAC. In a similar vein, for prosecutors who later returned to their original jurisdictions, their stint at the AAC counted as lost time, because they had been uprooted from their local environment and missed opportunities to participate in more recent investigations. Because they had to catch up again once they returned to their original posts, they perceived their chances of promotion to be lower than those of their peers who had remained.[19]

More Surveillance, Less Accountability

The Ma administration instructed Taiwan's watchdog institutions to produce concrete measures that would demonstrate the success of their anticorruption efforts, such as concurrently increasing the number of anticorruption investigations and the conviction rate. These orders incentivized anticorruption agents to increase their activity, but it also led to declines in political and legal accountability. For example, there was tangible evidence that prosecutors abused the power vested in them by engaging in dragnet wiretapping and deliberately targeting the political opposition.

This section first provides insights into the widespread practice of wiretapping during the Ma administration and highlights the virtual absence of accountability measures for this practice. It then examines the number of indictments and the ratio between indictments and convictions, benchmarks set by Ma Ying-jeou himself. As will be seen, heightened surveillance did not produce the promised results.

Increased Use of Wiretaps

The frequency of wiretapping increased dramatically during the Ma era.[20] Drawing on data from the Judicial Yuan, the *Taipei Times* reported that "from 2007 to August this year [2013], investigators received approval to tap 500,000 [phone] lines."[21] I was unable to locate statistics that document wiretapping to this extent, and it might be possible that the paper's reporters counted all wiretapping applications, including new ones and the extension of existing ones, into the reported sum. That said, the number of authorized wiretaps did increase steeply after Ma took power, as Figure 8.1 shows.

Figure 8.1 illustrates two different kinds of information. The line at the bottom of the graph indicates the number of cases for which wiretapping was approved, and the line at the top shows how many phone lines were tapped each year. The stacked bars provide information on the duration of these wiretaps. They show for each year the percentage of wiretaps that were in operation for up to one month, up to three months, up to six months, up to nine months, up to one year, and more than one year.

The figure reveals several interesting trends. It is clear that wiretapping became a favored instrument for prosecutors during the Ma years. The number of approved wiretaps increased from almost none during the Chen era to nearly 26,000 lines in the first year of the Ma administration. Two years later, that figure had almost doubled, with 46,000 wiretaps authorized in 2010 alone.

Furthermore, there is a wide discrepancy between the number of cases and the number of wiretaps, indicating that during these years local prosecutors tapped four phones for each case on average. It is also noteworthy that the average number of lines tapped in each case declined significantly after 2013. This might be the result of the Legislative Yuan wiretapping scandal in that year. What the graph does not reveal, however, is that judges checked on only a small fraction of these cases—about 150 to 250 wiretaps each year.[22] It should also be noted that most of these wiretaps were not corruption-related. "Investigating corruption" was only the fourth most frequent reason that local

Figure 8.1 Approved Wiretapping Warrants: Cases, Lines, and Duration, 2007–2014

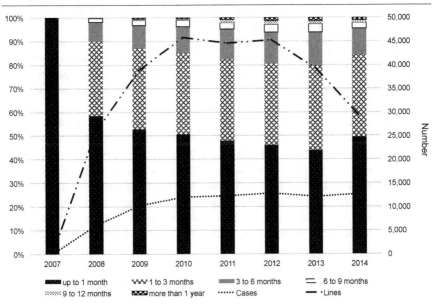

Source: Judicial Yuan, 2019, "Duration of Completed Electronic Surveillance Cases by the District Courts—by Year and Organization."

prosecutors gave when applying for a wiretap warrant, behind drug trafficking, fraud, and the possession of illegal weapons.[23]

In 2015, prosecutors applied for 2,119 wiretaps to target 184 persons. Out of these cases, 149 applications were approved, 15 partially approved, and 20 dismissed. For these cases, 1,855 phone lines were wiretapped, an average of more than 10 phone lines per targeted person. This is by far the largest ratio of lines to cases among all categories listed in the table provided by the Judicial Yuan.[24] Given that, as shown in the next section, the number of judicial indictments on charges of corruption was largely constant, hovering around the 400 mark, wiretaps in this year were approved for one in two cases that later led to an indictment. As regards the number of indicted persons, the ratio is the opposite: for each indicted person, two wiretaps were authorized.

Unfortunately, we lack vital information to contextualize these figures—for example, statistics from previous years or from other countries, interviews with prosecutors and judges, or case studies that illustrate the decisionmaking process regarding which lines to tap. Still, the available information is very disconcerting given what we know about Taiwan's prosecutorial system.

First, the numbers clearly indicate that if the prosecutor's aim was to tap as many lines as possible, obtaining a warrant for suspected corruption would be the way to go. Second, prosecutors were not a part of the judicial but rather the executive branch of government. Although they were required to be neutral in their investigations, what they investigated was decided by their superiors. The fact that political appointees had great influence over who would be wiretapped made partisan bias a very real danger. As judges performed checks to prevent abuse of power in not even one in every forty cases during the Ma era, such abuse was not very likely to be detected.

Third, Taiwan has very strict anticorruption laws, which means that it is comparatively easy to make the case for a wiretap warrant. This is especially true for politicians and legislators, whose frequent dealings with constituencies and interest groups makes it quite easy to argue that transactions might be corrupt. Fourth, while a conscientious judge would demand hard evidence before issuing a wiretapping warrant, it is another worrying sign that barely one in ten applications for a corruption-related warrant was refused by district judges. This suggests that judges were quite amenable to issuing wiretapping warrants and not likely to check on possible abuses of power. Taiwan's actual performance in bringing individuals involved in political corruption to trial notwithstanding, these findings raise the question of whether the investigations were conducted in an impartial fashion, and if enough was being done to "watch the watchers."

Indictments and Convictions

What effect did these measures have? When making his anticorruption promises, President Ma provided two benchmarks: the number of indictments and the ratio between indictments and convictions.[25] Neither increased during his tenure. As regards investigations, Figures 8.2 and 8.3 reveal that the number of indictments even decreased slightly, albeit not significantly, after Ma was sworn into office in 2008. At the same time, the number of indicted persons dropped to its third-lowest since 1994.

In terms of the occupational composition of those indicted, visualized in Figure 8.3, we see no difference between the Chen and Ma eras. Similarly, the amount of money recovered after the successful conclusion of corruption cases continued its downward trend during the Ma administration.

The conviction rate also remained constant throughout the Chen and Ma eras. Judged by the benchmarks set by President Ma, Taiwan's integrity policies during the Ma era were a continuation of the status quo, despite significantly higher investments in anticorruption bodies. At best, the Ma administration could claim that its investments into the prevention of corruption—for example the production of educational DVDs, pamphlets and advertisements—had paid off,[26] but this claim is difficult to verify. It should be noted that most of the advertising was directed toward ordinary citizens,

Figure 8.2 Indictments on Political Corruption Charges: Cases and Persons, 1994–2015

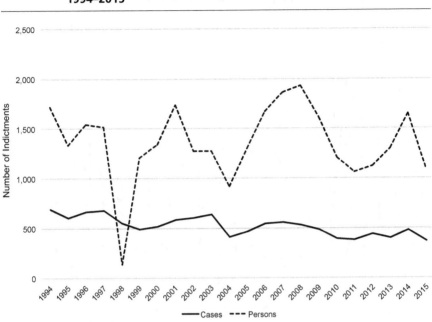

Source: Ministry of Justice, "Cases Investigated and Prosecuted by District Court Prosecutors," various years, http://www.rjsd.moj.gov.tw.

of whom, according to the Global Corruption Barometer, only a fraction (around 3 percent) were ever involved in a corrupt act.[27] Public education might have helped to prevent administrative corruption, which was not a big problem in Taiwan, but not political corruption, which was.

The Control Yuan, which could not operate fully under the Chen presidency because the KMT-dominated legislature refused to confirm Chen's appointees, again became fully operational under Ma. To reiterate, its main responsibilities were the impeachment of officials and the enforcement of the so-called Sunshine Laws. According to its reports, it performed random checks to find out if officials had fully reported their incomes, and followed up on reports of violations of the Conflict of Interest Prevention Law.[28] The Lobbying Law continued to remain toothless under the Ma administration. It was passed by the Legislative Yuan in 2008 to prevent undue influence of economic and private actors on political decisions, but not a single lobbying activity was registered in the entire history of the law's existence. Although contacts between politicians and domestic and foreign businesspeople, which were considered lobbying activities under the law, occurred

Figure 8.3   Indictments on Political Corruption Charges: Position of Indicted Persons and Involved Sums, 1994–2015

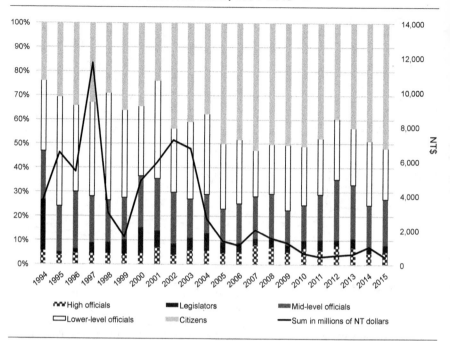

Source: Ministry of Justice, "Cases Investigated and Prosecuted by District Court Prosecutors," various years, http://www.rjsd.moj.gov.tw.

frequently and regularly, not a single politician or legislator reported such activities to the Control Yuan.[29]

Information: Watching the Watchers

Taiwan's watchdog organizations vary considerably in the information they provide. As will be shown, lack of information is a major impediment in allowing outside observers to judge the performance of Taiwan's watchdog institutions.

Information about the Control Yuan comes in the form of downloadable yearbooks that introduce the organization and its functions. The yearbooks are available in both Chinese and English and provide statistical information about its activities during the reported year. Unfortunately, the information is very sketchy. For example, the Control Yuan accepts petitions on judicial matters, but does not provide detailed information about what types of petitions it receives and how it acts on them.

The work of the AAC, the Control Yuan, and the MoJIB is reasonably well-documented, but that of the Special Investigation Division and the prosecutors less so. It is true for all watchdog institutions in Taiwan, however, that information is often not easy to find and does not come in formats amenable to statistical analysis. There is no database to query, and instead of making statistical data available in a readable format, they tend to be delivered as PDF files, sometimes even in the form of scans.

These restrictions notwithstanding, the AAC is the best performer when it comes to accountability, even though it makes only part of its information available in English. On its website, detailed budget reports, performance statistics, and even reports on many of its cases are available for download. In addition, the website summarizes the agency's activities and visions, and offers access to educational material.

The Judicial Yuan also has a website that provides yearly statistical data. For example, the information on wiretap warrants summarized earlier was downloaded from that website. This information is available in both Chinese and English, but only in the form of PDFs that need to be converted into a machine-readable format first. The amount of available information provided by the Judicial Yuan increased steadily during the Ma administration. Wiretapping statistics became more informative, and the 2015 data for the first time contained information on the kinds of crimes for which wiretap warrants were applied.

The data supplied by the prosecutors offices at the various levels are not nearly as detailed. For example, data on conviction rates is hard to find, and the work of the SID is hardly documented at all, raising additional concerns about the accountability and transparency of that body. The website of the supreme prosecutor's office provides only crude statistics on the number of cases handled by the SID during its decade-long existence, and merely summaries of the dozen or so cases considered most important by the office.

Things are better with respect to the MoJIB, which publishes annual yearbooks in Chinese and English. Apart from this, the MoJIB is known for not seeking the attention of the media. In the Ma era, this habit led to conflicts with the more media-savvy AAC. MoJIB agents complained that the AAC's self-portrayal tended to be overly positive, thereby overshadowing the more substantial achievements of the MoJIB.[30] In operations where the two organizations cooperated, the AAC often took the credit, according to an agent I interviewed. This rivalry led to unhealthy competition between the two bodies, in which both organizations strove to snatch those cases that were likely to result in a conviction.

Finally, the websites of the high- and division-level prosecutors offices generally provide an introduction into their responsibilities, and most of them have valuable performance data for many areas of operation.

However, anticorruption investigations do not tend to be among the areas that are documented particularly well.

In any case, those interested in the overall performance of the Taiwanese government in fighting corruption need stamina. They need first to search the website of each watchdog institution and then download all available information, which is often sparse and poorly organized. Many of these documents do not provide summaries, so it is necessary to leaf through all of them. For time-series performance statistics, the PDFs need to be converted into a machine-readable format, which involves either painstaking copy-and-pasting or writing macros to automate this work. Hence, the accountability of watchdog institutions could be improved in two obvious ways: making more information available and making existing information more accessible.

Accusations of Partiality

An objective assessment of the efficiency and effectiveness of watchdog institutions is notoriously difficult. The information that we have on the performance of these institutions is far less than what we need for such an assessment. For example, we do not know if an increase in corruption cases is the result of increased corruption or better anticorruption measures. In a similar vein, we cannot say if there would be more corruption had a certain institution not been created.

That said, the public perception of an increase or decrease in corruption, or the perceived efficacy of an anticorruption agency, has a great impact on the public's support for a particular administration. Arguably, publicly addressing widespread doubts about the impartiality of the system should be a part of anticorruption policy, but the Ma administration failed to do so in several instances.

Ambiguous Special Expenditure Accounts

First, although there was no doubt that Chen Shui-bian, Ma's predecessor, engaged in corrupt practices, legal experts were at a loss to explain the harshness of the life-term prison sentence Chen received.[31] The Ma administration did not invest much energy into proving to the public that this long sentence was not politically motivated. Second, and related, the judiciary came under suspicion for its rulings on the use of special discretionary funds. Judging from the publicly available evidence, politicians of both the DPP and the KMT had long treated such funds as subsidies to their salaries.[32] In 2009, however, Chen was sentenced to life imprisonment because he allegedly embezzled US$5 million from a special presidential fund.[33] Ma Ying-jeou, however, was acquitted for very similar charges—he had wired half of his discretionary funds as mayor of Taipei to his wife's bank account and used the money to pay for personal expenses. Later, other politicians from both parties were charged for the same crime. Ultimately, all were acquitted of the charges, but the fight was tougher for DPP politicians, who were investigated by the SID. In 2010, Taiwan's High Court also acquitted Chen Shui-bian of other embezzlement charges, the reason given being that there was not enough evidence to prove Chen's guilt.[34] Assuming that the sentence would have stood if there had been enough evidence, this raises the question of why the same act carried a life sentence in one instance and no punishment at all in others. If the cases were significantly different from each other, neither the government nor the media did a good job of explaining these differences.

The SID Wiretapping Scandal

The second instance of the Ma administration failing to address the system's partiality occurred when a wiretapping scandal unfolded in September 2013. It began when Wang Jin-pyng, the speaker of the Legislative Yuan, was accused of influence-peddling. This accusation was based on evidence obtained from the wiretapped phone of a DPP legislator, Ker Chien-ming, who was suspected of having engaged in bribery.[35] It was later discovered that not only had the legislators' phone lines been wiretapped, but also the switchboard of the Legislative Yuan itself.[36] Follow-up investigations by DPP legislators revealed that wiretapping had become a common practice under the Ma administration, with local courts quick to approve wiretapping requests by local prosecutors with little judicial oversight to prevent the violation of privacy rights.[37] Observers did not fail to make note of the fact that Wang was a political opponent of Ma, giving rise to allegations that Taiwan's watchdog institutions had been abused for political purposes. Huang Shih-ming, the supreme prosecutor at the time, stepped down from his post as a consequence of the scandal.[38] The SID's controversial role in the dust-up between Ma and Wang in 2013–2014 also made it a target for the DPP, and after Tsai Ing-wen took office in 2016 the DPP majority in the legislature voted to abolish it and return corruption investigations to regular prosecutors offices.[39]

Lack of Public Information

The third instance was when controversy surrounded the indictment and eventual conviction of Lin Yi-shih, the former secretary-general of the Executive Yuan and a close ally of Ma, on bribery charges. That the AAC began investigating this case only after allegations of corruption had been published in Taiwan's *Next* magazine led to the (unfair) accusation that Taiwan's watchdog institutions were ineffective at best, biased at worst.[40] This impression was hardened not only by the fact that the newly created agency did not have much to show for its efforts at the time, despite a sizable amount of money being spent on rewarding whistleblowers, but also because it had engaged in an unfortunate publicity stunt that brought it much ridicule: celebrating the first year of its existence by organizing a marathon through Taipei.[41]

Add to this the indictment of a senior prosecutor for soliciting prostitutes during his working hours, and the conviction of three High Court judges in 2010 on charges of judicial corruption,[42] and it is not difficult to see why a sizable part of the public was cynical about the quality of Taiwan's judicial system. Again, I do not make reference to these incidents because I agree with this viewpoint, but to highlight the narratives on which people based their skepticism. That the reality was more complex, and that Taiwan's accountability institutions functioned better than these accounts would suggest, was exactly the problem.

Many misunderstandings about the performance of Taiwan's watchdog institutions could be ameliorated by providing better access to vital information and, perhaps just as important, providing explanations to counter the widespread perception of judicial unfairness. Also, neither the government nor the media used the available information to help laypersons better understand Taiwan's integrity policies. During the Ma administration, information on anticorruption came either in the form of overly optimistic reports by the AAC, or as overwhelmingly negative newspaper reports. For example, I was unable to find a single balanced account of the legal status of special expenditure accounts or the differences in the various cases pertaining to the special accounts that were up for trial in 2010.

Hence, instead of stating that evaluating anticorruption during the Ma era is difficult because of often confusing information on the subject, it is more appropriate to conclude that the Ma administration could have done a better job of explaining its policies, achievements, and shortcomings.

Conclusion

The performance sheet for anticorruption during the Ma administration is not impressive. When Ma took office, anticorruption was clearly not a priority despite the fact that political corruption was a major concern among the Taiwanese public. A further improvement in Taiwan's integrity institutions would have not only demonstrated responsiveness to public concerns, but also helped to address the increasing cynicism displayed by many Taiwanese toward what they considered to be a self-serving political class. Instead, the Ma administration's integrity policies were largely a continuation of the previous administration's. When the corruption of three High Court judges caused a public backlash, Ma attempted to show resolve by establishing a specialized anticorruption agency. This move backfired, not the least because competition between the AAC and other watchdog organs such as the MoJIB hampered Taiwan's fight against corruption. Judging from the raw number of indictments for corruption, the Ma administration was not able to improve over its predecessor.

Even worse, the Ma administration was widely perceived as having turned the erstwhile Black Gold Investigation Center into a task force for imprisoning senior politicians of the previous administration on charges of corruption. At the same time, wiretaps became a new tool that local prosecutors were able to draw on liberally—approvals were easy to get, and judicial checks on the practice minimal. In sum, the Ma administration's integrity policies achieved little besides perhaps maintaining the status quo, but came at a huge cost to the accountability of the judicial apparatus.

Why did Ma fail to further consolidate Taiwan's watchdog institutions? One explanation is political expediency. Anticorruption was not popular among the rank-and-file of the KMT, who typically did not campaign on policy positions but rather by relying on social capital and personal relationships. Ma was removed from his post as minister of justice during the Lee Teng-hui administration because he took anticorruption investigations too far, and he may have decided not to take the risk again.

Another explanation is related to the agenda-setting process. Ma came into office promising that he would rejuvenate the economy, and most of his political capital was spent on improving relations with the PRC. Anticorruption might have made it onto the agenda if it had been the preference of his ministers of justice. However, the Ministry of Justice was very unstable during his presidency and deeply divided on the question of the death penalty. Ma's first minister of justice resigned over this question. Her successor became entangled in the SID wiretapping scandal and was forced to resign after three and a half years in office. With the Ma administration in disarray after that point, it arguably would have been difficult for Ma's third minister of justice to push such an agenda, especially considering that Ma's second term ended barely two and a half years later.

Notes

For valuable comments, I am grateful to T. J. Pempel and participants in the 2017 "Annual Conference on Taiwan Democracy" at Stanford University.

1. The sentence was later reduced to seventeen and a half years. Both Chen and his wife were able to leave prison on medical parole in 2016, after serving less than a year.

2. "Kindness and Hatred Between Lee and Ma: From Fervent Support to Forced Abdication," *Apple Daily,* March 23, 2008, http://www.appledaily.com.tw/appledaily/article/headline/20080323/30379953.

3. "Public Funds Paid to Ma Still 'Unaccounted For,'" *Financial Times,* December 1, 2006, https://www.ft.com/content/66f18816-809c-11db-9096-0000779e2340.

4. William Wan, "Taiwan's President, Ruling Party Hit by Scandal, Rifts, Anger over Wiretapping," September 12, 2013, http://www.washingtonpost.com/world/asia_pacific/taiwans-president-ruling-party-hit-by-scandal-rifts-anger-over-wiretapping/2013/09/12/355ed3a8-1bb8-11e3-8685-5021e0c41964_story.html.

5. Ko, Su, and Yu, "Sibling Rivalry Among Anti-Corruption Agencies in Taiwan."

6. *Organic Law of the Control Yuan,* https://law.moj.gov.tw/ENG/LawClass/LawAll.aspx?pcode=A0010071.

7. Ko, Su, and Yu, "Sibling Rivalry Among Anti-Corruption Agencies in Taiwan."

8. Göbel, "The Quest for Good Governance."

9. Ibid.

10. Ibid.

11. Because the SID was disbanded, the website is no longer available. A copy is stored at https://web.archive.org/web/20170313215822/http://www.tps.moj.gov.tw/ct.asp?xItem=221224&CtNode=30091&mp=002.

12. Ibid.

13. Author interview with BGIC prosecutor, October 2013.

14. Available at the SID website, archived at https://web.archive.org/web/20170313215822/http://www.tps.moj.gov.tw/ct.asp?xItem=221224&CtNode=30091&mp=002.

15. The organization's Chinese name translates as "Clean Government Division of the Ministry of Justice" (fawubu lianzhengshu).

16. Author interview with the director-general of the AAC, October 2014.

17. Author interview with MJIB agent, October 2014.

18. Ko, Su, and Yu, "Sibling Rivalry Among Anti-Corruption Agencies in Taiwan."

19. Ibid.

20. Hsieh, "Taiwan in 2013."

21. Rich Chang, "Ministry Discusses Discipline Against Huang Shih-ming," *Taipei Times,* December 1, 2013, http://www.taipeitimes.com/News/taiwan/archives/2013/12/01/2003578065.

22. Judicial Yuan, "State of Filings and Dispositions of Electronic Surveillance and Communication Access Cases by the District Court—by Year and Case," 2018, https://www.judicial.gov.tw/en/dl-64685-28fcad7396084d8fb76a759ad75ed8de.html.

23. Judicial Yuan, "Local Court Approvals of Communication Access Requests—by Issue," https://www.judicial.gov.tw/en/dl-794370-4089405860c74ab48adc8ef2a320647f.html.

24. Judicial Yuan, "Local Court Approvals of Communication Access Requests—by Case," 2015, https://www.judicial.gov.tw/en/dl-79439-93b759bcd8ff40fb838ed944860ae446.html.

25. Office of the President, Republic of China (Taiwan), "President Ma Holds Press Conference to Announce Plans for Anti-Corruption Agency," July 20, 2010, https://english.president.gov.tw/NEWS/3376. See also "President Ma Announces New Anti-Corruption Agency," *Taiwan Today,* July 21, 2010, https://taiwantoday.tw/news.php?unit=2,23,45&post=1316.

26. See the expenditures on a promotional movie and other educational items in the AAC's 2014 *Annual Budget Report,* https://www.aac.moj.gov.tw/media/57141+/83298405624.pdf?mediaDL=true.

27. Transparency International, "Global Corruption Barometer 2017: Results for Asia Pacific," https://www.transparency.org/files/content/publication/2017_GCB_AsiaPacific_RegionalResults.xls.x

28. See the reports at https://www.cy.gov.tw/EN/News.aspx?n=253&sms=8937.

29. Author interview with an adviser to former minister of justice Chen Ding-nan.

30. Author interview with MJIB agent, October 2013.

31. Jerome A. Cohen, "A Work in Progress: The Trial of Chen Shui-bian Highlights the Shortcomings of a Legal System in Transition," *South China Morning Post,* September 17, 2009.

32. "DPP Leaders Indicted on Corruption Charges, Accused of Embezzling Allowance Funds," *Taiwan Today,* September 28, 2007, https://taiwantoday.tw/news.php?unit=10,23,45,10&post=14598.

33. Copper, *Democracy on Trial.*

34. Quah, *Curbing Corruption in Asian Countries,* pp. 153–197.

35. Rich Chang, "Prosecutor-General Resigns after Conviction," *Taipei Times,* March 22, 2014, http://www.taipeitimes.com/News/front/archives/2014/03/22/2003586252.

36. Rich Chang, "Ministry Discusses Discipline against Huang Shih-ming," *Taipei Times,* December 1, 2013, http://www.taipeitimes.com/News/taiwan/archives/2013/12/01 /2003578065.

37. Pei-lin Wang and Jake Chung, "Ma-Wang Showdown: Judges Rubberstamp Wiretap Applications: Lawmakers," *Taipei Times,* October 5, 2013, http://www.taipeitimes.com /News/taiwan/archives/2013/10/05/2003573774.

38. "Ma Faces Investigation in 24 Cases Against Him," *China Post,* May 21, 2016, http://www.chinapost.com.tw/taiwan/national/national-news/2016/05/21/466830/Ma -faces.htm.

39. Yu-fu Chen and Jake Chung, "SID Abolished As Legislature Hands Prosecutors Reins," *Taipei Times,* November 19, 2016, http://www.taipeitimes.com/News/front/archives /2016/11/19/2003659559.

40. "Ma's Government Cleanup in Doubt After Lin Bribery Case," *China Post,* July 4, 2012, http://www.chinapost.com.tw/editorial/taiwan-issues/2012/07/04/346596/Mas -government.htm.

41. Wen-chuan Chang, Yu-hsin Lee, and Jake Chung, "Corruption Agency Events Criticized as 'Meaningless,'" *Taipei Times,* July 12, 2012, http://www.taipeitimes.com /News/taiwan/archives/2012/07/12/2003537551.

42. "13 Indicted in Judicial Graft Probe," *China Post,* November 9, 2010, http:// www.chinapost.com.tw/taiwan/local/taipei/2010/11/09/279207/13-indicted.htm.

9

Managing the Economy

Pei-shan Lee

As Taiwan went through its first peaceful transfer of power in 2000, few people realized that it was also about to leave behind its traditional economic development paradigm. Active state-led management of the economy had delivered rapid growth and low inequality for many years, and it was a key factor behind the Taiwanese "economic miracle" that attracted so much admiration in the 1980s and 1990s. But by 2016, when Taiwan experienced its third peaceful transfer of political power, it was clear that the country's vibrant democracy had not been able to forge a pro-developmental coalition behind an alternative model of economic stewardship as effective as the old one. For the past two decades, wages in Taiwan have stagnated, economic growth has been sluggish, and strategic plans for industrial upgrading have repeatedly been undermined by politics.

Taiwan's democratization has somewhat obscured these signs of economic decline. While South Korea was forced to embark on painful economic restructuring and jumped headlong into the global economy in the wake of the 1997 Asian financial crisis, Taiwanese were focused on the victory of Chen Shui-bian in the 2000 presidential race, and the ascension of the Democratic Progressive Party (DPP) to power. During the Chen era (2000–2008), the DPP government prioritized the "Taiwanization" and localization of the democratic regime over steering industrial upgrading and fostering national competitiveness. Given the social foundations of the DPP's support base, welfare spending expanded, and anti-developmentalism became the fashion. With little public notice, in 2004 all manufacturing sites of laptop computers in Taiwan were shut down and moved to mainland China. The underlying structural problems that had contributed to capital flight, the deterioration of local investment conditions, and economic stagnation were not identified and addressed. Instead, the DPP government relaxed restrictions on outbound investment. A massive exodus of Taiwanese manufacturing business was the result—one that has never been reversed. Two decades later, Taiwan has ended up with hollowed-out industries, shortages of investment inputs, stagnant wages, and dormant entrepreneurship. Figures 9.1 and 9.2, on Taiwan's gross investment as a share of gross domestic product (GDP) and its foreign direct investment (FDI), reveal the striking fact that both have been declining and lag far behind counterparts in East Asia and Southeast Asia. In the 2017 report issued by United Nations Conference on Trade and Development (UNCTAD), Taiwan's FDI was ranked at the bottom around the globe.[1]

How has Taiwan's economy ended up suffering through two lost decades, during which investment, both domestic and foreign, has headed for other shores? Why was the previous developmental paradigm discarded?[2] The structural explanation for these patterns dates back to the post-authoritarian reconfiguration of Taiwan's political economy in the 2000s. Rather than trying to stem the exodus of business, the DPP government turned inward to try to reform the Kuomintang (KMT)-dominated governance structure. In an attempt to boost national competitiveness, President Chen Shui-bian picked the banking sector as a reform target and prioritized

Figure 9.1   Gross Domestic Investment in Taiwan, 2000–2017

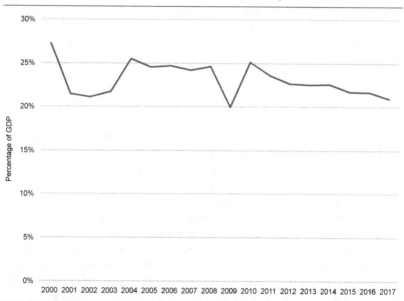

Source: Directorate-General of Budget, Accounting, and Statistics, Executive Yuan.

Figure 9.2   Foreign Direct Investment in Taiwan, 2000–2017

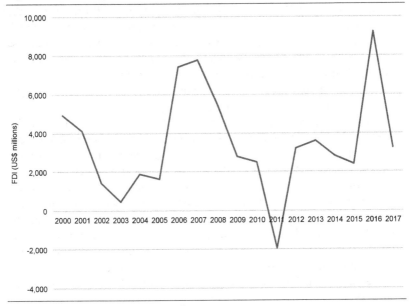

Source: National Development Council.

financial-sector mergers that created a few colossal financial holding companies. In practice, however, the merger of private and public banks turned out to be a political business. In the process, Chen's family members received bribes from interested private banks in return for meddling in bank mergers. The last two years of Chen's presidency were riddled with a series of scandals and investigations related to these so-called financial reforms. After the dishonorable departure of Chen Shui-bian in 2008, Ma Ying-jeou came into office on the heels of a sweeping victory, and in 2012 he won a second term while retaining a substantial majority in the legislature. His first election victory ended eight years of divided government during the Chen years, and he was expected to use his political mandate to overhaul Taiwan's distorted political economy. Nevertheless, Ma failed to find a cure for what I call the "Taiwan disease"—a structural mismatch between its political and economic institutions that has hindered industrial upgrading and accelerated the hollowing-out of manufacturing. The coalition of interest groups that has gradually consolidated majority support behind it over the last two decades has effectively paralyzed the ability of the state to steer economic development. As a consequence, Taiwan's economic policymaking system today is a form of "vetocracy," with many policy initiatives that would benefit the collective interests of the country blocked by narrow groups with either formal or informal veto power.

The nature of government-business relations in the Ma era and Ma's political and decisionmaking style made any further efforts to treat this "Taiwan disease" almost impossible. The most prominent economic breakthrough during Ma's two terms was the opening and normalization of cross-Strait economic interactions, which relied more on goodwill from Beijing than on his own political capabilities. The culminating events of Ma's rapprochement with the People's Republic of China (PRC) were the signing of the Cross-Strait Services Trade Agreement (CSSTA) in 2013 and a meeting between Ma and Xi Jinping in Singapore in 2015. The former was effectively blocked by the Sunflower Movement in 2014; the latter did not result in much domestic approval. The KMT was then defeated in the next presidential election as Ma's term ended in 2016, delivering an electoral rejection of Ma's approach to cross-Strait relations—and also revealing that Taiwan's traditional activist, state-led developmental model had hit a dead end. Simply put, developmentalist economic governance was smashed with the breakdown of the KMT-centered governing system in 2000, but a new model of economic governance has still not been created to replace it. Democracy and development have come into conflict, with democratic "deepening" occurring alongside a polarized political society, a fragmented civil society, and a listless economy.

The three peaceful transfers of power between the KMT and the DPP have not helped Taiwan escape from the limbo of this "paradigm lost." As GDP per capita in South Korea passes US$30,000, the equivalent figure for Taiwan today is only about US$25,000, and lagging farther behind each year. Taiwan's contemporary economic stagnation has its roots in the transition from authoritarian to democratic governance, in which an interest-group-centered, rights-based ideology gave rise to anti-developmentalist populism. It has become all but impossible to sustain a majority political coalition behind a long-term economic development strategy that would benefit the national interest.

The Taiwan Disease: Anti-Developmentalist Populism, Economic Dualism, and Social Fragmentation

The social foundations of the DPP's political support solidified in the early 2000s with the rise of a new anti-developmentalist orthodoxy and a fever for greater democratization of the political system. This orthodoxy remained dominant even after the KMT resumed power in 2008. The origins of Taiwan disease can be traced back to the breakdown of the KMT-dominated system of economic governance after Chen Shui-bian's victory in the 2000 presidential election. The KMT's defeat set the stage for a new approach to managing the economy. As the authoritarian statist model of development was undermined, a new ruling coalition was put in place, and it turned the previous power establishment upside down. The rise of this new orthodoxy in Taiwan, which is based on a US-style liberal democratic template, has occurred in tandem with the global promotion of neoliberalism by the United States in the post–Cold War world. Since the dawn of the twenty-first century, this coalition of interests has been politically dominant in Taiwan, in the sense that it can muster electoral majorities behind it. Though it exists only as a loose umbrella of splinter groups, any political party seeking to win and retain power must still cater to it. This coalition of interests collectively supported the replacement of the "authoritarian" ingredients of the ancien régime under the KMT with a different, politically correct foundation for post-authoritarian Taiwan.

The dominant ideology of this coalition is, by its nature, a blending of anti-authoritarianism with elements of Western liberalism and post-materialism. It is composed of ideologically driven activist groups who identify variously as anti–nuclear power, anti-development, anti-business, anti–free trade, anti–land expropriation, anti–death penalty, and anti-China, among others. These groups, most of which have an affinity with the DPP, have for the most part prevailed in debates about what a progressive democracy should look like. For instance, at the urging of environmental activist groups, Taiwan has introduced complicated environmental assessment procedures, which have then been used to block or sabotage local and foreign direct investment in new development projects. In effect, these activist groups have functioned as a "coalition of obstruction" in opposition to a "coalition for economic development."

The political atmosphere at the time of Chen Shui-bian's election implied that the overarching developmental model of the previous KMT era had to be demolished, no matter how successful it was, together with the party-state apparatus. However, the coalition that emerged in support of reform of Taiwan's political economy has had mutually conflicting interests and goals of its own. For example, anti–nuclear power activists have ignored the downsides of greater air pollution and increased carbon emissions when nuclear power plants are replaced by fossil fuel–burning thermal power plants. Thus, the most striking feature of this fractured coalition is that it offers only intransigent objections to traditional approaches to development, without suggesting alternative solutions to foster economic growth. By assembling single-issue protest groups to block proposals one by one, the dominant ruling coalition has successfully eroded the legitimacy of the previous developmentalist model under which the political leadership, the bureaucracy, and private firms collaborated to steer industrial upgrading. As Richard Doner and Ben Ross Schneider have argued, political obstacles to industrial upgrading are common for countries trapped "in a development nutcracker," "unable to compete with low-income, low-wage economies in manufactured exports and unable to compete with advanced economies in high-skill innovations."[3] Without effective state-business cooperation, countries caught in this "middle-income trap" can suffer economic stagnation and backsliding—a dilemma Taiwan now also finds itself in.

Apart from social activist groups, the most influential coalition partner in state-directed economic development has been the business sector. The realignment of business-government relations in Taiwan has been closely related to increasing economic integration with mainland China. As global manufacturing supply chains developed in both traditional labor-intensive and skill-intensive information technology industries across the Taiwan Strait, this has had two consequences for business-state relations. First, labor-intensive small and medium-sized enterprises have benefited from the economies of scale provided by China's vast markets and supplies of cheap labor. The survivors and winners among these firms have become much bigger and have grown to be embedded in global supply chains. Sustained by partnerships with leading global firms, they have shifted to exporting parts and goods from Taiwan, assembling them in mainland China, and then exporting the finished products to the rest of the world. The rising fortunes of these enterprises came from these triangular relationships rather than cooperation with the Taiwanese state, and thus the range of their potential political partnerships in Taiwan was broadened. Some pro-independence firms that were excluded from the ruling coalition in the KMT era aligned instead with the DPP and became important financial backers of the new ruling coalition. Some became more focused on cultivating their political and business connections in mainland China, while others clung to the KMT due to that party's traditional pro-business inclinations. After Chen Shui-bian became president, he set up parallel business associations to dilute the political influence of many of the existing peak business associations, which had been important sources of support for the KMT. The business sector therefore became more fragmented and was unable to speak with one voice in favor of its collective interests. As a consequence, beginning in the Chen administration, the Taiwanese business community ceased to act in a coordinated fashion as a partner with or consultant to the state. The diverging political affinities of different parts of the business sector have ended whatever cohesion used to exist in state-business relations.

The second consequence of the fragmentation of the business section has been the emergence of a new dualism in Taiwan's domestic economy—a bifurcation between businesses plugged into global production chains and those left outside them. The origins of this economic dualism can be dated to the late 1980s, when rising manufacturing costs drove many Taiwanese businesses to shift production to mainland China and later to Southeast Asia. Small and medium-sized firms that stayed in Taiwan faced daunting challenges. The lack of state-assisted upgrading efforts to orchestrate education, research and development, technological incubation, and market expansion confined local firms to the position of original equipment manufacturers (OEMs) for global production networks. With little government support for innovation, the profit margins for these local firms were thin, and competition with less developed countries severe. Their contributions to global value chains gradually became smaller and smaller, and local small and medium-sized enterprises gradually ceased to be the mainstay of economic growth in Taiwan.

This bifurcation between businesses with and without global connections has resulted in a marked contrast in terms of their employees. Big firms such as Foxconn hire many more Chinese than Taiwanese employees. One-third of production by large Taiwanese companies is located in mainland China. As a result, a significant proportion of GDP growth in Taiwan has been driven by overseas manufacturing. Exports to mainland China and Southeast Asia have primarily been for the purpose of assembly, so GDP and export growth do not tell the full story of the domestic economy. Instead, the domestic market and local wages have become increasingly disconnected from the growth of the export-oriented sector. As this has occurred, large firms that are taking part in global production networks and benefiting from globalization and mainland China's economic rise have come to dominate the coalition of businesses supporting the KMT, while the interests of small and medium-sized enterprises have been pushed aside. The traditional pro-KMT coalition of business interests has gradually narrowed to the point that it is made up primarily of large, globally connected firms. In sharp contrast, the DPP has enlarged its electoral base through populist-style mobilization against two kinds of business interests: Taiwanese businesspeople in China and privileged conglomerates in the domestic market.

As these transformations in the economy have occurred, Taiwanese society has become increasingly divided between the "haves" and "have-nots." Growing resentment against privileged economic elites has paved the way for the rise of a radicalized united front of groups opposed to capitalism, globalization, and China. But these political targets are merely scapegoats for people suffering from Taiwan's economic stagnation, whose resentment can be mobilized into political action via populist appeals. The outbreak of the Sunflower Movement in 2014 against further economic integration with mainland China was but the most obvious manifestation of these deeper undercurrents, which have been present in Taiwan now for almost two decades.

The emergence of a new economic orthodoxy contributed to a worsening investment climate in Taiwan. By doing so, it spurred even more outbound investment, feeding a vicious economic cycle. Before about 2010, Taiwanese capital invested in mainland China contributed to net increases in cross-Strait trade, but after 2010 investment-generated trade has gradually declined. The overall picture is that Taiwan has been losing both domestic and foreign direct investment due to its political climate. The rise of anti-developmentalist populism has reinforced economic dualism, which has in turn exacerbated differences between economic winners and losers in recent years. The winners reap the benefits from cross-border economic activity, while the losers can only seek local political solutions to their economic woes. Given that the losers outnumber the winners, politicians have to be more responsive to their demands in order to win elections—and so elected officials have incentives to support anti-developmentalist policies.

The radicalization and fragmentation of Taiwan's post-authoritarian ruling coalition have also empowered many single-issue groups. Protests, demonstrations, and litigation battles are seen as rightful resistance to injustices of various sorts. Unlike the forms of leftist populism commonly witnessed in Latin America and Southeast Asia, Taiwan's anti-developmentalist populism is based less on calls for material redistribution than on ideological battles. In the worldview of many of these groups, "the weak" in society have been exploited by political and social forces without necessarily being fairly compensated. The weak, being laborers or peasants, function as a weapon with which ideologues can attack the privileged in society. With the manipulation of ethnic cleavages and national identity now outdated in Taiwan, the ideological vacuum since the demise of authoritarianism has been filled instead with all manner of new leftist, post-materialist, and post-industrialist activist groups. In addition, the sweeping anti-statism that has infused the new political orthodoxy has prevented the forging of a new economic developmental model for the democratic era—especially any model that would require heavy state intervention in the economy, bureaucratic discretion, planning over long time horizons, and the persistence of policy decisions beyond a single leader's time in office.

When Ma Ying-jeou took office in 2008, he offered some promise of reversing these patterns, but hopes were soon dashed. Taiwan was first hit by the 2008 global financial crisis, and then in 2009, a flood caused by a typhoon further damaged public confidence in the Ma administration. The domestic economy continued to suffer from declines in investment, capital flight, and relocation of production to mainland China. To understand why Ma's electoral mandate quickly faded, and why he was unable to redress Taiwan's systemic economic weaknesses, we need to consider how state-business relations have changed since democratization.

Revisiting State-Business Relations in the Ma Era

Ma's Political Survival

With its original sin inherited from the authoritarian past, the KMT has had to face two notable challenges in the past two decades. First, the new dualist economy has rendered the KMT's allies in the Taiwanese business community—most of whom have prospered due to investments in mainland China—an almost permanent political minority in comparison to the electoral majority of economic losers in Taiwan. Second, the new orthodoxy of liberal democracy has further consolidated the DPP's appeal and empowered various social movements who are natural allies of that party. President Ma encountered a tough choice between securing votes in the short term and making politically unpopular decisions that would pay off for the economy only in the long term. At the beginning of Ma's presidency, he attempted to do both. He sought to incorporate pan-Green elements with his political appointments, and he was then criticized by his loyal supporters for being too accommodating to their rivals. He also sought to push economically sound but politically suicidal reforms such as energy price liberalization and pension reform. Unfortunately, his first economically correct decision, to adjust the prices of oil and electricity—set by the state via its control of state-owned enterprises—to track more closely the fluctuations in international energy markets, stirred up protests that severely damaged his approval rating. This setback left Ma feeling politically burned, and he shrank from making unpopular decisions about the economy for the rest of his time in office. In fact, this pattern of decisionmaking continued throughout his whole presidency: trying to please everyone, attempting to do the right thing, wavering and cowering in the face of populist opposition, and finally giving in.

Another instance of Ma retreating in the face of populist opposition can be seen in his handling of the Kuo-kuang Petrochemical Plant project, which had encountered local resistance from environmental activists. This classic case of anti-developmentalist politics provides a good illustration of the "Taiwan disease" in practice. The petrochemical project was officially proposed in 2005 by the DPP government, and it was actually approved and promoted by the premier and deputy premiers at the time, Su Tseng-chang and Tsai Ing-wen. However, the estimated NT$600 billion investment plan, orchestrated by a consortium led by the state-owned CPC Corporation, was delayed and then abandoned after the KMT resumed power in 2008, mostly because DPP politicians turned against the project and allied with local environmentalists to sabotage it. Activist groups, sometimes with overlapping membership, flocked to protest this project in the name of protecting white dolphins and wetlands, preserving irrigation water for farmers, preventing air pollution, and so forth. Protesters learned to make use of the judicial system to block executive action on the project, and central government authority was repeatedly hamstrung by decisions in environmental lawsuits. The prolonged disputes over the proposed sites and environmental impact assessments finally led President Ma to cancel the project in 2011. That an industrial investment project of this scale, and in particular one that began as a state-initiated program, could be nullified in such an arbitrary way caused great concern for interested investors, and it became a symbol of the heightened political risks and uncertainties of doing business in Taiwan.

Ma's handling of the dispute over whether to abandon the Fourth Nuclear Power Plant in Gongliao, New Taipei, provides another illustration of how he hesitated, faltered, and finally gave in to anti-developmentalist activists. The Fourth Nuclear Power Plant has long been a symbol of Taiwan's authoritarian developmental state. The use of nuclear power became politicized in the 1990s, as anti-nuclear activism became one of the weapons used to help undermine the legitimacy of state-led economic development, and opposition to nuclear power became sacred DPP doctrine. After Chen Shui-bian took office, he tried to follow through on one of the DPP's campaign promises by stopping construction of the Fourth Nuclear Power Plant, but his power to do so was challenged by the KMT-controlled legislature, and Chen eventually backed down while construction continued. Finally, in 2014, after three decades of travails, the Fourth Nuclear Power Plant was nearly complete and ready to begin initial operations. But then a prominent opposition figure, Lin Yi-hsiung, went on a hunger strike to demand that it be mothballed instead. Lin's anti-nuclear power stance quickly attracted support from the opposition DPP and social activists, who asserted that there was a popular consensus behind keeping the plant closed, regardless of the scientific and economic arguments for nuclear power. In the end, Ma gave in to this pressure and announced that the state-owned electricity provider and builder of the plant, Taiwan Power Corporation, would "seal" the Fourth Nuclear Power Plant and leave it for the next generation to make a decision about activating it. This unwise move reduced Taiwan's electricity margins and led to an excessive dependence on two other aging nuclear power plants, as well as an increase in carbon emissions and air pollution from oil-, gas-, and coal-fueled thermal power plants.

The abrupt decision not to open the plant once again demonstrates the catch-22 that Ma found himself in. Policy decisions that made economic sense in the long term, such as activating the Fourth Nuclear Power Plant and removing subsidies for oil and electricity, were political suicide in the short term, and his approval ratings dropped to dismally low levels. In addition, by attempting to please all constituencies, Ma managed only to alienate his core supporters while winning no friends among his opponents. Ma needed political determination and, most importantly, an ideologically coherent blueprint, both of which had been lacking since the end of the authoritarian era, to successfully break away from the dominant progressive orthodoxy. But his professional training and career path had not equipped him with the prerequisites for overhauling Taiwan's "vetocracy"—a term originally coined by Francis Fukuyama to describe the sources of political dysfunction and decay in the United States, but one that also applies to Taiwan's current impasse.[4]

Ma's Detachment from the Business Sector

"Business" is a tarnished term in the new orthodoxy that has emerged with Taiwan's democratization, and business influence over political decisions has been treated as nothing short of evil. Consciously or not, Ma's presidential style reflected this orthodoxy. He was obsessively proud of his own integrity and always kept himself at arm's length from the business sector. When he was still mayor of Taipei, he had been involved in the merger of Taipei City Bank and a private bank, which raised questions about possible conflicts of interest, and he appeared determined to avoid being put in a similar position while president. His training as a lawyer and academic further contributed to his detachment from the business world. All of this meant that state-business collaboration, a core ingredient of developmental governance, was quite limited during Ma's presidency. To fill his cabinet, Ma tended to favor technocrats, such as the first premier, Liu Chao-shuan, and scholars, such as Jiang Yi-huah. Nevertheless, career politicians such as Wu Den-yi, who served as premier in Ma's first term and then vice president in the second, appeared to be better suited to managing relations between the executive, KMT legislators, and their backers in the business world.

The central premise of Taiwan's traditional economic governance model was that the bureaucracy should be led by an apolitical premier capable of commanding divergent agencies, mediating between state and business, and engaging in far-sighted projects, all while maintaining trust as an impartial overseer. In contrast, no new developmentalist coalition has emerged to replace the old authoritarian model in Taiwan's present political system. Moreover, in tandem with the transition to democracy that began in the late 1980s, a new economic orthodoxy gradually took root in Taiwanese politics, discrediting the old model of state-business collaboration.

This new orthodoxy drew from US-style liberal democracy, under which strong rule of law and liberal corporate governance were held up as the template for business-state relations. In such a political atmosphere, Taiwan's bureaucracy became increasingly cautious about mediating directly between different economic interests, let alone undertaking proactive planning for industrial ventures and upgrades. Lawsuits were often filed against the bureaucracy, charging it with abuse of power, violations of administrative neutrality, lack of transparency, or even corruption. In the wake of the transition to democracy, the economic bureaucracy in Taiwan lost its pivotal position in development ventures and its ability to steer the long-term trajectory of the economy. Since the judiciary had to get involved in the policy process, lawsuits crippled the bureaucrats. They sought to remain passive unless directions were dictated from the top.

In the eyes of populists, the business sector in Taiwan has become dominated by a collection of well-connected conglomerates who enjoy special privileges provided by the state via regulatory concessions, favorable loans, tax breaks, and so on. Peak business associations, which once played a quasicorporatist role in the KMT era, lost their privileged monopoly position during the Chen Shui-bian era when he set up parallel industrial and business associations under the label "Taiwan" to compete with those operating under the label "Republic of China." These peak business associations were thus politicized and duplicated. The mechanisms of consultation and corporatist intermediation in business-state relations were thereafter weakened, and businesspeople increasingly turned instead to "individualistic," lobby-specific politicians, particularly legislators, to try to exert influence over crucial policy decisions concerning business interests.

As a consequence, during the Chen presidency, collective and corporatist arrangements waned, and specialized business interests became more and more aligned with individual legislators. On the surface, the new orthodoxy that Chen embraced resented big business of any kind, but in practice his economic policies, and particularly his changes to the tax structure, were actually quite friendly to business interests. For instance, collective bargaining rights and cross-industry coordination of wage negotiations, which might have better served the collective interest, were undermined, and the large conglomerates saw their influence over economic policy increase much more than that of small and medium-sized firms. But Ma had no intention of changing the business-state situation inherited from Chen, nor did he seek to strengthen the collective bargaining power of unions. From this perspective, not only did the KMT abandon the practice of quasicorporatist consultation with business that it had followed during the authoritarian era, but it also turned its back on workers. The business sector had long asked for the government to solve long-standing shortages of key inputs for industrial development: land, electricity, water, workers, and talent. When Ma did not take these matters seriously, his loss of popular support became difficult to reverse.

Ma's Economic Policies

Shortly after his inauguration, Ma had to face the challenge of responding to the 2008 global financial crisis. By assembling a team of experienced technocrats led by Premier Liu, Ma had apparently counted on having a development-minded cabinet to lead his government's response and help Taiwan weather the crisis. His administration issued a consumption voucher, which helped boost consumer and business confidence, and Taiwan's economy rebounded quickly after the initial shock of the downturn. But the technocrat-centered cabinet had lasted barely a year before Typhoon Morakot hit in August 2009, causing widespread flooding in southern Taiwan. The administration's slow and awkward management of flood relief efforts led to a popular outcry against his cabinet, and Premier Liu resigned in order to take responsibility, leading to a significant reshuffle of ministers. The highly politicized and populism-ridden political environment seemed to be incompatible with Ma's vision of a technocrat-centered administration, and he replaced Liu with the veteran KMT politician Wu Den-yi, who led the cabinet for the rest of Ma's first term.

Another challenge for Ma was how to revive domestic and foreign direct investment, which remained a deeply rooted structural problem with no easy answers. Ma frequently resorted to short-term changes to economic incentives, particularly tax-related stimulus measures, as his go-to solution to revive the economy. In hopes of spurring local investment, for instance, he reduced the inheritance tax from 50 to 10 percent. This change, however, had a much bigger impact on the stock exchange and real estate markets than it did on business investment, and it was mostly the wealthiest Taiwanese who benefited. In 2010, the Ma administration also cut the business tax from 25 to 17 percent. But this reform only continued a long-term shift in Taiwan's tax structure that has increasingly favored businesses over wage-earners. Beginning in 2004, a series of changes to the tax code have included not only tax cuts for business but also generous new deductions— for instance, Taiwanese firms can now deduct business taxes from their corporate income. This shift has come primarily at the expense of Taiwan's hourly employees and salaried workers—the backbone of its middle class— who continue to pay a marginal tax rate of up to 40 percent. As a consequence, over the past two decades, nearly 70 percent of Taiwan's total tax revenue has come from income tax paid by wage-earners, rather than business, corporate, capital gains, or inheritance taxes.

During Ma's presidency, the Legislative Yuan also passed amendments that permitted a broader range of businesses to take tax deductions. In an attempt to attract more foreign direct investment, the Ma administration lowered the capital gains tax rate for foreign investors to the point where it was 25 points lower than the rate for domestic investors. This gap incentivized local owners of capital to shift their money abroad and then reenter Taiwan's capital market through foreign shell companies. By using tax cuts in this way to try to boost investment, Ma actually followed in Chen Shui-bian's footsteps. Yet tax incentives alone provided no remedy for the deterioration of investor confidence in the real economy. Whether local or foreign, investors continued to be more interested in putting their money into Taiwan's stock and real estate markets rather than making direct investments in the local economy. At the end of his second term, Ma finally decided to impose a tax on stock exchange gains and apply a luxury tax on housing speculators in response to the overwhelming discontent over inequality and soaring housing prices. Nevertheless, Ma's high disapproval ratings for his handling of economic policy persisted until the end of his presidency.

Another example of Ma turning to short-term economic measures to boost the economy occurred in 2012, when his administration announced a wage subsidy program for young college graduates. This program, called the "22K wage policy," provided payments to employers to raise the wage for entry-level jobs for college graduates to at least NT$22,000. But it, too, turned out to be counterproductive—it was later widely criticized for benefiting employers more than employees and creating a de facto ceiling on entry-level wages. The subsidy program did not prevent younger college graduates from turning broadly against the KMT government, along with many other workers and farmers. In his second term, especially, Ma struggled to fend off portrayals of his government as serving only the interests of big business and wealthy capitalists. In such a hostile political and economic climate, the emergence of a new pro-developmental majority coalition stood little chance.

The Breakdown of Executive-Legislative Relations

The Ma administration also suffered from a breakdown of coordination between the executive and legislative branches. Ostensibly, the KMT held a secure legislative majority in each of Ma's two terms. In practice, however, the legislature was under the thumb of the longtime KMT speaker, Wang Jin-pyng, and Ma's legislative priorities were constantly threatened by the affinity between Wang and the DPP party caucus. Wang had also maintained strong connections with KMT legislators from local factions, with whom Ma had never been especially close. As a consequence, Ma had to rely on Wang to steer his agenda through the legislature. To support Wang, Ma even revised the KMT's nomination rules to allow Wang a continuous presence at the top of the party list for legislative elections, ensuring his reelection. But it appears that Ma did not seek to maximize his power over the legislative branch, and he had no particular strategy to directly confront the populist orthodoxy he inherited. By distancing himself from the messiness of local politics, as he did with business, Ma avoided possible charges of collusion from local factions and their special interests. Instead, Wang acted as a power-broker between Ma and the KMT's local party bosses. The power imbalance in favor of the legislative branch resulted in constant dismembering of legislation proposed by the Ma administration. The special "party negotiation mechanism," which the legislature routinely used to resolve interparty disputes, gave minority parties tremendous veto power and a disproportionate ability to insert preferred amendments into important legislation. As the largest party in the legislature, the KMT frequently fell victim to backroom negotiations between individual legislators and the opposition parties.[5] The DPP and other party caucuses enjoyed the privilege of proposing alternative versions of bills in competition with the bills introduced by the Ma administration, making it harder to secure a legislative majority in support of the original proposals. Widespread popular distrust of the lawmaking process and negative perceptions of legislators were indicators of the poor quality of democratic governance resulting from this system.

Ultimately, Ma's reliance on Speaker Wang to coordinate between the executive branch and the legislature was also his Achilles' heel, as Wang blocked Ma's preferred method for winning approval of the CSSTA with the PRC. The conflict between Ma and Wang over this issue triggered the outbreak of the Sunflower Movement protests and the end of cross-Strait normalization efforts during Ma's presidency.

Cross-Strait Normalization Sparks a Political Backlash

During Ma's tenure, cross-Strait normalization reached a historic high. Tourists from mainland China poured in, and direct flights across the Strait increased alongside busy trade and cultural exchanges. In 2009, President Ma proposed the idea of normalizing cross-Strait trade in goods and services, investment protections, and dispute settlements. In 2010, the cross-Strait Economic Cooperation Framework Agreement (ECFA) was signed, which set the terms for the economic negotiations that followed. In 2013, the most far-reaching of these agreements, the Cross-Strait Services Trade Agreement (CSSTA), was signed and sent to the legislature, but its approval was delayed there for more than eight months, until March 2014. When the KMT caucus finally attempted to force through passage of the agreement, it triggered the eruption of the Sunflower Movement, a combination of a social movement and student protest that occupied the legislature for over three weeks. The Sunflower Movement started a massive political backlash against Ma's cross-Strait policies, effectively halting the rapprochement with Beijing.[6]

At the root of the massive demonstrations against the CSSTA was deep fear of mainland China. Protesters feared that service jobs in Taiwan could be taken by workers from the PRC, and they also feared that Ma's cross-Strait agreements would lead to an irreversible abdication of national sovereignty. The CSSTA became the target of sweeping attacks, as opponents claimed that it would harm Taiwanese workers and farmers, sacrifice less competitive industries, and increase Taiwan's economic dependence on the PRC. The agreement became a scapegoat for all of Taiwan's economic ills.

The political unpopularity of Ma's cross-Strait policies was due in part to perceptions that he was too pro-China and not concerned enough about the downsides of accelerated integration with the mainland Chinese economy. The perceived threats of this integration overshadowed the potential benefits that ordinary people might obtain, such as the economic activity generated by millions of mainland tourists visiting Taiwan every year. In addition to the hollowing-out of industry and the rising dependency on trade with the mainland—both long-term trends that long predated Ma's presidency—domestic service workers also became panicked about potential job losses in service industries. Unfounded rumors that Ma wanted to seek unification before the end of his term found a receptive audience among people already deeply suspicious of closer relations. The 2015 Xi-Ma meeting and the possibility of a peace agreement looming on the horizon made the public even more frightened by rumors of a "sellout" of Taiwan to the PRC, and the DPP encouraged this rising Sinophobia in hopes that it would reap electoral benefits. In this environment, rational public discussion that objectively weighed the costs and benefits of specific agreements became impossible. In hindsight, the Sunflower Movement represented the end of rapprochement between Taiwan and the

PRC, and it also effectively ended the KMT's monopoly as the broker of cross-Strait affairs.

Ironically, Taiwan's trade dependence on mainland China peaked during Chen Shui-bian's presidency rather than Ma's. The most tangible impact Ma had on cross-Strait relations was the huge influx of Chinese tourists, which provided some economic gains but also raised collective anxiety about Taiwan's future if it continued down a path of economic integration with the giant country across the Strait. Making the situation worse, the agreement to liberalize trade in services was negotiated and signed ahead of the agreement on trade in goods. This order put liberalization in some of the most politically sensitive industries, such as publishing, up for approval first, where it was bound to stir up fierce resistance against the extension of PRC business practices into more parts of the economy. In addition, there was even a downside to the unilateral concessions that Beijing granted in the form of "early harvest" agreements to purchase Taiwanese agricultural goods: by highlighting the absence of any policy to protect or support Taiwan's manufacturing industries, the purchase agreements reinforced feelings of economic insecurity. The political normalization and economic integration that Ma was promoting could easily be interpreted as being possible only through subordination to Beijing and the sacrifice of national security. This Taiwan-centered argument neglected the fact that cross-Strait economic relations were in fact embedded in regional production networks, in which Taiwanese firms operated in supply chains that were competing with networks in other countries and regions. As PRC-based firms embarked on building their own local supply chains, Taiwanese firms would increasingly focus on producing manufactured parts and semi-finished goods in Taiwan again. The Ma administration did not do enough to explain this trend to people and to sell the potential long-run economic benefits of this regional integration to Taiwan's economy.

After the Sunflower Movement occupation of the legislature ended, the CSSTA was shelved and the trade in goods agreement negotiations were called off. After Tsai Ing-wen won the 2016 presidential election and succeeded Ma, official cross-Strait relations were frozen, yet the stream of Taiwanese professionals, students, and white-collar workers emigrating to mainland China, following the previous wave of Taiwanese businesspeople, did not let up. The industrial clusters nurtured by the PRC's development plans over the years have continued to attract semiconductor engineers, banking and financial managers, high school graduates, and other young people to establish startup firms on the mainland. The anti-China fever that spiked during the Sunflower Movement seems to have receded and been replaced with a well-reasoned and well-calculated west-bound surge of people. For those who stay in Taiwan, protectionist attitudes, together with a strong fear of job losses, are gaining currency in domestic politics. Thus,

Taiwan continues to be divided by national identity, ethnicity, economic bifurcation, class antagonism, and an array of other ideological issues such as same-sex marriage and the death penalty.

Reframing the Taiwan Paradox: A Taiwanese Variant of Capitalist Democracy

Taiwan today presents a paradox. Outsiders often praise Taiwan's democracy, freedom, and protection of human rights. Many insiders, by contrast, argue that Taiwan's democracy has become an obstacle to economic development, effective governance, social cohesion, and national integration. The crux of this paradox is a mismatched political economy. Taiwan's current economic policies are strongly pro-capitalist and pro–big business in practice, but anti-developmentalist populism has come to dominate the political system. This fundamental contradiction is manifested in the tax structure, which reflects a systemic preference for investment capital rather than labor, and in the housing market, where soaring prices reflect the abundance of domestic capital that stands in stark contrast to low rates of domestic and foreign direct investment in the broader economy.

The transition to liberal democracy in Taiwan has also led to an emasculated state and a fragmented society. The Taiwanese state can no longer provide effective administrative leadership to steer industrial planning and upgrading over the long term. Society has become increasingly divided by complex political cleavages, and ideological fights have become an unavoidable feature of daily politics. Since democratization, Taiwan's politics have also turned increasingly populist and anti-developmentalist. And worse still, the island has no overarching sense of shared national identity to help unify its many warring political factions.

This is why Taiwan's path of democratization has diverged from that of its East Asian neighbors Japan and South Korea. Japanese politics have never been as liberal or as populist as Taiwan's. South Korea's developmentalist paradigm remains intact, with the state guiding the economy through a process of "managed globalization." Taiwan's emulation of American-style liberal democracy, by contrast, has given rise to a mismatched political economy configuration that blends a rightist capitalist economy and a leftist populist democracy. This mismatch has persisted because Taiwan's economy has become highly embedded in global and regional production networks, whereas its politics have become infused with an anti-developmentalist populism. Taiwan's environmental regulations were set up with a clear intention to mimic US environmental law, but its much-harsher review procedures have in practice created a de facto barrier to investment from within and without. The economic recession and governance crises that the Ma administration faced were inevitable consequences of Taiwan's political gridlock, which both the KMT and the DPP have had to confront while in power. To this point, neither party has had much success in getting the political economy right.

When he took office in 2008, President Ma inherited a mismatched political economy, and despite enjoying majority support in the legislature and a strong mandate for change, he ultimately did little to change economic governance. At the individual level, Ma's legal background led him to keep the business sector at arm's length. His major economic policy tools were tax cuts, consumption vouchers, special budgets, and wage subsidies to the young. He did not have the advisers he needed to attempt to recreate a state-centered developmental model in Taiwan.

From a structural perspective, the nature of Taiwan's political economy will make fundamental economic reform difficult as long as the economic "losers" continue to outnumber the winners. Politicians will still be constrained by their need to maintain electoral support from the majority of the electorate, which is now skeptical of both greater integration with the regional and global economy and of a return to state-guided economic development. The new political orthodoxy, which has gradually become dominant in Taiwan over the past two decades, is based on disdain for the KMT's old developmentalist model, authoritarian past, elitist inclinations, and China-friendly stance. This new political orthodoxy filled the ideological vacuum left in the wake of the transition to democracy, and it has been embraced by the DPP as part of its exclusive political brand. It is a historical irony that the DPP has now replaced the KMT and risen to become the largest party in the party system. The decline of the KMT has not only made possible the DPP's current rule as a single-party majority, but also has eliminated the possibility that a pro-developmentalist coalition might ever be rejuvenated. Taiwan's populist democracy, hollowed-out economy, and relentless hostility toward the PRC appear irreversible. What can be expected for the foreseeable future is unchallenged DPP dominance of the political system, the endurance of the new political orthodoxy, and the persistence of the Taiwan paradox.

Notes

1. From 2000 to 2017, FDI inflow to Taiwan was on average 15 percent of GDP, significantly lower than the global average of 39.24 percent. Singapore registered as high as 282 percent of FDI during the same period. South Korea was at a similar level as Taiwan in terms of FDI, but its domestic capital formation was around 31 percent of GDP, much higher than Taiwan's at about 23 percent. See World Bank Database, "Foreign Direct Investment, Net Inflows," https://data.worldbank.org/indicator/BX.KLT.DINV.CD.WD.

2. On Taiwan's developmental state after its democratization, see Lee, "Dismantling Developmentalism in Taiwan"; and Wu, "Taiwan's Developmental State."

3. Doner and Schneider, "The Middle-Income Trap," p. 609.

4. Fukuyama, "America in Decay."

5. Chu, "Who Is to Tame the Legislature?"

6. Lee and Chu, "Cross-Strait Economic Integration, 1992–2015."

10

Assessing Support
for Democracy

Yu-tzung Chang and Yun-han Chu

Against the backdrop of a major corruption scandal in Chen Shui-bian's second term, Ma Ying-jeou won the 2008 presidential election with an overwhelming majority, beating his rival, Frank Hsieh, by more than 2 million votes. A poll conducted by *Commonwealth Magazine* on the day of Ma's inauguration showed that 64.2 percent of respondents expressed confidence in the Ma administration and only 15.6 percent stated they had no confidence.[1] Public expectations for Ma Ying-jeou's presidency were high.

The first major challenge that Ma's new administration encountered was the onslaught of the 2008–2009 global financial crisis, which in many ways was more severe even than the 1997 Asian financial crisis. His government took extraordinary measures to keep the financial crisis from spreading into the local financial system and used effective countercyclical fiscal policy to pump up domestic demand. Taiwan's economy weathered the economic crisis largely unscathed, and this crisis-management performance helped sustain his popularity until mid-2009.

However, in August 2009, Taiwan experienced unprecedented rainfall and flooding as a result of Typhoon Morakot, and the Ma administration was accused of reacting too slowly to the disaster, causing a sharp fall in the president's popularity. Although Taiwan and mainland China signed the cross-Strait Economic Cooperation Framework Agreement (ECFA) in 2010 in the hope that, under World Trade Organization (WTO) principles, barriers to cross-Strait trade and investment would be eliminated, Ma received little credit for this achievement. According to a poll carried out by Taiwan Indicators Survey Research on May 10, 2012, before the end of his first term,

221

60.6 percent of respondents felt that Ma Ying-jeou was "over-packaged," 53.3 percent felt that he was "overhyped," and 38.5 percent felt that he was a "deteriorating expired product."[2]

Despite this, Ma managed to defeat Tsai Ing-wen in the 2012 presidential election and win a second term. However, not long into his second term, in June 2012, a bribery scandal emerged involving one of Ma's top aides, Lin Yi-shih. In July 2013, another scandal broke out following the death of a military conscript, Hung Chung-chiu, leading to allegations of abuse of power within the military apparatus. Hung's death sparked large protests and further undermined support for the president. A TVBS poll at the time found that 69 percent of respondents were dissatisfied with Ma Ying-jeou and only 15 percent were satisfied.[3] As Ma's popularity fell, rivals within the ruling Kuomintang (KMT) began to make waves. The conflict between Ma and Legislative Yuan speaker Wang Jin-pyng that erupted in September 2013 is a case in point. Ma Ying-jeou seized on a clear case of obstruction of justice to try to force Wang out of the speaker's position. However, after the entire Democratic Progressive Party (DPP) Legislative Yuan caucus as well as many KMT legislators rushed to protect the speaker, the attempt failed, and the president's power base was further undermined. Subsequently, an opinion poll conducted by *ERA News* showed that only 9.2 percent of respondents were satisfied with Ma's performance.[4]

The deadliest political blow to Ma was the Sunflower Movement, which first erupted on March 18, 2014. As the KMT rushed the Cross-Strait Service Trade Agreement (CSSTA) through the committee stage after it had been upheld by the DPP's disruptive tactics for over eight months, students and social movement leaders who vehemently opposed further cross-Strait economic integration staged a demonstration outside the Legislative Yuan, which quickly turned into a large-scale movement to occupy the legislature. The sit-in received widespread social support, forcing Ma to make concessions and agree to an item-by-item review, which essentially killed the agreement for good. The most direct political consequences of the Sunflower Movement were the Kuomintang's defeat in the December 2014 local elections and Tsai Ing-wen's victory in January 2016. When Ma left the presidential office in May 2016, according to a TVBS poll, only 23 percent of respondents were satisfied with his performance over his eight years in office, while 58 percent were dissatisfied.[5] Following the pattern of Chen Shui-bian's eight years in office, Ma Ying-jeou started his presidency with high expectations, which gradually gave way to disillusion and disappointment. Unfortunately, a similar downward spiral of declining popular support and widespread disillusionment is currently also dragging down Tsai Ing-wen's political fortunes with even greater velocity.

Is Democratic Legitimacy Damaged by Bad Governance?

Taiwan has in the past two decades peacefully undergone three rotations of power (in 2000, 2008, and 2016) between the Kuomintang and the Democratic Progressive Party. In addition, the DPP won the majority in the Legislative Yuan for the first time in 2016. So in terms of Samuel Huntington's "two-turnover test" for democratic consolidation, Taiwan's nascent democracy passed this simple litmus test in 2008.[6]

While there is little doubt that Taiwan's political regime fully meets the democratic principles of popular sovereignty featuring free and fair elections, universal adult suffrage, and multiparty competition, the island's young democracy is still facing some daunting challenges on its way to consolidation. One might even argue that it has shown some worrisome signs of deconsolidation, as the Sunflower Movement set an ominous precedent of forcing a shutdown of the Legislative Yuan, the single most important democratic institution in Taiwan, for three weeks, successfully depriving the KMT-controlled legislature of the power to ratify a trade agreement on cross-Strait services. On the domestic front, an increasingly turbulent, volatile, and polarized social and political climate has damaged both the legitimacy and the governing capacity of the democratic system; it has become nearly impossible for any democratically elected government to effectively cope with the island's pressing economic and social challenges—a looming fiscal crisis, a shrinking and rapidly aging population, deteriorating economic competitiveness and protracted wage stagnation, and increasing marginalization in the process of regional economic integration.[7]

As countries in the West face the possible erosion of the popular foundation of their democracies, we should also consider whether Taiwan's democracy has shown signs of deconsolidation. It is against this backdrop that we have conducted four waves of the Asian Barometer Survey (ABS) in Taiwan since 2001 (see Table 10.1). A longitudinal public opinion survey such as the ABS plays a crucial role in the study of the state of democracy. It enables an empirical assessment of the extent of normative commitment to democracy among the public at large, and thus tells us much about how far the political system has really traveled toward democratic consolidation. It also helps identify what factors enhance popular support for democracy and what undermine it. Furthermore, public opinion surveys offer a valuable vantage point from which to see if the citizenry think that political institutions produce an acceptable degree of democracy and deliver an acceptable level of good governance. No matter how well or poorly international donors or academic think tanks rate democracy in a given country, this form of regime will be consolidated only if ordinary people themselves believe that democracy of acceptable quality is being supplied. The citizens are the final judges of the quality of democracy in terms of freedom, rule of

Table 10.1   Four Waves of the Asian Barometer Survey in Taiwan

First Wave	Second Wave	Third Wave	Fourth Wave
June–July 2001	January–February 2006	January–February 2010	June–October 2014
Chen Shiu-bian's first term	Chen Shiu-bian's second term	Ma Ying-jeou's first term	Ma Ying-jeou's second term
Divided government	Divided government	Unified government	Unified government

law, equality, accountability and transparency, participation and competition, and responsiveness.

We put forward a multidimensional and multilevel conceptualization of democratic legitimacy, which is very useful for disentangling citizen orientations toward a political system. We will highlight some of the more interesting findings over the four waves and then discuss their meanings. We begin with an explanation of the importance of democratic legitimacy for democratic consolidation and outline three measures of democratic legitimacy: trust in political institutions, detachment from authoritarianism, and support for democracy. Next we examine trust in political institutions, followed by the preferences of people for democracy and authoritarianism, and then analyze how people support democracy.

Democratic Legitimacy and Consolidation

Consolidation involves questions about whether the democratic regime is sustained and deepened.[8] A majority of democracy researchers argue that party alternation is an extremely important indicator of the consolidation of new democracies.[9] However, to use an analogy borrowed from economics, these studies focus on the supply side, while ignoring the demand side. In addition to a strong consensus among political elites over the design of an appropriate and workable constitutional system, there must also be a great majority of citizens who believe that democracy is "the only game in town" and that further political changes must be based on democratic procedures, and that democracy must not be abandoned even in times of political and economic crisis.[10] When democratic institutions enjoy widespread and deep-rooted legitimacy, we should be able to find empirical evidence showing that a majority of citizens are resiliently loyal toward democracy, that most people are willing to actively protect and defend democracy, and that it will be difficult for any other alternatives to democracy to gain wide acceptance. Furthermore, if any political group tries to overthrow democracy through illegal means, they will face strong resistance from society. In addition, even if a nondemocratic regime is established by force, it will face a serious crisis of legitimacy. Democratic legitimacy is an indispensable condition for the consolidation of democracy.

It is important to differentiate normative legitimacy from empirical legitimacy. Normative legitimacy is the rightness of the regime's claim to rule. Behavioral or empirical legitimacy is the level of the relevant public's diffuse support for the regime. In contemporary times, normative political theory typically expects democratic regimes to be more legitimate than authoritarian regimes because democracy is built on the consent of the ruled and universal suffrage. In a democracy, diffuse regime support is supposed to remain robust over time because citizens understand that the regime is accountable and the authorities or their policies can be changed if they perform poorly and displease the citizens. Empirically, however, a measure of popular support can be found in states with many different kinds of regimes, some democratic and some not—a point often overlooked by theories that concentrate exclusively on democratization.[11] Ample survey data have shown that the public's diffuse support for the regime varies considerably across democracies, and the observed level of regime legitimacy under nondemocratic regimes may be substantially higher than that of emerging democracies.[12]

Much of the empirical research on democratic legitimacy builds on this conceptual distinction between different aspects of the regime. For instance, Russell Dalton distinguishes between three objects of regime support: principles, norms and procedures, and institutions.[13] Pippa Norris classifies three objects of regime support: principles (the core values of a political system), performance (the functioning of a political system), and institutions (actual state institutions such as parliament, courts, the police, political parties, and the military).[14] Similarly, John Booth and Mitchell Seligson differentiate between three dimensions of regime legitimacy: core regime principles, regime performance, and regime institutions.[15]

Despite these conceptual clarifications and theoretical distinctions, researchers have had difficulty distinguishing empirically between different types or modes of democratic legitimacy. Nonetheless, a multidimensional and multilevel conceptualization of democratic legitimacy is useful for disentangling citizen orientations toward a political system. We outline three measures of democratic legitimacy: trust in political institutions, detachment from authoritarianism, and support for democracy. By specifying the targets of support, we should be able to better understand the nature of democratic legitimacy, its sources, and its consequences.

Trust in Political Institutions

Trust in political institutions has been widely used as an indicator of political support for a regime at the institutional level. To function effectively, democracies rely on myriad political institutions.[16] Previous studies on trust in political institutions have focused on the executive, legislative, and judicial branches as well as the key components of the state apparatus, including trust in the civil service, military, and police. However, political parties, which act as an intermediary between government and citizens, have been mentioned less frequently. This chapter uses ABS data to measure trust in the executive, legislature, judiciary, military, and political parties, assessing which factors affect the public's trust in political institutions.

From the results of the four waves of the ABS, Figure 10.1 shows an overall downward trend in the nine objects of institutional trust. In particular, respondents have very low levels of trust in political parties, parliament, the president, the courts, and the central government. Most notable, the level of public trust in political parties dropped sharply to below 17 percent during Ma's first term and to below 13 percent in his second. We witnessed a parallel drop in the trust level of parliament (the Legislative Yuan), which plummeted to a depressingly low level of 21 percent in 2010 and to 18 percent in 2014.

In contrast to political institutions such as parliament, the president, the courts, and political parties, respondents have consistently higher trust in

Figure 10.1   Trust in Political Institutions

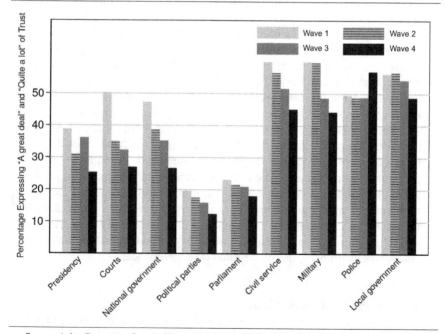

Source: Asian Barometer Survey, Waves 1–4 (2001–2003, 2006–2008, 2010–2012, 2014–2016).

nonpolitical institutions such as the police, civil service, and the military. But even these institutions have suffered an erosion of public trust. The most noticeable slide is trust in the courts, which were perceived as just as untrustworthy as the president and national government by the time we conducted the fourth wave of the survey in 2014. The judicial system has rapidly lost public trust probably for two reasons. First, many corruption scandals involving judges and prosecutors have come under public scrutiny. Second, the courts have been burdened with many politically explosive legal disputes that can easily provoke partisan backlash no matter the verdicts.

Our findings also show that the performance of elected national leaders affects trust in political institutions, and that once people withdraw their trust in political institutions it is difficult for the state to win back popular confidence. If we compare the administrations of Chen Shui-bian and Ma Ying-jeou, we find that the first noticeable fall in the trust level of political institutions occurred between Chen Shui-bian's first and second terms. This drop was probably due to the corruption scandal in 2006. Ma's approval rate suffered a nosedive after mounting criticism of his administration's handling of the response to Typhoon Morakot in 2009, and consequently the trust level in the president remained low throughout his two terms.

As Figure 10.2 indicates, the steep decline in the trust of the president happened across all age cohorts. But the sharpest drop was among the younger generation, those under age thirty-five. It happened twice in a strikingly similar pattern, between Chen Shui-bian's first and second terms, and between those of Ma Ying-jeou. This low level of institutional trust and the corresponding rise of distrust set the stage for the outbreak of the Sunflower Movement, targeted against the KMT-dominated legislature in 2014.

In many young democracies, the legitimacy of the democratic regime is often eroded by polarized conflict between contending parties.[17] The losing camp may not consent to the outcomes of democratic competition and may question the integrity of the electoral system as well as the openness and fairness of the entire system. The losing camp may also question the impartiality of the state bureaucracy, which could easily become susceptible to the influence of incumbent elected officials seeking to advance a partisan agenda. Our data suggest that Taiwan's young democracy is also suffering from the corrosive effects of the loser-winner syndrome, and show a familiar pattern of a dramatic swing of the pendulum in terms of political trust in the president after the two power rotations of 2000 and 2008. During both Chen Shui-bian's and Ma Ying-jeou's tenures, institutional trust among the losing camp plunged, while political trust among the voters of the winning camp surged. The most glaring contrast usually took place in the second term. For the measure of trust in the president, the gap between pro-DPP voters and pro-KMT voters was a huge 40-plus percent during Chen Shui-bian's second term (based on the second wave of the ABS). The swing of

Figure 10.2   Trust in Political Institutions by Age Cohort

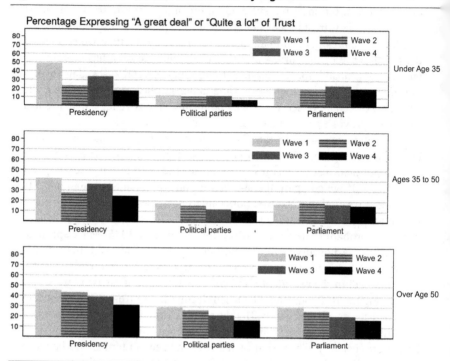

Source: Asian Barometer Survey, Waves 1–4 (2001–2003, 2006–2008, 2010–2012, 2014–2016).

the trust pendulum was just as dramatic when we conducted the fourth wave of the ABS in 2014. This is in part because the proportion of citizens who still identifed themselves as either pro-DPP or pro-KMT shrunk in the president's second term. These hardcore supporters exhibited a strong tendency to circle the wagons around their leader just when the incumbent was suffering a depletion of popular support. However, there was no such dramatic fluctuation when it comes to the measure of trust in the Legislative Yuan, Taiwan's parliament. Across the political spectrum, when the popular trust in the legislative body has already reached such a low level, it cannot go much further down.

As Taiwan has been deeply embroiled in a polarized conflict over national identity, it is not surprising to find that the fluctuation of trust in the president and the parliament was closely intertwined with people's ethnic self-identity as well as their preference over the divisive issue of unification versus independence. This became most evident when an incumbent president entered his second term with dwindling popular support. Only the most loyal supporters offered their unwavering trust on the basis of ideological solidarity. Our data provide empirical evidence for this dramatic contrast. During Chen Shui-bian's second term, the highest level of trust in the president came from people who identified themselves as "Taiwanese" (instead of "both Taiwanese and Chinese" or "Chinese") and from people who favored independence (over either "maintaining the status quo" or "unification"). Many loyalists did not withdraw their trust despite the outbreak of the corruption scandal. At the same time, the same group of people registered the lowest level of trust in parliament, which was still dominated by the KMT. We found a mirror image of this identity-based political divide during Ma Ying-jeou's second term. People who identified themselves as "Chinese" registered the highest level of trust in the president, followed by people with "both Taiwanese and Chinese" as their ethnic identity.

However, during Ma's second term, the KMT-controlled parliament lost the trust of even people with Chinese identity or favoring unification. This is probably because in the eyes of pro-unification loyalists, the KMT-controlled parliament under the influence of Speaker Wang Jin-pyng made too many concessions to the DPP.

Detachment from Authoritarianism

Democracy cannot be judged in isolation from other regimes. Richard Rose put forward the "Churchillian hypothesis," which suggests that we should cast democratic legitimacy in a comparative and competitive light.[18] If people who have personally experienced the shortcomings of both democratic and nondemocratic regimes opt in favor of the former, then the Churchillian hypothesis stands. If, however, those people prefer the nondemocratic alternatives to the imperfections of democracy, then the Churchillian hypothesis is false: democracy falls short of even the "lesser evil" threshold.

Therefore, support for democracy should be the opposite side of detachment from authoritarianism. Asian citizens' attitudes toward these two seemingly opposite political setups pose a great challenge to the existing democratic theories: Why do firm supporters of democracy still not let go of authoritarianism? Why does life under democracy fail to take people away from authoritarianism? Why are people resistant to some types of authoritarian rule but not others?

With the exception of Japan, all the countries in the region have recent experience of authoritarian rule. Taiwan and South Korea transitioned from authoritarianism during the third wave of democratization; prior to this they had been ruled by one-party or military authoritarian regimes. Mongolia was a client state of the Soviet Union and underwent its democratic revolution only in 1990. Indonesia and the Philippines were subject to strongman rule, and even after democratization remain trapped in low-quality and unstable democracy. Thailand has suffered many democratic breakdowns and is still trapped in a vicious cycle of recurring military coups. In addition, Malaysia, Singapore, and Hong Kong have been classified as electoral authoritarian regimes due to a failure to meet international standards for free and fair elections. In Cambodia, politics in the country is dominated by Prime Minister Hun Sen, who has been in power since a disputed election in 1998. Finally, Vietnam and China are authoritarian one-party regimes. We expect that genuine supporters of democracy will also reject these authoritarian alternatives. In the fourth wave of the ABS, we measured detachment from four types of authoritarian rule: strongman rule, military rule, rule by experts, and one-party rule.[19] Three of these types of authoritarian rule have been practiced in East Asia (strongman rule, rule by experts, and one-party rule), and while no country has been a pure technocracy, experts have wielded extensive policy influence under other types of regime, notably in the developmental states of Japan, South Korea, and Taiwan, and more recently in electoral authoritarian systems such as Malaysia and Singapore.

Although Taiwan has experienced authoritarian rule in the past, it has now been more than three decades since its democratic transition, and Taiwanese society is supposed to increasingly reject all authoritarian alternatives. Our findings support this strong optimism. If one applies the Churchillian hypothesis, democracy has clearly passed the "lesser evil" threshold in Taiwan, as it has proven more attractive than nondemocratic alternatives. The proportion of the people who express attachment to at least one of the four authoritarian alternatives has steadily declined, dwindling from around 16 percent to less than 10 percent (see Figure 10.3).

In order to present a clearer historical pattern of changes in detachment from authoritarianism and of the factors affecting these changes, we apply principal component analysis to extract one underlying common factor out of the four indicators of detachment from authoritarian alternatives. By looking at the three dotted average lines in Figure 10.4, which show the central tendency of three age cohorts, we can see that young people are more likely to object to authoritarian rule, while respondents aged fifty or older are relatively more likely to support authoritarian rule, across all four waves of the ABS. Moreover, the difference between different age groups is becoming increasingly wide. This means that authoritarian nostalgia has steadily dwindled with generational turnover. But it still lingers on among the older generation. Looking at the tendency of dispersion (i.e., the spread of the two tail-ends of the distribution), the distribution does not vary much across different waves of the ABS, which suggests that the hardening of authoritarian detachment took place across all age cohorts over time.

The relationship between level of education and detachment from authoritarianism is similar to that for age. Our data show that in all four survey waves, more-educated people are more likely to oppose authoritarian

Figure 10.3   Detachment from Authoritarianism in Taiwan

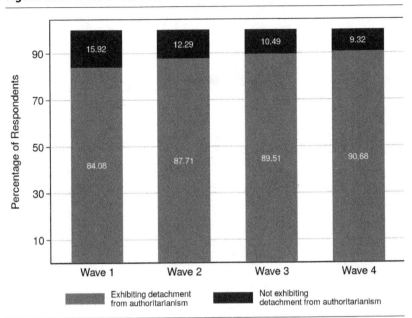

Source: Asian Barometer Survey, Waves 1–4 (2001–2003, 2006–2008, 2010–2012, 2014–2016).

rule, while respondents with a lower education are relatively more likely to embrace authoritarian rule. Moreover, the difference between different levels of education has become increasingly wide as people with higher education have steadily moved in the pro-democracy direction over time.

Looking at the tendency of dispersion, in the 2001 survey the differences in detachment from authoritarianism between respondents with different levels of education are not that obvious. However, in the following three waves of the ABS since 2006, there has been a marked shift due to level of education. Respondents with higher levels of education are more likely to oppose authoritarian rule with ever stronger resolve. This suggests that in Taiwan, living under a democratic regime has had the expected socializing effect by undermining the appeal of authoritarian alternatives. Another reason for the waning of the appeal of authoritarian alternatives is the fact that Taiwan's international environment has become more conducive to democratic development by making authoritarian rule an increasingly unrealistic and unthinkable option.

The fluctuation in the strength of authoritarian detachment across the partisan divide is very salient. Over time, the movement toward stronger objections to authoritarian alternatives has taken place in all three groups: pro-DPP,

Figure 10.4   Detachment from Authoritarianism by Age Cohort

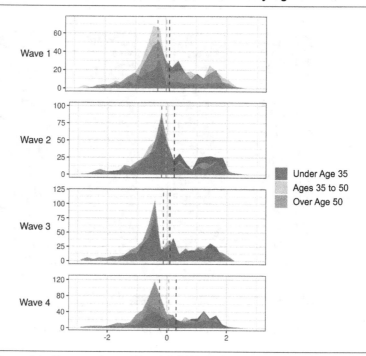

Source: Asian Barometer Survey, Waves 1–4 (2001–2003, 2006–2008, 2010–2012, 2014–2016).

pro-KMT, and nonpartisan. However, beneath this encouraging trend, there have been some counter-currents. Although the observed pattern of dispersion is very different from that of institutional trust, which has swung back and forth between pan-Blue and pan-Green supporters, partisanship has still left behind some visible footprints. During Chen Shui-bian's administration, there was little difference in detachment from authoritarian rule between pan-Blue and pan-Green supporters. However, during Ma Ying-jeou's administration, pan-Blue supporters and nonpartisans became relatively more likely to embrace authoritarian alternatives than pan-Green supporters. Our data suggest that there was a rise of nostalgia for authoritarianism among pan-Blue and nonpartisan voters after 2008. They became disillusioned after witnessing the ineffectiveness and indecisiveness of Ma Ying-jeou despite his strong popular mandate and the KMT's absolute parliamentary majority. Some pan-Blue voters lamented that the second power rotation in 2008 did not bring about the changes that many pan-Blue voters had expected. This subtle change in attitudes also manifested itself in the widening of dispersion within the pan-Blue and nonpartisan camps, with a visibly longer left tail-end (in the direction of a stronger tendency to embrace nondemocratic alternatives) than what was witnessed during the Chen Shui-bian era.

Support for Democracy

Over the years, the Asian Barometer Survey has employed a multifaceted approach to measuring popular support for democracy. The ABS instrument has taken into account David Easton's important distinction between diffuse support (support for the regime or constitutional order and the political community) and specific support (how members of a political community evaluate the political authorities).[20] Our instrument has also taken into consideration what Russell Dalton, and Michael Bratton and Robert Mattes, have called for to distinguish between instrumental support for democracy (support for a democratic regime based on the delivery of certain desirable goods) and intrinsic support for democracy (support for democracy as an end in itself).[21] Our support-for-democracy battery also represents an improvement over the World Values Survey, which measures both support for democracy as an ideal form of government and support for the democratic regime itself.[22] Our version of the direct measure employs four items that ask about democracy as a preferred political system, a desired political system, a suitable political system, and an efficacious system.[23]

In addition, the ABS also provides an indicator showing how ordinary citizens assess the progress of democratic development that the country has actually achieved. The respondents are asked to place the country's current state of democratic development on a 10-point scale, with 1 standing for completely undemocratic and 10 for completely democratic. This useful indicator gives us a sense of how the people evaluate the level of democratic development that the country has achieved and how far away the current system is from being a full democracy. We can combine this evaluation with the item asking respondents where they prefer the country to be on the same 10-point scale. This comparison shows whether the democratic demand meets the democratic supply (where the current political system is perceived to be).

Figure 10.5 shows that in the eyes of Taiwan's citizens, the mismatch between democratic demand and supply has steadily become greater. On the one hand, across the four waves of the ABS, Taiwanese voters have maintained rather modest expectations, expressing their wish (on average) that Taiwan's political system ought to be around 8 on a 10-point scale. This expectation has stayed nearly at the same level for the past fifteen years. Intuitively, this is akin to wanting Taiwan's democracy to be B+. On the other hand, their collective assessment of the country's young democracy has gradually but visibly declined, from a rating of 7.4 in 2002, to 7.0 in 2006, 6.7 in 2010, and 6.5 in 2014. This means that by 2014, many Taiwanese citizens believed that the real-world democratic system they were

Figure 10.5   Democratic Demand vs. Supply in Taiwan

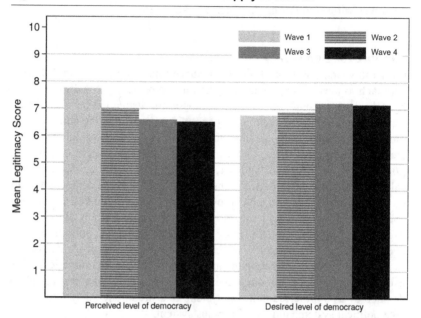

Source: Asian Barometer Survey, Waves 1–4 (2001–2003, 2006–2008, 2010–2012, 2014–2016).
Note: Scored on a 10-point scale with 1 meaning completely undemocratic and 10 meaning completely democratic.

experiencing was just barely above the passing grade (6.0) and that the country was moving further away from full democracy.

This rather discouraging evaluation of how much progress Taiwan's democratic development has made has probably led many Taiwanese to withhold their unequivocal embrace of democracy as the most preferable political system in all circumstances. On this measure of preference for democracy, Taiwan in 2014 registered the lowest level of unequivocal support for democracy among all East Asian young democracies.

The lowest level of popular belief in democracy as the most preferable system was observed during Chen Shui-bian's first term. In our 2002 survey, only 45 percent of respondents chose "democracy is always preferable under all circumstances," while the remaining 26 percent and 29 percent chose "sometimes an authoritarian regime can be more preferable" or "for people like me it does not matter," respectively. It is possible that the confusion and chaos that came with the historic rotation of power in 2000 and the protracted political gridlock under divided government dampened popular faith in democracy. Nevertheless, the popular preference for democracy recovered somewhat during Chen Shui-bian's second term as Taiwan's citizenry became more accustomed to democracy's unpredictable and conflict-ridden nature. The level of preference for democracy reached 52 percent, a temporary peak, after the second power rotation. But it suffered a visible slide again as voters were disappointed by a protracted record of sluggish performance no matter which party was in power or whether Taiwan had a divided or unified government. By this most widely used measure of democratic support, the legitimacy of Taiwan's democracy remains very fragile. Our survey data also suggest that many Taiwanese people have not completely abandoned authoritarianism and that there is still nostalgia for Taiwan's economic miracle and the more equitable income distribution and government efficiency that occurred under one-party authoritarian rule (see Figure 10.6).[24]

On two other measures of support for democracy, Taiwan comes out looking slightly better. On the question of whether democracy is suitable for Taiwan, the popular assessment has steadily but slowly improved, from 6.8 in 2002 (on a 10-point scale from completely unsuitable to completely suitable) to 7.2 in 2014 (see Figure 10.7). On the question of whether respondents believe that "democracy is capable of solving the problems the country is facing," 58 percent thought democracy was capable in 2002 (see Figure

Figure 10.6 Preference for Democracy in Taiwan

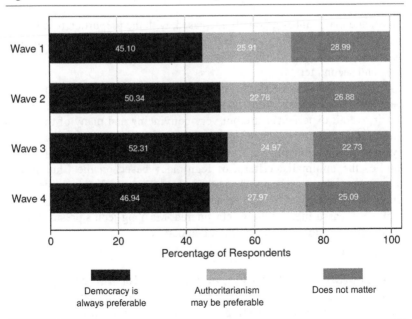

Democracy is always preferable	Authoritarianism may be preferable	Does not matter

Source: Asian Barometer Survey, Waves 1–4 (2001–2003, 2006–2008, 2010–2012, 2014–2016).

Figure 10.7   Suitability of Democracy for Taiwan

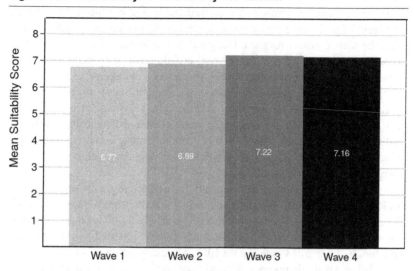

Source: Asian Barometer Survey, Waves 1–4 (2001–2003, 2006–2008, 2010–2012, 2014–2016).
Note: Scored on a 10-point scale with 1 meaning completely unsuitable and 10 meaning completely suitable.

10.8), and that number gradually increased, with the proportion reaching 65 percent during Ma's first term. But, in a familiar pattern witnessed before, this measure of democratic efficacy suffered a visible slide between Ma's first and second terms.

In sum, Taiwan's people have adjusted their belief in and evaluation of democracy on the basis of the real-world democracy they have experienced. Their overall experiences are not very convincing and many of them still harbor some reservation and doubt about the superiority of a democratic system of government. So, Taiwan's democracy looks resilient if one applies the minimalist criteria of legitimacy based on the Churchillian hypothesis, but the system looks not so robust if one applies multiple measures of direct support for democracy. For the latter, the trend lines do not look very reassuring. All things considered, Ma Ying-jeou's presidency did very little to restore popular faith in democracy.

Age, Education, Partisanship, and Support for Democracy

In order to detect patterns of change in support for democracy in Taiwan, and uncover the factors affecting these changes, we use principal component analysis to condense the four-item battery into one composite index.

Figure 10.8 Efficacy of Democracy in Taiwan

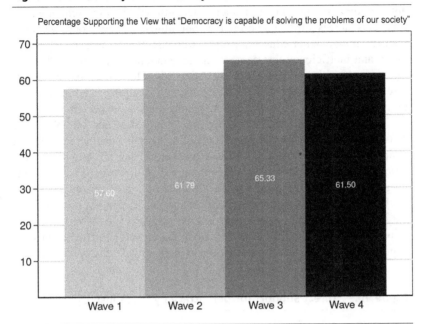

Percentage Supporting the View that "Democracy is capable of solving the problems of our society"

Source: Asian Barometer Survey, Waves 1–4 (2001–2003, 2006–2008, 2010–2012, 2014–2016).

Our data show that age is not associated with large variations in support for democracy. In addition, looking at the tendency of dispersion, the difference between survey waves is not large. This suggests that neither demographic trends nor generational turnover have had much impact on people's normative commitment to democracy. The driving force behind the downward trend observed in the two indicators, one on democratic rating and the other on preference for democracy, is the ineffective performance of elected leaders and the political system as a whole.

The results by education and age are similar initially, but subsequently show variation. Our data show that during the first term of Chen Shui-bian's administration, regardless of level of education, there was little variation in direct support for democracy. The distributions for the three levels of education are very similar. However, during the Ma administration, and especially during Ma's second term, more-educated respondents tended to show greater support for democracy while less-educated respondents had lower levels of support. Looking at the tendency of dispersion, the distribution varies considerably between different survey waves. In 2001, there was little variation according to level of education, but after 2006 differences began to emerge.

Also, we observe a visibly tilted left-hand tail (reaching the far end of the anti-democratic pole) among respondents with only a grade school education. This suggests that the normative commitment to democracy was more resilient among better-educated people, who could better tolerate the uncertainty and inefficiency that came with the democratic system. At the same time, people with lower levels of education might have been more prone to lose their faith in the superiority of democracy when the two historic rotations of power did not bring about the results they had expected.

Figure 10.9 shows that during the first term of the Chen administration, pan-Green supporters had higher levels of support for democracy than did nonpartisan or pan-Blue supporters. However, during the Ma administration, and especially during Ma's second term, the three camps steadily converged on an equilibrium of a moderate level of democratic support, with negligible difference between pan-Blue and pan-Green supporters and a very similar pattern of dispersion across the partisan aisle. After two rounds of power rotation, the followers of the pan-Green and pan-Blue camps had experienced the ups-and-downs of the electoral cycle and were probably

Figure 10.9   Direct Support for Democracy by Partisanship

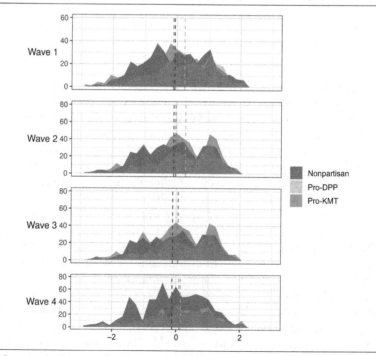

Source: Asian Barometer Survey, Waves 1–4 (2001–2003, 2006–2008, 2010–2012, 2014–2016).

equally disappointed by the political system's overall performance, albeit at different points in time and for different reasons.

The Cultural Foundation of Democratic Legitimacy

The Asian Barometer Survey also employed another battery of questions to probe further into the substance and depth of popular commitment to democracy. All items in this battery carry no mention of "democracy." They tap into respondents' value orientations toward some fundamental organizing principles of liberal democracy, namely political equality, popular accountability, political liberalism, horizontal accountability (checks-and-balances), and political pluralism. This battery is an important supplement to the direct measurement of people's support for democracy. Democratic values incorporate the basic principles of democratic governance; in other words, they tell us by what principles people believe a democracy should be run.[25] Sometimes, people's overt support for democracy might indicate only their expressive values—the way they want to be perceived by others, regardless of whether they understand what democracy really is or truly believe in its intrinsic values.[26] Therefore, the battery of democratic value orientation is an effective indirect measure of democratic legitimacy, one that in many ways is superior to direct measures.[27] Unlike direct measures, which calculate expressed support for democracy without asking what the citizen thinks democracy is, indirect measures look at the substance of political beliefs held by citizens as a way of assessing normative commitment to liberal democracy.

In what follows, we present the empirical results of a 9-item battery for measuring liberal democratic value orientation. There are two items measuring political equality: "Women should not be involved in politics as much as men," and "People with little or no education should have as much say in politics as highly educated people." A "disagree" answer to the first question or an "agree" answer to the second question indicates a pro-liberal democratic orientation. We use the following two items for measuring normative commitment to popular accountability: "Government leaders are like the head of a family; we should all follow their decisions," and "If we have political leaders who are morally upright, we can let them decide everything." For both items, a "disagree" answer points to a pro-liberal democratic orientation. There is only one indicator for measuring the acquisition of the value of political liberty: "The government should decide whether certain ideas should be allowed to be discussed in society." Again, it takes a "disagree" answer to reveal a pro-liberal democratic orientation. For measuring the normative commitment to the principle of horizontal accountability and checks-and-balances, we employ the following two items: "When judges decide important cases, they should accept the view of the executive branch," and "If the government is constantly checked [i.e., monitored and supervised] by the legislature, it cannot possibly accomplish great things." For both items, a "disagree" answer indicates a pro-liberal democratic orientation. Last, we tap the normative commitment to political pluralism with the following two indicators: "Harmony of the community will be disrupted if people organize lots of groups," and "If people have too many different ways of thinking, society will be chaotic." Again, respondents reveal their pro-liberal democratic orientation by registering disagreement with the two statements.

Our data (see Figure 10.10) show that the cultural foundation of Taiwan's democracy is robust and has gained strength steadily over the past fifteen years, albeit with movement along the five dimensions remaining very uneven and with each dimension following its own momentum. The growth of liberal democratic value orientations in Taiwan has taken the path of pattern-maintaining change. The acquisition of some liberal democratic values—such as political equality and popular accountability—was facilitated by these values' intrinsic compatibility with the traditional notion of good governance that Taiwanese society had inherited. There is overwhelming support for the principle of political equality. And the pro-

Figure 10.10 Democratic Value Orientations: Indirect Support for Democracy

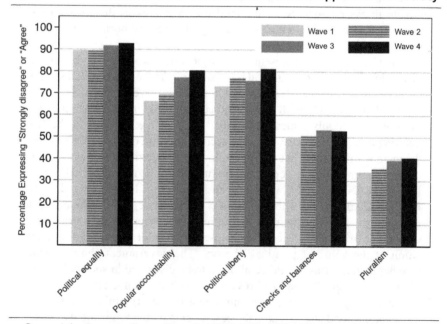

Source: Asian Barometer Survey, Waves 1–4 (2001–2003, 2006–2008, 2010–2012, 2014–2016).

portion of respondents embracing the principle of popular accountability has steadily risen, from 66 percent in 2002 to almost 81 percent in 2014. A great majority of Taiwanese people no longer believe in bestowing enormous power on patriarchic or charismatic leaders. The acquisition of the norm of political liberty has been propelled by the socializing effect of living under a liberal democratic regime. However, the acquisition of the principles of horizontal accountability (checks-and-balances) and political pluralism has turned out to be the slowest and most difficult due to both the lingering influence of traditional values in favor of a strong state and harmonious society, and people's growing disenchantment over the declining capability of the political system.

Overall, Taiwan's democracy rests on a robust cultural foundation. The normative commitment to many organizing principles—such as political equality, popular accountability, and political liberty—has been internalized by the great majority of Taiwan's citizenry. There is still some lingering resistance to embracing the principles of horizontal accountability and political pluralism. Nevertheless, the trend lines are basically upward, although they started from a rather low baseline and have moved upward at a rather slow pace.

Conclusion

In assessing the consolidation of Taiwan's democracy on the basis of how citizens orient themselves toward the political system, we have uncovered some worrisome trends but also spotted some positive signs. The most reassuring empirical findings lie in the long-term evolution of people's political values. The normative commitment to many organizing principles—such as political equality, popular accountability, and political liberty—has steadily become internalized by the great majority of Taiwan's citizenry. This robust cultural foundation should provide Taiwan with a strong defense against the threat of democratic deconsolidation.

The most alarming trend is the rapid depletion of public trust in some key democratic institutions, such as the president, the central government, the legislature (parliament), and political parties. By the time of Ma Yingjeou's second term, none of these institutions enjoyed a trust level above 30 percent. Furthermore, Taiwan's young democracy has also suffered from the corrosive effects of the loser-winner syndrome. The recurring pattern of dramatic swings of the pendulum in terms of political trust in the president and legislature after each rotation of power has done a lot of damage to the foundational legitimacy of the democratic regime.

The institutions that constitute the permanent components of the state apparatus still enjoy substantially higher levels of trust. But even these institutions, which are supposed to be above partisan politics, have also suffered from the poisonous effects of political polarization, which has made the impartiality of the state apparatus increasingly difficult to sustain. The most worrisome trend is the steep drop of public confidence in the courts, which are supposed to be the arbitrators of last resort in resolving political conflicts when all the existing conflict-resolution mechanisms in a democracy fail. Given this sagging public trust, it is an open question whether the courts would be able to decisively resolve a high-stakes conflict triggered by a disputed election or a constitutional confrontation between the executive and the legislative branches. Another worrisome trend is that the popular assessment of the overall quality of Taiwan's democracy is heading steadily downward. In the eyes of citizens, Taiwan's real-world democracy is moving further away from a full democracy, and the gap between the supply of and demand for democracy has widened. This perception of slow democratic backsliding has probably led many among Taiwan's electorate to withhold their unequivocal embrace of democracy as the most preferable political system in all circumstances. For this widely used measure of the preference for democracy, Taiwan in 2014 registered the lowest level of unequivocal support for democracy among all the young East Asian democracies.

Although Taiwan scores high on the detachment from authoritarianism indicator, this is probably a result of the residual nostalgia for authoritarian rule going dormant rather than evaporating. The nostalgia for Taiwan's economic miracle and the more equitable income distribution, and seemingly higher government efficiency that occurred under one-party authoritarian rule is still lurking in the background when people evaluate the performance of present-day democracy, which has failed to live up to people's high expectations despite three rotations of power. Ma Ying-jeou's presidency did not greatly undermine support for democracy, but his administration did not do much to restore popular faith in the superiority of democracy, either, despite his convincing electoral victory and the KMT's legislative majority.

Some of the long-term factors that Robert Foa and Yascha Mounk have identified as contributing to worrisome signs of democratic deconsolidation in established Western democracies also are present in Taiwan.[28] First, with a depletion of public trust in political parties, we detect a simmering popular backlash against the political establishment. The numbers of both DPP and KMT party identifiers have declined in recent years, while there is growing popular interest in "nonmainstream" alternatives exemplified by the meteoric rise of Ko Wen-je, who as a total novice in politics and without party affiliation delivered a stunning victory over his KMT opponent in the Taipei mayoral race of 2014. He is also now widely regarded as the most popular politician island-wide and potentially a strong contender in the 2024 presidential race. This anti-establishment sentiment could trigger a political earthquake in Taiwan's two-party system.

Next, resentment against the widening income and wealth gap is becoming more intense, especially among the millennial generation. The issue of redistributive justice could become a source of political rupture in the future. The strong resistance to advance cross-Strait economic integration has been propelled not only by Taiwanese nationalism and the growing apprehension about the political consequences of economic dependency but also by the local manifestation of grassroots anti-globalization populism.

Taiwan also has its fair share of native nationalism, which could turn anti-democratic if the long-running political polarization over cross-Strait relations escalates. It is too early to tell what will be the long-term political legacy of the Sunflower Movement, which crippled arguably the most important institution in a representative democracy for almost a month and substantially derailed the presidency of democratically elected Ma Ying-jeou for the remaining two years of his second term.

Finally, Taiwan's democracy, much like its counterparts in the West, has repeatedly failed to convince its citizens that the system can eventually break the cycle of great expectations becoming great disappointments. Following the pattern of Chen Shui-bian's eight years in office, Ma Ying-jeou started his presidency with high expectations, which soon gave way to disillusion and disappointment. Unfortunately, a similar downward spiral of declining popular support and widespread disillusionment is currently also dragging down Tsai Ing-wen's political fortunes with even greater velocity.

Notes

1. Global Views Monthy Poll Center, "First Poll After Ma Ying-jeou's Inauguration, 66.4% Have Confidence in Ma Ying-jeou," *Global Views Monthly*, June 1, 2008, https://www.gvm.com.tw/article/12470.

2. Chris Wang, "Survey Reflects Ma's Falling Popularity," *Taipei Times*, May 11, 2012, http://www.taipeitimes.com/News/front/archives/2012/05/11/2003532523.

3. TVBS Poll Center, "Ma Ying-jeou's Approval Ratings over Eight Years," May 2016, https://cc.tvbs.com.tw/portal/file/poll_center/2017/20170602/0505041.pdf.

4. Liberty Times, "Ma Ying-jeou's Approval Rating only 9.2%," *Liberty Times*, September 15, 2013, https://news.ltn.com.tw/news/politics/breakingnews/869716.

5. TVBS Poll Center, "Ma Ying-jeou's Approval Ratings over Eight Years," May 2016, https://cc.tvbs.com.tw/portal/file/poll_center/2017/20170602/0505041.pdf.

6. Huntington, *The Third Wave*.

7. Chang and Chu, "Democratization in East Asian in Comparative Perspective."

8. Schedler, "What Is Democratic Consolidation?"

9. Przeworski et al., "What Makes Democracies Endure?"

10. Linz and Stepan, *Problems of Democratic Transition and Consolidation*.

11. Mishler and Rose, "Learning and Re-Learning Regime Support."

12. Norris, *Democratic Deficit*.

13. Dalton, *Democratic Challenges, Democratic Choices;* Park and Chang, "Regime Performance and Democratic Legitimacy."

14. Norris, "Introduction: The Growth of Critical Citizens."

15. Booth and Seligson, *The Legitimacy Puzzle in Latin America.*

16. Chang, Chu, and Park, "Authoritarian Nostalgia in Asia."

17. Anderson, *Loser's Consent.*

18. Rose, Mishler, and Haerpfer, *Democracy and Its Alternatives.*

19. On detachment from authoritarianism, the ABS third wave asks respondents if they agree with the following statements: "We should get rid of parliament and elections and have a strong leader decide things." "Only one political party should be allowed to stand for election and hold office." "The army (military) should come in to govern the country." "We should get rid of elections and parliaments and have experts make decisions on behalf of the people." Reponses are given on a four-point scale, which we code into positive and negative answers.

20. Easton, *A Systems Analysis of Public Life;* Easton, "A Re-Assessment of the Concept of Political Support."

21. Dalton, *Democratic Challenges, Democratic Choices;* Bratton and Mattes, "Support for Democracy in Africa"

22. Klingemann, "Mapping Political Support in the 1990s," pp. 35–36.

23. Shin, "Democratization"; Chu et al., *How East Asians View Democracy;* Chu and Huang, "The Meanings of Democracy."

24. Chang, Chu, and Park, "Authoritarian Nostalgia in Asia."

25. Thomassen, "Democracy Values."

26. Chu and Huang, "The Meanings of Democracy."

27. Schedler and Sarsfield, "Democrats with Adjectives."

28. Foa and Mounk, "The Democratic Disconnect"; Foa and Mounk, "The Signs of Deconsolidation." See also Plattner, "Liberal Democracy's Fading Allure."

11

Trends in Public Opinion

Ching-hsin Yu

Taiwan has frequently been praised as a successful democratic model when compared with other third-wave democracies.[1] Regular and peaceful power alternations have made Taiwan a consolidated democracy. Yet behind these accomplishments, challenges remain. An increasingly intense partisan competition for power, rising tension among ethnic (and sub-ethnic) groups, and a deep divide over national identity have emerged since democratization, and these continue to be the core issues in Taiwan's political development.

This chapter begins with a discussion of people's long-term party affiliations, self-identity, and preferences on the topic of unification versus independence. The two major political parties, the Kuomintang (KMT) and the Democratic Progressive Party (DPP), have jointly consolidated a two-party system in Taiwan. Unfortunately, instead of policy debates, the differences in the parties' ideologies and stances on the issue of unification versus independence drive party competition. This situation is further complicated by the increase in Taiwanese identity that penetrates the parties' social bases, and the impact of this identity on preferences for unification versus independence. The experience with alternation of power, by contrast, has had less influence than we might expect on the development of Taiwanese identity and on preferences for unification versus independence. For instance, during the Ma years (2008–2016), neither Chinese identity nor pro-China attitudes increased among Taiwanese citizens, despite the ruling KMT's more China-friendly positions and policies. Longitudinal survey results suggest that the increase in Taiwanese identity over the Ma years has more to do with the long-term consequences of Taiwan's democratization than with which party is in power. This increase in Taiwanese identity should not necessarily be interpreted as an increase in support for independence, either, though the two measures are correlated.

Trends in Party Identification: A Changing Party System

The concept of party identification refers to a long-term psychological attachment to, or affinity for, a specific political party.[2] Examining the changes in and continuities of the electorate's party identification is crucial to understanding how Taiwan's party system operates.[3] As indicated in Figure 11.1, a plurality of Taiwanese do not identify with a specific political party. Since 2000, approximately 40 percent of Taiwanese indicated they had no affinity with any political party; however, these nonpartisans are not necessarily inactive in politics, and many vote in elections. This situation is partly responsible for the relatively high voter turnout and the significant swings that can occur in Taiwan's party system from election to election.

In addition to the nonpartisans, the KMT had comparatively more partisans than the other parties before 2000, when approximately 25 to 33 percent

Figure 11.1   Party Identification in Taiwan, 1994–2016

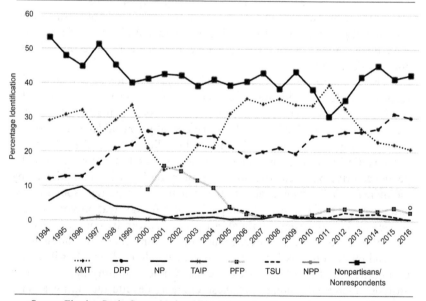

Source: Election Study Center, National Chengchi University.
Note: DPP = Democratic Progressive Party, KMT = Kuomintang, NP = New Party, NPP = New Power Party, PFP = People First Party, TAIP = Taiwan Independence Party, TSU = Taiwan Solidarity Union.

of people identified with it. Partisan affinity for the KMT dropped sharply after 2000, when it lost the presidential election, and it fell to a historic low in party identification until 2005, when Ma Ying-jeou became the party's chairman. Under Ma's leadership, the KMT gradually won back popular support between 2005 and 2011, but its popularity began to decline again after 2011, and it has continued since then to suffer from a decline in partisans as a share of the overall electorate. Compared with the KMT, the DPP started with a relatively small base of partisan identifiers in the 1990s, which grew slowly until its candidate won the presidential election of 2000. With the collapse in identification with the KMT, DPP partisans became the biggest group in the electorate for several years. However, in 2005 the KMT recovered its position as the party with the largest number of identifiers, which it maintained for almost the next decade, while DPP partisans dropped below 20 percent of the electorate until 2010, when its popularity gradually started to recover. In 2013, the DPP's partisan support base grew large enough to overtake the KMT's again, contributing to its victory in the presidential election of 2016.

Minor parties also have played a significant role in Taiwan. The China-friendly and mainlander-dominated New Party was created by former KMT members over ideological disputes in 1993, undermining the KMT's predominance in the party system, and the People First Party (PFP) and the Taiwan Solidarity Union (TSU) both split from the KMT after the 2000 presidential election. Similar to the New Party in the 1990s, the PFP was a reform-oriented party and opposed KMT leader Lee Teng-hui's tolerance of Taiwanese independence. By contrast, the TSU was formed after the 2000 presidential election under Lee's leadership. Unlike the PFP, the TSU supported independence and opposed the idea of unification with China. The PFP and the TSU performed well in the 2001 and 2004 legislative elections, but their popularity began to fade in the late 2000s. After the Sunflower Movement in 2014, some of the participants in those protests formed the New Power Party (NPP), which focused on social reform and adopted a more hostile stance against the People's Republic of China (PRC). This platform helped the party surpass the New Party, PFP, and TSU in the 2016 legislative election, and it became the third-largest party in the Legislative Yuan.

Since the 2000 election, Taiwan's party system has developed into a "two-party-plus" system, with the KMT and DPP joined by several minor parties. This party system has mainly evolved along with and been shaped by the dynamics of cross-Strait issues: the KMT, New Party, and PFP share a pro-unification platform, while the DPP, TSU, and NPP have consistently supported Taiwan's independence. This "China issue" has driven the creation of two-camp coalitional politics in Taiwan: the pro-unification pan-Blue camp includes the KMT, New Party, and PFP; the pro-independence pan-Green camp includes the DPP, TSU, and NPP.

The KMT's rising appeal in the mid-2000s rejuvenated its electoral prospects and made it the favorite to win the 2008 presidential election. That election gave the party control of both the executive and legislative branches, which it retained in 2012. But this favorable political aura disappeared soon after Ma won a second term, and his signature cross-Strait policy was strongly challenged by Taiwanese society. A series of controversial events and social movements, including the Dapu land exproporiation incident in Miaoli in 2010, the death of military conscript Hung Chungchiu in July 2013, the KMT's internal feud between Ma and Legislative Yuan speaker Wang Jin-pyng that broke into the open in September 2013, and the Sunflower Movement in March 2014 all further eroded the KMT's popularity.[4] The DPP benefited from the declining popularity of the Ma administration and regained power in the presidential election of 2016. The DPP had previously experienced its own devastating electoral defeat in the presidential election of 2008, when Ma received more than 58 percent of the popular vote, suggesting how quickly political fortunes can change in Taiwan's party system.

Trends in Preferences for Unification vs. Independence: Dominance of the Status Quo

Taiwan independence versus unification with the mainland (sometimes shortened to the "TI-UM issue") has been a contentious topic in Taiwan's domestic politics and cross-Strait relations for decades.[5] Positions on Taiwan's relationship with the People's Republic of China have developed dynamically along with the development of Taiwan's party politics, in particular the political competition between the pro-unification and pro-independence camps, and the distinct platforms of parties within those camps. The TI-UM issue has turned into the most crucial partisan divide in Taiwanese politics. Party competition, in turn, has increased the complexity of the reasoning behind people's preferences for unification, independence, or maintaining the status quo. Notably, the broad trends show that these preferences have been relatively stable over the long term, but when examined in detail, subtle but important changes can be observed in each group.

As Figure 11.2 indicates, the option to "maintain the status quo, decide at later date" has been the most widely held preference since the mid-1990s, followed by "maintain the status quo indefinitely." Together, these pro–status quo positions are favored by the majority of all Taiwanese. Next are "maintain status quo, move toward independence" and "maintain status quo, move toward unification." These positions are in competition with each other. For the first fifteen years after democratization, "maintain status quo, move toward unification" had more support than "maintain status quo, move toward independence"; yet the latter took the lead in 2003. The posi-

Figure 11.2 Preference for Unification vs. Independence in Taiwan, 1994–2016

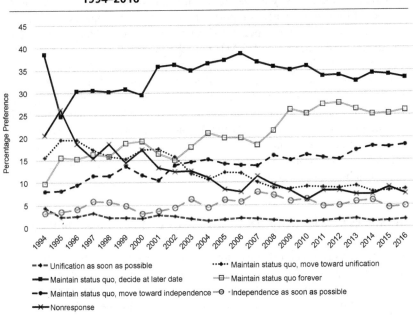

Source: Election Study Center, National Chengchi University.

tions "independence as soon as possible" and "unification as soon as possible" are comparatively less often chosen by Taiwan's people, and have consistently been favored by less than 10 percent of all respondents. In addition, the non-response rate was relatively high in the early surveys but has gradually declined, suggesting the TI-UM question is no longer a difficult one for the majority of Taiwanese to answer.

These distributions clearly show the preferences of Taiwanese for unification versus independence: for now, the majority of people would prefer to maintain the status quo and neither unify with China nor declare independence. Neither of the totals of the two pro-unification items ("maintain status quo, move toward unification" and "unification as soon as possible") or the totals of the two pro-independence items ("maintain status quo, move toward independence" and "independence as soon as possible") is very large. Instead of choosing either unification or independence, the majority tends to support maintaining the status quo and deciding Taiwan's future at a later date, or maintaining the status quo forever: over the past two decades, survey respondents on average chose one of these two items approximately 55 percent of the time.

Judging from these survey data, the status quo appears to be a desirable situation for the majority of people in Taiwan in comparison with the alternatives. More importantly, support for the status quo appears to be quite stable and not affected much by short-term political changes, as it has remained similar across both KMT and DPP governments. When the KMT was in power—that is, before 2000 and between 2008 and 2016—support for unification did not increase significantly. Notably, there was a subtle, gradual increase in support for maintaining the status quo, with independence later, when the KMT was in power between 2008 and 2016. This finding suggests that the policies of the Ma administration did not lead to an increase in support for unification. This gradual decline in the popularity of unification has continued for two decades, regardless of which political party has been in power in Taiwan.

Trends in Self-Identity: The Supremacy of Taiwanese Identity

The development of Taiwanese self-identity has been extensively studied.[6] Either as a causal factor that explains political orientations and behavior, or as an outcome shaped by various other socioeconomic and historical variables, the importance of self-identity to politics in Taiwan is obvious.

The evolution of the self-identity of Taiwanese has been closely related to Taiwan's democratic transition. Democratization ensured full political rights for the once politically underrepresented "native" Taiwanese, also known as *benshengren* ("local provincials"), whose ancestors lived in Taiwan before 1945, in contrast to mainlanders (*waishengren*) who emigrated with the KMT from mainland China after 1945 and initially dominated the political system. As the majority of *benshengren* enjoyed increasing opportunities to participate in politics, it was only natural that identity-related issues would become more salient. In addition, the "retake the mainland" mission advocated by the KMT regime during the authoritarian period appeared increasingly unrealistic, and by the time of the transition to democracy, devotion to the vision of a unified China under ROC rule had faded away. Instead, more public attention was directed toward a vision of a separate future for Taiwan, and the preexisting connections between Taiwan and mainland China were no longer taken for granted. Meanwhile, the sharp differences between Taiwan's new democracy and the authoritarian political system in the PRC further highlighted the impracticality of political integration between the two sides in the near future. For many of Taiwan's people, China is different from Taiwan in many respects, and the identification with the island of Taiwan, geographically, culturally, and politically, is a matter of course.

Since the early 1990s, Taiwanese have been regularly asked in surveys how they self-identify: as Taiwanese, Chinese, or both? The general trends in these self-identity surveys over the past two decades are documented in Figure 11.3. The most discernible trend is the strong growth of exclusive Taiwanese identity. Although it was second to dual Taiwanese-Chinese identity before 2000, the share of respondents expressing an exclusive Taiwanese identity increased significantly to the point where it drew even with dual identity in 2007, at approximately 45 percent of all Taiwanese. It then surpassed dual identity and continued to increase steadily, rising to as high as 60 percent in 2014, and it now is expressed by a clear majority of Taiwan's people. Before 2000, most people identified as both Taiwanese and Chinese, but these dual identifiers gradually declined as a share of the population, and in 2007 they were surpassed for the first time by those identifying exclusively as Taiwanese. The subsequent decline in dual identity between 2007 and 2014 is apparent in the data, though this decline appears to have paused, if not reversed, in recent years—an inflection point that is probably temporary but worth keeping an eye on in the future.

As for exclusive Chinese identity, it continuously declined during the same period: approximately 20 percent of all respondents identified only as Chinese before 1996, but less than 10 percent did after 2001, and less than 5 percent did in 2008. During the Ma years between 2008 and 2016, the

Figure 11.3   Self-Identity in Taiwan, 1994–2016

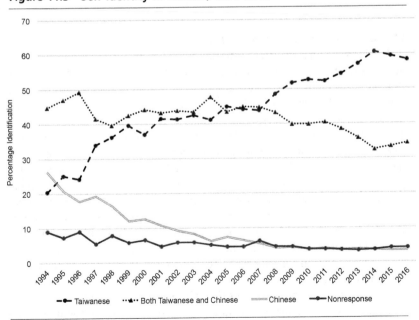

Source: Election Study Center, National Chengchi University.

share of people identifying exclusively as Chinese did not change much, and remained a very small minority.

Taiwanese identity has shown robust strength in the past two decades. It grew rapidly between 1996 and 2000, when the KMT was in power; continued to grow between 2000 and 2008, though more gradually, when the DPP was in power; and grew even stronger between 2008 and 2016, when the KMT returned to power. It appears that the political party in power has had only a limited effect, if any, on the increase in Taiwanese identity over the past twenty years. It is true that the DPP has regularly used the identity issue to challenge the KMT, and that Taiwanese identity has been either implicitly or explicitly part of the DPP's "brand" and therefore a political asset. Nonetheless, during the more China-friendly KMT government of the Ma era, Taiwanese identity still grew rapidly. To some extent, then, Taiwanese identity now cuts across party lines. It is also reasonable to suggest that the concept of Taiwanese identity, as understood by Taiwan's people, now simply refers to the broadly defined group of "people who live in Taiwan," including mainlanders who arrived with the KMT regime and their descendants, and even more recent immigrants, rather than reflecting the older *benshengren* connotation. Identifying exclusively as Taiwanese might still carry some political implications, but it also increasingly reflects the idea that the people of the island have become socialized to a common culture, set of languages, lifestyle, value system, and so forth.

Moderate Associations Between Self-Identity and Political Parties

As we saw in the previous section, Taiwanese self-identity has increased dramatically in the past two decades. The political implications of this growth are of special importance, particularly if we look at the effects across the Green-Blue divide rather than at individual parties.[7] As Figure 11.4A shows, since the mid-1990s, Taiwanese identifiers have been more likely to call themselves either pan-Green supporters or nonpartisans. The national identity and party camp identity variables have tracked one another fairly closely across time. As early as the late 1990s, the plurality of respondents who identified as exclusively Taiwanese also supported the pan-Green camp. Identification with the pan-Green camp among this group peaked at more than 48 percent in 2003, and then declined substantially until 2009 before bouncing back in 2010. In 2015, support was as high as 48 percent again, making affinity for the pan-Green camp the most common one among Taiwanese identifiers.

Nonpartisan Taiwanese identifiers also show ups-and-downs, and these fluctuations echo the increases and decreases of identification with the pan-Green camp. As we might expect, Taiwanese identifiers were least likely to

Figure 11.4 Self-Identity and Partisan Support in Taiwan, 1994–2016

A   Taiwanese Identifiers and Partisan Support

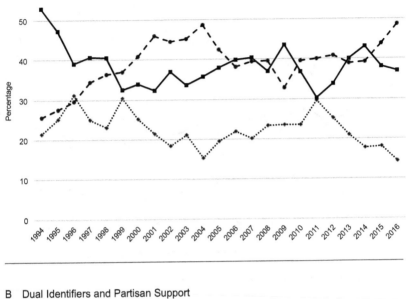

B   Dual Identifiers and Partisan Support

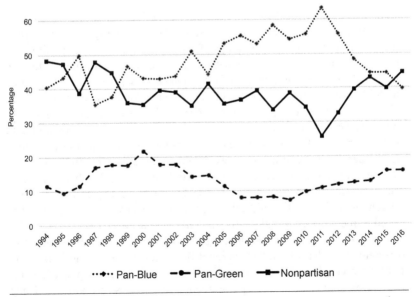

continues

Figure 11.4   Continued

C   Chinese Identifiers and Partisan Support

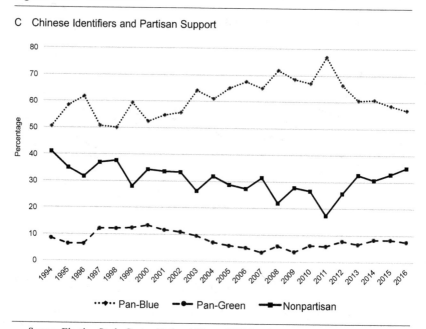

Source: Election Study Center, National Chengchi University.

express an affinity for the pan-Blue camp, but this group is still significant, and changes in its size have been closely related to changes in the relative political fortunes of the two camps. This share hit a low of only about 15 percent in 2004 when Chen Shui-bian won reelection, but then gradually increased to almost 30 percent of all Taiwanese identifiers in 2011, when the KMT was dominant. The trend then reversed again, and identification with the pan-Blue camp has since decreased sharply among this group, falling to an all-time low of 14 percent in 2016. Obviously, the dominant partisan affinity of Taiwanese identifiers has been with the pan-Green camp, not the pan-Blue. Nonetheless, these data do not indicate that the connection between Taiwanese identifiers and the pan-Green camp has been unbreakable. The share of pan-Green partisans among this group fell over fifteen percentage points in the mid-2000s, probably because the ruling DPP had failed to meet the expectations of Taiwanese identifiers.

As Figure 11.4B shows, dual identifiers' partisan affinity is markedly different from that of Taiwanese identifiers. Respondents who indicated a dual national identity were more likely to call themselves pan-Blue supporters or nonpartisans than pan-Green supporters. The majority of dual identifiers expressed an affinity for the pan-Blue camp between 2005 and

2013, but by 2014 they were just as likely to claim to be nonpartisan. Support for the pan-Green camp from dual identifiers was moderate and relatively stable over the past twenty years. It increased to as high as 20 percent in 2000, but dropped to as low as 8 percent between 2006 and 2010, before rising a bit again to 15 percent in 2016.

Most Chinese identifiers have consistently supported the pan-Blue camp ever since the mid-1990s. As shown in Figure 11.4C, the amount of support among this group was most impressive between 2008 and 2012, with 65 to 77 percent of dual identifiers expressing an affinity for the pan-Blue camp. Nonetheless, the share of pan-Blue partisans among this group also trended downward after 2012. Most Chinese identifiers who did not express a pan-Blue affinity claimed they were nonpartisan, and the two categories have moved in opposite directions over the years: as the share of pan-Blues has risen, the share of nonpartisans has fallen, and vice versa. As we might expect, pan-Green camp partisans have been much rarer among Chinese identifiers, at roughly 10 percent over the long term.

The long-term correlations between national self-identity and partisan affinity make clear that Taiwanese identifiers have tended to support the pan-Green rather than the pan-Blue camp. Taiwanese identity has grown so much in recent years that a majority of all adults now identify this way, more than both the dual and Chinese identity categories combined. Recognizing this pattern helps us to decode the growth of pan-Green partisans, especially those who support the DPP. Although a considerable number of Taiwanese identifiers have expressed an affinity for the pan-Blue camp, this share has not been stable over time, and it declined significantly during Ma Ying-jeou's second term. Dual identifiers, in contrast, generally have preferred pan-Blue to pan-Green; however, beginning in 2011, pan-Blue affinity declined among this group as well, while pan-Green affinity increased and grew to over 15 percent in 2016. The strongest pan-Blue supporters are those whose national identity is exclusively Chinese, but their share of the overall electorate is now too small to significantly boost support for pan-Blue parties in elections.

These public opinion data are consistent with the idea that the pan-Green camp has gradually gained the upper hand in the electorate due to rising Taiwanese identity. But the electoral story is actually more complicated than that. The pan-Blue camp, particularly the KMT, enjoyed strong popular support before the mid-1990s, but affinity for the pan-Blues weakened thereafter as Taiwanese identity grew. The KMT's return to power in 2008 occurred despite this increase, and appears linked instead to rising pan-Blue partisanship across the electorate. Even 20 percent of Taiwanese identifiers that year also identified with the pan-Blue camp. In fact, from 2004 to 2008, identification with the pan-Blue camp increased by 8 to 10 percent in all three national identity categories: Taiwanese, dual, and Chinese. But this increase did not last long. From 2012 to 2016, pan-Blue partisanship declined by roughly 15 percent across the board, and the KMT lost power again in 2016.

Support for the Status Quo Cuts Across Party Lines

Preferences for unification versus independence are a policy choice about the overall political arrangement across the Taiwan Strait. This policy choice has naturally been affected in the long term by the differing stances advocated by the KMT and DPP. The KMT was originally a pro-unification party, and the DPP a pro-independence party; however, since democratization, neither of these outcomes has appeared feasible or likely in the near future. Consequently, the intermediate position between these two extremes, maintaining the "status quo," has emerged as a pragmatic compromise and is embraced by many people who do not support, or are unwilling to accept the potential costs associated with, the realization of either unification or independence. Since the transition to democracy, maintaining the "status quo" has therefore provided a convenient political position between unification and independence.

After facing overwhelming public support for maintaining the status quo, the major political parties both moderated their official positions on cross-Strait policy but approached this idea differently in their electoral campaigns. For example, the purpose of the "new middle way" proposed by the DPP's 2000 presidential candidate, Chen Shui-bian, was to persuade the electorate that he and the DPP would not take any action toward Taiwanese independence. Similarly, in 2008, the KMT's Ma Ying-jeou put forward his "three no's" declaration: "no unification, no independence, and no use of force" to assure the electorate that he and the KMT would try their best to maintain the status quo without advancing unification or independence. These efforts continued when the DPP's 2016 presidential candidate, Tsai Ing-wen, announced her cross-Strait stance of "maintaining the status quo" during her campaign. Consequently, the term "status quo" has had a special political interpretation in Taiwan. Although definitions of the status quo may differ among Taiwan's people, the term is sufficiently ambiguous to allow the political parties some flexibility in elaborating their cross-Strait policies.

Figure 11.5 shows the linkage between preferences on the TI-UM issue and party identification. It is clear that most respondents who hold preferences for "unification as soon as possible" and "maintaining the status quo and unification later" have also tended to identify with with the pan-Blue camp. Affinity for the pan-Blues among this group ranged from 50 to 60 percent between 1997 and 2004, surged after 2005, continued to as high as 71 percent in 2011, and then declined, reaching a low of 47 percent in 2016. Most pro-unificationists who do not identify with the pan-Blue camp are nonpartisans. With the exception of 2011, between 25 and 35 percent

Figure 11.5 Preference for Unification vs. Independence and Partisan Support in Taiwan, 1994–2016

A Preference for Unification and Partisan Support

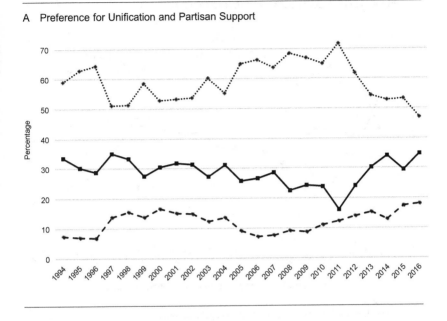

B Preference for Status Quo and Partisan Support

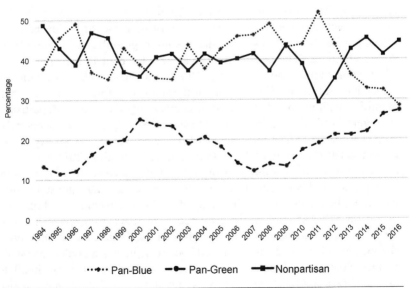

····◆··· Pan-Blue   ─●─ Pan-Green   ─■─ Nonpartisan

continues

Figure 11.5   Continued

C   Preference for Independence and Partisan Support

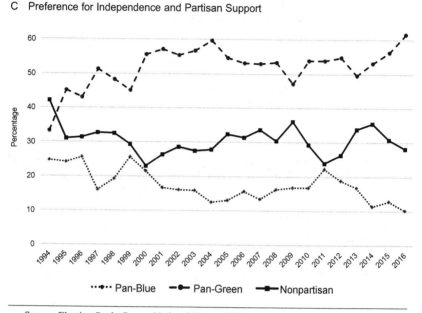

···◆··· Pan-Blue   ●Pan-Green   ■Nonpartisan

Source: Election Study Center, National Chengchi University.

have consistently expressed no party affiliation among this group. As we might expect, few people who support unification identify with the pan-Green parties. Nevertheless, this share is not negligible, and it more than doubled between 2006 and 2016, from about 7 to about 18 percent.

Among people who chose one of the status quo options, "maintain the status quo, decide later" or "maintain the status quo forever," most either identified with the pan-Blue camp or claimed that they were nonpartisan. As Figure 11.5B shows, for most of the survey period, status quo supporters who expressed an affinity for the pan-Blue camp and those who expressed no partisan affinity were each 35–45 percent of the total. In 2011, there was a relative spike in pan-Blue partisans, along with a corresponding drop in nonpartisans, but beginning in 2012, fewer and fewer status quo supporters have identified with the pan-Blue camp, dropping to a record low of only 28 percent in 2016. Affinity for the pan-Green camp among this group has historically been much lower; it hit a high of about 25 percent in 2000, then slumped to as low as 12 percent in 2007 before beginning a gradual rebound. In a development with potentially long-term political implications, in 2016 the pan-Green partisans were nearly even with the pan-Blues among status quo supporters for the first time.

As we might expect, most people who express support for the position "maintain the status quo, move toward independence" or "independence as soon as possible" also identify themselves as pan-Green supporters. As Figure 11.5C shows, with the exception of 2009 and 2013, at least half of all independence supporters have expressed an affinity with the pan-Green camp ever since 2000. In Ma Ying-jeou's second term this share steadily increased to over 60 percent. On average, about 30 percent claimed to be nonpartisan over the previous two decades. It may be somewhat surprising to see that a small but still significant share of independence supporters has consistently identified with the pan-Blue camp. This share dropped from as high as 25 percent in 1999 to as low as 12 percent in 2004, but it has never fallen below 10 percent. In fact, during the Ma era, affinity for the pan-Blue camp actually increased at first among this group, rising to 22 percent of all independence supporters by 2011. From 2012 to 2016, however, identification with the pan-Blues dropped by half, and at the end of Ma's term it was at a record low.

Overall, the survey data presented in Figure 11.5 show a close connection between preferences on the TI-UM issue, on the one hand, and partisanship on the other. In particular, supporters of unification and independence clearly have different partisan tendencies: the pro-unification people tend to be pro-pan-Blue, and the pro-independence people tend to be pro–pan-Green. However, toward the end of the Ma era, identification with pan-Blue parties declined moderately even among pro-unificationists, while identification with pan-Green parties gradually increased among the pro-independence people. Beginning in 2012, the pan-Blue camp suffered declines among supporters of all three positions. The most dramatic decline, however, was among supporters of the status quo. In 2011, these people were 2.5 times more likely to identify with the pan-Blue camp, but by 2016 they were almost equally likely to identify as pan-Green. This shift among status quo supporters was politically very important, because they made up the largest share of the electorate. The disappearance of the pan-Blue lead among this group probably contributed to the weak electoral performance of the KMT and other pan-Blue parties in 2016.

Associations Between Self-Identity and Preference for Unification vs. Independence

It is widely recognized that there is a close correlation between increasing Taiwanese identity and support for independence.[8] Given this correlation, it is often assumed that support for independence will continue to rise as a larger and larger share of Taiwan's people identify exclusively as Taiwanese. This pattern has more or less held true over the past two decades. There have also been clear effects on partisan attachments, as the relative majority of people who identify as Taiwanese have tended to support pan-Green parties, and these parties in turn have advocated in various ways for Taiwan's independence.

Nevertheless, it is an oversimplification to equate the increase in Taiwanese identity with an increase in support for independence. Not everyone who identifies as Taiwanese also supports independence. Likewise, it is not self-evident that the dual identifiers—people who identify as both Taiwanese and Chinese—should support unification or the status quo over independence. Even those who identify exclusively as Chinese are not obviously pro-unification and might instead prefer to maintain the status quo for various reasons. The point here is that the association beween national identity and preference on the TI-UM issue needs to be evaluated empirically. A cross-tab of the two variables can help clarify this relationship. The results are shown in Figure 11.6.

Figure 11.6A shows the preferences of people who identified exclusively as Taiwanese between 1994 and 2016. Since the 1990s, the most popular TI-UM option among this group has been "maintain status quo, decide later." This was also the pattern for the general Taiwanese population, so at first glance, at least, Taiwanese identifiers did not actually appear to be exceptionally supportive of independence. Support for "decide later" also was quite stable during the Ma presidency between 2008 and 2016.

The second-most-favored option among Taiwanese identifiers has varied over time. Before 2009, it was "maintain the status quo, move toward independence." But since then, support for "maintain the status quo forever" has been at a roughly similar level, at between 25 and 30 percent. The surge since 2008 in support for "status quo forever" is a striking development, and it appears to have come in part at the expense of support for "independence as soon as possible," which dropped from a high of over 15 percent of Taiwanese identifiers in 2007 to roughly 5–6 percent in 2016. Thus, while there continues to be support among this group for independence, it is now running neck and neck with support for the status quo forever. By 2016, about three-fourths of people who favored independence also supported maintaining the status quo for the present. Somewhat counterintuitively, there also used to be a significant number of Taiwanese identifiers—as high as 13 percent in 2001—who supported unification, either immediately or in the future. But this share declined rapidly after 2001, during Chen Shui-bian's first term, and that share remained at only about 5–7 percent through 2016. Thus, it is not an oversimplification to say that almost everyone who identifies as exclusively Taiwanese also opposes unification.

What about dual identifiers—those who said that they were both "Taiwanese and Chinese"? Figure 11.6B shows the patterns of support among this group for unification versus independence. As is immediately clear

Figure 11.6 Self-Identity and Preference for Unification vs. Independence in Taiwan, 1994–2016

A Taiwanese Identity and Preference for Unification vs. Independence

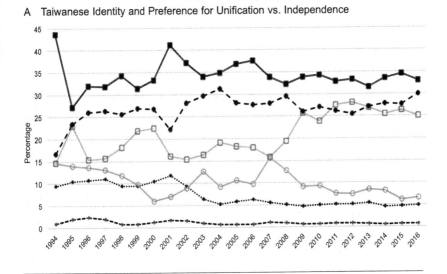

B Dual Identity and Preference for Unification vs. Independence

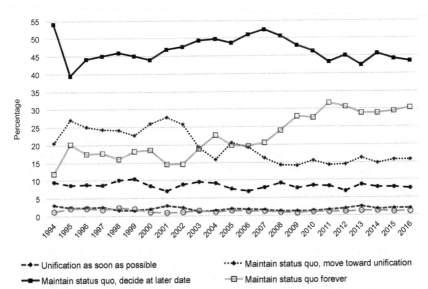

- ◆ Unification as soon as possible
- ■ Maintain status quo, decide at later date
- ● Maintain status quo, move toward independence
- ◆ Maintain status quo, move toward unification
- □ Maintain status quo forever
- ○ Independence as soon as possible

continues

Figure 11.6   Continued

C   Chinese Identity and Preference for Unification vs. Independence

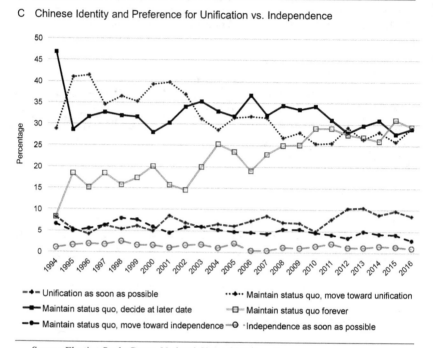

Legend:
- ━◆━ Unification as soon as possible
- ••◆•• Maintain status quo, move toward unification
- ━■━ Maintain status quo, decide at later date
- ━□━ Maintain status quo forever
- ━●━ Maintain status quo, move toward independence
- ⊖ Independence as soon as possible

Source: Election Study Center, National Chengchi University.

from the data, dual identifiers have overwhelmingly supported some version of the status quo: since the mid-1990s, at least 60 percent have consistently chosen "maintain status quo forever" or "maintain status quo, decide at later date." This combined share has risen further since about 2003 and has remained above 70 percent since 2006. That rise has come mostly at the expense of support for unification in the future, which declined by nearly half, from almost 28 percent in 2001 to only about 15 percent in 2016. This subtle but lasting shift among dual identifiers from unification to "decide at a later date" may have important long-term political implications, as it represents a gradual weakening of support for unification, regardless of the cross-Strait situation. In contrast, there has been little change in support for independence, now or later, among dual identifiers; support for either of the pro-independence positions has remained steady at roughly 10 percent over the last two decades. It is also worth noting that support for either of the most extreme positions, immediate independence or immediate unification, was consistently low from 1994 to 2016 and never exceeded 5 percent of the dual identifiers.

The TI-UM preferences of the third national identity group, those who identify exclusively as Chinese, have varied more dramatically over time than those of the other two groups. Before 2003, support for "maintain the status quo, move toward unification" was the most popular option among this group, reaching a high of 40 percent as late as 2001. However, support for moving toward unification in the future dropped by about 15 points over the 2000s, reaching a low of 25 percent in 2010, before fluctuating between 25 and 30 percent during the Ma era. The other option to show significant swings in support was for "maintain the status quo forever." Less than 20 percent of Chinese identifiers preferred this option before 2002, but after 2002 that share gradually increased to 30 percent or more, becoming one of the three major preferences of this group during Ma's second term. As we might expect, "unification as soon as possible" received much more support from Chinese than Taiwanese or dual identifiers, but even among this group, only at most 10 percent endorsed this option over the past two decades. Likewise, support for the independence options, either now or in the future, was quite low among this group, and remained well below 10 percent through the end of the Ma era.

These general associations between self-identity and TI-UM preference reveal some important clues about the consequences of shifting national identity in Taiwan. First, by the end of the Ma era, support for one of the two status quo options—maintain forever, or decide at a later date—was favored by clear majorities of people in all three identity categories: Taiwanese, Chinese, and both. Nevertheless, each group arrived at this high level of support for the status quo through a different process of evolution. Among Taiwanese identifiers, this majority preference has persisted alongside a rise in support since 2007 for moving toward independence in the future, rather than immediately. Given the increase in the share of people who identified exclusively as Taiwanese, this shift represents a big part of the rise in support for independence in the future during the Ma era.

A similar tendency toward support for the status quo occurred among the Chinese identifiers, but with different implications. In the 1990s, support among this group for moving toward unification in the future was significant, but beginning in the 2000s it gradually lost ground to the two neutral status quo categories. Clearly, Chinese identifiers were unlikely to favor independence, yet as a group, they moderated their position on the TI-UM issue away from support for unification. The reasons behind this shift are worth exploring further in future research.

The TI-UM preferences of dual identifiers look similar to Taiwanese identifiers, but with some crucial differences in how they evolved over time. By the end of the Ma era, large majorities in both groups expressed support for one of the two neutral status quo categories. But among the dual identifiers, this support grew at the expense of support for future unification, especially after about 2006. By 2016, roughly 75 percent of all respondents who held dual identity expressed no support for independence or unification, either now or in the future. In other words, pro-unification attitudes declined among dual identifiers, and as they switched to support for maintaining the status quo, this group became firmly committed to stability in the cross-Strait relationship.

It is obvious that Taiwanese and Chinese identifiers have consistently held different preferences on the TI-UM issue. What is less immediately obvious is the dramatic difference in the number of people in the two identity categories. As we saw earlier, Chinese identity steadily declined for many years, so that by the beginning of the Ma era in 2008, this group was only about 5 percent of the population and of limited electoral importance. Nevertheless, because they represented an expansive definition of Chinese nationality and the promise of unification, they remained politically relevant for many years despite their small numbers.

Today, the continued marginal status of Chinese identity has given dual identity a new meaning in Taiwan. The dual Taiwanese-Chinese identity is a compromise between two competing, exclusive visions of the Taiwanese people: as a distinct nation that should pursue political independence from China, and as part of a larger Chinese nation that remains divided and should seek political reunification. Neither of these visions is appealing to most dual identifiers. Given the decline in exclusive Chinese identity, it is possible that we are seeing the emergence of a new and important, though subtle, distinction between the preferences of dual identifiers and Taiwanese on the TI-UM issue. Dual identifiers who support the status quo are still more likely to favor "decide at a later date" than "maintain forever." Taiwanese identifers who support the status quo, by contrast, have become more likely to favor either "maintain forever" or "move toward independence." As the number of dual identifiers continues to decline relative to exclusive Taiwanese, we may see three moderate options emerge as the most widely supported choices on the TI-UM issue: "maintain status quo, decide later," "maintain status quo forever," and "maintain status quo, move toward independence."

Effects on Preference for Unification vs. Independence by Power Alternation

Of the various choices on the TI-UM issue, for decades clear majorities of Taiwanese have consistently expressed support for maintaining the status quo. However, this consensus in favor of the status quo has coexisted with the alternation of governments with markedly different ideologies on cross-Strait issues. The pro-independence DPP replaced the pro-unification KMT in 2000, the DPP was replaced by the pro-unification KMT in 2008, and the

DPP secured power again in 2016. This rotation raises an interesting theoretical question: does the ideological position of the government affect preferences for unification versus independence?

The increase in support between 2000 and 2008 for independence, particularly the "maintain the status quo, move toward independence" option, is consistent with the argument that the DPP government successfully shifted preferences on the TI-UM issue. But if Chen Shui-bian was able to increase support for independence, then by the same logic we should expect to see the KMT rally support behind unification when it was in power between 2008 and 2016. In particular, Ma Ying-jeou promoted extensive socioeconomic exchanges with mainland China, which many people, including in Ma's administration and in Beijing, expected to strengthen pro-China attitudes among the Taiwanese public.[9] In practice, however, these interactions did not increase support for unification in Taiwan. On the contrary, the Ma era witnessed a strong increase in Taiwanese identity and a moderate increase in support for independence. The impact of power alternation between pro-independence and pro-unification parties in Taiwan on TI-UM atittudes appears to be inconsistent and warrants a closer examination.

A reasonable method to evaluate the impact of power alternation is to trace and compare preferences for unification versus independence during the different periods of party control. In the first power alternation, after the DPP came to power in 2000, the Chen administration took increasingly pro-independence positions until 2008. This pro-independence stance was replaced when the KMT returned to power in 2008, and a policy of positive engagement with mainland China was adopted by the Ma administration. Consistent and friendly interactions between the two sides evolved from 2008 to 2016. The different prevailing attitudes toward cross-Strait relations of the two governments could have had very different impacts on public opinion on the TI-UM issue. Similarly, as we saw earlier, the patterns of self-identification and preferences for unification or independence tend to be very different between pan-Blue supporters, pan-Green supporters, and nonpartisans. These three groups were likely to have been affected differently by the power alternation. The analysis that follows provides a closer examination of how this power alternation was related to preferences for unification versus independence.

Table 11.1 shows the results of two logistic regression models, one predicting support for unification (immediate or in the future), and the other predicting support for independence (immediate or in the future). The baseline for each is support for the status quo in 2004. There are several significant findings about the impacts of power alternation. Compared to 2004, pan-Blue partisans tended to be more supportive of the status quo (and less of unification) in 2012, but not in 2008 or 2016, and they were no more supportive of independence in any of the other three years. The pattern for nonpartisans is a bit different. Compared with 2004, nonpartisans in 2008 and 2012 tended to be more supportive of the status quo. They were not, however, any more supportive of independence between 2004 and 2016. There is no evidence that pan-Green partisans became more likely to support unification between 2004 and 2016, but they were more likely to support independence in 2012, though not 2008 or 2016.

Table 11.1 also confirms the importance of national identity. Pan-Blue identifiers with Taiwanese identity preferred the status quo to unification, but pan-Blue identifiers with Chinese identity preferred otherwise. Taiwanese identity shows a similar effect on nonpartisans and pan-Green identifiers. Chinese identity strongly boosted support for unification among pan-Blue partisans. There is also a moderate effect on the pan-Green partisans with Chinese identity. The impact of Taiwanese identity on the preference for independence against the status quo is particularly apparent. Across all partisan groups—pan-Blues, nonpartisans, or pan-Greens—Taiwanese identity was associated with a strong preference for independence over the past two decades. Other significant factors included gender and age: females were less inclined to support either unification or independence, and older people were also less supportive of independence, compared with the baseline case.

Most importantly, these results indicate that the power alternation had no significant impact on self-identity or on preferences for unification versus independence. In fact, if we reflect back on the election campaigns during this period, Ma was clearly aware of the increase of Taiwanese identity and the decrease of Chinese identity in Taiwan. He also understood that solid majorities favored maintaining the status quo over either independence or unification. Hence, he proposed "no unification, no independence, and no use of force" as a campaign theme in the 2008 presidential election campaign. This proposal sounded conservative and defensive at the time. Yet, Ma did push for extensive socioeconomic cross-Strait interaction once he assumed the presidency in 2008, and various talks and agreements between the two sides were concluded.[10]

Ma's strategy was to avoid impulsively trying to sell unification to the general public. Indeed, Ma intended to create a benevolent environment in cross-Strait relations that would generate constructive engagements, with unification a possible but not inevitable outcome of these interactions. The cross-Strait peace and economic benefits helped Ma to win the 2012 presidential election, but these fruits did not lead to increasing support for unification in Taiwan, nor did they ultimately increase the KMT's support in the electorate and help it remain in power after 2016. The opposition camp contended that it was only KMT-related enterprises, not the general public, that significantly benefited from Ma's cross-Strait efforts. The Ma administration was portrayed by the opposition (and pan-Green media) as a government serving only the rich. Together with the surprising emergence of the Sunflower Movement and other sociopolitical events such as the Ting-Hsin

Table 11.1 Impacts of Power Alternation on Preference for Unification vs. Independence

Pro-unification/Status quo	Pan-Blue B	Pan-Blue S. E.	Nonpartisans B	Nonpartisans S. E.	Pan-Green B	Pan-Green S. E.
Female	−0.403***	0.107	−0.532**	0.177	−0.399	0.211
Age	0.009*	0.004	0.001	0.007	0.020*	0.008
Education	−0.007	0.052	−0.088	0.085	0.181	0.098
Career (base = high-middle white collar)						
Middle-low white collar	−0.027	0.129	−0.131	0.244	−0.180	0.283
Farming and fishing	0.044	0.277	0.070	0.355	−0.407	0.460
Blue collar	−0.021	0.151	0.169	0.244	0.219	0.273
Others	0.267	0.226	0.195	0.377	−0.934	0.565
Provincial origins (base = Minnan)						
Hakka	−0.079	0.154	0.119	0.264	−0.192	0.295
Mainlanders	0.266	0.170	0.358	0.345	−0.199	0.622
Aboriginals	−0.216	0.424	0.588	0.725	0.759	1.172
Self-identity (base = dual identity)						
Taiwanese	−0.604***	0.134	−0.845***	0.182	−0.638**	0.210
Chinese	0.872***	0.158	0.593	0.328	0.992*	0.482
Approval rating	0.050	0.149	0.005	0.177	0.110	0.235
Year (base = 2004)						
2008	−0.268	0.140	−0.615**	0.226	−0.134	0.288
2012	−0.401*	0.182	−0.789**	0.256	−0.017	0.300
2016	−0.221	0.182	−0.241	0.231	−0.145	0.328
Constant	−0.934*	0.383	−0.806	0.621	−2.639***	0.750

Pro-independence/Status quo	B	S. E.	B	S. E.	B	S. E.
Female	−0.238	0.161	−0.117	0.136	−0.052	0.100
Age	−0.030***	0.007	−0.003	0.006	0.008	0.004
Education	0.031	0.088	0.103	0.071	0.106*	0.049
Career (base = high-middle white collar)						
Middle-low white collar	−0.113	0.205	−0.431*	0.197	0.060	0.136
Farming and fishing	0.252	0.443	0.158	0.269	0.202	0.210
Blue collar	0.170	0.235	−0.055	0.194	−0.115	0.141
Others	0.338	0.309	−0.339	0.305	−0.105	0.198
Provincial origins (base = Minnan)						
Hakka	−0.119	0.230	−0.095	0.199	−0.006	0.163
Mainlanders	−0.355	0.292	−0.653	0.367	−0.150	0.340
Aboriginals	−0.613	0.660	−0.185	0.713	−0.253	0.804
Self-identity (base = dual identity)						
Taiwanese	1.078***	0.165	1.152***	0.159	1.557***	0.141
Chinese	−0.711	0.602	0.439	0.441	−0.650	0.656
Approval rating	0.284	0.218	0.100	0.139	0.165	0.120
Year (base = 2004)						
2008	−0.046	0.232	−0.243	0.187	−0.230	0.143
2012	−0.213	0.283	−0.279	0.197	−0.435**	0.158
2016	0.072	0.280	−0.133	0.199	−0.242	0.165
Constant	−1.169	0.636	−1.734**	0.528	−1.550***	0.394

N	2,267		1,566		2,059	
Log likelihood	−1,758.139		−1,230.139		−1,679.458	
LR X²	277.930		170.03		248.34	
p < 0.001	< 0.001		< 0.001			
Pseudo R²	0.0730		0.0646		0.0688	

Source: Taiwan's Election and Democratization Study 2004P, 2008P, 2012, 2016.
Note: * = $p < .05$; ** = $p < .01$; *** = $p < .001$.

Group food safety scandal, the death of military conscript Hung Chung-chiu, and the Chou Tzu-yu apology incident, Ma's achievements in cross-Strait relations were overshadowed by mounting criticism that he was yielding Taiwan's sovereignty to the PRC.

The Ma administration did ease the tension in cross-Strait relations that existed during the previous Chen administration. Yet Ma's China-friendly stance did not encourage a substantial increase in pro-unification attitudes among the Taiwanese public. It was true that the majority of voters supported Ma's approach of constructive engagement with the PRC in the 2008 and 2012 presidential elections. But this support eroded quickly after the Sunflower Movement. The overall attitude toward Ma's China policy was one of ambivalence, with the general public perceiving that close interaction with the PRC would threaten Taiwan's economic competitiveness, national security, and sovereignty.[11]

A related indicator of people's ambivalence was their attitudes toward the pace of cross-Strait interaction. Since the late 1980s, the Mainland Affairs Council has regularly conducted public opinion surveys to measure popular attitudes on cross-Strait relations. From 1989 to 2015, these surveys consistently found that the relative majority of Taiwanese perceived the pace of economic interaction between the two sides to be just right (not too fast, not too slow). However, the surveys also revealed a clear difference between administrations: the proportion thinking interactions were too slow was higher than the proportion of too fast during the Chen era (between 2000 and 2008), while the reverse was true during the Ma era (between 2008 and 2016).[12] These patterns suggest that most Taiwanese share the view that cross-Strait interaction is necessary, but at a moderate speed. When the DPP was in power, people were cautious about the party's anti-China mentality, thinking it would put Taiwan in direct confrontation with Beijing; and when the KMT was in power, people were also concerned that the KMT's pro-China stance would make Taiwan's economy too dependent on the PRC. The popular consensus on cross-Strait interaction is that it should be step-by-step, not too fast and not too slow.

Conclusion

Taiwan has frequently been praised as a successful democratic model when compared with other third-wave democracies.[13] Regular and peaceful power alternations have made Taiwan a consolidated democracy. Yet behind these accomplishments, challenges remain. The significant changes in the party system since the 1980s, for example, imply that there is a not-so-stable social base for major political parties. The KMT's comfortable victory in 1996 soon evaporated in 2000. Likewise, its successor, the DPP, was in power for only eight years and embarrassingly replaced by the KMT, which won a landslide victory in the 2008 presidential election. Then the KMT's popularity collapsed again, and it ended up suffering through a disastrous electoral defeat in the 2016 presidential election. It has been observed that a type of two-party system has taken root in Taiwan. However, the forces behind the operation (and power alternations) of this two-party system have less to do with good (or bad) performance of the party in power and more with changing national identity and ideological issues.

The growth of Taiwanese identity is essentially one of the side effects of Taiwan's democratization and a key factor behind the DPP's recent political gains. The DPP has portrayed itself as genuinely representing the interests of Taiwan's people. The increase in Taiwanese identity has thus benefited the DPP as well. By contrast, the KMT has remained committed to a position of eventual unification, and improving cross-Strait relations has been its top priority—even at the cost of being accused of acting as Beijing's agent. The increase in Taiwanese identity has been detrimental to the KMT's political appeal, and it has made it much harder for the party to argue that active and positive engagement with the PRC would benefit Taiwan. These factors fundamentally shaped the setting, goals, and strategies for the Ma administration between 2008 and 2016.

During the Ma era, the KMT government maintained a stable and peaceful relationship with Beijing, and the social and economic interaction between the two sides benefited Taiwan. However, in addition to these legacies, political attitudes related to cross-Strait issues did not conform to the KMT's expectations—or to Beijing's. Taiwan's people overwhelmingly have continued to identify not as Chinese but as Taiwanese. Moreover, survey results indicate that 50 to 60 percent of Taiwanese consistently viewed the Chinese government as hostile toward the Taiwanese government, even when the KMT was in power between 2008 and 2016. These percentages were relatively lower than under the DPP government between 2000 and 2008; however, they were still high and did not change much.[14]

The increase in Taiwanese identity has also influenced preferences on unification versus independence, although the effect is not as straightforward as we might imagine. Support for the status quo is the majority position among all three national identity groups—those who identify as Taiwanese, Chinese, and both—and support for unification has declined among all three. Among partisan groups, there is very little support for unification among pan-Greens, and it has also declined among nonpartisans and even pan-Blues. Put simply, the choice that most Taiwanese make today is between support for some version of the status quo and eventual independence. Unification now or in the future has ceased to be a competitive option.

To be fair, it is premature to declare that we know all the impacts of the Ma era on self-identity and preferences for unification versus independence. Taiwan has undergone a very rapid and broad sociopolitical transformation.

The PRC has also experienced grand economic modernization over the same period. Economic interaction remains important for the development of cross-Strait relations. Nonetheless, political interaction will still be at its core. The topic of unification versus independence remains an open question in Taiwan, with different possible options for its future; yet this is not the case in the PRC. Worse still, the Beijing government rigidly insists on the eventual unification option and has unrelentingly curbed Taiwan's international space. The lack of a flexible and convincing formula for unification, and the repeated suppression of Taiwan's status, has only served to alienate Taiwan's people further from the idea of unification. Beijing's pressure has also made it politically more challenging to support China-friendly policies in Taiwan, and it represents a long-term problem for the KMT.

Notes

1. Cheng and Haggard, *Political Change in Taiwan;* Tsang and Tien, *Democratization in Taiwan.*
2. Campbell et al., *The American Voter.* The term *party identification* is sometimes used interchangeably with *partisanship* or *party affiliation.* In this chapter, we use "party identification" to refer to a psychological affinity for a political party, rather than formal membership in that political party.
3. Fell, *Party Politics in Taiwan;* Yu, "The Evolving Party System in Taiwan"; Lin, "The Evolution of Party Images and Party System in Taiwan."
4. For more on these incidents and the related social movements, see Chapter 12 in this volume.
5. Hsieh and Niou, "Salient Issues in Taiwan's Electoral Politics"; Chu and Lin, "Political Development in 20th Century Taiwan."
6. Gold, "Taiwan's Quest for Identity in the Shadow of China"; Wachman, "Competing Identities in Taiwan"; Hsieh, "Ethnicity, National Identity, and Domestic Politics in Taiwan"; Stockton, "National Identity, International Image, and a Security Dilemma"; Achen and Wang, *The Taiwan Voter.*
7. Schubert, "Taiwan's Political Parties and National Identity"; Rigger, *Taiwan's Rising Rationalism.*
8. Chu, "Taiwan's National Identity Politics and the Prospect of Cross-Strait Relations"; Huang, "Dimensions of Taiwanese/Chinese Identity and National Identity in Taiwan."
9. Schubert and Braig, "How to Face an Embracing China?"; Wu, "The Evolution of the KMT's Stance on the One China Principle."
10. See the full list of cross-Strait talks and interactions at the website of the Mainland Affairs Council, https://www.mac.gov.tw/en/News.aspx?n=A25A31DE8D66F1C6&sms=7D28EA87CFA26186.
11. Lee and Chu, "Cross-Strait Economic Integration."
12. The full list of public opinion polls is available on the Mainland Affairs Council website, https://www.mac.gov.tw/en/Content_List.aspx?n=2A0F1393B67987D2.
13. Cheng and Haggard, *Political Change in Taiwan;* Tsang and Tien, *Democratization in Taiwan.*
14. Ibid.

12

The Impact of
Social Movements

Dafydd Fell

When historians look back on the Ma Ying-jeou era (2008–2016), they are likely to focus on a handful of key developments. The three that I believe will be most stressed will be the breakthroughs in cross-Strait relations, the failure of the Kuomintang (KMT) to engage in domestic reforms despite such large legislative majorities, and the impact of social movements. During this period, social movements went from being a marginal issue to becoming one of the most popular topics for researchers in Taiwan studies. As someone who teaches on Taiwan's politics, I have seen a surge in student interest. For instance, social movement–related public events have been extremely popular, and many students have chosen to examine social movements in their dissertations. I have also found that the topic of social movements has allowed me to make Taiwan interesting and understandable to audiences that originally were not familiar with it. When I am trying to persuade prospective students to take my courses on Taiwan's politics, I often tell them about the Sunflower occupation, the LGBTQ movement's promotion of marriage equality, and Taiwan's anti-nuclear movement. At the end of my courses I have often heard students tell me that the thing they most admire about Taiwan's democracy is the fact that protest actually matters.

The Ma era appears to be one of the most important eras in the history of social movements in Taiwan. In Chapter 13, Min-hua Huang and Mark Weatherall place it among the four most important waves of protest, along with the period leading up to the Kaohsiung (Formosa) Incident (1979), the Wild Lily Movement (1990), and the Red Shirt anticorruption protest (2006). Hsin-huang Michael Hsiao and Yu-yuan Kuan's overview of the development of Taiwan's civil society organizations reaches a similar conclusion about the importance of the Ma era.[1]

Although the majority of my research has focused on political parties, I was fortunate to be involved in a number of research projects related to Taiwan's social movements during the Ma era. In particular, in June 2014 we hosted an international conference on social movements at my university. When I first began planning for the conference in the middle of Ma's first term, I had no idea just how important this topic would soon become. The conference papers would later become the basis of a book I edited titled *Social Movements in Taiwan Under Ma Ying-jeou: From the Wild Strawberries to the Sunflowers.*[2] I also have been working on a project looking at the development of one of Taiwan's social movement–linked political parties, the Green Party Taiwan (GPT).[3] Taken together, these two projects exposed me to both activists in a wide range of movements as well as scholars working on social movements in Taiwan.

One issue that came up repeatedly in discussions during our 2014 conference was how to evaluate the success of social movements in Taiwan.[4] Discussions of protests often focus on the scale of mobilization. It is clear that the scale of protests progressively expanded over the Ma era. However, one of the conclusions emerging from the research of Michael Cole was that in this period the numbers of people joining protests were not necessarily decisive in determining impact. Instead, he showed how size did not always matter, as at times smaller protests were actually much more threatening to the government.[5] Naturally, the Sunflower Movement's ability to stall the controversial Cross-Strait Services Trade Agreement (CSSTA) is often taken as proof of the strength and success of Taiwan's civil society. But we also should remember that the achievements of the core social movements were never inevitable. Even within civil society prior to the Sunflower occupation, there was widespread pessimism about its ability to constrain the Ma administration's agenda. For instance, in Kevin Lee's documentary *Self-Censorship,* sociologist Wu Rwei-ren recalled how "by 2013 all the major western discourses believed it was the end of Taiwan." He noted how the Sunflower Movement "didn't just knock down the KMT and allow the Taiwanese local party to regain power, it even turned the tables on East Asian geopolitics."[6]

How should we best assess the impact of Taiwan's social movements? Although success is something many studies touch upon, it has rarely been addressed systematically.[7] In this chapter, I employ a revised version of an analytical framework for assessing the impact of social movements proposed by Neil Carter.[8] He suggests that we first distinguish between internal and external impacts. By internal impacts, he is referring to the degree to which involvement in social movements affects the identities of its participants. He next distinguishes between four types of external impacts: sensitizing impacts, procedural impacts, structural impacts, and substantive impacts. Sensitizing impacts mainly refer to the ability of movements to get their issues on the political agenda, as well as changing public opinion. Procedural impacts refer to the degree to which movements are given access to decisionmaking bodies. Structural impacts refer to changes in institutions and the alliance structures. These might include the creation of a relevant new government agency, alliances between movements and with political parties, as well as shifts in mainstream party positions. Finally, by substantive impacts he is referring to actual material results, such as whether a relevant piece of legislation is passed or a polluting factory is closed down. In addition, I have added the dimension of political impact to the framework. Here we can look at how well social movement–linked political parties perform in elections, as well as the fortunes of the allied and least-favored mainstream parties.

Internal Impacts

Of all the elements of this framework, internal effects are the hardest to measure. There are not surveys available that allow us to systematically assess patterns of politicization of social movement supporters. However, we can reach some tentative conclusions about such effects. Prior to the Ma era, protests had become associated with older citizens, while the younger generation—the so-called Strawberry Generation, named because they were supposedly delicate and bruised easily—had been stereotyped as being uninterested in politics. However, as Huang and Weatherall show in Chapter 13, the activism in 2014 was quite different from the protests led by older citizens in 2006. They note how it was dominated by the two youngest generations, those who completed high school education between 1987 and 2001 and those who finished after 2002. In other words, the Ma years saw the emergence of a new generation of younger and much more active protesters than had been seen since 2000.

It also appears that activists who first joined protests in Ma's first term gradually became involved in a much wider range of movements in his second term. In other words, many protesters initially started off joining relatively focused protest movements, such as the Wild Strawberry Movement (2008) and the environmental movement against the Kuo-kuang Petrochemical Plant (2010–2011). However, over time they become involved in much more diverse types of movements that focused on issues such as land justice, media systems, constitutional reform, and LGBTQ rights. One way we can get a sense of such changes among activists is by viewing the documentaries of Chiang Wei-hua. His first film, *Right Thing*, tells the story of the Wild Strawberry Movement and its activists. He followed up on this project in his later film called *The Edge of Night*, which examines what these activists did in the subsequent years. Michael Cole offers a similar understanding of the politicization process, writing about "the cross-pollination of various movements that had mobilised over a number of disparate issues, from the monopolization of the media to forced evictions, which fostered an environment in which activists could learn from each other."[9]

Another way we can see the politicization effect is in changing patterns of partisan attitudes of activists. By the end of the Ma era there were clear signs of much higher levels of youth voter turnout and political interest, including a new willingness of social movement activists to actually run for office as candidates in 2014 and 2016. In 2008, the KMT actually enjoyed an advantage among the younger generation of voters, but following their involvement in numerous protest movements against KMT policies, these activists appeared by the end of the Ma era unlikely to support the KMT in future elections. Although the Democratic Progressive Party (DPP) was the primary short-term beneficiary of the rise of social movements, the emergence of a new generation of activists has also helped create a market that movement parties such as the New Power Party (NPP), the Green Party Taiwan (GPT), and the Social Democratic Party (SDP) have appealed to.

Sensitizing Impacts

In order to achieve their substantive goals, a crucial challenge for social movements is to get their issues placed on the public and political agenda. Changing public opinion and values toward those held by social movements is of course a goal in itself, but it is also a key ingredient for putting pressure on governments to respond to social movement demands. Such changes in agenda-setting and public opinion are what Carter calls sensitizing effects, and on this dimension social movements during the Ma presidency were remarkably successful.[10]

An initial sign of the changed political agenda is in media reports featuring the term "social movement." A search of *United Daily News* database reports shows that the high point of such reports came in Ma's second term, with three of the highest annual numbers of reports coming in 2014, 2015, and 2016.[11] An analysis of numerous social movement case studies also reveals how protests were able to push previously marginal issues onto the public and political agenda. Key examples include successes in placing the issues of media ownership and LGBTQ rights firmly in the public eye. At times, public interest initially appeared quite limited, but protesters were able to make what seemed at first to be niche issues into mainstream ones. When the CSSTA was signed in the summer of 2013, for instance, the public reaction was quite muted, but sustained protest made it a central issue of public concern by the spring of 2014. Early in Ma's second term, protests against the attempt of Tsai Eng-meng

(Cai Yanming) to extend the influence of his Want Want China Times Group over Taiwan's media market were initially quite small-scale, but they eventually developed into the largest-ever rallies related to media politics. The anti-media monopoly movement brought unprecedented visibility to the issue of media reform and put it squarely on the political agenda.[12] Protests against the controversial Fourth Nuclear Power Plant being constructed in Gongliao, New Taipei, followed a similar pattern. In this case, the issue had declined in salience after 2001, but following the Fukushima nuclear accident in Japan in 2011, environmentalists were able to revive public concern about the plant and place heavy pressure on political society to respond.[13]

The sensitizing effect of social movements also shows up in public opinion survey data. One of the major successes of Taiwan's social movements in this era was their ability to maintain strong public support, even when protesters were using quite radical methods. The Sunflower Movement's twenty-three-day occupation of Taiwan's legislature would have been impossible without broad public backing. For example, a survey taken between March 20 and 21, 2014, showed 48 percent of respondents supported the student occupation of the Legislative Yuan, and by March 24 the support rate had risen to 51 percent.[14] Moreover, the protesters were able to keep public opinion on their side throughout the occupation, despite attempts by the KMT and affiliated media to demonize the movement. Following the ending of the occupation, a survey found that 49 percent of respondents also hoped that Taiwan's courts would be lenient in how they treated the student occupiers.[15] In fact, another survey found that 65 percent of respondents believed that the Sunflower Movement had helped the development of Taiwan's democracy.[16] These results are in clear contrast to the case of the Umbrella Movement in Hong Kong, which took place at about the same time. There, public opinion was much more divided, and less supportive of protesters.

Although we cannot prove a direct causal relationship, there is a clear pattern of public opinion moving closer to the positions of key social movements during this period, including views about nuclear power, economic relations with China, and marriage equality. In all three cases, not only was there a rise in the salience of the issues, but also there were dramatic shifts in public opinion. When the Chen Shui-bian administration attempted to stop construction of the Fourth Nuclear Power Plant in 2000–2001, for instance, one of the reasons that it did not push harder for a national referendum was that public opinion was broadly supportive of the project. By Ma's second term, there had been a clear swing in public opinion against nuclear power, with almost 60 percent of respondents supporting a shift toward a nuclear-free homeland in surveys conducted in 2011, 2012, and 2016.[17] When voters were asked in 2014 whether the fate of the

Fourth Nuclear Power Plant should be determined by a referendum, 69 percent agreed. When asked how they would vote in such a referendum, 73 percent in 2013 and 60 percent in 2014 stated they would vote to stop construction of the plant.[18]

Public opinion about cross-Strait agreements followed a similar pattern. Although the KMT did not consider holding a referendum on the Economic Cooperation Framework Agreement (ECFA), if there had been one it probably would have passed, as public opinion in Ma's first term was initially broadly supportive of closer cross-Strait economic ties. For instance, President Ma was widely regarded as having won the televised debate over the ECFA against DPP chairwoman Tsai Ing-wen in April 2010.[19] Similarly, the two surveys held immediately prior to the signing of the ECFA in April 2010 and May 2010 revealed that 41 percent of respondents were supportive (compared to 33–34 percent opposed).[20] If such a referendum had been held in Ma's second term, however, it probably would have been soundly defeated, as public opinion became more concerned about the dangers of rapid economic liberalization with mainland China. Surveys on the CSSTA in late 2013 and March of 2014 reveal this shift in the public mood. In the former survey, 32 percent supported the CSSTA, while 43 percent were opposed, while in March 2014 only 21 percent were supportive compared to 48 percent opposed.[21] Protest movements appear to have contributed to public opinion change toward cross-Strait relations during this period.

Although polling data are not so abundant on the issue of marriage equality, there has been a gradual trend toward first tolerance and more recently support of LGBTQ rights. In Taiwanese popular culture, for instance, gay relationships have increasingly been portrayed sympathetically. Following the precedent of Ang Lee's *Wedding Banquet* (1993), large numbers of popular Taiwanese feature films addressed the issue in the 1990s and since 2000, such as *Vive L'Amour* (1994), *Murmur of Youth* (1997), *Blue Gate Crossing* (2002), and *Formula 17* (2004). Moreover, many of these gay-themed films have received public subsidies and have been promoted by Taiwan's government in overseas film festivals. Since the Ma era, surveys have tended to show that approximately half of respondents are supportive of legalizing gay marriage, with less than 30 percent opposed and many indifferent. Moreover, when the figures are broken down by age group, it is clear that generational change is a major factor, with those in the age group of twenty to twenty-nine most supportive (63 percent). Even with the respondents in the age groups of thirty to thirty-nine, and forty to forty-nine, there are clear majorities in support, and only among voters over age fifty is there a majority in opposition.[22] The fact that Tsai Ing-wen came out so strongly in support of marriage equality in the 2016 campaign suggests that she saw this position as a vote-winner.

Procedural Impacts

Out of all the impact dimensions of social movements in the Ma era, the weakest effects were in the area of procedural impacts. During the Chen presidency, civil society groups gained new access to decisionmaking bodies. Former environmental activists such as Edgar Lin and Chang Kuo-long served as environment ministers, and activists were openly welcomed on a range of consultative bodies. One such body was the Environmental Impact Assessment Committee (EIAC), which featured record numbers of civil society figures. However, by the end of the Chen presidency, environmental activists had become dissatisfied and quite critical of the DPP administration; as environmental lawyer and former member of the EIAC Robin Winkler explained to me, "We had such a negative experience with the DPP."[23]

The picture was very different for most social movements in the Ma era. The KMT government worked on the assumption that social movements were working with the DPP, and so largely shut them out of decisionmaking processes and refused to engage in dialogue. The KMT's large majorities in the legislature also gave it the confidence it could govern without needing to consult with either civil society or the political opposition—such as during the Wild Strawberry Movement in 2008, and especially during the lead-up to the Sunflower Movement and anti–nuclear power demonstrations in 2014. Where dialogue did occur, it was as if the two sides were speaking different languages, as when Premier Jiang Yi-huah met with Sunflower Movement leaders, as well as when DPP chairman Su Tseng-chang and Ma met to discuss how to resolve the crisis over Lin Yi-hsiung's hunger strike over the Fourth Nuclear Power Plant.[24]

Due to its ability to gain cross-party support, the procedural impact of Taiwan's women's movement under Ma should have been rather different from other movements that were more closely allied with the DPP. Under both Lee Teng-hui and Chen Shui-bian, an impressive range of legislation was passed that contributed to greater gender equality in Taiwan.[25] A key reason for this policy success was the access that feminist leaders gained to government decisionmaking and consultation bodies. After Chen Shui-bian won the presidency, models of public consultation and engagement that he had first introduced to the Taipei City government (1994–1998) during his time as mayor were brought to the national level in the form of the cabinet-level Commission on Promotion of Women's Rights and the Ministry of Education's Commission on Gender Equality Education. Huang Chang-ling calls this alliance between the state and the feminist movement an example of "state feminism."[26] She argues that during the more conservative government of the Ma era it "had become really fragile or nearly broken."[27] While environmentalists were immediately shut out by the Ma administration, Huang argues that state feminism initially survived in what she calls an "uneasy alliance." She notes how there was a gradual increase in more conservative members on the Commission on Promotion of Women's Rights. A turning point came in January 2014, when the Ministry of Education appointed two members to the Commission on Gender Equality Education who had been involved in the campaign against same-sex marriage.

Among all of Taiwan's social movements, one exception to the overall pattern of growing exclusion from decisionmaking were migrant support groups. These groups, particularly those representing Chinese spouses, had been treated with some hostility during the Chen era. In fact, Isabelle Cheng argues that they were treated as the "enemy within."[28] The government attempted not only to prolong the time required for Chinese spouses to gain citizenship from eight to eleven years, but also to deny them the right to form social organizations and the right to assembly.[29] In contrast, there was a positive sea change after the Ma administration took office. Lara Momesso and Isabelle Cheng argue that the KMT was motivated by the desire to secure the votes of Chinese spouses and their Taiwanese husbands. They note how the mode of interaction between the government and activist groups was transformed from one of public confrontation to face-to-face negotiations that became routinized, so that the Marriage Association of Two Sides of China "became one of the major communication channels between the state and PRC spouses."[30]

Structural Impacts

The two key dimensions of Carter's structural impacts are changes in the institutional and alliance structures. The patterns on these two dimensions in the Ma era are starkly different. A range of social movement–related government bodies and committees were established during the Lee and Chen presidencies. However, in the Ma era, the climate changed quite radically due to the KMT's hostility toward social movements. Often, as we saw in the previous section on procedural impacts, the Ma administration attempted to affect the functioning of government-related bodies such as the Commission on Promotion of Women's Rights by changing their composition toward more conservative membership. Ming-sho Ho notes that the pattern was very similar in the case of the Human Rights Advisory Committee.[31] Another approach was to close down bodies completely, such as the Nuclear-Free Homeland Commission, which was suspended immediately after Ma came into office.[32] One exception to this generally negative trend was the establishment of the Department of Gender Equality in 2012, with its core stated goals of gender mainstreaming and implementing the Convention on the Elimination of All Forms of Discrimination Against Women and the New Gender Equality Policy Framework. However, Huang suggests that the new department did not have a transformative impact. She argues that "under the progressive government, when a large number of activists were appointed as commissioners, the feminist movement network was brought into the government. Under the conservative government, however, some of the feminist activists stayed on as commissioners, but the feminist movement network was no longer in the government."[33] Ming-sho Ho comes to a similar conclusion to Huang, arguing that civil society faced an increasingly "narrowed policy channel" under Ma.[34]

In contrast, the impact of social movements on alliance structures during the Ma era was much more positive. This was not the case at the outset of the period. Chiang Wei-hua's film *Right Thing,* about the Wild Strawberry protests, gives viewers the impression that the movement was isolated and underresourced. Robin Winkler offered a similar comment when he recalled the GPT's hopes of widespread civil society support when it joined the 2009 legislative by-election for Da-an District, but found that "nobody rallied around us. We had very little support. . . . Because I was thinking the people from Hualien are going to come up who are against the Su-hau highway, the people from the Lo Sheng Sanatorium, are going to come and all these groups."[35] In the end, however, these groups, who each had engaged in environmental protests during the Chen era, did not come to support the GPT candidate in Taipei.

The key trend in subsequent social movements in the Ma era was how they were able to develop broad and diverse alliances, which became critical to their increased impact on a range of areas. For example, the pressure for marriage equality advanced significantly, as an alliance developed that involved feminist groups, LGBTQ rights groups, Sunflower-linked movements, movement parties such as the GPT, NPP, and SDP, and individual politicians within the two mainstream parties. The classic alliance case of the period, though, has to be the diverse coalition of twenty-two civil society organizations that made up the Democratic Front Against the CSSTA, which played a central role in the Sunflower Movement.[36] Szu-chien Hsu's study reveals that they varied a great deal, ranging from older, larger, and more institutionalized nongovernmental organizations (NGOs) with rich movement experience to others that were quite new, small, and less politicized. Many of the groups in the alliance had not worked together in the past and were actually quite suspicious of each other due to ideological differences. Hsu argues that the cross-Strait, pro-democracy/human rights and anti-globalization paths were what brought together these disparate groups to unite against the CSSTA.

Substantive Impacts

Social movements generally do not achieve their substantive goals, especially when they are facing strong governments. Carter notes that "most of the British roads that were the subject of an extensive anti-roads direct action campaign during the 1990s were eventually built."[37] However, what makes the Ma era especially interesting is the fact that it is perceived as a period when social movements were victorious. I will attempt to address the substantive impact of social movements by looking at a number of prominent movement cases in Ma's first and second terms.

The first movement to consider is the Wild Strawberry Movement of 2008. Apart from seeking government apologies for police treatment of protesters and the resignation of the National Police Agency's director-general, its most important goal was liberalization of the Parade and Assembly Law. Despite the movement's occupation of Liberty Square from November 6 to December 11, 2008, it did not get any government response on any of its substantive goals. Although many of the movement's activists would go on to join other more successful social movements, the predominant view among civil society activists was that the Wild Strawberry Movement failed. This sense of the movement's failure is revealed in Chiang Wei-hua's remarkable documentary *Right Thing*.

In contrast, the best-known movement success in Ma's first term was the canceling of the Kuo-kuang Petrochemical Plant on the coastline of Changhua County in 2011. In this case, the project had originally been strongly supported by the Ma administration, as well as the local KMT-led government, and the DPP was largely silent. However, an alliance of local residents, environmental NGOs, and cultural figures were able to build up sufficient movement momentum, such that first the DPP's local politicians and then its national leaders came out against the plant. The pressure on the KMT grew as the campaign for the 2012 presidential election started, and it was clear that central Taiwan, where the plant was located, would be a critical battle ground. The central government came under growing pressure to back down. Eventually, on April 22, 2011, Ma announced at a press conference that the plan was being dropped and that the government instead supported wetland conservation.[38]

One movement that cut across both Ma's first and second terms was the campaign against legalizing casinos. In 2009, the Offshore Development Act legalized gambling activities on the condition that they be approved by local-level referendums. The first local jurisdictions to hold referendums seeking approval of casinos were the offshore island archipelago of Penghu in 2009, followed by the Matsu islands (Lienchiang County) off the Fujian coast in 2012. Since earlier, nonbinding referendums in 2002 and 2003 had resulted in victories for casinos in Penghu, and local politicians were almost universally supportive, it looked inevitable that the referendum drive would be successful. The prospects for a successful referendum were even greater in Matsu, as the level of KMT dominance there was much higher than in Penghu, and civil society was also much weaker.

Nevertheless, in both Penghu and Matsu, local activists and civic groups were able to build up alliances with national-level NGOs to campaign against the pro-casino groups. In Penghu, the anti-casino vote won 56.4 percent against 43.6 percent in support, while in Matsu the referendum was successful, with 57.2 percent in favor and 42.8 percent opposed. Yet even though the referendum passed in Matsu, no further progress was made on actually establishing casinos, and the key promoter of gambling in the islands, the county magistrate, Yang Sui-sheng, lost his reelection attempt in 2014. The anti-gambling movement in Penghu demonstrated its strength a second time when, after the DPP won control of Penghu in 2014, the new county magistrate called a second casino referendum in 2016. This time, there was a landslide vote against the casino proposal, with over 81 percent voting no.[39]

The anti-media monopoly movement was the first large-scale social movement to emerge in Ma's second term. It revolved around protests aimed at preventing the Want Want China Times Group from expanding its influence over Taiwan's media market, and it pushed for legislation to prevent media-ownership monopolies. There was a clear China factor behind this movement, because Want Want's *China Times* newspaper and its television channels, CTV and CtiTV, all took very pro–People's Republic of China (PRC) editorial lines, something quite new to Taiwan's media. Moreover, both were relentlessly hostile toward the DPP and civil society. This movement had both successes and failures. The bid of Want Want chairman Tsai Eng-meng to acquire one of Taiwan's largest cable television operators, China Network Systems, as well as the Next Media Group, both eventually fell through. However, even though legislation to prevent media monopolies was drafted and discussed at the committee stage in the Legislative Yuan, the KMT was not willing to support its passage, and it was set aside until Tsai Ing-wen and the DPP took power in 2016.[40]

The Sunflower Movement is generally taken as the representative case of movement success in the Ma era. Although it clearly has had numerous long-term impacts on Taiwanese politics, if we consider the movement's stated goals at face value, its substantive impact appears rather mixed. The Sunflower Movement's core goals were that the government withdraw the CSSTA, and that further negotiations with the PRC be postponed until legislation establishing greater oversight of cross-Strait negotiations had been passed. The KMT had hoped that as with the Strawberries, the Sunflowers would run out of steam and the public mood would swing against activists. However, in the end, the KMT was forced to compromise when Legislative Yuan Speaker Wang Jin-pyng announced that cross-party negotiations on the CSSTA would not restart until after the oversight legislation had been passed. This promise was enough to persuade the Sunflowers to end their occupation of the legislature. However, a closer look at the movement's core goals shows that the impact was mixed. The Ma administration never officially withdrew the CSSTSA and continued to trumpet its benefits for Taiwan's economy until he left office. Similarly, although a number of different drafts of oversight legislation were proposed, none came close to being approved by the legislature. Interestingly, since the DPP came to power, it too has not prioritized legislation strengthening cross-Strait oversight, despite the fact that it has the necessary majority to force this change through.

The Sunflower Movement also managed to promote discussion of a very wide range of political issues beyond the immediate goal of blocking the CSSTA. One such issue concerned the fate of the controversial Fourth Nuclear Power Plant.[41] Although this issue had again become politically salient in the aftermath of the 2012 election, the Ma administration did not call the referendum that it had proposed at the height of the controversy, and construction on the plant continued. The decisive moment occurred two weeks after the Sunflower occupation ended, when former political prisoner and DPP chairman Lin Yi-hsiung began a hunger strike against the continued construction of the plant on April 22, 2014. Thousands of protesters came out in support of Lin. As had been the case with the Kuo-kuang Petrochemical Plant in 2011, with elections on the horizon the Ma administration reluctantly backed down in the face of the protest. On April 27, the government announced it was mothballing the plant and that it would require approval in a referendum before the plant was put into operation. Although the Ma administration was not exactly canceling the plant and did not rule out the possibility of it coming into operation once the conditions were right, this outcome was still a major environmental-movement success. The KMT had promoted the project as a major government policy since the late 1980s, but shortly before completion it had canceled it. As it is unlikely that a future government will allow the mothballed nuclear plant to go into operation, or that further new nuclear power plants will be considered, this result was a major achievement for Taiwan's anti-nuclear movement.

The women's movement has long been regarded as the most successful of all of Taiwan's many social movements. What sets the women's movement apart is that it has tried to avoid becoming associated with any political party, and that it has been more elitist, focusing more on gaining cross-party support than mass protests in the streets.[42] One issue that became a priority for many feminist groups in the Ma era was LGBTQ rights, in particular marriage equality. It was joined on this front by an increasingly active LGBTQ rights movement. The Ma era saw both progress but also a significant conservative counter-movement against LGBTQ rights on the marriage issue, and also in the realm of gender education.[43] In October 2013, a Taiwan Alliance to Promote Civil Partnership Rights draft bill to legalize same-sex marriage was submitted to the Legislative Yuan by a DPP legislator, and it passed its first reading. However, protests mobilized by the Alliance for Protecting Families, together with intensive lobbying of both KMT and DPP legislators, were enough to stall the bill.[44] As with many of the other issues promoted by civil society, the battles over same-sex marriage and LBGTQ rights were carried over into the Tsai presidency. In May 2017, the Council of Grand Justices, Taiwan's constitutional court, ruled that the civil law banning same-sex marriage was unconstitutional, and gave the legislature two years to either revise the law or create a new law legalizing same-sex marriage. This decision put extra weight behind President Tsai's quiet support for marriage equality, and despite considerable opposition even from parts of the DPP the legislature approved a new law in April 2019, making Taiwan the first Asian country to legalize same-sex marriage.

Another issue that was reintroduced onto the political agenda by social movements was constitutional reform. Rather than adopt a brand new constitution, Taiwan went through a period of gradual constitutional revisions from the early 1990s through until 2005. By the Ma era, though, the topic had largely fallen off the political agenda, and despite its large majorities the KMT showed no interest in making additional constitutional changes. This changed after the Sunflower Movement. One of the causes of the movement was a sense that party politics were not responsive to the demands of younger voters and civil society.[45] Therefore, one of the proposals that gained momentum was for lowering the voting age to eighteen and reducing the 5 percent threshold for small parties to enter the Legislative Yuan on the party list. In June 2015 there appeared to be cross-party support for these reforms. Both main parties hoped to use reforms as a means to improve their electoral prospects, so for instance the KMT tried to attach provisions to allow absentee voting to the reform package. However, in the end the KMT, perhaps fearing a further backlash from more newly enfranchised young voters, got cold feet. It withdrew its support and the reforms were again aborted.[46] Interestingly, since the DPP has come to power, it too has been quite cautious about constitutional reforms. The voting age remains at twenty, and the long-delayed Political Parties Act, passed in November 2017, only reduced the vote share needed to gain government subsidies from 3.5 to 3 percent, leaving intact the 5 percent threshold to win seats in the legislature.[47]

Two threads appeared to unite most social movements during the Ma era: a desire to protect Taiwan's democracy, and a concern that rapid economic integration with the PRC could undermine its way of life. Although these are not easily measured, there is clear evidence that social movements did have a substantial impact on both fronts. A number of scholars have made the argument that recent social movements have served to revitalize or deepen Taiwan's democracy at a time when it had previously been in crisis. For instance, Ming-yeh Rawnsley has suggested that key civic movements such as the anti-media monopoly movement and the Sunflower

Movement contributed to further democratization in Taiwan, or what she has termed "a second wave of democratisation (following the initial wave under Lee Teng-hui)."[48] Similarly, Ketty Chen writes that these movements were "significant in Taiwan's democratic consolidation in two ways. First, the Sunflower Movement inspired a much-needed societal and political debate on the constitution of 'democracy' and 'citizen participation' in Taiwan. Secondly, the Sunflower Movement signifies the ripening of a distinct Taiwan-centric identity."[49] If a strong and critical civil society is one of the three core components of democratization, as democratic theorist Jean Grugel has argued, then Taiwan's experiences under during the Ma era should be regarded as strengthening its democracy.[50]

The impact of social movements on cross-Strait relations has perhaps been even greater. There were numerous protests against Ma's cross-Strait policies since the start of his first term, but for a long time it appeared that noting could derail rapprochement with the PRC. Ma started his second term seeking to make progress on an ambitious agenda that included establishing mutual representative offices, a meeting between himself and Xi Jinping, and signing and approval of the CSSTA as well as the parallel Cross-Strait Trade in Goods Agreement, and it appeared likely he would attempt to revive his earlier proposal for a cross-Strait peace treaty. However, he was only able to achieve his historic meeting with Xi, and even in this case the meeting had no lasting impacts. By that stage of Ma's presidency, the damage had been done. Following the Sunflower Movement, there was no longer the prospect of approval of any further cross-Strait agreements. In other words, the movement had an impact not only on the final two years of the Ma era but also on the subsequent DPP government.

Political Impacts

Much of the focus on the political effect of social movements in the Ma era has focused on three areas: the electoral success of the DPP, the collapse of the KMT, and the breakthrough into the Legislative Yuan of the New Power Party. I will address these political effects and show how when we look in more detail, these effects are more complex than they first appear.

The DPP was of course the big winner in the 2014 and 2016 elections. In the past, the party had a close working relationship with many of Taiwan's social movements, particularly in the democratic transition period.[51] KMT members such as Alex Tsai and Chiu Yi tried to argue that the Sunflowers and other movements were led by the DPP. Although the DPP did undoubtedly benefit from the rise of social movements, we should be cautious about characterizing the DPP's return to power as a social movement success. Many social movement activists remained bitter after the experience of the previous DPP administration under President Chen Shui-bian. Environmental activists, in particular, were disillusioned by the DPP's failure to live up to its anti-nuclear promises, and viewed the party as having compromised too much with big business in putting economic development ahead of environmental concerns.[52] The younger generation of social movement activists also tended to try to either retain autonomy or at least keep their distance from the DPP. As Cole noted in 2015, "the new generation of activists that has taken on the government is not only highly suspicious of *all* political parties, but well-organized, resourceful, and intelligent enough to accomplish great things without being 'subsidized' by any political parties."[53]

The political impact of social movements on the DPP shows up in Ma's second term both in the party's changed nomination strategy and in its campaign appeals. The DPP nominated record numbers of civil society figures for its party list in 2016, including two former GPT convenors, Chen Man-li and Karen Yu (Yu Wan-ju), as well as Frida Tsai (Tsai Pei-hui) of Taiwan Rural Front. Moreover, the DPP chose to highlight these social movement–linked candidates in the final stage of the election campaign in both its television and newspaper ads as a means to counter the electoral threat from the NPP.[54] Its issue appeals followed a similar pattern. In its 2016 television ads, the DPP made reference to "black box" negotiations (a euphemism for the CSSTA), land justice issues such as the Dapu eminent domain case in Miaoli County, nuclear energy, and marriage equality.[55] In an ad that ran in September 2015, there were images of police using water cannons against protesters.[56] Similarly, as both party chair and the DPP's presidential candidate, Tsai Ing-wen issued a number of ads showing her support for marriage equality.[57] Four years earlier, the DPP had largely ignored social movement activists and their issues. The most obvious case was on LGBTQ issues, which were completely absent from the DPP's campaign materials in 2012. In other words, the rise of social movements pushed the main opposition party to take positions closer to the movements and adjust its nominations to absorb activists.

The electoral collapse of the KMT, first at the local level in 2014 and then at the national level in 2016, was unprecedented. It suffered its worst-ever local and national elections results in just over a year. Many social movement activists and groups contributed to and celebrated the fall of the KMT. Broadly, these results can be interpreted as an electoral punishment for Ma's promotion of policies that triggered an unprecedented scale of social protests. The enemy of the majority of social movements had been kicked out of office.

Political campaign material provides some support for the argument that the defeat of the KMT was a triumph for social movements. In both 2014 and 2016, the KMT ran a series of television ads that offered a critique of social movements. For instance, in one of the KMT's 2014 ads, it appealed to a silent majority supposedly opposed to protest movements.

The narrator says, "Because you do not go out in the streets to protest, you are wrong. Because you do not snatch the microphone, you are wrong." The ad ends with a call to voters to hold on "tightly to your votes and on November 29 to let us quietly speak out loudly."[58] The KMT adopted a very similar message in a much discussed "I'm Fifth Generation" television ad in 2016. In one scene, the middle-aged protagonist walks past protest banners while the narrator speaks for him complaining that "the court of law is theirs, 'resident justice' is theirs, economic justice is theirs. My justice is nowhere." Later he states: "Who stirs up hatred, he is the real bad guy." The ad ends with his resolution that "I will vote. I will vote for the values and country I believe in." At the time, a number of analysts argued that this ad was an attempt by the KMT to stir up intergenerational conflict.[59] A similar and even more direct attempt to demonize protests appeared in Hung Hsiu-chu's campaign ad explaining her support for Eric Chu. In this ad, protest banners appear with the slogan "Oppose locking up the country, liberalization"—a clear reference to the Sunflower Movement, which the ad blamed for preventing Taiwan from enjoying the economic benefits of free trade.[60] In short, given the KMT's stress on critiquing social movements in both 2014 and 2016, the party's defeat in those elections can be interpreted at least in part as a rejection of that message.

On the individual level, activists successfully targeted politicians with a reputation for opposition to social movements. For instance, KMT legislator Chang Ching-chung, who had been at the center of the KMT's bid to push the CSSTA through the Legislative Yuan, lost his seat in 2016. He had won with a majority of about 20,000 votes in 2012, but four years later lost to the same DPP politician by a margin of 25,000. Another target was KMT legislator Alex Tsai, a hated figure in movement circles due to his frequent criticism of protesters in the media. Activists collected enough signatures to hold a recall vote against Tsai in February 2015. Although an overwhelming majority voted for his recall, the turnout rate was only 23 percent—not enough to meet the 50 percent turnout requirement for the recall to be valid. Nevertheless, Tsai's reputation was sufficiently damaged that he did not seek reelection in 2016.

In addition to the KMT, other parties appealed to voters with an anti-social movement message in 2016. The New Party, for instance, made clear its appeal by nominating prominent social movement critic Chiu Yi to head its party list. One of its television ads, which ran on January 2, 2016, opened with a cartoon scene of demonstrators holding placards showing the words "protest" (*kangyi*). The protesters were demonized by giving them demon's eyes. They were then contrasted with social elites (represented by Chiu), who would stand up to this "evil force" (*xie'e shili*). Another case was the emergence of the Faith and Hope Alliance, which campaigned on opposition to marriage equality in its first election. Another of the highest-spending smaller parties to run candidates in this election was the Chinese Unification Promotion Party (CUPP). It had gained notoriety among civil society figures when it led a group of supporters to confront the Sunflower Movement protesters during the occupation of the legislature. In 2016 all three anti–social movement parties failed to gain the necessary five percent to enter the Legislative Yuan.

For some observers, the ability of the NPP to enter the legislature was a key sign of the success of social movement activism. The party had placed heavy emphasis on its social movement roots in its campaign materials. For instance, its party-list election ad showed scenes from a range of Ma-era social movement protests.[61] It particularly chose to highlight the Sunflower occupation of the Legislative Yuan in this advertisement. Moreover, the majority of its candidates, such as Sunflower leader Huang Kuochang, were from social movement backgrounds. Nevertheless, some social movement activists questioned whether the NPP was a genuine movement party due to its preelectoral coalition with the DPP.[62] The DPP yielded three districts and allowed NPP candidates to stand against the KMT with DPP support. This DPP-NPP alliance is apparent in an NPP party-list ad in which NPP leader Huang appears hand-in-hand onstage at a campaign rally with Tsai Ing-wen.

In contrast, other parties preferred to keep their distance from the DPP, including the GPT, SDP, and Trees Party. However, these movement parties, despite running well-funded campaigns, were able to achieve only limited electoral gains. In 2014 the GPT won two local assembly seats, and in 2016 the GPT/SDP Alliance was able to increase its vote share to 2.5 percent from 1.6 percent in 2012. In the aftermath of the GPT's failure to enter the legislature, there was a great deal of disappointment among the party, and some of its politicians withdrew from party politics or switched to the NPP.[63]

Despite the fact that there has been much negative media coverage of the NPP since 2016, it cannot be denied that it introduced a new dynamic into the Legislative Yuan quite unlike that of the old-style splinter parties such as the Taiwan Solidarity Union (TSU) and the People First Party (PFP). In the legislature, the NPP has continued to press the DPP to live up to its electoral promises on issues such as marriage equality. It was able to build on its initial breakthrough in local elections in 2018, winning sixteen council seats around Taiwan, but it faced a much bigger test in 2020, when its members had to decide whether to maintain its semi-alliance with the DPP or make a clear break with the Tsai administration and attempt to become a true "third force" in Taiwanese politics. In the end, this issue became so divisive that it split the party—two of its legislators, Freddy Lim and Hung Tzu-yung, left the NPP and endorsed Tsai Ing-wen for reelection. Nevertheless, the NPP still managed to increase its party-list vote share by almost two points in the 2020 elections, and it holds three seats in the new legislative term.

Conclusion

During the Ma Ying-jeou administration, Taiwan's social movements had a transformative impact on the political scene. From being marginalized and isolated political actors at the outset of the Ma era, social movements became a force to match political parties by the end of his second term. In this study, I have tried systematically to examine the impact of social movements through a number of dimensions using a revised framework of analysis proposed by Neil Carter. On some dimensions, I found the impact to have been especially significant. Social movements were remarkably successful at setting the political agenda as well as changing public opinion on issues such as nuclear power and LGBTQ rights. Social movements were also very successful at developing diverse alliances, such as the Democratic Front Against the CSSTA, that were critical to their ability to achieve concrete policy goals. Although social movements rarely achieve their substantive objectives, in this period they were remarkably successful, especially when we consider how strong the KMT-led government was at the time. Key social movement successes included the mothballing of the Fourth Nuclear Power Plant, blocking of Want Want Group's media acquisitions, and of course preventing the legislative approval of the CSSTA. However, the impacts went much beyond these specific cases. Social movements were able to derail what had seemed to be an unstoppable economic and political integration process with the PRC, something that had eluded the largest opposition party, the DPP. At a time when some observers thought democracy in Taiwan was in crisis, social movements served to revive confidence in and deepen it. Civil society was less successful in achieving legislative goals, but activists were able to lay the foundations for a range of progressive bills that the Tsai administration has been under pressure to pass, most notably marriage equality. Finally, I outlined a number of key political impacts, including the electoral success of the DPP, the DPP's shift toward social movement issues, the resounding defeat of civil society's bitter enemy, the KMT, and the emergence of social movement–linked political parties in the 2014 and 2016 elections. It is likely that historians will judge the legacy of social movements in this period to have been equal to, and probably even to have exceeded, earlier waves of social activism.

Notes

1. Hsiao and Kuan, "The Development of Civil Society Organizations in Post-Authoritarian Taiwan."
2. Fell, *Taiwan's Social Movements Under Ma Ying-jeou.*
3. Fell and Peng, "The Electoral Fortunes of Taiwan's Green Party."
4. Cole, "Was Taiwan's Sunflower Movement Successful?"
5. Cole, "Civic Activism and Protests in Taiwan."
6. Wu Rwei-ren, quoted in Kevin Lee's film *Self Censorship,* available at https://www.youtube.com/watch?v=dpHFVZX2TuA&t=4499s.

7. One study that does address the question of social movement impact is by Da-chi Liao and Yueh-ching Chen, but this focuses on whether social movements can affect their representative deficit. See Liao and Chen, "The Effect of Social Movements on Representative Deficit."

8. Carter, *The Politics of the Environment*, pp. 164–168. Carter is using this framework for environmental movements, but it translates well for movements broadly.

9. Cole, "Civic Activism and Protests in Taiwan," p. 21.

10. Carter, *The Politics of the Environment*, p. 165.

11. See https://udndata.com.

12. For details see Ebsworth, "Not Wanting Want."

13. For details see Grano, *Environmental Governance in Taiwan*, pp. 60–91.

14. TVBS Poll Center, "Survey on CSSTA and Student Occupation of the Legislative Yuan," March 21, 2014; TVBS Poll Center, "Survey of Student Occupation of the Executive Yuan," March 24, 2014. All TVBS poll results are available in PDF format at the poll center website, https://www.tvbs.com.tw/poll-center.

15. TVBS Poll Center, "Survey After Sunflowers Leave the Legislative Yuan," April 10, 2014.

16. TVBS Poll Center, "Survey on Students Announcing They Will Leave the Legislative Yuan and CSSTA," April 8, 2014.

17. TVBS Poll Center, "Survey on Pollution and Nuclear Power Issues," March 8, 2018. Interestingly, the most recent survey, in 2018, showed reduced enthusiasm for the nuclear-free goal.

18. TVBS Poll Center, "Survey on the Fourth Nuclear Power Station Referendum," April 25, 2014.

19. TVBS Poll Center, "Poll After the Ma-Tsai ECFA Debate," April 25, 2010.

20. TVBS Poll Center, "Survey on ECFA Referendum," May 31, 2010.

21. TVBS Poll Center, "Survey on CSSTA Issue and Student Occupation of Legislative Yuan," March 21, 2014.

22. TVBS Poll Center, "Survey on Attitudes Towards Homosexuality," April 19, 2012.

23. Author interview, Taipei, July 27, 2013.

24. For a video of the public dialogue between Premier Jiang and Sunflower Movement leaders, see https://www.youtube.com/watch?v=-MDY53wP2aM. For the dialogue between President Ma and DPP chairman Su Tseng-chang, see https://www.youtube.com/watch?v=Ra85R1b_YIA.

25. See Fan and Wu, "The Long Feminist March in Taiwan," pp. 313–325.

26. Huang, "Uneasy Alliance."

27. Ibid., p. 258.

28. Cheng, "Making Foreign Women the Mother of Our Nation."

29. Tseng, Cheng, and Fell, "The Politics of the Mainland Spouses' Rights Movement in Taiwan."

30. Momesso and Cheng, "A Team Player Pursuing Its Own Dreams," p. 230.

31. Ho, "The Resurgence of Social Movements," p. 111.

32. Ibid.

33. Huang, "Uneasy Alliance," p. 266.

34. Ho, "The Resurgence of Social Movements," pp. 110–112.

35. Author interview, Taipei, July 27, 2013.

36. Hsu, "The China Factor and Taiwan's Civil Society in the Sunflower Movement."

37. Carter, *The Politics of the Environment*, p. 167.

38. Ho, "Resisting Naphtha Crackers."

39. For details on these cases, see Tsai and Ho, "The Tale of Two Off-Shore Islands."

40. For an overview of this movement's trajectory, see Ebsworth, "Not Wanting Want."

41. For details see Grano, *Environmental Governance in Taiwan*, pp. 60–91.

42. See Fan and Wu, "The Long Feminist March in Taiwan," pp. 313–325.

43. On the countermovement, see Cole, *Black Island,* pp. 89–146.

44. Huang "Uneasy Alliance," pp. 268–269.

45. Rawnsley, "New Civic Movements and Further Democratisation in Taiwan."

46. Alison Hsiao, "Activists Assail the KMT over Failed Reform," *Taipei Times,* June 18, 2015, http://www.taipeitimes.com/News/front/archives/2015/06/18/2003620958.

47. Sean Lin, "Act to Block Gangs from Politics," *Taipei Times,* November 11, 2017, http://www.taipeitimes.com/News/front/archives/2017/11/11/2003682051/1.

48. Rawnsley, "New Civic Movements and Further Democratisation in Taiwan."

49. Chen, "This Land Is Your Land?" p. 92.

50. Grugel, *Democratization,* pp. 64–67.

51. Ho, "Politics of Anti-Nuclear Protest in Taiwan."

52. Fell and Peng, "The Electoral Fortunes of Taiwan's Green Party."

53. Cole, "Two Myths About Taiwan's DPP That Need to Be Laid to Rest."

54. See DPP newspaper ad (print edition), *Liberty Times,* January 5, 2016, p. A1.

55. For details on the Dapu case, see Chen, "This Land Is Your Land?"

56. Available at https://www.youtube.com/watch?v=V1TKb1FX4kA&list=PL2q-00FomLN8EWwUyZy19ybYJuWhSFcm.

57. For example, see https://www.youtube.com/watch?v=xLv3wL73RnM&t=4s.

58. Available at https://www.youtube.com/watch?v=KFUSbbErFdA.

59. See Tumin, "The KMT's Recent Campaign Ad and the Minguo Fifties Generation," *New Bloom Magazine,* January 6, 2016, https://newbloommag.net/2016/01/06/kmt-intergenerational-conflict-ad.

60. KMT's Hung Hsiu-chu television ad available https://www.youtube.com/watch?v=zw1srbkvHsw.

61. NPP party-list television ad available at https://www.youtube.com/watch?v=O6p8i5Fx1Gg.

62. For instance, I have termed it a "hybrid" party, with both mainstream-party and movement-party characteristics. See Fell, "Small Parties in Taiwan's 2016 National Elections?"

63. See also Chapter 5 in this volume.

13

Who Are the Protesters?
Why Are They Protesting?

*Min-hua Huang and
Mark Weatherall*

Since the 2000 presidential election and the subsequent formation of the rival pan-Blue and pan-Green camps, Taiwanese politics has experienced two major protest movements against the incumbent government. The first wave of protests were directed against the administration of Chen Shui-bian, beginning in the aftermath of the president's highly contested victory in the 2004 election and culminating with mass street protests against alleged corruption by the president and members of his family in late 2006. The second wave of protests were directed against the administration of Ma Ying-jeou, and reached their climax in March and April 2014 when student protesters occupied the Legislative Yuan for twenty-four days to protest the passage of the Cross-Strait Services Trade Agreement (CSSTA) by the ruling Kuomintang (KMT) without a full legislative review. In both cases, the protesters called into question the very foundation of the government's democratic legitimacy—claiming that it was either elected illegitimately and abusing state power for personal enrichment in the case of the Chen administration, or riding roughshod over democratic processes to force a highly unpopular trade agreement through the Legislative Yuan with little oversight in the case of the Ma administration. The two waves of protests were major contributing factors to devastating electoral defeats suffered by the ruling parties in subsequent elections. However, Taiwan's democratic institutions have shown significant resiliency in the face of worsening polarization and mass protests, even as protesters called into question the legitimacy of democratic institutions by refusing to accept the president's electoral victory and by occupying the nation's highest legislative body.

Despite the importance of these two waves of protest in the context of Taiwan's democratic consolidation, there have been few attempts to provide empirical answers to some of the important questions raised by the protests. For instance, who were the protesters in each wave of protests? How did their demographic and ideological profiles differ from the wider society? What factors can account for the resilience of Taiwan's democratic institutions in the face of these waves of protests? What are the similarities and differences between the two waves of protest activity? This chapter attempts to answer these questions using data from four waves of the Asian Barometer Survey (ABS), focusing on two peaks of protest activity identified in the ABS second wave (carried out between January and February 2006) and the fourth wave (carried out between June and November 2014).

Political Protest During Taiwan's
Democratic Transition and Consolidation

The mobilization of civil society forces in Taiwan can be traced back to the 1980s, when social actors first tried to force the government to move beyond its focus on economic growth and political stability and address the many serious social and environmental problems faced by the island.[1] Following the lifting of martial law in 1987, there was a sharp increase in protest activity, with a flourishing civil society taking advantage of the more liberal political atmosphere to launch movements demanding reform across a range of issues including women's rights, workers' rights, environmental protection, and transitional justice.[2]

Amid this upsurge in civil society activity, two protest movements had a defining impact on Taiwan's political development and its eventual democratization. The first was the pro-democracy demonstrations held in the southern city of Kaohsiung on December 10, 1979, to mark Human Rights Day, and the subsequent government crackdown, which later became known as the Kaohsiung or Formosa (Meilidao) Incident. The protests ended with the arrest and trial of leading opposition figures, but they also consolidated political opposition to the ruling KMT, which continued to strengthen through the 1980s. Many of the participants in the Kaohsiung Incident went on to become leading opposition figures—one of the defense lawyers was Chen Shui-bian, who went on to serve as president between 2000 and 2008, while his vice president, Annette Lu, served a five-and-a-half-year prison sentence for her role in the protests. The second was the Wild Lily student movement, which took place between March 16 and March 22, 1990. The Wild Lily protests were instrumental in pushing for constitutional reforms that introduced direct elections for the president and vice president and full elections to legislative bodies (the Legislative Yuan and the National Assembly) for the first time since the KMT's retreat to Taiwan in 1949. As with the Kaohsiung Incident, some of the student leaders of the Wild Lily Movement, including Lin Chia-lung and Cheng Wen-tsan (who later served as mayors of Taichung City and Taoyuan City, respectively), later became prominent figures within the Democratic Progressive Party (DPP).

Notwithstanding the prominent role that many of the leaders of the Kaohsiung Incident and the Wild Lily protests later went on to play within the DPP, the genesis of the two movements was markedly different. In 1979, Taiwan was still under martial law, and new parties were banned. Instead, opposition figures cooperated under an "outside the party" (*dangwai*) banner. The Kaohsiung Incident protests were organized by *Formosa Magazine* (*Meilidao Zazhi*), a publication set up by the *dangwai* under the direction of veteran opposition legislator Huang Hsin-chieh, which was intended to act as a vehicle for an island-wide quasi-party.[3] However, while the Kaohsiung Incident protests were organized by a quasi-party organization (*dangwai*), the Wild Lily student protests were organized outside of the opposition DPP. Although the DPP subsequently mobilized large demonstrations in support of the students on March 18 and 19, and the students shared many of the same demands with the DPP, the Wild Lily protesters steadfastly maintained their independence from party politics.[4]

Although civil society movements strove to maintain their independence from the DPP prior to 2000, activists saw new opportunities to work within political institutions to achieve political change when Chen Shui-bian was elected president. However, once in power, the priorities of the DPP administration, which was constrained by the continued KMT majority in the Legislative Yuan, gradually turned toward ensuring stability rather than delivering on its promises of major reform. Furthermore, the economic slowdown during Chen's first term compelled the government to revert to KMT-style developmentalism at the expense of environmental protection and social welfare, further marginalizing the social movements that previously had such high expectations of the DPP government.[5] Despite the disappointment that many social movements felt toward Chen once he took office, the 2000 election marked an important turning point. For the first time, civil society leaders held positions within the government, and could to some extent pursue their agendas within formal political institutions. The KMT also actively courted civil society organizations who felt excluded by the new administration, albeit with varying degrees of success.

At the same time, with the growing polarization of Taiwanese politics between pan-Green and pan-Blue camps, protest activities became increasingly partisan in nature, with civil society at most playing only a supporting role. In 2003, the KMT organized the first mass protests against the Chen administration, rallying against the so-called three highs (high tuition fees, high health insurance premiums, and high unemployment).[6] Following the contested election in 2004, which Chen won by less than 30,000 votes out of 13 million cast amid opposition claims of voting irregularities and doubts about an apparent assassination attempt on Chen on the final day of the campaign, KMT supporters launched large-scale and often violent protests against the result. The demonstrations came to a climax on March 27, when as many as half a million protesters gathered in front of the presidential office to demand a vote recount and an investigation into the disputed shooting incident on the eve of the election.[7] Partisan mobilization was not limited to the pan-Blue side. In 2005, following the passage of the Anti-Secession Law by the National People's Congress of the People's Republic of China (PRC), formalizing Beijing's long-standing policy to use "non-peaceful" means to prevent Taiwan from establishing formal independence, pan-Green parties together with civic groups mobilized large anti-China demonstrations.[8] However, pan-Green mobilization based on appeals for Taiwan's independence did not halt the tide of pan-Blue protests, which culminated in 2006 with massive protests demanding the resignation of Chen for alleged involvement in corruption.

In 2008, after Ma Ying-jeou won back the presidency for the KMT, civil society–led protest movements underwent a revival.[9] The visits of the PRC's top Taiwan affairs negotiator, Chen Yunlin, in 2008 and 2011 generated violent protests. The police crackdown on the 2011 protests against Chen's travels around the island led to the student-led Wild Strawberry Movement. The Strawberries were unsuccessful in their demands, but the organizational skills developed during the protests laid the foundation for the Sunflower Movement three years later. That movement began at 9:00 P.M. on March 18, 2014, when student protesters stormed Taiwan's Legislative Yuan to protest the KMT's attempt to approve the Cross-Strait Services Trade Agreement[10] without a full legislative review. The occupation of the Legislative Yuan eventually lasted twenty-three days, and the protesters also briefly occupied the Executive Yuan (the office of the premier). Though the protesters eventually withdrew from the Legislative Yuan on April 10, the movement was ultimately successfully in blocking the passage of the CSSTA and contributed to the KMT's devastating election defeat less than two years later.

From these four landmark movements, we can identify two main sources of protest. The first is partisan mobilization, meaning protests against the incumbent government mobilized by opposition parties. Although the DPP had not yet been founded in 1979, the Kaohsiung Incident protests belonged to this type, since they were organized by the quasi-party *dangwai* under the leadership of veteran opposition legislator Huang Hsin-chieh. The wave of protests that took place following Chen Shui-bian's contested electoral victory in 2004 and culminated with massive protests demanding Chen's resignation in 2006 were also partisan in their genesis, even though the 2006 protests were fronted by former DPP leader Shih Ming-teh. The second source of protest is civil society organizations. Since the 1980s, Taiwan has witnessed numerous protests by a wide range of civil society groups, including environmental protection groups, women's rights groups, and workers' rights groups. However, the two most important civil society protests movements in terms of their long-term impact—the Wild Lily and Sunflower Movements—were both organized by students. The success of these student movements in redirecting Taiwan's political trajectory can be attributed to their politically privileged status: in culturally Chinese societies, students are assumed to be pure and not motivated by personal greed or self-interest. The student-led protest movements fought hard to hold on to this "moral" advantage by resisting the involvement of outside groups—particularly the opposition DPP.

Previous Research on Civil Society Activism and Protest Events in Taiwan

Since civil society activism and protest events played a critical role in Taiwan's democratic transition and consolidation, they have been the subject of considerable academic interest from scholars. These studies have contributed significantly to our understanding of a number of important topics, including the historical origins and social and political context of rising civil society activism and protest movements in Taiwan, the strategies and backgrounds of activists, the relationship between activists and other political actors in Taiwan, and the impact of civil society activism and protest events on Taiwan's democratic transition and consolidation.

Early research on civil society and protest movements coincided with the beginnings of Taiwan's democratic transition in the late 1980s and early 1990s. This work generally understood social movements as arising in opposition to the hegemonic party-state in the context of a rapidly modernizing society, while rejecting class-based accounts of social movements. For example, Michael Hsiao has argued that although protest movements pursued a "depoliticized" strategy by deliberately maintaining their independence from the opposition DPP, they ultimately arose out of and were defined by their opposition to the dominant KMT party-state.[11] However, as Ming-sho Ho points out with regard to Taiwan's anti-nuclear movement, social movements were often dependent on the DPP to achieve policy goals.[12] Thomas Gold has also taken a state-centered approach, explaining the emergence of social movements as a challenge to the hegemony and dominant ideology of the KMT party-state.[13] Shui-yan Tang and Ching-ping Tang have also looked at the rise of environmental protest movements during Taiwan's democratization, arguing that such protests were increasingly effective because the retreating authoritarian regime was no longer able to ignore local environmental concerns in pursuit of economic growth.[14] Teresa Wright has argued that the emergence of student-led protest movements after the 1980s was facilitated by a change in the political opportunity structure caused by the decision of political elites to ease restraints on political expression.[15]

The first peaceful transfer of power, in 2000, marked an important turning point for civil society in Taiwan, because it replaced the previously dominant KMT with a DPP administration that was expected to be more sympathetic to the demands of civil society. Researchers turned their focus to the relationship between civil society and the new administration, showing how that relationship changed from confrontational in the 1980s and 1990s to more cooperative after 2000.[16] However, researchers found that the ability of civil society to influence government policy was in fact quite limited, as the new administration largely adopted the same growth-orientated developmentalist policies of the old regime.[17] Following the return of the KMT to power in 2008, researchers turned to confrontations between the state and a resurgent civil society, marked by major protest movements including the Wild Strawberry protests of 2008, the anti–media monopoly protests of 2012, and the Sunflower Movement of 2014. The civil society protests during the Ma era have been the subject of extensive academic study, including an edited volume covering protests ranging from those of national significance (such as the anti–media monopoly protests and the Sunflower protests) to more localized civil society movements (such as anti-casino movements in Penghu and Matsu).[18]

Although these studies have contributed to our understanding of the relationship between social movements and the state, and the role of social movements in Taiwan's democratic transition and consolidation, they suffer from some limitations. First, they tend to focus on protest movements arising from civil society organizations, which are generally assumed to be relatively independent from party politics. However, many of the most successful protest movements during the last three decades were in fact heavily influenced by, and even organized by, political parties, even when parties did not assume a formal leadership role so the movement could claim nonpartisan support from across society. Even in cases such as the Sunflower Movement that were organized by genuinely autonomous civil society organizations, the durability of these movements can be in large part attributed to the tacit (and sometimes explicit) support of the opposition DPP. Second, studies of protest movements tend to focus on the choices of the major actors within the movements and their interactions with the state and other political actors using research methods such as in-depth interviews and participant observation. However, because of this focus on the major actors in civil society movements, the importance of the ordinary participants (who were often not members of any of the groups participating in the protest) and support from the wider society are often overlooked. For example, in addition to their effective organization and experience accumulated from previous protest movements, the relatively small numbers of core participants in the Sunflower Movement were bolstered by the presence of the protesters who subsequently gathered outside of the Legislative Yuan in support of the occupation. The students also enjoyed the support of important segments of society, including some parts of the media,[19] many academics,[20] and a large number of ordinary people.[21] Without the legitimation and financial resources that these supporters provided to the movement, the occupation would not have been possible.

Who Is Protesting? Participants in Political Activism

The Asian Barometer Survey has completed four survey waves in Taiwan. The first wave was completed between June and July 2001, the second between January and February 2006, the third between January and February 2010, and the fourth between June and November 2014. The first and third waves of the survey were completed during the first terms of President Chen Shui-bian and President Ma Ying-jeou, respectively. In 2001, civil society was still adapting to a new administration that was potentially more sympathetic to their concerns, while the pan-Blue camp remained in turmoil following Chen's unexpected victory. In sharp contrast, civil society protests against the Ma Ying-jeou administration started early in his term, the most prominent being the Wild Strawberry Movement protests of 2008. However, during this period, civil society protests were still confined to relatively small groups of political activists, with a majority of society continuing to adopt a "wait-and-see" attitude toward the direction of the new government, whereas early 2006 and middle-to-late 2014 were periods of widespread participation in protest movements from across society. In early 2006, President Chen Shui-bian was still facing a series of protests following his contested election victory two years earlier, while in middle-to-late 2014 the administration of Ma Ying-jeou was struggling with the political aftermath of the Sunflower Movement protests.

The two peaks in protest are reflected in the results from the ABS over the four survey waves. In Figure 13.1 we show political activism, measured as whether the respondent had participated in a protest or a march in the past three years, over the four waves of the survey. Since we are interested in identifying the background of participants in political activism, we divide the population into five generations. The first is the pre-1949 generation, those who had reached elementary school age prior to the KMT's retreat to Taiwan. The second generation completed high school before 1971, the year of the Republic of China's withdrawal from the United Nations. This generation experienced both oppressive authoritarian rule and rapid economic development during their initial period of political socialization. The third generation, who completed high school between Taiwan's withdrawal from the United Nations and the end of martial law, grew up in a period of what scholars of Taiwan have referred to as "soft" authoritarianism[22] (in contrast to the "hard" authoritarianism of the 1950s and 1960s), and enjoyed the benefits of increasing economic opportunities provided by the island's continued rapid economic growth. The fourth generation completed their high school education after the lifting of martial law in 1987, enjoying the political freedoms offered by the island's emerging democracy, but often suffering financially as economic growth slowed. The fifth generation completed their high school education after the abolition of the joint entrance examination in 2001, and were socialized in a period of comprehensive educational reform that transformed the school curriculum in Taiwan.

Comparing political activism between generations over the four waves of the survey, we find that between 2001 and 2006, the 1950–1971 generation, followed by the pre-1949 generation, showed the most dramatic increase in political activism. In contrast, political activism among the 1987–2001 generation barely increased at all over the same period. This finding demonstrates that participation in political activism during Chen's second term was dominated by older citizens, in particular the generation who completed high school between 1950 and 1971 and were socialized during the period of the Kuomintang's "hard authoritarianism." In 2010, activism fell across the population as a whole, most dramatically among the 1950–1971 generation, although activism continued to increase among the pre-1949 and 1987–2001 generations. In 2014, levels of political activism recovered, but the profile of activists in 2014 was very different from the peak of 2006, with a significant rise in activism among the youth and a decline in activism among the older generations.

Figure 13.1   Activism in Taiwan

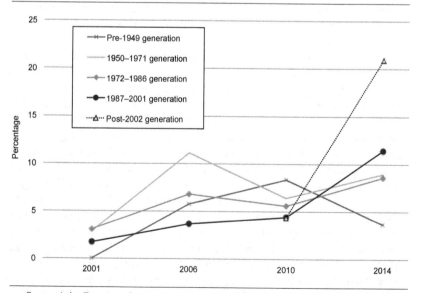

Source: Asian Barometer Survey, Waves 1–4 (2001–2003, 2006–2008, 2010–2012, 2014–2016).

In Figure 13.2 we divide participation in political activism for each generation by level of education, distinguishing between citizens with at least a university education and those educated only to high school or lower. Previous research has shown that educational attainment is positively associated with political participation.[23] Our data show that participation in Taiwan is consistent with the findings of the empirical literature, with the two spikes in political activism both dominated by citizens with at least a university-level education, despite the substantial differences in patterns of political mobilization in 2006 and 2014. In 2006, there was a dramatic increase in participation in political activism among those educated to at least university level in the pre-1949 and 1950–1971 generations, while levels of political activism among those without a university education remained low. In 2014, there were substantial increases in participation among those educated to university level in the 1987–2001 and post-2002 generations, while political activism among their counterparts without a university education remained at very low levels.

Why Are They Protesting? The Political Views of Activists

In the preceding section we showed that protesters in the 2001 and 2006 surveys were likely to come from the better-educated members of the older

Figure 13.2 Fluctuating Activism by Education and Generation

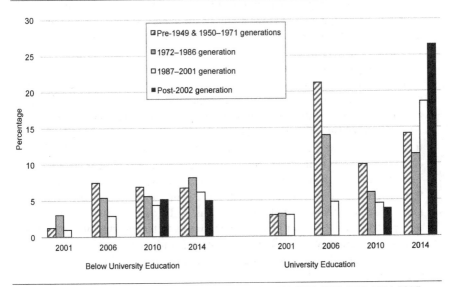

Source: Asian Barometer Survey, Waves 1–4 (2001–2003, 2006–2008, 2010–2012, 2014–2016).

generations, while those in the 2010 and 2014 surveys were still highly educated but on average much younger than in the earlier surveys. In Table 13.1 we show the results of an ANOVA analysis comparing the political attitudes of each of these demographic groups in 2006 and 2014, respectively, with the attitudes of other demographic groups.

The top half of Table 13.1 shows a comparison of the political attitudes of the older generations with a university degree when compared with the younger generations with a university degree (Group A) and all generations without a university degree (Group B) across the four waves of the survey. In 2006, when activism among the older better-educated citizens peaked, there was no significant difference between this demographic group and the younger generations with a university degree on the first five items listed (defend our own way of life, Taiwanese identity, pan-Green partisanship, satisfaction with the Chen government, and corruption), but there was a significant negative difference with all generations without a university degree on all of the items with the exception of corruption. The only consistent finding was a significant positive difference with the other demographic groups on the perception that the last election was unfair. Therefore, in early 2006, the consistent factor leading to discontent among the better-educated members of the older generations was the perceived unfairness of the previous presidential election, rather than corruption, which only became the dominant issue later in the same year.

The bottom half of Table 13.1 compares the political attitudes of the younger generations with a university degree with the older generations with a university degree (Group C) and all generations without a university degree (Group D) across the four waves of the survey. Interestingly, given the prominence of the potentially adverse effects of the PRC's growing influence on Taiwan during the Sunflower protests, in the 2014 survey we found no statistically significant difference between the attitudes of the better-educated members of the younger generations, who were the main participants in political protests over this period, and the other demographic groups. In addition, despite the attempts to link the Sunflower protests to the DPP, there was no significant difference in the level of pan-Green partisanship between the better-educated members of the younger generations and the less-educated. However, the better-educated members of the younger generations were more likely to be pan-Green partisans than their peers in older generations. Finally, we found that the better-educated members of the younger generations consistently had greater levels of Taiwanese identity and were more likely than the other demographic groups to believe that national officials were corrupt. We also found that this generation was consistently more likely than the other demographic groups to hold both of these orientations at the same time.

The findings of the ANOVA analysis show that Chen's fiercely contested reelection in 2004 was a crucial rallying point for protests among

Table 13.1 ANOVA Means Comparison

Comparing the oldest generation with at least a university education to Groups A and B

Variables	W1 A	W1 B	W2 A	W2 B	W3 A	W3 B	W4 A	W4 B
Defend our own way of life	—	—	—	/	—	—	—	—
Taiwanese identity	—	/	—	/	—	/	\	/
Pan-Green partisanship	—	/	—	/	—	—	\	/
Satisfaction with the Chen/Ma government	—	/	—	/	—	—	—	—
Corruption	\	—	—	—	\	/	\	/
China's influence does more harm than good	n/a	n/a	n/a	n/a	—	—	—	—
Last presidential election was unfair	n/a	n/a	⬭ (circled)		—	—	—	—

Comparing the youngest generation with at least a university education to Groups C and D

Variables	W1 C	W1 D	W2 C	W2 D	W3 C	W3 D	W4 C	W4 D
Defend our own way of life	—	—	—	/	—	—	—	—
Taiwanese identity	/	—	/	—	/	—	⬭ (circled)	
Pan-Green partisanship	/	—	/	—	—	—	/	—
Satisfaction with the Chen/Ma government	/	—	—	/	—	—	—	—
Corruption	—	—	/	\	/	\	⬭ (circled)	
China's influence does more harm than good	n/a	n/a	n/a	n/a	/	—	—	—
Last presidential election was unfair	n/a	n/a	\	—	—	—	—	/
Taiwanese identity & Corruption	/	—	/	—	/	—	⬭ (circled)	

Source: Asian Barometer Survey, Waves 1–4.

Notes: ANOVA tests were conducted using SPSS. The reported results do not assume equal variances between groups. The level of significance is set at $p \leq 0.05$ for the contrast tests.

In the left-hand columns (A and C), an upward-sloping line indicates that the measured group is significantly higher than either Group A or Group C, while a downward-sloping line indicates that the measured group is significantly lower than either Group A or Group C.

In the right-hand columns (B and D), an upward-sloping line indicates that the measured group is significantly lower than either Group B or Group D, while a downward-sloping line indicates that the measured group is significantly higher than either Group B or Group D.

The circled results indicate "peaks" where the measured group is significantly higher than both of the two comparison groups.

Flat lines indicate no significant finding.

Group A refers to other younger generations with at least a university education. Group B refers to all generations with a high school or lower education. Group C refers to other older generations with at least a university education. Group D refers to all generations with a high school or lower education.

better-educated and older voters against the president in the early years of his second term. Figure 13.2 shows that there was a spike in participation in 2006 in protests among the pre-1949 and 1950–1971 generations educated to university level. Figure 13.3 shows that in 2006 a majority (56 percent) of respondents in these groups believed that the "last election was unfair," while only around a third or less of the other demographic groups held the same view. The belief that Chen had "stolen" the 2004 election was widespread among older and better-educated voters, but not among older and less-educated voters, or among young voters regardless of their level of education.

The ANOVA analysis also shows that younger and better-educated citizens were more likely to identify as Taiwanese and to believe that most national officials were corrupt. Unlike the 2004 election, Ma Ying-jeou's two election wins in 2008 and 2012 were relatively free of controversy. However, throughout Ma's presidency, there was increasing tension between growing Taiwanese identity, particularly among young people, and Ma's efforts to improve relations with Beijing. Furthermore, the claimed "peace dividend" from improved cross-Strait relations was perceived to benefit

Figure 13.3   Share of Respondents Who Thought Last Presidential Election Was Unfair

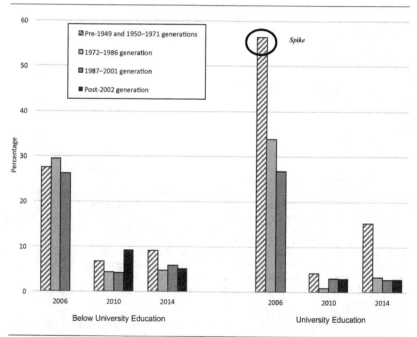

Source: Asian Barometer Survey, Waves 2–4 (2006–2008, 2010–2012, 2014–2016).

almost exclusively a narrow and corrupt business and political elite. To capture the intersection of these two items, we measure the proportion of respondents who both identified as Taiwanese and perceived most national officials to be corrupt. As Figure 13.4 shows, this view was increasingly held among young people (both the 1987–2001 and post-2001 generations) in the two surveys conducted during Ma's presidency, but was most apparent among the youngest and best-educated generation in the 2014 survey: 74 percent of the university-educated post-2014 generation both identified as Taiwanese and believed that most national officials were corrupt.

Mass Protest and Democratic Resilience

The mass protests in 2006 and 2014 were not only a challenge to the incumbent regime. At a more fundamental level they also raised questions about the legitimacy of Taiwan's democratic institutions. In the period leading up to the 2006 survey, protesters repeatedly challenged the legitimacy of Chen's 2004 election victory, and by extension Taiwan's ability to hold free and fair elections; in the period leading up to the 2014 survey,

Figure 13.4 Taiwanese Identity and Perceived Corruption

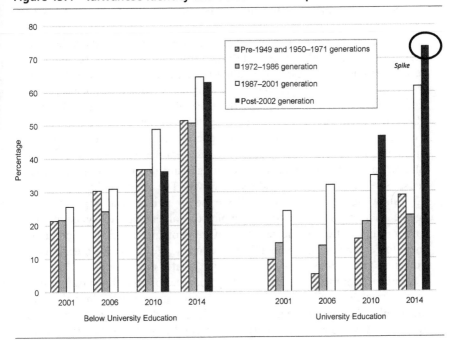

Source: Asian Barometer Survey, Waves 1–4 (2001–2003, 2006–2008, 2010–2012, 2014–2016).

protesters challenged the legitimacy of the legislative process, arguing that the failure to follow correct procedures was serious enough to justify the unprecedented occupation of the Legislative Yuan. Yet, ultimately, both crises were defused peacefully and the institutions of democracy survived. This was because, at least in part, despite the protesters' criticisms of the functioning of democratic institutions, discontent with how the institutions of democracy worked in practice did not undermine the reservoir of support for democracy as a preferred political system or lead discontented citizens toward authoritarian alternatives.

In Table 13.2 we show items from the ABS measuring support for democracy, rejection of authoritarianism, belief in procedural norms, and political efficacy across the four survey waves. We are interested in comparing whether attitudes on these dimensions showed the same peak-shaped co-variation between the demographic groups who were most likely to be involved in political protests, namely the better-educated of the older generations, who believed in 2006 that the previous election (in 2004) was unfair, and the better-educated of the youngest generation, who in 2014 had a strong Taiwanese identity and who believed that most officials were corrupt. If we find that these groups had weaker democratic orientations when compared to the population as a whole, this may be an indication that these groups were less committed to democracy, suggesting that the protests challenged not only the government but also the continued sustainability of democracy in the country.

First, we compare the attitudes of the better-educated of the older generations who believed in 2006 that the previous election was unfair with the rest of the population. Since we do not have any items in the first wave of the ABS that capture perceived fairness of the previous presidential election, we have only the most recent three waves of data to identify the variables that show the same co-variation pattern, which can help us identify the factors behind the 2006 protests. Specifically, we need to identify the attitudinal deviation of the targeted groups from the remainder of the population in the second survey wave, suggesting divergent findings from those observed in the third and fourth waves. The middle column of Table 13.2 shows three findings that indicate the potential causal impact related to the sudden peak in activism among the older educated generations: preferability, efficacy, and rejection of dictatorship. In terms of commitment to democracy, the preferability measure suggests that the older better-educated generations in general had a far greater rate of approval (around 20 percent) compared to the rest of the population, but this measure was largely reduced to a level similar to the rest of the population in the second wave (plus 2 percent). Regarding the efficacy of democracy, this measure was far lower (minus 19 percent) in the second wave for these groups than the rest of the population, deviating from the increase seen in the last two

Table 13.2 Means Comparisons of Targeted Groups for Democratic Attitudes

Target Group (vs. Rest)	Older generations + University education + Unfair election			Youngest generation + University education + Taiwan identity + Perceived corruption			
Wave	W2	W3	W4	W1	W2	W3	W4
Support for democracy							
• The extent you want our country to be democratic in the future. (desirability)	−3% (89%)	−4.0% (88%)	−6% (86%)	+2% (89%)	+1% (93%)	+3% (95%)	+1% (93%)
• Democracy is suitable for our country. (suitability)	−15% (61%)	−14% (65%)	−16% (65%)	−7% (65%)	+1% (76%)	+5% (84%)	+9% (88%)
• Democracy is always preferable to any other kind of government. (preferability)	+2% (53%)	+20% (71%)	+23% (69%)	+17% (61%)	−4% (47%)	+9% (61%)	−1% (46%)
• Democracy is capable of solving the problems of our society. (efficacy)	−19% (45%)	−4% (62%)	+9% (71%)	+6% (63%)	+5% (66%)	+13% (78%)	+12% (72%)
Rejection of authoritarianism							
• We should get rid of parliament and elections and have a strong leader decide things. (reject dictatorship)	+2% (84%)	−12% (73%)	−5% (80%)	+7% (86%)	−3% (80%)	+6% (89%)	+3% (87%)
• No opposition party should be allowed to compete for power. (reject one-party rule)	−6% (83%)	+0% (91%)	−6% (85%)	+3% (85%)	−2% (87%)	+4% (94%)	+1% (92%)
• The army should come in to govern the country. (reject military rule)	−5% (89%)	+0% (96%)	−5% (91%)	+4% (96%)	+3% (96%)	+1% (96%)	+3% (99%)
Belief in procedural norm							
• When the country is facing a difficult situation, it is not okay for the government to) disregard the law in order to deal with the situation. (reject disregard the law)	+4% (79%)	+4% (76%)	−5% (76%)	−7% (60%)	−3% (70%)	+15% (87%)	+3% (83%)
Political efficacy							
• People like me have influence over the government. (influence government)	—	+8% (39%)	−3% (33%)	−1% (32%)	—	−3% (28%)	+20% (53%)
• People have the power to change the government. (change government	−6% (59%)	+11% (70%)	−15% (44%)	—	+5% (69%)	−2% (58%)	−5% (54%)

Source: Asian Barometer Survey, Waves 1–4.

Notes: Entry is the means difference of the targeted vs. remaining groups. Numbers in parentheses are the percentages of the targeted group. Because we are interested in trends over time rather than a particular value at a specific point in time, we do not report the result of significant tests.

waves. However, for the rejection of dictatorship, our findings show that these groups had around the same level of liberal democratic orientations (plus 2 percent) compared to the rest of the population, which runs counter to the trend in later waves. These findings suggest that the 2006 protesters might have had a weaker commitment to democracy as well as less confidence that democracy could solve societal problems, but simultaneously may have been less likely to consider dictatorship as an alternative to democracy. In other words, while the 2006 protests might be associated with weaker commitment to and confidence in democracy among the older better-educated generations, this group exhibited the same level of rejection of dictatorship.

Second, we look at the democratic attitudes of the better-educated respondents of the youngest generation, who were most likely to identify exclusively as Taiwanese and who believed that most national officials were corrupt. Of the four dimensions the 2014 protest might have impacted, support for the suitability of democracy and the two measures of political efficacy show peak-shaped co-variation. In terms of the suitability of democracy, this group showed an even stronger belief that democracy was suitable for Taiwan than did the rest of the population. In fact, attitudes among this group flipped over the four waves: in 2001, they were on average less likely than the rest of the population to believe that democracy was suitable for Taiwan (at minus 7 percent), but in 2014 they were more likely to hold this view (plus 9 percent). For the two measures of political efficacy, this group showed two apparently conflicting psychological orientations: on the one hand, they were much more likely to believe that they could exert influence over the government (plus 20 percent) than the rest of the population; but on the other hand, they were less likely to believe that they had the power to change the government (minus 5 percent). In fact, such conflicting orientations were very salient only in the fourth wave, and this belief that their actions could influence the government was likely a powerful motivating factor for the protesters.

Overall, the findings from the co-variation analysis of the two protests in 2006 and 2014 show the same message: those who protested were more apprehensive about the state of Taiwan's democracy and were more frustrated with the incumbent government. For 2006, we find eroding democratic legitimacy, in terms of the preferability and efficacy of democracy, for the better-educated members of the older generations, who tended to believe that the last election was unfair. At the same time, respondents in this group were more aware of the political risks of dictatorship. In 2014, apprehension about Taiwan's democracy was more apparent among the better-educated of the youngest generation, who were most likely to identify as Taiwanese and to perceive government officials as corrupt. This group showed stronger belief for the suitability and efficacy of democracy than the population as a whole, and were simultaneously more pessimistic about whether they could actually change the government but optimistic about whether they could exert influence over the government.

Conclusion

Political protests, from the Kaohsiung Incident in 1979, to the growing civil society movements in the 1980s, to the Wild Lily Movement of 1990, have been central to Taiwan's transition from an authoritarian single-party regime to its current vibrant, multiparty democracy. As Taiwan's democracy has consolidated, political protests have continued to play a key role. However, despite the extensive research on civil society and political protest in Taiwan, there have been few attempts to investigate how the demographic profiles of the protesters or their ideological orientations differ from the wider society. We find that for the protests against the presidency of Chen Shui-bian, those people who participated tended to be older and well-educated and were motivated by a belief in the illegitimacy of Chen's 2004 electoral win. In contrast, for the protests against the presidency of Ma Ying-jeou, those who participated were younger and well-educated and were more likely to identify as Taiwanese and to believe that politicians were corrupt. Interestingly, however, these younger well-educated citizens were no more likely than the population as a whole to view the influence of the PRC in adverse terms. Finally, the democratic orientations of these groups were not generally weaker than those of the population as a whole, and indeed in 2016, protesters had stronger democratic orientations than the population as a whole on a number of measures. Therefore, although the protesters were challenging core institutions of Taiwan's democracy, they did not reject democracy as their preferred political system or consider authoritarian alternatives to democracy. This deep reservoir of support for democracy can help us explain how both crises were defused peacefully and the institutions of democracy were eventually able to resume normal functioning.

Although the two waves of protests were defining features of the Chen and Ma presidencies, their political effects proved to be short-lived. Ma Ying-jeou swept to power in 2008 on the back of public anger against the alleged corruption of the Chen Shui-bian regime, and Ma successfully won reelection in 2012. Yet this initial wave of popular support and enthusiasm eventually evaporated as the Ma administration faced multiple domestic challenges and criticism of its handling of cross-Strait relations. The controversy over the CSSTA was of course one of the factors critical to the rise of civil society protests against the KMT government. However, although Tsai Ing-wen and the DPP benefited from popular anger against President Ma and demands for change, particularly from young people, President Tsai has also faced domestic and international challenges. In particular, controversial amendments to the Labor Standards Act were widely criticized for favoring employers over employees. The Tsai administration has also struggled to provide solutions to issues of concern to young people, such as low salaries and unaffordable housing. These issues have the potential to produce another wave of protests in the future, perhaps condemning Tsai to the same fate that befell her two predecessors.

Although this study can help us understand more about who was protesting and why they were protesting, there are a number of limitations due to the data we have available. First, although protests in Ma's second term were largely anti-government, during Chen's second term the government was actually also effective at mobilizing its own protests, most notably against the passage of the PRC's Anti-Secession Law in 2005, which formalized Beijing's threat to use "nonpeaceful" means against Taiwan in the event of a declaration of independence. To test for the effect of pro-government protesters, we look at whether protesters supported the winning or losing side in the preceding election. In the second wave of the ABS, supporters of the losing side (pan-Blue) were much more likely to participate in protests than supporters of the winning side (pan-Green) among the oldest generation (born before 1949). However, this gap was less apparent among the 1950–1971 generation, who made up the largest group of protesters at the time of the second-wave survey. For the fourth-wave survey, young people who supported the losing side (pan-Green) in the most recent election were much more likely to participate in the protests than their peers who supported the winning side (pan-Blue), lending support to our observation that protests during the second term of the Ma presidency were largely anti-government. Overall, although protesters were more likely to be opponents of the government (based on their vote in the previous election), we cannot entirely rule out the effect of pro-government protests. Second, the timing of the surveys may be an issue. The fourth-wave survey was conducted between June and November 2014 after the Sunflower protests, effectively covering the major protest movement of Ma's presidency. However, the second-wave survey was conducted in early 2006, prior to the large anticorruption protests against Chen later in the same year. If the survey had been carried out later in the year, we might expect to find some different results with regard to the ideological orientations of the protesters, in particular a greater focus on the problem of corruption in the central government.

Notes

1. Hsiao, "Emerging Social Movements and the Rise of a Demanding Civil Society in Taiwan."
2. Ho, "Understanding the Trajectory of Social Movements in Taiwan."
3. Rigger, *Politics in Taiwan*, p. 117.
4. Smith and Yu, "Wild Lilies and Sunflowers."

5. Ho, "Taiwan's State and Social Movements Under the DPP Government."

6. Ibid.

7. Caroline Gluck, "Police End Taiwan Ballot Protest," *BBC News,* March 28, 2004, http://news.bbc.co.uk/2/hi/asia-pacific/3575875.stm.

8. "Taiwan Rallies Against China Law," *BBC News,* March 26, 2005, http://news .bbc.co.uk/2/hi/asia-pacific/4382971.stm.

9. Fell, *Taiwan's Social Movements Under Ma Ying-jeou.* See also Chapter 12 of this volume.

10. The CSSTA is an agreement between the PRC and Taiwan on the liberalization of trade in services. The agreement was signed in June 2013 but remained unratified by the Legislative Yuan at the end of the Ma presidency.

11. Hsiao, "Emerging Social Movements and the Rise of a Demanding Civil Society in Taiwan."

12. Ho, "The Politics of Anti-Nuclear Protest in Taiwan."

13. Gold, "Civil Society and Taiwan's Quest for Identity."

14. Tang and Tang, "Democratization and Environmental Politics in Taiwan."

15. Wright, "Student Mobilization in Taiwan."

16. Hsiao and Ho, "East Asia's New Democracies."

17. Ho, "Taiwan's State and Social Movements Under the DPP Government."

18. Fell, *Taiwan's Social Movements Under Ma Ying-Jeou.*

19. The movement benefited from (often favorable) twenty-four-hour coverage on cable television, while also making adept use of social media.

20. For example, a group of presidents from fifty-two universities issued a statement on March 21 urging Ma Ying-jeou to respond to student demands. Many academics also voiced support for the movement. See Yi-ching Chen and Rachel Lin, "University Heads Call on Ma to Respond to Occupiers," *Taipei Times,* March 23, 2014, http://www .taipeitimes.com/News/front/archives/2014/03/23/2003586323.

21. A TVBS poll on March 20–21 showed that 70 percent of respondents agreed with the protesters' demand for a line-by-line review of the CCSTA, and 48 percent of respondents supported the occupation of the Legislative Yuan (with 40 percent opposed). See Ho, "Occupy Congress in Taiwan," p. 71.

22. Winckler, "Institutionalization and Participation on Taiwan."

23. La Due Lake and Huckfeldt, "Social Capital, Social Networks, and Political Participation"; Putman, "Bowling Alone"; Berinsky and Lenz, "Education and Political Participation."

14

Social Media and Cyber-Mobilization

Eric Chen-hua Yu and Jia-sin Yu

In Taiwan, we often hear the term "cyber-warriors" (*wangjun*). In this usage, cyber-warriors are not military personnel out to damage the information systems of the enemy or to hack confidential information, but instead are civilian Internet users purposely seeking attention on social media to promote specific political issues or viewpoints. During the Ma Ying-jeou years (2008–2016), whenever there was a major political or social incident, opinion leaders on the Internet often expressed their viewpoints via social media, exerted influence on the press, and in turn stirred up political sentiments among the general public. This phenomenon occurred during many different social movements and political campaigns over this era. Thus it is of great interest to scholars to examine whether the Internet (and especially social media) provided a new path to political mobilization in Taiwan during the Ma years.

In 2008, Ma Ying-jeou won the presidential election with 7.65 million votes (58.5 percent), the highest total a presidential candidate had ever won until Tsai Ing-wen's reelection in 2020. Nevertheless, he struggled with low public approval ratings for much of his eight years in office. One of Taiwan's major media groups, TVBS, tracked President Ma's public support over his two terms, as shown in Figure 14.1. As measured in these surveys, Ma's approval rating (that is, his popularity or satisfaction rating) started at only 41 percent in June 2008, one month after he took office. Though it bounced around during his first three years in office, by December 2011, right before the 2012 presidential election, Ma managed to record a satisfaction rating of around 40 percent, similar to where he began. But then, although Ma was reelected with 6.89 million votes (51.6

Figure 14.1   Approval/Disapproval Ratings of President Ma

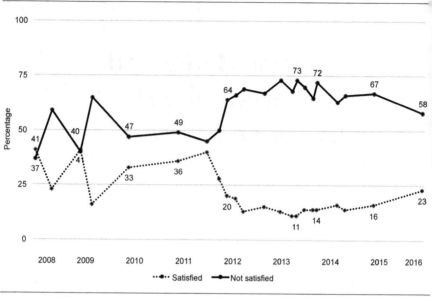

Source: TVBS.

percent) in January 2012, his popularity declined sharply at the beginning of his second term. In September 2013, due to a political conflict between President Ma and Kuomintang (KMT) Legislative Yuan speaker Wang Jin-pyng, his approval rating dropped even further, and it remained low from then until the end of his time in office.

President Ma's disapproval rating is even more revealing. Two things are worth noting about disapproval trends over Ma's two terms. First, when major scandals or political missteps occurred, such as a food safety scandal in October 2008, the bungled government response to the Typhoon Morakot flood disaster in August 2009, and the row over US beef imports to Taiwan in March 2012, the president's disapproval rating went up. After a controversy broke over allowing US beef imports into Taiwan, for instance, Ma's disapproval rating stood as high as 60 percent at the beginning of his second term in May 2012, and it never fully recovered until the very end of his presidency. Second, Ma's high and lasting disapproval ratings made him especially vulnerable to opposition criticism, fed anti-Ma and anti-KMT protests, limited his ability to push through new government policies, and eventually contributed to the KMT's defeat and a transfer of political power to the opposition Democratic Progressive Party (DPP) in 2016.

During Ma's eight years in office, numerous social movements occurred, and their scale and scope became larger and larger, in particular during his second term. These social movements shared a common feature—they all relied heavily on cyber-mobilization of participants initiated via social media. In this chapter, we consider the connections between widespread dissatisfaction with President Ma, social movement mobilization, and usage of social media. We consider how opposition forces were able to take advantage of widespread anti-Ma sentiment and harness the power of social movements to achieve Taiwan's third democratic transfer of power, in 2016, and we consider the online habits and other characteristics of participants in these movements.

We begin by highlighting some major characteristics of Internet and social media users in Taiwan over the past few years. Second, we focus on anti-Ma sentiment on the Internet and discuss the social movements that were closely tied to social media and cyber-mobilization. Third, we use survey data to elaborate on the relationships among social media, social movements, and elections during the Ma era. Fourth, we consider the links between anti-government sentiment, cyber-mobilization, and social movements, and we discuss the future development of party competition by exploring whether the KMT might be able to come back to power by copying the DPP's cyber-mobilization model.

Internet Usage and Political Communication

In their analysis of protests in Taiwan between 1996 and 2008, Tse-min Lin and Yen-pin Su found that increases in the frequency of social and political protests were correlated with increases in access to the Internet. However, they found no significant association between the electoral strength of the political opposition (that is, the vote share of the opposition parties) and the number of protests held. In other words, the increasing penetration rate of Internet access had a positive and significant impact on the number of protests, but no significant impact on the size of vote shares won by the opposition party. Lin and Su suggest that new forms of media and information accessed via the Internet have become critical for mobilizing protests, regardless of the size of the political opposition.

Dissatisfaction with any government tends to increase the longer that government is in power. This pattern is also reflected online: it is easy to express one's negative sentiments on the Internet since it has a free flow of information along with some degree of anonymity. Lin and Su's analysis covers a period when the Internet penetration rate was increasing and the use of social media was expanding rapidly.[1] In this environment, a closer relationship between Internet access and protest was to be expected. In short, it was not the opposition party that used the Internet as a tool to mobilize protests; instead, the Internet itself provided a new platform to express and discuss dissatisfaction with the government, which in turn led online "netizens" to be more likely to participate in protests. The key to the link between Internet usage and political mobilization lies in how such negative sentiment was turned into real action against the government.

When we consider who has been better able to link the use of social media and political campaigning, we normally think of supporters of the DPP (or the pan-Green coalition led by the DPP) as well as the younger generations.[2] After examining the 2008, 2012, and 2016 post-election survey data from Taiwan's Election and Democratization Study (TEDS), we found a rising percentage of voters "who used the Internet to access to election news," and indeed the youth demonstrated a higher propensity than other age groups to do so (see Figure 14.2). In 2017, when no election was held, TEDS data also showed that voters between the age of twenty and twenty-nine years old were more likely than other age groups to use the Internet as their main source of "political news" (see Figure 14.3). This result is consistent with previous findings that Taiwanese youth are the most active Internet users, and that they are more likely to go online to acquire almost all types of information.

In addition to electoral and political news, the youth tended to use the Internet to learn about candidates by going directly to candidates' official

Figure 14.2   Online News Readership During Presidential Campaigns by Age, 2008–2016

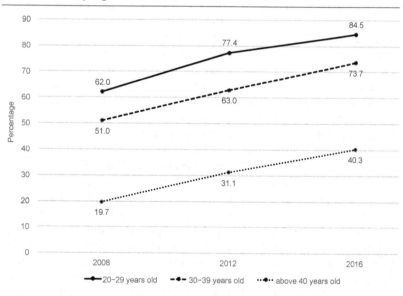

Source: Taiwan's Election and Democratization Study 2008, 2012, and 2016.

Figure 14.3   Online News Readership in an Off-Election Year, by Age, 2017

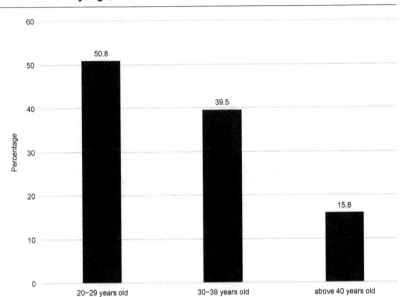

Source: Taiwan's Election and Democratization Study 2017.

websites and social media sites. This trend became more apparent after 2008 (see Figure 14.4). We assume this phenomenon is tied to the development of social media. Plurk was founded in 2008 and Facebook launched its traditional Chinese version the same year. Most people used these two platforms when social media first became popular in Taiwan. Due to the vastly expanded networks available through social media, users could access candidate information via many different sources. Thus, in this chapter we ask, as social media gradually penetrated people's daily lives and increased their access to new information flows, how did it affect the patterns of political mobilization?

To answer this question, we must first look at the role of political parties. As documented by Po-chung Chuang, the DPP significantly outperformed the KMT in online campaigning in the 2000 presidential election.[3] As a result, the KMT started following the DPP's approach by increasing their own campaign outreach on the Internet. In 2012, the campaign activities of the parties shifted again in response to the growing popularity of social media, and leaders of both the KMT and DPP created their own campaign pages on Facebook for the first time. The expanding use of social media disrupted the DPP's traditional advantage online. For instance, when President Ma used his Facebook page to connect with voters, it was praised by the KMT as a tool to

Figure 14.4   Share of Respondents Who Visited Candidate Homepages or Social-Networking Services, by Age, 2008–2016

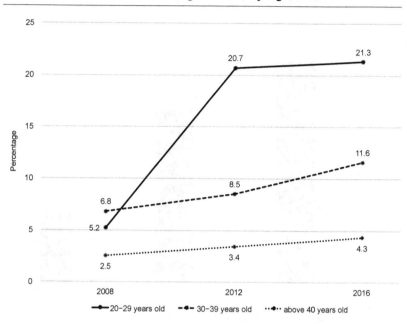

Source: Taiwan's Election and Democratization Study 2008, 2012, and 2016.

"balance" the dominance of DPP's online influence.[4] In her empirical analysis of the 2012 presidential election, Tai-li Wang found that online supporters of the pan-Blue camp (the KMT and People First Party [PFP]) were more likely to cast a vote than their pan-Green counterparts (supporters of the DPP and Taiwan Solidarity Union [TSU]), suggesting that the pan-Green camp no longer enjoyed a significant advantage over the pan-Blues in the online space.[5] But, because the contexts of the past few elections have varied a lot, it is not easy to determine which camp has ultimately benefited more from the growing use of social media over the long term. We should be cautious in interpreting Wang's findings, which view any type of user behavior on social media only through a partisan lens.

Figure 14.5 shows data from the 2014 Taiwan Social Change Survey (TSCS) describing the extent to which social media users engaged with politics or public affairs. Regarding various types of social media usages about political information, pan-Blue supporters were more likely to engage in observational behavior (e.g., watch and read posts) online than their pan-Green counterparts. Yet they were less likely to join in social groups or networks, become followers, share and post information, or participate in political events than pan-Green supporters. Thus these 2014 data suggest that pan-Green supporters were on average more politically active on social media.

Additionally, TEDS data show that a consistently higher percentage of pan-Green supporters use the Internet to access to candidate information (see Figure 14.6, top). While Internet use in the pan-Green camp gradually increased from 2008 to 2016, it increased among pan-Blues from 2008 to 2012 but then fell in 2016. In hindsight, it appears that pan-Blue supporters, perhaps due to the change of their presidential candidate in the middle of the campaign period, lacked enthusiasm for the electoral campaign in 2016 in general.

Data on the use of the Internet to acquire election news show slightly different patterns (Figure 14.6, bottom). Supporters of both party camps showed a increasing propensity to acquire election news online. Yet while the pan-Green camp's number (33.4 percent) was about ten points lower than that of the pan-Blue camp (43.1 percent) in 2008, this situation has reversed in recent years, with the pan-Green's number (60.2 percent) rising to surpass the pan-Blue's (57.9 percent) by two points in 2016.

Figure 14.5 Use of Social Media to Engage with Political Issues, by Party, 2014

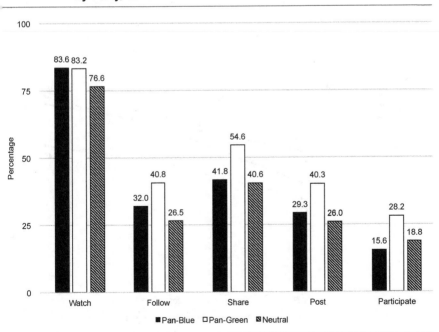

Source: Taiwan Social Change Survey 2014.

Figure 14.6 **Share of Respondents Who Visited Candidate Homepages or Social-Networking Services (top); Online News Readership During Presidential Campaign (bottom), by Party, 2008–2012**

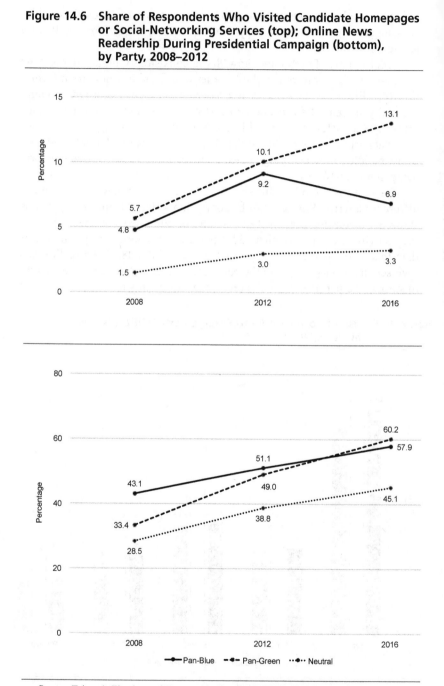

Source: Taiwan's Election and Democratization Study 2008, 2012, and 2016.

Are pan-Green supporters more likely to use the Internet to acquire political information than their pan-Blue counterparts? If the patterns just shown represent long-term and stable trends, data acquired later should show the same result. Yet the 2017 data do not necessarily support the aforementioned pattern. TEDS 2017 data show that among supporters of Taiwan's major parties that obtained seats in the Legislative Yuan, 27.3 percent of KMT supporters used the Internet to obtain political news, compared to 69.2 percent of New Power Party (NPP) supporters, 50.0 percent of People First Party supporters, and only 18.6 percent of DPP supporters. If we classify the supporters into their respective party camps (i.e., the DPP and NPP as pan-Green and the KMT and PFP as pan-Blue), the total percentage of pan-Green supporters who used the Internet to obtain political news was only 24.0 percent, while the number for pan-Blue supporters was 28.7 percent (see Figure 14.7). In other words, the 2017 data do not support the pattern we observed during the 2016 election campaign.

Indeed, the recent data do not support the claim that the DPP and pan-Green camp have enjoyed an advantage over their political competitors in disseminating political information simply because more of their supporters are Internet users. As suggested by the data, the supporters of opposition parties in general, whether pan-Green or pan-Blue, seem to be more likely to use the Internet to obtain political information than supporters of the ruling

Figure 14.7 Online News Readership in an Off-Election Year, by Party, 2017

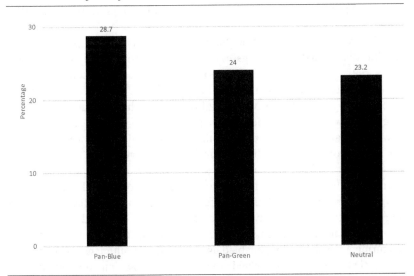

Source: Taiwan's Election and Democratization Study 2017.

party. We may analyze such phenomena from the viewpoint of resource availability. That is, unlike the ruling party, opposition parties may lack resources or channels to disseminate their information. The ruling party can easily reach out to voters because commercials can be broadcast and sponsored by the government, or the media can be invited to join press conferences and shadow public officials on their itineraries. The opposition parties simply do not have such advantages. Due to this lack of resources, they may be motivated to seek quicker and cheaper methods of political communication. If the goal is to communicate cheaply with potential supporters, the Internet should be regarded as the ideal tool for opposition parties to engage in outreach to their voters and to facilitate political campaigning. If we assume that Internet users self-select the information they are willing to obtain, the higher percentages of opposition supporters who acquire information via the Internet may be due to the relatively strong supply of online information disseminated by opposition parties or related groups, relative to the ruling party. The next question then becomes how they do so.

Chi-ying Chen and Shao-liang Chang highlight three important periods of Taiwan's online political communication: "blogs more frequently used" prior to 2009, "blogs and microblogs used together" starting in 2010, and "microblogs more frequently used" after 2012.[6] They show that the impact of social media increased over time during the Ma era. During the early period, when blogging had matured but microblogs were not yet in wide use, more than 80 percent of candidates for elected office gave up websites and used blogs instead, because of their low cost and simple structure. When microblogs became more widespread, political figures set up Facebook pages as well in order to appeal to young voters, in particular first-time voters.

In addition, the general public was more likely to trust political information disseminated by blogs compared to microblogs on social media. Thus, politicians were incentivized to use social media to interact with their voters, but to put important information on blogs. By 2013, however, the popular blog *The Wretch,* which had once been the most active blogging site in Taiwan, had terminated its services—a sign of the rapid move toward social media. Even though other blogging platforms were still available, much of Taiwan's online political commentary moved onto Facebook instead. The major advantage of traditional blogs over social media platforms was their searchability and clear record of posts, but Facebook, after several upgrades to its platform, offered most of the same functions, eroding whatever remaining advantage blogs might have offered.

Social media platforms such as Facebook also had the advantage of featuring a news feed that enabled users to follow politicians' posts by indicating that they were "interested" in that politician. Compared to traditional blogging services, in which users needed to conduct searches on their own, social media provided a more convenient option for online followers to obtain political information of interest. Essentially, social media, especially Facebook, had better functionality compared to blogs.

As a result, social-networking platforms gradually became the primary medium for online communication during the Ma era, and by 2016 almost all politicians used them to disseminate policy and campaign information and to communicate with voters. Another advantage for politicians was that social media was generally cheaper than blogging—a particular concern for political figures in the opposition who did not have many resources to maintain a public presence online. While the ruling KMT had government resources to disseminate information via news reports and regular advertising channels, the opposition parties needed to find more cost-effective ways to communicate with the general public. Thus, during the Ma era, supporters of opposition parties tended to be more likely to obtain information from the Internet than those who supported the KMT.

Cyber-Mobilization and Social Movements

Along with the growing penetration rate of the Internet and social media services in Taiwan, it is not surprising that social movements used social media to mobilize supporters. In this section we compare the patterns of online mobilization across three important social movements that occurred during the Ma era: the Wild Strawberry Movement in 2008, the White-Shirt Army movement in 2013, and the student-led protests against the Cross-Strait Service Trade Agreement (CSSTA), known as the Sunflower Movement, in 2014. We also examine the impact of online communication on elections by looking at two other high-profile events: the online mobilization behind the so-called Appendectomy Project to recall pan-Blue legislators, and the infamous apology by Taiwanese singer Chou Tzu-yu for waving a Taiwanese flag, which became the dominant news story on the day of the 2016 presidential and legislative elections.

The Wild Strawberry Movement in 2008 was the first social movement mobilized almost entirely online.[7] When People's Republic of China (PRC) official Chen Yunlin, head of the semiofficial Association for Relations Across the Taiwan Strait (ARATS), visited Taiwan for the first time in November 2008, a significant number of protesters shadowed him during his visit. Chen was protected by a large police presence and unusually restrictive policies that kept protesters far away from him and even forbade the waving of Republic of China (ROC) flags during his events. Several demonstrations took place at locations he was scheduled to visit, with protesters asserting that the Ma administration was sacrificing the nation's dignity to please a Chinese Communist Party (CCP) official from mainland China. In some conflicts between the police and protesters, the police were accused of taking extreme measures that violated protesters' civil rights, which in turn sparked the first large-scale social movement of the Ma era, the Wild Strawberry Movement.

The Wild Strawberry Movement used Taiwan's largest and most popular bulletin board system to mobilize protesters. Unlike conventional social movements, the Wild Strawberry Movement built its "virtual ecosystem" with bulletin board features.[8] Although members of this online system did not know each other, they shared common user experiences and developed trust in one another. Without being bound by the spatial limitations of traditional organizations (such as communities, social clubs, or other offline groups), the movement gathered momentum within a very short period of time and organized demonstrations in several cities against the PRC, the Ma administration, and the restrictions in the Parade and Assembly Act used as the legal basis for detaining protesters.

Nevertheless, the Wild Strawberry Movement also proved to be a weak movement: it did not stop visits from PRC officials, it failed to achieve passage of amendments to the Parade and Assembly Act, and it faded away by January 2009. A key reason was that it was mobilized almost entirely online, and it was a flat organization without clear leadership. Previous research on social movements has found that the interpersonal networks that develop in offline organizations such as political parties, churches, and unions usually are critical to sustaining movement momentum.[9] These offline relationships serve to legitimize the authority of the leaders of social movements, even if actual mobilization of group members takes place mostly online. A strong leadership group, in turn, is important for forging a group consensus and making binding decisions when there are differences of opinion within the movement.[10] In contrast, if online mobilization is not based on offline relationships, even though it may help intensify and enlarge participation in the movement, a lack of clear leadership can result in situations where any consensus within the movement can be reached only by means of direct democracy. If so, the movement's goals and tactics can easily shift or become muddled due to inefficient or contentious decisionmaking processes. Although the Wild Strawberry Movement lasted long enough to show what online mobilization could do, it also quickly faded away when it did not achieve its initial demands. The collapse of Strawberries suggested that interpersonal networks would still be necessary as a basis for any successful social movement.

Another prominent social movement to spring up during the Ma era was the White-Shirt Army movement. This movement took place beginning in July 2013 in response to the death of a young conscripted solider, army corporal Hung Chung-chiu, after he was detained and physically disciplined for a minor rules violation. This incident of military "abuse" aroused enormous public attention and outrage. On July 20, a protest was launched that drew about 5,000 people demanding that the government provide further information about Hung's death. The Ministry of National Defense did not respond to the demand in any quick or proper way, sparking further public anger and triggering a much larger protest and memorial demonstration on

August 3, which attracted 250,000 people. The movement demanded that the Ministry of National Defense release all information about the circumstances surrounding Hung's death, and it insisted that the Ma administration conduct a special investigation into the case. Political pressure from the movement resulted in the rapid passage of a bill that moved military criminal justice proceedings to civilian courts—a swift and fundamental change to Taiwanese military laws.

Ming-sho Ho describes the White Shirts as "a movement mobilized without the participation of political parties and social movement organizations."[11] In fact, at the beginning of the Hung Chung-chiu incident, thirty-nine professionals from various fields formed the "Citizen 1985" (*gongmin 1985*) alliance to take charge of planning and preparation of the movement's subsequent activities. In other words, this incident gave birth to a new social movement organization. After the White-Shirt Army movement, this new alliance not only monitored the legislative process of amending military laws but also expanded its scope to track the performance of the Legislative Yuan as a whole and spawned a new independent organization, the Congress Investigation Corps.

The Citizen 1985 alliance used both PTT and Facebook to call for the participation of dissatisfied online users, and it managed to boost the number of protesters to a new high for a demonstration in the Ma era. At the time, the movement turned so many people out onto the streets that some media referred to it as a Taiwanese version of the Jasmine Revolution in Tunisia.[12] One commentator writing at the time asserted that online mobilization had been the direct cause of this offline political action,[13] but others explained the protest turnout by noting that anti-government sentiment was already high, and that online mobilizers already had a large pool of angry citizens to appeal to. Run-hsin Ho, for instance, asserted that "instead of arguing that the White Shirt Army movement has built a successful online social movement model, we should say that society's dissatisfaction with the mishandling of the Hung incident reached a boiling point that led to such powerful online mobilization."[14] We agree with both arguments and posit that without both widespread anger and the Internet, this social movement would not have been so successful.

In an important study of cyber-mobilization in environmental movements in Taiwan done at about this time, Wei-ching Wang, Chi-han Ma, and Chao-wei Chen concluded that the success or failure of a movement depended not on online mobilization but instead on building grassroots organizations and realization of organizational objectives.[15] When social movements went online, they found, they were actually less likely to succeed due to their decentralized and disorganized nature. In general, when a social movement utilizes online mobilization, it inevitably incorporates three coexisting but different types of forces: conventional civil organizations, intellectuals and activists, and Internet users (in Chinese, *xiangmin* or "netizens"), who are relatively easy to mobilize toward different kinds of goals. Netizens need direction and tend to follow core organizers at the beginning of a movement. Later on, however, netizens and intellectuals may themselves emerge as new movement organizers as their involvement in movement activities increases. If a social movement itself has a clear objective that satisfies its potential online participants and provides an appropriate channel for actual participation, it will be well-positioned to attract and organize netizens for activities that stretch beyond a single movement. Once a social movement builds up the organizational capacity that can attract netizens to become frequent participants, it can mobilize demonstrators more easily in the future.

The findings of Wang, Ma, and Chen provide a way to compare the effectiveness of the Wild Strawberry and White-Shirt Army protests. It is clear that the two movements were organized differently. The White-Shirt Army movement had an organizational structure centered on Citizen 1985, and voluntary workers acted as the "duty team" at protest sites to keep order. This type of social movement model matches the concept of "organization" put forward by Wang, Ma, and Chen. In contrast, the lack of such an organizational structure limited the scope of the Wild Strawberry Movement. Additionally, the purpose and goals of the White-Shirt Army movement reflected the wide dissatisfaction with the Ma administration at that time. Unlike the Wild Strawberry Movement, which urged supporters to contribute time, money, and expertise to the movement, the White Shirt Army movement only asked for a very simple form of participation: going onto the street and protesting. In sum, a solid offline organization with clear appeals and objectives contributed to the success of the White-Shirt Army movement.

The most important social movement during the Ma years was the student-led anti-CSSTA movement. On June 21, 2013, after Ma's government signed the CSSTA with the PRC, sporadic protests occurred due to numerous concerns about the possible impacts of the agreement on Taiwan's future economic security. Thus, the approval of the agreement was held up by the legislature for a significant period of time. On March 17, 2014, the KMT-led legislature advanced the measure out of committee to a final vote in less than thirty seconds. Some student activists and civil groups were greatly upset by this legislative maneuver. They started calling for a protest in front of the Legislative Yuan, and more than 400 people came to participate on very short notice. The next night, some student protesters broke into the Legislative Yuan and occupied the chamber to start the so-called Sunflower Movement.

This was the first time that Taiwan's Legislative Yuan had ever been occupied by protesters. The incident began around 10 P.M. on March 18, and the media immediately started live-broadcasting. Although the protestors were raising concerns widely held among the public, the number of participants at the beginning was actually low. The protesters probably could have easily been expelled if the government had used riot police. But legislators from the opposition parties, the DPP and TSU, along with KMT speaker Wang Jin-pyng, used their authority to stop the police from entering the legislature. Protesters on-site quickly used social media such as PTT, YouTube, and Facebook to live-stream the developments in the chamber and request further assistance. Within twenty-four hours, more than 10,000 protesters had gathered outside the Legislative Yuan.

The effective use of live-streaming on social media was one of the major factors that contributed to the success of the Sunflower Movement.[16] Because conventional-media reporters were not able to get into the Legislative Yuan during the occupation, they tended to use the content on social media as a primary news source. Thus, live-streaming on social media not only affected reporting by the conventional media, but also expanded the time, space, issues, and receivers of communication. Additionally, because the protesters could use social media to broadcast directly to viewers online, the relations among conventional media, government, and political parties also shifted. That is, information about the occupation was directly disseminated via social media, while conventional media were reduced to playing the role of transmitting news and were no longer in the role of an agenda-setter. The popular use of social media also limited the capacity of the government and political parties to disseminate their own interpretation of events.

What were the motives of the participants in the Sunflower Movement? Wan-chi Chen and Su-jen Huang conducted a survey on-site during the occupation, and their findings undercut some of the common assumptions about the participants. The majority were college students and youth. The students came from many different regions, departments, and institutes, while the non-student participants came from various professional fields—they included office workers, managers, and even business owners. Although the Internet was the most important channel for participants to receive information, fewer than 7 percent said that they had decided to participate in the movement due to messages they had received online. Instead, about half indicated that they had "voluntarily participated" without being mobilized by other groups.[17] (This high rate of voluntary participation may reflect the self-centered, self-managed model of social media usage and can be regarded as a feature of new Internet-based social movements.) In addition, netizens who voluntarily participated in the movement were more likely to remain at the demonstration in front of the Legislative Yuan than those participants mobilized by family and friends. Demonstrators who received most of their political information via the Internet tended to stay longer, and heavy users of social media stayed the longest of all respondents.[18]

This survey helps us better understand the participants in the Sunflower Movement. It shows that they tended to be young people with diverse backgrounds who used social media as their major source of political information and regarded themselves as voluntary participants. But it does not tell us why many participants were willing to stay at the demonstration for such a long period of time. As we noted earlier, the success of social movements depends a great deal on effective organization, and the Sunflower Movement was indeed very well organized.

Traditional social organizations (e.g., Taiwan Association for Human Rights, Taiwan Labor Front, Green Citizens Action Alliance, Taiwan Referendum Alliance, Taiwan Rural Front, and Judicial Reform Foundation), political parties (the DPP and TSU), and newly emerging social associations (Black Island Nation Youth Front, Citizen 1985, g0v [pronounced "Gov-Zero"], and Taiwan Citizens Union) all participated in this movement. At the very beginning of the occupation of the Legislative Yuan, a core decision-making team led by Huang Kuo-chang, Chen Wei-ting, and Lin Fei-fan was formed. The members of this leadership team surely had different opinions about how to proceed, and as a result of intra-leadership conflicts, some fellow members decided to lead a new occupation of the Executive Yuan, the location of the premier's office and other critical government functions, on March 23. A number of serious confrontations occurred that night when the police were called in to expel the demonstrators, and dozens were injured in the crackdown. The relatively harsh measures used by the police were effective in ending the occupation of the building, but they also may have increased public sympathy toward the movement. Demonstrators posted the attempted occupation and police crackdown on the Internet to draw the attention of foreign media.[19] The protesters created a Sunflower Movement page on Facebook, and wrote their own press releases in various languages to disseminate their views to foreign media outlets. They also set up fundraising websites not only to raise money but also to collect materials for a possible long-term occupation.[20] By the time the movement managed to draw 500,000 people to a street demonstration in support of the student-led occupation on March 30 (see Figure 14.8), different types of voluntary groups and activities such as a duty team, medical group, media group, and lectures on democracy had been operating around the clock for almost two weeks.

After examining the three major social movements during the Ma administration, two common features can be identified. First, all these movements used social media to effectively mobilize Internet users. Certainly, the use of social media was a great help, and the combination of social media and audiovisual media was especially sophisticated and powerful during these movements.[21] Second, the main opposition party, the DPP, was a participant but not a leader in these movements. That is, all three social movements were initiated from the grassroots and organized by social groups, and the DPP never took center stage.

One thing we can learn from these Ma-era social movements is that offline organization was the key to success. Although the Internet could play an effective role in mobilizing people who were concerned about or dissatisfied with a certain issue to take to the street to protest, without any

Figure 14.8   Scale of Three Social Movements

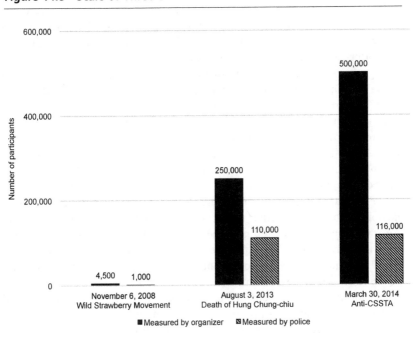

Source: Compiled by authors.

solid organization to direct them, a movement could lose its focus when more people joined in, and it would not be able to reshape public opinion in an effective and efficient way. The Wild Strawberry Movement lacked a strong organization. The White-Shirt Army movement was organized by a newly invented organization. And the Sunflower Movement successfully incorporated traditional social organizations with new groups under a strong leadership team. The Wild Strawberry Movement successfully used social media to issue a call for participants, but without a solid organization to take the leadership role, a feeling of solidarity among participants was hard to create as people came and went easily.

It is important to note that the lack of momentum for the Wild Strawberry Movement could also simply be due to its timing in 2008, when Ma Ying-jeou still enjoyed relatively strong support. As President Ma's popularity waned, the White Shirt Army movement and Sunflower Movement benefited from a surge in anti-Ma sentiment. Nevertheless, the success of the latter two movements probably is due mostly to their solid leadership organizations and effective use of the Internet to unify different appeals, actions, and participants.

Cyber-Mobilization and Elections

Taking their inspiration from the Sunflower Movement, some activists attempted a new movement to recall three unpopular KMT legislators who had been especially harsh critics of the Sunflower Movement and public supporters of the Ma administration and of rapprochement with the PRC. A new group was formed to fulfill that purpose, and its founders adopted the name Appendectomy Project—a play on the words for "appendix" and "pan-Blue legislators" (*lanwei*), which are homonyms in Chinese. The Appendectomy Project first put out a call online for a possible recall election to remove either Alex Tsai, Lin Hung-chih, or Wu Yu-sheng from the Legislative Yuan. Because a recall against Alex Tsai received the highest number of online votes, he was the first legislator that the Appendectomy Project attempted to remove.

This was the first time in twenty years a recall election against a legislator had been held. Other recent removal attempts had failed to qualify for a vote because they did not meet the high signature requirement specified in the recall law. The Appendectomy Project successfully tapped anti-KMT sentiment in the electorate and the momentum built up by the Sunflower Movement to promote the recall petition, and they were able to meet the signature requirement. Nevertheless, the activists soon discovered that the recall law also prohibited open campaigning for a legislator's recall, or even for people to sign the recall petition. These restrictions presented an interesting twist: how to advocate for something without actually "campaigning" for it.

Because no other recent recall petition had met the requirements, the activists did not initially understand the restrictions on campaigning in recall elections when they started the project. Once they realized the restrictions imposed by the law, they found loopholes in the regulations and extensively used social media to advocate for Legislator Tsai's recall. For example, they promoted the statement "campaigning for the recall election of Tsai is prohibited." Then the restriction itself became a topic to help draw public attention to the recall election. In the end, although the recall attempt failed because turnout did not meet the 50 percent required under the recall law, and Tsai kept his seat,[22] the Appendectomy Project nevertheless demonstrated that heavy reliance on online campaigning could at least mobilize supporters and sympathizers to sign petitions. These activists also managed to initiate the first legislative recall petition in twenty years that met the requirements for a special recall election.

As noted earlier, cyber-mobilization would not have been so successful without the high level of dissatisfaction with the Ma administration and the ruling KMT among the public. But on the other hand, without the help of the tools of cyber-mobilization, this offline dissatisfaction would not necessarily have been transformed into real-world action in a rapid way. In this new era of cyber-mobilization, it turned out that protesters could be mobilized literally overnight to join a demonstration against a new outrage.

Before the 2016 elections were held on January 16 of that year, Chou Tzu-yu, a seventeen-year-old Taiwanese singer, was familiar only to those who paid close attention to Korean popular entertainment. But on the eve of the elections, she suddenly became a household name all over Taiwan. Chou had been developing her entertainment career in Korea for several years. In 2015, she was accused by Chinese netizens of waving the ROC flag on a Korean entertainment program and was labeled a supporter of "Taiwan independence." JYP Entertainment Corporation, her agency, had been boycotted by Chinese audiences ever since. In an act whose timing was more than just a coincidence, on January 15, the night before the elections, JYP released a video featuring Chou bowing her head and reading out a Chinese script: "I'm Chou Tzu-yu. . . . [T]here's only one China. The mainland and Taiwan are together. I'm proud of being Chinese, and I feel very, very sorry for the inappropriate behavior and words that I displayed as a Chinese during activities abroad."

On the screen, poor Chou appeared to most Korean, Japanese, and Taiwanese viewers to have been forced by JYP to make a public apology. On the night before the election, this video was repeatedly broadcast on Facebook, YouTube, and PTT, before spreading to traditional media outlets and being shown repeatedly on election day on news channels. The contents of this video touched directly on the sensitive issue of cross-Strait relations between mainland China and Taiwan, and many Korean and Japanese Internet users voiced their dissatisfaction with JYP and called for support for Chou online. This call reached Taiwan and triggered widespread public anger at the PRC, which spilled over into criticism of the China-friendly KMT. Messages such as "How can we vote for the KMT?" or "We shall give the KMT a lesson in tomorrow's election" were posted on social media all night long.

It is difficult to measure the extent to which the angry reaction to this video affected the vote. But the Chou Tzu-yu incident undoubtedly had at least a short-term impact on voting intentions. A post-election study that used text analysis, for instance, found that social media users indeed linked this incident to cross-Strait relations.[23] The KMT was tagged with many more negative comments than the DPP online, and by midnight on January 16, about 300,000 netizens had responded to this incident on various social media platforms. More important, most of these Internet users cared about the election—that is, among those netizens who were concerned about the Chou incident, about 61 percent had read information related to the presidential election within the two weeks prior to election day.

The defeat of the KMT in the 2016 presidential race was foreseeable for weeks prior to the election. The turnout rate for this election, at 66.3 percent, was the lowest ever for a direct presidential election in Taiwan. The

DPP's candidate, Tsai Ing-wen, won 6.89 million votes, a record for her party. The record-low turnout rate and record-high vote share for the DPP suggest that anti-KMT voters came out in large numbers to cast their votes, while a greater proportion of KMT supporters stayed home. Nevertheless, studies drawing on Taiwanese survey data have not found clear links in the 2016 election between the use of social media and voting behavior.[24] Rather than being the straw that broke the camel's back, the Chou Tzu-yu incident likely made little difference to the overall outcome of the election. The long-simmering anti-Ma and anti-KMT sentiment in the electorate, expressed in and reinforced through a series of social movements in the years leading up to the 2016 elections, was probably the primary driving force behind the KMT's defeat. Only through organized social movements could such negative sentiment toward the incumbent government and ruling party be sustained and articulated in a politically impactful way. Unlike previous social movements organized and mobilized by political parties, individual candidates, or well-established social groups, those occurring in the Ma era were primarily organized at the grassroots by newly founded groups, and mobilized via new communication technologies. In elections, this new model of social movement not only helped the opposition party to generate political momentum behind a change in the ruling party in 2016, but also contributed to the creation of an innovative campaign model that helped a candidate without any previous political experience or background, Ko Wen-je, to make a successful bid for mayor of Taipei in 2014.

Cyber-Mobilization and the Formation of New Alliances

In the early 2000s, anyone who wanted to run for elected office in Taiwan would create an official website to appeal to voters.[25] Nowadays, however, politicians in Taiwan almost always use social media rather than a personal website to communicate with voters, and in particular to get connected to the youth. Tsai Ing-wen was one of the first political figures to create an official Facebook page for her campaign, in 2010, when she ran in the New Taipei City mayoral race that year. President Ma started his Facebook page in January 2011 as part of his preparation for his 2012 reelection campaign. Over the past decade, politicians have gradually come to realize that having their own official websites to disseminate information is not enough, and that a social-networking platform is in fact a better medium for political communication, as it facilitates two-way information flows between candidates and voters. By the end of the Ma era, the vast majority of Taiwanese elected officials had their own professional Facebook pages, and the most prominent political figures had millions of followers. For instance, in September 2018, President Tsai Ing-wen had about 2.19 million followers, Ma Ying-jeou had 1.87 million, and Taipei City mayor Ko Wen-je had 1.89 million. Politicians who had a high number of Facebook fans and followers could sometimes become a sort of "personal media outlet" capable of controlling information flows and even directing the reporting angles taken by the traditional media.

Ko Wen-je did not begin his Facebook page in order to run in the 2014 Taipei mayoral election, but instead started writing commentaries on his public page to express his thoughts after an organ-transplant incident. Ko was a pioneering doctor as well as the chair of the Trauma Department at National Taiwan University Hospital, Taiwan's most prestigious medical facility. In 2011, the Control Yuan opened an investigation into a case Ko had overseen, in which the organs from an HIV-positive patient in a coma were transplanted into other patients. Its report resulted in the university taking disciplinary action against Ko in August 2013. Ko argued on his Facebook page that the entire investigation was unfair to him, and he subsequently announced in January 2014 that he would run for Taipei mayor. After winning a polling primary against the DPP's Yao Wen-chih, Ko was supported by the DPP but ran as an independent. In December 2014, he won the election easily, beating the KMT's candidate, Sean Lien, and ending the KMT's twenty-year hold on the city.

Given his large margin of victory in 2014, it is interesting to consider whether Ko benefited more than other candidates from his online profile and activities. Were Ko's supporters more likely to spend time online and consume news via the Internet? TEDS survey data for the 2014 Taipei City mayoral election indicate that Ko's supporters seemed to be more likely to use social media, YouTube audiovisual streaming channels, and electronic bulletin boards than KMT candidate Sean Lien's supporters, though the gap between the two was modest.[26] Regarding unconventional political participation (such as campaigning and donations via any channel), Ko's supporters were also more active than Lien's, as Figure 14.9 shows.

In addition, we can classify political social media usage into four categories—none, watching and following, sharing and posting, and real participation—to see if there was any difference between Ko's and Lien's supporters. Figure 14.10 shows that although their supporters did not differ much in terms of watching and following political campaigns, Ko's supporters tended to be more willing than Lien's to share or post campaign information and to participate in actual rallies or campaign activities. Yet only a very small proportion of people who really were politically mobilized in this way were activated via social-networking services. In sum, Figures 14.9 and 14.10 suggest that a higher percentage of Ko's supporters used social media, and they were also more likely than Lien's supporters to use social media for political activities.

Negative campaigning is a common strategy implemented by candidates, particularly by those who trail behind in an election. Yet, negative campaigning online can be initiated not only by candidates but also by voters. Sometimes, based on their perception toward candidates, voters themselves

Figure 14.9   Proportion of Social-Networking-Service Use and Mobilization by Supporters of Taipei City Mayoral Candidates in 2014

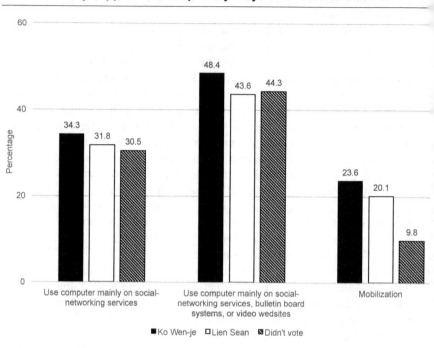

Source: Taiwan's Election and Democratization Study 2014.

may engage in negative attacks online. Again, we use TEDS 2014 survey data to examine the negative perceptions toward the two candidates in the 2014 Taipei City mayoral election, Ko Wen-je and Sean Lien, based on respondents' different types of social media usage (see Figure 14.11). We find that Sean Lien's main negative image was his "political family." Even among those engaging in no political activities via social media, 46 percent perceived that Lien was from a political family, and among those who used social-networking services to participate in political activities, 60 percent linked Lien's image to his political-family background.

In contrast to Lien, among the respondents who had never engaged in any political activity via social-networking services, 49 percent expressed no negative opinion toward Ko. Nevertheless, among those who used social-networking services to participate in political activities, 38 percent directly linked Ko to a research fund scandal during his time at National Taiwan University Hospital (see Figure 14.12).[27] By comparing Figures 14.11 and 14.12, we find that Ko's negative image was not as strong as Lien's across different types of users of social-networking services. In the final phase of

Figure 14.10   Degree of Use of Social-Networking Services for Political Activities by Supporters of Taipei City Mayoral Candidates in 2014

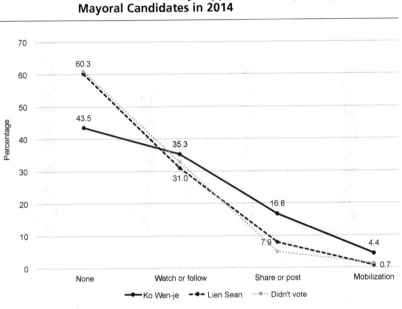

Source: Taiwan's Election and Democratization Study 2014.

the race, Ko's campaign featured various social media celebrities and filmed relatively low-cost campaign advertisements with them. By doing so, he not only gained the advantage of high visibility on social media but also reinforced his positive image among users of social-networking services. Overall, people who used social-networking services to engage in political activities seemed to be more likely to have negative perceptions of the candidates. This might have been due to the fact that they had stronger political interests or political efficacy and were more willing to express their political opinions as well as to participate in politics. That Ko effectively built up a better image than Lien among users of social-networking services may also have contributed to the success of his campaign.

Negative perceptions of one or the other candidate probably had a significant effect on the 2014 Taipei City mayoral election. But dissatisfaction with the KMT, rather than online campaigning, should be regarded as the primary factor that set up an unfavorable environment for Lien and the rest of the KMT candidates, especially after the Sunflower Movement. Based on TEDS 2014 survey data, about 51.9 percent of Taipei citizens considered the movement to have contributed positively to Taiwan's democracy, while only about 34.2 percent agreed that the movement had been harmful to

Figure 14.11   Negative Image of Sean Lien by Type of Social Media Usage in Taipei's 2014 Mayoral Election

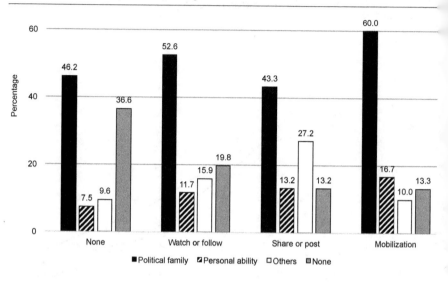

Source: Taiwan's Election and Democratization Study 2014.

Figure 14.12   Negative Image of Ko Wen-je by Type of Social Media Usage in Taipei's 2014 Mayoral Election

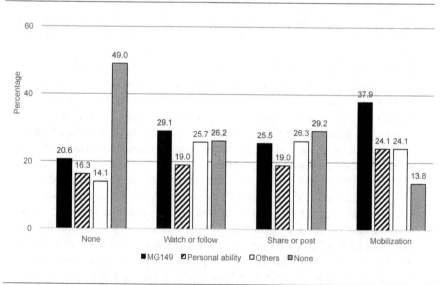

Source: Taiwan's Election and Democratization Study 2014.

democracy. Of those who gave a positive assessment of the Sunflower Movement, 76.3 percent voted for Ko, but only 7.3 percent voted for Lien (see Figure 14.13). In other words, Ko successfully exploited anti-KMT sentiment in the electorate and portrayed himself as a nonpartisan reformer in the post–Sunflower Movement era. Thus, even in Taipei, which had been a KMT bulwark since the late 1990s, the Sunflower Movement boosted momentum for Ko and shook up the traditional political landscape.

In addition, inspired by the Sunflower Movement, several new political parties were formed in 2015, including the New Power Party and the Social Democratic Party (SDP). Both parties participated in the 2016 Legislative Yuan elections, and some of their candidates were well-connected to various social movements over the preceding years.[28] For example, two important figures of the White-Shirt Army Movement, Hung Tzu-yung, the sister of Hung Chung-chiu, and Chiu Hsien-chih, Hung's attorney, became NPP district-level legislative candidates. One of the Sunflower Movement leaders, Huang Kuo-chang, became the NPP's chairman and also ran in the legislative elections in a district in New Taipei. And the SDP's legislative candidates, such as Jennifer Lu and Miao Poya, were main figures in Taiwan's LGBTQ movement. In other words, the social movements that had tapped into anti-Ma sentiment among the public appeared to contribute to a new dynamic of party competition in Taiwan, reflecting a transformation of

Figure 14.13 Image of the Sunflower Movement by Respondent Vote Choice in Taipei's 2014 Mayoral Election

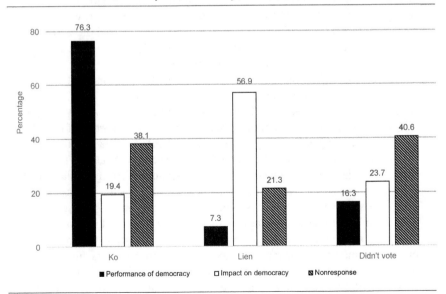

Source: Taiwan's Election and Democratization Study 2014.

these movement tactics from fighting external battles to seeking to take power and promote internal reform.

These newly emerging political parties had a significant impact on the traditional political landscape dominated by the KMT and DPP. In the 2016 Legislative Yuan elections, the DPP and the newly founded social movement parties shared a common goal: to defeat the KMT. The DPP negotiated pre-electoral coalitions with the new parties, yielding districts and encouraging its traditional supporters to vote for them.[29] In other words, the DPP managed to incorporate the social forces generated by the social movements in the Ma era into its campaign, and it became the leader of the anti-KMT alliance in the 2016 elections, even though in those social movements, the DPP was just one of the participants.

Conclusion

It is no surprise that dissatisfaction with the ruling party built up over the length of Ma's two terms in office. This happened in both the Chen Shui-bian (2000–2008)[30] and Ma Ying-jeou (2008–2016) eras, and it may well also prove to be the case with Tsai Ing-wen. The emergence of social media as an important source of political information has increased the speed at which political criticism and anti-government sentiment spreads, and it has made it easier for ordinary citizens to mobilize offline protests. Nevertheless, while cyber-mobilization can be extremely quick, substantial real-world organizational structures are still essential to lead movements to success and to maintain pressure on the government. The most effective social movements during the Ma era were led not by political parties but by a joint effort of traditional and newly emergent social associations, though the DPP was able to acquire political power after 2014 by forging an effective alliance with social movement organizations.

It is important to note that the DPP did not have a dominant political advantage in cyberspace. The key to its successes in 2014 and 2016 lay in dissatisfaction with the ruling KMT and President Ma, but those who were upset with the KMT government online were not necessarily supporters of the DPP. As the primary opposition party at the time, the DPP was in fact quite good at manipulating and enhancing the level of dissatisfaction with the KMT government, particularly on social media. Two major features of social media—quick information flows and anonymity—made it especially easy to disseminate many types of negative political sentiment. Thus, any opposition party should have been able to take advantage of social media to expand negative sentiments toward the incumbent government. During the second term of Ma's presidency, major protests repeatedly occurred due to the successful combination of anti-government sentiment and cyber-mobilization. But in the end, it was the DPP that consolidated all the negative sentiments toward the KMT government behind its successful campaign to take power.

The last question to consider is: Could the KMT duplicate this path to get back into power? Our answer is yes, but the KMT needs to overcome more hurdles than the DPP. Over President Tsai Ing-wen's first term, dissatisfaction with her and the DPP gradually built up among the public. Anti-government sentiment grew particularly strong online. Yet the KMT lacked the ability to take full advantage of such anti-DPP sentiment due to its weak linkages with civil society organizations. In a series of events including reforms of pensions and labor policies, the DPP took policy positions similar to those of the previous Ma administration, and further undercut the KMT's attempts to mobilize anti-DPP political sentiment. Unlike the DPP, the KMT failed to form alliances with major social forces, and it could not exercise much influence over online commentary. Compared to the KMT, the NPP was probably better-positioned to make use of online appeals to grow into a more powerful opposition party. Yet the NPP also targeted its appeals primarily at the new, younger generation of supporters of Taiwan's independence (the so-called naturally independent generation).[31] Thus, although the NPP maintained strong connections with various issue advocacy groups, it was not clear at the end of Tsai Ing-wen's first term whether the party would eventually be able to appeal to those voters in the middle of the political spectrum to increase its electoral support.

The KMT's failure to build up strong connections with grassroots organizations meant that it was not effective at converting anti-DPP sentiment into large-scale social movements like those that occurred during the Ma era. Although it was able to mobilize its traditional supporters to participate in demonstrations against the Tsai administration, the KMT was not able to make use of cyber-mobilization to expand its appeal to disaffected swing voters or other grassroots organizations, or to prevent the DPP from winning a second term in power.

Notes

1. According to the Taiwan Network Information Center, among the population aged twelve years and older in 2003, 57.2 percent used the Internet, while in 2008 and 2017 the percentages grew to 68.5 and 78.8, respectively. At the same time, the percentage of mobile Internet users grew from 25.0 in the initial study to 87.4 in 2017.

2. Chuang, "Online Campaign Strategies of the KMT for the 2004 Presidential Election."

3. Ibid.

4. Yan and Huang, "Add Word 'President' to Prevent Tricks: Ma's Facebook Online" (in Chinese), *Apple Daily,* January 28, 2011, https://tw.appledaily.com/headline/daily/20110128/33147052.

5. Wang, "Facebook Election?"

6. Chen and Chang, "From Blogs to Microblogs."

7. Hsiao, "How the Internet Impacts Social Movements."

8. Ibid.

9. For example, see Ho, "Taiwan's State and Social Movements Under the DPP Government."

10. Hsiao, "How the Internet Impacts Social Movements."

11. Ho, "Civil Movement and Civil Disobedience," p. 19.

12. For example, see Paul Lin, "People Must Battle to Change Military," *Taipei Times,* July 28, 2013, http://www.taipeitimes.com/News/editorials/archives/2013/07/28/2003568323.

13. Yan-lin Wu, "Letter from Taiwan: Outcry from the White-Shirt Army," *BBC News China,* July 25, 2013, http://www.bbc.com/zhongwen/trad/taiwan_letters/2013/07/130725_twletter_white_shirts.

14. Run-hsin Ho, "The Healing Effect of the White Shirt Army" (in Chinese), *Commonwealth Magazine,* August 22, 2013, https://www.cw.com.tw/article/article.action?id=5051584.

15. Wang, Ma, and Chen, "The Social Movements in the Internet Age."

16. Liu and Su, "Mediating the Sunflower Movement: Hybrid Media Networks in a Digital Age."

17. Chen and Huang, "Outcry Outside the Legislature." Chen and Huang also compared their findings with other studies of Sunflower Movement participants, which suggested that the respondents in their own survey had tended to overreport their voluntary level of participation.

18. Chen, Chang, and Huang, "The Coming of Networked Social Movements?"

19. See http://4am.tw.

20. Tabata, "Material Resources Raising Mechanism of Sunflower."

21. Ho, "Occupy Congress in Taiwan."

22. However, Legislator Tsai did not run for reelection in 2016, at least in part because of the negative attention he attracted by being targeted in a recall election.

23. Su et al., "Online Communication Network for Disseminating Emotion-Provoking Events."

24. Wang, "Facebook Election?"; Wang, "The Political Use of Social Media and Civic Engagement in Taiwan."

25. Chuang, "Online Campaign Strategies of the KMT."

26. See Huang, "Taiwan's Election and Democratization Study."

27. Ko was accused by a KMT legislator of money laundering and tax evasion through a research fund, MG149, that he had set up for National Taiwan University Hospital's Surgical Intensive Care Unit when he headed the team. Ko was later cleared by the hospital of any improper use of the account. See Tu-min Chu and Jake Chung, "NTUH Head Stands Firm on Legitimacy of MG149," *Taipei Times,* October 7, 2014, http://www.taipeitimes.com/News/front/archives/2014/10/07/2003601472.

28. The NPP and SDP are political parties that developed from one of the groups that participated in the Sunflower student movement, the Taiwan Citizens Union.

29. For example, the DPP in the 2016 legislative elections created the Capital Progressive Alliance to cooperate with candidates from small parties in districts in Taipei.

30. According to TVBS opinion polls, when Chen Shui-bian took office his satisfaction rate was 77 percent, but by the end of his presidency in 2008 it had dropped to only 13 percent.

31. According to a measure of unification and independence attitudes utilized in TEDS 2016 (i.e., 0 represents quick independence and 10 refers to quick unification with the PRC), the average score of the respondents was 4.39; for the pan-Blue camp, those who identified with the KMT scored 7.36, and with the PFP, 5.88; among pan-Green supporters, those who identified with the DPP scored 3.12 and the NPP scored 2.95. The average voter was slightly closer to the DPP's position than the KMT's on the unification-independence scale, and the NPP was more pro-independence than the DPP.

15

Cross-Strait Relations

Szu-yin Ho

After eight years of relative tranquility in the Taiwan Strait during the Ma era, relations between the People's Republic of China (PRC) and Taiwan (Republic of China [ROC]) were once again thrown into uncertainty. After serving out his second term as president, Ma Ying-jeou was constitutionally barred from standing for reelection in Taiwan's January 2016 presidential election. Tsai Ing-wen, chair of the opposition Democratic Progressive Party (DPP), won the presidency by a wide margin over her Kuomintang (KMT) opponent, Eric Chu. The KMT was also trounced in the concurrent legislative elections by the opposing DPP, which won a majority in the Legislative Yuan for the first time ever. Many observers interpreted the 2016 elections as bringing about a realignment of Taiwan's domestic political forces, in which the rapprochement-oriented KMT gave way to the Taiwan independence–minded DPP and a younger generation of voters.[1] The sour note for the KMT had wide repercussions for security not only in the Taiwan Strait but also across East Asia.

In this chapter, I first examine the Ma administration's efforts to find a formula to anchor its relationship with the PRC. Next, I discuss the conduct of cross-Strait policy during the Ma era. In the third section I assess possible developments in cross-Strait relations under a DPP administration in Taiwan. The last section offers some concluding thoughts. A caveat should be in order here. I served as the deputy secretary-general of the National Security Council in the first two years of the Ma administration, and after my departure I was still involved with the administration in various ways. I write this chapter as a participant-observer, which means I will be unable to footnote some events described in what follows. But I have made conscious efforts to avoid biases, as any social scientist should do under these circumstances.

Creation of the "1992 Consensus"

In general, small states neighboring great powers have two grand-strategic choices, bandwagoning or balancing.[2] Small states like the Melos during the Peloponnesian War, the United Provinces facing a rising England,[3] Finland in its long and sometimes bloody history with Russia/Soviet Union,[4] and contemporary Commonwealth of Independent States (CIS) countries in their relations with Russia[5] have often struggled to settle on a grand strategy for dealing with their powerful neighbors. Taiwan is no exception. During the Cold War years, it was convenient for Taiwan to choose a balancing strategy against the PRC, since its security was aligned with the interests of the United States. When United States–China relations began to thaw in the early 1970s, Taiwan's strategic position became more difficult. It was still engaged in a zero-sum struggle with the PRC, but Washington had already made strides in improving relations with Beijing through the 1970s and 1980s. Seeing Taiwan's international position worsen, President Chiang Ching-kuo made two strategic decisions before his death in 1988. First, he opened up Taiwan's political system by acquiescing to the formation of the DPP, despite the fact that a party ban was still in place. Second, by allowing some old soldiers who had moved to Taiwan with Chiang Kai-shek's KMT government in 1949 to visit their hometowns in mainland China, Chiang Ching-kuo allowed a trickle of people-to-people exchanges with the PRC to begin to flow. This trickle later became a flood of commercial and cultural exchanges between the two sides of the Strait. Ever since then, two competing forces in Taiwan—the Taiwan-first force represented by the DPP and the force that wants to have smooth relations with Beijing as represented by the KMT—have vied with each other to determine Taiwan's grand strategy.

From Lee Teng-hui, who succeeded Chiang Ching-kuo as president in 1988 and won Taiwan's first direct presidential election in 1996, to the DPP's Chen Shui-bian (2000–2008), to the KMT's Ma Ying-jeou (2008–2016), Taiwan's policy toward the PRC has followed a clear zigzag pattern. In the first four years of the Lee administration, both sides of the Taiwan Strait were gingerly sizing each other up, as cross-Strait people-to-people exchanges increased dramatically. In March 1993, Taiwan's representative Koo Chen-fu met with his mainland Chinese counterpart, Wang Daohan, in Singapore over ostensibly mundane people-to-people affairs. The meeting, though "unofficial," was full of symbolic significance, because it was the first such meeting between Taiwan and the PRC since 1949. Following that meeting, however, cross-Strait relations worsened and then took a nosedive after President Lee's visit to his alma mater, Cornell University, in June

1995. Lee's speech at Cornell University was representative of Taiwan's newfound self-assertiveness. In the speech Lee mentioned Taiwan sixteen times, but did not bother to mention China even once. Worse, in the eyes of Beijing, Lee's visit also meant that Washington had broken its tacit promise that no high officials from Taiwan would visit the United States. From the summer of 1995 to March 1996, when Taiwan held its first direct presidential election, Beijing employed a variety of scare tactics, including launching missiles into waters near the island, that only made Taiwanese even more resentful of the PRC. In September 1996, Lee initiated his "Show Restraint, Go Slow" policy, trying to slow Taiwan's increasing trade with and investment in mainland China, an economic statecraft move that Beijing resented a great deal. In a July 1999 interview with a foreign reporter, Lee claimed that the relationship between Taiwan and the PRC was one between two states, a claim bordering on a formal declaration of de jure Taiwanese independence. This triggered an angry response from Beijing, and Washington intervened. Lee backtracked under US pressure,[6] and a new pattern of power politics emerged in the triangular relationship between the PRC, Taiwan, and the United States: when Taipei introduced policies that smacked of outright de jure independence and ruffled feathers in Beijing, Washington would get involved to prevent the crisis from escalating.

President Chen continued Lee's legacy. As president-elect in 2000, Chen promised a more open economic policy toward the PRC under the slogan "Active Opening, Effective Management." The new slogan was compatible with Chen's pledge of a "Five No's" policy to guide cross-Strait relations, which he laid out in his inaugural speech in May 2000.[7] But by 2002, when President Chen felt that his goodwill had not been reciprocated, he changed course and proposed the idea of "One State on Each Side (of the Taiwan Strait)." On the economic front, in 2006, Chen twisted his 2000 policy slogan around to "Active Management, Effective Opening," giving it a strong anti-China flavor. In the run-up to the 2008 presidential election, President Chen and the DPP initiated a referendum to be held together with the presidential vote, the formal title of which was "Joining the United Nations Under the Name of Taiwan." In promoting this vote, the DPP government was not so naive as to be unaware that a successful referendum does not a UN membership make. Rather, the aim was to stake out support for an independent Taiwan for a domestic audience, with a maximum dose of legal formality. This time Beijing did not throw its usual tantrums, largely because Ma Ying-jeou, the KMT presidential candidate, was considered to be a shoo-in in the upcoming presidential election.

Behind all these zigzags in policy is the necessity for every presidential administration in Taiwan to find a formula to define itself vis-à-vis China— who are "we" and who are "they." This formula then serves to anchor Taiwan's cross-Strait policies, laws, and regulations. In a sense, the search for a consensus on a formula for cross-Strait relations has been ongoing ever since Taiwan's transition to democracy started in the late 1980s. Political discourse and mobilization revolve around this never-ending quest. During the martial law era, Taiwanese were told they were Chinese, no matter what. But the freedom of expression that came with political democratization naturally opened up space for different ways for Taiwanese to self-identify, and accordingly widened the spectrum of possible relations (in the legal sense) that Taiwan could have with mainland China. Complicating the matter is that how one sees oneself sometimes depends on how others see oneself. Given Taiwan's long political separation and its increasing diplomatic isolation as a consequence of PRC pressure, it was only natural for many Taiwanese to feel alienated from mainland China. President Lee's "State-to-State" theory, President Chen's "One State on Each Side" slogan, and many other counter-proposals uttered by high political figures, public intellectuals, and salient social groups (I count no less than thirty-four distinct positions on the spectrum, ranging from immediate reunification to immediate de jure independence) are all parts of the incessant search for a foundation on which Taiwan can base its relations with the PRC. Beijing's unwavering position that Taiwan is part of one and the same China as the mainland (the one-China principle) makes it necessary for Taiwanese to consider both realpolitik and irredentism in their search for such a foundation. But an equilibrium point has been elusive. Lee's and Chen's proposals never really got off the ground. In the end, President Lee could vent his frustration and anger only in books he published in retirement advocating immediate Taiwanese independence. And President Chen could only lament about declaring de jure independence that "I can't do it, I just can't."[8]

Putting the Consensus to Work

Ma Ying-jeou was elected president in 2008. It now was Ma's turn to find and define the formula. From the very beginning of his political career, Ma had been deeply immersed in the Taiwan government's mainland affairs portfolio. His chief policy adviser in this issue area was Su Chi, an international relations scholar by training. Su's government experience was also focused on mainland affairs. The formula that Ma ended up adopting for cross-Strait relations was the "1992 Consensus."

The term "1992 Consensus" was coined by Su in 2000 during the government transition from the KMT to the DPP. Su was hoping that the nebulous nature of the newly created term would be more palatable to the DPP, and hence cross-Strait relations would not further deteriorate under the incoming DPP administration. The term refers to a sequence of signals exchanged between representatives from Taipei and Beijing in 1992. Both sides were then engaged in talks over the validation of legal papers (birth certificates, household registration cards, marriage certificates, and the like) issued by the other side's government. The issue was much more important to Beijing than to Taipei. For the PRC, the issue was how to ensure that acceptance of ROC government-issued legal papers would not constitute a formal acceptance of the separate sovereignty or independence of Taiwan's government. Beijing insisted upon inserting the one-China principle into the accord, but the Taiwan representatives did not like the idea. Negotiations over this major political issue, which had escalated from a minor procedural issue, quickly stalemated. To break the deadlock, on October 30, Taiwan's Straits Exchange Foundation (SEF) proposed that "each side orally express, respectively, its position on the issue." On November 3, the PRC's Association for Relations Across the Taiwan Strait (ARATS), in the form of a Xinhua News Agency press release, responded to this overture by stating that "ARATS is willing to respect and accept that both ARATS and SEF, respectively, use oral statements to express the 'One-China' Principle."[9] Based on these exchanges, Taiwan's SEF chairman Koo and the PRC's ARATS president Wang met in Singapore the next year (1993), the first time since 1949 that high-level representatives from the two sides of the Taiwan Strait had met in person. Taipei then gradually moved to a position of "one China, respective interpretations." Beijing did not think this was the right formulation of what came out of the exchanges in 1992. From the PRC's point of view, the formation should have been both sides "respectively expressing a 'one-China' principle." As one important Beijing think tank director told me, the Taiwan side's formulation connotes separation, while the PRC's connotes reunion. But Beijing never chose to object publicly to Taipei's position.

Based on these exchanged signals, the term "1992 Consensus" introduced even more ambiguity into the formula of "one China, respective interpretations." For the incoming Chen administration in 2000, the term deleted "China" from the slogan, presumably making it more palatable to the DPP. For the KMT, the ROC still lurked in the background through "respective interpretations." And Beijing could still add its own addendum to the consensus—"the gist of the consensus is that both sides of the Strait belong to one and the same China"—whenever it saw fit. In the parlance of rational choice theory, the term "1992 Consensus" expanded the intersection of choice sets for both Taipei and Beijing. The DPP immediately rejected this newest formulation of Taiwan's relations with the PRC lest any acceptance of it preclude other alternatives for Taiwan (meaning, in particular, Taiwanese independence). The term was therefore put into hibernation during the eight years of the Chen administration. But with all the ambiguities, denotations, connotations, and historical interpretations built into only four Chinese characters, the "1992 Consensus" (read in Chinese as *jiu'er gongshi*) would later come back to become the foundation of Ma's mainland policy, a jinx for the DPP, and a focus of attention for both the PRC and the United States.

Ma faced an international environment that was even more daunting than his two predecessors had faced. First, the power gap between the PRC and Taiwan continued to widen. According to the World Bank, in 1996 mainland China's gross domestic product (GDP) was 2.94 times Taiwan's. The figure grew to 3.66 in 2000, 10.93 in 2008, and 19.55 in 2014. Second, Taiwan's National Security Council (NSC) was leery of Chinese military modernization. Prodded by the presence of two aircraft-carrier groups deployed by the United States in the final days of the 1995-1996 Taiwan Strait crisis, the People's Liberation Army (PLA) embarked upon an intensive modernization program. Most important of them all, in the assessment of Ma's first NSC, was the PLA's increasing anti-access/area denial (A2AD) capabilities, which would presumably give the United States second thoughts about initiating the kind of naval deployment that it undertook during the 1996 crisis, should a future situation in the Taiwan Strait require it.[10] The NSC also believed that the United States, now bogged down in the Middle East and preoccupied with the economic turmoil of the global financial crisis, simply would not have much of an appetite for forceful intervention in the Taiwan Strait. Third, the NSC observed that the United States had many interests that overlapped with China's. A troublemaking Taiwan would damage US national interests, thus undercutting US support for Taiwan's cause. This assumption could also apply to other countries that had substantial relationships with Taiwan. Fourth, Beijing would never give up its national goal of reunification, but it would also not put the issue high on its agenda in the near term as it faced tremendous domestic difficulties. The NSC decided that Beijing really meant it when it said that its development depended on regional peace and stability. From these realities a conclusion was drawn: rapprochement with the PRC was both possible and necessary.

Ma's NSC gradually developed the "1992 Consensus" into an integrated edifice. The edifice has three constitutive parts—a declaratory, symbolic supra-structure; a holistic operational mode; and many nuts and bolts—all meant to buttress the Ma administration's reputation for not being a trouble-maker in international politics in East Asia. The building of the declaratory supra-structure started right from the beginning of the Ma administration. In his inaugural speech, Ma maintained that

> under the principle of "no unification, no independence and no use of force," as Taiwan's mainstream public opinion holds it, and under the framework of the ROC Constitution, we will maintain the status quo in the Taiwan Strait. In 1992, the two sides reached a consensus on "one China, respective inter-pretations." Many rounds of negotiation were then completed, spurring the development of cross-strait relations. I want to reiterate that, based on the "1992 Consensus," negotiations should resume at the earliest time possible.[11]

This paragraph includes all the major elements of Ma's cross-Strait policy for the next eight years: the "Three No's," the ROC constitution, the status quo, "one China, respective interpretations," and the 1992 Consensus. In this carefully worded paragraph, two features are worth highlighting. First, regarding the "Three No's," "no unification" comes before "no independence," apparently for domestic consumption. And the binding together of "no independence and no use of force," with no comma in between, implied a kind of quid pro quo. Second, "one China, respective interpretations," the KMT's characterization of the exchanges in 1992, was mentioned before the more encompassing term "1992 Consensus," with the two terms being separated by a full sentence. This ordering reflected the new administration's dual need to have a viable position on which to anchor Taiwan's relations with mainland China, on the one hand, and to forge a common ground with Beijing so that the two sides could engage in future negotiations, on the other.[12]

Ma elaborated further on this declaratory supra-structure throughout his two terms. In his second inaugural speech, in 2012, Ma proposed the idea of "mutual non-recognition of sovereignty and mutual non-denial of jurisdiction." In an address in 2013 to commemorate the twentieth anniversary of the Koo-Wang meeting in Singapore, Ma reiterated that his administration would not promote a two-Chinas principle; a one-China, one-Taiwan principle; or Taiwanese independence. All these statements were aimed at providing assurances and reassurances to the PRC—and the United States—that Ma intended to maintain peace and stability in the Strait. The underlying message was that Taiwan should be accordingly rewarded.

At the operational level, Ma's first NSC, under the aegis of Su Chi, had used a holistic thinking mode to mull over Taiwan's mainland China policy. From day one the NSC thought of the Ma administration's cross-Strait policy not just in terms of Taiwan's interactions with the PRC, but also in terms of how these interactions would influence its relationships with third parties in the international community (mainly the United States) and, vice versa, how Taiwan's international relations (again mainly with the United States) would have boomerang effects on Taiwan's relations with Beijing. Then there was the domestic audience. The analogy in the NSC was that the Ma administration was like a player having to play three chess games all at the same time, and each game would simultaneously influence the other two games. Moreover, two players—China and the United States—on the other sides of the tables had much deeper strategies, and the third player, Taiwan's domestic politics, could well be a wild card. Hardly a fair game—but then again the NSC felt that fairness was beyond reach for a small state facing great powers. President Ma therefore in his public speeches and interviews with foreign guests tirelessly promoted the idea of win-win-win results in the triangular relations between Taiwan, the PRC, and a third country. To achieve win-win-win results (a draw for Taiwan would be good enough in certain circumstances) in any round of the games, the NSC just had to have better skills, a better sense of timing, a better feel for balance, and sometimes just better luck.

Let me use an event to illustrate the NSC's holistic thinking mode. On December 31, 2008, Chinese president Hu Jintao, in commemorating the thirtieth anniversary of the "Open Letter to Compatriots in Taiwan," which the PRC had promulgated on the eve of its establishment of formal diplomatic relations with the United States (January 1, 1979), publicized six points as Beijing's policy guidelines toward Taiwan: (1) sticking to a one-China principle to increase mutual trust, (2) promoting economic cooperation to further cross-Strait development, (3) championing Chinese culture to strengthen the spiritual bond across the Taiwan Strait, (4) increasing personnel exchanges to facilitate communications in all walks of life, (5) safeguarding national sovereignty so that both sides can negotiate over (Taiwan's) external affairs, and (6) ending any remaining hostilities across the Strait by signing a peace accord. How the Ma administration should respond to the six points needed serious thought.

Taiwan was clearly able to accept the second, third, and fourth points, as these were mainly economic and cultural issues. The first point was exactly what the 1992 Consensus was designed for. The fifth was hard to respond to because Beijing held the key to Taiwan's participation in international space. Without negotiation over this issue, Taiwan's efforts to increase its international standing were likely to be stonewalled. But the Ma administration could not afford to be accused of "Finlandizing Taiwan," as the opposition would surely launch this accusation. The sixth point was the most difficult issue. A peace accord with Beijing may have had some prima facie value. But the PRC as an authoritarian regime just could not provide the kind of "democratic commitments" needed by Taiwan.[13] And the United States could not be expected to underwrite the accord. In addition, would Beijing use the peace accord to pressure the United States not to sell necessary defensive arms to Taiwan? If the United States did decide to scale down arms sales to Taiwan, a quintessential part of its commitment to Taiwan's national security, would Beijing still honor the accord? But saying no to the peace accord proposal would be like shooting oneself in the foot, as Ma did mention a "possible" peace accord in his inaugural speech. Alternatively, the Ma administration could not simply respond selectively to the six points (yes to the second, third, and fourth, no to the rest), for doing so would look self-serving and possibly dampen the enthusiasm in Beijing for starting a better relationship with the new administration. On top of these considerations, the NSC had to calculate possible reactions both from the international community and politically at home. The ultimate decision on this issue was that the Ma administration would not respond to Hu's six points at all. Among other things, the decision was informed by a lesson from the Cuban missile crisis that the NSC's scholars-cum-officials had learned well during their graduate studies in US universities. On October 26, 1962, day eleven of the crisis, Premier Khrushchev wrote a letter to President Kennedy in a significantly conciliatory tone. But the next day—the most dangerous day in the whole crisis, before the administration had the chance to discuss the offer from the Kremlin the previous day—Khrushchev upped the ante in a Moscow Radio message. The Kennedy administration ultimately decided to respond only to the conciliatory message of October 26 and to ignore the hardline message of October 27, thus sending a clear signal to the Kremlin. By learning this lesson in a different way, Ma's NSC hoped to send a signal to Beijing—"not so fast, let's start from scratch."[14] Since there was never a response from the Ma administration to Hu's six points, foreign observers, in particular those from the United States and China, kept asking when the Ma administration might produce one.

At the next level were many nuts-and-bolt issues. But these issues were by no means small matters in cross-Strait relations, loaded as they were with symbolic significance. Examples abound. How the PRC was to be referred to in official government statements was a significant issue. In the Chen administration, "China" was called just that, implying that it was a separate country from Taiwan. The Ma administration would call China "mainland China" to be consistent with the ROC constitution, which with its 1991 amendment stipulates that the ROC is constituted of two areas, the Taiwan area and the mainland area. Then there were other issues: Taiwan's official stance on the Diaoyu Islands; the Ministry of Education's issuance of a guideline for editing high school history textbooks (which became a salient ideological issue in 2015); the instructions given to Taiwan's diplomats about how to proceed given that a tacit diplomatic truce between Taiwan and the PRC was happening in some parts of the international community, but not in other parts; the use of the term "responsible stakeholder" in Ma's interviews with foreign guests;[15] and so on. To walk a tightrope in all these specific situations required a strong sense of balance. Let me use a speech by Ma to illustrate the kind of balancing act the NSC strained to achieve. The speech was given in a video conference with Harvard's Fairbank Center on April 5, 2010. The following excerpts are the leading paragraphs of the speech, both of which are worthy of lengthy quotation:

> It heartens me to be once again addressing the excellent faculty and student body of Harvard University. This moment brings back a rush of nostalgia because it was here I became a proud father for the first time before I even got my doctoral degree. . . . I also feel nostalgic on a deeper level. When I think of a long litany of historic events, figures, and institutions—John Hay's Open-Door Policy, Boxer Rebellion, American Indemnity Scholarships for China (with all its recipients, like Hu Shih and Chien Shih-liang), Tsinghua University, Yenching University,

May Fourth Movement, Flying Tigers, Pearl Harbor, John Leighton Stuart, 1949 Korean War, United States–Republic of China Mutual Defense Treaty, Fairbank Center, the Quemoy and Matsu Crisis, Cultural Revolution, Shanghai Communiqué, Taiwan Relations Act, mainland China's Reform and Open [*sic*] Policy, US arms sales to Taiwan, and so on—I cannot help but think of the far-reaching impact that America has had on China's, and later on Taiwan's, convoluted path to modernization. I cannot help but think my time at Harvard was not only a personal academic journey, but also a microcosm reflecting a people's long search for a modern nation.

The late venerable Benjamin Schwartz, who as you know had been a prominent member of the Fairbank Center, [wrote] that the evolution of modern China has been a journey in search of wealth and power. Given the rise of mainland China's economic power and military strength over the last thirty years, it seems that it has achieved those goals to a considerable degree. However, I believe a society that is truly modernizing should not be limited to wealth and power but must also include the foundations for freedom and democracy. For it is only through the active participation and free choice of one's citizens that government truly serves the welfare of the people; only then can a government sustain, and a nation thrive. So I am proud to say that the Republic of China on Taiwan has in fact achieved all these three pillars. The ROC has since become a thriving nation with a robust economy, viable military and a truly open and vibrant democracy. With so much already achieved, the roadmap of my administration is quite straightforward: namely to strengthen the foundation of these three pillars so as to safeguard the future of Taiwan's posterity, and to share with mainland China our values and way of life.[16]

From all the efforts to put the 1992 Consensus into practice, the Ma administration was able to sign twenty-three agreements with the PRC. It was also able to improve relations with the United States and many other countries, and it lost no diplomatic allies to Beijing. Not a small feat.

The 1992 Consensus on the Domestic Front

A country's grand strategy needs the support of a domestic base.[17] The rapprochement with the PRC pursued by the Ma administration certainly boded well for peace and stability, and it appeared to be good for business too. Increased direct flights between cities across the Strait (up to 890 flights per week), the large number of Chinese tourists to Taiwan (4.23 million in 2015), and Chinese purchases of Taiwanese products and manufactured goods were all positive results from the rapprochement policy. When the free trade Economic Cooperation Framework Agreement (ECFA) was signed with Beijing in 2010, in which the PRC made major concessions to Taiwan, opposition parties accused the Ma administration of making Taiwan an economic hostage to the mainland. But the government prevailed. Ma was able to hold together a domestic coalition to win a second term, from 2012–2016. Starting in 2012, however, the opposition sharpened its attacks on his grand strategy. It began to frame the cross-Strait business exchanges in terms of wealth distribution, against the backdrop of rising global inequalities in the wake of the Great Recession. The opposition also pushed harder for Taiwan's independence, emphasizing all the differences between Taiwan and the PRC and hence eroding the legalism embedded in the term "1992 Consensus." The Ma administration's rebuttal against this one-two punch from the opposition was ineffective at best. After all, it is hard to argue against reality. Taiwan's fast-rising real estate prices (a result of very low interest rates in the wake of the Great Recession) put the dream of owning a house beyond the reach of many people, especially the youngest generation. Salaries and wages stagnated. And to be sure, Confucius's teaching that "a state need not fear scarcity but should fear inequality" was still the social ethos: when things go wrong, the government is to blame. The calls for Taiwan's independence were even more difficult to defend against. The romantic appeal to declare a new nation with its own creole origins stirred emotions, especially among the young, who tended to identify as Taiwanese rather than Chinese. In contrast, Ma's grand strategy as represented in the 1992 Consensus was based on realist calculations. It was sophisticated and cold, and about maintaining the status quo, which unlike revolution was hardly appealing to young hearts and difficult to explain to ordinary people. To the degree that politics is about symbolic action,[18] Ma's outside-in grand strategy was at a disadvantage to the opposition's inside-out strategy.

The twenty-three agreements signed between Taiwan's SEF and the PRC's ARATS during Ma's two terms are illustrative of this political dynamic. Table 15.1 shows that the Legislative Yuan dealt with the twenty-three agreements in four different ways. In increasing order of intensity of review, these were file-for-reference, approve-by-default without joint committee reviews, approve-by-default after joint committee reviews, and delay indefinitely. On the surface the Legislative Yuan seemed to have an institutionalized process for making trade policy. And one would expect that for a trading state like Taiwan, where international trade accounts for over 100 percent of GDP, it should have already had a reliable legislative mechanism through which the costs and benefits of an international trade agreement could be debated and then voted on, a mechanism something like the 1934 Reciprocal Trade Agreements Act of the United States.[19] Instead, the legislative review process for cross-Strait trade agreements was full of uncertainties. For one thing, the Executive Yuan did not know for sure what method the Legislative Yuan would employ in processing cross-Strait agreements, because there is no specific step-by-step legislative guideline for both the legislative and executive branches to follow. Of course the executive branch would consult with the KMT party caucus in the Legislative Yuan before it sent the bill to the legislature. But the promises

Table 15.1   Cross-Straight Agreements Signed During the Ma Era, 2008–2016

Agreement Title	Signing Date	Legislative Yuan Decisions
Agreement on Travel by Mainland Residents to Taiwan	June 13, 2008	July 4, 2008: Filed for reference.
Minutes of Talks on Cross-Strait Charter Flights	June 13, 2008	July 4, 2008: Filed for reference.
Agreement on Direct Sea Transport	November 4, 2008	December 4, 2008: After committee review, Committee of the Whole passed by default.
Agreement on Direct Flights	November 4, 2008	December 4, 2008: After committee review, Committee of the Whole passed by default.
Agreement on Food Safety Cooperation	November 4, 2008	December 4, 2008: After committee review, Committee of the Whole passed by default.
Agreement on Postal Service	November 4, 2008	December 4, 2008: After committee review, Committee of the Whole passed by default.
Agreement on Justice Cooperation	April 26, 2009	June 10, 2009: After committee review, Committee of the Whole passed by default.
Supplement Agreement on Direct Flights	April 26, 2009	June 10, 2009: After committee review, Committee of the Whole passed by default.
Agreement on Financial Cooperation	April 26, 2009	June 10, 2009: After committee review, Committee of the Whole passed by default.
Agreement on Fishing Affairs	December 12, 2009	January 7, 2010: After committee review, Committee of the Whole passed by default.
Agreement on Agricultural Product Quarantine and Inspection	December 22, 2009	January 7, 2010: After committee review, Committee of the Whole passed by default.
Agreement on Standards, Metrology, Inspection, and Accreditation	December 22, 2009	January 7, 2010: After committee review, Committee of the Whole passed by default.
Economic Cooperation Framework Agreement	June 29, 2010	August 17, 2010: Committee of the Whole passed by default.
Agreement on Intellectual Property Rights Protection	June 29, 2010	August 17, 2010: Committee of the Whole passed by default.
Agreement on Medical and Health Cooperation	December 21, 2010	December 31, 2010: After committee review, Committee of the Whole passed by default.
Agreement on Nuclear Power Safety Cooperation	October 20, 2011	November 25, 2011: After committee review, Committee of the Whole passed by default.
Agreement on Investment Guarantee	August 9, 2012	October 5, 2012: After committee review, Committee of the Whole passed by default.

continues

Table 15.1 Continued

Agreement Title	Signing Date	Legislative Yuan Decisions
Agreement on Customs Cooperation	August 9, 2012	October 5, 2012: After committee review, Committee of the Whole passed by default.
Agreement on Trade in Services	June 21, 2013	Delayed indefinitely.
Agreement on Meteorological Information Exchanges	February 27, 2014	May 2, 2014: After committee review, Committee of the Whole passed by default.
Agreement on Seismic Monitoring Cooperation	February 27, 2014	May 2, 2014: After committee review, Committee of the Whole passed by default.
Agreement on Taxation Cooperation	August 25, 2015	Delayed indefinitely.
Agreement on Aviation Safety	August 25, 2015	December 31, 2015: After committee review, Committee of the Whole passed by default.

Source: Mainland Affairs Council.

and consensus coming out of the Executive Yuan–KMT caucus meetings may not have held in the informal cross-party discussion that had final say on the legislative agenda. Even for those legislative agendas approved via cross-party discussion, individual legislators could still use disruptive tactics (e.g., occupying the speaker's podium or taking away his gavel) to stall the agenda. This lack of legislative institutionalization and norms introduced a high degree of uncertainty and randomness into Taiwan's making of cross-Strait trade policy.

The first eighteen agreements, including the much-ballyhooed ECFA, were all approved by the Legislative Yuan, one way or another. But when the Cross-Strait Services Trade Agreement (CSSTA) was finally discharged from committee and set for a vote in March 2014, students mobilized to occupy the floor of the Legislative Yuan for twenty-three days, backed by encouragement and logistical support from the DPP. This student movement (later called the Sunflower Movement) had two appeals: it opposed the CSSTA (or any future agreement with the PRC) and supported Taiwan's independence. By the end of the occupation, the Sunflower Movement had captured the full attention of the media. In the year-end local elections, the KMT was routed. The momentum of an anti-China, pro-independence social ethos continued into the 2016 presidential election and the concurrent legislative elections. The KMT lost again in a landslide. Not only did it lose the presidency, but it also ceded to the DPP majority control of the Legislative Yuan for the first time ever.

Several factors led to this watershed event. For one thing, the personality conflict that emerged between President Ma and Speaker Wang prevented the ruling party from forming a unified front against the student movement and DPP coalition. Second, as mentioned earlier, the Legislative Yuan never had an institutionalized process for handling cross-Strait agreements. If there had been such a process, the political repercussions of the CSSTA might have been ameliorated.[20] Third, in sharp relief with ECFA, the CSSTA caused a deep sense of insecurity in Taiwanese society. The ECFA was nothing but a roadmap for better economic relations between Taiwan and mainland China, sweetened by a list of early harvests for trade in manufactured goods. For the average person, the roadmap was quite abstract, and the early harvests were all gains, no pains (because the PRC lowered its tariffs much more than Taiwan did). In contrast, the CSSTA was detailed and specific, with both sides making concrete commitments to trade-in-services. It soon became a contentious public issue. Both the general public and demagogic politicians showed a clear trade policy preference: they wanted the benefits of trade with mainland China but were not willing to bear any costs from that trade. Last, the politics of trade could easily transform into the politics of identity. For example, the publishing industry asserted that any concessions to PRC publishers (though mutual) would be tantamount to mainland Chinese culture invading Taiwanese culture (though there is huge overlap between the two). In the aftermath of the Sunflower Movement, all negotiations with Beijing came to a halt. Taiwanese politicians went back to square one in their collective efforts to define Taiwan's status vis-à-vis China.

The 1992 Consensus: Still Alive?

Since the Sunflower Movement, the KMT has been gradually sidelined in Taiwanese politics, but the 1992 Consensus has not. The chess game is now being played between the DPP and Beijing. Commenting on the Sunflower Movement in July 2014, then–DPP chair Tsai said: "Taiwan independence is a natural ingredient of the young generation."[21] When the PRC was holding its 2015 annual "Two Conferences" (National People's Congress and National Committee of the Chinese People's Political Consultative Conference [CPPCC], both nominally part of the PRC parliament), Chinese president Xi Jinping had this to say on March 4: "China regards the '1992 Consensus' as the foundation of China's exchanges with Taiwan . . . the core meaning of which is 'both Taiwan and the mainland belong to one and the same China.' . . . If the foundation no longer exists, then the earth will move and the mountains will shake."[22] As a presidential candidate, Tsai gave a speech at the Center for International and Security Studies (CSIS) in Washington, DC, on June 4, 2015, reiterating her "position of maintaining the status quo" and saying that if elected president, she would "push for the peaceful and stable development of cross-Strait relations in accordance with the will of the Taiwanese people and the existing ROC constitutional order."[23] On November 7, 2015, Xi met with Ma in Singapore, with both leaders reiterating the importance of the 1992 Consensus. On December 27, 2015, in a presidential debate, Tsai said that "the 1992 Consensus is an option, but not the only option for Taiwan."[24] In a postelection interview president-elect Tsai gave to Taiwan's *Liberty Times* on January 21, 2016, she laid out the "existing political foundation" in terms of four "key elements."[25] The first was the historical fact of the SEF-ARATS discussions of 1992 and that both sides had agreed to set aside differences and seek common ground. The second was the Republic of China's current constitutional order. The third was the accumulated results of more than twenty years of cross-Strait negotiations, exchanges, and interactions. The fourth was Taiwan's democratic principles and the general will of the Taiwanese people. Chinese foreign minister Wang Yi, in the question-and-answer session after a speech he gave at the CSIS on February 25, 2016, said that "what we care about . . . is whether she [Tsai] will recommit [to] the political foundation of cross-Strait relations. . . . The One China Principle is what we care about. . . . I hope that she will accept the provision in Taiwan's own constitution that the mainland and Taiwan belong to one and the same China. . . . She is elected on the basis of the current constitution of Taiwan, which still recognizes the mainland and Taiwan as one and the same China."[26] During the 2016 "Two Conferences," Chinese president Xi Jinping, premier Li Keqiang, and CPPCC chair Yu Zhengsheng (the fourth-ranking Chinese Communist Party [CCP] Politburo member) all reiterated China's determination to stick to the 1992 Consensus and oppose Taiwan's independence. Premier Li repeated this determination yet again in the closing speech of the National People's Congress. Current and formal officials and think-tank interlocutors all joined the chorus during this time. A commentator's article in *People's Daily* makes the Chinese position crystalclear: "When one refers to the '1992 Consensus,' he has to be very clear on two points—first, he has to recognize the consensus as a historical fact, and, secondly, he has to recognize the core meaning of the consensus is that cross-Strait relations are neither state-to-state nor one-China, one-Taiwan relations."[27] On March 14, 2016, the CPPCC passed a resolution stipulating that the 1992 Consensus was necessary to continue cross-Strait interactions and that the PRC strongly opposed Taiwan's independence.[28]

Beijing has since upped the ante. With the Ma administration, the PRC's representatives would speak of the "1992 Consensus" without attaching to it the "core connotation" extension—that Taiwan and the mainland belong to one and the same China. Likewise, the Ma administration would mention the consensus without the "respective interpretations" rider. When the circumstances on one side required the addendum to be stated, the other side would have its addendum stated at some other time. This norm of reciprocity was first established in the second half of the 1990s. It is the ambiguity built into the term "1992 Consensus" and the manner in which the term was used that made it useful as the political foundation for cross-Strait negotiations. If one side intended to push the envelope in clarifying the term, the term would lose its usefulness and the two sides would have to go back to square one—that is, defining in clear terms the relations between the two sides of the Strait. When Tsai and the DPP did not recognize even the existence of the "1992 Consensus," all the ambiguities embedded in the term vanished, and Beijing had to reset the bar high enough to make its intentions clear.

And Beijing has not hesitated to back its words with deeds. Since Tsai was sworn into office, the PRC has cut the number of Chinese tourists to Taiwan. It has pried away seven of Taiwan's diplomatic allies, ending the diplomatic truce during the Ma years and reducing the number of Taiwan's diplomatic allies to fifteen. It has denied Taiwan's participation in some international organizations that the Ma administration was allowed to take part in. Militarily, it has taken a much more aggressive posture toward Taiwan that has not been seen since the 1958 Quemoy crisis. For example, after the CCP's Nineteenth Party Congress, held in October 2017, the PLA let it be known that military pressure had been put on Taiwan by posting on its official *Weibo* page on December 12 a video titled "Cruising Around the Island."[29] This military patrol by air and sea was in play again on April 19, 2018, this time announced by a PLA air force spokesperson.[30] On the civilian front, China initiated a number of concrete measures to appeal to the hearts and minds of Taiwan's people.[31] All of these concrete measures are purported to give Taiwan's people the national treatment enjoyed by PRC citizens (such as equal opportunity employment and equal treatment in opening a bank account). Key to these measures is the PRC State Council's announcement that Taiwanese can apply for a PRC "residence card," which will treat Taiwanese applicants as PRC nationals.[32] As Chinese interlocutors like to say, "The hard hand gets harder; the soft hand gets softer."[33] As of this writing, Tsai administration still has yet to find an effective counterstrategy for Beijing's moves.

The PRC's credibility in making good on the 1992 Consensus was established by Xi's meeting with Ma in Singapore. In this move, Xi was sending a costly signal of reassurance about the 1992 Consensus not only to Taiwan but also to the international community.[34] Xi was telling the international community that his meeting with Taiwan's leader, which was anathema to high political leaders of the PRC, was based on the 1992 Consensus. If Taiwan disregarded the consensus and moved decidedly toward de jure Taiwanese independence, he could be severely compromised in China's domestic politics. Given Xi's domestic situation, this "hand-tying" tactic might just work. Xi's ever-widening anticorruption campaign, announcement to cut 300,000 PLA personnel, and mishandling of a slowing Chinese economy, together with increasing labor unrest, do not bode well for the PRC's social stability, the top concern of the CCP. The Ninteenth

Party Congress of the CCP in 2017 made Xi the PRC's permanent leader. Xi will have to bear all the responsibility for a breakaway Taiwan. Further down the road will be the centennial anniversary of the CCP in 2021,[35] a milestone that may require some action on Taiwan.[36] Furthermore, the many position-taking reiterations that followed the Singapore meeting, especially those made during the holding of the "Two Conferences" in mid-March 2016, are a kind of institutional commitment, Chinese style. Beijing may have another two credibility-related concerns. One is that the KMT may have electoral incentives to give up the 1992 Consensus so as to be more able to compete with the DPP's nativism. If that were to be the case, the PRC would encounter even more difficulties in peacefully reunifying with Taiwan, as the director of the Institute of Taiwan Studies at the Chinese Academy of Social Sciences, the PRC's leading think tank on Taiwan research, pointed out in a major speech.[37] The second concern is that should the KMT come to power again, it may renege on the consensus on the grounds that if Beijing looked the other way when the DPP was trashing the 1992 Consensus, then it could certainly look the other way again when the KMT is in power. Beijing has an incentive to prevent Taiwan's political parties from "racing toward the bottom" on cross-Strait issues.

Will President Tsai budge then? I think not. First, Tsai's hands are tied by three DPP documents: the clause in the party platform that calls for de jure Taiwanese independence (1991), the party resolution on the self-determination of Taiwan's future (1999), and the party resolution on normalizing Taiwan's statehood (2007). Second, Tsai's winning coalition consists of many a social and political group in favor of Taiwan's independence. Third, her own ideology does not allow her to cave in to Chinese pressure. And last, as mentioned, Beijing has already raised the bar. For the PRC, it is now not enough for Tsai just to reendorse the term "1992 Consensus." She also has to specify the core meaning of the term as stipulated by Xi Jinping. She has had to restrict symbolic actions on Taiwanese independence on many occasions (e.g., a bill introduced by a DPP legislator to denounce the status of Sun Yat-sen as the founding father of the ROC), and she has had to refrain from implementing her campaign promise to change the writing guidelines for high school history textbooks to fit the historiography of Taiwanese independence. In a nutshell, if Tsai were to make concessions on the consensus, her winning coalition would collapse.

So then what might happen? Many people in Taiwan, especially those of the DPP's ideological ilk, tend to believe there is only so much Beijing can do. If Tsai sticks to her promise to maintain the status quo, she will not offer any excuse for the PRC to use force against Taiwan. Others think Beijing can do a number of things. It can gradually strangle Taiwan's international space by taking away its remaining diplomatic allies, further limiting its already-miniscule participation in international organizations, hampering the ability of its citizens to take part in nongovernmental organizations (NGOs), and so on.

Beijing will certainly not consider Taiwan for membership in the Regional Comprehensive Economic Partnership (RCEP).[38] Furthermore, Taiwan's competitiveness in the mainland Chinese market, its largest export market, will be reduced. This is not merely because the trade-in-services agreement with the PRC has already been stopped mid-track in the Legislative Yuan, or because further trade-in-goods liberalization, once promised by Beijing, is nowhere to be seen, but rather because of the PRC–South Korea free trade agreement that will give South Korea, Taiwan's main trade competitor, an insurmountable advantage over Taiwan in the vast Chinese market.

Another measure by Beijing may look fine for the time being, but it may have tremendous consequences for Taiwan. On August 26, 2015, the head of the mainland's Taiwan Affairs Office, Zhang Zhijun, alluded to the possibility that "without the '1992 Consensus' as the common political foundation for both sides, the extant institutionalized mechanism will collapse."[39] The PRC has now suspended communications between its ARATS and Taiwan's SEF, and those between the mainland's Taiwan Affairs Office and Taiwan's Mainland Affairs Council. Should anything happen between the two sides, there is always the possibility that it could be blown out of proportion if communication channels that serve to de-escalate tensions no longer exist. For example, what would happen if a Taiwanese fishing boat captain hurt a mainland Chinese fisherman he employs in his fishing boat? Or vice versa?

I surmise that Beijing is unlikely to use force against Taiwan should President Tsai stay true to her promise of maintaining the status quo and not recognizing the 1992 Consensus. But the PRC can still adopt a "constrictor" strategy to keep Taiwan on edge. On economic fronts, this constrictor strategy will sap Taiwan's economic strength, causing long-term damage to its competitiveness. But what if Tsai caves under Beijing's pressure? In that case, Tsai would lose her reputation, an invaluable asset in international politics,[40] and Beijing may think it can gain more by being even tougher on Taiwan. Most likely Tsai and the DPP's pushback will be limited to measures that fall into the category of what Beijing calls "cultural Taiwan independence," such as resuming the drive to United Nations membership, or promoting the idea in history textbooks that Taiwanese and Chinese are two separate peoples, or saying the Diaoyu Islands are not Chinese territory. These de-Sinicization measures will in no way hurt the PRC's material well-being, but will certainly anger Beijing. Cross-Strait relations may well be set in a cold peace for a long time to come.

Postscript

Ma's policy toward the PRC has come to an end. Taiwan's current DPP administration simply could not accept the concept and edifice of the 1992 Consensus, as it is at odds with the DPP's fundamental principle—Taiwanese independence. Beijing, after failing to cajole the DPP administration to follow Ma's formula, has now stripped the concept of its deliberate ambiguities by specifically saying that "the core of the Consensus is the One-China principle," making it even more unpalatable to the DPP government. As a result, the situation across the Taiwan Strait is a stalemate. And the stalemate is very slowly turning into a downward spiral, much to the detriment of Taiwan.

For the decades between the 1972 Shanghai Communiqué and the end of the Obama administration in early 2017, the United States played a pivotal role in stabilizing cross-Strait relations. As cross-Strait relations have been inevitably couched in the larger game between the United States and the People's Republic of China, what happens in Taiwan—with or without the 1992 Consensus—is of minor importance compared to America's China policy in shaping cross-Strait relations. In this sense, the Trump administration's foreign policy is adding uncertainties to cross-Strait relations. From Taiwan's perspective, it is not that the Trump administration has mistreated Taiwan. In fact, the Trump administration has enhanced United States–Taiwan relations by signing the Taiwan Travel Act of 2018 and maintaining arms sales to Taiwan, among other things. It is, rather, the general thrust of President Trump that causes some anxieties in Taiwan.

First of all, President Trump likes to boast about his ability to make a deal. Many in Taiwan fear that if Taiwan ever becomes a "bargaining chip," then the "Taiwan chip" could be exchanged with the PRC's "North Korea chip," for example. This fear is embedded in Trump's "hug-the-thug, flick-off-friends" worldview. This fear also has to do with the Trump administration turning its back on democracy and human rights in world affairs. Second, Taiwan's security and prosperity are couched in the security and free trade framework in East Asia that the United States has cultivated since the end of World War II. But now the Trump administration, in pursuit of its "America First" policies, has snubbed friends and foes alike on both security and trade issues. As a result, all major players in East Asia are less committed to collective security and prosperity. Taiwan suffers in this poisonous environment. Third, the Trump administration has a poor record of staffing the national security apparatus. If a crisis happens across the Taiwan Strait, it is doubtful the United States currently has the bureaucratic capability to stabilize the situation. Fourth, since the Trump administration has treated China as a "strategic competitor," rather than a "strategic partner,"[41] Beijing has an incentive to be more competitive—putting more pressure on other countries to be more friendly to the PRC. This is, indeed, the alliance politics that great powers have played so well in their rivalry since the time of the Peloponnesian War. Taiwan will almost certainly encounter further pressure from the PRC. If Taiwan's leader for some reason (for instance, to mobilize nationalistic emotions to win a presidential election) decides to push back against pressure from Beijing by moving decidedly toward de jure independence, not just inching toward it, then all bets on a peaceful Taiwan Strait will be off. It is only at this juncture that people in Taiwan might feel nostalgic about the 1992 Consensus and the stability it once brought to the Taiwan Strait.

Notes

1. For more on the 2016 election, see Chapters 3–5 of this book.

2. A more conventional term for this strategic dyad is "bandwagoning versus balancing." See Walt, *The Origins of Alliances,* pp. 17–21, 27–32. For small states' practices of these two grand strategies, see Schweller, "Bandwagoning for Profits." In this chapter I use "rapprochement/confrontation" in place of the "bandwagoning/balancing" terms found in international relations literature because the former fits better with Taiwan's domestic polemics.

3. Israel, *The Dutch Republic,* pp. 700–862.

4. See, for example, Singleton, "The Myth of 'Finlandisation.'"

5. See Abdelal, *National Purpose in the World Economy.*

6. For the origin and management of the crisis caused by the "state-to-state" theory, see Bush, *Untying the Knot.* Bush was a key figure in the de-escalation of the crisis. For an insider's account (in Chinese) of the Taiwan government's scrambling over this issue, see Su, *To the Brink,* pp.71–122. An English version of this book, with roughly the same content, is Su, *Taiwan's Relations with Mainland China,* pp. 30–85.

7. The "Five No's" are no declaration of de jure Taiwan independence, no change of Taiwan's national title (Republic of China), no constitutional amendment based on Lee Teng-hui's "state-to-state" theory, no referendum on Taiwanese independence/reunification that could change the status quo, and no abrogation of the National Unification Guidelines and National Unification Committee.

8. Author teleconference with members of the European Parliament, March 1, 2005.

9. "Strait Group Agrees to State Positions 'Orally,'" *Central News Agency,* Taipei, November 18, 1992.

10. Many of the military security issues considered at the time by the NSC that had serious implications for cross-Strait relations are elaborated in Montgomery, "Contested Primacy in the Western Pacific." Several other articles on Taiwan's military security published by RAND Corporation and other US think tanks also caught the eyes of the NSC, such as Murray, "Revisiting Taiwan's Defense Strategy." Though not everyone would agree on the many technical issues with regard to Taiwan's defense, the general thrust of this body of research is unmistakable—that Taiwan is lagging further and further behind China's military capabilities given the PLA's military modernization programs.

11. An English-language translation of Ma's inauguration speech is available at the website of the US-China Institute, University of Southern California, https://china.usc .edu/ma-ying-jeou-"taiwan's-renaissance-presidential-inauguration-address"-may-20 -2008.

12. This arrangement of "one China, respective interpretations" and "1992 Consensus" was immediately noticed by an experienced US scholar who called me right after Ma delivered his inaugural speech. Several Chinese interlocutors also mentioned this to me in the following weeks.

13. The term is from Martin, *Democratic Commitments.*

14. Later this incrementalist approach was summarized into a twelve-character policy guideline, "Go Fast with the Most Urgent Issues, the Easiest Issues, and the Economics Issues." As later developments show, China picked up on the signal.

15. The term "responsible stakeholder" was used by US deputy secretary of state Robert Zoellick as a description of the role the United States would expect China to play in world affairs. Zoellick mentioned the term in a speech titled "Whither China: From Membership to Responsibility," delivered at the National Committee on United States– China Relations on September 21, 2005. He was responding to an article titled "China's

'Peaceful Rise' to Great Power Status," published by Zhen Bijian, then president of the Chinese Communist Party School, in *Foreign Affairs* in the fall of 2005. Zoellick's signal was picked up by Qian Qichen, former vice premier and minister of foreign affairs of the PRC, in an article that appeared on the front page of the *People's Daily,* overseas edition, on November 21, 2005, titled "Peaceful Development Is China's Strategic Choice." Having Ma use this term sent a signal to both the United States and China that Taiwan would be a responsible stakeholder in the international community as well, leaving behind its image as a troublemaker during the Chen administration.

16. The full text of this speech is available at the Mainland Affairs Council website, https://www.mac.gov.tw/en/News_Content.aspx?n=C62A6E4BD490D38E&sms=F56AA 93EEC16ECD5&s=9F66855954073B97.

17. Rosecrance and Stein, *The Domestic Bases of Grand Strategy.*

18. Two books by Murray Edelman are especially useful for viewing politics in this light: *Symbolic Uses of Politics* and *Politics as Symbolic Action.*

19. The Reciprocal Trade Agreements Act sets up an institutional design that strikes a balance between the executive (presumably representing the national interest) and the Congress (representing constituency interests), and between the United States and its trading partners. See Haggard, "The Institutional Foundation of Hegemony." As I have argued elsewhere, the lessons of the Reciprocal Trade Agreements Act can be useful for Taiwan. After Taiwan moved away from the previous pattern of authoritarian-bureaucratic policymaking, the Legislative Yuan became so assertive that Taiwan's trade negotiators seemed unable to make any meaningful concessions in trade negotiations with trading partners. See Ho, "Trade Politics in Taiwan."

20. At the time the Sunflower Movement ended, seventeen different bills had been introduced to establish a set of legislative procedures in future trade talks with China. Twelve of them, introduced by the DPP or its political allies, smacked of outright Taiwanese independence, while those introduced by the KMT and its allies still defined cross-Strait relations in terms of the 1992 Consensus. There was still no intersection between these two sets of political choices; hence the Legislative Yuan was still not able to agree on any institutionalized process to govern trade policy deliberations with the PRC.

21. Weng Jung-hsuan, "To Freeze or Not to Freeze? Tsai Ing-wen: Independence Is Already a Natural Ingredient, How Can It Be Frozen?" (in Chinese), *Newtalk News,* July 14, 2014, https://newtalk.tw/news/view/2014-07-19/49377.

22. A summary of Xi's remarks in English is available at "Xi Jinping: Cross-Strait Relations to Return to Turbulence Without 1992 Consensus," *KMT News Network,* March 5, 2015, http://www.kmt.org.tw/english/page.aspx?type=article&mnum=112& anum=15874.

23. The video and transcript of this speech can be found at "Tsai Ing-wen 2016: Taiwan Faces the Future," Center for Strategic and International Studies, June 3, 2015, https://www.csis.org/events/tsai-ing-wen-2016-taiwan-faces-future.

24. "Respect Taiwan's Democratic Way of Life: DPP Chief Tsai Ing-wen," *Straits Times,* December 28, 2015, https://www.straitstimes.com/asia/east-asia/respect-taiwans -democratic-way-of-life-dpp-chief-tsai-ing-wen.

25. For the English-language translation, see "Interview: Tsai's Cross-Strait Policy to Rest on Democratic Will," *Taipei Times,* January 22, 2016, p. 1, https://taipeitimes.com /News/front/archives/2016/01/22/2003637766.

26. Video and transcript available at "Statemen's Forum: Wang Yi, Minister of Foreign Affairs, PRC," Center for Strategic and International Studies, February 25, 2016.

27. Ren Chengqi, "The Core Connotation of '1992 Consensus' Cannot Be Avoided," *People's Daily,* March 8, 2016, p. 3.

28 For a thorough review of the exchanges across the Strait up to this point in time, see Romberg, "The '1992 Consensus': Adapting to the Future?"

29. Jonathan Chin, "Chinese Air Force Conducts an 'Island Encirclement' Patrol," *Taipei Times,* December 13, 2017, https://taipeitimes.com/News/front/archives/2017 /12/13/2003683885.

30. "PLA Appears Again! PLA Spokesman: Testing Combat Ability and Safeguarding National Sovereingty" (in Chinese), *Storm Media,* April 19, 2018, https://www.storm.mg/article/426946.

31. Aaron Tu, Jonathan Chin, and Jake Chun, "China Extends 'Unprecedented' Benefits to Taiwanese," *Taipei Times,* March 1, 2018, p. 1, https://www.taipeitimes.com/News/front/archives/2018/03/01/2003688463.

32. See the PRC State Council announcement, at http://www.gov.cn/zhengce/content/2018-08/19/content_5314865.htm.

33. I also speculate that China's high-handedness toward the Tsai administration is not just because of Tsai's position on the 1992 Consensus. Tsai's clear intention to use US and Japanese support to counterbalance China probably does not sit well with Xi.

34. I use the term "reassurance" in the same manner as Andrew Kydd conceptualizes it. See Kydd, *Trust and Mistrust in International Relations.*

35. Many also believe that the huge difficulties Xi faces on the domestic front are the driving force behind China's increasingly strict censorship regime. See *ChinaFile,* March 15, 2016, https://www.chinafile.com/conversation/whats-driving-current-storm-chinese-censorship.

36. Xi's meeting with Ma was an attempt to deter the DPP from undercutting the consensus. As Thomas Shelling suggests, any deterrence attempt also contains some form of reassurance—that is, if the target does not cross the red line as specified by the deterrence initiator, then the initiator guarantees that the target will not be punished. Shelling, *Arms and Influence,* p. 74.

37. Zhou Zhihuai, "Opening Remarks," Second Forum of Cross-Strait Think Tanks, Chongqing City, October 12, 2015. Interestingly, a high-level PRC official informed the head of the Taiwan delegation in private that Zhou's speech had been cleared by the "highest level."

38. Now that US president Trump has formally withdrawn the United States from the TPP, the TPP in its most expansive form might be dead for good, even though other TPP member countries have pushed ahead without the United States. But there is still another irony for Taiwan: Tsai and the DPP may also have squandered an opportunity for Taiwan to enhance its economic relations with the United States. Ma's NSC in 2009 knew that opening Taiwan's market to US beef imports was crucial to enhancing economic relations with the United States. Copying a page from the playbook of South Korea's anti-American beef movement, which toppled South Korean president Lee Myung-bak's first cabinet, the DPP mobilized strongly on the streets and in the Legislative Yuan to force the Ma administration to change the contents of an agreement that Taiwan's representative to the United States had signed with the AIT office in Washington, which pledged to open Taiwan's market to American beef. As a consequence, the Ma administration gained a reputation in Washington, DC, as a bad-faith negotiator. For the remaining seven years of Ma's two terms, United States–Taiwan economic relations were stalled. If the DPP had not been so eager to topple the cabinet or score political points on the beef issue, United States–Taiwan trade relations might have been stronger than they are at present. At the time, the United States was very supportive of Taiwan on economic fronts. After Tsai became president, her administration floated the idea of expanding US beef imports, but this move was threatened by what the DPP had sowed back in 2009. The Tsai administration ultimately did not make any moves on American beef imports during her first term.

39. Alan Romberg, "Consolidating Positions."

40. On how reputation functions in international politics, see Mercer, *Reputation and International Politics.*

41. From the United States 2019 National Defense Authorization Act (NDAA). This is indeed a watershed moment in Sino-American relations, the most significant shift since President Nixon pursued rapprochement with the People's Republic of China in 1972.

16

In the Shadow of Great Power Rivalry

Dean P. Chen

Under the Kuomintang (KMT) administration of President Ma Ying-jeou, the Republic of China (ROC) regime on Taiwan attempted to pursue well-calibrated foreign and cross-Strait policy strategies to maintain positive and balanced relations with the United States, mainland China, and Japan. Since 2010, the growing assertiveness of the People's Republic of China (PRC) in maritime conflicts over the East and South China Seas has caused a heightening of tension between Beijing, Washington, and Tokyo. Nevertheless, as Taipei's security and economic well-being rely heavily on these three major powers, the Ma government faced a dilemma that could be translated into the following conundrum: how to deepen socioeconomic relations with the PRC on the basis of a 1992 Consensus or "one China, respective interpretations" stance without creating the impression that Taiwan was cozying up so intimately with Beijing as to threaten its ties with Washington and Tokyo, the two major security backers of the island. To address that, President Ma came up with a delicate formula—to seek peaceful relations with China, friendly relations with Japan, and close relations with the United States. Essentially, Ma employed a hedging strategy toward the PRC with three main elements: binding engagement, limited bandwagoning, and soft balancing.[1]

The deterioration of Sino-American and Sino-Japanese relations after 2010 undermined Taipei's efforts to create a détente with Beijing, even though leaders in Washington and Tokyo initially praised the dramatic improvement in cross-Strait relations after 2008. The aphorism "my enemy's enemy is my friend" rings true in the anarchic system of international politics, where balance of power and zero-sum competition are the norm.[2]

Conversely, one can note as well that "my enemy's friend is my enemy," by similar reasoning. Thus, when rivalry between the United States, Japan, and China intensified, the KMT's ideological commitment to a single Chinese nation—a position it shared with the Chinese Communist Party (CCP), though the KMT was careful to insist that its support for "one China" referred to the ROC—essentially placed Taiwan in a pan-Chinese union with the PRC. The Ma administration's positions on maritime territorial disputes in the East and South China Seas were largely consistent with those of the PRC, even though Taipei explicitly refused to cooperate with the Beijing to assert these common claims. In contrast, Washington's and Tokyo's positions on these disputes were closely aligned and followed from their common security interests. Though the Barack Obama administration remained firmly committed to the long-standing "one China" policy of the United States (also known as strategic ambiguity) and to the maintenance of peace and stability across the Taiwan Strait, the Ma government's rapprochement with the PRC contradicted, to some extent, the strategic posture of the United States in the Asia Pacific.[3]

I agree with the argument of Yun-han Chu and Yu-tzung Chang (in Chapter 6) that President Ma Ying-jeou should be credited for improving cross-Strait relations and putting them on a more solid and peaceful footing. Years of confrontational policies implemented by Ma's predecessors, Lee Teng-hui and Chen Shui-bian, had strained ties with both Beijing and Washington; between 1995 and 2008, the Taiwan Strait was a potential flashpoint for conflict.[4] Thus, the United States and the international community welcomed Ma's conciliatory moves to mend fences with Beijing and repair their relations by promoting deeper socioeconomic cooperation through various official and unofficial venues. Moreover, as cross-Strait tensions subsided between 2008 and 2016, Taiwan's international profile, to some extent, was also elevated as Taipei restored confidence with its major allies and economic partners around the world.

Nevertheless, I wish to underscore in this chapter how the heightening of Sino-American competition ultimately hindered Ma's rapprochement efforts. While supporting Ma's peaceful overtures, Washington, especially in the later Obama years, assumed a more cautious attitude toward the 1992 Consensus, which in effect placed Taiwan unequivocally into a "one China" framework.

To rectify the de-Sinification and nativization policies pushed by former presidents Lee and Chen, Ma Ying-jeou felt an imperative to restart the KMT's own nation-building projects in order to shore up the ROC's legitimacy and strengthen the national, historical, economic, and cultural bonds between Taiwan and mainland China.[5] Being a staunch follower of Sun Yat-sen (the founding father of the ROC), Ma never wavered in his conviction that the republic represented the only legitimate heir to the "one China" legacy, which included a history of strenuous fighting and great sacrifices during World War II to recover lost territories, including Taiwan, from Imperial Japan. Thus, cross-Strait relations, Ma contended, were "not inter-state relations" because Taiwan and the mainland were two regions within one Chinese nation, albeit separated since the KMT-CCP civil war. The successful democratic model of the ROC, rather than the autocratic one of the PRC, should be the blueprint for a future united China encompassing both Taiwan and the mainland. Ma also emphasized the shared Chinese roots and heritage among the compatriots on both sides of the Taiwan Strait.[6]

Yet the KMT president underestimated the vehemence of the backlash against cross-Strait rapprochement that would be unleashed by societal and political forces sympathetic to the cause of Taiwanese nationalism and independence. Young social activists and college students, nurtured by years of Lee and Chen's Taiwanization and de-Sinification campaigns, became more predisposed to support the Democratic Progressive Party (DPP). In addition, this new generation's genuine fear and discontent about the PRC's rising economic influence and coercive power over Taiwan also fueled their skepticism and anxiety toward the KMT-CCP détente. Facilitated by the instantaneous organizational and mobilizing capacity of social media, they marshalled for an all-out offensive to challenge and constrain Ma's endeavors to deepen cross-Strait ties. Consequently, the discrepancy between Ma's China-centric nationalism and the changing national identity among the Taiwanese youth, who increasingly perceived themselves to be Taiwanese rather than Chinese and worried about Taiwan's increasing economic dependency on the PRC,[7] ultimately dealt the KMT enormous political setbacks in the 2014 and 2016 elections.

This chapter proceeds by surveying United States–Taiwan relations after the KMT won back power under Ma Ying-jeou in 2008, and then by examining the Obama administration's responses to cross-Strait rapprochement in light of increasing frictions in the East and South China Seas. It concludes with a brief discussion of how the arguments presented here may be applicable to the DPP government's policies toward the PRC and the United States under President Tsai Ing-wen.

Taipei's Relations with Washington, DC, After 2008

When the KMT regained political power in Taiwan in March 2008, the strategic relations of the United States with the PRC were much more benign and cooperative than they have been since 2010. President Ma Ying-jeou initially enjoyed strong US support for deepening cross-Strait socioeconomic ties on the basis of the 1992 Consensus. Shortly after Ma's electoral victory on March 22, 2008, PRC leader Hu Jintao said in a telephone conversation with President George W. Bush that both China and Taiwan should "restore consultation and talks on the basis of the '1992 consensus,'" under which "both sides recognize there is only one China, but agree to differ on its definition."[8] President Bush, according to his national security adviser, Stephen Hadley, welcomed the Chinese leader's flexibility.[9]

President Obama, in his visit to mainland China in November 2009, declared, "I am very pleased with the reduction of tensions and improvement in cross-strait relations, and it is my deep desire and hope that we will continue to see great improvement between Taiwan and the People's Republic in resolving many of these issues."[10] Testifying before Congress on October 4, 2011, Kurt Campbell, US assistant secretary of state for East Asian and Pacific Affairs, praised President Ma's embrace of the 1992 Consensus and his "no reunification, no independence, and no war" pledge in his inaugural address for contributing to the "remarkable progress in cross-strait relations."[11] For Taiwan, whose security, autonomy, and democracy have long depended so heavily upon Washington's political support and defense commitments, the interests of the United States and its attitude toward Beijing are vital determinants of Taiwan's relations with the mainland.[12] Indeed, the cross-Strait relationship, in the words of Hu Weixing, is never a "purely bilateral relationship between Beijing and Taipei" but is "overshadowed by the competitive and cooperative relations between the United States and China."[13]

Beginning about 2010, however, the PRC's increasingly assertive foreign policy started to raise anxiety among its regional neighbors and prompted Obama's "rebalancing" policy toward the Asia Pacific.[14] Beijing's determined drive to advance claims in disputed maritime territories in the East and South China Seas suggested that the Chinese leadership might be forsaking its peaceful-development grand strategy in favor of nationalistic expansionism, thereby raising the chances of a military confrontation that could involve the United States.[15] Consequently, the intensification of Sino-American competition called into question whether the KMT's China-friendly policy would continue to be compatible with Washington's security interests in the region.

The growth of the PRC's relative power along with the amelioration of cross-Strait tensions sparked a major debate within the Obama administration about whether the United States should distance itself from Taiwan in order to protect US interests.[16] Those advocating for "abandoning" Taiwan advanced two arguments. First, a Taiwan choosing to bandwagon with an autocratic and belligerent China could abandon its democratic values as well as undermine the strategic and economic interests of the United States across the Asia Pacific.[17] Second, with a warming of cross-Strait relations and the receding prospect of military conflict, Washington could be more at ease and less concerned about Beijing's security threats to Taiwan.[18] However, the dissenters stressed that appeasing Beijing over Taiwan would only serve to sharpen the PRC's appetite and embolden its aggressive impulses. This could endanger the security of the United States and its allies in the Pacific, with the latter losing faith in the former's resolve and credibility.[19] Therefore, an array of US congressional representatives, specialists, and commentators urged the Obama White House to step up America's security, diplomatic, and economic relations with Taiwan in order to more forcefully balance against China's rise and to frustrate Beijing's territorial ambitions in the East and South China Seas.[20] From the perspective of these critics, the Obama administration was too timid in the face of the PRC's rising assertiveness. The United States should, instead, cultivate stronger ties with Taipei to "balance against China's expansionism" or to show "negative costs for China's interests if it pursues its salami slicing in nearby disputed territories."[21] Taiwan, in other words, would be the "cork in the bottle" if the "United States needs to shore up radars, defenses, and other anti-China military preparations along the first island chain running from Japan through Taiwan to the Philippines."[22]

The Obama administration nevertheless repeatedly reaffirmed its commitment to cross-Strait peace and stability and its endorsement of Ma's policy of rapprochement, citing the foundations of the US "one China policy" as articulated in the three Sino-American joint communiqués and the Taiwan Relations Act.[23] The Obama administration thus dispelled any speculation that Washington would sacrifice Taiwan as it strengthened relations with Beijing or that the United States would use the island strategically to counterbalance or deter the PRC.[24] President Obama reiterated this approach during President Xi Jinping's state visit in September 2015.[25] Susan Thornton, deputy assistant secretary of state for the Bureau of East Asian and Pacific Affairs, called Taiwan a "vital partner for the United States in Asia" and noted that "an important ingredient" of the close relationship between Washington and Taipei in recent years had been "the stable management of cross-strait ties."[26] The US government sought to "treat Taiwan matters in ways that do not undermine" President Ma's approach, which was "to reassure China and avoid bringing the Taiwan issue to the top of the American policy agenda with China once again."[27] In keeping with this logic, the Obama administration refrained from explicitly mentioning Taiwan in its Asia rebalancing strategy to keep from provoking Beijing's ire.[28]

In fact, since the 1950s, Taiwan has always been a sensitive issue in America's China policy. Knowing that reunification with Taiwan plays an essential role in the Chinese quest for national unity and territorial integrity, US policymakers preferred to support the island through less obtrusive means, fearing that unequivocal positions would instigate Chinese anti-Americanism, encourage Taiwan's unilateral provocations, and jeopardize United States–China relations.[29] The Obama administration inherited this same set of considerations.[30]

Nevertheless, the Obama administration's support for cross-Strait rapprochement was not unconditional. Indeed, as the Ma government became closely attached to Beijing and polarized Taiwan's domestic politics through its attempts to rehabilitate a Sino-centric nationalist paradigm, Taipei began to depart from the cross-Strait equilibrium maintained under Washington's "one China" or strategic ambiguity policy framework.[31] Under this policy, which was institutionalized by the three Sino-American joint communiqués of 1972, 1978, and 1982, the Taiwan Relations Act in 1979, and President Ronald Reagan's "Six Assurances to Taiwan" in 1982, the United States aims to deter both parties from unilaterally upsetting cross-Strait peace and stability (such as Taipei declaring de jure independence or Beijing coercing reunification) in order to preserve Taiwan's self-defense and freedom without impinging upon Beijing's "one China" principle. The United States also vows to respect any resolution of the conflict between Taiwan and the PRC as long as it is peaceful, consensual, and free of coercion.[32] As well, because Taiwan has become a full-fledged liberal democracy, the US government also emphasizes that the Taiwanese people's preferences should be taken seriously prior to reaching any cross-Strait agreements.[33] While satisfying Washington's security imperatives, strategic ambiguity also strives to fulfill the fundamental liberal objective of the United States in preserving the de facto autonomy and security of Taiwan, whose experience—transitioning from a Leninist party-state to a multiparty democracy—could also help foster democratic political change in the PRC.[34]

As US policy opposes any attempt by Beijing to coerce reunification, so it also does not support formal Taiwanese independence, and not just for reasons of strategic stability. In addition to the potential to spark a conflict, an unqualified endorsement of Taiwan's separation from China would "retard the hope for political reform on the mainland because democracy would be associated with the breakup of the nation, and political reformers would seem like dupes or even agents of the United States and the Taiwan traitors who declared independence."[35] Strategic ambiguity, in short, is an ambiguous means toward the unambiguous ends of preserving security and stability in the region, ensuring that the cross-Strait impasse is resolved only peacefully and consensually, fostering China's political and economic liberalization.[36]

Indeed, as cross-Strait ties warmed during the Ma era, there were signs of growing qualms in the Obama administration about the 1992 Consensus. The KMT's and CCP's common identification with a Chinese nation, whether the ROC or PRC, put Taiwan in a "pan-Chinese union" with the mainland and placed some of the island's strategic and economic interests at odds with those of the United States and its allies in Asia. Moreover, the

KMT and CCP have relied on similar historical claims to assert Chinese sovereignty over contested island territories in the East and South China Seas. As cross-Strait military and economic balances have shifted in the PRC's favor, Taiwan's freedom of action has diminished, threatening to force Taipei down a path leading to accommodation of and eventual unification with mainland China.[37]

Critics in the United States charged that Ma's emphasis on closer economic integration was enhancing Beijing's leverage over Taiwan and causing an erosion of the island's democracy. They cited the escalation of sociopolitical polarization and partisan conflicts as well as the lack of oversight of negotiations between top KMT and CCP authorities. Taiwan's domestic political opposition and civil society groups subsequently gained momentum in questioning and challenging Ma's cross-Strait policies, as the student-led occupation of the Legislative Yuan in March 2014 to block the Cross-Strait Services Trade Agreement (CSSTA) demonstrated.[38] In August 2015, hundreds of high school students stormed the Ministry of Education to protest the government's initiatives of "fine-tuning" history textbooks and curricula, accusing the KMT of attempting to "brainwash" them into accepting a "one China" view of history. The November 2015 summit between Xi Jinping and Ma Ying-jeou, the first meeting since 1949 between the top leaders of the two sides, aimed to further consolidate the one-China core of the 1992 Consensus and bolster the KMT's fading electoral prospects. Yet the Ma-Xi meeting did not improve the standing of the KMT's presidential candidate, Eric Chu, who was soundly defeated by Tsai Ing-wen in the presidential election of January 2016. The DPP also won a decisive majority in the Legislative Yuan, ushering in an age of unified DPP control over both the executive and legislative branches that continued even after the 2020 elections.

The reaction of the United States to the Ma-Xi summit, though welcoming, was once again based on a note of prudence.[39] Hence, just as Washington took the side of Beijing toward the end of Chen Shui-bian's presidency to "temper provocative Democratic Progressive Party moves toward formal independence,"[40] the United States found it necessary to pay more deference to Taiwanese nationalism in order to stem the KMT's "tilt" toward the PRC. For instance, although the United States reiterated its neutrality in Taiwan's 2016 presidential election, Washington's high-profile treatment of the DPP candidate, Tsai Ing-wen, during her visit to the United States in June 2015 raised eyebrows in China and among the KMT leadership. To be sure, this did not mean that Washington was abandoning its long-standing balanced posture on the cross-Strait conflict. Rather, it judged that within this framework, pulling Taiwan away from the PRC orbit would be more compatible with US interests and with its rebalance toward the Asia Pacific.

Rising US and Japanese Wariness
of the KMT's "One China" Policy

To safeguard and promote its national interests, the United States, like all great powers, has attempted to shape the domestic politics and decisionmaking of its allies and adversaries, particularly allies as strategically situated as Taiwan. Richard Bush, the former chairman of the American Institute in Taiwan (AIT), stated in September 2014 that the United States would "express its views on . . . how our interests will be affected by Taiwan's elections. To say nothing, which some in Taiwan might want us to do, is actually meant as a statement as well."[41] Though Bush's remarks were immediately refuted by US officials as merely his personal and unofficial views,[42] they were understood as a more candid reflection of the reality. Recall that the George W. Bush administration rebuked Chen Shui-bian's referendum initiatives in the late 2000s and sternly cautioned Taipei against taking any moves that would jeopardize its security relations with the PRC and the United States.[43] The Hu-Bush conversations in March 2008 were repeatedly cited by President Ma Ying-jeou to underscore the joint endorsement of the 1992 Consensus by the United States and the PRC.[44]

When Tsai Ing-wen traveled to the United States in September 2011 in the midst of the campaign for her first presidential election bid in 2012, an anonymous senior Obama administration official told the *Financial Times* that the DPP candidate's election "could raise tensions with China," adding that "she left us with distinct doubts about whether she is both willing and able to continue the stability in cross-strait relations the region has enjoyed in recent years."[45] Washington's "vote of no confidence," although indirect, clearly played a role in the DPP's defeat in 2012, by sending the message that a Tsai administration would derail cross-Strait peace and stability. These incidents took place when Sino-American relations were much more benign and cross-Strait rapprochement on the basis of the 1992 Consensus was not in apparent tension with the national interests of the United States.

As mentioned earlier, international power relations between Washington (as well as Tokyo, the staunchest US security ally in Asia) and Beijing have grown more adversarial in recent years, particularly after tensions spiked over territorial disputes in the East and South China Seas. Given the nearly complete overlap between the Ma administration's sovereign claims over these areas and those of Beijing, Taiwan's role in these disputes also became complicated, leading Washington to eschew some of its previous support for the KMT-CCP détente.

The Senkaku/Diaoyu Islands in the East China Sea

In recent years, Sino-Japanese relations have deteriorated over their competing territorial claims to the Senkaku/Diaoyu Islands in the East China Sea. As the two countries have ramped up contestation over sovereignty, their interactions in the area have turned more adversarial. In September 2010, the Japanese coast guard detained a Chinese fishing boat captain and its crew after the latter's trawler struck two Japanese coast guard vessels near one of the Senkaku/Diaoyu Islands, and Beijing reacted sharply to the standoff.[46] The Japanese authorities released the entire crew except the captain, announcing he would be subject to a judicial proceeding. The PRC retaliated by arresting four Japanese businessmen in western China and banning the export to Japan of rare-earth minerals, which were vital for Japanese electronics and digital product assembly.[47] Although Tokyo relented and released the captain, this showdown not only rekindled Sino-Japanese rivalry over the Senkaku/Diaoyu Islands but also, in the words of Jeffrey Bader, demonstrated to the world that Beijing would be ready to "upend global trading arrangements and practices . . . in retaliation for what looked like a bilateral dispute and to give it international consequences."[48]

The Ma government struck a more anti-Japanese tone on the issue than did DPP politicians, even though Taipei's official stance was to remain neutral in these great power rivalries. Indeed, as China and Japan deepened their clashes over the Senkaku/Diaoyu Islands beginning in 2012, sometimes edging close to military conflict, the ROC government unequivocally reaffirmed its "sovereignty" over the island islets and its nearby waters, thereby revealing Taipei's determination not to "cede even an inch of territory" and implicitly buttressing the Chinese position.[49] This was despite Ma's vow, in his East China Sea Peace Initiative, not to team up with Beijing to counter Tokyo's claim over these territories.[50]

Since the KMT has long asserted maritime claims similar to the CCP over the East and South China Seas, Taipei and Beijing are actually "on the same side" in dealing with these territorial issues.[51] In September 2012, after Japan's Noda government nationalized three of the eight Senkaku/Diaoyu Island islets, the ROC government lodged a strong protest and recalled its chief representative to Tokyo, who was ordered to return to Taiwan immediately. President Ma even flew out to Pengjia Island in the vicinity of the Senkaku/Diaoyu island chain to declare that Taipei would back up its commitment to defend ROC sovereignty and safeguard the security of fishermen. Taiwan's coast guard vessels were even dispatched to escort several Taiwanese fishing boats and, on several occasions, faced minor standoffs with the Japanese coast guard, resulting in a few hours of water-cannon fire.[52]

Beijing "welcomed Taiwan's assertiveness, not only because it supports China's historically based claims to the territory in question but because of the potential merger of Chinese and Taiwanese national identities."[53] Ma's "one China" stance created such an impression even though he was keenly aware that "any explicit move or coordination with China would put Taiwan awkwardly between China's hope of using the dispute as opportunity to mold its 'one China' principle into Taiwan's policy discourses on the one side and the

U.S.-Japan anxiety of Taiwan's drifting inches closer to China's embrace on the other side."[54] In order to prevent Taiwan from further bandwagoning with the PRC, Japan negotiated a fisheries agreement with Taipei in April 2013 to accord benefits and protections to Taiwan's fishermen.[55] Though Washington persistently claimed that it did not take any position on the question of sovereignty, the Obama administration also stated that the Senkaku/Diaoyu Islands would fall under Article 5 of the US-Japanese Security Treaty, which authorizes the United States to help defend areas and territories under Japanese administration.[56] As tensions mounted, the Ma government refrained from getting involved. For instance, in November 2013, Taipei issued a rather tepid condemnation of Beijing's recently imposed air defense identification zone, disappointing both Washington and Tokyo.[57]

The South China Sea Dispute:
The "Nine-Dashed Line" vs. Freedom of Navigation

In the early and middle 2000s, Beijing wished to assure the regional and international community that its rise would be peaceful and cooperative, conducive to regional stability, and an economic "win-win" for all, while seeking to dampen suspicions incurred from its aggressive behavior in the Taiwan Strait and South China Sea territorial competition during the mid-1990s.[58] The crisis that briefly arose in late 1994 over China's occupation of Mischief Reef (located just west of Palawan and claimed by the Philippines) abated when both the PRC and the Association of Southeast Asian Nations (ASEAN) decided to de-escalate. This thereafter resulted in the "most constructive of all periods in South China Sea diplomacy,"[59] with Beijing and Hanoi reaching agreement on their land border (1999) as well as on their maritime boundary in the Gulf of Tonkin (2000). China and ASEAN agreed in 2002 on a declaration of conduct that included a pledge to "refrain from action of inhabiting on the presently uninhabited islands, reefs, shoals, cays, and other features."[60]

However, probably due to its renewed confidence after emerging relatively unharmed from the 2008 global financial crisis and its success in hosting the Summer Olympics, Beijing began to talk about America's "declining power." The Chinese leadership felt that the PRC "did not need to suppress its ambitions. It should assume a leadership role. It should use the leverage provided by its wealth, not least in relation to the United States, which owed it over a trillion dollars. It should utilize the military assets it had begun to develop over the past two decades to project Chinese strength abroad and to undercut American influence."[61] The increasingly contentious relations between the United States and China and a spike in tensions in Asia after 2010 raised questions about whether an ascending China would continue its policy of peaceful development or embrace a more confrontational approach toward regional and international affairs.[62]

The Obama administration was wary of Beijing's reluctance to more actively cooperate with Washington in addressing their economic policy disagreements, Iran and North Korea's nuclear ambitions, climate change, and humanitarian crises in Libya and Syria. Both Washington and Seoul, for instance, were dismayed by Beijing's failure to pressure North Korea to account for its sinking of the South Korean ship *Cheonan* in March 2010 and its bombardment of Yeonpyeong Island (where South Korean troops were stationed) in November 2010. These episodes resulted in South Korean military and civilian casualties.[63]

In the South China Sea, in March 2009, Chinese vessels "shadowed and aggressively maneuvered" in dangerously close proximity to the USNS *Impeccable,* an oceanic surveillance ship, to harass it while it was conducting routine operations in China's exclusive economic zone off Hainan Island.[64] Washington maintained the legality of its mission under the United Nations Convention on the Law of the Sea (UNCLOS) while Beijing claimed a violation of its sovereignty. Similar near-miss encounters have occurred regularly ever since, as US naval ships have continued operations in the South China Sea. Beijing also started to take more belligerent actions against fishing boats from Vietnam and other nearby states in the region.[65]

In May 2009, for the first time, the PRC attached to an official diplomatic communication to the UN its map with the "Nine-Dashed Line" to promote its territorial and maritime claims over almost the entire South China Sea. This initiative generated protests from many nearby Southeast Asian countries asserting their own respective claims, including Malaysia, Vietnam, Indonesia, Brunei, and the Philippines.[66] Responding to Beijing's acts, the Obama administration opted for a more hardline position toward China. At the July 2010 ASEAN Regional Forum meeting in Hanoi, Secretary of State Hillary Clinton pushed back against China's intransigence by affirming America's interest in ensuring freedom of passage through international waters and peaceful resolution of sovereignty disputes, warning Beijing that "it should not assume its material advantage over smaller ASEAN states would enable it to get its way in settling the disputes bilaterally."[67]

Furthermore, on November 17, 2011, President Obama, in a speech to the Australian parliament, announced America's rebalancing or "pivot" to the Asia Pacific after winding down the decade-long US war on terrorism in Iraq and Afghanistan.[68] In a *Foreign Policy* article, Secretary Clinton summarized the "pivot," writing that it would proceed along "six key lines of action: strengthening bilateral security alliances; deepening [US] working relationships with emerging powers, including with China; engaging with regional multilateral institutions; expanding trade and investment; forging a broad-based military presence; and advancing democracy and human rights."[69] The "pivot," then, was a multifaceted grand strategy encompassing security, economic, diplomatic, and normative dimensions.[70]

Without a doubt, Washington was targeting China as a rising power.[71] The United States resorted to a balancing or hedging strategy to "protect, and whenever possible to expand, the extant U.S. advantages in relative power." A key component was to "support the rise of other Asian powers located along China's periphery."[72] At the same time, the Obama administration repeatedly reassured Beijing that the United States "does not seek the containment of China."[73]

Because Beijing's "Nine-Dashed Line" assertion of sovereignty over the South China Sea is built upon a Chinese map published in 1947 (though it was called the "Eleven-Dashed Line" then), when Chiang Kai-shek was still ruling the Chinese mainland,[74] the PRC and ROC are actually on the same page regarding these issues. The KMT's and CCP's shared commitment to China's historical claim can be seen by Chiang using the term "national humiliation" as a unifying idea to bring the country together and to assert sovereignty over territories that China claims were ceded to foreign imperialist powers.[75] The Ma government's position was quite ambivalent. On the one hand, in conforming to the UNCLOS, Taipei advanced much more limited claims than Beijing, restricted to islands from three to twelve nautical miles off its adjacent waters.[76] On the other hand, the KMT administration also suggested that Taiwan's sovereignty over the South China Sea, based on the 1947 map, was more expansive, covering all the islands, reefs, and shoals as well as their surrounding waters.[77] In a December 2014 report, the US State Department challenged the "Nine-Dashed Line," claiming it "does not accord with the international law of the sea."[78]

Moreover, the United States rejected any effort by Beijing (or Taipei) to use history as the basis of maritime jurisdiction, except in a narrow category of near-shore "historic bays" and "historical title" in the context of territorial-sea boundary delimitation.[79] Indeed, the complexity of competing historical claims among the regional states over the South China Sea makes it highly unlikely that history can ever prevail over international legal arguments, which must be based on concrete evidence of continuous and effective occupation of the territorial and maritime features.[80] Thus, if Taiwan were to take the more restrained approach, by following the UNCLOS, it would be more in tune with Washington's interests toward the South China Sea issue, and help delegitimize Beijing's open-ended position.[81] Nevertheless, while being ambiguous to avoid antagonizing Beijing or Washington,[82] President Ma did not go so far as to explicitly renounce the "Nine- or Eleven-Dashed Line," since doing so would have repudiated the one-China core of the 1992 Consensus.[83]

In 2014 and 2015, Beijing's land-reclamation initiatives on islands and reefs in the South China Sea escalated the prospect of military confrontations with claimants in the region, and they threatened to drag the United States into the fray.[84] By late October 2015, less than two weeks before the

Ma-Xi summit, the Obama administration dispatched a guided-missile destroyer, the USS *Lassen,* to travel within twelve nautical miles of the Chinese-controlled Subi Reef in the South China Sea on a freedom-of-navigation patrol to challenge the PRC's "Nine-Dashed Line."[85] Meanwhile, the Permanent Court of Arbitration in The Hague also accepted the case brought forward by the Philippines challenging the legality of the Chinese "Nine-Dashed Line" under the UNCLOS.

The Ma administration staunchly stood by the 1992 Consensus as the bedrock foundation for dealing with Beijing. But the KMT won itself no plaudits from the United States by continuing to adhere closely to the "Dashed Line" position. On January 28, 2016, the US State Department and the AIT registered a rare harsh response when President Ma visited Itu Aba (known in Chinese as Taiping Island) in the Spratly Island archipelago of the South China Sea. The KMT leader sought to make an initiative for peace while reaffirming the island as indisputably part of the ROC's sovereignty territory. As the Philippine legal challenge was proceeding, Ma wanted to prove to the Permanent Court of Arbitration in The Hague that Taiping was an island capable of sustaining human habitation and economic life.[86] If this were so, Taipei claimed, the ROC enjoyed "full rights associated with territorial waters, a contiguous zone, an exclusive economic zone, and continental shelf in accordance with UNCLOS."[87] The United States, however, called Ma's visit "disappointing" and "unhelpful" to resolving the dispute in the region.[88] As Beijing was allegedly "militarizing"[89] some of the land features in the South China Sea by placing surface-to-air missiles and radar systems on them,[90] the United States was dismayed by any unnecessary provocations that could threaten to escalate confrontations.[91] On July 12, 2016, the PCA ruled against the PRC's "Nine-Dashed Line" claim over the South China Sea and also found the Taiwan-controlled Taiping Island to be merely a "rock," hence repudiating Taiwan's right to a 200-nautical-mile exclusive economic zone.

Against this backdrop, many US domestic actors, such as congressional elites, scholars, and commentators, attempted to "push against the White House's restraint," calling on the Obama government to "reinforce U.S. interests in Taiwan."[92] These included recommendations for selling more-advanced weapons to Taiwan and more vocal US support of the DPP and other opposition parties in Taiwan's 2016 elections.[93] The US Congress urged the Obama administration in various ways to support Taiwan's democracy, to meet its self-defense needs, and to assist with its bid to participate in regional economic integration and international organizations, including the US-backed Trans-Pacific Partnership (TPP) free trade agreement. Furthermore, the number and stature of US congressional members visiting Taiwan increased.[94] In 2015, the US Congress urged the Obama administration to permit active-duty US generals and flag officers to visit Taiwan and to step up military cooperation with Taiwanese military officials. In 2016, both the House of Representatives and the Senate formally incorporated, for the first time, both the Taiwan Relations Act and President Reagan's "Six Assurances" into a concurrent congressional resolution reaffirming US commitments to the defense of Taiwan's security and democracy.[95]

On the South China Sea territorial disputes, many US analysts and former government officials called on the ROC government to behave more responsibly on the matter. Jeffrey Bader, for instance, argued that the ROC government on Taiwan—as the creator of the original Eleven-Dashed Line in the late 1940s to designate Chinese claims over most of the South China Sea—should "reevaluate its position in line with existing international law." If Taiwan were to do that, "it would demonstrate the extremity and unreasonableness of China's current claim, pushing Beijing to do a similar reevaluation."[96] Nonetheless, as already noted, Ma showed little interest in clarifying the ROC's "Dashed Line" position, for fear of aggravating China and compromising the legitimacy of the KMT's own "one China" stance. In October 2015, the KMT's presidential candidate for the 2016 election, Eric Chu, also noted that he and his party would not "stand behind the United States" on the South China Sea dispute. In contrast, Tsai Ing-wen sounded more in tune with America's position on the matter, suggesting that "all parties should put forth their proposals and state their stances based on the legal principles of the United Nations Convention on the Law of the Sea."[97] The Kuomintang's passivity and halfhearted efforts to defend against an assertive PRC disappointed some longtime US supporters of Taiwan and reinforced the view of others that the island would inevitably capitulate to Beijing's economic and military power.[98]

The Obama Administration's Pushback Against the 1992 Consensus

The Obama administration responded to concerns about Taiwan's security and China's increasing belligerence by displaying growing unease with the KMT's peaceful overtures to Beijing. US officials admonished Taipei for leaning too eagerly toward Beijing at the expense of Taiwan's interests and security. Assistant Secretary of State Daniel Russel warned that cross-Strait bilateral exchanges should be done "at a pace acceptable to people on both sides of the strait" and "free from coercion."[99] In an interview with Taiwan's *Business Weekly* in June 2014, former secretary of state Hillary Clinton warned that President Ma's push for closer cross-Strait relations could "lead to Taiwan losing its economic and political independence and becoming vulnerable to overreliance on China."[100] She advised Taiwan to decide on its relations with China "carefully and smartly." President Obama expressed his support for greater cross-Strait contacts but emphasized that they should be carried out "on the basis of dignity and respect."[101]

At the Ma-Xi summit, President Xi repeatedly talked about the importance of upholding the 1992 Consensus, and such insistence has continued since Tsai Ing-wen became president in May 2016. Although Beijing has never endorsed the KMT's interpretation of "one China" as the ROC, the Ma administration's acceptance of "one China" as a foundational premise for cross-Strait engagements was "good enough" for the CCP.[102] The DPP charged that the KMT was effectively folding Taiwan into Beijing's "one-China framework" by conceding and limiting the island's sovereignty and presence on the international stage.[103]

Washington declined to take a clear stance on the 1992 Consensus.[104] Refuting President Ma's claim that the 1992 Consensus was recognized and agreed upon by mainland China, Taiwan, and the United States,[105] the American Institute in Taiwan (the de facto US embassy in Taiwan) affirmed that "the scope and nature of cross-strait interaction is for the two sides to decide. . . . The U.S. takes no position on the substance of such matters."[106] In her speech at the Brookings Institution on May 21, 2015, Susan Thornton responded to a reporter's query about the 1992 Consensus by stating: "We want to see the continued stable foundation and continuation of stable cross-strait ties. . . . [But] as to the name given to that foundation, I don't think it's really appropriate for the U.S. to either favor or disfavor."[107]

It is interesting to note as well that the Obama administration exhorted Beijing to demonstrate greater "flexibility and restraint" in managing a peaceful and stable cross-Strait relationship with Taiwan.[108] The implication of this statement was that Beijing should not impose the 1992 Consensus as a stringent precondition for deepening cross-Strait ties, especially given that the "one China" rubric was not widely accepted on the island.[109] Thus, in the later years of the Obama administration, the United States adopted a more reserved position on the 1992 Consensus, holding that there could be other possible formulas under which cross-Strait peace and stability could be maintained, and that the specific means should be decided upon by the people on both sides of the Taiwan Strait themselves.[110]

Tsai Ing-wen and the Future of United States–Taiwan Relations

In hindsight, President Ma's conciliatory cross-Strait policies to a great extent enhanced Beijing's perception (or increased its confidence) that the United States was no longer interested or relevant in deterring China from coercing Taiwan into political unification. Therefore, the US encouragement of cross-Strait rapprochement could be construed as Washington's acquiescence to the PRC's sovereign claim over Taiwan. Thomas Christensen insightfully pointed out that "cross-strait détente [was] generally welcomed in Washington. Ironically, however, the lack of tensions in relations across the Taiwan Strait deprived the Obama Administration of the opportunities afforded to the Clinton and Bush Administrations to reassure the PRC about U.S. strategic intentions without appearing overly weak or compromising in the process."[111]

Despite President Tsai Ing-wen's seemingly more moderate and centrist cross-Strait approach, as compared to Chen Shui-bian's, Tsai's refusal to accept the 1992 Consensus has led, from the PRC's point of view, to the current suspension and worsening of cross-Strait interactions. The United States, however, has placed most of the blame for the downturn on Beijing, faulting it for unreasonably pressuring Taipei to accept a formula that is not supported by a majority of the Taiwanese public. In contrast to Ma Ying-jeou's strategic stances, Tsai's closer alignment with Washington and Tokyo has also deepened Beijing's distrust of her and suspicion that Taiwan is joining in an anti-PRC encirclement campaign, especially in light of US president-elect Donald Trump's unprecedented call with Tsai on December 2, 2016.[112] Trump then even suggested that his incoming administration might break with the decades-old US "one China" policy if Washington and Beijing could not bridge over a range of security and economic differences.

Nonetheless, although the Republican president eventually reaffirmed the US government's commitment to "honor the one-China policy" in his call with Xi Jinping on February 9, 2017, Trump's mercurial and transactional decisionmaking style has surely introduced greater uncertainty into cross-Strait relations. Furthermore, as US-PRC strategic and economic rivalries have intensified, the Trump administration has not only explicitly designated China as America's "strategic competitor" but also elevated Washington's relations with Taipei by pushing forward, in cooperation with the US Congress, many pro-Taiwan initiatives and legislation. These have included the Taiwan Travel Act and TAIPEI Act signed by President Trump in March 2018 and March 2020, respectively, intended to help strengthen Taiwan's security, expand its international space, and raise its democratic profile.[113] The Trump administration has been less inclined to rigidly follow all the traditional strictures of the "one China" policy than the Obama White House, and it has found ways to gradually and creatively enlarge the scope and depth of the partnership with Taiwan. In addition to signing Taiwan-friendly legislation passed by Congress, the administration has regularly dispatched US warships to sail through the Taiwan Strait, approved six arms sales packages (including the August 2019 sale of 66 F-16V fighter jets, valued at $8 billion), and criticized China's attempts to disrupt Taiwan's democratic process via coercion and disinformation campaigns. Top executive branch officials from the State Department and National Security Council have routinely praised Taiwan for its positive role in democratic governance and contributions to regional peace and stability, including the island democracy's stellar management of the coronavirus pandemic, and Washington voiced stronger support for Taiwan's participation in the World Health Organization (WHO).[114]

Both Presidents Ma and Tsai pledged that their administrations would seek to maintain the cross-Strait status quo and not unilaterally jeopardize relations with Beijing. However, there are also distinct differences between Ma and Tsai's definitions of "status quo." The KMT leader's cross-Strait position rested upon a clear acceptance of the 1992 Consensus. Tsai, by contrast, though acknowledging the "historical fact of the 1992 talks," has not endorsed the 1992 Consensus and its underlying "one China" principle, to the chagrin of Beijing. To be sure, however, Beijing has been responsible for the Tsai administration's unrelenting rejection of the 1992 Consensus. In January 2019, for instance, Xi reiterated that the only future acceptable to the PRC for Taiwan would be unification with China under the "one country, two systems" formula, effectively equating that model with the 1992 Consensus and denying the existence of the ROC as an alternative interpretation of "one China" (the way Ma and the KMT had described). Beijing's intransigence and mishandling of the Hong Kong protests beginning in June 2019 further discredited the "one country, two systems" model and deepened Taiwan's fear for its security, sovereignty, and democracy. These factors contributed to Tsai's successful reelection bid in January 2020.[115]

Even though Tsai has not embraced overt and direct confrontation with the PRC, she still appears to have pursued a more implicit or subtle de-Sinification strategy. For instance, the DPP government has been seeking to recover KMT party assets that it alleges were illegally taken or stolen by the KMT regime on Taiwan after 1945. To be sure, the KMT's one-party dominance during the authoritarian era precluded any transparent due-process mechanism for acquiring many of its financial holdings and properties. There is, however, reasonable skepticism about whether the DPP is using appropriate formal legal and constitutional channels to investigate and retrieve the KMT's ill-gotten assets. Adding to the controversy, the KMT has accused the DPP of using the issue to try to destroy it through extralegal and partisan means, to which the DPP has responded with its own fierce words about the KMT's sixty years of misuse of wealth and inability "to right a wrong."[116]

Furthermore, some DPP legislators and their political allies in the Legislative Yuan have floated proposals to remove Sun Yat-sen's portraits from government, schools, and other public institutions, dismantle the last traces of Chiang Kai-shek's mementos and legacies, and revise Taiwanese history textbooks to bring them in line with a more separatist interpretation—all in the name of transitional justice. At the same time, the DPP has tended to depict in a much more favorable light Taiwan's colonial past under Imperial Japan, while downplaying inhumane and authoritarian aspects of Japanese rule. If these initiatives are pushed forward in a more partisan and incendiary manner, the Tsai government could end up undermining its promise to handle cross-Strait affairs on the basis of the ROC constitutional order, and end up overseeing divisive de-Sinification projects similar to those pursued by Chen Shui-bian.[117] Taiwan cannot afford to squander more time and energy on these partisan fights. Although recognizing past crimes committed by the KMT is important for political reconciliation, transitional justice also needs to be pursued legally, truthfully, and objectively.

The DPP and the KMT, encumbered by their respective national visions, each lacks the ability on its own to evaluate Taiwan's external environment rationally and implement sound national security policies. Under Ma, the KMT's pro-China prerogatives pushed the island into much closer relations with Beijing, possibly at the cost of sacrificing Taiwan's autonomy. In contrast, the DPP's push for de-Sinification has also unnecessarily aggravated the PRC and provoked ethnic animosity in Taiwan. Yun-han Chu probably said it best:

> Taiwanese nationalists advocate a separate Taiwanese national identity and seek permanent separation from China, while Chinese nationalists oppose movement toward Taiwan independence and favor eventual reunification with China. In the end, the state became the arena. The competing forces strove to gain control of the governing apparatus and use its power to steer cross-strait relations, erect a distinct cultural hegemony, and impose their own vision of nation-building, either in the direction of Taiwanization or Sinicization.[118]

Neither direction, when taken to the extreme, is conducive to Taiwan's interests and well-being.

As Taiwan becomes a more consolidated and mature democracy, the majority of its citizens are also more inclined to exercise their civil rights and voting power to punish irresponsible and demagogic political leaders (whether they are KMT or DPP), as they have done in every election for the past twelve years. Although it is true that there is a rising Taiwan-centric identity and consciousness, especially among the youth, observers have explained that this new identity or civic nationalism is, in fact, an inclusive one that includes "not just ethnic Taiwanese but all residents of Taiwan and [is] based on Taiwan's particular [democratic] values and institutions."[119] It essentially has replaced the Chinese identity imposed by the KMT and the exclusively ethnic identity that some Taiwanese nationalist and independence advocates are trying to establish. In a sense, Taiwan's median voters and its younger generations cherish their liberal democratic "way of life" and reject the PRC authoritarian system as well as Beijing's pressing attempts to stifle Taiwan's political autonomy and international space. Yet it would be an oversimplification to characterize such attitudes as "anti-Chinese" or "non-Chinese."[120] For the most part, the Tsai government has sought the middle ground on this China question. Hopefully, it will continue to strive for a balanced and reasonable posture to manage Taiwan's domestic politics and cross-Strait and foreign policies.

Notes

1. Wu, "Taiwan's Hedging Against China." See also Leng and Liao, "Hedging, Strategic Partnership, and Taiwan's Relations with Japan."
2. Morgenthau, *Politics Among Nations*, pp. 373–374.
3. These arguments are advanced more fully in Chen, *U.S.-China Rivalry and Taiwan's Mainland Policy*.
4. Templeman, Diamond, and Chu, "Taiwan's Democracy Under Chen Shui-bian," pp. 10–11.
5. Hughes, "Revisiting Identity Politics Under Ma Ying-jeou"; Cabestan, "Cross-Strait Integration and Taiwan's New Security Challenges," pp. 292–293; Chang and Holt, *Language, Politics, and Identity in Taiwan*.
6. Rigger, *Why Taiwan Matters*, p. 7; Copper, *The KMT Returns to Power*, p. 20.
7. See Lin, *Taiwan's China Dilemma*, pp. 169–205.
8. "Chinese, U.S. Presidents Hold Telephone Talks on Taiwan, Tibet," *Xinhua News*, March 27, 2008, http://news.xinhuanet.com/english/2008-03/27/content_7865209 .htm. Although the *Xinhua* website did display this news article, it was immediately taken down and never appeared again in the Chinese media. Thus, Beijing probably felt "it was a mistake" to give any official credence to "one China, respective interpretations."
9. Brown, "Taiwan Voters Set a New Course," p. 4.
10. "Remarks by President Barack Obama at Town Hall Meeting with Future Chinese Leaders," White House Office of the Press Secretary, November 16, 2009, https://www .whitehouse.gov/the-press-office/remarks-president-barack-obama-town-hall-meeting -with-future-chinese-leaders.
11. "Why Taiwan Matters," pt. 2, testimony by Kurt Campbell, assistant secretary, Bureau of East Asian and Pacific Affairs, before the House Foreign Affairs Committee, October 4, 2011, http://www.state.gov/p/eap/rls/rm/2011/10/174980.htm.
12. Benson and Niou, "Public Opinion, Foreign Policy, and the Security Balance in the Taiwan Strait." See also Hsu, "Between Identity Quest and Risk Aversion."
13. Hu, introduction to *New Dynamics in Cross-Taiwan-Strait Relations*, pp. 8, 3.
14. Shambaugh, *China Goes Global*, pp. 77–78.
15. Sutter, "More American Attention to Taiwan amid Heightened Competition with China," p. 5.
16. Bush, "U.S.-Taiwan Relations Since 2008," pp. 221–224.
17. Nadia Tsao, "Rohrabacher to Leave Taiwan Caucus Position," *Taipei Times*, March 15, 2009, http://www.taipeitimes.com/News/taiwan/archives/2009/03/15/2003438534.
18. See Gilley, "Not So Dire Straits." See also Glaser, "A U.S.-China Grand Bargain?"
19. Tucker and Glaser, "Should the United States Abandon Taiwan?"
20. Sutter, "More American Attention to Taiwan amid Heightened Competition with China," pp. 8–9.
21. Ibid., p. 10.
22. Ibid., pp. 10–11.
23. The three Sino-American joint communiqués of 1972, 1978, and 1982 essentially affirmed Washington's "acknowledgment" of Beijing's one-China principle, in which Taiwan is part of mainland China. The Taiwan Relations Act of 1979, conversely, assured Taipei that the United States would maintain unofficial diplomatic, security, and economic ties with the ROC. The United States would also continue its arms sales to Taiwan in order to help the island defend against PRC challenges. In the 1982 joint communiqué, the United States suggested that it would eventually end arms sales to Taiwan, but the Taiwan Relations Act and Reagan's "Six Assurances" (1982) actually committed the United States to not setting a deadline to end arms sales and to not pushing Taipei into any political negotiations with Beijing. These contradictions have generated perplexities and ambiguities that serve to prevent either side (ROC or PRC) from recklessly instigating tension and confrontation. See Bush, *At Cross Purposes*.
24. Bush, "U.S.-Taiwan Relations Since 2008," p. 224.

25. "Remarks by President Obama and President Xi of the People's Republic of China in Joint Press Conference," White House Office of the Press Secretary, September 25, 2015, https://www.whitehouse.gov/the-press-office/2015/09/25/remarks-president -obama-and-president-xi-peoples-republic-china-joint.

26. "Taiwan: A Vital Partner in East Asia," US Department of State, May 21, 2015, http://www.state.gov/p/eap/rls/rm/2015/05/242705.htm.

27. Sutter, "More American Attention to Taiwan amid Heightened Competition with China," p. 15.

28. Ibid., p. 9.

29. Tucker, *Strait Talk,* pp. 11–16.

30. Sutter et al., "Balancing Acts," p. 21.

31. Tucker, *Strait Talk.*

32. Rigger, *Why Taiwan Matters.*

33. Author interview with a former US government official responsible for US Taiwan Strait policy, February 2016.

34. Phillips, "Why Taiwan?" pp. 165–169.

35. Christensen, "The Contemporary Security Dilemma," p. 19.

36. Chen, *U.S. Taiwan Strait Policy: The Origins of Strategic Ambiguity.*

37. Sutter, "More American Attention to Taiwan amid Heightened Competition with China," pp. 6–7.

38. Jonathan Sullivan, "The Battle for Taiwan's Soul," *National Interest,* May 3, 2015, http://nationalinterest.org/feature/the-battle-taiwans-soul-the-2016-presidential -election-12790.

39. "White House Cautions on Historic China-Taiwan Meeting," *Associated Foreign Press,* November 3, 2015, http://news.yahoo.com/white-house-cautious-historic-china -taiwan-meeting-200700481.html. See also David Brunnstrom, "U.S. Says Unclear If Tai-wan-China Meeting Will Influence Taiwan Elections," *Reuters,* November 4, 2015, http:// www.reuters.com/article/2015/11/05/us-taiwan-china-usa-idUSKCN0SU07920151105.

40. Dittmer, "Taiwan's Narrowing Strait," p. 19.

41. "U.S. to Have Voice in Taiwan's 2016 Presidential Election: Bush," *Focus Tai-wan News,* September 13, 2014, http://m.focustaiwan.tw/news/aipl/201409130014.aspx.

42. "Washington Says Bush's Taiwan Remarks His Own," *Taipei Times,* September 18, 2014, http://www.taipeitimes.com/News/taiwan/archives/2014/09/18/2003599986.

43. "A Strong and Moderate Taiwan," Thomas Christensen, deputy assistant secretary for East Asian and Pacific Affairs, US Department of State, September 11, 2007, http:// 2001-2009.state.gov/p/eap/rls/rm/2007/91979.htm.

44. "1992 Consensus Verified by History: Ma," *China Post,* May 15, 2015, http://www.chinapost.com.tw/taiwan/china-taiwan-relations/2015/05/15/436072/1992 -Consensus.htm.

45. "U.S. Concerned About Taiwan Candidate," *Financial Times,* September 15, 2011, http://www.ft.com/intl/cms/s/0/f926fd14-df93-11e0-845a-00144feabdc0.html #axzz3bm75hK48.

46. Keith Bradsher, "In Dispute, China Blocks Rare Earth Exports to Japan," *New York Times,* September 23, 2010, p. B1.

47. Bader, *Obama and China's Rise,* pp. 106–107.

48. Ibid., p. 108.

49. Cheng, "Taiwan-U.S. Relations," p. 381.

50. Interview with Mainland Affairs Council official who requested to remain anony-mous, August 2014.

51. Dittmer, "Taiwan's Narrowing Straits," p. 23. Chung, *Domestic Politics, Inter-national Bargaining, and China's Territorial Disputes,* pp. 28–31. This point was also confirmed by a DPP official who requested to remain anonymous during my interview in July 2014.

52. Lee, "A Quartet in Disharmony."

53. Dittmer, "Taiwan's Narrowing Straits," p. 24.

54. Lee, "A Quartet in Disharmony," p. 105.

55. Sahashi and Cabestan, "Japan-Taiwan Relations Since 2008."

56. Cheng, "Taiwan-U.S. Relations," p. 381. See also "Joint Press Conference with President Obama and Prime Minister Abe of Japan," White House, April 24, 2014, http://www.whitehouse.gov/photos-and-video/video/2014/04/24/president-obama-holds -press-conference-prime-minister-abe-japan#transcript.

57. Shannon Tiezzi, "Why China's Air Defense Identification Zone Is Terrible for Cross-Strait Relations," *The Diplomat*, November 28, 2013, http://thediplomat.com /2013/11/why-chinas-air-defense-identification-zone-is-terrible-for-cross-strait-relations.

58. Hayton, *The South China Sea*, pp. 86–89.

59. Tonnesson, "The South China Sea," p. 469.

60. Ibid.

61. Bader, *Obama and China's Rise*, p. 81.

62. Goldstein, "U.S.-China Interactions in Asia," pp. 263–264.

63. Ibid., p. 270.

64. "U.S. Accuses the Chinese of Harassing Naval Vessel," *New York Times*, March 9, 2009, http://www.nytimes.com/2009/03/09/world/asia/09iht-ship.3.20710715.html?_r=0.

65. Lin, "Behind Rising East Asian Maritime Tensions with China," p. 485.

66. Tonnesson, "The South China Sea," p. 464.

67. Goldstein, "U.S.-China Interactions in Asia," p. 273.

68. "Remarks by President Obama to the Australian Parliament," White House Office of the Press Secretary, November 17, 2011, http://www.whitehouse.gov/the-press -office/2011/11/17/remarks-president-obama-australian-parliament.

69. Hillary Clinton, "America's Pacific Century," *Foreign Policy*, November 2011, http://www.foreignpolicy.com/articles/2011/10/11/americas_pacific_century.

70. Sutter et al., "Balancing Acts," pp. 11–16.

71. Chris Buckley, "Xi Jinping's Rapid Rise in China Presents Challenges to the U.S.," *New York Times*, November 11, 2014, http://www.nytimes.com/2014/11/12 /world/asia/president-xi-jinping-makes-it-his-mission-to-empower-china.html.

72. Tellis, "Balancing Without Containment," pp. 111–112.

73. Bader, *Obama and China's Rise*, p. 69.

74. See US Department of State, Bureau of Oceans and International Environmental and Scientific Affairs, "Limits in the Sea no. 143, China: Maritime Claims in the South China Sea," December 5, 2014, http://www.state.gov/documents/organization/234936.pdf.

75. Hayton, *The South China Sea*, p. 53.

76. Lynn Kuok, "Tides of Change: Taiwan's Evolving Position in the South China Sea and Why Other Actors Should Take Notice," East Asia Policy Paper no. 5 (Washington, DC: Center for East Asia Policy Studies at Brookings Institution, May 2015), p. 6. See also "Joining the Dashes," *The Economist*, October 4, 2014, http://www.economist.com /news/asia/21621844-south-china-seas-littoral-states-will-fight-museums-archives-and.

77. Kuok, "Tides of Change," p. 7.

78. US Department of State, "Limits in the Sea," p. 24.

79. Ibid., pp. 19–22.

80. Hayton, *The South China Sea*, p. 99. See also US Department of State, "Limits in the Sea."

81. "Joining the Dashes."

82. Kuok, "Tides of Change," p. 9. Shannon Tiezzi, "Taiwan Will Not Cooperate with China in South China Sea," *The Diplomat*, May 15, 2014, http://thediplomat .com/2014/05/taiwan-will-not-cooperate-with-china-in-south-china-sea.

83. Kuok, "Tides of Change," p. 13.

84. "South China Sea: Try Not to Blink," *The Economist*, May 30, 2015, http:// www.economist.com/news/asia/21652348-china-asserts-itself-naval-and-air-power-and -america-responds-risks.

85. Helene Cooper, "Challenging Chinese Claims, U.S. Sends Warships Near Artificial Island Chain," *New York Times*, October 26, 2015, http://www.nytimes.com/2015

/10/27/world/asia/challenging-chinese-claims-us-sends-warship-near-artificial-island
-chain.html.

86. Ralph Jennings and Julie Makinen, "Taiwan President Makes Waves with South China Sea Visit," *Los Angeles Times,* January 28, 2016, http://www.latimes.com/world /asia/la-fg-taiwan-south-china-sea-20160128-story.html.

87. "Taiping Island Is an Island, Not a Rock," press release, Ministry of Foreign Affairs, Republic of China (Taiwan), January 23, 2016, http://www.mofa.gov.tw/en /News_Content.aspx?n=1EADDCFD4C6EC567&s=542A8C89D51D8739.

88. "U.S. 'Disappointed' over Ma's Taiping Island Visit," *Focus Taiwan News,* January 28, 2016, http://focustaiwan.tw/news/aipl/201601280007.aspx.

89. "Pacific Command Chief Urges New Capabilities As Tensions Mount with China," *Navy Times,* February 24, 2016, http://www.navytimes.com/story/military /2016/02/23/pacom-harry-harris-china-militarizing-south-china-sea/80796756.

90. Shannon Tiezzi, "South China Sea Militarization: Not All Islands Are Created Equal," *The Diplomat,* March 1, 2016, http://thediplomat.com/2016/03/south-china-sea -militarization-not-all-islands-are-created-equal.

91. Interview with a former US government official responsible for Taiwan Strait policy, February 2016. This person commented that although President Ma made a long and good speech on Taiping, there was no reason why he couldn't make the same speech in Taiwan. Although the ROC has established a permanent presence and administration on the Taiping since 1956, the island was also claimed by the PRC, Vietnam, and the Philippines.

92. Robert Sutter, "Hardening Competition with China: Implications for U.S. Taiwan Policy," *China & U.S. Focus Digest,* September 5, 2014, http://www.chinausfocus.com /foreign-policy/hardening-competition-with-china-implications-for-us-taiwan-policy.

93. Sutter, "More American Attention to Taiwan amid Heightened Tension with China," p. 12.

94. Ibid.

95. William Lowther, "U.S. Senate Reaffirms TRA, 'Six Assurances,'" *Taipei Times,* July 9, 2016, http://www.taipeitimes.com/News/taiwan/archives/2016/07/09/2003650668.

96. Bader's remarks paraphrased from Sutter, *Chinese Foreign Relations,* p. 167. See also Jeffrey Bader, "The U.S. and China's Nine-Dash Line: Ending the Ambiguity," February 6, 2014, http://www.brookings.edu/research/opinions/2014/02/06-us-china-nine -dash-line-bader.

97. "KMT, DPP Presidential Candidates Comment on South China Sea Strategy," *Focus Taiwan News,* October 28, 2015, http://focustaiwan.tw/news/aipl/201510280032.aspx.

98. Mearsheimer, "Taiwan's Dire Straits," *National Interest,* March–April 2014, pp. 29–39.

99. "Testimony of Daniel R. Russel, Assistant Secretary of State, Bureau of East Asian and Pacific Affairs, U.S. Department of State, Before the Senate Committee on Foreign Relations Subcommittee on East Asian and Pacific Affairs," April 3, 2014, http:// www.foreign.senate.gov/imo/media/doc/Russel_Testimony1.pdf.

100. Jason Pan, "Reliance on China Makes Taiwan Vulnerable: Clinton," *Taipei Times,* June 25, 2014, http://www.taipeitimes.com/News/front/archives/2014/06/25/2003593606. For the original interview transcript, see *Business Weekly* no. 1389 (June 30, 2014–July 6, 2014), pp. 58–73.

101. "Remarks by President Obama and President Xi Jinping in Joint Press Conference," White House Office of the Press Secretary, November 12, 2014, http://www .whitehouse.gov/the-press-office/2014/11/12/remarks-president-obama-and-president -xi-jinping-joint-press-conference.

102. "Xi-Chu Meeting Consolidated Sino-Taiwanese Cooperation Framework," *Deutsche Welle,* May 4, 2015, http://www.dw.de/xi-chu-meeting-consolidated-sino -taiwanese-cooperation-framework/a-18428392.

103. "Opposition Party Raises Alarm over Chu-Xi Meeting," *Focus Taiwan News,* May 4, 2015, http://focustaiwan.tw/news/aipl/201505040034.aspx.

104."Daily Press Briefing by Jeff Rathke," US Department of State, May 4, 2015, http://www.state.gov/r/pa/prs/dpb/2015/05/241844.htm#CHINA.

105. "1992 Consensus Verified by History: Ma," *China Post*, May 15, 2015, http://www.chinapost.com.tw/taiwan/china-taiwan-relations/2015/05/15/436072/1992-Consensus.htm.

106. "U.S. Takes No Stance on '1992 Consensus': AIT Spokesman," *China Post*, May 16, 2015, http://www.chinapost.com.tw/taiwan/china-taiwan-relations/2015/05/16/436153/US-takes.htm.

107. "Stable Cross-Strait Ties Key to Taiwan-U.S. Relations: U.S. Officials," *China Post*, May 22, 2015, http://www.chinapost.com.tw/taiwan/national/national-news/2015/05/22/436643/Stable-cross-strait.htm. On Thornton's full speech transcript, see "Taiwan: A Vital Partner in East Asia," US Department of State, May 21, 2015, http://www.state.gov/p/eap/rls/rm/2015/05/242705.htm.

108. Thornton, "Taiwan."

109. Romberg, "Squaring the Circle," p. 13.

110. Interview with a former US government official responsible for US Taiwan Strait policy, February 2016.

111. Christensen, *The China Challenge*, p. 296. Christensen served from 2006 to 2008 as deputy assistant secretary of state for East Asian and Pacific affairs, with responsibility for relations with China and Taiwan.

112. Under Tsai, Taiwan and Japan are forging closer economic and political relationships. See Yasuhiro Matsuda, "Japan-Taiwan Relations in the New DPP Era," February 11, 2016, http://www.eastwestcenter.org/system/tdf/private/apb334.pdf?file=1&type=node&id=35524.

113. Sutter, *The United States and Asia*, pp. 109–110. See also Gingrich, *Trump vs. China*.

114. As the novel coronavirus (COVID-19) pandemic spread around the world in early 2020, the Trump administration also commended Taiwan's measured and effective responses to manage the contagion and stepped up rhetoric in favor of Taiwan's meaningful participation in the World Health Organization (WHO). Taiwan's successful "mask diplomacy" in the face of the pandemic, and the intense criticism of both the PRC and the WHO coming from many quarters of the US political system, has brought Taiwan's interests even more in line with those of the United States.

115. Ishaan Tharoor, "The End of Xi Jinping's Taiwan Dream," *Washington Post*, January 14, 2020, https://www.washingtonpost.com/world/2020/01/14/end-xi-jinpings-taiwan-dream.

116. "KMT Threatens Protest over Assets," *Taipei Times*, September 7, 2016, http://www.taipeitimes.com/News/front/archives/2016/09/07/2003654642.

117. Templeman, Diamond, and Chu, "Taiwan's Democracy Under Chen Shui-bian," pp. 20–21.

118. Chu, "Taiwan's National Identity Politics and the Prospect of Cross-Strait Relations," pp. 498–499.

119. Lin, *Taiwan's China Dilemma*, p. 31.

120. Ibid.

Bibliography

Abdelal, Rawi. *National Purpose in the World Economy: Post-Soviet States in Comparative Perspective.* Ithaca: Cornell University Press, 2001.

Achen, Christopher H., and T. Y. Wang, eds. *The Taiwan Voter.* Ann Arbor: University of Michigan Press, 2017.

Aggarwal, Vinod K. "Bilateral Trade Agreements in the Asia-Pacific." In *Bilateral Trade Agreements in the Asia-Pacific: Origins, Evolution, and Implications,* edited by Vinod Aggarwal and Shujiro Urata, 19–42. New York: Routledge, 2006.

Ahn, Byung-jun. "A Study of the Determinants Influencing the Legislative Success of a Government-Proposed Bill in Korea." Graduate capstone, Martin School of Policy and Administration, Lexington, KY, 2017.

Alchian, Armen, and Harold Demsetz. 1972. "Production, Information Costs, and Economic Organization." *American Economic Review* 62, no. 5 (1972): 777–795.

Aldrich, John H. *Why Parties? The Origin and Transformation of Political Parties in America.* Chicago: University of Chicago Press, 1995.

Anderson, Christopher. *Losers' Consent: Elections and Democratic Legitimacy.* Oxford: Oxford University Press, 2007.

Andeweg, Rudy B., and Lia Nijzink. "Beyond the Two-Body Image: Relations Between Ministers and MPs." In *Parliaments and Majority Rule in Western Europe,* edited by Herbert Döring, 152–178. Frankfurt: Campus, 1995.

Arian, Asher, and Michal Shamir. "Two Reversals in Israeli Politics: Why 1992 Was Not 1977." *Electoral Studies* 12, no. 4 (1993): 315–341.

Armigeon, Klaus, and Kai Guthmann. "Democracy in Crisis? The Declining Support for National Democracy in European Countries, 2007–2011." *European Journal of Political Research* 53, no. 3 (2014): 423–442.

Bader, Jeffrey. *Obama and China's Rise: An Insider's Account of America's Asia Strategy.* Washington, DC: Brookings Institution, 2012.

Batto, Nathan F. "The KMT Coalition Unravels: The 2016 Elections and Taiwan's New Political Landscape." In *A New Era in Democratic Taiwan: Trajectories and Turning Points in Politics and Cross-Strait Relations,* edited by Jonathan Sullivan and Chun-yi Lee, 10–34. London: Routledge, 2018.

——. "Sources and Implications of Malapportionment in Taiwan." *Taiwanese Political Science Review* 20, no. 2 (2016): 263–307.

Batto, Nathan F., Chi Huang, Alexander C. Tan, and Gary W. Cox, eds. *Mixed-Member Electoral Systems in Constitutional Context: Taiwan, Japan, and Beyond.* Ann Arbor: University of Michigan Press, 2016.

Batto, Nathan F., and Hsin-ta Huang. "Executive Competition, Electoral Rules, and Faction Systems in Taiwan." In *Mixed-Member Electoral Systems in Constitutional Context: Taiwan, Japan, and Beyond,* edited by Nathan Batto, Chi Huang, Alexander C. Tan, and Gary W. Cox, 102–134. Ann Arbor: University of Michigan Press, 2016.

Batto, Nathan F., and Yun-chu Tsai. "Storming the Podium: Parliamentary Brawls as a Dilatory Tactic in the Taiwanese Legislature." Paper presented at the annual meeting of the Midwest Political Science Association, Chicago, April 6–9, 2017.

Benson, Brett, and Emerson Niou. "Public Opinion, Foreign Policy, and the Security Balance in the Taiwan Strait." *Security Studies* 14, no. 2 (2005): 274–289.

Berinsky, Adam J., and Gabriel S. Lenz. "Education and Political Participation: Exploring the Causal Link." *Political Behavior* 33, no. 3 (2011): 357–373.

Booth, John A., and Mitchell A. Seligson. *The Legitimacy Puzzle in Latin America: Political Support and Democracy in Eight Nations.* New York: Cambridge University Press, 2009.

Bowler, Shaun, David M. Farrell, and Richard S. Katz. "Party Cohesion, Party Discipline, and Parliaments." In *Party Discipline and Parliamentary Government,* edited by Shaun Bowler, David M. Farrell, and Richard S. Katz, 3–22. Columbus: Ohio State University Press, 1999.

Bratton, Michael, and Robert Mattes. "Support for Democracy in Africa: Intrinsic or Instrumental?" *British Journal of Political Science* 31, no. 3 (2001): 447–474.

Brown, David G. "Taiwan Voters Set a New Course." *Comparative Connections* 10, no. 1 (April 2008), http://cc.pacforum.org/2008/04/taiwan-voters-set-new-course.

Brunner, Martin. *Parliaments and Legislative Activity: Motivations for Bill Introduction.* Mannheim: Springer, 2013.

Buchanan, James, and Gordon Tullock. *The Calculus of Consent.* Ann Arbor: University of Michigan Press, 1967.

Burnham, W. D. *Critical Elections and the Mainsprings of American Politics.* New York: Norton, 1970.

Bush, Richard C. *At Cross Purposes: U.S.-Taiwan Relations Since 1942.* New York: Routledge 2004.

———. *Untying the Knot: Making Peace in the Taiwan Strait.* Washington, DC: Brookings Institution Press, 2005.

———. "U.S.-Taiwan Relations Since 2008." In *Political Changes in Taiwan Under Ma Ying-jeou,* edited by Jean-Pierre Cabestan and Jacques deLisle, 217–231. New York: Routledge, 2014.

Cabestan, Jean-Pierre. "Cross-Strait Integration and Taiwan's New Security Challenges." In *Taiwan and the "China Impact,"* edited by Gunter Schubert, 282–300. New York: Routledge, 2016.

Campbell, Angus. "Surge and Decline: A Study of Electoral Change." *Public Opinion Quarterly* 24, no. 3 (1960): 397–418.

Campbell, Angus, Philip E. Converse, Warren E. Miller, and Donald E. Stokes. *The American Voter.* Chicago: University of Chicago Press, 1960.

Campbell, James E. "The Revised Theory of Surge and Decline." *American Journal of Political Science* 31, no. 3 (1987): 965–979.

Carmines, Edwin G., and Michael W. Wagner. "Political Issues and Party Alignments: Assessing the Issue Evolution Perspective." *Annual Review of Political Science* 9 (2006): 67–81.

Carter, Neil. *The Politics of the Environment: Ideas, Activism, Policy.* Cambridge: Cambridge University Press, 2007.

Casar, María Amparo. "Executive-Legislative Relations: The Case of Mexico (1946–1997)." In *Legislative Politics in Latin America,* edited by Scott Morgenstern, Benito Nacif, and Peter Lange, 114–146. Cambridge: Cambridge University Press, 2002.

Central Election Commission. *Election Archives.* http://db.cec.gov.tw.

Chang, Hsiang-yi. "Taiwan's Unfair Tax System: Helping the Rich Get Richer." *Commonwealth Magazine,* September 20, 2012. https://english.cw.com.tw/article/article.action?id=649.

Chang, Hui-ching, and Richard Holt. *Language, Politics and Identity in Taiwan: Naming China.* New York: Routledge, 2015.

Chang, Yu-tzung, and Yun-han Chu. "Democratization in East Asia in Comparative Perspective: Viewing Through the Eyes of the Citizens." In *Routledge Handbook on East Asian Democratization,* edited by Tun-jen Cheng and Yun-han Chu, 19–39. London: Routledge, 2018.

Chang, Yu-tzung, Yun-han Chu, and Chong-min Park. "Authoritarian Nostalgia in Asia." *Journal of Democracy* 18, no. 3 (2007): 66–80.

Chang, Yu-tzung, Mark Weatherall, and Jack Wu. "Democracies Under Stress: The Dwindling Public Trust in Asian Political Institutions." *Global Asia* 10, no. 3 (2015): 106–111.

Chen, Chi-ying, and Shao-liang Chang. "From Blogs to Microblogs: A Long-Term Study of Applying Social Media for Political Communication" (in Chinese). *Journal of Information Communication* 5, no. 1 (2014): 1–24.

Chen, Dean. *U.S.-China Rivalry and Taiwan's Mainland Policy: Security, Nationalism, and the 1992 Consensus.* New York: Palgrave Macmillan, 2017.

———. *U.S. Taiwan Strait Policy: The Origins of Strategic Ambiguity.* Boulder, CO: Lynne Rienner, 2012.

Chen, Fang-yu, and Wei-ting Yen. "Who Supports the Sunflower Movement? An Examination of Nationalist Sentiments." *Journal of Asian and African Studies* 52, no. 8 (2017): 1193–1212.

Chen, Hong-ming. "Competition over Party Chairmanship and the Types of Party Organization: A Case Study of the Democratic Progressive Party" (in Chinese). *Taiwanese Journal of Political Science* 63 (2015): 91–128.

———. "The President's Position Taking of Bills and His Influence on Legislation Under Semi-Presidentialism: The Experience of President Ma Ying-jeou" (in Chinese). *Soochow Journal of Political Science* 30, no. 2 (2012): 1–71.

Chen, Ian Tsung-yen, and Da-chi Liao. "The Rise of the New Power Party in Taiwan's 2016 Legislative Election: Reality and Challenges." In *Taiwan's Political Realignment and Diplomatic Challenges,* edited by Wei-chin Lee, 71–96. Cham: Palgrave Macmillan, 2019.

Chen, Ketty. "This Land Is Your Land? This Land Is *MY* Land: Land Expropriation During the Ma Ying-jeou Administration and Implications on Social Movements." In *Taiwan's Social Movements Under Ma Ying-jeou: From the Wild Strawberries to the Sunflowers,* edited by Dafydd Fell, 92–112. London: Routledge, 2017.

Chen, Tain-jy. "Taiwan's Middle-Income Trap: No Escaping Without Services." *Global Asia* 8, no. 1 (Spring 2013): 120–123.

Chen, Wan-chi, Heng-hao Chang, and Su-jen Huang. "The Coming of Networked Social Movements? Social Ties and Social Media in the Sunflower Movement" (in Chinese). *Journal of Social Sciences and Philosophy* 28, no. 4 (2016): 467–501.

Chen, Wan-chi, and Su-jen Huang. "Outcry Outside the Legislature: A Portrait of Sunflower Movement Sit-In Demonstrators" (in Chinese). *Taiwanese Sociology* 30 (2015): 141–179.

Cheng, Isabelle. "Making Foreign Women the Mother of Our Nation: The Exclusion and Assimilation of Immigrant Women in Taiwan." *Asian Ethnicity* 14, no. 2 (2013): 157–179.

Cheng, Tuan. "Taiwan-U.S. Relations: Close but Uncertain." *China Report* 49, no. 4 (2013): 371–384.

Cheng, Tun-jen, and Stephan Haggard. *Political Change in Taiwan.* Boulder: Lynne Rienner, 1992.

Cheng, Tun-jen, and Yung-ming Hsu. "Issue Structure, the DPP's Factionalism, and Party Realignment." In *Taiwan's Electoral Politics and Democratic Transition: Riding the Third Wave,* edited by Hung-mao Tien, 137–173. Armonk, NY: Sharpe, 1996.

———. "Long in the Making: Taiwan's Institutionalized Party System." In *Party System Institutionalization in Asia: Democracies, Autocracies, and the Shadows of the Past,* edited by Allen Hicken and Eric Kuhonta, 108–135. New York: Cambridge University Press, 2015.

Christensen, Thomas. *The China Challenge: Shaping the Choices of a Rising Power.* New York: Norton, 2015.

———. "The Contemporary Security Dilemma: Deterring a Taiwan Conflict." *Washington Quarterly* 25, no. 4 (2002): 5–21.

Chu, Yun-han. "Coping with the Global Financial Crises: Institutional and Ideational Sources of Taiwan's Economic Resiliency." *Journal of Contemporary China* 22, no. 82 (2013): 649–668.

———. "The Political Implications of Taiwan-Mainland Economic Integration." *Global Asia* 7, no. 1 (Spring 2012): 120–125.

———. "Taiwan's Election and Democratization Study, 2009–2012." Pt. 3, "Survey of the Presidential and Legislative Elections, 2012 (TEDS2012)." Taipei: National Science Council, 2012.

———. "Taiwan's National Identity Politics and the Prospect of Cross-Strait Relations." *Asian Survey* 44, no. 4 (2004): 484–512.

———. "Unraveling the Enigma of East Asian Economic Resiliency: The Case of Taiwan." In *Two Crises, Two Outcomes,* edited by T. J. Pempel and Ken'ichi Tsunekawa, 64–89. Ithaca: Cornell University Press, 2015.

———. "Who Is to Tame the Legislature?" (in Chinese). *Commonwealth Magazine,* Issue 594 (30 March, 2016), https://www.cw.com.tw/article/article.action?id=5075463.

Chu, Yun-han, Larry Diamond, Andrew Nathan, and Dol C. Shin, eds. *How East Asians View Democracy.* New York: Columbia University Press, 2008.

Chu, Yun-han, and Min-hua Huang. "The Meanings of Democracy: Solving an Asian Puzzle." *Journal of Democracy* 21, no. 4 (2010): 114–122.

Chu, Yun-han, and Jih-wen Lin. "Political Development in 20th Century Taiwan: State-Building, Regime Transformation, and the Construction of National Identity." *China Quarterly* 165 (2001): 102–129.

Chu, Yun-peng, and Gee San. "Taiwan's Industrial Policy and the Economic Rise of the PRC: Opportunities and Challenges." In *Taiwan's Democracy: Economic and Political Challenges,* edited by Robert Ash, John W. Garver, and Penelope Prime, 125–145. New York: Routledge, 2011.

Chuang, Po-chung. "Online Campaign Strategies of the KMT for the 2004 Presidential Election: A Perspective of Action Research" (in Chinese). *Journal of Electoral Studies* 12, no. 2 (2005): 79–109.

Chung, Chien-peng. *Domestic Politics, International Bargaining, and China's Territorial Disputes.* New York: Routledge, 2004.

Cole, J. Michael. *Black Island: Two Years of Activism in Taiwan.* CreateSpace Independent Publishing Platform, March 27, 2015.

———. "Civic Activism and Protests in Taiwan: Why Size Doesn't (Always) Matter." In *Taiwan's Social Movements Under Ma Ying-jeou: From the Wild Strawberries to the Sunflowers,* edited by Dafydd Fell, 18–33. London: Routledge, 2017.

———. *The Hard Edge of Sharp Power: Understanding China's Influence Operations Abroad.* Ottawa: Macdonald-Laurier Institute for Public Policy, October 2018.

———. "Two Myths About Taiwan's DPP That Need to Be Laid to Rest." *The Diplomat,* August 6, 2015. https://thediplomat.com/2015/08/two-myths-about-taiwans-dpp-that-need-to-be-laid-to-rest.

———. "Was Taiwan's Sunflower Movement Successful?" *The Diplomat,* July 1, 2014. https://thediplomat.com/2014/07/was-taiwans-sunflower-movement-successful.

Copper, John F. *The KMT Returns to Power: Elections in Taiwan, 2008–2012*. Lanham: Lexington Books, 2012.

———. *Taiwan's Democracy on Trial: Political Change During the Chen Shui-bian Era and Beyond*. Lanham: University Press of America, 2010.

Cox, Gary W. "The Organization of Democratic Legislatures." In *The Oxford Handbook of Political Economy*, edited by Barry Weingast and Donald Wittman, 141–161. Oxford: Oxford University Press, 2006.

Cox, Gary W., and Mathew D. McCubbins. *Legislative Leviathan: Party Government in the House*. Berkeley: University of California Press, 1993.

———. *Setting the Agenda: Responsible Party Government in the U.S. House of Representatives*. Cambridge: Cambridge University Press, 2005.

Croissant, Aurel, and Philip Völkel. "Party System Types and Party System Institutionalization: Comparing New Democracies in East and Southeast Asia." *Party Politics* 18, no. 2 (2012): 235–265.

Dalton, Russell J. *Democratic Challenges, Democratic Choices: The Erosion of Political Support in Advanced Industrial Democracies*. New York: Oxford University Press, 2004.

———. "Political Support in Advanced Industrial Democracies." In *Critical Citizens: Global Support for Democratic Government*, edited by Pippa Norris, 57–77. New York: Oxford University Press, 1999.

Davidson, Roger. "The Two Congresses and How They Are Changing." In *The Role of the Legislature in Western Democracies*, edited by Norman J. Ornstein. Washington, DC: American Enterprise Institute, 1981.

Davidson, Roger H., and Walter J. Oleszek. "Adaptation and Consolidation: Structural Innovation in the U.S. House of Representatives." *Legislative Studies Quarterly* 1, no. 1 (1976): 37–65.

DeLisle, Jacques. "Taiwan's 2012 Presidential and Legislative Elections: Winners, Losers, and Implications." Foreign Policy Research Institute E-Note, January 2012. https://www.fpri.org/article/2012/01/taiwans-2012-presidential-and-legislative-elections-winners-losers-and-implications.

Diamond, Larry, and Orville Schell. *Chinese Influence and American Interests: Promoting Constructive Vigilance*. Stanford: Hoover Institution Press, 2018.

Diaz-Bazan, Tania. *Measuring Inequality from Top to Bottom*. Washington, DC: World Bank Group, 2015.

Director General of Budgeting, Accounting, and Statistics. *DGBAS Database*. Republic of China (Taiwan). https://eng.dgbas.gov.tw/mp.asp?mp=2.

Dittmer, Lowell. "Taiwan's Narrowing Strait: A Triangular Analysis of Taiwan's Security Since 2008." In *The U.S. Strategic Pivot to Asia and Cross-Strait Relations*, edited by Peter Chow, 15–29. New York: Palgrave Macmillan, 2014.

Doner, Richard, Ben Ross Schneider. "The Middle-Income Trap: More Politics Than Economics." *World Politics* 68, no. 4 (2016): 608–644.

Döring, Herbert. "Parliaments, Public Choice, and Legislation." Paper presented at the Project Conference, University of Heidelberg, 1993.

Doshi, Rush. "Hu's to Blame for China's Foreign Assertiveness?" January 22, 2019. https://www.brookings.edu/articles/hus-to-blame-for-chinas-foreign-assertiveness.

Easton, David. "A Re-Assessment of the Concept of Political Support." *British Journal of Political Science* 5, no. 4 (1975): 435–437.

———. *A Systems Analysis of Political Life*. New York: Wiley, 1965.

Ebsworth, Rowena. "Not Wanting Want: The Anti-Media Monopoly Movement in Taiwan." In *Taiwan's Social Movements Under Ma Ying-jeou*, edited by Dafydd Fell, 71–91. Abingdon: Routledge, 2017.

Edelman, Murray. *Politics as Symbolic Action: Mass Arousal and Quiescence*. New York, San Francisco, and London: Academic Press, 1971.

———. *The Symbolic Uses of Politics*. Urbana-Champaign: University of Illinois Press, 1967.

Evans, Geoffrey, and Pippa Norris, eds. *Critical Elections: British Parties and Voters in Long-Term Perspective*. London: Sage, 1999.

Fan, Yun, and Wei-ting Wu. "The Long Feminist March in Taiwan." In *Routledge Hand-book of Contemporary Taiwan,* edited by Gunter Schubert, 313–325. London: Routledge, 2016.

Feigenbaum, Evan. "China and the World: Dealing with a Reluctant Power." *Foreign Affairs* 33 (January–February 2017): 33.

Fell, Dafydd. "Do Party Switchers Pay an Electoral Price? The Case of Taiwan." *Parliamentary Affairs* 70 (2017): 377–396.

———. *Government and Politics in Taiwan.* 2nd ed. London: Routledge, 2018.

———. "Merger and Takeover Attempts in Taiwanese Party Politics." *Issues and Studies* 53, no. 4 (2017): 1–28.

———. *Party Politics in Taiwan: Party Change and the Democratic Evolution of Taiwan, 1991–2004.* London: Routledge, 2006.

———. "Should I Stay or Should I Go? Patterns of Party-Switching in Multiparty Taiwan." *Journal of East Asian Studies* 14 (2014): 31–52.

———. "Small Parties in Taiwan's 2016 National Elections: A Limited Breakthrough?" *American Journal of Chinese Studies* 23, no. 1 (2016): 41–58.

———. "Success and Failure of New Parties in Taiwanese Elections." *China: An International Journal* 3, no. 2 (2005): 212–239.

———, ed. *Taiwan's Social Movements Under Ma Ying-jeou: From the Wild Strawberries to the Sunflowers.* Abingdon: Routledge, 2017.

———. "Was 2005 a Critical Election in Taiwan? Locating the Start of a New Political Era." *Asian Survey* 50, no. 5 (2010): 927–945.

Fell, Dafydd, and Yen-wen Peng. "The Electoral Fortunes of Taiwan's Green Party: 1996–2012." *Japanese Journal of Political Science* 17, no. 1 (2016): 63–83.

Field, Bonnie N. *Why Minority Governments Work: Multilevel Territorial Politics in Spain.* New York: Palgrave Macmillan, 2016.

Figueiredo, Argelina Cheibub, and Fernando Limongi. "Presidential Power, Legislative Organization, and Party Behavior in Brazil." *Comparative Politics* 32, no. 2 (2000): 151–170.

Fiorina, Morris P. "Comment: Alternative Rationales for Restrictive Procedures." *Journal of Law, Economics, and Organization* 3, no. 2 (1987): 337–343.

Foa, Roberto Stefan, and Yascha Mounk. "The Democratic Disconnect." *Journal of Democracy* 27, no. 3 (2016): 5–17.

———. "The Signs of Deconsolidation." *Journal of Democracy* 28, no. 1 (2017): 5–15.

Foxall, Andrew, and John Hemmings, eds. *The Art of Deceit: How China and Russia Use Sharp Power to Subvert the West.* London: Henry Jackson Society, December 19, 2019.

Friedberg, Aaron. *A Contest for Supremacy: China, America, and the Struggle for Mastery in Asia.* New York: Norton, 2012.

Froman, Lewis. "Organization Theory and the Explanation of Important Characteristics of Congress." *American Political Science Review* 62, no. 2 (1968): 518–526.

Fu, Hu, and Yun-han Chu. "Neo-Authoritarianism, Polarized Conflict, and Populism in a Newly Democratizing Regime: Taiwan's Emerging Mass Politics." *Journal of Contemporary China* 5, no. 11 (Spring 1996): 23–41.

Fu, Yang-chih, Ying-hwa Chang, Su-hao Tu, and Pei-shan Liao. "Taiwan Social Change Survey 6-5." Taipei: National Science Council, 2015.

Fukuyama, Francis. "America in Decay: The Sources of Political Dysfunction." *Foreign Affairs,* September–October 2004. http://www.foreignaffairs.com/articles/united -states/2014-08-18/america-decay.

Fuller, Douglas B. "ECFA's Empty Promise and Hollow Threat." In *Political Changes in Taiwan Under Ma Ying-jeou: Partisan Conflict, Policy Choices, External Constraints, and Security Challenges,* edited by Jean-Pierre Cabestan and Jacques deLisle, 85–99. New York: Routledge, 2014.

Gasiorowski, Mark J., and Timothy J. Power. "The Structural Determinants of Democratic Consolidation: Evidence from the Third World." *Comparative Political Studies* 31, no. 6 (1998): 740–771.

Gilley, Bruce. "Not So Dire Straits: How the Finlandization of Taiwan Benefits U.S. Security." *Foreign Affairs* 89, no. 1 (2010): 44–56.

Gingrich, Newt. *Trump vs. China: Facing America's Greatest Threat.* New York: Center Street, 2019.

Glaser, Bonnie, and Brittany Billingsley. "Taiwan's 2012 Presidential Elections and Cross-Strait Relations: Implications for the United States." November 2011. https://www.csis.org/analysis/taiwan's-2012-presidential-elections-and-cross-strait -relations.

Glaser, Charles. "A U.S.-China Grand Bargain? The Hard Choice Between Military Competition and Accommodation." *International Security* 39, no. 4 (2015): 49–90.

Göbel, Christian. "The Quest for Good Governance: Taiwan's Fight Against Corruption." *Journal of Democracy* 27, no. 1 (2016): 124–138.

Gold, Thomas. "Civil Society and Taiwan's Quest for Identity." In *Cultural Change in Postwar Taiwan,* edited by Stevan Harrell and Chun-chieh Huang, 47–68. Boulder: Westview, 1994.

———. "Taiwan's Quest for Identity in the Shadow of China." In *In the Shadow of China: Political Development in Taiwan Since 1949,* edited by Steve Tsang, 169–192. Honolulu: University of Hawaii Press, 1993.

Goldstein, Avery. "U.S.-China Interactions in Asia." In *Tangled Titans: The U.S. and China,* edited by David Shambaugh, 263–292. Lanham: Rowman and Littlefield, 2013.

Grano, Simona A. *Environmental Governance in Taiwan: A New Generation of Activists.* London: Routledge, 2015.

Grugel, Jean. *Democratization: A Critical Introduction.* London: Palgrave Macmillan, 2002.

Haggard, Stephan. "The Institutional Foundations of Hegemony: Explaining the Reciprocal Trade Agreements Act of 1934." *International Organization* 53, no. 4 (1988): 669–698.

Hawang, Shiow-duan. "Executive-Legislative Relations Under Divided Government." In *Taiwan's Democracy Challenged: The Chen Shui-bian Years,* edited by Yun-han Chu, Larry Diamond, and Kharis Templeman. Boulder: Lynne Rienner, 2016.

Hayton, Bill. *The South China Sea: The Struggle for Power in Asia.* New Haven: Yale University Press, 2014.

Hedlund, Ronald D. "Organizational Attributes of Legislative Institutions: Structure, Rules, Norms, Resources." In *Handbook of Legislative Research,* edited by Gerhard Loewenberg, Samuel C. Patterson, and Malcolm E. Jewell, 321–394. Cambridge: Harvard University Press, 1984.

Hedlund, Ronald D., and Patricia K. Freeman. "A Strategy for Measuring the Performance of Legislatures in Processing Decisions." *Legislative Studies Quarterly* 6, no. 1 (1981): 87–113.

Heller, William B. "Making Policy Stick: Why the Government Gets What It Wants in Multiparty Parliaments." *American Journal of Political Science* 45, no. 4 (2001): 780–798.

Hicken, Allen D. *Building Party Systems in Developing Democracies.* New York: Cambridge University Press, 2009.

Hicken, Allen, and Eric Kuhonta, eds. *Party System Institutionalization in Asia: Democracies, Autocracies, and the Shadows of the Past.* New York: Cambridge University Press, 2015.

Ho, Ming-sho. "Civil Movement and Civil Disobedience: Two Paths of Recent Taiwan Social Movements" (in Chinese). *New Society for Taiwan* 30 (2013): 19–22.

———. "From Organizational Mobilization to Contingency: Enlightenment of Sunflower Student Movement." Presentation at the twentieth-anniversary academic seminar "Student Movement and Social Justice," Institute of Sociology, Taipei, 2015.

———. *Introduction to Social Movements* (in Chinese). Taipei: San Min, 2005.

———. "Occupy Congress in Taiwan: Political Opportunity, Threat, and the Sunflower Movement." *Journal of East Asian Studies* 15, no. 1 (2015): 69–97.

———. "Politics of Anti-Nuclear Protest in Taiwan." *Modern Asian Studies* 37, no. 3 (2003): 683–708.

———. "Resisting Naphtha Crackers: A Historical Survey of Environmental Politics in Taiwan." *China Perspectives* 99 (2014): 5–14.

———. "The Resurgence of Social Movements Under the Ma Ying-jeou Government." In *Political Changes in Taiwan Under Ma Ying-jeou,* edited by Jean-Pierre Cabestan and Jacques deLisle, 100–119. London: Routledge, 2014.

———. "Taiwan's State and Social Movements Under the DPP Government, 2000–2004." *Journal of East Asian Studies* 5, no. 3 (2005): 401–425.

———. "Understanding the Trajectory of Social Movements in Taiwan (1980–2010)." *Journal of Current Chinese Affairs* 39, no. 3 (2010): 3–22.

Ho, Run-hsin. "The Healing Effect of the White-Shirts Army" (in Chinese). *Commonwealth Magazine,* August 22, 2013. https://www.cw.com.tw/article/article.action?id=5051584.

Ho, Szu-yin. "Trade Politics in Taiwan." In *From ECFA to TPP* (in Chinese), edited by Tien-zi Chen and Daniel Liu, 255–283. Taipei: The Prospect Foundation, 2014.

Horton, Chris. "Taiwan's Ex-President Ma Ying-jeou Indicted in Wiretapping Case." *New York Times,* March 14, 2017. https://www.nytimes.com/2017/03/14/world/asia/taiwan-president-ma-ying-jeou-charged.html.

Hsiao, Hsin-huang Michael. "Emerging Social Movements and the Rise of a Demanding Civil Society in Taiwan." *Australian Journal of Chinese Affairs* 24 (1990): 163–180.

Hsiao, Hsin-huang Michael, and Ming-sho Ho. "East Asia's New Democracies: Deepening, Reversal, Non-Liberal Alternatives." In *Civil Society and Democracy Making in Taiwan: Reexamining the Link,* edited by Yin-wah Chu and Siu-lun Wong, 61–82. London: Routledge, 2010.

Hsiao, Hsin-huang Michael, and Yu-yuan Kuan. "The Development of Civil Society Organizations in Post-Authoritarian Taiwan (1988–2014)." In *Routledge Handbook of Contemporary Taiwan,* edited by Gunther Schubert, 253–267. London: Routledge, 2016.

Hsiao, Yuan. "How the Internet Impacts Social Movement: A Case Study of the Taiwan Wild Strawberry Movement" (in Chinese). *Taiwan Democracy Quarterly* 8, no. 3 (2011): 45–85.

Hsieh, John Fuh-sheng. "Continuity and Change in Party Politics in Japan, Taiwan, and South Korea." *East Asian Policy* 5, no. 76 (2013): 76–85.

———. "Ethnicity, National Identity, and Domestic Politics in Taiwan." *Journal of Asian and African Studies* 40, no. 13 (April 2005): 13–28.

———. "Taiwan in 2013: Stalemate at Home, Some Headway Abroad." *Asian Survey* 54, no. 1 (2014): 145–150.

———. "Taiwan's General Elections of 2016." In *Taiwan's Political Re-Alignment and Diplomatic Challenges,* edited by Wei-chin Lee, 49–65. London: Palgrave Macmillan, 2019.

Hsieh, John Fuh-sheng, and Emerson M. S. Niou. "Salient Issues in Taiwan's Electoral Politics." *Electoral Studies* 15, no. 2 (1996): 219–235.

Hsieh, Jui-ming. "Democratic Progressive Party's Factionalism: 2000–2008." PhD dissertation, Graduate School of Political Science, Chinese Culture University, Taipei, 2013.

Hsu, Philip. "Between Identity Quest and Risk Aversion: Lessons from the Chen Shui-bian Presidency for Maintaining Cross-Strait Stability." *Journal of Contemporary China* 19, no. 66 (2010): 693–717.

Hsu, Shih-hsien. "Gender Gap and Voting Behavior: Comparison Between the Three Presidential Elections." Master's thesis, Department of Political Science, National Chengchi University, Taipei, 2005.

Hsu, Szu-chien. "The China Factor and Taiwan's Civil Society in the Sunflower Movement." In *Taiwan's Social Movements Under Ma Ying-jeou: From the Wild Strawberries to the Sunflowers,* edited by Dafydd Fell, 134–153. London: Routledge, 2017.

Hsu, Yung-ming, and Houng-chang Chen. "Intra-Party Factional Competition and the Fate of the Party Election: A Case Study of the Democratic Progressive Party" (in Chinese). *Taiwan Journal of Political Science* 31 (2007): 129–174.

Hu, Fu. *Political Culture and Political Life* (in Chinese). Taipei: Sanmin, 1998.

Hu, Weixing. Introduction to *New Dynamics in Cross-Taiwan-Strait Relations*, edited by Hu Weixing, 1–9. New York: Routledge, 2013.

Huang, Chang-ling. "Uneasy Alliance: State Feminism and the Conservative Government." In *Taiwan's Social Movements Under Ma Ying-jeou: From the Wild Strawberries to the Sunflowers*, edited by Dafydd Fell, 258–272. London: Routledge, 2017.

Huang, Chi. "Dimensions of Taiwanese/Chinese Identity and National Identity in Taiwan." *Journal of Asian and African Studies* 40, nos. 1–2 (2005): 50–70.

———. "Generation Effects? Evolution of Independence-Unification Views in Taiwan, 1996–2016." *Electoral Studies* 58 (2019): 103–112.

———. "Taiwan's Election and Democratization Study, 2012–2016." Pt. 3, "Survey of the Nine-in-One Local Elections, 2014 (TEDS2014)." Taipei: Ministry of Science and Technology, 2014.

———. "Taiwan's Election and Democratization Study, 2012–2016." Pt. 4, "Survey of the Presidential and Legislative Elections, 2016 (TEDS2016)." Taipei: Ministry of Science and Technology, 2016.

———. "Taiwan's Election and Democratization Study, 2016–2020." Pt. 1, "Quasi-Experiment on Two Sampling Frames for Face-to-Face Survey (TEDS2017)." Taipei: Ministry of Science and Technology, 2017.

Huang, Chi, and T. Y. Wang. "Presidential Coattails in Taiwan: An Analysis of Voter- and Candidate-Specific Data." *Electoral Studies* 33 (2014): 175–185.

Huang, Shih-hao. "How Formal Parliamentary Negotiation Affects Policymaking: Evidence from Taiwan." *Parliamentary Affairs* 72, no. 3 (2019): 702–723.

Hughes, Christopher. "Revisiting Identity Politics Under Ma Ying-jeou." In *Political Changes in Taiwan Under Ma Ying-jeou*, edited by Jean-Pierre Cabestan and Jacques deLisle, 120–136. New York: Routledge, 2014.

Hung, Rudy. "The Great U-Turn in Taiwan: Economic Restructuring and a Surge in Inequality." *Journal of Contemporary Asia* 26, no. 2 (1996): 151–163.

Huntington, Samuel P. *The Third Wave: Democratization in the Late Twentieth Century.* Norman: University of Oklahoma Press, 1991.

Inglehart, Ronald. *Cultural Evolution: People's Motivations Are Changing, and Reshaping the World.* Cambridge: Cambridge University Press, 2018.

Inglehart, Ronald F., and Pippa Norris. "Trump, Brexit, and the Rise of Populism: Economic Have-Nots and Cultural Backlash." Faculty Research Working Paper no. RWP16–26. Cambridge: Kennedy School of Government, Harvard University, April 2016.

International Monetary Fund. *World Economic Outlook Database.* https://www.imf.org /external/pubs/ft/weo/2019/02/weodata/index.aspx.

Israel, Jonathan Irvine. *The Dutch Republic: Its Rise, Greatness, and Fall, 1477–1806.* Oxford: Oxford University Press, 1995.

Ker, Chien-ming. *Big Picture, Major Responsibility* (in Chinese). Taipei: Third-Nature, 2017.

Key, V. O. "A Theory of Critical Elections." *Journal of Politics* 17, no. 1 (1955): 3–18.

Kiewiet, D. Roderick, and Mathew D. McCubbins. *The Logic of Delegation: Congressional Parties and the Appropriations Process.* Chicago: University of Chicago Press, 1991.

Kinkel, Jonathan, and William Hurst. "Review Essay—Access to Justice in Post-Mao China: Assessing the Politics of Criminal and Administrative Law." *Journal of East Asian Studies* 11, no. 3 (2011): 467–499.

Klingemann, Hans-Dieter. "Mapping Political Support in the 1990s: A Global Analysis." In *Critical Citizens: Global Support for Democratic Government*, edited by Pippa Norris, 31–56. New York: Oxford University Press, 1999.

Ko, Ernie, Yu-chang Su, and Chilik Yu. "Sibling Rivalry Among Anti-Corruption Agencies in Taiwan." *Asian Education and Development Studies* 4, no. 1 (2015): 101–124.

Krehbiel, Keith. *Information and Legislative Organization.* Ann Arbor: University of Michigan Press, 1992.

Kriesi, Hanspeter, and Takis S. Pappas, eds. *European Populism in the Shadow of the Great Recession.* Colchester: ECPR, 2015.

Kuan, Ping-yin. "Generational Differences in Attitudes Toward Cross-Strait Trade." Paper presented at the conference "Political Polarization in Taiwan," Stanford University, March 2014.

Kurlantzick, Jonathan. "Why the 'China Model' Isn't Going Away." *The Atlantic,* March 21, 2013. https://www.theatlantic.com/china/archive/2013/03/why-the-china-model -isnt-going-away/274237/.

Kydd, Andrew. *Trust and Mistrust in International Relations.* Princeton: Princeton University Press, 2005.

La Due Lake, Ronald, and Robert Huckfeldt. "Social Capital, Social Networks, and Political Participation." *Political Psychology* 19, no. 3 (1998): 567–584.

Lee, Pei-shan. "Dismantling Developmentalism in Taiwan." Paper presented at the conference "Dismantling Developmentalism: Japan, Korea, Taiwan," organized by Institute of East Asian Studies, University of California, Berkeley, October 23–24, 2015.

Lee, Pei-shan, and Yun-han Chu. "Cross-Strait Economic Integration, 1992–2015." In *Routledge Handbook of Contemporary Taiwan,* edited by Gunther Schubert, 409–424. New York: Routledge, 2016.

Lee, Wei-chin. "A Quartet in Disharmony: Taiwan, Japan, China, and the U.S. in the Diaoyu (Tai)/Senkaku Islands Dispute in the 2010s." *American Journal of Chinese Studies* 21 (2014): 95–109.

Leng, Tse-kang, and Nien-chung Chang Liao. "Hedging, Strategic Partnership, and Taiwan's Relations with Japan Under the Ma Ying-jeou Administration." *Pacific Focus* 31, no. 3 (2017): 357–382.

Liao, Da-chi, and Yueh-ching Chen. "The Effect of Social Movements on Representative Deficit: A Study of Two Taiwanese Cases." *Taiwan Journal of Democracy* 13, no. 2 (2017): 73–106.

Lin, Chung-chu. "The Evolution of Party Images and Party System in Taiwan, 1992–2004." *East Asia: An International Quarterly* 23, no. 1 (2006): 27–46.

Lin, Shirley. *Taiwan's China Dilemma: Contested Identities and Multiple Interests in Taiwan's Cross-Strait Economic Policy.* Stanford: Stanford University Press, 2016.

Lin, Thung-hong. "Cross-Strait Trade and Class Cleavages in Taiwan." In *Taiwan and the "China Factor": Challenges and Opportunities,* edited by Gunther Schubert, 174–195. London: Routledge, 2016.

Lin, Tse-min, and Yen-pin Su. "Flash-Mob Politics in Taiwan: New Media, Political Parties, and Social Movements" (in Chinese). *Taiwan Democracy Quarterly* 12, no. 2 (2015): 123–159.

Lin, Tsong-jyi, and Ching-hsin Yu. "Party Image and Voting Behavior of Taiwanese Voters: Analysis of the Presidential Elections, 1996–2008" (in Chinese). In *2008 Presidential Election,* edited by Lu-huei Chen, Ching-hsin Yu, and Huang Chi, 178–208. Taipei: Wu-nan, 2009.

Linz, Juan J., and Alfred Stepan. *Problems of Democratic Transition and Consolidation: Southern Europe, South America, and Post-Communist Europe.* Baltimore: Johns Hopkins University Press, 1996.

Liu, Shih-chun, and Herng Su. "Mediating the Sunflower Movement: Hybrid Media Networks in a Digital Age" (in Chinese). *Journal of Information Society* 33 (2017): 147–188.

Mainwaring, Scott, and Timothy R. Scully, eds. *Building Democratic Institutions: Party Systems in Latin America.* Stanford: Stanford University Press, 1995.

Manion, Melanie. *Information for Autocrats: Representation in Chinese Local Congresses.* New York: Cambridge University Press, 2016.

Martin, Lisa L. *Democratic Commitments: Legislatures and International Cooperation.* Princeton: Princeton University Press, 2000.

Mattson, Ingvar. "Private Members' Initiatives and Amendments." In *Parliaments and Majority Rule in Western Europe,* edited by Herbert Döring, 448–487. Frankfurt: Campus, 1995.

Mayhew, David. "Electoral Realignments." *Annual Review of Political Science* 3 (2000): 449–474.

Mearsheimer, John J. "Taiwan's Dire Straits." *National Interest* 130, no. 1 (2014): 29–39.

Mercer, Jonathan. *Reputation and International Politics.* Ithaca: Cornell University Press, 2010.

McAllister, Ian. "Democratic Consolidation in Taiwan in Comparative Perspective." *Asian Journal of Comparative Politics* 1, no. 1 (2016): 44–61.

Milanovic, Branko. *Globalization and Inequality.* Cambridge: Harvard University Press, 2016.

Minzner, Carl. *End of An Era: How China's Authoritarian Revival Is Undermining Its Rise.* Oxford: Oxford University Press, 2018.

Mishler, William and Richard Rose. "Learning and Re-Learning Regime Support: The Dynamics of Post-Communist Regimes." *European Journal of Political Research* 41, no. 1 (2002): 5–36.

Momesso, Lara, and Isabelle Cheng. "A Team Player Pursuing Its Own Dreams: Rights-Claim Campaign of Chinese Migrant Spouses Before and After 2008." In *Taiwan's Social Movements Under Ma Ying-jeou: From the Wild Strawberries to the Sunflowers,* edited by Dafydd Fell, 219–235. London: Routledge, 2017.

Montgomery, Evan Braden. "Contested Primacy in the Western Pacific: China's Rise and the Future of U.S. Power Projection." *International Security* 38, no. 4 (Spring 2014): 115–149.

Morgenthau, Hans. *Politics Among Nations.* New York: McGraw-Hill, 1985.

Murray, William S. "Revisiting Taiwan's Defense Strategy." *Naval War College Review* 61, no. 3 (2008): 12–39.

Muyard, Frank. "Taiwan Elections 2008: Ma Ying-jeou's Victory and the KMT's Return to Power." *China Perspectives* no. 1 (January 2008): 79–94.

Nachman, Lev. "Misalignment Between Social Movements and Political Parties in Taiwan's 2016 Election." *Asian Survey* 58, no. 5 (2018): 874–897.

Nalepa, Monik. "Party Institutionalization and Legislative Organization: The Evolution of Agenda Power in the Polish Parliament." *Comparative Politics* 48, no. 3 (2016): 353–372.

Newton, Kenneth. "Institutional Confidence and Social Trust: Aggregate and Individual Relations." In *Political Disaffection in Contemporary Democracies: Social Capital, Institutions, and Politics,* edited by Mariano Torcal and José R. Montero, 81–100. London: Routledge, 2006.

Norris, Pippa. *Democratic Deficit: Critical Citizens Revisited.* New York: Cambridge University Press, 2011.

———. "Introduction: The Growth of Critical Citizens." In *Critical Citizens: Global Support for Democratic Government,* edited by Pippa Norris, 1–30. New York: Oxford University Press, 1999.

Olson, David M., and Philip Norton. "Legislatures in Democratic Transition." *Legislative Studies* 2, no. 1 (1996): 1–15.

Organization for Economic Cooperation and Development. "Review Statistics for Asian and Pacific Economies 2019: The Philippines." https://www.oecd.org/countries /philippines/revenue-statistics-asia-and-pacific-philippines.pdf.

———. "Revenue Statistics 2019: Tax Revenue Trends in the OECD." https://www .oecd.org/tax/tax-policy/revenue-statistics-highlights-brochure.pdf.

Park, Chong-min, and Yu-tzung Chang. "Regime Performance and Democratic Legitimacy." In *Democracy in East Asia: A New Century,* edited by Larry Diamond, Marc F. Plattner, and Yun-han Chu, 48–71. Baltimore: Johns Hopkins University Press, 2013.

Passarelli, Gianluca, ed. *The Presidentialization of Political Parties: Organizations, Institutions, and Leaders.* New York: Springer, 2015.

Phillips, Steven. "Why Taiwan? ROC Leaders Explain Taiwan's Strategic Value." In *The U.S. Strategic Pivot to Asia and Cross-Strait Relations,* edited by Peter Chow, 159–177. New York: Palgrave Macmillan, 2014.

Plattner, Marc F. "Liberal Democracy's Fading Allure." *Journal of Democracy* 28, no. 4 (2017): 5–14.

Przeworski, Adam, Michael Alvares, Jose A. Cheibub, and Fernando Limongi. "What Makes Democracies Endure?" In *Consolidating the Third Wave Democracies,* edited by Larry Diamond, Marc Plattner, Yun-han Chu, and Hung-mao Tien, 295–311. Baltimore: Johns Hopkins University Press, 1997.

Putnam, Robert. "Bowling Alone: America's Declining Social Capital." *Journal of Democracy* 6, no. 1 (1995): 65–78.

Quah, Jon S. T. *Curbing Corruption in Asian Countries: An Impossible Dream?* Bingley, UK: Emerald Group, 2011.

Rasch, Bjorn Erick, and George Tsebelis. "Norway: Institutionally Weak Governments and Parliamentary Voting on Bills." In *The Role of Governments in Legislative Agenda Setting,* edited by Bjorn Erik Rasch and George Tsebelis, 254–273. New York: Routledge, 2011.

Rawnsley, Ming-yeh T. "New Civic Movements and Further Democratisation in Taiwan." April 29, 2014. https://cpianalysis.org/2014/04/29/new-civic-movements-and-further -democratisation-in-taiwan.

Rich, Timothy S. "Coattails and Mixed Electoral Systems: Evidence from Taiwan's 2016 Election." *Journal of East Asian Studies* 18 (2018): 47–66.

Rigger, Shelley. *From Opposition to Power: Taiwan's Democratic Progressive Party.* Boulder: Lynne Rienner, 2001.

———. "Party Politics and Elections: The Road to 2008." In *Taiwan's Democracy Challenged: The Chen Shui-bian Years,* edited by Yun-han Chu, Larry Diamond, and Kharis Templeman, 29–50. Boulder: Lynne Rienner, 2016.

———. "Political Parties and Identity Politics in Taiwan." In *New Challenges for Maturing Democracies in Korea and Taiwan,* edited by Larry Diamond and Gi-wook Shin, 106–132. Stanford: Stanford University Press, 2014.

———. *Politics in Taiwan: Voting for Reform.* New York: Routledge, 1999.

———. "Taiwan's Presidential and Legislative Elections." *Orbis* 52, no. 4 (2008): 689–700.

———. *Taiwan's Rising Rationalism: Generations, Politics, and "Taiwanese Nationalism."* Washington, DC: East-West Center, 2006.

———. *Why Taiwan Matters: Small Island, Global Powerhouse.* Lanham: Rowman and Littlefield, 2013.

Rodrik, Dani. *The Globalization Paradox: Democracy and the Future of the World Economy.* New York: Norton, 2012.

———. "Populism and the Economics of Globalization." *Journal of International Business Policy* 1, nos. 1–2 (2018): 12–33.

Rolland, Nadège. "China's Eurasian Century? Political and Strategic Implications of the Belt and Road Initiative." Washington, DC: National Bureau of Asian Research, 2017.

Romberg, Alan. "Consolidating Positions." *China Leadership Monitor* no. 48 (Fall 2015), https://www.hoover.org/research/consolidating-positions.

———. "The '1992 Consensus'—Adapting to the Future?" *China Leadership Monitor* no. 49 (Winter 2016), https://www.hoover.org/research/1992-consensus-adapting-future.

———. "Squaring the Circle: Adhering to Principle, Embracing Ambiguity." *China Leadership Monitor* no. 47 (Summer 2015), https://www.hoover.org/research/squaring -circle-adhering-principle-embracing-ambiguity.

———. "The 2012 Taiwan Election: Off and Running." *China Leadership Monitor* no. 35 (Summer 2011), https://www.hoover.org/research/2012-taiwan-election-and-running.

Rose, Richard, Willian Mishler, and Christian Haerpfer. *Democracy and Its Alternatives: Understanding Post-Communist Society.* Baltimore: Johns Hopkins University Press, 1998.

Rosecrance, Richard, and Arthur A. Stein, eds. *The Domestic Bases of Grand Strategy.* Ithaca: Cornell University Press, 1993.

Rowen, Ian. "Inside Taiwan's Sunflower Movement: Twenty-four Days in a Student-Occupied Parliament, and the Future of the Region." *Journal of Asian Studies* 74, no. 1 (2015): 5–21.

———. "Tourism as a Territorial Strategy: The Case of China and Taiwan." *Annals of Tourism Research* 46 (2014): 62–74.

Sahashi, Ryo, and Jean-Pierre Cabestan. "Japan-Taiwan Relations Since 2008: An Evolving Practical, Non-Strategic Partnership." In *Political Changes in Taiwan Under Ma Ying-jeou,* edited by Jean-Pierre Cabestan and Jacques deLisle, 232–246. New York: Routledge, 2014.

Samuels, David J., and Matthew S. Shugart. *Presidents, Parties, and Prime Ministers: How the Separation of Powers Affects Party Organization and Behavior.* New York: Cambridge University Press, 2010.

Sanborn, Howard. "Democratic Consolidation: Participation and Attitudes Toward Democracy in Taiwan and South Korea." *Journal of Elections, Public Opinion, and Parties* 25, no. 1 (2015): 47–61.

Schattschneider, E. E. *The Semisovereign People: A Realist's View of Democracy in America.* New York: Holt, Rinehart, Winston, 1960.

Schedler, Andreas. "Measuring Democratic Consolidation." *Studies in Comparative International Development* 36, no. 1 (2001): 66–92.

———. "What Is Democratic Consolidation?" *Journal of Democracy* 9, no. 2 (1998): 91–107.

Schedler, Andreas, and Rodolfo Sarsfield. "Democrats with Adjectives: Linking Direct and Indirect Measures of Democratic Support." *European Journal of Political Research* 46, no. 5 (2007): 637–659.

Schmitter, Philippe C. "Crisis and Transition, but Not Decline." *Journal of Democracy* 26, no. 1 (2015): 32–44.

Schubert, Gunter. "Taiwan's Political Parties and National Identity: The Rise of an Over-arching Consensus." *Asian Survey* 44, no. 4 (2004): 534–554.

Schubert, Gunter, and Stefan Braig. "How to Face an Embracing China? The DPP's Identity Politics and Cross-Strait Relations During and After the Chen Shui-bian Era." In *Taiwanese Identity in the Twenty-First Century,* edited by Gunter Schubert and Jens Damm, 72–94. New York: Routledge, 2011.

Schweller, Randall L. "Bandwagoning for Profits: Bringing the Revisionist State Back In." *International Security* 19, no.1 (1994): 72–107.

Shambaugh, David. *China Goes Global: The Partial Power.* New York: Oxford University Press, 2013.

Shelling, Thomas. *Arms and Influence.* New Haven: Yale University Press, 1966.

Sheng, Shing-yuan, and Shih-hao Huang. "Decentralized Legislative Organization and Its Consequences for Policymaking." Paper presented at the 2015 Stanford Taiwan Democracy Project annual conference, Stanford University, October 26–27, 2015.

———. "Party Negotiation Mechanism: An Analysis Through the Lens of Institutionaliza-tion" (in Chinese). *Soochow Journal of Political Science* 35, no. 1 (2017): 37–92.

Sheng, Shing-yuan, and Hsiao-chuan (Mandy) Liao. "Issues, Political Cleavages, and Party Competition in Taiwan." In *The Taiwan Voter,* edited by Christopher H. Achen and T. Y. Wang, 98–138. Ann Arbor: University of Michigan Press, 2017.

Shepsle, Kenneth A., and Barry R. Weingast. "Structure-Induced Equilibrium and Leg-islative Choice." *Public Choice* 37, no. 3 (1981): 503–519.

Shiao, Yi-ching. "The Seniority System in the Legislative Yuan in Taiwan: Change of the Transfers Among Committees and the Convener's Seniority" (in Chinese). *Taiwanese Journal of Political Science* 25 (2005): 105–134.

Shih, Yen-ting. "Timing of Elections, Party Presidentialization, and Party System Nation-alization: A Case Study of the DPP (2008–2016)" (in Chinese). Master's thesis, Department of Political Science, National Taiwan University, Taipei, 2016.

Shin, Doh C. "Democratization: Perspectives from Global Citizenry." In *The Oxford Handbook of Political Behavior,* edited by Russell J. Dalton and Hana-Dieter Klingemann, 259–282. New York: Oxford University Press, 2007.

Shugart, Matthew S., and John Carey. *Presidents and Assemblies: Constitutional Design and Electoral Dynamics.* New York: Cambridge University Press, 1992.

Shullman, David. "Protect the Party: China's Growing Influence in the Developing World." January 22, 2019. https://www.brookings.edu/articles/protect-the-party-chinas-growing -influence-in-the-developing-world.

Shyu, Huo-yan. "Trust in Institutions and the Democratic Consolidation in Taiwan." In *Taiwan's Politics in the 21st Century: Changes and Challenges,* edited by Wei-chin Lee, 69–100. Hackensack, NJ: World Scientific, 2010.

Sia, Ek-hong Lajavakaw. "Nationalist Dealignment in 2014, Realignment in 2016?" *Thinking Taiwan,* November 11, 2014. http://thinking-taiwan.com/nationalist-dealignment -in-2014-realignment-in-2016.

Singleton, Fred. "The Myth of 'Finlandisation.'" *International Affairs* 57, no. 2 (1981): 270–285.

Smith, C. Donovan. "The Coming Collapse of the KMT?" *China Policy Analysis,* May 14, 2015. https://cpianalysis.org/2015/05/14/the-coming-collapse-of-the-kmt.

Smith, Stephen, and Ching-hsin Yu. "Wild Lilies and Sunflowers: Political Actors' Responses to Student Movements in Taiwan." Paper presented at the fifty-sixth annual conference of the American Association for Chinese Studies on China, Hong Kong, Taiwan, and the Chinese Diaspora, Washington, DC, 2014.

Stanley, Harold W. "Southern Partisan Changes: Dealignment, Realignment, or Both?" *Journal of Politics* 50, no. 1 (1988): 64–88.

Stockmann, Daniela. *Media Commercialization and Authoritarian Rule in China.* Cambridge: Cambridge University Press, 2013.

Stockton, Hans. "National Identity, International Image, and a Security Dilemma: The Case of Taiwan." In *The "One China" Dilemma,* edited by Peter Chow, 99–115. New York: Palgrave Macmillan, 2008.

Strøm, Karre. "Parliamentary Committees in European Democracies." *Journal of Legislative Studies* 4, no. 1 (1998): 21–59.

Stromseth, Jonathan R., Edmund J. Malesky, and Dimitar D. Gueorguiev. *China's Governing Puzzle: Enabling Transparency and Participation in a One-Party State.* New York: Cambridge University Press, 2017.

Su, Chi. *Taiwan's Relations with Mainland China: A Tail Wagging Two Dogs.* London and New York: Routledge, 2008.

———. *To the Brink: From Two State Theory to One Country on Each Side* (in Chinese). Taipei: Bookzone, 2003.

Su, Herng, Tai-ta Kuo, Jin-gu Pan, Yan-heng Cao, and Bing-yi Chen. "Online Communication Network for Disseminating Emotion-Provoking Events During the Taiwanese Presidential Elections of 2016: An Analysis of Online Political Discussions." Paper presented at the annual conference of Chinese Communication Society, Chiayi, Taiwan, 2016.

Sullivan, Jonathan, and Michael Thim. "Here Comes Taiwan's Big Political Realignment." *National Interest,* December 3, 2014. http://nationalinterest.org/feature/here-comes -taiwan's-big-political-realignment-11774.

Sun, Ying. "Municipal People's Congress Elections in the PRC: A Process of Cooptation." *Journal of Contemporary China* 23, no. 85 (2014): 183–195.

Sundquist, J. L. *Dynamics of the Party System: Alignment and Realignment of Political Parties in the United States.* Washington, DC: Brookings Institution, 1973.

Sutter, Robert. "More American Attention to Taiwan amid Heightened Competition with China." *American Journal of Chinese Studies* 22, no. 1 (2015): 1–16.

Sutter, Robert, Michael Brown, Timothy Adamson, Mike Mochizuki, and Deepa Ollapally. *Balancing Acts: The U.S. Rebalance and Asia-Pacific Stability.* Washington, DC: Sigur Center for Asian Studies, Elliott School of International Affairs, George Washington University, 2013.

———. *Chinese Foreign Relations: Power and Policy Since the Cold War.* Lanham: Rowman and Littlefield, 2016.

———. *The United States and Asia: Regional Dynamics and Twenty-First Century Relations.* Lanham: Rowman and Littlefield, 2020.

Tabata, Mayumi. "Material Resources Raising Mechanism of Sunflower: Social Media and Social Capital." Presentation at the twentieth-anniversary academic seminar "Student Movement and Social Justice," Academia Sinica, Institute of Sociology, Taipei, 2015.

Taiwan Network Information Center. *Taiwan Internet Experience Survey.* 2017. https:// www.twnic.net.tw/webstatistic.php.

Tang, Shui-yan, and Ching-ping Tang. "Democratization and Environmental Politics in Taiwan." *Asian Survey* 37, no. 3 (1997): 281–294.

Tellis, Ashley. "Balancing Without Containment: A U.S. Strategy for Confronting China's Rise." *Washington Quarterly* 36, no. 4 (2013): 109–124.

Templeman, Kharis. "Blessings in Disguise: How Authoritarian Legacies and the China Factor Have Strengthened Democracy in Taiwan." *International Journal of Taiwan Studies* 2, no. 2 (2019): 230–263.

Templeman, Kharis, Larry Diamond, and Yun-han Chu. "Taiwan's Democracy Under Chen Shui-bian." In *Taiwan's Democracy Challenged: The Chen Shui-bian Years,* edited by Chu Yun-han, Larry Diamond, and Kharis Templeman, 1–28. Boulder: Lynne Rienner, 2016.

Thomassen, Jacques. "Democracy Values." In *The Oxford Handbook of Contextual Political Analysis,* edited by Russell J. Dalton and Hans-Dieter Kligemann, 418–434. New York: Oxford University Press, 2007.

Tonnesson, Stein. "The South China Sea." *Asian Survey* 55, no. 3 (2015): 455–477.

"The Transpacific Partnership and Taiwan's Future Development Strategy." Conference report. Taiwan Democracy Project, Stanford University, January 2014.

Tsai, I-lun, and Ming-sho Ho. "The Tale of Two Off-Shore Islands: Anti-Casino Movements in Penghu and Mazu." In *Taiwan's Social Movements Under Ma Ying-jeou: From the Wild Strawberries to the Sunflowers,* edited by Dafydd Fell, 54–70. London: Routledge, 2017.

Tsang, Steve, and Hung-mao Tien, eds. *Democratization in Taiwan: Implications for China.* London: Macmillan, 1999.

Tsebelis, George. *Veto Players: How Political Institutions Work.* Princeton: Princeton University Press, 2002.

Tseng, Yu-chin, Isabelle Cheng, and Dafydd Fell. "The Politics of the Mainland Spouses' Rights' Movement in Taiwan." In *Migration to and from Taiwan,* edited by Dafydd Fell, Kuei-fen Chiu, and Ping Lin, 205–226. London: Routledge, 2013.

Tucker, Nancy. *Strait Talk: United States–Taiwan Relations and the Crisis with China.* Cambridge: Harvard University Press, 2009.

Tucker, Nancy, and Bonnie Glaser. "Should the United States Abandon Taiwan?" *Washington Quarterly* 34, no. 4 (2011): 23–37.

TVBS Poll Center. https://www.tvbs.com.tw/poll-center/1.

van der Horst, Linda. "The Rise of Taiwan's 'Third Force.'" *The Diplomat,* January 6, 2016. http://thediplomat.com/2016/01/the-rise-of-taiwans-third-force.

Wachman, Alan M. "Competing Identities in Taiwan." In *The Other Taiwan: 1945 to the Present,* edited by Murray Rubinstein, 17–80. Armonk, N.Y.: Sharpe, 1994.

Walt, Stephen M. *The Origins of Alliances.* Ithaca: Cornell University Press, 1987.

Wang, Austin Horng-en. "Democratic Progressive Party's Online Campaigning Strategy, 1990–2016." Paper presented at the International Workshop on Parties online conference "New Party Organizational Strategies in 8 Democracies," National Sun Yat-sen University, Kaohsiung, Taiwan, December 14–16, 2016.

Wang, Austin Horng-En, and Fang-yu Chen. "Extreme Candidates as the Beneficent Spoiler? Range Effect in the Plurality Voting System." *Political Research Quarterly* 72, no. 2 (2019): 278–292.

Wang, James W. Y., Sheng-mao Chen, and Cheng-tian Kuo. "Restructuring State-Business Relations." In *Taiwan's Democracy Challenged: The Chen Shui-bian Years,* edited by Yun-han Chu, Larry Diamond, and Kharis Templeman, 241–266. Boulder: Lynne Rienner, 2016.

Wang, Song-in. "The Political Use of Social Media and Civic Engagement in Taiwan" (in Chinese). *Journal of Information Society* 3 (2017): 83–111.

Wang, Tai-li. "Facebook Election? The Impact of Social Media on Political Participation in Taiwan's 2012 Presidential Elections" (in Chinese). *Soochow Journal of Political Science* 31, no. 1 (2015): 1–52.

Wang, Te-yu, Wei-chin Lee, and Ching-hsin Yu. "Taiwan's Expansion of International Space: Opportunities and Challenges." *Journal of Contemporary China* 20, no. 69 (2011): 249–267.

Wang, Wei-ching, Chi-han Ma, and Chao-wei Chen. "The Social Movements in the Internet Age: Taiwan's Environmental Movement Organizations as an Example" (in Chinese). *Journal of Information Society* 25 (2013): 1–22.

Wang, Yuhua. *Tying the Autocrat's Hands: The Rise of Rule of Law in China.* New York: Cambridge University Press, 2015.

Wang, Zheng. "Chinese Discourse on the 'Nine-Dashed Line.'" *Asian Survey* 55, no. 3 (2015): 502–524.

Weber, Wiebke, and Willem Saris. "Explaining Trust in Political Institutions—Before and After Correction for Measurement Error." Paper presented at the WAPOR conference "Political Trust in Contemporary Representative Democracies," Barcelona, November 24–25, 2016.

Wei, Hao, and Zheng Chen. "ECFA: Its Impact on the Economy of Taiwan and Mainland China and Development Outlook." *Asia-Pacific Economic Review* 4 (2010): 1–25.

Weingast, Barry R., and William Marshall. "The Industrial Organization of Congress." *Journal of Political Economy* 96, no. 1 (1988): 132–163.

Winckler, Edwin A. "Institutionalization and Participation on Taiwan: From Hard to Soft Authoritarianism?" *China Quarterly* 99 (September 1984): 481–499.

Wright, Teresa. "Student Mobilization in Taiwan: Civil Society and Its Discontents." *Asian Survey* 39, no. 6 (1999): 986–1008.

Wu, Charles Chong-han. "Taiwan's Hedging Against China: The Strategic Implications of Ma Ying-jeou's Policy." *Asian Survey* 56, no. 3 (2016): 466–487.

Wu, Sara, Monique Hou, and Hsiang-yi Chang. "Taiwan Needs Radical Tax Reform." *Commonwealth,* June 11, 2014. https://english.cw.com.tw/article/article.action?id=392.

Wu, Yan-lin. "Letter from Taiwan: Outcry from the White-Shirt Army." *BBC Chinese,* July 25, 2013. http://www.bbc.com/zhongwen/trad/taiwan_letters/2013/07/130725 _twletter_white_shirts.

Wu, Yu-shan. "Appointing the Prime Minister Under Incongruence: Taiwan in Comparison with France and Russia." *Taiwan Journal of Democracy* 1, no. 2 (2005): 103–132.

———. "The Evolution of the KMT's Stance on the One China Principle: National Identity in Flux." In *Taiwanese Identity in the Twenty-First Century,* edited by Gunter Schubert and Jens Damm, 51–71. New York: Routledge, 2011.

———. "From Identity to Distribution: Paradigm Shift in Taiwan Politics—A First Cut." Paper presented at the American Association of Chinese Studies Annual Conference, Rutgers University, Oct 11–13, 2013.

———. "Taiwan's Developmental State: After the Economic and Political Turmoil." *Asian Survey* 47, no. 6 (November–December 2007): 977–1001.

Yang, Wan-ying, and Pei-ting Lin. "Do Women Transfer Their Votes to Tsai? The Change of Gender Gap from 2008 to 2012 Presidential Election" (in Chinese). *Electoral Studies* 20, no. 2 (2013): 37–71.

Yu, Ching-hsin. "The Evolving Party System in Taiwan, 1995–2004." *Journal of Asian and African Studies* 40, nos. 1–2 (2005): 105–123.

———. "Taiwan's Election and Democratization Study, 2005–2008." Pt. 4, "The Presidential Election, 2008 (TEDS2008P)." Taipei: National Science Council, 2008.

Yu, Eric. "Partisanship and Public Opinion." In *Taiwan's Democracy Challenged: The Chen Shui-bian Years,* edited by Yun-han Chu, Larry Diamond, and Kharis Templeman, 73–94. Boulder: Lynne Rienner, 2016.

Zhen, Bijian. "China's 'Peaceful Rise' to Great Power Status." *Foreign Affairs* 84 (September–October 2005): 18–24.

Zucchini, Francesco. "Italy: Government Alternation and Legislative Agenda Setting." In *The Role of Governments in Legislative Agenda Setting,* edited by Bjorn Erik Rasch and George Tsebelis, 288–325. New York: Routledge, 2011.

The Contributors

Nathan F. Batto is an associate research fellow at the Institute of Political Science, Academia Sinica, and at the Election Study Center, National Chengchi University.

Yu-tzung Chang is professor and chair of the Department of Political Science at National Taiwan University.

Dean P. Chen is associate professor in the Department of Political Science, Ramapo College, New Jersey.

Yun-han Chu is professor of political science at National Taiwan University, distinguished research fellow at the Institute of Political Science at Academia Sinica, and president of the Chiang Ching-kuo Foundation.

Larry Diamond is senior fellow at the Freeman Spogli Institute for International Studies and the Hoover Institution, Stanford University.

Dafydd Fell is a reader in comparative politics and director of the Centre of Taiwan Studies, School of Oriental and African Studies, University of London.

Christian Göbel is the deputy head of the Department of East Asian Studies and University Professor of Modern China Studies at the University of Vienna.

Szu-yin Ho is professor in the Graduate Institute of Strategic and International Affairs, Tamkang University, Taiwan.

Isaac Shih-hao Huang is a postdoctoral fellow in the Department of Political Science, National Chengchi University.

Min-hua Huang is professor in the Department of Political Science, National Taiwan University.

Pei-shan Lee is professor in the Department of Political Science, National Chung Cheng University, Taiwan.

Shelley Rigger is the Brown Professor of Political Science at Davidson College.

Shing-yuan Sheng is professor in the Department of Political Science, National Chengchi University.

Kharis Templeman is an adviser to the Project on Taiwan in the Indo-Pacific Region at the Hoover Institution, Stanford University.

Austin Horng-En Wang is assistant professor in the Department of Political Science at the University of Nevada, Las Vegas.

Mark Weatherall is a postdoctoral fellow at the Hu Fu Center for East Asia Democratic Studies, National Taiwan University.

Ching-hsin Yu is a research fellow at the Election Study Center, National Chengchi University.

Eric Chen-hua Yu is an associate research fellow at the Election Study Center and associate professor in the Department of Political Science at National Chengchi University.

Jia-sin Yu holds a master's degree from National Chengchi University.

Index

403

About the Book

During the Ma Ying-jeou presidency in Taiwan (2008–2016), confrontations over relations with mainland China stressed the country's institutions, leading to a political crisis. Nevertheless, its democracy proved to be resilient. The authors of *Dynamics of Democracy in Taiwan* explore key aspects of the complicated Ma era, including party politics and elections, the sources of Ma's governance challenges, changing public opinion, protest movements, and shifts in the regional balance of power.

Kharis Templeman is adviser to the Project on Taiwan in the Indo-Pacific Region at the Hoover Institution, Stanford University. **Yun-han Chu** is professor of political Science at National Taiwan University, Distinguished Research Fellow at the Institute of Political Science at Academia Sinica, and president of the Chiang Ching-kuo Foundation. **Larry Diamond** is senior fellow at the Freeman Spogli Institute for International Studies and the Hoover Institution, Stanford University.